To my Wife

in remembrance of our visits to Rome

TABLE OF CONTENTS

PREFACE TO THE SECOND EDITION

This book appeared for the first time, in 1958, as a major part of Volume V of the series *Sacrum Poloniae Millennium* which had been published in Rome from 1954 to 1966. That part was also printed separately, but in a limited number of copies. Most of them have been distributed in the United States by Fordham University Press. Since that edition is now completely exhausted, a new one was very desirable for two reasons which have to be briefly explained.

First of all, in view of the ecumenical movement which is so rapidly developing especially in the relations between Western and Eastern Christendom, any contribution to the better understanding of the historical background of those relations seems more welcome than ever before. And since it remains one of the most important controversial problems whether regional unions between Rome and individual Eastern Churches were steps in the right direction, the connection which leads from the union with all these Churches concluded in 1439 at the ecumenical Council of Florence to the union with only the Ruthenian Church concluded in 1596 at the local synod of Brest and surviving until our time, deserves general attention.

Furthermore, the purely scholarly interest in the whole matter is also growing, as evidenced by many publications of the last decade. The new contributions which I have tried to make myself, are listed in the second appendix to the present edition of my book. No rewriting was needed, except the correction of minor errors and printing mistakes in the original text. But I wanted to indicate to the specialists those of my latest articles in which I developed some points made ten years ago in various chapters of the book and in its general conclusions.

More important is the first appendix to which the reader is specifically referred in the changed footnote 42 to Chapter II of Part III, though some points raised in Chapter V of the same part—as noted in its footnote 38— are also clarified, thanks to the new document which I discovered in 1962. The article in which I published that document with detailed comments, is reprinted in the appendix with some abridgments. Only the decisive paragraph of the document itself is quoted verbatim because it clearly answers the question which was very doubtful before, namely, why the preparations of the Ukrainian hierarchy for reunion with Rome started precisely in 1590, but were kept secret for several years. It is hardly necessary to point out the significance of the revealing information that this decision was taken because Jeremiah II, one of the most eminent patriarchs of Constantinople, had approved and encouraged it a few months before at a first synod in Brest, of course confidentially, being himself under Turkish control.

I was very glad to have this contribution included in one of the very valuable and numerous publications of the Ukrainian Order of Saint Basil the Great, appearing in Rome. That symposium[1] was published in 1963 on the occasion of the 500th anniversary of the death of Cardinal Isidore, the Metropolitan of Kiev who so strongly supported the Union of Florence; It contains no less than 24 articles and miscellanea,[2] of which the four by M. Wawryk and the three by A. G. Welykyj must be particularly commended here.

The former has discovered and published[3] the full text of a document which had been noted before only in an inadequate summary and now adds a very important point to the story of the ecclesiastical separation of Kiev from Moscow in 1458.[4] There was indeed a moment, early in 1459, when Cardinal Isidore, hoping to promote the Union of Florence in both places, committed Moscow also to his disciple and successor Gregory. Eventually he was recognized in Kiev only, as it had been anticipated from the outset. But the very fact that an enlargement of the regional reunion was considered, is instructive from an ecumenical point of view, just like the point which has been discussed above in connection with the Union of Brest.

In another article[5] Wawryk supports not only my opinion that Metropolitan Gregory, in spite of his relations with Constantinople, remained faithful to the Union of Florence, but also the basic thesis of my book that there is a link of continuity between that ecumenical union of 1439 and that of Brest, in 1596, which was one more revival of the Florentine tradition in the region where it had never been obliterated through the XVth and even the XVIth century.

---

[1] *Miscellanea in honorem Cardinalis Isidori*, in two parts, being volume IV of Series II, Section II, of the general collection *Analecta Ordinis S. Basilii Magni*.

[2] In one of the articles (pp. 79–94), G. Mykoliw gives new arguments in favor of the opinion that Peter Arcudius who is so frequently mentioned in my book, not only cooperated in the writing of *Antirrhesis*, a contemporary defense of the Union of Brest (see my footnote 1 to Part IV, Chapter IV), but was its sole author. In the miscellanea (p. 513–526), L. Wynar, writing about the mission of Komulovich to the Cossacks (see in my book Part III, Chapter IV, particularly footnote 47), tries to prove that their leader with whom the papal diplomat established contacts but whose name is not given in the sources, must have been the famous Nalyvayko.

[3] In his article "Quaedam nova de provisione metropoliae Kioviensis et Moscoviensis Ann. 1458–1459" (pp. 9–26). The decisive documents are published on pp. 18–21.

[4] See in my book Part I, Chapter IV (particularly footnotes 1 and 24), where the reader should now take the new information into consideration.

[5] "Florentisjki unijni traditsii v kyivs'kij mitropolij" (pp. 329–362; see particularly p. 329 and 361f.).

Turning to Welykyj's contributions which concern also the XVIth and XVIIth centuries, the one which explains the sources of Ukrainian Catholicism[6] is also in substantial agreement with my interpretation of the Union of Brest in two controversial matters. Although he certainly does not underrate the role of Prince Constantine Ostrožskyj, (Ostrogski), quoting a report that in 1587 he had serious chances of being elected king of Poland,[7] Welykyj comes to the conclusion that it was not that opponent to the Union of Brest, but its initiators, the bishops of Eastern rite, who served the real interests, both religious and national, of the Ukrainian people. And, calling the Union not a humiliation but a triumph of the Ukrainian Church, he wonders that there are still serious historians who repeat the slogans that it should have been rejected.

Welykyj does not name any of these historians but only three years before his article in 1960, there appeared a scholarly monograph in which a German professor, Eduard Winter,[8] studying the relations between Russia and the papacy, presented the Union of Brest as a particularly shocking example of the hostile and degrading treatment of the Eastern Slavs by the popes and their agents, especially the Jesuits. Strangely enough, Winter started his chapter on Brest by complaining how difficult the study of the Union is because in the Vatican Archives the sources for the period 1593–1608 have allegedly been lost. He failed, however, to notice that the main source, the reports and instructions of the Nuncio to Poland, missing indeed in the series *Nunziatura di Polonia*, can easily be found in other files of the same Archives, chiefly in the *Fondo Borghese*. These and many other sources had been abundantly used and quoted in my book in 1958[9] when most of them were still unpublished. In the following year Welykyj rendered a great service to all scholars by editing the *Littera nuntiorum apostolicorum historiam Ucrainae illustrantes*[10] and starting with the period 1550–1620 which is most important for the origin and development of the Union of Brest. In his article of 1963 he also used some additional material, discovered in the State Archives of Rome.

Without listing here all the other recent contributions of Ukrainian

---

[6] "Alle fonti del cattolicesimo ucraino" (pp. 44–78; see particularly pp. 49, 65, 68, 77f.).

[7] *Ibidem*, p. 46f.

[8] *Russland und das Papsttum*. Teil I: *Von der Christianisierung bis zu den Anfängen der Aufklärung*, Berlin 1960. The chapter "Die Union von Brest" is on pp. 253–273.

[9] This book is quoted on p. 253, note 2, but has not been used, probably because it came too late; but already in 1954 I gave in *Sacrum Poloniae Millenium*, vol. I, p. 72f, notes 5–9, a detailed list of the manuscripts in the Vatican Archives, the Vatican Library, and other Roman collections, where the correspondence of Nuncio Malaspina and Legate Caetani at the time of the Union of Brest is preserved.

[10] In the Series II, Section III of the *Analecta Ordinis S. Basilii Magni*. In that same section he published in 1953–1954 the two volumes of *Documenta Pontificum Romanorum historiam Ucrainae illustrantia* (1075–1953) which I found very helpful when writing my book.

historians, it must be noted that one of them, Nicolaus Čubatyj, published in 1965 the first volume of a comprehensive history of Christianity in Rus'-Ukraine.[11] That truly imposing volume covers, however, only the period from the origins to the middle of the XIVth century, and therefore we have to wait for the next one before being able to discuss his views on the developments leading from Florence to Brest which are only briefly touched upon in his general introduction.

It is, on the other hand, indispensable to pay a tribute here to another Roman center of studies, the Pontifical Oriental Institute, whose publications, including the well-known series *Orientalia Christiana Periodica* and *Orientalia Christiana Analecta,* which proved already invaluable when the first edition of this book appeared, continue to offer new material. As far as the Union of Florence is concerned, one of the professors of that Institute, Joseph Gill, S.J., published in 1959 a brilliant synthesis of the history of the Council of Florence,[12] where in the chapter on "The reception of the Union in the East" he wrote not only about the Byzantine Empire but also about the Orthodox of Poland, Lithuania, and Moscow, going in the "Epilogue" as far as 1472 and the prospects for the Union of Brest. It was gratifying to find his views in full agreement with my own. He also contributed an interesting article to the symposium quoted above.[13]

I should like to conclude this preface by explaining that in a few footnotes of the first edition new bibliographical references could be added, though the publications of the last decade would hardly require any change in the text. Some of them rather confirm the views which I expressed in 1958. This is particularly important in two cases where controversial questions were discussed. What has been said, in Part I, Chapter V, on Moscow's aggressive policy against Lithuania at the time of Ivan III, has now been substantiated in the highly objective book, based mainly on Russian material, which the British historian J. L. I. Fennell published in 1961 on that outstanding ruler.[14] The Protestant influence on the Orthodox opposition against the Union of Brest, which I noted time and again, in Parts III and IV, has been equally emphasized, in 1959, by a French specialist, A. Jobert.[15] The Polish historian P. Skwarczyński has not directly touched that question in his quite recent studies on the history

[11] *Istorija Khrystyjanstva na Rusy-Ukraini,* vol. I (to the year 1353), Rome and New York 1965. See my review in *The American Historical Review,* vol. LXXII (July 1967) p. 1364 f.

[12] *The Council of Florence* (Cambridge University Press, 1959); see particularly pp. 332f, 358–394f., and the excellent bibliography where he listed among others the volumes of the Institute's outstanding publication *Concilium Florentinum: Documenta et Scriptores,* which, however, is not yet entirely completed.

[13] "Isidor's Encyclical letter from Buda," *Miscellanea in honorem Card. Isidori,* pp. 1–8, where the Russian version of that message, quoted in my book, p. 56 n. 51, its English translation, and a commentary are given.

[14] *Ivan the Great of Moscow,* New York 1961.

[15] In his article "Aux origines de l'Union de Brest. Le Protestantisme en Ruthénie," *Księga pamiątkowa 150-lecia Archiwum Głównego,* Warsaw 1959, pp. 371–382.

of the Reformation in East Central Europe,[16] but added very interesting information on the relations between the Protestants and the Eastern Churches in the Baltic region, Moldavia, Transylvania, the Balkans, and Constantinople, another issue of ecumenical significance.

———————

I am very obliged to Fordham University Press, particularly to its Director, Rev. Edwin A. Quain, S.J., for technical facilities which proved of great help in the preparation of this second edition of my book.

The first edition was dedicated to my beloved wife who had been so deeply interested in my work. She did not live to see the present one which can be dedicated only to her memory.

———————

[16] *Szkice z dziejów Reformaeji w Europie środkowo-wschodniej*, London 1967; see pp. 49–56.

PREFACE

Forty years ago, in the academic year 1917-1918, I gave at the Jagellonian University in Cracow a lecture course on the Unions of Florence and Brest. My interest in that problem continued ever since, but I worked chiefly on the political union between Poland, Lithuania, and the Ruthenian lands, as well as on the earlier relations between the Latin and the Greek Churches. Among the various books which in the meantime discussed the projects of religious union within the limits of the Polish-Lithuanian Commonwealth, the excellent work of my late colleague and friend Kazimierz Chodynicki proved particularly valuable and helpful, but approached the problem as part of the history of the Orthodox Church in the Commonwealth, and being published in 1934, could not use the rich material which the Papal Oriental Institute in Rome has made available during the last quarter of a century. Furthermore, there remained a vast amount of unpublished sources to be studied, especially as I wanted from the outset to present the problem in connection with the whole eastern policy of the Papacy.

A serious attempt in that direction was made possible to me only in 1952-1953 when, thanks to the grant of a Fulbright scholarship by the United States Government and of a sabbatical year by Fordham University, I could do again extensive research work in the archives and libraries of Italy. Among those who helped me in exploring the treasures of the Vatican Archives — by far the most important, though inseparable from the manuscript collections of the Vatican Library — I remember with deepest gratitude their late Custodian, Mons. Angelo Mercati. Invaluable was the kind assistance and advice which I received from two professors at the Papal Oriental Institute, Fathers A. M. Ammann and G. Hofmann, S. J., the latter of whom unfortunately passed away last year. I also want to acknowledge the friendly reception which I experienced at the Roman Archives of the Society of Jesus and other Roman institutions, including the Croat and Greek Colleges and the Libraries Casanatense and Vallicelliana, as well as in the State Archives of Venice where my difficult investigations were greatly facilitated by Dr. Francamaria Tiepolo.

I fully realize that, in spite of the help received from all these institutions and their expert staff, it was impossible to exhaust the whole material in a comparatively short time. I tried to supplement these new sources through additional research in the libraries of New York and in the Polish Library of Paris, avoiding, however, to repeat once more what has been said, though sometimes from a different point of view, in earlier publications, if it was not indispensable for the general picture. Nor did I repeat all that I wrote myself in a few articles published in preparation of the present book which in turn will lead, as I hope, to further discussions of the many controversial issues which had to be raised.

Two of my preparatory essays appeared in earlier volumes of the *Sacrum Poloniae Millennium*, and I am very happy and grateful indeed that, thanks to the kind interest of H. E. Archbishop J. Gawlina, the whole work has been included in that truly monumental series which is edited on his initiative in order to commemorate the approaching anniversary of Poland's Christianization in 966. I am deeply obliged, too, to the Secretary of the Editorial Committee, Msgr. J. Manthey, for his special care in having my monograph printed as rapidly and accurately as possible, and for his permission to make some last minute changes and additions based upon my most recent investigations.

That supplementary research work, undertaken in connection with the preparation of another book, has been greatly facilitated by a fellowship granted to me by the John Guggenheim Memorial Foundation in 1957.

In view of the wide scope of this study, it appeared practically impossible to add a systematic bibliography to the references in the numerous footnotes. An exception has been made only for the unpublished primary sources : they proved so important, particularly for the chapters dealing with the later sixteenth century and also for a better understanding of the general background, that all manuscripts which have been consulted in various archives and libraries are listed with their specific numbers.

FROM LYONS TO KREVO AND CONSTANCE 1245-1418

The regional union of one of the Eastern Churches with Rome, which was concluded at the Synod of Brest in 1596, was a return to the tradition of the general union between Western and Eastern Christendom, which had been achieved at the Council of Florence in 1439. It is, therefore, only in connection with that earlier achievement to which all the sources regarding the Union of Brest continuously refer, that the momentous decision of the Ruthenian hierarchy and its approval by the Holy See can be properly understood. But the Union of Florence itself had not been the first reconciliation between Rome and Constantinople. It had been preceded by a similar union at the second Council of Lyons in 1274. Furthermore, while the Union of Brest came long after that of Florence as its revival in a strictly limited region, the Union of Lyons had been preceded by a limited union in practically the same region, a union whose origin can be traced back to the first Council of Lyons in 1245.

Therefore, without going back to the first attempts of reunion which started almost immediately after the schism of 1054 and before its earliest repercussions in Kiev,[1] the study of the developments which led from Florence to Brest requires as an introduction a survey of the tradition of both Councils of Lyons. Without any specific reference to that remote tradition, the idea of combining a universal religious union with a local initiative coming from the Ruthenian lands reappeared at the very end of the Council of Constance in 1418. Hence that earlier background comes very close to the new phase of negotiations with the East which directly prepared the Union of 1439.

There are at least two striking analogies between the period of 173 years

---

[1] The Cerularian Schism has recently been studied, with all its implications, in the symposium 1054-1954 *L'Eglise et les Eglises*, 2 vol., Chevetogne : Collection Irenikon, 1954, where the problem of the repercussions in Kiev is briefly discussed by P. Kovalevsky, " L'Eglise russe en 1054, " I, 475-483. Particularly important for the understanding of Kiev's continued relations with Rome after 1054 is V. Meysztowicz, " L'Union de Kiev avec Rome sous Grégoire VII, " *Studi Gregoriani*, V (1956), 83-108 ; see also his publication of the " Manuscriptum Gertrudae, " *Antemurale*, II 1955), 97-157.

which can be considered merely a preparation for future achievements, and the period of almost equal length which separates the Council of Basel-Ferrara-Florence-Rome from the Union of Brest.

In both cases, in spite of the ultimate failure of unions between West and East which were supposed to be universal, projects of religious reunions of a territorially limited character but not without prospects of extension could reappear with serious chances of success, because political unions had more or less intimately included large populations of Greek-Orthodox religion in a federal system under Catholic leadership. The road from Lyons to Constance led through the distant and obscure place of Krevo where, in 1385, a treaty was signed which associated not only the Lithuanian but also the Ruthenian lands with the Kingdom of Poland. On the road from Florence to Brest — in this case even in the geographical sense — was the city of Lublin where, in 1569, the Polish-Lithuanian union received its final constitution including momentous changes in the position of the Ruthenian lands. Both political unions had far reaching cultural and especially religious implications which were connected with the contemporary crises of the Western Schism and of the Protestant Reformation. Religious unions seemed, therefore, indispensable supplements and highly desirable contributions to the unity of the federation.

In both periods, too, they were considered contributions to not only the unity but also to the defense of Christendom. As far as the general religious union is concerned, it is well known that almost all the negotiations between Rome and Constantinople had the desire of cooperation against the enemies of Christendom at least as an additional motive. Only the situation of 1274 is an exception, because the Byzantine Empire was then afraid not of an Asiatic but of a western invasion. [2] On the contrary, the first Council of Lyons confirms the rule, not only because the final loss of Jerusalem in 1244 made the Asiatic danger particularly evident, but also because the Mongol invasion, having reached in 1241 the very heart of Europe, was a serious warning that the danger was approaching on two different ways: from the Near East in the direction of the Straits and from Central Asia through the open gate of Europe north of the Black Sea.

The Ruthenian lands which seemed ready for a regional union with Rome, even independently of the simultaneous negotiations with the Greek Empire of Nicaea, were then threatened by the Mongols only. That danger from the Tartars — as the invaders of Eastern Europe were called later — remained a serious concern at the time of the federal unions of Krevo and

---

[2] Among the most recent contributions to the history of the Union of Lyons and of its background see D. J. Geanakoplos, " Michael Palaeologos and the Union of Lyons, " *Harvard Theological Review*, 1953, 73-89 (with bibliography), and " On the Schism of the Greek and Roman Churches, " *The Greek Orthodox Theological Review*, I (1954), 16-24.

Lublin and long after the Union of Brest. But around 1596 the Tartar danger was only part of a much larger problem : the simultaneous defense against Moscow in the north-east and Turkey in the south-east. In order to understand that critical situation, it must be traced back not only to the time of the Union of Florence, but far into the preceding period : to the rise of Muscovite and Ottoman power from the beginning of the fourteenth century. And this is indeed a problem not of any particular region, but of general European history.

In that history the rise of the Ottoman Empire made reappear the old problem of the crusades in the form of a defensive anti-Turkish league [3] in cooperation with the Greeks or, after 1453, with a view to liberating them along with the other Balkan populations which had been conquered by the Turks. Since practically all these populations were Orthodox, the problem of their union with Rome proved inseparable from that of the new crusade, as it had been at the time of the crusades in the earlier Middle Ages. Entirely new, on the contrary, was the question whether the young power of Moscow could be gained for participation in the struggle against the Turks, or for religious union, or for both.

That question, vital for Moscow's Catholic neighbors from the outset, became of serious interest for all Europe and particularly for the Holy See [4] as soon as Moscow, even before the final fall of the Golden Horde, seemed to be free from Tartar control, that is, already at the time of the Union of Florence. On the contrary, at the first Council of Lyons an entirely different question had to be considered in a similar connection. The distant Volga region where Moscow, a city hardly mentioned in the middle of the thirteenth century, was to emerge as leading center at the beginning of the next, soon appeared to be lost to the Mongol conquerors with no chance of joining a crusade against them. But could not a part at least of the old Kievan State, in spite of the fall of Kiev itself in 1240, still be saved and on the same occasion gained for reunion with the Catholic West ? That question, which was to reappear in 1596 when Kiev was a border city of a Catholic power, was in 1245 put before Innocent IV, a pope very deeply interested in all eastern problems. [5]

It is, unfortunately, impossible to determine whether the otherwise unknown bishop Peter who supplied Pope and Council with detailed information on the Mongol danger, really was a metropolitan of Kiev, so that he

---

[3] A. S. Atiya, author of the basic book on *The Crusades in the Later Middle Ages*, London, 1938, has recently touched this problem in his article, " The Crusades : Old Ideas and New Conceptions, " *Journal of World History*, II (1954), 469-475.

[4] Best evidenced by P. Pierling, *La Russie et le Saint-Siège* Vol. I, Paris, 1896, whose interpretations will be discussed many times in the course of the present study.

[5] See J. Umiński, *Niebezpieczeństwo tatarskie w połowie XIII w. i papież Innocenty IV* (The Tartar danger in the middle of the XIII century and Pope Innocent IV), Lwów, 1922.

could be called a precursor of Metropolitan Isidore [6] who contributed so much to the Union of Florence. It is even more uncertain whether Peter acted on behalf of Prince Michael of Chernigov who indeed was to prove more courageous than the others in defying the Mongol conquerors but only to be executed at the order of Batu Khan in the very year 1245. There remained, however, Michael's equally outstanding rival, Prince Daniel of Halich, whose brother Vasilko of Volhynia so friendly received the papal mission which under the leadership of the Franciscan John of Plano Carpini was sent from Lyons to Mongolia. Daniel himself, to whom his younger brother referred them in the matter of a possible religious union with Rome, was then at Batu's camp trying to appease the Mongols. But the representatives of Innocent IV, whose mission to Karakorum naturally ended in failure, met Daniel on their way back, in 1247, after his own return to Halich, and found him as anxious as Vasilko to enter into relations with the Holy See.

The negotiations which followed [7] and after six years resulted in a formal union and in the coronation of Daniel, by a papal legate, as Catholic king, in 1253, are instructive for various reasons. They confirmed indeed that in Halich and Volhynia, in the southwestern border region of the old Kievan State which Daniel had hoped to restore, there was a serious chance for restoring also the religious unity with Rome which had existed at least until the beginning of the twelfth century. At the given moment three circumstances favored such a reunion. First, the relations with Daniel's western Catholic neighbors, with Poland and Hungary, both of whom had attempted to conquer his patrimony in his early youth, had greatly improved. And while the danger of an enforced Catholic domination by foreign rulers had hardly served the cause of religious union, exactly as it had happened in Constantinople after the Latin conquest of almost the same years, [8] friendly relations with the nearest Catholic powers [9] removed the main reason for resistance and suspicion against the West. Secondly, Rome's relations with the Greeks, whose influence continued to be strong

---

[6] This is the suggestive hypothesis of S. Tomašivsky, " Predteča Isidora, Petro Akerovič " (A precursor of Isidore, Peter Akerovič), *Analecta Ordinis S. Basilii M.*, Vol. II, 1926.

[7] Described, among others, by N. Čubaty, " Zachidna Ukraina i Rym v XIII v. " (The Western Ukraine and Rome in the XIII century), *Zap. Nauk. Tov. Ševčenka*, Vol. 123-124, 1917. The papal bulls in that matter are collected in *Documenta Pontificum Romanorum Historiam Ucrainae illustrantia* (ed. A. G. Welykyj), Vol. I, Rome, 1953, Nr. 11-32.

[8] See the introduction to Th. Haluščynskyj, *Acta Innocentii Papae III*, Rome, 1944.

[9] The Polish part in the negotiations with Daniel has been recently explained by B. Szcześniak, " Benoit le Polonais, dit le Vratislavien, et son rôle dans l'union de la Ruthénie de Halicz avec Rome en 1246, " *Antemurale*, I (1954), 39-50 ; see also his latest article : " The Mission of Giovanni de Plano Carpini and Benedict the Pole of Vratislavia to Halicz, " *Journal of Ecclesiastical History*, VII, 12-20.

among the Ruthenians, had also substantially changed. Innocent IV no longer supported unconditionally the Latin Empire of Constantinople as his great predecessor Innocent III had done after some initial hesitation, but conducted negotiations with the Greek Empire of Nicaea, [10] which were parallel to those with Daniel of Halich. In 1253, an agreement with Emperor John Vatatzes seemed imminent, especially as Rome proved ready to recognize the Eastern rite, as it had already done in the Ruthenian case in 1247. [11] Last but not least, Daniel hoped to gain through his union with Rome Catholic support against the Mongols.

That third reason which could seem the decisive one proved, however, the most deceiving for both sides. As usualy, political expediency appeared insufficient to promote a lasting agreement in the religious sphere. Daniel who even in the course of his preliminary negotiations, in 1248, showed some temporary hesitation under Mongol pressure, turned away from the West when soon after his coronation, in 1255, a change in Mongol leadership increased the danger from the East, [12] while no substantial help came from the Catholic side. Even the promising cooperation with the new Catholic kingdom of Lithuania, which Innocent IV had established simultaneously with that of Halich, ended in failure and disappointment. [13] Great too, was, of course, the disappointment of the Holy See when both recently converted kings at the border of Europe for political reasons, different in either case, gradually abandoned their Catholic orientation, with Lithuania returning to paganism and the State of Halich and Volhynia to the Greek schism which remained unchanged in Nicaea too. For, the simultaneous death of Innocent IV and John Vatatzes, in 1254, postponed indefinitely the agreement which had seemed so near, [14] and the unique opportunity for reaching at the same time an understanding with the Greek Patriarchate and with the Ruthenian Church was not to repeat itself for a long time.

Even in the hopeful years when Innocent IV was making good progress in his negotiations with both Nicaea and Halich, there was not the slightest chance for extending the prospects of religious union to the new colonial Russia of the Volga region. It is true according to Plano Carpini that even Grand Prince Yaroslav of Vladimir, whom the papal envoy had met in Mongolia before he was poisoned there, seemed desirous to get in touch with

---

[10] W. Norden, *Das Papsttum und Byzanz*, Berlin, 1903, 359-378 ; see also app. Nr. XII, 756 ff.

[11] In his bull of August 27, 1247 ; *Documenta Pontificum Romanorum*, Vol. I, Nr. 22.

[12] G. Vernadsky, *The Mongols and Russia*, New Haven, 1953. 149 f., 157.

[13] H. Paszkiewicz, *The Origin of Russia*, London, 1954, 206, notes 1 and 2 where the sources and earlier studies of the reign of Mindaugas, King of Lithuania, are quoted.

[14] V. Laurent, " Le pape Alexandre IV et l'Empire de Nicée, " *Echos d'Orient*, Vol. 38 (1935), 31-34.

Rome. But when the Pope, in 1248, invited Yaroslav's famous son, Alexander Nevsky, to unite with the Catholic Church, he received no answer at all, and it is well known that Alexander's policy combined persistent hostility against the Catholic West with systematic appeasement of the Mongols. [15] Even the temporary rapprochement between his brother Andrew and Daniel of Halich, in 1251-52, did not affect that general picture which is easy to explain.

In the Russia of Suzdal and Vladimir which rose to power long after the Eastern schism, there was no tradition at all of any original unity with Rome. The relations with Catholic neighbors, both the Swedes whom Alexander defeated on the Neva, thus gaining his surname, and the German knights of Livonia whom he equally had to repulse, were always hostile. And, since their anti-schismatic crusades were mainly directed against Novgorod whose defense Alexander assumed before being made Grand Prince of Vladimir by the Khan, even the western ties of this semi-independent republic could not improve the chances for an understanding with the Catholic world. Much nearer to Saray — the capital of the Khanate of Kypchak — than was Daniel's realm, Alexander was even more exposed to Mongol pressure and realistic enough to see that no agreement with distant Rome, contrary to his religious conviction, would be of any political use. [16]

For all these reasons, Great Russia — as the Suzdal region soon was to be called in the Greek sources — though continuing to maintain close ecclesiastical relations with the Greek Patriarchate — retransferred in 1261 from Nicaea to Constantinople — did not follow the Greeks at all when in 1274 they concluded the Union of Lyons with Pope Gregory X. [17] On the contrary, in that same year an important synod of all bishops of northeastern Russia took place in Vladimir, [18] trying to consolidate the Church of that region through its own forces in spite of the difficult conditions of Mongol domination. That synod took place in the presence of the Metropolitan of Kiev, Cyril II, who had started his ecclesiastical career as bishop of Chełm (Kholm) at the western border of Daniel's principality, where he had met in 1245 the papal envoys. He seems to have followed Daniel's policy, [19] and the fact that he was consecrated as metropolitan in Nicaea

[15] A. A. Ammann, *Abriss der ostslavischen Kirchengeschichte*, Wien, 1950, 55 ; also: *Kirchenpolitische Wandlungen im Ostbaltikum bis zum Tode Alexander Newskis*, Rome, 1936. A different interpretation has been recently given by J. J. Zatko " The Union of Suzdal 1222-1252 ", *Journal of Eccles. History*, VIII, 33-52.

[16] G. Vernadsky, *op. cit.* 147 ff.

[17] W. Norden, *op. cit.*, 528 (see also p. 717 his comparison with the Union of Florence) has overestimated the universal significance of the Union of Lyons for the whole East.

[18] A. A. Ammann, *Abriss ...*, 59, 74 f.

[19] See, however, the different opinion of Ammann, *op. cit.*, 58 f.

by the Greek Patriarch does not prove that he was then, in 1250, opposed to a union with Rome which at the same time was considered by the Greeks themselves. Even later, in 1265, there is some evidence that he favored the separate position of the dioceses of " Little Russia, " as the State of Halich and Volhynia was called in the Greek sources, and though already Cyril II showed an equal interest in the northeastern region, it was only his successor, Maxim, who in 1300 transferred his residence from Kiev to Pereyaslav near Vladimir. [20]

The transfer to Moscow followed not before 1326, under Metropolitan Peter, but already at the turn of the century the rise of Moscow to a leading position in the Volga region had started, [21] and at the same time started the repeated efforts of Daniel's successors to obtain from the Patriarchs of Constantinople the recognition of a separate metropolitan see in Halich. [22] This had nothing to do with any desire to restore the religious union with Rome which, only a few years after the second Council of Lyons had been abandoned in Constantinople also. And throughout the fourteenth century the Greek Patriarchs remained undecided whether or not they should admit a division of the ecclesiastical province of " all the Russias. " [23] Nevertheless, the claims for such a division were highly significant. The metropolitans who resided in Moscow, in close cooperation with princes under Tartar control, had no contact whatever with the Catholic world, while the western part of the old Kievan State was soon to have new opportunities for entering once more into relations with Rome.

It is true that most of these western principalities were gradually liberated from Tartar domination by Lithuania which in spite of various projects of conversion to the Catholic faith still remained pagan and in conflict with her Catholic neighbors. When, therefore, those pagan Grand Dukes of Lithuania, just like the Orthodox rulers of Halich and Volhynia, wanted separate metropolitans for their Ruthenian acquisitions which already in 1330-31 reached as far as Kiev itself, [24] it was not for any religious reasons, but only to oppose the influence of the rival power of Moscow. But soon after 1340 Halich and parts of Volhynia came under the rule of Catholic Poland, and King Casimir the Great, who safeguarded the traditional autonomy of his Ruthenian lands, followed his Orthodox predecessors in favoring the definite establishment of a metropolitan see in Halich under the Patriarch of Constantinople. [25] It may seem astonishing why that Catholic King,

---

[20] *Ibidem*, 79.

[21] See the discussion of the various interpretations of the causes of that rise by Paszkiewicz, *op. cit.*, 310 ff.

[22] K. Chodynicki, *Kościół prawosławny a Rzeczpospolita polska* (The Orthodox Church and the Polish Commonwealth), Warszawa, 1934, 3-7.

[23] *Ibidem*, 11-25 ; H. Paszkiewicz, *op. cit.*, 219 f., 226 f.

[24] Paszkiewicz, *op. cit.*, 211.

[25] Chodynicki, *op. cit.*, 7-11.

who founded in these lands the first Catholic bishoprics of Latin rite,[26] did not try to promote the reunion of the Ruthenian hierarchy with Rome. But it must be remembered that in his time Constantinople itself had resumed negotiations with the Holy See in that matter, negotiations which had started as soon as the growing danger from the Ottoman Turks had made the Greeks realize how badly they needed western support.[27]

It is important to note that these negotiations, dictated mainly by political motives and never sincerely favored by the patriarchs, resulted at least in the conversion to Catholicism of Emperor John V Palaeologus during his visit in Rome in 1369-1370,[28] i. e., at the very moment when Casimir the Great sent to Constantinople his formal request for a separate metropolitan in Halich.[29] In that same year of 1370, Casimir's death opened in Poland a succession crisis which, after the interlude of a brief Polish-Hungarian union, was to lead in 1386 to a lasting union of Poland and Lithuania.[30] That union included, of course, all the Ruthenian lands of both Poland and Lithuania where Catholicism was finally introduced in the following year, so that all what is called today the Ukraine and Byelorussia or White-Ruthenia was placed under Catholic leadership.

Such a result of the Treaty of Krevo of August 14, 1385,[31] in which Jagello (Jogaila) of Lithuania, before receiving in marriage Queen Jadwiga of Poland, had promised the conversion of his country, was indeed a great success for the Catholic Church in the midst of the crisis of the Western Schism. That new schism of course, had, created a situation which seemed most unfavorable to any attempts at ending the old Eastern Schism.[32] Nevertheless these attempts were not given up by the Roman popes, and just at the time of the conclusion of the Polish-Lithuanian union delegates of Urban VI were again in Constantinople[33] where John V, in spite of all political vicissitudes and the increasing Ottoman pressure, remained faithful to Rome though his individual conversion had never been followed by any real union.

[26] W. Abraham, *Powstanie organizacji Kościoła łacińskiego na Rusi* (The Origin of the Organization of the Latin Church in Ruthenia), Lwów, 1904, 238-254.

[27] O. Halecki, *Un Empereur de Byzance à Rome*, Warszawa, 1930, Chapter I.

[28] *Ibidem*, 205 ; this was, as generally recognized now, no union of the Western and Eastern Churches, but only a personal conversion to Catholicism of the Latin rite.

[29] *Acta Patriarchatus Constantinopolitani*, Vol. I, Vindobonae, 1860, 577-578 ; see the comments of Chodynicki, *op. cit.*, 9, note 1.

[30] O. Halecki, " From the Union with Hungary to the Union with Lithuania, " *The Cambridge History of Poland*, Vol. I, Cambridge, 1950, 188-209.

[31] *Akta Unji Polski z Litwą* (The Acts of Union between Poland and Lithuania, ed. J. Kutrzeba and W. Semkowicz), Kraków, 1932, Nr. 1, p. 2.

[32] O. Halecki, " Rome et Byzance au temps du grand schisme d'occident, " *Collectanea theologica*, Vol. 18, Lwów, 1937, 477-532.

[33] R. Loenertz, *Les recueils de lettres de Démétrius Cydonès*, Città del Vaticano, 1947, 93-101, where four letters of Cydones in that matter are published.

Such a union with Constantinople which would have included the whole Eastern Church, all followers of the oecumenical Patriarchate, was now even less probable than before. But the problem of a regional union could easily reappear since for the first time so many Orthodox people were living with an approximately equal number of Catholics in one body politic : the confederation under the rule of Jagello — after his baptism King Władysław II — and his saintly wife Queen Jadwiga. The idea which had inspired her when she decided to accept him as husband[34] and which he himself proved anxious to serve was indeed the spread of Catholicism towards the East. And though it was understood that only those Lithuanians who still remained pagan would have to be baptized in the Catholic Church, following the example of their ruler and his brothers,[35] strict measures were taken at once in order to stop the trend which in earlier years had made many Lithuanians, including members of the dynasty, join the Eastern Orthodox Church of the Ruthenians. The freedom of worship of the latter remained untouched and there was in practice little if any real discrimination against them,[36] but the new civic rights and liberties which were granted to the Lithuanian boyars on the pattern of the Polish constitution were restricted to Catholics only. And since among the Orthodox individual conversions to Catholicism of the Latin rite remained rather exceptional, only a union similar to that which King Daniel once had concluded in part at least of the territory under question could remove the religious differences within the limits of the confederation. Desirable from the point of view of the Catholic Church, such a union could also contribute to the unity of a realm which was composed of heterogeneous parts, hitherto frequently hostile to each other.

It is, therefore, no wonder that such a project appeared as soon as the internal political conditions and the international relations of the new federal State were stabilized, not later than ten years after its formation, in 1396.[37] The plan was officially sponsored by Jagello and by his cousin Vitold (Vytautas) whom he had entrusted four years before with the administration of Lithuania and of the Ruthenian lands attached to her. That Queen Jadwiga, who had called to Cracow from Bohemia Benedictines of the Eastern rite,[38] must have been deeply interested and perhaps even the real initiator, seems only natural. But surprising is that what was envisaged

---

[34] W. Maciejewska, *Jadwiga, Królowa polska* (Jadwiga, Queen of Poland), Kraków, 1934, 54.

[35] " Cum omnibus fratribus suis nondum baptisatis, " according to the act of Krevo, cited above, note 31.

[36] Chodynicki, *op. cit.*, 77 f.

[37] The project is known only thanks to the answers which the Patriarch of Constantinople sent in January 1397 to the King of Poland and to the Metropolitan of Kiev ; see *Acta Patriarchatus Constantinopolitani*, Vol. II, Vindobonae 1862, 280-285.

[38] W. Maciejewska, *op. cit.*, 129 f.

was more than a merely regional union with the Ruthenian hierarchy under a metropolitan of unusual ability and versatility : the Bulgarian Cyprian. Through that metropolitan, who, without giving up his authority over all Russias, including Moscow, at that time resided in Kiev, the Patriarch of Constantinople himself was approached in due course with a view of achieving a union which would have been practically universal, a return to the union of Lyons and to the original projects of John V Palaeologus, though this time with the effective and even leading participation of the Ruthenian followers of the Eastern Greek Church.

Their participation had become of outstanding importance for two different reasons. On the one hand, the Greek Empire was now so much weaker than in 1274 or even before 1369. Its territory was practically reduced to the nearest environs of Constantinople which remained under a quasi-permanent Ottoman blockade, and to the important but geographically isolated Despotate of Mistra. [39] The new emperor, Manuel II, after trying in vain to appease the Turks, was looking for Latin support, but divided by the Western schism and their political rivalries, those Catholic powers, which in the past had been leading in the crusading movement, were unable to revive it on an adequate scale. The crusade of 1396, even before it ended in the catastrophe of Nicopolis, [40] had to be undertaken without the usual papal initiative, because Burgundy — the only part of France which in spite of the crisis of the Hundred Years War continued to be actively interested in the eastern problem — sided, along with the French king, with the antipope at Avignon, and because Venice would not cooperate with her traditional rival, the King of Hungary. On the other hand, Venice was first to realize that for a complete success of any anti-Ottoman action the participation of the new great power which had emerged in Eastern Europe, thanks to the Polish-Lithuanian union, was of primary importance. [41] And that leads to the second reason why the Polish-Lithuanian project of a religious union was so significant at that crucial date.

Poland, too, was in tense relations with Sigismund of Luxemburg and, therefore, not prepared to participate in a crusade under the leadership of the King of Hungary who could enlist only the support of individual Polish knights. [42] But a restoration of religious unity between West and East would have been another valuable contribution to the defense of the latter, in the interest not only of Jagello's realm, the outpost of the West in north-

---

[39] P. Charanis, " The Strife among the Palaeologi and the Ottoman Turcs 1370-1402, " *Byzantion*, XVI (1942-43), 286-314 ; D. A. Zakythinos, *Le despotat grec de Morée*, Vol. I, Paris, 1932.

[40] A. S. Atiya, *The Crusade of Nicopolis*, London, 1934.

[41] *Monumenta Slavorum Meridionalium*, vol. IV, Zagreb 1874, 343.

[42] See the list of the crusaders of 1396 in Delaville Le Roux, *La France en Orient au XIV-e siècle*, Paris, 1886, appendix 20.

eastern Europe, but also of the Byzantine Empire, so badly threatened from the southeast. And while a merely regional union of the Ruthenians with Rome would have deprived the Patriarchate of Constantinople of a most urgently needed source of financial support, an invitation to join with that most numerous group of Orthodox people free from Ottoman control, who were much more interested in the approaching Ottoman danger than was faraway Moscow, certainly deserved serious attention.

Such an attention is indeed evidenced in the answer of Patriarch Antonius II which certainly was drafted in agreement with Emperor Manuel II. The main objection was not of a religious character, but written in 1397, already after the defeat of Nicopolis, the Greek reply suggested to put first things first, viz., to consider first the urgent necessity of military defense against the Turks and to wait for conditions more favorable to negotiations in religious matters. The Polish project had, of course, taken into consideration that in the given political situation an oecumenical council which, as experience had shown, was indispensable for conducting such negotiations, could not meet in or near Constantinople. And since the religious situation in the West was hardly ripe for a convocation of such a council there, where the Western Schism was the first thing to be considered, Jagello and Vitold had made the suggestion to hold such a council for discussing the reunion with the Eastern Church somewhere in their own Ruthenian lands. That unusual idea which would have increased their prestige as well as that of Metropolitan Cyprian was, however, hardly acceptable to the Patriarch: never had any of his predecessors visited these lands in person, and his successors would not do it before the end of the sixteenth century, at the time of their deepest humiliation under Ottoman rule. The Greek reluctance to accept a proposal which seemed to transfer to Kiev and its region the center of the Eastern Church and which, if known at all in the West, must have raised much surprise even there, was an additional reason why the far reaching project of 1396 — exactly two hundred years before the Union of Brest — could not materialize and seems to have been abandoned very soon.

It was completely abandoned in Constantinople where, instead of sending the Patriarch among the Ruthenians for concluding a union with the Catholic Church, new efforts were made to gain unconditional financial assistance from faithfully Orthodox Moscow, [43] while the Emperor himself was preparing for a spectacular journey, but to Western Europe, as far as Paris and London, and without any religious objectives. [44] As far as the papacy was concerned, Manuel II was ready to approach on that occasion both Rome and Avignon — an attitude which could not but discourage

---

[43] *Acta Patriarchatus Constantinopolitani*, II, 359-361 ; see also *Polnoe sobranie russkikh letopisei*, IX (1897), 168.

[44] Particularly well described by G. Schlumberger, " Un Empereur de Byzance à Paris et à Londres, " *Byzance et les Croisades*, Paris, 1927, 87-147.

Boniface IX in his efforts to do something in favor of the Byzantine Empire. [45] But the imperial visitor was well aware that in view of the Western Schism the Holy See was powerless anyway, and the political powers far from making religious reunion a condition of assisting the Greeks.

Eventually it was not the very limited French assistance, [46] but the crushing defeat which in 1402 the Turks suffered from Tamerlane, that saved the Empire of Constantinople for the time being. During the following decade no advantage was taken of the chaotic situation of the Ottoman State with a view of obtaining lasting guarantees of security, and it seemed even less necessary from the Greek point of view to achieve a religious reconciliation with the Latins. Even the election of a pope of Greek origin by the Council of Pisa, in 1409, [47] could hardly impress the Eastern Orthodox Church since that election, of highly doubtful legitimacy, only increased the confusion in the West where now three popes were rivaling with each other.

Poland which so long had been loyal to the Roman popes and had only a limited part in the Council of Pisa [48] was now adopting an attitude of neutrality and was looking forward to another council which would at last put an end to the Western Schism. But Jagello and Vitold, though absorbed by so many political problems, were also aware that such a council, if universally recognized and successful, could at the same time deal with the Eastern Schism, a problem which was so vital for Poland and Lithuania. Before, however, returning to an initiative similar to that of 1396, they wanted to prepare it more carefully and to improve their methods of action. Such an action was not easy to coordinate with the policy of Constantinople as represented by both the Emperor and the Patriarch. [49] Their policy remained largely determined by the Turkish advance which did not yet directly affect either Poland or Lithuania except, to a certain degree, in

---

[45] See in addition to the material in the Vatican Archives which I discussed in " Rome et Byzance au temps du grand schisme d'Occident ", 516-518, the notice of S. C. Estopanan, " Ein Chrysobullos des Kaiser Manuel II Palaiologos für den Gegenpapst Benedikt XIII vom 20 Juni 1402, " *Byzantinische Zeitschrift*, Vol. 44 (1951), 89-93.

[46] G. Schlumberger, " Jean de Châteaumorand et la défense de Constantinople, " *Byzance et les Croisades*, Paris, 1927.

[47] N. Valois, *La France et le Grand Schisme d'Occident*, Vol. IV, Paris, 1902, 105 ff. ; see also L. v. Pastor, *Storia dei Papi*, Vol. I, Rome, 1942 (revised Italian edition by A. Mercati), 199 n. 1.

[48] W. Abraham, *Udział Polski w soborze pizańskim* (Poland's part in the Council of Pisa), Kraków, 1905, 130-143.

[49] O. Halecki, " La Pologne et l'Empire byzantin, " *Byzantion*, VII, (1932), 41-67. That Poland was not yet really threatened by the Ottoman Empire has been stressed by B. Stachoń, *Polityka Polski wobec Turcji i akcji antitureckiej w XV. w.* (Poland's policy towards Turkey and the anti-Turkish action in the XVth century), Lwów, 1931, and J. Skrzypek, *Polityka Jagiełły wobec Turcji* (Jagiello's policy towards Turkey), Kraków 1936.

— 27 —

connection with their Moldavian fief. On the contrary, the Muslim and
Asiatic danger was represented for them by the Tartars who at the time of
Tamerlane had been, though indirectly and involuntarily, the saviors of
the Byzantine Empire, while they had inflicted upon Vitold the defeat on the
Vorskla, in 1399, and even after Tamerlane continued to be a source of
trouble at the border of the Ruthenian lands. Furthermore, that same
border was already threatened by the rival power of Moscow which Constantinople did not want to alienate by any means, especially in the delicate
matter of the appointments to the metropolitan see of Kiev.

Even Cyprian who after 1397 seems to have lost his interest in the idea
of reunion with the Latin Church proved anxious until his death, in 1406,
to maintain friendly relations with both the Polish-Lithuanian State and
Moscow and to be recognized by both powers as pastor of their Orthodox
populations. [50] After his death, the Emperor and the Patriarch of Constantinople decided against the candidate of Vitold, Theodosius, Bishop
(recently made Archbishop) of Polotsk, and appointed instead a native
Greek of the almost symbolic name of Photius who soon proved a partisan
of Moscow and seemed to neglect the interests of the western part of his
metropolitan area which was under Polish-Lithuanian control. [51] It was,
however, not before their victory over the Teutonic Order, in 1410, and
another strengthening of the political union between Poland and Lithuania,
in 1413, that Jagello and Vitold turned again to the problem of the Eastern
Church.

First, they raised once more the issue of a separate metropolitan for
their own Orthodox subjects. Though the question of a metropolitan see
in Halich which had created an additional difficulty during the abortive
negotiations of 1396-97 [52] was not touched this time, even the request for
a metropolitan of Kiev, other than Photius whose authority would have
been restricted to Moscow, seemed unacceptable in Constantinople where
the Emperor's eldest son and heir presumptive, the future John VIII, had
recently married a daughter of Basil I of Moscow, [53] a success which the
latter probably owed to Photius. For Vitold, who was Basil's father-in-law
— hence the grand-father of the princess — but in tense relations with him,
this was one more reason to eliminate the influence of Photius from his own
territory, and the candidate whom he wanted to be made metropolitan of
the Ruthenian dioceses within the limits of Lithuania and Poland, with his
permanent residence in Kiev, was a nephew of the late Cyprian, Gregory
Tsamblak, a prominent theologian, representing the best traditions of Tir-

[50] K. Chodynicki, *op. cit.*, 25 f.
[51] *Ibidem*, 35 (see particularly note 2).
[52] *Ibidem*, 28-33.
[53] O. Halecki, " La Pologne et l'Empire byzantin, " *loc. cit.*

novo. [54] Most probably he also represented the trend toward reunion with the Catholic West, though that question was not raised immediately when Vitold requested his appointment from Patriarch Euthymius II of Constantinople. Even so the Patriarch refused twice, and through his representatives which crossed Lithuanian territory on their way back from a mission to Moscow, tried at least to postpone any decision. Yet, on November 15, 1415, a synod of the Eastern hierarchy of the whole Jagellonian federation, held at Novogrodek, elected Gregory as metropolitan. Photius, of course, excommunicated his opponent, and his sentence was confirmed not only by Patriarch Euthymius, but, when he died the following year, also by his successor, Joseph II. [55]

This was the same patriarch who 22 years later was to come to the Council of Ferrara, and therefore the question arises whether his opposition to the projects of Jagello and Vitold was irreductible. The political relations between them and Emperor Manuel II were, in any case, excellent, and it was precisely in the same year, 1415, that in answer to a Greek embassy they sent grain from their Black Sea ports to Constantinople, again seriously threatened by the Turks. [56] Under the impression of that danger from Mohammed I who since 1412 was the uncontested master of Bayezid's heritage, Manuel II sent twice, in 1415 and in 1416, ambassadors to the Council of Constance, and the representative of Jagello and Vitold, whom they met there as spokesman of religious reunion, was another Greek from Constantinople, the Vicar General of the Dominican missionary society, Theodore. [57] The Chrysoberghes family to which he belonged was prominent among those Greeks who, following the example of Demetrius Cydones and of Manuel Chrysoloras, favored the union with Rome so much that, pending its general acceptance by the Eastern Church, they made their individual conversion to Catholicism, probably keeping their eastern rite.

Before being sent to Constance in the fall of 1415, Theodore Chrysoberghes visited the Dominican monasteries of Poland and Lithuania right at the time of the Synod of Novogrodek, and working for the conversion of the Ruthenians, he probably discussed the possibilities of religious union not only with the rulers of the country but also with the new Metropolitan of Kiev. [58] The union which that Greek envisaged was certainly universal,

[54] See his (Russian) biography by A. I. Yatsimirsky, *Grigoriy Tsamblak*, Petersburg 1904.

[55] Chodynicki, *op. cit.*, 36-41 ; A. A. Ammann, *op. cit.*, 123.

[56] J. Długosz, *Historiae Polonicae libri XIII*, Vol. IV, Cracoviae, 1889, 188.

[57] R. Loenertz, " Les Dominicains byzantins Théodore et André Chrysobergès et les négociations pour l'Union des Eglises grecque et latine de 1415-1430, " *Archivum Fratrum Praedicatorum*, IX (1939), 5-62. The first to discover the role of the Chrysoberghes family in that matter was Cardinal J. Mercati, *Notizie di Procoro e Demetrio Cidone*, Rome, 1931, 100 f., 482 f., 490 f.

[58] Rightly observed by A. A. Ammann, *loc. cit.*, who, however, overstresses the

and when in January 1418 the King of Poland sent to the Council of Constance Gregory Tsamblak himself, at the head of a large delegation from all Ruthenian lands, it was certainly not in opposition to Constantinople. On the contrary, in another letter to the Council which Jagello and Vitold had written a little earlier on August 24, 1417, [59] they clearly expressed the hope that, after the return to the Catholic Church of those eastern schismatics who were under their political control, all Greeks would follow, especially as they themselves had for a long time similar aspirations. In that same letter the two cousins, with a view of facilitating the reception of their Ruthenian subjects into the Catholic Church, requested the Council to permit that this be done without rebaptizing those Ruthenians, a concession which was demanded by the Ruthenian hierarchy in order to remove a serious obstacle to reunion. The problem whether or not the baptism in the Eastern Church, separated from Rome, was to be considered valid, reappeared time and again in the future, and the conciliatory attitude taken and recommended by Jagello and Vitold, probably at the request of Metropolitan Gregory Tsamblak, gives serious evidence of their desire to facilitate the religious union and to prepare it at home before the departure of the metropolitan for Constance.

It was, however, not only that obvious need of careful preparation which delayed his mission. It was clear that before the Council could take up the problem of the Eastern Schism, the Western Schism had to be finally healed. Therefore, Jagello and Vitold were waiting for the election of a universally recognized pope before sending to Constance a Ruthenian delegation in the matter of reunion. That delegation had been preceded by outstanding Catholic representatives from Poland and Lithuania who under the leadership of Nicolaus Trąba, the Archbishop of Gniezno who then was made Primate of Poland, were playing an important part in all activities of the Council. [60] Thanks to them, the Council was fully aware of the role of the Polish-Lithuanian federation at the eastern border of Christendom, and had not only entrusted the conversion of pagan Samogitia — that Lithuanian province which had been freed at last from the Teutonic Order — to the Archbishop of Lwów and to the Bishop of Wilno, but also named Jagello and Vitold general vicars " in rebus temporalibus " for all Ruthenian lands, including even the Republics of Novgorod and Pskov. [61] It was,

---

difference between the intentions of Jagello and Vitold, and those of Theodore and Tsamblak.

[59] J. H. Baxter, *Copiale Prioratus Sancti Andreae*, Oxford, 1930, 38-41.

[60] See the bibliography in the study of St. Belch, " Magistri Pauli Vladimiri ... scriptum denunciatorium ... Concilio Constantiensi datum, " *Sacrum Poloniae Millennium*, Vol. II, Rome, 1955, 165 f., notes 2 and 3, written in preparation of his forthcoming biography of the most prominent member of the Polish delegation, Paulus Vladimiri (Włodkowic) Rector of the University of Cracow.

[61] A. A. Ammann, *op. cit.*, 125, where the sources are quoted.

therefore, no surprise that the Metropolitan of Kiev who arrived with their recommendation and attracted general attention by celebrating mass according to the eastern rite [62] asked at once for an audience in order to submit to the newly elected pope, Martin V, his ideas of religious reunion.

That memorable audience took place on February 24, 1418, one week after Gregory's arrival, and his address, [63] which was translated into Latin by a Czech priest, showed indeed his full readiness for reunion under papal authority. When he expressed the hope that such a reunion would include also the Greeks, he was acting in complete agreement with Jagello's and Vitold's intentions. They had indeed the right to expect that their initiative, concerning primarily the Ruthenians of their own realm, would have the approval of the Emperor of Constantinople whom the Metropolitan of Kiev called a neighbor and relative of the King and of the Grand Duke. For, even before Tsamblak's arrival, the Greek ambassadors, led by Nicolaus Eudemonojoannes, who had been waiting in Constance for the election of a universally recognized pope, had seized the opportunity of the coronation of Martin V to stress in public the Emperor's desire for a union between the Eastern and Western Churches. [64]

There are indications that these Greek representatives, particularly their leader who, before coming to the Council, had offered to Venice the mediation of Byzantium in the conflict of the Republic with Sigismund of Luxemburg, were in contact with the latter at Constance, exactly as the earlier diplomatic agents of Manuel II, Manuel Chrysoloras and his nephew John had been before the Council. [65] And the King of the Romans who, in general, wanted to play a leading part at the Council was always anxious to show his interest in the matter of religious reunion with the Greeks also. But, recalling later the endeavors which had been made at Constance with a view to reunite the Greeks " and the other peoples and churches of the East " with the Church of Rome, Pope Martin V praised the cooperation not only of Sigismund who was present in person, but also of other kings and princes who had sent their representatives. [66] In that connection, it is important to note that Eudemonojoannes was seconded at the papal coronation by Andrew Chrysoberghes who in his speech proved particularly enthusiastic about the prospects of reunion. Andrew, the future bishop of Rhodes,

[62] *Ulrichs von Richental Chronik des Constanzer Conzils* (ed. Buck), Tübingen 1882, 188 ff.; the most interesting pictures are reproduced in the reprint (Müller et Co. Verlag, Potsdam ed. 1924) of the 1483 edition, printed in Augsburg by Anton Sorg.

[63] H. Finke, *Acta Concilii Constanciensis*, II, Münster 1923, 166.

[64] R. Loenertz, *op. cit.*, 30.

[65] *Ibidem*, 11-13; see also Chodynicki, *op. cit.*, 44, who, however, goes too far in considering the influence of Sigismund of Luxemburg on Jagello's projects of reunion with the Greeks. (45 note 1).

[66] *Epistolae pontificiae ad Concilium Florentinum spectantes* (ed. G. Hofmann), I, Romae, 1940, Nr. 11, p. 7 (Martin V to the Archbishop of Cologne, Aug. 21, 1420).

recalled himself at the Council of Basel that at Constance he had translated the long statement — thirty-six articles — in the matter of reunion which the Greek representatives had submitted to the pope in the presence of Sigismund of Luxemburg. [67] But being a brother of Theodore Chrysoberghes, who had been sent to Constance from Poland by King Ladislas Jagello, and cooperating with that brother so closely that both were rewarded by Martin V almost as the same time, shortly before Tsamblak's arrival, for the services rendered to the cause of religious union, [68] Andrew, as well as Theodore, must have been in contact with the Polish delegation also.

That delegation used the Polish and Lithuanian efforts in the matter of the reunion of the Ruthenians, as well as the efforts of Christianizing Samogitia, as an evidence of the services which the Jagellonian federation was ready and in a position to render to the Catholic Church, contrary to the charges and suspicions of the Teutonic Order. The representatives of that Order at Constance, who from the outset, in 1415, had tried to discredit Jagello's and particularly Vitold's announcements in both matters, were the first to point out that Tsamblak's mission had no success and merely ended in " shame for the Poles. " [69] As a matter of fact, it is true that the spectacular audience of the Metropolitan of Kiev seems not to have been followed by any further negotiations with him, and that soon after his return from Constance Tsamblak disappeared, maybe retiring to a Moldavian monastery. [70] The reason of such an apparent failure was, however, neither a request of the Council that the Ruthenians abandon their oriental rite nor their unwillingness to accept any change at all, as stressed in the German sources. A first obstacle was, of course, the lack of time, since the Council after more than three years of strenuous labors was anxious to adjourn. Furthermore, an unexpected disagreement between the Polish delegates and Martin V who refused to condemn as heretical the violently anti-Polish writings of a German Dominican hired by the Teutonic Order spoiled the otherwise excellent impression which the Poles had made at Constance and even led to a regrettable incident at the very end of the Council. [71] Yet, their work in defense of Lithuania against German aggression and in favor of integrating with the Western world the Ruthenians of the whole federa-

[67] *Ibidem*, III, Rome, 1946, 40 ; this important note by G. Hofmann refers to all the earlier discussions of the part played by Andrew Chrysoberghes.

[68] R. Loenertz, *op. cit.*, 32-34, and the bull of Jan. 26, 1418, published in the Appendix on p. 61.

[69] *Scriptores rerum Prussicarum*, III, 376 ; see Loenertz, *op. cit.*, 21 (where an unpublished letter of Oct. 25, 1415, is used), 40.

[70] This is the hypothesis of Yatsimirsky (see above, note 54) ; see also Chodynicki, 47 note 4.

[71] A. A. Ammann, *op. cit.*, 126.

tion, though unfinished, was a promising basis for further developments which were to affect the destinies of the Union of Florence. [72]

That union itself, viz., the agreement between Rome and Constantinople, can also be traced back to the last months of the Council of Constance. There was no time for completing the negotiations with the Greek representatives who were disappointed in their hopes to get at once actual assistance against the Turks, or at least a promise that an oecumenical council would be convoked, as always requested by the Greek side as prerequisite condition for reunion. They only received on April 6, 1418, a bull of Martin V [73] who at the request of Emperor Manuel II permitted his sons to marry Catholic princesses, and most probably also granted indulgences to all those who would defend the Hexamilion — the wall erected by the Emperor in protection of the Peloponnesus — against Ottoman onslaughts. [74] At the same time just before the end of the Council, the Pope wrote to Manuel II, to his son and heir presumptive John VIII and Patriarch Joseph II, inviting them to a religious union, [75] but the project of sending to Greece as papal legate the Cardinal John Dominici of Ragusa, which was considered as early as February 1, 1418, did not materialize. [76] When the cardinal died on June 20, 1419, the project was not yet given up, but the replies which Martin V received from Constantinople at the beginning of the year and which insisted upon the convocation of a universal council in that city [77] had already changed the situation. These replies clearly proved the necessity of further negotiations before the union between the Western and the Eastern Churches could be concluded at a new, truly oecumenical council. And since the Metropolitan of Kiev, favorable to the union, had also requested that it be concluded in the regular, traditional way, i. e., by the convocation of a council where qualified experts from both sides would explore the differences which separated them, [78] it could be expected that just like at Constance representatives of the Ruthenians would participate in these negotiations.

[72] See the comments by R. Loenertz, *op. cit.*, 41, on that " réalité nouvelle " and the vain (" impuissante ") opposition of the Teutonic Knights.
[73] *Epistolae pontificiae ad Concilium Florentinum spectantes*, I, N. 2.
[74] *Ibidem*, N. 3-4.
[75] *Ibidem*, N. 3-4, 5.
[76] *Ibidem*, N. 1.
[77] *Ibidem*, N. 6, 7 ; see R. Loenertz, *op. cit.*, 42 f.
[78] H. Finke, *Acta Concilii Constanciensis*, II, 166.

PART I

THE UNION OF FLORENCE AND ITS AFTERMATH AMONG THE RUTHENIANS

CHAPTER I

THE ORIGIN OF THE UNION OF FLORENCE AND THE RUTHENIAN PROBLEM

From the point of view of the Holy See, the oecumenical council which the Greeks joined at Ferrara, in February 1438, and which resulted in the Union of Florence of July 6, 1439, was a continuation of the Council which had started at Basel on July 23, 1431, but had been transferred to Italy by Pope Eugene IV on September 18, 1437[1]   But even independently of that legal interpretation, no aspect of the Union of Florence can be properly understood without going back to the discussions with the Greek representatives who as early as 1434 came to Basel.   This is particularly true with regard to the attitude of the Ruthenian Church towards the project of reunion with Rome.   For, at the same time when the famous Greek Isidore, who was to attend the Council of Ferrara and Florence as Metropolitan of Kiev, appeared at Basel as one of the Greek delegates, his predecessor in Kiev was planning to come to that same place in connection with one more project of religious union which then was considered in the Grand Duchy of Lithuania.   The very failure of that project explains to a large extent the absence in Ferrara and Florence of any representatives from the Ruthenian lands of Lithuania and Poland.

But the study of the immediate origin of the Union of Florence cannot be limited to the early phase of the Council of Basel, when that assembly, in spite of its recurrent conflicts with Eugene IV, was still the only council of these years, representing the Catholic Church as a whole.   An important Greek delegation arrived there because such a meeting between the representatives of Western and Eastern Christendom had been contemplated and

---

[1] For the general background see N. Valois, *La crise religieuse du XVe siècle. Le Pape et le concile*, 2 vol., Paris, 1909.

3

prepared in the negotiations between Rome and Constantinople which immediately followed the Council of Constance.

These negotiations were first conducted through an exchange of letters between the Emperor and the Patriarch of Constantinople on one side and Pope Martin V on the other. The latter hesitated at first to accept the Greek condition regarding the convocation of a new council where both sides would be duly represented, and it was only in March 1420, writing for the third time to Manuel II and Patriarch Joseph II that he agreed to the holding of such a council in Constantinople and instructed Cardinal Peter Fonseca to go there as papal legate. [2]

That decision was taken under the impression of another Greek mission to the Holy See : Nicholas Eudemonojoannes and Theodore Chrysoberghes, both well known to Martin V since their participation in the Council of Constance, now had brought him new letters from Constantinople and promised in advance that at the planned council in the East the union would be concluded " simpliciter secundum Romanam ecclesiam. " [3] Whether at the given moment the Emperor was really ready for such an agreement, is rather doubtful. But it is certain that he had entrusted to Eudemonojoannes also a political mission, since on his way to the papal Curia the ambassador stopped in Venice to offer once more a Greek mediation in the conflict with Sigismund of Luxemburg to whom another Greek envoy, present at the discussions with the Venetian Senate, was sent soon after. [4] This was Manuel Philanthropenos, possibly also a former imperial representative at Constance, [5] who now proceeded from Sigismund's court to that of Jagello and Vitold. Through Poland where he appeared in August 1420, he came to Novogrodek in Lithuania and met there not only the Grand Duke but also that same Metropolitan Photius who five years before had been deposed by a synod in that very city but now was recognized again in the Ruthenian lands of Lithuania and Poland. [6] It, therefore, seems obvious that the mission of Philanthropenos, exactly as that of Eudemonojoannes, had both a political and a religious purpose, an interpretation which is confirmed by the letter which the King of Poland sent to Manuel II in the summer of 1420 [7] expressing his pleasure that the Emperor favored the union of the Churches. It remains, however, very doubtful, whether there was any chance, or even any serious attempt, to gain for the idea of religious reunion the successful

---

[2] *Epistolae pontificiae ad Concilium Florentinum spectantes*, I, Nr. 8-10.

[3] See R. Loenertz, " Les Dominicains byzantins ... " (as quoted above in note 57 to the Introduction), 43, 46.

[4] N. Iorga, *Notes et extraits pour servir à l'histoire des croisades au XVe siècle*, Vol. I, Paris, 1899, 300.

[5] See O. Halecki, " La Pologne et l'Empire byzantin, " 49, and Loenertz, *op. cit.*, 28, n. 79.

[6] Halecki, *op. cit.*, 55 ; Chodynicki, *Kościół prawosławny*, 48, n. 1.

[7] *Codex epistolaris Vitoldi* (ed. A. Prochaska), Kraków, 1882, Nr. 985.

rival of Gregory Tsamblak : until his death in 1431, Photius identified himself with the policies of Moscow where Vitold's political influence was growing before and after the death of Basil I, in 1425, but not the slightest inclination toward Rome could possibly be discovered. [8]

Yet, the very fact that Manuel II conducted parallel negotiations with Rome and the western powers on the one hand and with the Jagellonian monarchy and its Orthodox hierarchy on the other hand, [9] gives clear evidence that he was fully aware of the role which Poland and Lithuania including the Ruthenian lands could play in both matters which he was discussing with the Holy See : religious reunion and defense against the Turks. It is true that the direct relations between Martin V and the Polish-Lithuanian State [10] concerned then and in the following years entirely different problems : the Teutonic Order and the Hussite wars, i. e., those northern and western troubles of the " Christian Republic " which Martin V himself so clearly distinguished from the eastern when writing to Manuel II. [11] Nevertheless, even in Western Europe the attitude of Jagello and Vitold was considered in connection with the various aspects of the Greek problems also. Soon after the Treaty of Troyes of 1420, which was supposed to prepare a dynastic union between France and England, both kings decided to send a joint ambassador to Eastern Europe, the famous Burgundian knight Gilbert de Lannoy who had visited Poland and Lithuania as early as 1414. [12] Now, in 1421, the ultimate goal of his mission was Constantinople where he had to assure Emperor Manuel II that both Charles VI of France and Henry V of England " had the desire to promote the union between the Roman and the Greek Churches. " [13] But choosing the rather unusual way through Polish and Lithuanian territory, the ambassador, before reaching Constantinople, visited once more, this time officially, Jagello and Vitold with the obvious purpose to gather information on the whole situation in the East, which would help him to accomplish his mission.

That mission did not prove successful, though Gilbert de Lannoy met at the imperial court an envoy of Martin V. This was not Cardinal Fonseca whose legation had been first delayed by financial difficulties [14] and then given up in view of the obvious impossibility of holding a council in Constantinople under the growing threat of Turkish aggression. For that very

---

[8] For the ecclesiastical situation in Moscow see E. Golubinsky, *Istoria russkoi tserkvi* (History of the Russian Church), vol. II-1, Moscow, 1907, 387 f.

[9] See Loenertz, *op. cit.*, 44.

[10] Described in detail by H. Bellée, *Polen und die römische Kurie in den Jahren 1414-1424*, Berlin, 1914.

[11] *Epistolae pontificiae*, I, Nr. 17, p. 12.

[12] O. Halecki, " Gilbert de Lannoy and his Discovery of East Central Europe, " *Bulletin of the Polish Institute of Arts and Sciences in America*, II (1944).

[13] Ch. Potvin, *Oeuvres de Ghillebert de Lannoy*, Louvain, 1878, 67.

[14] *Epistolae pontificiae*, I, Nr. 11-14 ; see Loenertz, *op. cit.* 45 notes 27, 28.

reason the Franciscan Anthony de Massa who finally was sent from Rome to Constantinople in June 1422, [15] could not persuade the Emperor to conclude any religious union. [16]   On the contrary, Manuel II declared that the promises made by his envoys two years earlier went beyond their instructions, and being disappointed that in spite of the papal appeals and promises he did not receive any real help from the Catholic West, he did not even permit the Anglo-French ambassador to participate in the war against the Turks. [17]   After succeeding in defending Constantinople without any foreign assistance against the Ottoman onslaught in August, [18] the Emperor became even less interested in the negotiations in religious matters, though the Pope sent him another message at the end of the same year. [19]   And when a little later, in 1423-24, Manuel's son and co-emperor, John VIII, went in person to the West in order to secure some effective cooperation, he disregarded the invitation which he probably received from the Council of Siena [20] and visited only Venice and Buda, the capitals of the nearest powers which seemed to be directly interested in the military action against Murad II. But the persistent hostility between the Venetians and Sigismund of Luxemburg, as well as the Hussite wars which prevented the latter from concentrating his forces in the direction of the Balkans, made the whole journey practically useless. [21]   The old emperor felt obliged to appease the Turks and gave evasive answers to another papal proposal regarding reunion and close cooperation. [22]   The plan of convoking an oecumenical council with Greek participation was, however, reconsidered by both sides as early as 1425, and it is highly improbable [23] that Manuel, before dying on July 21 of that year, warned his son never to treat the problem of religious union with the Latins seriously.

As a matter of fact, negotiations in that matter were soon resumed when John VIII became sole emperor.   The new mission [24] which in reply to his proposals Martin V, in June 1426, sent to him and to Patriarch Joseph

---

[15] *Ibidem*, Nr. 15 (where the other sources concerning his mission and his report submitted to the Council of Siena, are quoted), 16.

[16] *Ibidem*, Nr. 17 ; in this letter sent to Manuel II on Oct. 8, 1422, the pope described all his efforts to secure help against the Turks and renewed his appeal to religious union.

[17] Concilium Florentinum A III/3, *Orientalia documenta minora* (ed. G. Hofmann), Nr. 1 ; Ch. Potvin, *loc. cit.*

[18] About the sources regarding the siege of Constantinople in 1422, see L. Bréhier, *Vie et mort de Byzance*, Paris, 1944, 483.

[19] *Epistolae pontificiae*, I, Nr. 18, 19 (Nov. 6, 1422).

[20] This important trip has not yet been studied in detail, though many sources have been indicated by N. Iorga, *Notes et extraits* (see above, note 4).

[21] Loenertz, *op. cit.*, 49, note 45.

[22] See R. Guilland in *Histoire générale* (ed. G. Glotz), IX/1, 356f.

[23] As pointed out by Loenertz, *op. cit.*, 19, note 54.

[24] *Epistolae pontificiae*, I, Nr. 23-25 ; see Loenertz, *op. cit.*, 51-56, who also discusses briefly, 57-58, Andrew's subsequent mission to Poland.

II, was headed by the Greek Dominican Andrew Chrysoberghes of Constantinople, now Vicar General of the missionary society of his Order after his brother Theodore with whom he had cooperated at the Council of Constance, when Theodore was sent there by the King of Poland and the Grand Duke of Lithuania, in preparation of Tsamblak's mission. It is, therefore, highly significant that before Andrew's discussions in his place of origin led to any concrete result and before the idea of another universal council materialized, the prominent Dominican of Greek origin participated as papal legate in a congress of political character which was held in the Polish-Lithuanian realm and had on its comprehensive agenda the problem of religious union also.

That congress which Vitold, in January 1429, received in his Volhynian city of Lutsk, in the presence of Jagello, was attended in person by Sigismund of Luxemburg, King of the Romans, of Hungary, and of Bohemia, while the Greek Emperor, King Eric of Denmark who was at the same time King of Norway and Sweden, the Teutonic Order, Basil II of Moscow, Vitold's grandson, along with other Russian princes and Tartar Khans, and the prince of Moldavia, all had representatives at that unusual meeting. [25] Even an English ambassador was sent to the King of Poland and to the Teutonic Order about the same time, [26] though the congress was dealing primarily with problems of Central and Eastern Europe.

These problems were then numerous and complex enough to absorb the attention of the delegates, and though the growing Ottoman pressure which in the following year was to lead to the fall of Tessalonika, then held by the Venetians, [27] seemed to interest Latins and Greeks alike and to recommend their political and religious union, the Hussite question, that painful division in the Latin world, continued to be of more direct concern to Sigismund of Luxemburg. Unable to solve that question himself, he came to distant Lutsk with a view of preventing any intervention in that matter by the Polish-Lithuanian federation, then at the height of its power. The moderate wing of the Hussites had always been looking for a peaceful settlement through Polish and Lithuanian assistance [28] and after the failure of so many anti-Hussite crusades under German leadership the Pope himself was turning towards the King of Poland and his cousin. Though they opposed the penetration of Hussite doctrines into their domains, contacts had been established by the revolted Czechs with the Ruthenians of Poland and

---

[25] The sources concerning the Congress of Lutsk are discussed by A. Prochaska, *Król Władysław Jagiełło*, Kraków, 1908, vol. II, appendix I : as to the general background see L. Kolankowski, *Dzieje W. Ks. Litewskiego za Jagiellonów* (History of the Grand Duchy of Lithuania under the Jagellonians), Warszawa, 1930, I, 153-155.

[26] British Museum, Ms. *Nero* B II, fol. 78.

[27] See L. Bréhier, *op. cit.*, 487.

[28] See F. G. Heymann, *John Žižka and the Hussite Revolution*, Princeton 1955, 116, 269 ff., 319 ff.

Lithuania [29] who all belonged to the Eastern Church and therefore enjoyed the privileges in rite and discipline which the Hussites were claiming, particularly communion under both species by the laity and the use of the Slavic tongue in liturgy.

It was in that connection that Sigismund of Luxemburg, when the relations with the Greek Orthodox were discussed, apparently made a cynical remark about " the beards and wives of their clergymen. " [30] He wanted to discourage any serious consideration at Lutsk of either the Hussite or the Greek problem, since in the given situation the role of the hosts of the congress, his political rivals, would have been prominent if not decisive in both matters. And since he did not succeed in creating trouble for them in connection with the role of the Teutonic Order and with a suggested partition of Moldavia, [31] Sigismund decided to divide the Poles and the Lithuanians. His proposal to grant a royal crown to Vitold in order to make him independent from Poland and closely associated with the Holy Roman Empire, resulted indeed in confusion and suspicion. The congress of Lutsk had to be adjourned without any decisions taken, and among others, an opportunity to advance the cause of union between Western and Eastern Christendom, with Poland and Lithuania acting as intermediaries as it had been planned in 1396 and during the Council of Constance, was again completely lost.

On the contrary, the Polish-Lithuanian conflict which had been provoked by Sigismund's interference, turned soon after Vitold's death, in 1430, into a long civil war within the limits of the Jagellonian federation, its Ruthenian Greek Orthodox provinces being one of the objects of controversy and practically the main battlefield. [32] And through a strange coincidence, in 1431, when the actual fighting started, a parallel civil war began in Moscow [33] where Metropolitan Photius died and Basil II lost his main supporter against the opposition of his uncle and cousins. Therefore, the Greek Orthodox Eastern Slavs, whether the Ruthenians of Poland and Lithuania or the Great Russian Muscovites, were torn by their own political problems at the very moment when the chances for negotiations between Rome and Constantinople considerably improved. For already in 1430 an agreement between Martin V and the Greeks in the matter of a meeting somewhere in Italy with the participation of the Emperor and all Eastern patriarchs, had been drafted not without the cooperation of Andrew Chrysoberghes who in the meantime had returned from Poland, [34] and the new Council which in 1431 gathered

---

[29] A. V. Florovsky, *Čekhi i vostočnye Slavyane* (The Czechs and the Eastern Slavs), Praha 1935, 300-305 (about one of the Ostrogskis), 300 ff.

[30] J. Dlugosz, *Hist. Pol.*, IV, 368.

[31] *Ibidem*, 367.

[32] The most detailed account remains A. Lewicki, *Powstanie Świdrygielly* (The insurrection of S.), Kraków 1892.

[33] Best described by A. A. Presniakov, *Obrazovanie velikorusskago gosudarstva* (The formation of the Great Russian State), Petrograd 1918, 376-394.

in Basel, was expected to be joined by the Greeks and to see the union concluded.

One of the reasons which from the outset led to repeated conflicts between that council and the new pope, Eugene IV, was the question whether the Greeks should be invited to come to the very city of Basel or whether the council should be transferred to a place more convenient for the eastern guests, that is to a city of Italy,[35] since the project of holding a council in Constantinople was hardly realistic. However, both sides were in full agreement as to the urgency of ending the eastern schism, and even in rivalry with each other as to which side would more successfully negotiate with the Greeks. And both sides, too, were fully aware how desirable it was that the Greeks, when concluding the union with Rome, be followed by all eastern Orthodox peoples who recognized the Patriarch of Constantinople as their religious leader, in the first place by the Ruthenians who were under a Catholic government. When, therefore, as early as October 1431 the Council of Basel, through its envoy, requested Eugene IV to write to the Greek Emperor inviting him to send representatives to the council for negotiations in matter of reunion, the request was added that the Pope should write also to the King of Poland and to the Grand Duke of Lithuania, advising them to work for the reunion of the Ruthenians and to get in touch with the Council in that matter.[36] Since the Emperor and the Patriarch were really decided to enter into such negotiations, one of the reasons why after the death of Photius they chose as metropolitan of Kiev and all Russia not Moscow's candidate, Bishop Iona of Riazan, but the candidate of Lithuania, Bishop Harasim of Smolensk,[37] was certainly the opinion that the latter, much more than the former, would be inclined to participate in these negotiations with the Latins.

That opinion proved entirely correct, but unfortunately the Grand Duke of Lithuania, Vitold's successor Svidrigello who had recommended Harasim, though a brother of King Ladislas Jagello who approved his election, was already in war with the Poles in connection with the interpretation of the union charters — the question raised at the congress of Lutsk — and with territorial disputes. He had even allied himself with the Teutonic Order, and since the truce concluded with him on September 1, 1431, proved of no avail, the Poles exactly one year later opposed to Svidrigello another Grand Duke, Vitold's brother Sigismund.[38] The civil war now changed from a Polish-Lithuanian struggle into an internal

---

[34] *Epistolae pontificiae*, I, Nr. 26; see Loenertz, *op. cit.*, 58-60.

[35] *Ibidem*, Nr. 29-31 (bulls of Nov. 12 and Dec. 18, 1431, regarding the transfer of the Council from Basel to Bologna).

[36] *Concilium Basiliense* (ed. J. Haller), Vol. II, Basel 1897, 550 (appendix Nr. 1).

[37] Chodynicki, *op. cit.*, 49, n. 1.

[38] See his (Ukrainian) biography by B. Barvinsky, *Zygimont Keistutovych*, Zovkva, 1905.

conflict in the Grand Duchy, and since, in general, Lithuania proper with its predominantly Catholic population sided with Sigismund, while Svidrigello was supported by the autonomous Ruthenian lands of Orthodox faith, their rivalry has been frequently considered a religious conflict. Yet Svidrigello was himself a Catholic, baptized together with Jagello, in 1386, under the name of Boleslas, and along with his partisans who included Catholics also, he brought his claims before the Pope and the Council, exactly as did Sigismund and his Polish patrons. Therefore, in March 1433, a meeting of Svidrigello's supporters held in Vitebsk, one of the main cities of White Ruthenia, addressed a message to the Council of Basel, refuting the charges that the Grand Duke had deserted the Catholic Church, and declaring that they all desired a religious union with the Latins. [39] Furthermore, Svidrigello, after sending an embassy to Basel where the Vitebsk document bearing the seals of his partisans was formally submitted on June 16, 1433, [40] along with a letter of his ally, the Grand Master of the Teutonic Order, and after realizing the strong Polish influence at the Council, decided to send another embassy directly to the Pope. Welcoming this initiative, Eugene IV, then in Florence, granted on October 20 a safe-conduct to the envoys of " Boleslaus, " Grand Duke of Lithuania, who were expected to arrive " in important matters regarding our Christian faith and the Roman Church. " That these words referred as usually on similar occasions to negotiations in view of religious reunion, is best evidenced by the fact that on the same day Eugene IV gave a safe-conduct also to " the metropolitan of the Ruthenians " and to his companions up to the number of forty. [41]

Instead, however, of coming to the papal Curia together with Svidrigello's envoys, Harasim in July of the following year, 1435, perished in Smolensk where he was burned at the stake on Svidrigello's order. In spite of the form of his punishment, usually applied to heretics, there could not possibly be any religious reason for his trial and execution. Neither could he be considered a martyr of the cause of reunion, since the Grand Duke himself favored and even needed such a union ; nor could he be punished for any opposition against reunion, since he was ready to go to Italy, and even if at the last minute he had changed his mind, Svidrigello could not kill the Metropolitan for that reason without alienating the Orthodox majority of his supporters. There is, on the contrary, ample evidence that the Grand Duke's wrath was provoked by the suspicion, justified or not, that Harasim was involved in the plots against Svidrigello which even in the Ruthenian lands, not only in Smolensk but also in Kiev, manifested themselves in the fall of 1434 and in the spring of 1435, among many of his supporters who

---

[39] *Veterum Scriptorum arrplissima collectio* (ed. E. Martène and U. Durand), Vol. VIII, Paris 1733, 575.
[40] *Concilium Basiliense*, II, 430 f.
[41] *Epistolae Pontificiae*, I, Nr. 44.

now decided to pass over to his rival Sigismund. [42]   For that rival Grand Duke had been wise enough to issue a charter on May 6, 1434, [43] which confirming most of the rights granted, in 1387 and 1413, to the Catholics of Lithuania proper, not only enlarged those rights but also extended them without any religious discrimination to the autonomous Ruthenian lands of the Grand Duchy.   However, though Svidrigello was losing now more and more of his partisans and suffered a crushing defeat on September 1, 1435, soon after Harasim's death, his resistance continued in some border regions, and the situation remained confused when a new metropolitan of Kiev had to be chosen.   Yet Constantinople rejected once more the Muscovite candidate, Iona, recommended by Basil II whose position in the Great Russian civil war had improved and who apparently had never recognized Harasim. The successor of Svidrigello's victim was a Greek, the abbot of St. Demetrius in Constantinople, Isidore. [44]

The new metropolitan of Kiev and all Russia was already well known not only as a distinguished humanist but also a sincere promotor of religious reunion with the Latins, having played a leading role among the Greek delegates who in July 1434 arrived at the Council of Basel.   Furthermore, when he replied there to the speech of welcome of Cardinal Cesarini, then President of the Council, Isidore, emphasizing both the favorable prospects of reunion and its importance, he pointed out that the jurisdiction of the Patriarch of Constantinople extended, among others, over the immense territory of Russia as far as the " hyperborean " mountains. [45]   He must have, therefore, been interested in Russia already before his nomination as metropolitan and convinced of the importance of Russia's participation in the reconciliation between Rome and Constantinople.   When he left the imperial city for his new field of activities early in 1437, everybody seemed to be certain that along with the Emperor and the Patriarch, all countries which were obedient to the Greek Church would send ambassadors to the Council : [46] not only the Asiatic lands of Trebizond and Georgia, and the Balkan countries of Serbia and Wallachia, but also far away Russia.

The name " Russia, " in Greek Ῥωσία, covered, as usual, both the original Kievan Rus, now connected with the Polish-Lithuanian federation, and the new, colonial, northeastern Russia, which the Greeks sometimes called Great Russia (Μεγάλη Ῥωσία) in contradistinction to the Little Russia

---

[42] The political background of these events is explained by Kolankowski, *op. cit.*, 202-205.

[43] *Codex epistolaris saeculi XV* (ed. A. Lewicki), Vol. III, Cracoviae, 1894, Appendix, Nr. 22.

[44] There does not exist any exhaustive biography of Isidore ; rich in information is G. Mercati, *Scritti d'Isidoro il Cardinale Ruteno*, Roma, 1926.

[45] *Concilium Basiliense*, Vol. III, Basel 1900, 148, 151 f. ; Vol. V, Basel 1904, 97.

[46] *Ibidem*, Vol. I, Basel 1896, 377 (in the report of John of Ragusa, sent to Basel from Constantinople on February 13, 1437).

(Μικρὰ 'Ρωσία) of the southwest, and which, though not yet completely united under Moscow's domination, was largely under its influence. [47] Men of Isidore's experience must have been aware that the chances for religious union with Rome were much better in the former area which was under Catholic rulers and where such trends had so clearly appeared in a recent past, particularly during the Council of Constance. Nevertheless, the new metropolitan, without stopping at all in that much nearer part of his domain, went directly to Moscow. [48] It is, however, understandable that after Harasim's tragic experience he did not want to go to Kiev, the old metropolitan see, which still was in Svidrigello's hands, nor take sides in the continuing struggle between the two Lithuanian Grand Dukes of whom Sigismund, busy with eliminating his rival, showed no interest in the problem of religious union. Comparatively small were the Ruthenian provinces of Poland where Jagello had died in 1434, while his son and successor, Ladislas III, was a minor and the problem of regency highly controversial. Under such conditions it could seem advisable to start the preparatory work for the East Slavic participation in the Council precisely in Moscow where it was most difficult, but where for that very reason a success would be most important and decisive. And after a few months which he spent in the capital of Basil II, it could seem indeed to the enthusiastic and optimistic Greek that he had gained such a success.

After lengthy discussions with the Grand Duke and his clergy, which unfortunately have been recorded exclusively by the Russian chroniclers, [49] the metropolitan received the desired permission to go to the council where the Greeks and Latins would meet. But that permission to represent the Russian Church was granted reluctantly, since Basil II recalled to Isidore that according to the traditional doctrine, as interpreted in Moscow, only the seven oecumenical councils which had been held in the East were legitimate and any eighth council would be inadmissible. Furthermore, the metropolitan had to swear not to agree to any change nor to bring back to Moscow any innovation. Even if such a condition was accepted by Isidore, its interpretation was necessarily controversial, since it depended on the question whether the Latin West had really changed the original authentical doctrine of the Church through innovations, which the East was now supposed to

---

[47] These problems of terminology, as far as they are connected with the structure of the Grand Duchy of Lithuania, have been discussed by O. Halecki, *Litwa, Ruś i Żmudź jako części składowe W. Ks. Lit.* (Lithuania, Rus and Samogitia as constituent parts of the Grand Duchy of Lith.), Kraków, 1916, 219-223.

[48] See A. Lewicki, *Unia florencka w Polsce* (The Union of Florence in Poland), Kraków, 1899, a posthumously published, unfinished study which in spite of some controversial interpretations of this (see p. 216) and a few other points remains of basic importance.)

[49] Among the many accounts based on these sources, that of P. Pierling, *La Russie et le Saint Siège*, I, 16 ff. is the most vivid; see the Russian interpretation by E. Golubinsky, *Istoria russkoi tserkvi*, II, 414-440.

admit. And it is obvious that Isidore, even before participating in the discussions at Ferrara and Florence, had in that respect views entirely different from those of the Russians who in a fairly large number, over two hundred, decided to accompany him. In addition to those, including the bishop of Suzdal Avraam, who did it on Basil's order, the delegation was joined also by a representative of the Grand Duke of Tver who formally was still independent of Moscow and even used to look, as his predecessors, for Lithuanian support, but in religious matters seemed to agree with the Muscovite center of Great Russia.

When leaving Moscow with these companions and a few Greeks, including his faithful collaborator, Gregory, who was later to be his successor, Isidore still believed that the council where he would meet the other representatives of the East would continue to work at Basel. It was only on his way that he was informed of the transfer of the council by Eugene IV to Ferrara and of the final decision of the Greeks to embark on the papal galleys and to negotiate with the Pope in that Italian city, much more convenient for them, rather than to join the opposition which remained at Basel. [50] But whichever city was the goal, the shortest and most direct way from Moscow would lead, of course, through Lithuania and Poland, and the Metropolitan was anxious to get on that occasion in touch with the clergy and the people of the Ruthenian lands, as well as with their Catholic rulers. Such a contact which he had not established on his way to Moscow, would have been highly desirable, because it would have enabled Isidore to get a formal mandate from the western part of his metropolitan realm also. It would have been much easier there than in Moscow to secure an approval of his projects regarding reunion, as well as to gather prominent representatives of these lands, which would have accompanied him on his further journey along with those he brought from Moscow and from Tver. The Metropolitan must have perfectly realized all this, because he tried to travel directly by land and asked Sigismund, Grand Duke of Lithuania, for a safe-conduct. Unfortunately, as he wrote from Riga to Basel after a delay of several months, on March 20, 1438, [51] Sigismund refused his request and prohibited him from travelling through Lithuanian territory. He could, therefore, not reach the Polish territory either, and had to ask instead for safe-conducts from the Landmaster of Livonia and his superior, the Grand Master of the Teutonic Order in Prussia, both for himself and his party of two hundred men " or a little more, " feeling obliged to make a long detour and to travel from Riga to Lübeck by sea.

---

[50] On the reasons for the choice of the Greeks see D. J. Geanakoplos, " The Council of Florence, " *Church History*, XXIV (1955), particularly note 40.

[51] The text of this letter, preserved in a contemporary copy in the Archives nationales in Paris K 1711, fol. 414 a, is discussed by O. Halecki, " W drodze na sobór florencki " (On the way to the Council of Florence), *Oriens*, VII (1939), 66-70.

Sigismund's opposition was obviously dictated by political motives. Victorious in the civil war, but as suspicious of any possible opposition as his defeated rival who had not yet lost all his partisans especially among the Ruthenians, the new Grand Duke who really was to be killed two years later by dissatisfied members of the Lithuanian and Ruthenian aristocracy, was doubtful what attitude the metropolitan would take and whether he would not get involved in these controversies exactly as his predecessor Harasim had been. And though Sigismund's party in Lithuania was rather on Basil's side in the Muscovite civil war, he was not too anxious to give to the numerous guests from Moscow an opportunity to observe his own still precarious position in the Grand Duchy.

On the other hand, the well known sympathy of Sigismund and of the Catholic hierarchy of Lithuania with the Council of Basel in opposition to Eugene IV, similar to the attitude of State and Church in Poland, could not have anything to do with the difficulties made to the metropolitan. For, at the critical moment and even after the Grand Duke's refusal, Isidore was still planning to go to Basel where his letter of March 20 was sent and read on May 16, after a letter of the Teutonic Grand Master, another supporter of the Council, dated March 4. [52] It was not before reaching Lübeck that he heard from the local bishop to whom the Council of Basel had recommended the Metropolitan but who himself passed to the papal side, about the momentous developments of the preceding months : the formal transfer of the Council by Eugene IV from Basel to Ferrara, on September 18, 1437, and the arrival of the Greeks in that latter city, on February 26, 1438, when Isidore was still in faraway Riga.

It is, of course, easy to understand that after getting such information, he did not hesitate to follow the example of his countrymen, including the Emperor and the Patriarch, whom he was supposed and desired to join as soon as possible. He must have also heard that the most prominent members of the Council followed the papal orders, among them that same Cardinal Cesarini who as President of the Council had welcomed him at Basel four years before, when Isidore was still one of the Greek delegates. The attitude of those whom he represented now could not influence the choice of the Metropolitan. Moscow was hardly informed and not interested in the internal disputes among the Latins, and with the Ruthenians of Lithuania and Poland nor with their Catholic fellow-citizens and rulers no contact had been established. Isidore could not possibly know in advance that he would not find in Italy any delegates from the Jagellonian States, who would have facilitated the negotiations in the matter of religious reunion as they had done at the time of the mission of Metropolitan Gregory Tsamblak to the Council of Constance. But it was to prove one more obstacle to that

---

[52] *Concilium Basiliense*, V, 147, 162.

cause that the Catholic elements in the part of Isidore's sphere of action where the prospects of reunion were so much better than in Moscow, were to have no share in the work of Ferrara and Florence, deciding for official neutrality in the open conflict between Eugene IV and those who remained in Basel, and being in genuine sympathy with the latter [53].

[53] On the many controversial problems concerning Isidor's journey to the Council, see in addition to Lewicki *op. cit.*, 220-224, also P. Karge in *Altpreussische Monatschrift*, vol. 31 (particularly annex II) and Ad. Ziegler, *Die Union des Konzils von Florenz in der russischen Kirche*, Würzburg 1938, 81-84.

CHAPTER II

THE ATTITUDE OF POLAND, LITHUANIA, AND MOSCOW TOWARDS THE COUNCIL OF FLORENCE

After almost exactly one hundred years of inconclusive negotiations[1] the Union between the Western and the Eastern Churches was at last proclaimed on July 6, 1439, in Florence where the oecumenical council had been transferred from Ferrara. This was one hundred and sixty-five years — even to the day — after the similar union which had been concluded at the second Council of Lyons. One of the weaknesses of that earlier union had been the lack of preparation through thorough theological discussions such as those which were conducted for many months in Ferrara and Florence.[2] Another reason of the failure of the Union of Lyons was the fact that the agreement with the Holy See did not bring to Emperor Michael Palaeologus who made it for exclusively political motives, the expected advantages in his relations with the Catholic powers none of which was represented at the Council of 1274. Furthermore, the break between Rome and Constantinople which followed only a few years later, completely destroyed the Union of Lyons, since it had been concluded with Greek representatives only and never accepted in any of the other Orthodox countries, the wide regions of the various Russias having in particular remained completely untouched by the agreement.[3]

With regard to the representation of Catholic powers the situation was hardly better at the Council of Ferrara-Florence and their absence even more disappointing for the Greeks who this time were in such an urgent need of help against the onslaught of the Ottoman Turks which could not be foreseen in 1274. As a matter of fact, in spite of the appeals of Eugene IV[4] only one Western ruler took through his envoys an active part in the

---

[1] They can be traced back to the mission to Avignon of Barlaam of Calabria, in 1339; see, for ex., D. J. Geanakoplos, " The Council of Florence, " *Church History*, XXIV (1955), note 25.

[2] An excellent survey of these discussions has been given by G. Hofmann in *Orientalia Christiana Periodica*, III (1937) 110-140, 403-455, and IV (1938), 157-188, 372-422.

[3] See above, Introduction, p. 20.

[4] *Epistolae Pontificiae*, I, Nr. 91-94, 98, 99, 111; II, Nr. 115, 123, 134.

Council which had been moved from Basel to Italy. This was the Duke of Burgundy, Philip the Good, whose two representatives signed the Union bull immediately after the Cardinals and Western Patriarchs, [5] and who received a special copy of that memorable document and later an additional papal notification. [6] It is true that Burgundy, though a minor and distant power, used to show a special and active interest in the defense of Eastern Christendom against the Turks, as evidenced before the Union in the crusade of Nicopolis and soon after the Union in the crusade of Varna, in both of which Burgundian forces participated. Nevertheless, the cooperation of Philip's delegates could not be a compensation for the restrained attitude of so many other, more powerful and geographically closer monarchs who, in spite of the rise of papal prestige through the arrival of the Greek delegation headed by the Emperor himself, persisted in their attitude of neutrality in the growing conflict between Eugene IV and Basel.

One of these monarchs, the Western Emperor Sigismund of Luxemburg who always had shown so much concern with the Eastern problems, died before the deliberations at Ferrara started, and at Basel there was even some fear that if the electors would chose a successor unfriendly to Eugene IV, the Pope would " transfer the Empire from the Germans to the Greeks, "[7] since the Emperor and the Patriarch of Constantinople were already with him at Ferrara. These were, of course, wild rumors, and Eugene IV had nothing against the election of Sigismund's son-in-law, Albrecht II of Habsburg to whom he sent a legate before his election and before he gained the Bohemian and Hungarian successions, trying to get him interested in the negotiations with the Greeks. [8] Unfortunately, amidst all the difficulties of his short reign, Albrecht II hardly could deal with the problem of religious reunion, though the inseparable problem of cooperation with the Turks touched him directly as King of Hungary. It is true that soon after the German electors and the King of Aragon, also the newly elected King of the Romans sent his envoy to Ferrara, but the same diary of the Council [9] which briefly noted these arrivals, pointed out, when mentioning the legation of the Duke of Burgundy, that no other Christian ruler had shown the same active interest in the great work of reunion with the Greeks, though no western prince should have missed the opportunity of meeting and encouraging them. Nothing is known indeed of any participation of the other envoys

[5] *Ibidem*, II, Nr. 176, p. 73.
[6] Preserved in the Archives of the Dukes of Burgundy (now the departmental " Archives de la Côte-d'Or "), B 11 687, with the coats of arms of both the Pope and the Duke ; see also V. Boudet, *Notice sur les Archives de la Côte d'Or*, Dijon, 1828.
[7] *Concilium Basiliense*, V, 151 (March 13, 1438).
[8] *Epistolae Pontificiae*, I, Nr. 112 (end of Dec. 1437) ; see also Nr. 104, 107.
[9] *Concilium Florentinum - Fragmenta Protocolli, Diaria privata, Sermones* (ed. G. Hofmann), Rome, 1951, 43-44 ; see the sermon preached at Ferrara, in Nov. 1438, by one of the Burgundian delegates, *ibidem*, 63-70, and the introduction, p. xxxii f.

in that work and none of them, except the Burgundians, signed the Bull of Union. And as far as in particular the " King of the Romans, Hungary and Bohemia " was concerned, news came to Ferrara during the discussions with the Greeks, that he was engaged in the struggle against the " Bohemian heretics, " [10] viz., the Hussite party which once more tried to oppose to a German candidate a member of the Jagellonian dynasty.

The position of that dynasty which continued to rule over Poland and Lithuania, was hardly less important with regard to any larger anti-Ottoman action and much more important, or rather of decisive importancè, with regard to the union with the Eastern Church which had so many followers in their Ruthenian lands. It was difficult to expect that any delegates would come to Ferrara, or later to Florence, from Lithuania, where Grand Duke Sigismund felt so insecure. But even the King of Poland himself, Ladislas III, did not send any representatives to Italy nor did the Polish hierarchy, though its head, the Archbishop of Gniezno and Primate of Poland, received twice special invitations from Eugene IV. [11]

One of these invitations was sent to that Archbishop, Vincent Kot of Dembno, before the arrival of the Greeks, the other one soon after their arrival on April 9, 1438, the very day of the first joint session of the Council, in which Emperor John VIII, the Patriarch of Constantinople and so many other representatives of the Eastern Church duly participated. Expressing his conviction that the Archbishop of Gniezno would show his pleasure in view of the impending union, the Pope repeated his request that he should come to that truly oecumenical Council himself, cooperating in such a great work, and instruct all his subordinates to do the same. Unfortunately, Vincent of Dembno, along with the powerful Oleśnicki and most of the other members of the Polish hierarchy and clergy, continued to be in sympathy with the Council of Basel, even when it definitely ceased to be legitimate and elected an anti-Pope, [12] and while there always remained in Basel at least a few Poles, though now only persons of secondary importance, [13] almost nobody of them appeared at Ferrara or Florence. The only exception was just one theologian, Sędziwoj of Czechel, [14] but his presence was purely personal and unofficial, and being associated with the University of Cracow which supported to the very end the ideas of Basel, and which Eugene IV had invited in vain to send representatives to Ferrara to meet there the

---

[10] *Ibidem*, 46.

[11] *Epistolae Pontificiae*, II, Nr. 126, 136.

[12] The most detailed treatment of that problem is given by J. Fijałek, *Jakób z Paradyża*, I, Kraków, 1900 ; see also N. Valois, *La crise religieuse du XV-e siècle*, II, 259-261.

[13] See, f. ex., *Concilium Basiliense*, VI, Basel 1926, 428, 724, etc., about Derslaus of Borzymów, active in Basel at the time of the Union of Florence.

[14] A. Lewicki, *Unia florencka*, 213 note 2. See also K. Morawski, *Historia Uniwersytetu Jagiellońskiego* (History of the Jagellonian University), Kraków 1900, I.

Greek delegation, [15] he did not play any active part in the Pope's Council. There could be some hope that at least the new Bishop of Poznań, Andrew of Bnin, whom Eugene IV himself had recently elevated to that position, would come to Ferrara, where the Pope on June 23, 1438, [16] decided that the revenues of that bishopric in the current year would be reserved for the papal treasury to cover a part of the expenses for the maintenance of the Greek delegation to the Council and for the defense of Constantinople. That decision seems to indicate that the new bishop was considered interested in the union with the Eastern Church though his diocese was far away from the Ruthenian lands. But in any case even he remained in Poland while the Union of Florence was concluded, [17] and only the Union with the Armenians, which followed that with the Greeks on November 22 of the same year [18], was concluded with the participation of representatives of one of the bishops of Poland, the Armenian Bishop of Lwów, Gregory, whom the Pope on December 15 informed of that event. [19]

The Union with the Greeks was, of course, signed by Metropolitan Isidore who even made an unusual comment adding to his signature two words which stressed his pleasure and wholehearted agreement. [20] He signed it one of the first after the Emperor, among the personal representatives of the Eastern patriarchs, because he had been appointed " the substitute of the apostolic throne of the most holy Patriarch of Antioch. " And it is well known that no other Greek except the illustrious Metropolitan of Nicaea, Isidore's lifelong friend Bessarion, contributed more efficiently to the success of the negotiations which he had prepared already on the occasion of his earlier mission to Basel. It can be even pointed out that while Bessarion himself had to be convinced at the Council of the correctness of the Latin point of view, particularly in the most controversial issue of the procession of the Holy Gost, [21] Isidore arrived at Ferrara [22] with the well established conviction that the union had to be concluded according to the Latin interpretation of all dogmatic problems. [23] It is, therefore, of the utmost

---

[15] *Epistolae Pontificiae*, I, Nr. 95 (Sept. 23, 1437).

[16] *Ibidem*, II, Nr. 145.

[17] That he cannot be identified with " Andreas episcopus Rossinensis (Possaniensis?) " who signed the Union with the Greeks, has been demonstrated by I. Nowacki in *Oriens*, VII (1939), 112 f.

[18] *Epistolae Pontificiae*, II, Nr. 224.

[19] *Ibidem*, II, Nr. 236 ; see the special study of S. Obertyński, quoted there.

[20] *Ibidem*, II, Nr. 176, p. 77 : " στέργων κὰι συναινῶν ὑπέγραψα."

[21] See E. Candal, " Bessarion Nicaenus in Concilio Florentino, " *Orientalia Christiana Periodica*, VI (1940).

[22] The date, August 20, 1438, is given in *Concilium Florentinum-Fragmenta Protocolli* ... (see note 9), 43.

[23] It is true that even he did not always satisfy the Catholic theologians in his interpretation ; see E. Candal in his introduction to Ioannes de Torquemada, *Apparatus super decretum Florentinum*, Rome, 1942, p. xxx, n. 5. On his prominent role

importance that this prominent Greek came to the Council as " Metropolitan of Kiev and all Russia, " a title which in his signature came first.

The fact that Isidore officially represented Kiev and all Russia was duly stressed for a special reason. Though the union was supposed to be concluded with all the Orthodox churches which were under the supreme authority of the Patriarch of Constantinople, besides Kiev only one more of those churches outside the Eastern Empire and its former possessions, viz., the Church of Moldavo-Wallachia was represented at the Council and among the signatories of the Union bull. [24] And this was indeed a much less important and ancient see than Isidore's. But can it be said that he really, not only formally, represented the Orthodox of Kiev and the various Russias ?

To answer that question and to decide whether it is possible to speak of a real participation of the Eastern Slavs in the Council of Ferrara-Florence, a clear distinction must be made once more between Muscovite Russia and the Ruthenian lands of Poland and Lithuania. The former was indeed represented not only by the Greek Isidore but also by his Russian companions from Moscow and Tver, and the one of them who was a member of the hierarchy, Avraam, Bishop of Suzdal, signed indeed the bull of July 6, in the Russian language and in cyrillic letters, [25] right before the substitutes of the Metropolitan of Moldavo-Wallachia who like the Metropolitan himself and all the others signed in Greek. Avraam's Slavic signature, the only one on the charter of the Union of Florence, could give the impression that, after all, Metropolitan Isidore was not completely isolated, as supporter of the union, in the vast area under his ecclesiastical jurisdiction. Unfortunately, all that is known about the Russians present at the Council including the Bishop of Suzdal, rather seems to indicate that they merely created trouble to their Greek leader.

Nothing is known at all of any participation of Avraam nor of the other Russians in the theological discussions for which they were hardly prepared. One of them, it is true, left an account of their impressions during their unprecedented journey through Central Europe and their even more exciting stay in Italy, but only to evidence their amazement and lack of understanding with regard to the whole alien atmosphere which surrounded them, as well as their inveterate prejudice against that Western, Latin world which they were supposed to join. [26] According to the Russian interpretation of

---

see *Concilium Florentinum*, B V, Rome 1953, 399, 400; B VI, Rome 1955, 33, 251, *et passim*.

[24] *Epistolae Pontificiae*, II, Nr. 176, p. 78, 79 ; there were, of course, representatives of the Greek Orthodox Church in formerly Byzantine Bulgaria, headed by the Metropolitan of Tirnovo, *ibidem*, 78. About the delegates of eastern rulers (Serbia, Trapezunt, Georgia and Wallachia) see *Concilium Florentinum*, VI, 30.

[25] *Ibidem*, 79.

[26] See the most recent discussion of these Russian accounts by I. Ševčenko, " Intellectual Repercussions of the Council of Florence, " *Church History*, XXIV (1955), Chapter X.

what happened in Florence, the Bishop of Suzdal was simply forced to sign the Union bull by order of his Metropolitan who put him in jail for eight days.

That detail is not confirmed by any other sources, not even by the well known and violently anti-Latin story of the Union of Florence, which was written by the Greek ecclesiastical dignitary Sylvester Syropulus[27] and repeatedly complains of the pressure which was exercised against the Greek opposition. An even more distinguished Greek who later was to be the leader of their opposition against the Union, Gennadius Scholarius, who had only contempt for the ignorance of the Russians in theological matters, refers to the bribery which Metropolitan Isidore had to use in order to get their assent.[28] And there cannot be any doubt that Isidore, even if he did not resort to so drastic measures as imprisonment, had difficulties in making at least the Russian bishop sign the decisive document. For, as soon as the Russian delegation had left Florence and was on its way back to Moscow, one after the other of Isidore's companions not excepting Bishop Avraam, were to leave him secretly and to hurry home in order to warn the Grand-Prince against the consequences of the Metropolitan's policy.

On the other hand, that dangerous defection was not anticipated at the Council. Some of the Muscovites who later appeared most violent in their anti-unionism did not seem to be in such an intransigent mood while in Florence.[29] It is, therefore, understandable that until the departure of the whole group there were at the Council and at the papal Curia far reaching illusions as to the attitude toward the union which would be taken by the Russians and their rulers, illusions which Isidore most probably shared and fostered. Only a few weeks after the ceremony of July 6, Pope Eugene IV wrote to Grand Prince Basil[30] informing him of the conclusion of the Union and recommending the Metropolitan who had proved so helpful in the matter. And when Isidore with his companions including his Greek assistant Gregory left Florence in October, the Apostolic Chamber paid a special subsidy of 237 florins to the Bishop of Suzdal and to Thomas Mikhailovich, the boyar who represented the Grand Prince of Tver, as a contribution to their expenses at the Council and on their way to Venice.[31] The latter who at the liturgy following the conclusion of the Union had assisted in the

---

[27] See about Syropulus and the editions of his work D. J. Geanakoplos, " The Council of Florence, " *Church History*, XXIV (1955), note 16.

[28] See I. Ševčenko, *op. cit.*, notes 104, 106, 110. The anti-Latin account of Simeon of Suzdal has been analyzed by M. Cherniavsky. " The Reception of the Council of Florence in Moscow ", *Church History*, XXIV, 347-351.

[29] See *ibidem*, note 205.

[30] *Epistolae Pontificiae*, II, Nr. 204.

[31] *Acta Camerae Apostolicae ... de Concilio Florentino* (ed. G. Hofmann), Rome 1950, 82 ; both Abraham and Thomas are called " oratores Ruthenorum, " and sometimes (see Torquemada, *Apparatus*, 13) there are even references to the " oratores magni regis Russie " which is obviously not correct.

washing of the Pope's hands, [32] now received from Eugene IV a special safe-conduct and a message for his master, [33] perhaps in view of some expectations that the union would have better chances in Tver than in Moscow.

It must have been obvious that these chances would be even better in those parts of Isidore's metropolitan realm which were under Catholic rule, and therefore when on August 17, 1439, Isidore was made an apostolic legate, [34] he received the mission to propagate the union not only in " the provinces of all Russia, " but also in those of Lithuania and Livonia, as well as " in the cities, dioceses, lands and places of Lechia " which were under his metropolitan jurisdiction. Without discussing the wide powers which along with a comprehensive safe-conduct [35] were granted as usually to the new legate, the enumeration of the countries where he was sent must be carefully examined.

Livonia which had very few Orthodox inhabitants and was outside the jurisdiction of the metropolitan of Kiev, was probably mentioned only because of the possibility that Isidore might travel through that country on his return journey to Moscow as he had done it when coming from Moscow to Italy. But it was taken for granted that this time he would at least have an opportunity also to visit the Ruthenian lands of Lithuania and Poland. That the latter kingdom was designated as " Lechia, " a name quite unusual in Latin texts and obviously derived from the name of Poland and the Poles which was used in Russian and also in Greek sources, [36] can only be explained by Isidore's personal participation in the drafting of the papal bull. The lengthy reference to the parts of Poland with which he was concerned because of their Orthodox population, is another evidence of his special interest in that area where Catholic influence was strongest.

For that same reason, however, he as well as the Pope himself must have been disappointed that there was no Polish participation in the Council of Ferrara-Florence except only the delegates of the small Armenian community of Lwów whose attitude could hardly influence their much more numerous Ruthenian fellow citizens. The King of Poland was, of course, included in the list of Catholic rulers whom Eugene IV informed of the return of the Armenians to the unity with the Roman Church. [37] But that message simply supplemented an earlier one which notified to that same king the union with the Greeks. [38] In both cases the King of Poland was

---

[32] I. Ševčenko, op. cit., note 108.

[33] Epistolae Pontificiae, II, Nr. 225.

[34] Ibidem, Nr. 202.

[35] Ibidem, Nr. 203.

[36] For ex. in the Greek text of the letter of King Casimir the Great to Patriarch Philotheus, Acta Patriarchatus Constant., I, 577.

[37] Epistolae Pontificiae, II, Nr. 232.

[38] Ibidem, II, Nr. 193. Neither of these two papal bulls has been preserved : they are known only from the king's reply, dated March 20, 1440. They were probably brought to Poland by the messengers which the Holy See dispatched to the

indeed much more interested in the Pope's successful achievement than were the other rulers who received similar announcements. For he was the only one of them who had among his own subjects both a small group of the Armenian Christians scattered in so many parts of the world, and many more Ruthenians, followers of the Greek Orthodox Church. Whether the latter who were not at all represented at the Council of Ferrara-Florence, would follow the Greek Church in its momentous decision to reunite with Rome and to recognize the Pope's authority, that was a question of primary importance for Catholic Poland whose king could exercise a considerable influence in the matter.

Much depended, therefore, on the person of that king whose father and predecessor Ladislas Jagello, after converting his native Lithuania to the Catholic faith and uniting the whole Grand Duchy with the Crown of Poland, had shown so much interest in the union of his Ruthenian subjects, whether in Lithuania or in Poland, with the Roman Church. It was, however, difficult to foresee whether his son, Ladislas III, would follow this example, since at the time of the Union of Florence the young king was only fifteen years old. In Poland he was under the strong though not unopposed influence of Bishop Zbigniew Oleśnicki of Cracow who during the king's minority was at the head of the regency and whose opinion could be expected to prove decisive particularly in a religious question. In Lithuania, Grand Duke Sigismund who by that time had completely eliminated his rival Svidrigello, was formally recognizing the suzerainty of the King of Poland, but disregarding the repeated promises which he had made in that respect, [39] he was secretly conducting anti-Polish negotiations with Albrecht of Habsburg, King of the Romans, of Bohemia, and Hungary. [40]

This was an additional, though unknown reason why the unexpected death of Albrecht II, soon after the Union of Florence on October 27, 1439, influenced at least indirectly the general conditions in which that union was to come into force. That death seemed to affect even the journey of Metropolitan Isidore who on his way back to Russia had already reached Venice. There he was advised that in view of the troubles which might follow Albrecht's death it would be wiser not to continue his travel through German and Hungarian lands, but rather to go by sea to Constantinople and from there to reach Russia through ways suggested by the Greek Emperor. Writing in that sense to John VIII Palaeologus on November 28, [41] the Pope

---

King of Poland — the first of them also " ad alios prelatos dicti regni " — on September 5 and December 12, 1439. See *Acta Camerae Apost. ... de Concilio Florentino*, 77, 87.

[39] *Akta Unii Polski z Litwą*, Nr. 55, 59, 61, 63, 66.

[40] A. Lewicki, *Przymierze Zygmunta W. Ks. Lit. z. Królem rzymskim Albrechtem II* (The Alliance of Sigismund, Grand Duke of Lithuania, with Albert II, King of the Romans) Kraków, 1899.

[41] *Epistolae Pontificiae*, II, Nr. 233.

recommended to him Isidore very strongly, expressing the hope that the Metropolitan who had proved so helpful in obtaining the union, would also contribute to its conservation. In that connection it seems quite possible that the idea of making Isidore pass through Constantinople before returning to Russia, was also motivated by the conviction that he could help to make the union of Florence accepted by the Greeks as well as by the Russians, and also by the realization that the attitude of the Greeks and of their Emperor might be influenced, even more than Isidore's trip, by the sudden disappearance of Albrecht of Habsburg, whose assistance had been promised to John VIII only two months before. [42]

It is well known that many Greeks were inclined to accept the religious union with Rome chiefly, if not exclusively, because they hoped then to obtain the badly needed help of the Catholic world against the growing Ottoman danger. Even for John VIII, though his religious convictions seem to have been sincere, such political considerations were one of the strongest arguments, an argument which he frequently used particularly during the difficult negotiations in Ferrara and Florence, with a view of breaking the opposition against the union. [43] And it was obvious that any efficient action against the Turks depended on the participation of Hungary, the only Catholic land power which already was an immediate neighbor of the Ottoman Empire and was itself threatened by the Turkish onslaught. Albrecht of Habsburg, after succeeding his father-in-law Sigismund of Luxemburg not only in Germany and Bohemia but also in Hungary, had very well realized the necessity of opposing that onslaught and it was amid the preparations for an anti-Turkish campaign that he had been stricken by a deadly illness. Since he died without leaving an heir, though his wife Elizabeth was expecting a child, the question of the Hungarian succession was once more reopened and with it the question not only of Hungary's own defense but of the possibility of any anti-Ottoman action under adequate leadership. [44]

The importance of that question from the point of view of the whole future of the Union of Florence was so evident, that Metropolitan Isidore, who on December 18, 1439, was made a Cardinal of the Roman Church, along with Archbishop Bessarion of Nicaea, [45] gave up the idea of sailing from Venice to Constantinople and finally decided to continue his journey through Hungary in spite of, or rather because of the unsettled conditions in that country which he wanted to explore on his way. When he arrived at Buda early in March 1440, he could easily find out who was supposed to

---

[42] *Ibidem*, II, Nr. 217 (Sept. 23, 1439).

[43] See the comments of I. Ševčenko on that " terrestrial " argument of the pro-Unionists, *op. cit.*, Chap. IV and· V.

[44] The whole situation in Hungary is best described by J. Dąbrowski, *Władysław I Jagiellończyk na Węgrzech* (Ladislas I the Jagellonian in Hungary), Warszawa, 1923.

[45] J. Korzeniowski, *Analecta Romana*, Cracoviae, 1894, 31-33.

succeed Albrecht of Habsburg : the Hungarians had already elected the young king of Poland Ladislas III and after preliminary negotiations in Cracow which had settled the conditions of his election, were expecting his arrival from Poland. [46]

Among these conditions the most important was that the new king would resume Albrecht's plan to fight the Turks, and that Poland and Hungary would cooperate in that respect. The prospects of an efficient action in defense of Christendom seemed, therefore, even better than before, because Poland though herself not yet directly threatened, was alarmed by the Ottoman advance in view of her own expansion towards the Black Sea. The rival claims of Hungary and Poland in that region, particularly in Moldavia, were to be peacefully settled on the same occasion, thus removing the main obstacle to their cooperation, and since Lithuania too seemed to be interested in the problem in view of her relations with the Tartars, [47] a participation of that second Jagellonian state in the common front against the Muslims, Turks as well as Tartars, could be expected.

These possible expectations depended, however, on the simultaneous developments in the Lithuanian Grand Duchy, where the unreliable and unpopular Sigismund whom Eugene IV tried in vain to get interested in the Union of Florence, [48] was killed, probably before receiving the papal message, on March 30, by the leaders of the aristocracy, both Catholic Lithuanians and Orthodox Ruthenians. These leaders now turned to King Ladislas, first asking him to assume power in Lithuania himself and then, when he did not change his decision to go to Hungary, requesting him to send them his younger brother, Casimir. The latter was indeed elected Grand Duke and started his reign in Lithuania which was to last more than half a century. He started it in disagreement with the Poles who contrary to the union charters had not been consulted in the matter of his election. But in any case the two countries were now ruled by two brothers, both anxious to restore their friendly relations and cooperation. [49]

How this could be achieved, depended to a large extent on the influential Polish and Lithuanian advisers of the young Jagellonians who, in the critical year of 1440, were only sixteen and thirteen, respectively. In Poland, the influence of Bishop Oleśnicki was still to increase after the king's departure for Hungary, especially as the whole Hungarian project had originally been Oleśnicki's. Through the personal union with Hungary and the joint anti-Ottoman action the Bishop wanted, of course, to serve Poland's prestige but at the same time also the interests of the Catholic Church in-

[46] J. Dąbrowski, op. cit.

[47] O. Halecki, " La Pologne et l'Empire byzantin, " Byzantion, VII (1932), 62-63.

[48] Codex diplomaticus Cathedrae Vilnensis (ed. J. Fijałek and W. Semkowicz), Cracoviae, 1932, Nr. 161 (Feb. 27, 1440).

[49] O. Halecki, Dzieje Unii jagiellońskiej (History of the Jagellonian Union), Vol. I, Kraków 1919, 331-340.

cluding the cause of reunion with the Greeks. The trouble was, however, that in doing so he was thinking rather of the Council of Basel to whose lost cause he remained attached, than of Eugene IV to whose personal success, best evidenced in the Union of Florence, he was not at all anxious to contribute. Whether the young king of Poland and Hungary would follow Oleśnicki in his ecclesiastical policy, was another question, and equally uncertain was the attitude of the even younger Casimir and his Lithuanians among whom the Bishop of Wilno, Mathew, though politically opposed to the Bishop of Cracow, shared his views in the controversy between Eugene IV and Basel. [50]

All these intricacies of a situation which necessarily was to affect the chances of the Union of Florence among the Ruthenians of Poland and Lithuania, were hardly familiar to Cardinal Isidore. When still in Buda, he issued a message to the Slavs, not only the Russians but also those of the Balkan peninsula, inviting them to accept the Union of Florence. [51] But he must have realized the necessity of getting at last in touch with the powerful Oleśnicki, and therefore proceeded from Buda to Cracow to begin there, at the end of March, his discussion of both the position of the Ruthenians in Poland and the prospects of the anti-Ottoman action, equally important for the future of the religious union and for the defense of Constantinople.

Unfortunately, very little is known [52] about Isidore's first meeting with the two young Jagellonians and about his brief contact with Oleśnicki which probably was the last one. The Bishop of Cracow who was offered a cardinal's hat by both Pope Eugene IV and the anti-pope Felix V but waited before accepting it until the division within the Catholic Church was finally settled, received the newly appointed Cardinal of Eugene IV with perfect courtesy, faithful to his tactics of not openly taking sides in the whole painful issue. Favorable in principle to the idea of reunion with the Eastern Church, as were the Fathers who remained in Basel, Oleśnicki could not reject the Union of Florence which Cardinal Isidore came to promote ; [53] but he could not be enthusiastic about an achievement which was so obviously Eugene's nor about the activities of a Metropolitan who was so completely devoted to that Pope. Soon after his arrival on March 25, 1440, Isidore was permitted to celebrate mass according to the Eastern rite

[50] *Codex dipl. Cathedrae Vilnensis*, Nr. 157.

[51] *Polnoe sobranie russkikh letopisei* (Full collection of Russian chronicles), Vol. VI, St. Petersburg 1853, 159.

[52] The scarce material concerning Isidore's visit in Poland and Lithuania has been collected and analyzed by B. Bučynsky, " Studii z istorii tserkovnoi unii " (Studies about the history of the Union of the Churches), *Zap. Tov. im. Ševčenka*, Vol. 85-86, Lviv 1908, but in this posthumously published work the sources are not always quoted.

[53] See his letter to Cardinal Cesarini, *Codex epist. saec. XV*, I, Nr. 110.

in Oleśnicki's own cathedral at Cracow [54] and then to go from Poland's capital to her eastern provinces where he was to meet for the first time his Ruthenian faithful. But the leading Polish bishop and statesman, far from considering with his Greek guest the details of his Hungarian plans, his main concern at the given moment, was not too willing either to give his positive support to what Isidore would do in the Ruthenian lands for the Union of Florence, an issue which probably seemed to Oleśnicki of limited importance.

As to the Metropolitan, he remained in the Ruthenian provinces of the kingdom of Poland for about three months, [55] visited the three dioceses of Eastern rite and did his best to make them accept the Union of Florence and at the same time to safeguard their rights in the relations with the Latin hierarchy of the same region. That last point was intimately connected with a special difficulty which resulted from the fact that some times he found in the same place two bishops, a Ruthenian who hitherto had been an Orthodox and now had to be persuaded to join the Union, and a Catholic Pole who was not at all under Isidore's jurisdiction. At the Council of Florence similar situations which existed in the Greek East and particularly in Constantinople, where at the time of the Fourth Crusade a Latin patriarchate had been established besides the Greek, received due attention and it was decided that since now the Western and the Eastern Church were united, no double hierarchy was necessary : the vacancy which would occur first should not be filled but the surviving Patriarch, Archbishop, or Bishop, whatever his rite, should be the only one. [56] It seems that Isidore tried to apply that rule in the Ruthenian lands also, but it proved there even less acceptable than in Greece, and parallel hierarchies continued to exist side by side whether or not the Eastern one was united with Rome according to the Union of Florence.

Such was the case, for instance, in Przemyśl (Peremyšl in the Ruthenian language), the first city with an Eastern bishopric which Isidore visited coming from Cracow. He found that bishopric vacant and the Ruthenian cathedral in the hands of the Latin Polish bishop of the same place. However in spite, of Isidore's proclamation of the Union of Florence, which seems to have been accepted without opposition, the Ruthenians were not prepared to remain under the Polish bishop of Latin rite, and soon a bishop of Eastern rite would appear again in that city. [57] His attitude towards

---

[54] J. Długosz, *Hist. Pol.*, IV, 624.

[55] From April to July 1440. See Lewicki, *Unia flor.* 232, Ziegler, *op. cit.*, 90 ff.

[56] *Epistolae Pontificiae*, III, Supplem. Nr. 176 bis, with reference to the Patriarchate of Constantinople ; see the general remarks of W. Norden, *Das Papsttum und Byzanz*, 723-730.

[57] Bučynsky, *loc. cit.*, vol. 85, 28. See L. Sonevicki in *Analecta Ord. S Basilii M.* II (1954), 23 ff.

the union, as well as that of his successors, was, of course, to depend on the general situation in the Ruthenian lands.

That situation was particularly involved as far as the bishopric of Halich was concerned, which in the past had been elevated temporarily, on several occasions, to the rank of a separate metropolitan see, but now was under the direct control of the Metropolitan of Kiev, i. e., of Isidore himself, without any local bishop of Eastern rite. Practically, the center of that Ruthenian diocese was no longer in Halich itself but in the city of Lwów (Lviv in Ruthenian) which had become much more important and was the capital of the whole province. It also was, since 1375, the see of a Catholic Archbishop of Latin rite, [58] in addition to the Armenian Bishop of that same city who had accepted, for the time being, the union with Rome. Isidore, therefore, entered into negotiations with that Polish Archbishop of Lwów, John who belonged to the powerful family of the Odrowąż of Sprowa and was a brother of the Palatine (governor) of the province. Under Isidore's influence both of them seem to have recognized, in the summer of 1440, the authority of Pope Eugene IV, in spite of the Archbishop's sympathy with the Council of Basel, and already in May Isidore was able to proclaim the Union of Florence in the cathedral of Lwów. [59] Whether he took advantage of his comparatively long stay there in order to get in touch with the neighbor country of Moldavia which always was in close contact with the Lwów region and since 1387 under Polish suzerainty, and where at least formally the Union of Florence was recognized, [60] is impossible to ascertain. More probable is his concern with another Ruthenian province of Poland, that of Podolia, east of Lwów, which had a Latin but no Eastern bishopric, so that its Ruthenian population was under the see of Halich.

The Palatine of Podolia who belonged to the prominent Ruthenian family of the Kierdey's, happened to be at the same time Starosta (sheriff) of the land of Chełm (Kholm in Ruthenian), north of Lwów, where Isidore went in July, [61] finding again in the capital city of that small territory two bishoprics, a Latin and a Greek, one beside the other. After visiting also other places of that area to get in touch with the local nobility on whose support so much depended, the Metropolitan, on July 27, issued at Chełm an important charter which invoking the Union of Florence, stressed the equal rights of the Latin Church and the Eastern Church now reunited with Rome. Here, too, the coexistence of two hierarchies was to continue throughout the following centuries, but thanks to Isidore who spent more

---

[58] W. Abraham, *Powstanie organizacji Kościoła łacińskiego na Rusi*, I., 296.

[59] Bučynsky, *loc. cit.*, 29.

[60] C. Auner, " La Moldavie au Concile de Florence, " *Echos d'Orient*, VIII, 1905, 11[; about the ambassador of the " magnus voivoda Blachie " or " dominus Molduvlacie " at the Council of Florence, see now : Torquemada, *Apparatus super Decretum Flor.*, 13 ; *Acta Camerae Apost.*, 82 ; *Fragmenta Protocolli*, 30.

[61] Bučynsky, *loc. cit.*, 29-31.

than a fortnight in that important transition area between West and East, the Ruthenians, whether clergy or laymen, seemed to accept in Chełm, as in the previously visited provinces, the Union of Florence, while the Poles seemed to recognize the equal rights of the Ruthenian Church, which now was Catholic also.

The results of Isidore's visit of the Ruthenian provinces of Poland proved, therefore, quite satisfactory and encouraging. But a much more important task awaited him in the Grand Duchy of Lithuania which included much larger Ruthenian (Ukrainian) and all White Ruthenian lands, and where his own Metropolitan see of Kiev was situated. He, therefore, stayed there from August 1440 to March 1441, [62] travelling from one distant place to another, and probably well aware that his achievements in that eastern half of the Jagellonian confederation would affect subsequent developments in the Polish part also.

Without, however, realizing at first the differences of the respective situations, he started in Lithuania, just like in Poland, by visiting the capital and administrative center of the whole country, which also was the center of Catholic ecclesiastical life and organization, the city of Wilno, [63] though it would have been nearer to go from Chełm directly to the southern, Ruthenian provinces of the Grand Duchy. The first difference, unfavorable to his further activities, was in the attitude of the Catholic hierarchy : Bishop Mathias of Wilno was even more biased in favor of the Council of Basel than Oleśnicki and less diplomatic than the Bishop of Cracow, so that disregarding the authority of the Cardinal Legate of Pope Eugene IV, he did not permit him to proclaim in Wilno the Union of Florence. [64] However, though there were Orthodox Ruthenians even in that predominantly Catholic city and, in general, in the central part of Lithuania proper, their real majority was living in the eastern and southern borderlands of the Grand Duchy, and it was obvious that Isidore would have to visit in turn the main centers of these lands, after trying to prepare his action in Wilno.

But in that connection there appeared the second difference between the Polish and the Lithuanian situation. The Ruthenian (and White Ruthenian) lands of Lithuania enjoyed an even larger autonomy than those of Poland ; most of them were still governed by their own princes who belonged — it is true — to sidelines of the Lithuanian dynasty, but were mostly Greek Orthodox themselves ; and at the given moment, after the civil war of the thirties and the crisis of 1440, these lands and their local rulers were particularly anxious to affirm their practical independence from

---

[62] *Ibidem*, 32 f; Lewicki, 233 f; Ziegler, 93-95.
[63] On the growing role of Wilno in the ecclesiastical life of the Grand Duchy see *Codex diplomaticus Cathedrae Vilnensis*, I, Nr. 141-145 and *passim*.
[64] Bučynsky, *loc. cit.*, 33.

Wilno where in the name of the minor Grand Duke Casimir a group of purely Lithuanian lords was in full control. [65]   Therefore, on the one hand, Isidore's attempt to gain the support of the central authorities would have been in any case rather useless, while on the other hand, his failure in Wilno and especially in his relations with Bishop Mathias who belonged to the ruling group in Lithuania proper, did not prejudice at all of the reception which the Metropolitan would meet in the Ruthenian cities.

His visits in these various places kept him busy until the spring of 1441.   There is no positive evidence that he went to the important province of Volhynia where immediately after Sigismund's assassination his old rival Svidrigello had seized control, appearing again as pretender to the whole Grand Duchy, in opposition to his young nephew Casimir. [66]   But Svidrigello, a Catholic himself who had been interested in religious reunion and clashed with Metropolitan Harasim for merely political reasons, could be expected to be rather friendly toward the Union of Florence.   And there are indeed indications that the two Ruthenian bishops in Volhynia, the Bishop of Lutsk, Svidrigello's residence where also a Catholic bishop of Latin rite had his see, and particularly the Bishop of Volodymir (and Brest, north of the Volhynian border) sided at least temporarily with Isidore. [67]   The same seems to be true of one of the minor princes of Volhynia who were under Svidrigello's overlordship, Prince Fedor of Ostrog, an ancestor of the famous Ostrogskis of the following century : though he was of the Eastern rite himself and probably died as a monk of the Caves Monastery in Kiev — that old center of Orthodoxy — he founded in his town of Ostrog a Dominican convent under a prior from Bohemia. [68]

Whether Cardinal Isidore visited the less important bishopric of Turov and Pinsk in the rather isolated region of the Pripet Marches is very doubtful.   But there is a decisive document of February 5, 1441, [69] which proves that he not only came in person to the metropolitan city of Kiev, which was quite natural indeed, but also was eminently successful in being recognized there and making the Union of Florence accepted.   The document of that date which confirmed the Cardinal Legate in the complete control of all property of the metropolitan of Kiev, was issued by a cousin of Grand Duke Casimir, Prince Olelko (Alexander) who now, like his father had been before, was the autonomous ruler of the once glorious Duchy of Kiev.   That whole line of the Lithuanian dynasty was and remained particularly attached

---

[65] O. Halecki, *Dzieje Unii*, I, 340-343; L. Kolankowski, *Dzieje W. Ks. Lit.*, I, 228 ff.

[66] O. Halecki, *Ostatnie lata Świdrygiełły* (S's. last years), Kraków, 1915, 10-50.

[67] *Russkaia istorič. biblioteka* (Russian Historical Library), VI, Nr. 72.

[68] O. Halecki, *Ostatnie lata*, 138.

[69] *Akty istoričeskie* (Historical documents), I, St. Petersburg 1841, Nr. 259 ; as to the conflicting interpretations of this document see H. Jablonowski, *Westrussland zwischen Wilna und Moskau*, Leiden, 1955, 94.

to the Eastern Church, and in regular relations with Constantinople. [70]
But the very fact that it was precisely the Greek Empire which had concluded the Union of Florence, made Olelko inclined to welcome Isidore and
his policy. And the same position seems to have been taken by the monks
of the Monastery of the Caves.

From Kiev the Metropolitan moved again northward to Smolensk, then
a cultural and ecclesiastical center of the White Ruthenians second only to
Polotsk whose Archbishop was probably visited on the same occasion. Smolensk, the see of another bishop of Eastern rite, had then temporarily an
autonomous prince, just like Kiev, in the person of another cousin of Casimir, George, son of Lingven. His line, too, was Greek Orthodox, but it
seems that following Olelko's example, Prince George with his bishop received
Isidore well and recognized the Union of Florence. [71] Therefore, the general
conclusion would be that in spite of the unfriendly attitude of the Latin
Bishop of Wilno, that Union, thanks to Isidore's tireless efforts, was accepted,
at least for the time being, just like in Poland, by all the Orthodox of
the Grand Duchy of Lithuania. Ancient tradition of unity with Rome,
which never had entirely disappeared in the territory of the old Kievan
State, and recent association with a Catholic body politic, certainly contributed to that great success.

Smolensk which was not far from the frontier of Muscovite Russia and
which in earlier and later days was an object of controversy between
Lithuania and Moscow, now served to the Cardinal Legate as a basis or
stepping stone for approaching the most delicate stage of his mission : his
return to the court of Basil II. At the same time he took advantage of
the old relations between Smolensk, or rather the White Ruthenian lands
in general, and the Great Russian city-states of Novgorod and Pskov which
still were independent of Moscow and maintained contacts with the
Lithuanian Grand Duchy. The Metropolitan tried at least to counteract
there the propaganda against the Union of Florence which was to originate
from his Russian companions at the Council who had left him on his way
back from Florence in order to precede him in Russia. They too must
have travelled through the Ruthenian lands of Poland and especially of
Lithuania, but obviously did not succeed in creating any trouble there where
even the most energetic defenders of regional autonomy had nothing in
common with Moscow. While, however, Bishop Avraam of Suzdal who left
Isidore in Buda, seems to have hurried directly to Basil II, the monk Simeon
who probably was the Metropolitan's main Russian opponent and who along
with Thomas of Tver had left him even earlier, went first to Novgorod
where Lithuanian and Muscovite rivalry was traditional, the former having

---

[70] *Ibidem*, Appendix, note 40 ; see also E. Golubinsky, *Istoria russkoi tserkvi*, II,
450.

[71] Bučynsky, *op. cit.*, 34, 36 ; Jablonowski, *op. cit.*, 93.

been represented in the past by Prince Lingven, the father of George of Smolensk. [72] It was therefore to Smolensk that Isidore called back Simeon, perhaps with the assistance of the Archbishop of Novgorod, Euthymius. The latter must have been pleased by Isidore's decision to recall the special representative whom on his way to Italy, in 1437, he had left in Pskov, a city which the Archbishop of Novgorod considered to be under his own jurisdiction. [73] In any case, the Metropolitan, while still being in Lithuanian territory, established relations with the Orthodox of the two Russian city republics which continued to have close relations with the Catholic West and seemed to be easier to gain for the Union of Florence than Moscow whose control they still opposed.

When Isidore, on March 19, 1441, finally arrived in Moscow, taking with him, practically as a prisoner, the recalcitrant monk Simeon, he must have had from the outset serious doubts how he would be received by the Grand Prince and the local hierarchy. It is true that according to Russian sources [74] he left Florence with high hopes in this respect, assuring the Pope that there would be no opposition, since Basil II was young — actually already 21 — and the bishops mostly illiterate. But these Russian chronicles which pretend, among others, that the Metropolitan was expelled from Kiev by the people — a statement contrary to the facts — are definitely biased against him. Yet, they are the only sources which describe Isidore's attitude and experiences in Moscow, where he tried to act not only as Metropolitan of all Russia but also as Cardinal Legate of the Pope, exactly as he had done it in the Catholic States of Poland and Lithuania, but meeting this time with complete failure.

When preceded by a Latin cross he entered the Moscow Cathedral and during the solemn mass in the Eastern rite prayed first for Eugene IV and when at the end of the ceremony he ordered the bull of the Union of Florence to be read from the pulpit, the congregation, both the clergy and the boyars, remained silent. That silence did certainly not mean agreement nor acceptance of the Union. In view of the autocratic power which already then, and even in ecclesiastical matters, used to be exercised by the rulers of Moscow, they simply waited for Basil's decision. And it was that decision which was accepted without hesitation, a fact which in view of the exceptional importance of the matter greatly contributed to strengthen even more the authority of the Grand Duke. [75]

---

[72] Kolankowski, *op. cit.*, I, 242, 247.

[73] Lewicki, *op. cit.*, 220, 234.

[74] These sources have been critically analyzed by Pierling, *La Russie et le Saint-Siège*, I, 56-59 ; Golubinsky, *op. cit.*, 252 f. ; J. Koncevicius, *Russia's Attitude toward Union with Rome*, Washington, 1927, 120-123 ; A. Ziegler, *op. cit.* 96 f. ; M. Cherniavsky, *loc. cit.*, 353-356.

[75] See W. K. Medlin, *Moscow and East Rome*, Genève 1952, 75.

This decision was not only an absolute rejection of the Union of Florence, in spite of the recommendations by the Pope and even by the Emperor of Constantinople which Isidore had brought with him. Basil interrupted the reading of the bull and after a few days of reflection ordered the Metropolitan to be arrested and confined as a virtual prisoner in the Chudov Monastery at the Kremlin. This was, of course, a punishment which, in the opinion of the Grand Prince Isidore well deserved since contrary to his promise and to the condition on which he had been allowed to go to the Council, he brought back something which in Moscow was considered new and contrary to the Orthodox tradition. Such an interpretation of the decisions of Florence had been brought to Moscow without any doubt by Bishop Avraam of Suzdal and possibly also by some other members of the Russian delegation who came home before Isidore, and the Metropolitan's success in the rival country of Lithuania, which did not remain unknown in Moscow either, could only confirm Basil II in his absolutely negative attitude which following the Russian chronicles was inspired by God himself.

If there was any hesitation in that attitude, it concerned only the best way of dealing with the Metropolitan. As Cardinal and papal Legate he was, of course, not recognized at all, but even as the head of the Russian Church he could no longer be accepted nor any action of his tolerated by the State. While, however, imprisonment could seem the best way of stopping such an action immediately, it would have been rather embarrassing to keep Isidore indefinitely as a prisoner in Moscow. When, therefore, he could not be induced to abandon the union, the Grand Prince, without watching him too carefully, let him escape already in the following month of September. Probably [76] the Russian bishops planned to send a letter at once to the Emperor and Patriarch of Constantinople accusing their Metropolitan of apostasy and hoping perhaps to get in touch with the Greek opposition against the Union. Therefore, Isidore had to realize that he could not expect from them anything better than from the Grand Prince, and that the situation in Moscow was completely hopeless, for reasons which were both political and religious.

At least from the political point of view there seemed to be a better chance in Tver, that separate principality which remained traditionally opposed to Moscow's supremacy and in friendly relations with Lithuania. When, however, the Metropolitan with his faithful companion Gregory — later his successor in Kiev — succeeded in reaching that other Russian city, he was again imprisoned by the local ruler, Prince Boris. [77] The delegate of the latter, Thomas, who, too, had abandoned Isidore on his way back from Italy, must have reported to his master as unfavorably on the Union

---

[76] See A. A. Ammann, *Abriss der ostslawischen Kirchengeschichte*, 145.

[77] How particularly disappointing his attitude must have been to Isidore, is pointed out by Bučynsky, *op. cit.*, 39; see also Cherniavsky, *loc. cit.* 354 f.

of Florence as did the emissaries of Basil II, disappointing in a similar way the confidence of the Pope and his Legate. But in Tver, too, the purpose of those in power was only to make impossible any propaganda in favor of the Union of Florence, while it seemed even less desirable than in Moscow to keep the Metropolitan in jail. He could, therefore, again escape without difficulty or delay, but having lost all hope to influence the Great Russians in their negotiations with Constantinople, he simply returned to the Ruthenians of Lithuania.

This was, however, not before March 1442, and in the meantime, contrary to Isidore's expectations, in Lithuania, as well as in Poland, the attitude of both the government and most of the hierarchy had become even more favorable to the Council of Basel and accordingly opposed to Eugene IV. Nevertheless, the latter had not hesitated to write at the beginning of the year to the young Grand Duke Casimir and to one of his foremost Lithuanian advisers, asking them to help Isidore regain his liberty. [78] That appeal, however, cannot be interpreted as evidence that in Lithuania, too, the Cardinal Legate was imprisoned. [79] The papal intervention resulted obviously from the information about what had happened to Isidore in Russia and was supposed to make Casimir intervene in Moscow or in Tver, neighbor states with whom Lithuania was for the time being in peaceful, and in the case of Tver, even friendly relations. Furthermore, since one of Eugene's letters in that matter, the only one which has been discovered, found its way into the binding of a manuscript of the Vatican Library, it is highly probable that none of them was actually dispatched, but simply disregarded when it became known at the papal Curia that Isidore had recovered his freedom anyway.

But though there was no question of imprisoning him again in Catholic Lithuania, he really did not find there on his second visit any freedom of action. As he was to complain several years later, [80] Bishop Mathew of Wilno under whose influence Grand Duke Casimir on February 2, 1442, adhered to the Council of Basel, [81] this time did not even want to see Isidore without having consulted first that rump-council, and created him such difficulties that from Novogrodek in Lithuania, where the Metropolitans of exposed Kiev frequently took their residence, the Cardinal at the end of the year moved to Poland.

Here, too, the influence of Basel was increasing to such an extent that precisely the Archbishop of Lwów whose support Isidore particularly needed

[78] G. Mercati, *Scritti d'Isidoro il Cardinale Ruteno*, 158, has discovered and published that letter to " nobili viro Doldio Baroni dilecti filii nobilis viri Casimiri magni Lituanie Ducis consiliario, " most probably John Dowgird, Palatine of Wilno (see Chodynicki, *Kościół prawosławny*, 621).

[79] As seems to imply Ammann, *op. cit.*, 144; see also Lewicki, *op. cit.*, 238 note 1.

[80] Chodynicki, *op. cit.*, 52, note 1.

[81] Bučynsky, *op. cit.*, 40.

and obviously had enjoyed during his first visit, accepted the office of Legate of that Council and its anti pope Felix V, [82] so that his relations with the Cardinal Legate of Eugene IV must have become rather strained. These developments did not necessarily affect the attitude of the Ruthenian hierarchy and clergy, since the Latin hierarchy was not particularly nor directly opposing the idea of reunion with the East which the Council of Basel never ceased to favor in principle. Nevertheless, Isidore's activities must have been this time much more difficult than in 1440 when he first came to Poland, though it seems probable that precisely now he consecrated one or two Ruthenian bishops, at least that of Przemyśl. [83] There was, however, a special reason which made him leave soon the kingdom of Poland and, in general, the area of his metropolitan jurisdiction. He was not only anxious to return to the papal Curia to report to Eugene IV on his mission as Legate and to receive from him new instructions, but he saw a last chance to accomplish something very important for the future of the Union of Florence among the Ruthenians by trying to approach the King of Poland himself in his Hungarian residence, in Buda which was on Isidore's way to Italy.

King Ladislas after leaving Poland in the spring of 1440 never returned there from Hungary where he was absorbed both by his struggle with the partisans of the Habsburgs, i. e., of Albrecht's posthumous son, another Ladislas, and by the preparations for turning the defense of Hungary's frontiers against the Turks into a real crusade with a view to liberating the Balkans. [84] But all the time he remained, of course, in regular contact with the Poles whose cooperation he needed and many of whom sooner or later joined him at his Hungarian court. It is, therefore, obvious that already in Poland Isidore must have obtained some information regarding the king's policy which interested him for two different, but equally important reasons. First, he was anxious to see him start as soon as possible the planned crusade the success of which was a prerequisite condition for the success of the Union of Florence in Constantinople and, in general, in southeastern Europe. And secondly, it was vital for the survival of that same Union in northeastern Europe, in Isidore's own metropolitan area, at least in the part which was under Jagellonian rule, what attitude Ladislas III would take in the deplorable conflict between Eugene IV and the Council of Basel : whether he, too, like his younger brother Casimir of Lithuania, would yield to the influence of the partisans of that Council, particularly of Bishop Oleśnicki who had initiated the whole Hungarian project, or whether he would have his own different views in that matter.

---

[82] *Ibidem*, 41.

[83] *Ibidem*; it is, however, possible, that some of these ordinations were made by Isidore in later years, when he was already back in Rome; see Ammann, *loc. cit.*

[84] Dąbrowski, *op. cit.*

CHAPTER III

THE CRUSADE OF VARNA AND THE FALL
OF CONSTANTINOPLE

In spite of his tender age, King Ladislas III had never been completely under the influence of Oleśnicki's powerful personality to whom the Queen-Mother, Sonka, Jagello's last wife, a Lithuanian princess, remained strongly opposed along with her partisans. [1] The expedition to Hungary which, after securing the crown of St. Stephen, was to develop into an expedition against the enemy of Christendom, certainly appealed to the enthusiasm of the king ; but that did not mean that he would remain addicted to Oleśnicki's interpretation of the whole enterprise, keeping it independent of, if not opposed to the papal policy and making it serve at least indirectly, the interests of the Council of Basel. Even among the King's Polish followers who in increasing number were attracted to Buda in order to participate in the crusade, there were many who did not share the views of the Bishop of Cracow, and the situation in Hungary definitely requested agreement and cooperation with Eugene IV, in view of both problems which the young Jagellonian had to face.

In the civil war which followed the birth of Ladislas Posthumus and his recognition by some of the Hungarians, Eugene IV at first rather favored the Habsburgs whose cause was energetically defended by Albrecht's widow, Elizabeth. The Jagellonian king was, of course, fully aware of the importance of the Pope's support and of the impossibility of getting any valuable assistance from the Council of Basel. Furthermore, the very significant appeal which he sent to Eugene IV from his armed camp in Hungary on April 12, 1441, [2] seems to indicate that he was turning to the legitimate Pope not only for reasons of expediency but out of sincere religious conviction. Expressing his disappointment that Eugene IV had not shown him more favor " in his recent vocation and promotion to the government of this Kingdom " (*i. e.* of Hungary), he recalled his father's ardent devotion

---

[1] That situation is discussed in detail by E. Maleczyńska, *Spoleczeństwo polskie pierwszej polowy XV. wieku wobec zagadnień zachodnich* (The Polish society of the first half of the XV century with regard to the Western problems), Wrocław, 1947, Chapter V.

[2] British Museum, *Ms. Add.* 30.268, fol. 4-5.

and loyalty to the Holy See, and emphasized that he was decided to follow in that respect the example of his predecessor on the Polish throne. In evidence of this determination, he added that he had just written to an assembly of the Polish clergy informing them that he wanted the Kingdom of Poland to follow his own and Hungary's example in remaining united with, and obedient to Eugene IV. And he not only stressed his conviction that the Poles would not dare to dissent from the Holy Father, but throughout the following years until the eve of the crusade of Varna, in August 1444, he did not cease to admonish his Polish subjects through his letters and personal representatives to follow Pope Eugene IV.[3]

Already in his letter of 1441 he informed the Pope of his successes in fighting the partisans of Elizabeth whom he made responsible for breaking the peace, adding not without regret that Eugene IV had hitherto rather believed the reports of the other side. As a matter of fact, the Pope, though receiving contradictory information, was only to anxious to help in ending the civil war which badly delayed the crusade, and fully conscious that this crusade could not be undertaken under the leadership of Elizabeth and her infant child but only under that of Ladislas of Poland. Since the death of Albrecht of Habsburg there simply was no other leader available, and as the Pope's own contribution to the defense of Constantinople could not be but very limited, while the West in spite of all papal appeals remained indifferent, Eugene IV, though continuing to negotiate with his native Venice, as well as with Genoa and the Knights of Rhodus in view of a naval action,[4] decided to mediate between the two Hungarian parties to make possible, at last, the advance of their united forces, supported by those of Poland, against the Ottoman Empire.

The papal representative who after some earlier attempts successfully concluded that mediation between Ladislas the Jagellonian and the Queen-Widow Elizabeth in December 1442, was that same Cardinal Cesarini[5] who had played such an outstanding part in the conclusion of the Union of Florence. Nobody, therefore, could better realize the close connection between the cause of the crusade and that of the union. As to the former, in spite of Elizabeth's unexpected death which created new difficulties with the Habsburgs soon after the provisional agreement, far reaching preparations started at once: in Hungary, the Palatine of Transylvania, John Hunyadi, who had so well defended the country even before, was only waiting for the possibility to start the long delayed offensive action in cooperation with Cesarini. And as early as January 1, 1443,[6] an encyclical letter of Eugene

---

[3] N. Valois, *La crise religieuse du XVe siècle*, II, 261 note 1 (full text of the King's letter to Eugene IV, from Waradin, August, 28, 1444).

[4] See about all these efforts the Pope's letter to Christopher Garatoni, of Aug. 25, 1440, *Epistolae pontificiae*, III, Nr. 243, p. 18.

[5] His mediation is well described by J. Dąbrowski, *Władysław I Jagiell.*, 91 ff.

[6] *Epistolae pontificiae*, III, Nr. 261.

IV, outlining a systematic plan for the crusade, tried to mobilize the forces of all Christendom : in particular, the Bishop of Corona Christopher Garatoni who was playing such an important part in all the negotiations with the Greeks, was sent to " various princes and communities at the border of Hungary, Moldavia, Lithuania, Wallachia and Albania " to make them settle the problems of their regions and so to facilitate the crusade. In that brief sentence which follows immediately after a reference to the mission of Cardinal Cesarini as peace mediator between " the princes of Hungary and Poland and other neighbor countries, " it is rather surprising to find Lithuania mentioned besides Moldavia and Wallachia. Furthermore, recalling at the beginning of his bull the Union of Florence concluded with the Greeks, the Pope mentioned among their followers also the two Sarmatias which according to the classical and Renaissance terminology means all eastern Slavs at the border of Europe and Asia. And since at the time when this was written, the Holy See was already aware of the rejection of the Union by Moscow, it is clear that the Jagellonian king who had united Hungary and Poland and continued to be the suzerain of his brother's Lithuania, was practically the only powerful ruler of Eastern Europe who could respond to the urgent calls for help coming, as Eugene IV emphasized, from the Emperor and the Patriarch of Constantinople.

In view of that clear connection not only between crusade and union, but also between the defense of the imperial city, that " stronghold of the Christians in the East, " and the expected action of King Ladislas, it is highly significant that soon after the papal bull of January 1 reached Hungary and a few weeks before Cardinal Condulmer, a relative of Eugene IV, was sent as papal legate to Greeks, [7] notifying there the first victories over the Turks " in the regions of Hungary, Poland, and Wallachia, " the young King issued in Buda on March 22, 1443, a charter in recognition and support of the Union of Florence. [8]

The place where that document was drafted and the Hungarian magnates who were among the signatories are just additional indications how closely the subject matter was connected with the plans for the crusade which was discussed at that very moment in the same city and by the same men. But among the witnesses was also that Palatine of Podolia Hrytsko Kierdeyevich with whom Cardinal Isidore had been in touch during his first visit in the Ruthenian lands of Poland. [9] Most probably he now acted as an intermediary between the King whom he had joined in Hungary along with so many other Polish and Ruthenian lords in order to participate in the crusade, and the Metropolitan of Kiev who had reached the Hungarian capital on his way to Rome after trying once more to propagate the Union

[7] *Ibidem*, III, Nr. 264, May 8, 1443.
[8] Best edition in *Acta Regis Alexandri I* (ed. F. Papée), Cracow, 1927, Nr. 233.
[9] See the comments of B. Bučynsky, " Studii, " *Zap. Tov. Ševčenka*, Vol. 86, 5-6.

of Florence among the Ruthenians. In view of the more and more reserved, if not unfriendly attitude of those influential members of the Catholic hierarchy of Poland and Lithuania who were in sympathy with the Council of Basel, the official support of the King who remained loyal to Eugene IV and cooperated with him in the matter of the crusade, was highly desirable or rather absolutely necessary for that consolidation of the Union of Florence in the region where it had the best chances of success. The absence of Ladislas III from these lands was, of course, a serious handicap, but just as he tried to influence the Polish hierarchy through his messages from Hungary in the matter of their general relations with the papacy, so he decided now, undoubtedly on Cardinal Isidore's request, to clarify in Buda the official position of the Eastern Church within the limits of his Polish kingdom.

It is hardly necessary to stress that contrary to artificial misinterpretation in later times [10] the King was granting to that Eastern Church the privileges of the Buda charter in view of the Union of Florence which is specifically mentioned and on the implicit condition that that Union would be fully accepted and safeguarded by his subjects. These subjects who were to benefit from the charter were, of course, the Ruthenians, formerly of Greek Orthodox faith, now reunited with the Roman Church though permitted to retain their Eastern rite. But the question must be asked whether all Ruthenian lands of the Jagellonian realm were directly and immediately affected by the King's decision. There is no doubt indeed as to those provinces which were incorporated with the Kingdom of Poland and thus under the King's full and exclusive control. It is to them that he referred more particularly in the context of his documents speaking of " Russia and Podolia. " The separate mention of Podolia seems to signify that the name " Russia " which was being used in different meanings, was used here in its narrowest sense, meaning only the so called " Russian " Palatinate, sometimes also called the Palatinate, or province, of Lwów, which besides the Palatinate of Podolia was at that time the only one placed within the limits of the Polish kingdom. That Palatinate of " Russia " included the lands, or districts, of Lwów itself, of Halich, Przemyśl, and Sanok, and also the land of Chełm though the latter was almost entirely cut off from the others by the land of Bełz, then one of the royal fiefs which were in the hands of the Mazovian line of the old Piast dynasty and not incorporated with the Kingdom before 1462. However, from the point of view of ecclesiastic organization, Bełz was along with Chełm under the same Ruthenian bishop and therefore, that whole diocese most probably came with those of Przemyśl and Halich-Lwów (including Podolia also) under the provisions of the

---

[10] Briefly explained by K. Chodynicki, *Kościół*, 95 note 1 ; see also his remarks on Cardinal Isidore's influence in that matter, in note 2.

royal charter which set the pattern for the conditions in the Mazovian held duchy of Bełz. [11]

Much more important and at the same time much more doubtful is the question to what an extent the privilege which was issued in Buda by the King of Poland, affected the position of the Ruthenian Church in the lands which directly or indirectly belonged to the Grand Duchy of Lithuania. The federal union of that Grand Duchy with the Kingdom of Poland had been practically discontinued by the independent election of Prince Casimir, and even under the former union charters which thus had been disregarded, the Grand Duchy was autonomous in its internal constitution so that the laws of the Kingdom had no force there. It is true that during the crisis which followed the events of 1440 there was in Poland a trend to claim the control of some of the Ruthenian lands which had an autonomous position within the Grand Duchy, as for instance the controversial territory of Volhynia which now, under Svidrigello, was for several years in opposition to Wilno. [12] But these Polish claims were never enforced and the self-government of these lands, particularly of those which had their local princes, remained unchallenged. Furthermore, even without any new royal guarantees the position of the Eastern Church was entirely safe there, since it was to that church that most of the population, including most of the princes, traditionally belonged.

Nevertheless, in spite of all these considerations, whether legal or practical, it was not without importance even for the various territories of the Grand Duchy, that the King of Poland, the Grand Duke's elder brother who himself continued to use the title of " Supreme Duke of Lithuania, " recognized the full equality of the Eastern Church with the Polish Church of Latin rite, the equal privileges of both hierarchies and clergies. Particularly valuable were the provisions which guaranteed the ecclesiastical jurisdiction of the Ruthenian bishops, including matrimonial problems, as well as the property of their churches. It was a solemn recognition of the very principles on which the Union of Florence was based, and therefore an encouragement to accept that union, which must have had its repercussions in the whole Jagellonian federation and its lasting value for the future independently of the varying internal structure of that federation. Therefore, the original of the Buda charter was soon brought to Poland where it was kept by the Ruthenian Bishop of Chełm, while copies were to be found later in various other places, giving evidence even in much later days of the continuity of the Florentine tradition. [13] It is, of course, another question

[11] See about the subdivisions and administrative position of the various Ruthenian lands A. Jabłonowski, *Historia Rusi południowej* (History of Southern Ruthenia), Cracow, 1912.

[12] O. Halecki, *Dzieje Unii. jag.*, I, 339 f., where (345) also the connection of that project with the policy of the King himself is discussed.

[13] See my remarks in *Orientalia Christiana periodica*, 1953, 279 f.

how in the future, when that tradition faded away, the charter which so specifically made the Union of Florence and its full respect a prerequisite condition of all rights granted to the Ruthenian clergy, could be interpreted as protecting these rights even after their return to Greek Orthodoxy and separation from Rome. At the given moment, the momentous document of March 1443 made the head of the Jagellonian dynasty the formal protector of the Union of Florence among all Ruthenians whom his power or at least his influence could reach.

Such a new success of Cardinal Isidore, then Metropolitan of Kiev and all Russia who had felt obliged to leave the area of his jurisdiction and was never to return there, seemed the more precious and decisive, because the anti-Ottoman campaign which King Ladislas was preparing in the spring of that year of 1443, was to lead in the fall to a spectacular triumph.[14] Even before the Hungarian forces with their Polish and Serbian auxiliaries penetrated deep into the Balkans, raising high hopes both at the papal curia[15] and in Constantinople, Isidore met Eugene IV in Siena, and his report in the matters of both reunion and crusade seemed so satisfactory that when soon after his arrival, on July 11, the Pope received the alarming news of the death of the Patriarch of Constantinople, Mitrophanes, Isidore, on August 28, was sent once more on a mission which through his Greek country of origin was supposed to lead him to Russia again.[16]

Why the Ruthenian Cardinal, as he so frequently was called, never reached that ultimate goal and only from Constantinople communicated with the Ruthenian princes and hierarchy, that is understandable in the light of the rapidly changing situation of the following two years. Under the impression of the victorious advance of the crusaders, Eugene IV who, in 1443, in spite of all his efforts had not succeeded to get them any assistance from the western powers, became so optimistic that early in 1444 he took a rather surprising decision. In addition to Cardinal Condulmer who was entrusted with the command of the Christian navy but kept his position of Legate to Greece, in agreement with the uninterrupted negotiations between the Pope and Emperor John VIII,[17] another Legate to the Greek nation and the adjacent lands " beyond the seas " was appointed on February 12,[18] and this was the same Cardinal Cesarini, who as legate to Hungary, Poland, and all their neighbor countries dependent on King Ladislas, was preparing the land action against the Turks. For after his

---

[14] The whole campaign is best described by J. Dąbrowski, *op. cit.*

[15] See the memorandum submitted to the Pope by Beltramus de Mignanellis, published by J. Hoffman in *Concilium Florentinum - Fragmenta Protocolli* etc., Rome, 1951, 81-87, particularly 86 and the comments in the introduction, pp. XL-XLII.

[16] Eubel, *Hierarchia Catholica medii aevi*, II, Nr. 55 ; see A. M. Ammann, *Abriss*, 144.

[17] *Epistolae pontificiae*, III, Nr. 266-268.

[18] *Ibidem*, Nr. 274.

return from his campaign of 1443, the King was expected soon to undertake another and final one, so that after victory the two legates to Greece, one at the head of the navy, the other one with the Hungarian army, would meet in Constantinople, definitely liberated from the Turkish menace thanks to the assistance of the Catholic world.

It is only too well known that contrary to these expectations the great crusade of 1444 ended in the defeat of Varna where on November 11, 1444, the heroic King of Hungary and Poland as well as Cardinal Cesarini lost their lives. But contrary to a persistent legend the decision to undertake the second expedition, in spite of the peace proposals made by the Turks, was neither hopeless nor a break of faith.[19] It is true that Eugene IV was so anxious to mobilize all Christian forces against Murad II that he absolved one of the Albanian leaders from his oath to the Turks.[20] But King Ladislas had never taken any oath, because he did not ratify the peace treaty or rather the ten years truce which had been signed on not too favorable conditions in Adrianople on June 12.[21] On the contrary, in spite of a Turkish embassy sent to Szeged he openly proclaimed there on August 4, that he would proceed with the promised crusade. And while it is true that the separate peace concluded and ratified by the Despot of Serbia[22] reduced the forces of the crusaders, and that the Christian navy did not succeed in preventing the Turkish forces in Asia from crossing the Straits, the Greeks had no responsibility whatever in the failure of the crusade. On the contrary, the Emperor's brother and later successor, Constantine Palaeologus whom Eugene IV rightly considered even more loyal and faithful to the Union of Florence than John VIII himself,[23] moved from the Peloponnesus where he then was ruling, against the Turks, making a courageous and helpful diversion.

---

[19] I tried to prove this in my book *The Crusade of Varna. A Discussion of Controversial Problems*, New York, 1943, and in spite of the objections of some historians (see G. Ostrogorsky, *History of the Byzantine State*, Oxford, 1956, 503, note 1) who, in general, merely repeat the old arguments, I have not changed my opinion, especially as the leading specialist in Turkish history of that period, Franz Babinger, did not find any evidence that the Turks blamed King Ladislas for any break of faith. See his study " Von Amurath zu Amurath. Vor-und Nachspiel der Schlacht bei Varna, " *Oriens* (Journal of the International Society for Oriental Research), III (1950), 233-243, 251-254. The objections of J. Dąbrowski, *L'Année 1444*, Cracovie 1952, will be answered in my article now being printed in *Teki historyczne*, London 1958.

[20] This document, published already by O. Raynaldus, *Annales ecclesiastici*, 1444, Nr. 6, has been discussed for the first time by T. V. Tuleja, " Eugenius IV and the Crusade of Varna, " *The Catholic Historical Review*, XXXV (1949), 273 note 79.

[21] The documents are reprinted in the appendix to my *Crusade of Varna*, 82-93.

[22] It is only this separate peace with Serbia which is mentioned in the *Annales sultanorum Othmanidarum* where nothing is said about any treaty with the King of Hungary and Poland, and this fact, pointed out by L. Bréhier, *Vie et mort de Byzance*, 502, is a strong argument in favor of my interpretation.

[23] *Epistolae pontificiae*, III, Nr. 249, April 22, 1441.

He paid for his cooperation with the Latins when the Turks soon after their victory in the Balkans invaded once more the Despotate of Morea. But this was only a small part of the disastrous and far reaching consequences which the battle of Varna had for the two inseparable causes of the defense of all Christendom against the Turks and the reunion of the Eastern and Western Churches. As far as the fate of Constantinople and the chances of the Union of Florence among the Greeks and the Balkan Slavs are concerned, these consequences are obvious. Though the Union of Florence was not formally rejected in spite of the severe disappointment which the failure of the crusade was for the Greeks, and though less than one year after Varna, in July 1445, another Patriarch faithful to the union, Gregory Mammas, was elected in Constantinople and cooperated there with Cardinal Isidore, [24] the Union of Florence was not formally proclaimed either, and the opposition against it was steadily growing. And when Emperor John VIII who had been forced to appease the Turks once more after the battle of Varna, died on October 31, 1448, he may have known that a few days before the Hungarians under John Hunyadi who had resumed the struggle against the Turks, had been again defeated by them near Kosovo, the place where the Serbs had been crushed by Murad I in 1389. [25]

About the situation in Constantinople the Holy See was kept informed in detail by Cardinal Isidore. Thanking him for his frequent letters, Eugene IV, always deeply concerned with both " the union of the Churches and the destruction of the infidels, " encouraged him on June 11, 1445, [26] to serve the cause of the union as he had already done it before the Council of Florence. And it was Isidore's closest collaborator and successor as Abbot of St. Demetrius in Constantinople who was sent by the Emperor in the spring of 1448 to Pope Nicholas V [27] who the year before had succeeded Eugene IV and strictly continued his eastern policy.

But all this clearly shows that the Metropolitan of Kiev, remaining in Constantinople much longer than originally expected and dealing primarily with Greek problems, had given up the idea of proceeding to Russia. As far as Muscovite Russia was concerned, this was natural not only in view of his sad experience in 1441, but even more because of the continued hostility of Basil II against the Union of Florence. That opposition was so strong that it affected even Moscow's relations with Constantinople to which hitherto so much importance had been attached. Basil II, too, had his information, more or less accurate, about what was going on among the Greeks, and having probably heard that many of them were opposed to what had been promised in Florence, he decided not only in 1441, but again

---

[24] A. M. Ammann, *op. cit.*, 144 f.
[25] L. Bréhier, *Vie et mort de Byzance*, 506.
[26] *Epistolae pontificiae*, III, Nr. 282.
[27] *Ibidem*, Nr. 296 (papal safe-conduct of March 13, 1448).

in 1443, to get in touch with both Emperor and Patriarch in the matter of replacing Isidore by another metropolitan, faithful to what Moscow considered the Orthodox tradition. It seems that on both occasions the Grand Prince recalled his envoys, [28] having received news about the official attitude of the Empire and probably also about Isidore's presence in Constantinople. If, however, he hesitated to make his own candidate, Bishop Iona of Riazan, metropolitan of Russia even without Constantinople's agreement, it was not only because of his serious domestic troubles during the second phase of the civil war in which he even was temporarily deposed and blinded on his rival's order, [29] but also because he was waiting how the situation in Byzantium would develop in both the religious and the political sphere.

When in December 1448, at a synod convoked in Moscow, Iona was really elected Metropolitan without even any consultation with Constantinople, [30] it was not because of the recent change on the imperial throne and not only because Basil II had finally triumphed in the civil war in which the hierarchy and particularly Iona had supported him faithfully, but also because it seemed no longer necessary to reckon with the declining Greek Empire. The failure of the crusading movement in defense of the Greeks, obvious already after Varna and even more in 1448, must have confirmed Moscow in the opinion that the fall of Constantinople was imminent, and though Basil II a little later sent a letter of excuse to the new Emperor, Constantine XI, trying to explain why he had to appoint Iona without waiting for Constantinople's approval, [31] it is obvious that that appointment was a break with the Greeks who had betrayed Orthodoxy, just like Isidore himself, by concluding the Union of Florence, and a decisive step in making the Russian Church controlled by Moscow's ruler completely independent of Constantinople.

That same decision was, of course, a final confirmation of the Grand Prince's decision of 1441 to reject the Union of Florence absolutely. That decision was now confirmed by the hierarchy assembled in synod, giving clear evidence that they were ready to follow the ruler even in ecclesiastical matters. Confirmed also was that the Russian Church which already for centuries had been practically in complete separation from Rome, definitively rejected any papal interference with its affairs. And it was certain that Iona who recalled later that he had become Metropolitan of Russia

---

[28] Golubinsky, *Istoria*, II, 476-478.

[29] A. E. Presniakov, *Obrazovanie Velikorusskago Gosudarstwa*, Petrograd 1918, 400.

[30] The decisive importance of that well known fact for Moscow's relations with both Constantinople and Rome has been well explained by Ammann, *Abriss*, 146. See also about the growth of Moscow's " anti-Byzantine attitude " the remarks of I. Ševčenko, *loc. cit.*, 308, and M. Cherniavsky, *loc. cit.*, 353 f.

[31] Golubinsky, *op. cit.*, 458 f.

by the grace of God and the will of the Grand Prince,[32] would continue to support that prince in his policy of independence from the second Rome and hostility to the first one.

But it is equally obvious that the momentous decisions of the Synod of 1448 represented the attitude of only the Church of Great Russia, of the Muscovite State. Even the attitude of those Great Russian lands which were not yet completely dominated by Moscow, particularly of the Republic of Novgorod, could remain doubtful.[33] And as to the Ruthenian Church of the Jagellonian States, whose tradition and position towards Rome had always been quite different, it could even seem that the recent political tension between Lithuania and Moscow, though it resulted only in a minor war of comparatively little importance, in a Russian invasion of a frontier district in 1444 and a Lithuanian raid during the following winter,[34] would stress the opposition between the two powers in ecclesiastical matters also. But precisely when Grand Duke Casimir after that campaign against Moscow was staying in the White Ruthenian city of Polotsk, he was informed of his brother's death in the battle of Varna.[35]

That this tragedy would have far reaching consequences for Lithuania as well as for Poland was easy to foresee. Casimir was now the natural candidate to the vacant Polish throne which, though already elective in theory, was supposed to remain in the hands of the Jagellonian dynasty, were it only in order to continue the union with Lithuania. But the election of the Grand Duke of Lithuania as King of Poland necessarily led to protracted negotiations between the two countries regarding the conditions of their restored union, and the differences of interpretation in that matter were to absorb not only the candidate but also the lords of both nations for several years, even after Casimir's coronation in Cracow in 1447.[36] The problems of ecclesiastical policy in which the Bishop of Cracow and the Bishop of Wilno, though politically apart, had very similar ideas, received therefore, much less attention in these years, and the same is true, to a certain extent, of the problems of foreign policy.

Nevertheless, in that latter field two consequences of the battle of Varna and of the Polish election were soon to become apparent. First, as far as the struggle against the Turks was concerned, the defeat of Varna which did not yet directly affect the security of Poland but made her lose a promising young king and many gallant knights who had been fighting under his leadership, confirmed most of the Poles in their growing opposition against any participation in the projects of anti-Ottoman leagues. Already during

---

[32] *Russkaia istorič. biblioteka* (Russian hist. library), VI, Nr. 66, see also Nr. 64.
[33] Ibidem, Nr. 65.
[34] Kolankowski, *Dzieje W. Ks. Lit.*, I, 261.
[35] Halecki, *Dzieje Unii*, I, 352.
[36] *Ibidem*, I, 353-363.

the last years of Ladislas' reign in Hungary the Polish diets had claimed his return to his native country whose immediate interests seemed neglected, and Oleśnicki himself did not favor any longer an undertaking which was serving the policy of Eugene IV, contrary to the interests of the Council of Basel. [37]   Now, when after Varna the personal union between the kingdoms of Poland and Hungary was discontinued, there seemed to be no reason left for the former to participate in the latter's struggle against the Turks which in 1448 led to another defeat.   The hero of Varna had certainly not forgotten the interests of Poland nor even those of Lithuania : when planning his Turkish campaigns he had tried to strengthen the control of the Black Sea coast by the administration of Podolia and to improve the relations with the Tartars of the Crimea [38] whose invasions were a permanent threat to the Ruthenian borderlands of both the Kingdom of Poland and the Grand Duchy of Lithuania.   In that respect there was an obvious community of interest between the two States which now, under Casimir, were to be in a personal union.   But the main problem which Lithuania had to face, viz., the growing power of Moscow after Basil's final victory in the civil war, was hardly of any interest to the Poles who only exceptionally participated in the struggles at Lithuania's remote northeastern border. [39]   When, therefore, Grand Duke Casimir, succeeding his brother, became King of Poland, most of the time residing in Cracow and soon involved in the special problems of that country, a change in his policy with regard to Moscow was a natural consequence from which the prospects of the Union of Florence had to suffer in northeastern Europe just like they suffered in the Balkans from the failure of the anti-Ottoman action.

It is true that even in 1448 far reaching projects of replacing Basil II by another Russian prince more friendly to Lithuania seemed to be seriously considered. [40]   They had, however, no chances of success at all and were replaced the following year by a policy of appeasement which resulted in the important treaty of August 31, 1449, [41] apparently a turning point in the relations between Lithuania and Moscow. Recognizing his eastern neighbor as an equal, King Casimir divided with him the whole of eastern Europe into their respective spheres of interest and planned some kind of cooperation in political matters.   These matters were, as usual in these relations, inseparable from ecclesiastical issues, and it was highly significant that the treaty had been negotiated with the participation of the Metropolitan of Moscow, Iona, who once more appeared as Basil's closest adviser.   It is,

---

[37] Maleczyńska, *op. cit.*, 159.
[38] Halecki, *The Crusade of Varna*, 77.
[39] Halecki, *Dzieje Unii*, I, 368 f.
[40] *Ibidem*, I, 365.
[41] *Akty zapadnoi Rossii* (Documents concerning West Russia), I, Nr. 50.   On Iona's role in the negotiations see Chodynicki, *op. cit.*, 55, n. 3.

therefore, not surprising that there followed, in 1451, an agreement [42] in which Casimir recognized that same Iona as metropolitan of his own Ruthenian peoples disregarding the rights of Cardinal Isidore and the very existence of the Union of Florence to which Iona was so violently opposed. Among the members of the Lithuanian Council who are listed as witnesses of that agreement and obviously favored the appeasement of Moscow in both political and religious questions, there was not only a majority of Catholic lords but the Catholic Bishop of Wilno himself who, it is true, had never supported the Union of Florence, as Cardinal Isidore complained in Rome. Even the Ruthenian provinces of Poland seem to have been affected by that decision [43] which contrary to a long tradition accepted the control of all Ruthenian Orthodox by a metropolitan residing in Moscow and completely dependent on her political master.

For the time being nobody in Lithuania or Poland where spiritual and secular leaders were engaged in petty rivalries between the two countries with Casimir as patient mediator, [44] seemed to realize the serious political danger which was involved. But even Cardinal Isidore who from the point of view of Rome and according to the Union of Florence continued to be the rightful Metropolitan of Kiev and all Russia, did not react in those years against such a violation of his rights nor against the virtual repudiation of the Union in his whole metropolitan province. For he was then, after the defeat of Varna and before the fall of Constantinople, mainly concerned with the fate of his Greek country of origin and with the attitude of the Byzantine Empire in the matter of religious reunion, an attitude which was carefully observed by Moscow and by many Ruthenian leaders including the princes of Kiev. [45]

After returning to Rome, the " Ruthenian " Cardinal of Greek origin, joined his countryman Bessarion as adviser of the new Pope, Nicholas V who no less than his predecessor Eugene IV was interested in the acceptance of the Union of Florence by the whole Christian East and equally convinced that the attitude of Constantinople would prove decisive in that respect. Along with Isidore, Nicholas V tried to gain for reunion all Greeks, even those outside the Empire to whom he sent as Apostolatic Legate the experienced Andreas Chrysoberghes, now Archbishop of Nicosia. [46] But the Pope was, of course, particularly pleased when the new Emperor himself, Constantine XI, who had succeeded his brother John VIII in the fall of 1448, decided at last, after almost three years, to send to Rome an envoy

---

[42] *Russkaia istorič. biblioteka*, VI, Nr. 67.
[43] *Ibidem*, Nr. 68 III; see however, Chodynicki, *op. cit.*, 58.
[44] Halecki, *Dzieje*, I, 372 ff.
[45] Chodynicki, *op. cit.*, 56 f.
[46] *Epistolae pontificiae*, III, Nr. 291 (July 30, 1447); see also Nr. 299 and the papal appeals to Theodore Palaeologus, Nr. 293.

in order to explain why the Union of Florence had not yet been solemnly proclaimed in Constantinople. [47]

Nicholas V was indeed fully aware how strong there was the opposition against the Union, which eventually made the Patriarch Gregory Mammas abandon his see and come to Rome. [48] The request that he be recalled and universally recognized was, however, only the last point of a long message which the Pope, on September 27, 1451, sent to the Emperor in reply to his embassy. [49] Openly and strongly expressing his regret that both John VIII and Constantine XI had delayed the official proclamation of the Union of Florence, and even interpreting the decline of the once powerful Empire as divine punishment for the inveterate Greek schism, Nicholas V did not refer to any anti-unionistic synod which would have taken place in Constantinople. This is a conclusive argument that if such an assembly was held at all in the preceding year, it did not have the importance which was attributed to it by the adversaries of the Union of Florence. [50] As positive evidence of the world-wide significance of that Union, the Pope enumerated all the Christian countries to which copies of the decree of 1439 had been sent. The " glorious Kingdom of Poland " was included in that list along with the other Catholic powers but without any reference to its own Greek Orthodox population which had accepted the reunion with Rome, and this is just one more evidence that at the given moment the Holy See, trying to safeguard the great achievement of the Council of Florence, was chiefly if not exclusively concerned with the Greeks themselves.

This was, indeed, the last moment to have the Union formally and finally accepted by them, since the Ottoman threat which had been rapidly growing after the failure of the crusade of Varna, had become imminent in that very year of 1451 thanks to the accession of Mohammed II to the Turkish throne, [51] and since, on the other hand, many Catholics, even in Rome, were wondering whether the Greeks deserved the requested assistance in spite of the schism in which so many of them continued to persist.

Like so many of his predecessors, Nicholas V was decided to work for an anti-Ottoman league and for the defense of Constantinople without waiting for a complete settlement of the religious issue between the Greeks and the Latins, were it only for the obvious reason that it was easy to anticipate how with the conquest of Constantinople by the Turks any chance of reun-

---

[47] *Ibidem*, III, Nr. 304, p. 131 (reference in the papal reply).

[48] I. Ševčenko, *loc. cit.*, Chapter VI.

[49] *Epistolae pontificiae*, III, Nr. 304 ; see the important comments of the editor, p. 130 f.

[50] About the serious doubts regarding that antiunionist " Council " of 1450, see Norden, *Das Papsttum*, 719 n. 1, and R. Guilland in *Histoire du Moyen Age* (ed. G. Glotz), IX, 1 (Paris, 1945), 371, n. 14.

[51] See his latest biography by F. Babinger, *Mehmed der Eroberer und seine Zeit*, Munich, 1953.

ion with the Greeks would disappear. But it was equally realized in Rome that the chance of having the Union of Florence accepted was best at the moment when the Greeks needed so desperately the help of the Latins, and that the latter would be greatly encouraged to follow the papal appeals for such a help, if the Holy See could point at the final repudiation of the schism. And nobody was better qualified to obtain under these circumstances that long expected result than Cardinal Isidore who, therefore, at a time when he could hardly achieve anything in Moscow or even in Kiev, was sent once more to Constantinople. [52]

The main objective of his mission was indeed accomplished. On December 12, 1452, in the presence of the Emperor and surrounded by three hundred members of the clergy, the Greek Cardinal who had so much contributed to the success of the Council of Florence could solemnly proclaim its decision at St. Sophia's. [53] And it is quite possible that with the support of Constantine XI and thanks to his own familiarity with the conditions in his homeland which he understood so much better than those in Russia, Isidore would have succeeded also in appeasing the vociferous opposition against the Union, if he could have used the only argument which would have persuaded the overwhelming majority of the Greeks : an efficient assistance of the Latins against the Turks.

Unfortunately, the papal Legate brought with him from Rome only two hundred armed men, and that token of an auxiliary force was so insignificant, that he would later complain himself that he had left Rome " without bringing hence any assistance or help at all. " [54] It was not the Pope's fault that all that was done in that respect after Isidore's departure was too little and too late. But in any case when another legate, the Archbishop of Ragusa, Jacopo Veniero, was at last.sent to Greece by Nicholas V with " a certain fleet prepared according to the possibility of our power, " [55] that fleet of ten papal galleys and a few ships from Naples, Genoa and Venice could not arrive on time to Constantinople which was already besieged when the legate was named on April 29, 1453, and which was taken exactly one month later.

Among the many reports which brought that fateful event to the knowledge of the whole Christian world and shocked it so deeply, the most eloquent one was sent after hardly five weeks to Cardinal Bessarion by his friend and collaborator at the Council of Florence, Cardinal Isidore [56] who

---

[52] About the date of his arrival see G. Hofmann in *Orientalia Christiana Periodica*, XIV (1948), 406.

[53] L. Bréhier, *Vie et mort de Byzance*, 511 f. That the opposition was not so strong as usually supposed has been pointed out by I. Ševčenko, *loc. cit.*, 299 f. and note 57.

[54] In his letter to Bessarion, quoted below, note 56.

[55] *Epistolae pontificiae*, III, Nr. 306 (April 29, 1453), p. 141.

[56] Published by G. Hofmann, *loc. cit.*, 407-414.

almost lost his life in the battle of Constantinople along with the last Emperor, like Cardinal Cesarini had lost his in the battle of Varna along with Ladislas the Jagellonian. After " escaping the hands of the infidels " almost miraculously, the Greek humanist pointed out at the very beginning of his report that no fall and ruin of any other famous city, not even that of Troy nor the threefold destruction of Jerusalem, could be compared with the conquest and sack of his beloved Constantinople. And at the end of his description he warned of the imminent danger which now was threatening Italy. On the other hand, among all those who in the various Catholic countries commented upon the alarming news about the fall of the imperial city, nobody better summed up the significance of the catastrophe than the Polish historian Jan Długosz : [57] " Of the two eyes of Christendom — he wrote — one has been torn out and of its two hands one has been cut off. "

However, neither the Greek who did his best to propagate the Union of Florence not only among his countrymen but also among the Eastern Slavs, nor the Pole who under Oleśnicki's influence remained rather indifferent towards that union and towards its repercussions among the Ruthenians of the Polish-Lithuanian federation, seems to have realized at the given moment how deeply the conquest of Constantinople by the Turks was to affect the further destinies of the Union of Florence both in southeastern and northeastern Europe.

As a universal reunion between western and eastern Christendom the work of the Council of Florence received in 1453, fourteen years only after its completion, a deadly blow from which it was not to recover for centuries to come. Three of the eastern patriarchates were under Muslim domination already in 1439 and therefore unable to join the work of reunion except through the intermediacy of the Greek hierarchy. And for the same reason the unions with the dissident eastern Churches of Africa and Asia which were concluded in Florence and Rome during the later part of the Council, [58] could not really come into force. Now, however, the Eastern Empire itself, or rather what remained of it, was conquered by the most aggressive Muslim power, and the foremost of the eastern patriarchates, the last which had remained free, was dependent, not as in the past on a Christian Emperor, but on the much more autocratic Muslim sultan who took his place.

The shrewd Mohammed II was quick to understand that instead of openly persecuting his new Christian subjects and forcibly converting them to Islam, it was much wiser to take advantage of the opposition and prejudice of so many of them against Western Latin Christendom which the Turks still had to fight, and in particular against the Holy See who was

[57] *Hist. Pol.* V., 145
[58] *Epistolae pontificiae*, II, Nr. 224, III, Nr. 258, 278, 283.

taking the lead in organizing Christian resistance. The streets of Constantinople were still covered with the blood of thousands of Christian victims, when on June 1, 1453, the Sultan, exercising for the first time his imperial authority in the unhappy city, proceeded with the solemn investiture of a new Greek Patriarch. It was obviously under his influence that to that office nobody else was elected but the famous George Scholarius, better known under his monastic name of Gennadius who after seeming to favor the union with Rome now violently turned against it and was then the most prominent leader of the anti-Latin opposition. [59]

That first election, or rather appointment, of a Patriarch of Constantinople under Ottoman rule set a sad precedent. Not only was any free election made impossible and the candidate forced to pay an arbitrarily determined amount of money to the Turkish authorities in order to be confirmed, but the highest dignitary of the Greek Church was gradually turned into a tool of Turkish policy and forced to follow its directives of which the interdiction of any relations with the Holy See was the most important. Whenever a patriarch would try to enter into such relations, he would have to suffer the worst consequences, and any return to the Union of Florence was, of course, out of the question.

When Gennadius was installed by Mohammed II to remain Patriarch until 1457, the legitimate Patriarch of Constantinople loyal to the Union of Florence, Gregory Mammas was still residing in Rome as an exile. It is obvious that after 1453 he was even less able to exercise any authority among the Greeks, except perhaps some of those who in the Peloponnesus and on the Aegean islands were conquered by the Turks only a few years later. [60] It is equally uncertain whether during these last years of freedom there remained any traces of the Union of Florence in the Serbia of George Brankovich who thanks to the separate peace he concluded with the Turks on the eve of the crusade of Varna was left undisturbed until the fall of Constantinople. When after that catastrophe he realized that the ultimate struggle for survival was imminent, he asked for the support of Pope Nicholas V who already on October 24, 1453, [61] appealed in his favor to all Christians and stressed on that occasion that since Brankovich with his people was faithful to the Union of Florence, no pressure should be exercised upon them to abandon the Greek rite. But even before the Despot, as Brankovich used to be called, succumbed to Ottoman aggression, his Catholicism seemed rather doubtful and the successor of Nicholas V, Pope Calixtus III, received serious warnings in that respect. [62]

---

[59] R. Guilland, *op. cit.*, 408 ; see his biography (" Scholarius George ") by M. Jugie in *Dictionnaire de théologie catholique*, fasc. 130 (1939), 1521 f.

[60] On the conquest of the Peloponnesus see D. A. Zakythinos, *Le Despotat*, 247-274.

[61] *Epistolae pontificiae*, III, Nr. 307.

[62] See G. Hofmann, in *Papst Kalixt III und die Frage der Kircheneinheit im*

That same Pope had soon to consider the much more important problem of the eastern Slavs and their relations with Rome, a problem which had received little attention at the time of the Greek tragedy, but naturally reappeared in its lasting significance when the question had to be answered whether these numerous populations, untouched by the Ottoman danger, would once more follow the Greeks in recognizing a Patriarchate controlled by the Sultan or give to Rome another chance to propagate the Union of Florence in the only region of Eastern Christendom which could develop freely. That question was to influence for a long time the whole history of northeastern Europe and though primarily religious, was to have far reaching political implications.

In the light of the whole tradition of that part of Europe it was not difficult to foresee that the answer to that question would be different in old Kievan Ruś', now included along with Catholic Poland and Lithuania in one body politic, and on the other hand, in the new Muscovite Russia where the fall of Constantinople received an interpretation diametrically opposed to the Western. While the Catholic West saw in the tragedy of 1453 a punishment of the Greeks for not having completely and sincerely given up their schism, Moscow considered the same event a punishment for having at all concluded the Union of Florence. Politically, the only Orthodox power which survived could now pretend to be the legitimate heir of the destroyed Byzantine power. Even before the theory of the Third Rome, identified with Moscow, gradually emerged from that conception, [63] the Muscovite authorities both secular and spiritual would not even admit that the Patriarch of Constantinople, though now again decidedly opposed to the old Rome, had any rights over their Church. [64]

It was still during the pontificate of Calixtus III that the Holy See took a decisive step which was inspired by the full awareness of the difference between the conditions in Kiev and in Moscow, and which opened indeed new, though geographically limited possibilities of saving the Union of Florence notwithstanding the defeat of Varna and the fall of Constantinople.

Osten, Città del Vaticano, 1946, 26 (from a letter of the Pope to St. John of Capestrano), where, however, the papal letter of recommendation for the Despot of Serbia, issued in the same year 1455 is quoted (Vatican Archives, *Reg. Vat.* 437 f. 187 ; see there also f. 232, the privilege for one of George's advisors, June 8, 1455).

[63] See Cyril Toumanoff, " Moscow the Third Rome : Genesis and Significance of a Politico-Religious Idea, " *The Catholic Historical Review*, XL (1955), 411-447 ; and the symposium *Teoria tretioho Rimu* (The Theory of the Third Rome), by eight Ukrainan scholars, published in Munich 1952-1954.

[64] W. K. Medlin, *Moscow and East Rome*, 75 f.

CHAPTER IV

THE REVIVAL OF THE UNION OF FLORENCE IN KIEV [1]

Throughout his whole brief pontificate Pope Calixtus III, continuing the oriental policy of his predecessor and alarmed by the consequences of the fall of Constantinople, showed a deep concern with the problems of Eastern Christendom. [2] He seized every opportunity to promote a joint action of all Christian powers against the Ottoman onslaught and to encourage all those who in the East remained faithful to the idea of reunion with Rome. But it was not before the last months of his life that the Spanish Pope, while preparing a diplomatic conference at the Vatican in view of the organization of an anti-Turkish league, [3] considered the opportunity of reviving the Union of Florence where the chances seemed most favorable : among the numerous Ruthenian peoples of Poland and Lithuania who were under the rule of a Catholic king, Casimir the Jagellonian. A first step in that direction was made on January 16, 1458, but it was not before July 21 of that same year, only a fortnight before his death that Calixtus III took a decisive action the consequences of which he was not to see.

The decision was, of course, his own but it was based on such a thorough knowledge of the situation in Eastern Europe and the local developments during the two preceding pontificates that the initiative must have come from a well informed and experienced adviser. A certain role of Cardinal Bessarion who was so attached to the Florentine tradition and cooperated with one pope after the other in all questions concerning the East, is quite possible. And the exiled Patriarch of Constantinople, Gregory Mammas, must have been consulted before he was called to participate in a far reaching change of the ecclesiastical organization in a vast region which was under his supreme authority and jurisdiction. But it is even more certain that Cardinal Isidore whose own position was directly affected

---

[1] On this problem see also my articles, " The Ecclesiastical Separation of Kiev from Moscow in 1458, " *Studien zur älteren Geschichte Osteuropas*, II (Graz-Köln 1956), 19-32, and " Rome, Kiev et Moscou après la prise de Constantinople par les Turcs, " *Comptes-rendus de l'Académie des Inscriptions et Belles Lettres*, 1956.

[2] G. Hofmann, *Papst Kalixt III und die Frage der Kircheneinheit im Osten*, Città del Vaticano, 1946.

[3] L. v. Pastor, *Storia dei Papi*, I, 749.

and who alone had visited in the past that whole area, conceived the rather unexpected project and suggested the leading role of his closest collaborator in its realization.

Before, however, he persuaded Calixtus III to interfere with the whole structure of the metropolitan see of all Russia, he drew his attention to one diocese which " was once a large part of Kiev and the archbishopric of Russia, " which Isidore had received " in command " as metropolitan of Kiev, and which now, after a long vacancy was made again a cathedral see with its own bishop. This was the bishopric of Halich which for many centuries had been the ecclesiastical center of one of the main Ruthenian principalities and where both the last native rulers and later the kings of Poland, the last Piast and the first Jagellonian, had tried to establish, with the consent of the Patriarchs of Constantinople, a separate metropolitan see. While the political center of that territory had shifted to the city of Lwów, since 1375 the see of a Catholic archbishop of Latin rite, and also the see of an Armenian bishopric reunited with Rome at the Council of Florence, [4] Halich still remained the traditional religious center of those Ruthenians of Greek rite who were directly under the rule of the Polish Kingdom and therefore in closest contact with the Latin West. For that very reason it seemed easiest to revive the Union of Florence first in that very center where the metropolitan residing in far away Moscow, the violent opponent of the Union, Iona, could hardly have any influence in spite of significant attempts in that direction after the agreement with King Casimir in 1451. Now, on January 16, 1458, [5] a Basilian from the St. Cyprian Monastery of Constantinople, a certain Macarius of Serbia otherwise unknown, was chosen, obviously at Cardinal Isidore's suggestion, to be named bishop of Halich. On the same day the Pope wrote to the King of Poland, [6] recommending to him the new bishop and asking him to help Macarius in the exercise of his pastoral duties. In both papal documents it was, of course, taken for granted that the diocese of Halich was reunited with Rome according to the decision of the Council of Florence.

But Halich, though particularly rich in glorious traditions, was only one of the dioceses of Greek rite which were situated within the frontiers of Casimir's realm. Two others, those of Przemyśl and Chełm, belonged with Halich to the Ruthenian provinces of the Kingdom of Poland, while a much larger number, the Archbishopric of Polotsk, as well as the bishoprics of Briansk, Smolensk, Turov, Lutsk and Volodimir, were along with the metropolitan see of Kiev in the Grand Duchy of Lithuania, strictly speaking in its autonomous Ruthenian lands and principalities. The settlement regarding Halich was, therefore, only part of a much larger problem

---

[4] See above, Chapter II, p. 49.
[5] *Documenta Pontificum Romanorum Historiam Ucrainae illustrantia*, ᵀ, Nr. 78.
[6] *Ibidem*, N. 79.

which was decided by Calixtus III six months later without waiting to see whether Macarius of Serbia would receive the requested support of King Casimir and succeed in regaining the diocese of Halich for the Union of Florence. After consulting the College of Cardinals, in the first place indeed Isidore and probably Bessarion, the Pope divided on July 21, [7] Isidore's "Ruthenian province" in two parts : the "superior" and the "inferior," so called from the merely geographical point of view, the former being more remote than the latter. That division strictly corresponded to the political situation of the given moment to which the ecclesiastical organization was to be adapted.

Calixtus III fully realized, as it was clearly pointed out in the bulls of his successor, [8] that what he called "Superior Russia" or Moscovia was governed by a schismatic ruler whose name was not even mentioned, while the "inferior part" of the metropolitan area was under the rule of a Catholic, the King of Poland Casimir. He also knew that the schismatic Basilian monk, Iona of Moscow who in the papal documents received no title at all, was using the title of Archbishop-Metropolitan of Russia or Ruthenia in general and tried to intrude "into that whole region." Admitting, though not saying it in so many words, that nothing could be done for political reasons as far as Muscovite "Superior Russia" was concerned, the Pope left that distant and inaccessible part under the purely theoretical control of Cardinal Isidore, without even trying to interfere with its actual situation. On the contrary, the see of Kiev with all parts of Lithuania and "Inferior Russia" which had a population living according to the Greek rite under the obedience of "the Archbishop of the Ruthenians" and under the secular government of King Casimir of Poland, were separated from the Muscovite part which was "occupied by schismatics and rebels and in particular by the monk Iona, son of iniquity, who acted as Archbishop of all Russia." And that separated region, viz., "the Church of Kiev with the before mentioned inferior parts" was to be ruled and governed by its own Archbishop, it being understood that the schismatic Iona and his possible followers would be removed from that region. At the same time a candidate for the metropolitan see of Kiev was chosen in the person of Gregory, the abbot of the Basilian monastery of St. Demetrius in Constantinople.

The earliest record of that Gregory, most probably of Greek origin like Isidore himself, [9] seemed to give every possible guarantee that he would fully restore the Union of Florence in his metropolitan diocese and remain faithful and loyal to the Holy See. He had been indeed throughout the

[7] *Ibidem*, Nr. 82, p. 146.
[8] *Ibidem*, Nr. 82, 85.
[9] The doubtful tradition of his local origin will be discussed below, in Chapter V, p. 106n. 23; on his earlier record see above, pp. 43, 51, 63, 73.

vicissitudes of a quarter of a century the most intimate collaborator of Isidore to whom he succeeded as abbot of St. Demetrius, his inseparable companion on his two missions to Russia, and after their failure equally active, along with the Cardinal, in the attempts to make the Union of Florence acceptable in Constantinople. It is uncertain whether Gregory returned there after being sent to Rome by Emperor John VIII in 1448, but there is no doubt that after the fall of Constantinople he was living in Italy as an exile in close contact with Cardinals Isidore and Bessarion, as well as with Patriarch Gregory Mammas who soon after his election consecrated him as Archbishop-Metropolitan of Kiev, according to the Greek rite.

That consecration seems to have taken place already under the successor of Calixtus III who died on August 6, 1458, before even the papal bulls referring to his momentous decision could be written. The final settlement of the whole matter was one of the very first actions of Pius II [10] who as Cardinal Piccolomini had participated in making the decisions regarding Kiev and now, on the very day of his coronation, September 3, only two weeks after his election, issued a whole series of bulls with a view of putting in force the planned reform of Russia's ecclesiastical organization and of facilitating the task of the new Metropolitan in union with Rome.

One of these bulls was addressed to Gregory himself, [11] and after summarizing in detail the decision of July 21 and enumerating the nine dioceses which were to be under the see of Kiev as " suffraganeae, " requested the metropolitan to assume his duties, praising his religious zeal, literary culture, and purity of life, and wishing him full success. Two other bulls, [12] identical in part, were sent to the chapter, clergy, and people of the city and diocese of Kiev, including all " vassals " of the Kievan Church, and to the nine suffragan bishops whose individual names were, however, not given in the address. In both cases the addressees were urgently requested — the bishops even under the threat of excommunication — to obey Metropolitan Gregory, appointed by the Holy See, and not the schismatic Iona who in the letter to the nine bishops is called " intruder and heretic, " nor anybody who would act in his name.

Less conventional and therefore more important are the two bulls [13] which on the same day informed the King of Poland of the papal decision and asked for his support. It is not easy to explain why two such documents, partly repeating the same details, were drafted and simultaneously

---

[10] G. Hofmann, " Papst Pius II und die Kircheneinheit des Ostens, " *Orientalia Christiana Periodica*, XII (1946).

[11] *Documenta Pontificum Rom.*, I, Nr. 82, where the letter edited by G. Hofmann, *loc. cit.*, 230-232, is reprinted.

[12] *Ibidem*, Nr. 85, 86.

[13] *Ibidem*, Nr. 83, 84.

sent to Cracow though only one of them is recorded in the papal registers.[14] The main purpose of either message was, of course, to ask Casimir to receive favorably and, if necessary, to protect Rome's nominee, and not to permit the schismatic Iona to exercise any authority in the regions which were under the King's control. There are, however, two differences. While one of the letters was particularly strong in indicting Iona and requested Casimir to take concrete action against him or "others" who would come in the King's power, keeping them in jail until their condemnation by ecclesiastical courts, the other text added a specific warning against any other intruder who might arrive on behalf of the "profane Patriarch of Constantinople who has been installed by the lord of the Turks."[15] Such agitators should be removed from the King's realm and not permitted to pass through royal territory to Moscow.

The twofold danger which already then threatened the religious union of the Ruthenians with Rome from both Constantinople and Moscow was, therefore, clearly pointed out and the particular danger of an understanding between these two centers of opposition duly stressed. Pius II added that in all these matters he was sending to Casimir the nobleman Nicholas Zagupiti (sometimes spelled Jagupiti or Jagupi), knight and count of the Sacred Lateran Palace, who obviously was supposed to accompany the new metropolitan. Furthermore, the Pope who was so anxious that no representative of the schismatic Patriarch of Constantinople should go to Moscow through Polish territory, at once asked the King to assist Archbishop Gregory and his special lay envoy if together or separately they would have to proceed to the part of "Superior Russia" on behalf of the Holy See. Another effort to work for the Union of Florence even in Moscow was, therefore, not excluded, though the ecclesiastical division of all Russia in two parts was giving evidence that Rome was fully aware that in either region the chances of success were very different and different methods had to be applied.

It is not easy to explain the role of Nicholas Zagupiti whose origin is entirely unknown[16] and whose assignment does not seem to have been clearly determined from the outset. For only two days after the bulls regarding the appointment of Metropolitan Gregory, on September 5, 1458,[17] Pius II issued a safe-conduct for Cardinal Isidore's "familiares," Bishop Anthony of Carthage and Nicholas "Jacub," Count of the papal palace, who both were being sent by Isidore for the settlement of his affairs to

---

[14] The other one, with the reference to the Turkish danger and to the mission of Nicolaus Zagupiti, is known only thanks to the copy in the registers of the Polish Chancery; see below, note 24.

[15] *Documenta Pontificum Rom.*, I, Nr. 83, p. 147.

[16] Probably he was of oriental origin; see the documents in the Vatican Archives quoted in my article, "The Ecclesiastical Separation ...," 28 n. 45.

[17] *Documenta Pontif.*, I, N. 87.

various lands of Italy "and different other parts of the world." And
since the former Metropolitan of all Russia was made on that same day of
September 5 Archbishop of Corfu [18] and, in general, turned to entirely different problems, the mission which he intrusted to his "*familiares*" had
hardly anything to do with Kiev and Russia, but rather was to send Zagupiti, along with the Bishop of Carthage, to quite different countries.

Yet, it finally was decided that the enigmatic Count of the Lateran
Palace would go "to the lands of the Ruthenians" as papal nuncio, accompanying, as originally planned, the new Metropolitan Gregory. But their
departure was obviously delayed, because the new safe-conduct for Nicholas
"Jagupi" alone was not issued before January 17, 1459, [19] along with a
similar though more elaborate document for Gregory himself and his "*fami-
lia.*" And one month before that final expedition of both of them to the
Ruthenians, on December 18, 1458, [20] Pius II wrote a third letter to the
King of Poland, briefly repeating what he had said in the first two, of
September 3, but enlarging upon one significant point. While in his earlier
messages the Pope had only referred to the possibility that "perhaps"
another intruder might be sent to the Ruthenian lands from Constantinople,
he now had definite news that "the pseudopatriarch and profane head of
Constantinople, constituted by the Turkish tyrant" intended to give to the
Church of Kiev another pastor, in opposition to the legitimate one and to
the authority of the Holy See. The King was therefore once more requested,
as a Catholic ruler, to defend Gregory and not to permit to establish a
metropolitan "of the hostile blood and the faithless Turkish nation."

Nothing is known about any such initiative of the schismatic Patriarchate where about the same time Gennadius was succeeded by Isidore II
Xanthopulos. Furthermore, it is highly improbable that even a Patriarch
appointed by the Sultan would have sent to Kiev a metropolitan of Turkish
blood. But, even if the information received by the Pope and forwarded
to the King of Poland was inaccurate, it is understandable how alarming
it must have seemed to Pius II who was just preparing an international
congress at Mantua [21] in order to organize an anti-Ottoman crusade, inviting
all Catholic powers, Poland of course included, to participate, and planning
soon to leave Rome in order to attend himself that unusual assembly. It
is quite possible that Pius II made his point in the message to King Casimir with a view of showing the danger of Turkish interference to a country

[18] *Ibidem*, Nr. 88, see also Nr. 92.
[19] *Ibidem*, Nr. 93.
[20] *Ibidem*, Nr. 91. Two days later Gregory himself wrote to the King of Poland,
asking for his protection and explaining the delay in his journey to Kiev ; Patriarch
Mammas had written to the King in the same matter already on November 20. Both
letters have been published by A. Prochaska in the article quoted below, note 24.
[21] L. v. Pastor, *Geschichte der Päpste*, II, 18 f.

which remembered only too well the catastrophe of Varna where the king's own brother had perished, and which at the given moment was engaged in quite another war, the protracted struggle with the Teutonic Order for the control of Prussia and the access to the Baltic.[22] In any case, the close connection between the policy of the Holy See in the matter of religious reunion and that in the matter of defense against the Turks became once more well evident.

However, the concrete and immediate difficulties which Metropolitan Gregory had to face when in the course of 1459 he arrived in the Ruthenian lands, were of a different character. First of all, the dioceses of Greek rite in which he was supposed to revive the Union of Florence, were in a rather confused and neglected situation, since so many years had elapsed between Cardinal Isidore's last visit and the arrival of his successor. Even before Gregory left Rome, bad news had been received there from one of his suffragans, viz., Macarius of Serbia whom Calixtus III had named Bishop of Halich a few months before the general settlement of the Ruthenian ecclesiastic problem. After arriving at his episcopal see Macarius discovered that "some sons of iniquity, entirely unknown to him," had taken possession of all property of the Church of Halich, which he enumerated in detail asking for papal assistance. Therefore, on September 11, 1458,[23] Pius II had to write to the nearest members of the Polish hierarchy of Latin rite, the Archbishop of Lwów and the Bishop of Przemyśl, requesting them to secure the full restitution of everything that rightfully belonged to the Bishop of Halich of Greek rite. There is no reference in the papal letter to any responsibility of the Latin clergy in that whole matter. On the contrary, the Pope obviously expected that the hierarchy of Latin rite would loyally support Macarius. But on the other hand, it is equally doubtful whether any schismatic opposition could be blamed for the troubles of the Church of Halich, especially as precisely that diocese was remote from any possible interference of the Muscovite metropolitan Iona. If, however, such was the situation in the Ruthenian provinces of the Kingdom of Poland, it was easy to foresee that it would be much worse in the much larger Ruthenian section of the Grand Duchy of Lithuania and particularly in those dioceses which were in the neighborhood of Moscow and of her sphere of influence.

Much depended, therefore, on the attitude of Casimir the Jagellonian who in the papal bulls was simply called King of Poland but was responsible for the situation chiefly as Grand Duke of Lithuania. The relations with the papacy were indeed important for his realm as a whole, and it

---

[22] About the connection of these problems see M. Małowist, *Kaffa kolonia genueńska na Krymie i problem wschodni 1453-1475* (Caffa, a Genuese colony on the Crimea and the eastern problem), Warszawa, 1947, 143.

[23] *Documenta Pontif.*, I, Nr. 89.

was in the newly established registers of the royal Polish Chancery that the bulls received in the matter of the Ruthenian Church were carefully copied.[24] Yet, the main external danger which threatened the revival of the Union of Florence among the Ruthenians came from the old rival and neighbor of Lithuania, from Moscow.

Accordingly Casimir's decision was affected by two different factors. One of them was his desire to improve the relations with the Holy See. If these relations had suffered from the attitude of the Polish administration and hierarchy at the time of the conflict between the Papacy and the Council of Basel, that difficulty had disappeared with the end of that conflict and Poland's unreserved loyalty towards Nicholas V.[25] But already toward the end of his pontificate, in 1454, a new source of trouble had appeared when the subjects of the Teutonic Order in Prussia, in open rebellion against their oppressive masters, placed themselves under the protection of Casimir and under the authority of the Kingdom of Poland. In the war between Poland and the Order which followed Casimir's acceptance of that appeal and was to last for the next thirteen years, the Order was looking in turn for the protection of not only the Emperor but also the Pope who proclaimed indeed an interdict directed against the Prussian estates as rebels against an ecclesiastical power.[26]

That situation did not change during the pontificate of Calixtus III and became even more delicate after the election of Pius II who in view of his earlier political record was considered in Poland as pro-German[27] to such an extent that Casimir had opposed his appointment, when he still was Cardinal Piccolomini, to the important bishopric of Warmia (Ermeland) in war-torn Prussia. Furthermore, since Poland at the given moment was neither able nor willing to divert her efforts from the Prussian battlefields to the anti-Ottoman action planned by the Pope, new disagreements were to be anticipated and appeared indeed when not without delay a Polish delegation came at last in November 1459, to the Congress of Mantua.[28] In principle, its leader, the Rev. Jacobus of Sienno, could not but support in an eloquent speech the papal appeal for the defense of Christendom, but the only concrete suggestion that he made was the transfer of the Teutonic Order from Prussia where no infidels were to be fought any longer, to the strategic island of Tenedos in the Aegean Sea, where the German knights, like the Hospitalers of Rhodus, would have had ample opportunity to serve

[24] These copies have been published by A. Prochaska in the review *Ateneum Wileńskie*, I (1923), 64-73.

[25] K. Morawski, *Historia Uniwersytetu Jagiell.*, II.

[26] M. Małowist, *loc. cit.*

[27] See I. Zarębski, *E. S. Piccolomini stosunki z Polską i Polakami* (E. S. P.'s relations with Poland and the Poles), Kraków, 1939, 330-332.

[28] Długosz, *Hist. Pol.*, V, 299 f.

the Order's original purpose. Such a solution had, however, no chance of being accepted by the Teutonic Knights and could not satisfy Pius II who wanted the whole powerful Jagellonian realm to participate in the crusade. He expressed that hope in his closing address at the Congress, and even when granting personal spiritual privileges and dispensations to some of the leading Polish lords, he would specify that these concessions would he valid "whenever they would fight against the infidels in defense of Christendom."[29]

The large number of privileges which individual members of the Polish nobility and clergy received during the Congress,[30] obviously on the recommendation of the royal ambassador, seem to indicate that in spite of some disagreements in political matters a notable improvement in the relations between the new Pope and the King of Poland was achieved indeed. Particularly significant in that respect was a privilege for the Queen-Mother,[31] full of praise for her religious devotion, and since that former Princess Holszańska, of Lithuanian origin and Ruthenian culture, had already in the past appealed to the Holy See in favor of the many Ruthenians "of Greek obedience" whom she had at her court,[32] it was perhaps not without her intercession that the Pope succeeded in gaining Casimir's support for his project regarding the ecclesiastical organization of the Ruthenian lands.

Yet, there was another probably decisive reason which made the King accept the papal request to support Metropolitan Gregory and, through him, the restoration of the Union of Florence within the boundaries of his States. These boundaries were not yet directly threatened by the Ottoman Empire, and therefore the repeated references of Pius II to a possible interference from Constantinople were not the most convincing argument. But the situation was different as far as Moscow was concerned, the neighboring power which Casimir had hoped to appease when in addition to the political agreement of 1449 he had recognized in 1451 the Metropolitan of Moscow as spiritual head of his own Ruthenian subjects. In the following years it became apparent that, as usual, such a policy of appeasement did not pay. Grand Prince Basil II had been anxious to gain Lithuanian cooperation as long as his rival in the hardly terminated civil war, his troublesome cousin Dmitri Shemiaka, remained a possible threat. But as early as 1452 that irreconcilable opponent was poisoned, under mysterious circumstances, in Novgorod where he had hoped to find a haven and where now Moscow's influence rapidly increased. And when in 1456 Moscow forced upon the Republic of Novgorod, as first step to its conquest, the humiliat-

[29] *Vatican Archives, Reg. Vat.* 501, fol. 301-302, Nov. 16, 1459.

[30] *Ibidem,* fol. 51-51v, 420v-421, 423-436v ("Expectativae Polonorum," Dec. 21, 1459); see also *Reg. Vat.* 502, fol. 212, 241v-242v, and 503, fol. 127v-128v.

[31] *Ibidem, Reg. Vat.* 499, fol. 15v-16, Jan. 13, 1459.

[32] *Documenta Pontif.,* I, Nr. 63, April 5, 1434.

ing treaty of Yazhelbitsa, [33] this was a flagrant violation of the 1449 agreement with Lithuania which in one of its most important articles guaranteed the independence of the republic. Basil II was hardly more respectful of other clauses of the peace treaty, trying to control also the Principality of Tver which in 1449 had been recognized as being in the Lithuanian sphere of influence, and in general, taking advantage of Casimir's absorption by the Prussian problem. Under such circumstances, the authority which Metropolitan Iona, Basil's closest collaborator, was permitted to exercise among the Ruthenians of Lithuania and even of Poland, was no longer an ecclesiastical issue only but assumed alarming political implications. A change in that respect was, therefore, highly desirable, and the papal initiative offered a welcome opportunity in that sense.

Casimir's formal answer is, unfortunately, not known and may have been given orally through his envoy to the Congress of Mantua. In any case, Jacobus of Sienno could already report that Gregory had been well received by King Casimir who seems to have recognized him at once as lawful Metropolitan of Kiev and all his Ruthenian lands. Apparently the King who remained anxious to avoid an open break with Moscow in the midst of the Prussian war, tried to persuade even Basil II himself to recognize Gregory. [34] But such a solution was, of course, unacceptable to the Grand Prince, and though he too was not ready for any political showdown, there started immediately a propaganda campaign conducted by the two rival metropolitans with a view of securing the recognition of the Ruthenians.

This was much more than a personal rivalry between two candidates to the same see. On the contrary, two issues of lasting importance were involved. It was to be decided, first, whether one metropolitan would continue to control all dioceses of the Eastern Slavs of Greek rite in spite of the transfer of the metropolitan's residence from the original center of Kiev to the colonial Volga region and in spite of the division of the whole area between two rivaling powers, or whether the ecclesiastical administration should be adapted to that political division which corresponded more or less to the ethnic distinction between the Ruthenian and the Great Russian peoples. Furthermore, the Ruthenians were placed before the choice of a metropolitan hostile to the Union of Florence or of a candidate supported by the Holy See and entrusted by the Pope with the task of reviving that union where it still was possible, briefly speaking — between a schismatic and a Catholic.

There was, however, an additional consideration which facilitated Gregory's mission. As the Pope rightly stressed in recommending him, he had been consecrated according to the Greek rite by the Greek Patriarch of

---

[33] A. E. Presniakov, *Obrazovanie velikorusskago gosudarstva*, 411 f.
[34] *Russkaia istorič, bibl.*, VI, Nr. 87, 100.

Constantinople, a patriarch living as an exile in Rome but for that very reason independent of the Turkish conqueror who had placed the Church of Constantinople in such a humiliating position. It is true that for the Ruthenians it was difficult to find out which one of the two Greek Patriarchs was the legitimate successor of the former heads of the Greek Church to which they remained traditionally attached. But in any case that tradition was by no means broken by recognizing Gregory, the disciple and successor of the undoubtedly legitimate Metropolitan Isidore, who was ready to reside among them. On the contrary, Iona would continue to govern them from Moscow where at the end of the decisive year 1459 another synod, similar to that of 1448, completed the detachment from Constantinople under a metropolitan who never had been consecrated by any Patriarch and was fully dependent on the Grand Prince. [35]

Before convoking that synod Iona, acting as always in full agreement with Basil's policy, had tried hard to secure the participation of the Churches of Novgorod and Tver [36] which like the political authorities of these places hesitated between Lithuania and Moscow. Nevertheless, neither the Archbishop of Novgorod where Iona had the support of the monk Simon, one of Isidore's companions at Florence but a violent opponent of the union, nor the Bishop of Tver whose Grand Prince continued to look for Lithuanian support, decided to attend that assembly, preferring to remain neutral for the time being.

This being so, it is understandable that the Ruthenian hierarchy of Lithuania and Poland was even less inclined to follow Iona, and when in April 1460 a Lithuanian Diet which met in Brest, officially recognized Gregory as Metropolitan, [37] little opposition was to be expected. From among the nine Ruthenian dioceses which were within the limits of the Jagellonian federation and whose pastors had received the papal message in favor of Gregory, only one eventually passed over to Iona: this was the Bishopric of Briansk, [38] in Moscow's neighborhood, in an area which ethnically was of a mixed character and later was the first to be lost by Lithuania politically also. But even in Smolensk, another frontier region always coveted by Moscow, the bishop, though nominated by Iona a few years earlier, recognized Gregory not later than in 1461 and must have closely cooperated with the new Metropolitan since he was elected his successor a dozen of years later. [39]

---

[35] On the decisive importance of that synod see A. M. Ammann, *Abriss*, 158 f.
[36] On the interpretation of his messages (*Russkaia istorič. bibl.*, VI, Nr. 82, 86), and their results see E. Golubinsky, *Istoria russkoi tserkvi*, II, 1, and A. Ziegler, *Die Union des Konzils von Florenz in der russischen Kirche*, Würzburg, 1938, 135-138.
[37] Ammann, *op. cit.*, 159.
[38] *Russkaia istorič. bibl.*, VI, Nr. 89, p. 671 ; see also Nr. 88.
[39] About that bishop, Misael, see below, Chapter V.

Gregory did not succeed, however, in extending his authority beyond the eastern frontiers of the Grand Duchy of Lithuania. As far as Muscovite territory was concerned this was easy to foresee and even anticipated in Rome when the two Russia's, the " inferior " and the " superior " were divided from each other in a new ecclesiastical organization. The hope that Gregory or at least his companion on the trip from Rome to the East, Nicholas Zagupiti, could eventually continue their trip as far as Moscow was nothing but an illusion. Even when Isidore's and Gregory's personal opponent, Iona, died in 1461, nothing was changed in that respect. It is true that the new Metropolitan of Moscow, Theodosius, and his successor Philip I who was to survive Gregory, had even less chances than Iona himself to be recognized in Kiev which had never been under their control. [40] But it is equally evident that Gregory's recognition in any of the dioceses which were within the limits of the Muscovite State, continued to be out of the question, especially as one year after Iona's death Basil II who died after so many vicissitudes of his long reign, left the throne to his son Ivan III, an even more energetic and successful ruler, the real founder of Moscow's power.

It took a long time even for Ivan III to complete the conquest of Novgorod and Tver both of which remained quasi-independent states between Lithuania and Moscow throughout the lifetime of Gregory. Even there, however, he failed to be accepted as Metropolitan, though his recognition would have strengthened both States in the affirmation of their independence from Moscow. But it would have provoked for that very reason Moscow's wrath and therefore, independently of any religious consideration, was avoided in the hope that such a cautious attitude in the delicate ecclesiastical issue would help to maintain some kind of political neutrality also. As far as the case of Novgorod was concerned, which was by far the more important in view of the political role of the Archbishop in the life of the republic, Gregory tried time and again to counteract Moscow's propaganda [41] which everywhere branded him as an intruder who had betrayed the Orthodox faith. But in spite of Novgorod's close ties with the Latin West and the old influence of Lithuania whose political assistance was expected by the anti-Muscovite party in the city, Gregory's attempts to bring that old see under his authority were of no avail. The Archbishop of Novgorod, another Iona, was impressed by the stern warning he received from the Grand Prince of Moscow against not only Gregory himself but even the Patriarch who had consecrated him. [42] In Tver, the death of Grand Prince Boris Alexandrovich, Lithuania's ally, in 1461, permitted

---

[40] About Iona's successors see Golubinsky, *op. cit.*, and Ammann, *op. cit.*, 160.
[41] On the conflicting views about his attitude see now Horst Jablonowski, *Westrussland zwischen Wilna und Moskau*, Leiden, 1955, 95 f.
[42] *Russkaia istorič. bibl.*, VI, Nr. 91-96, 100.

Iona, Metropolitan of Moscow, shortly before his own death, to remove the bishop who had opposed him in 1459 and to appoint another candidate. [43]

It was, therefore, obvious that in spite of such fluctuations and hesitations in the intermediary zone between Lithuania and Moscow, and with the exception of the border region of Briansk, the ecclesiastical boundaries of the separate metropolitan province of Kiev would continue to coincide with the political frontiers of the Jagellonian federation. In that respect the project of dividing the metropolitan area of " all Russia " according to the political situation, a project probably conceived by Cardinal Isidore, approved by Calixtus III, carried out by Pius II, and accepted by King Casimir, was a complete success, and its importance for the whole future of Eastern Europe could hardly be overrated. The separation of the metropolitan sees of Kiev and of Moscow, which in the past had only been a temporary solution dependent on political contingencies, [44] now became permanent and the dividing line between the Ruthenians and the Great Russians clearly appeared in the field of ecclesiastical organization also, where in those days it was much more conspicuous and significant than any ethnic or linguistic differences.

The question arises, however, whether all this was merely a problem of organization and administration by different metropolitans or a difference of faith and of attitude towards the Papacy and towards the Union of Florence. For Rome this was the real issue indeed, and Isidore's disciple was sent to Kiev as a metropolitan independent of Moscow because he was supposed not only to remain himself a Catholic loyal to the Union of Florence but also to gain the whole Ruthenian population of Greek rite in the Archbishopric of Kiev and all the dioceses under that metropolitan see for a similar loyalty towards Rome and the Catholic Church. Such a solution was at the same time in the obvious interest of the Catholic power to which these Ruthenian lands belonged, viz., of the Jagellonian, Polish-Lithuanian federation whose religious unity had been the goal of the founders of the federation, of Queen Jadwiga, King Ladislas Jagello, and his cousin Vitold. Following their example, King Casimir had no intention whatever to impose such a unity by force. At a time when the cause of the Union of Florence seemed lost, that King, in agreement with the hierarchy and clergy of Latin rite, had favored the idea of simply propagating the Catholic religion in that rite through the missionary activities of religious orders and individual conversions. [45] But since that method had only a very limited success and since a new opportunity seemed to open before the Union of Florence, now limited to the territory of his own realm, it was

---

[43] See Ammann, *op. cit.*, 162.
[44] For example in 1435, see Chodynicki, *Kościół*, 40.
[45] See A. Lewicki, *Unia florencka w Polsce* (The Union of Florence in Poland), Kraków 1899, 208, 259, 265 f.

only natural for Casimir to return to the program of religious union as conceived by his father and his contemporaries, and supported by his brother King Ladislas III in the brief period between Florence and Varna.

Unfortunately it so happened that in the decisive years after Gregory's arrival the King was absorbed by the endless difficulties of his war against the Teutonic Order and the troubles he had with the opposition leaders in both Poland and Lithuania. In the Grand Duchy, the main of these leaders, the Catholic Lithuanian John Gasztold, had just died but was replaced by his son-in-law Prince Simeon Olelkovich, the elder son of the King's own cousin Alexander, usually called Olelko, [46] who as Duke of Kiev had played such an important part in the matter of religious reunion when Cardinal Isidore proclaimed there the Union of Florence. Simeon was permitted to succeed his father in 1455 as autonomous ruler of the Kiev province, but resented that Casimir did not recognize the hereditary rights of this side line of the dynasty to the throne of Kiev, and he even pretended to replace the Jagellonian king as Grand Duke of Lithuania. A formal request to entrust the whole Grand Duchy to that candidate was submitted to Casimir by the opposition party at the Diet of Wilno, in 1460. [47]

It was, therefore, of great importance how Prince Simeon would react in the matter of not only Gregory's metropolitan authority but also of the restoration of the Union of Florence. In spite of his Lithuanian origin, the Prince was a devoted adherent of the Eastern Greek Church and penetrated by Ruthenian culture, as was that whole branch of the dynasty. And it was only natural that he received special appeals from Moscow to remain loyal to Iona and to reject the papal candidate. [48] These appeals were, however, of no avail, and Simeon and his partisans had no intention to come under Moscow's influence whether political or religious. [49] But the tradition of religious dependency on Constantinople was very strong in Kiev and in Simeon's family, as well as, to a certain extent, among all Ruthenians of the Grand Duchy. It was, therefore, very harmful to the cause of Gregory and of the Union of Florence that already in 1459 Patriarch Gregory Mammas who had consecrated him, died in Rome as an exile. Pius II replaced him by Cardinal Isidore [50] who in turn, after his death in 1463, was replaced by Cardinal Bessarion, but neither of these two faithful supporters of the Union of Florence had ever resided in Constantinople nor could maintain any contact with the imperial city. And this explains why Kiev, without formally rejecting the Union with Rome, was now looking again towards the traditional see of the Greek Patriarchate, perhaps without

---

[46] Halecki, *Dzieje Unii*, I, 398 ff. ; Kolankowski, *Dzieje W. Ks. lit.*, I., 292 f.
[47] *Ibidem*, I, 403.
[48] *Russk. istorič. bibl.*, VI, Nr. 88.
[49] See H. Jablonowski, *op. cit.*, 122, 136.
[50] His appointment of April 20, 1459, in *Reg. Vat.* 470, fol. 463-464.

being fully aware how completely its present holders were under the control of the Ottoman Empire.

That trend which could not be but very dangerous to the Union of Florence, did not appear at once, and Gregory himself could hardly follow it as long as his lifelong master, Cardinal Isidore, was still alive. But even King Casimir, hoping perhaps to appease the political opposition of the Duke of Kiev, considered it desirable to have Gregory recognized as Metropolitan of Kiev by the Greek Patriarch of Constantinople also. A first attempt in that direction was made in 1466 when the King after making peace with the Teutonic Order turned again to the eastern problems. Rejected by Patriarch Simon of Trebizond that request was granted by his successor, Dionysius I, around 1470, [51] probably at the very moment when Casimir made another effort to strengthen Lithuanian influence, both political and ecclesiastical, in Novgorod on the eve of the gradual absorption of that republic by Moscow. It was the younger brother of the Duke of Kiev, Prince Michael Olelkovich, who was sent by the King to Novgorod early in 1470 but returned as soon as at the end of the year he was informed of the death of his brother Simeon whose place he wanted to take in Kiev. [52] This was not permitted by Casimir who seized that opportunity to make the former Duchy of Kiev a province of the Grand Duchy under his own governor and to limit the authority of the Olelkovich family to the petty Duchy of Slutsk in the Pripet region. But the political tension which followed that decision, might have been one more reason for satisfying the desire of many Ruthenians, including their leading family, to arrive at an understanding with the Patriarchate of Constantinople.

In any case Gregory shortly, before his death in 1472, was recognized by that Patriarchate as Metropolitan of Kiev, to the obvious dissatisfaction of Ivan III of Moscow as expressed in his warning to the people of Novgorod. [53] Whether that Greek recognition increased Gregory's chances to be accepted as Metropolitan in Novgorod, is rather doubtful and came too late anyway, since the fall of the Republic and the liquidation of the Lithuanian party there was already imminent. It would be much more important to know how Rome reacted to these relations between Gregory and the schismatic Patriarch of Constantinople, which could be interpreted as an abandonment of the Union of Florence by the very man who was supposed to assure its survival at least among the Ruthenians. There is no evidence, however, of any condemnation or even blame by the Holy See, and never, not even in the later tradition, was Gregory considered unfaithful to his mission. [54] It is true that under Pope Paul II (1464-1471) and at the

---

[51] *Russk. istorič. bibl.*, VI, Nr. 100, p. 710 ; see Chodynicki, *op. cit.*, 65 note 1.
[52] Halecki, *op. cit.*, I, 410 ; Jablonowski, *op. cit.*, 148-150.
[53] *Russk. istorič. bibl.*, *loc. cit.*
[54] A. Ziegler, *op. cit.*, 137-140.

beginning of the pontificate of his successor Sixtus IV the Holy See does not seem to have shown much interest in the problem of reunion with the Eastern Slavs, and when that interest reappeared in the very year of Gregory's death, it was in connection with a surprising project of gaining for the union with Rome Ivan III of Moscow, a project which seemed to reduce the importance of keeping the Union of Florence alive in Kiev. But is equally possible that without underestimating the importance of the attitude of the Ruthenians and their separate Metropolitan, and realizing the difficulty of their position, the Holy See did not consider it necessary nor expedient formally to object to their relations with Constantinople which, after all, were based upon a long tradition, and with a Patriarch whose own attitude in the matter of reunion could not be freely expressed in view of the strict control exercised by the Ottoman Empire and who not before the same decisive year of 1472 officially repudiated the Union of Florence. [55]

Since King Casimir was, from 1471, absorbed by the succession problem in Bohemia and Hungary, the future of that Union in his Ruthenian lands depended now on the peoples themselves, on the question whether Metropolitan Gregory, in spite of his final, rather enigmatic turn toward Constantinople, had succeeded in making them loyal to Rome, and ultimately on the choice of Gregory's successor and his recognition by the other Ruthenian bishops within the limits of the Polish-Lithuanian Commonwealth. One thing only was certain : these bishops along with the metropolitan see of Kiev would remain fully independent of, and separated from the metropolitan see of Moscow which would control only the dioceses under Moscow's political influence. This was the permanent result of the decision taken in 1458 by Popes Calixtus III and Pius II, a decision which remained unaffected by shortlived hopes of Sixtus IV, in 1472, regarding Moscow herself.

---

[55] See, f. ex., E. Winter, *Byzanz und Rom im Kampf um die Ukraine*, Leipzig 1942, 41.

CHAPTER V

THE METROPOLITANS OF KIEV FROM MISAEL TO JOSEPH I, 1473-1501

The history of the Ruthenian Church from 1458, when Kiev was separated from Moscow under a metropolitan appointed by the Holy See and loyal to the Union of Florence, until 1596 when one of his successors, after sending his representatives to Rome, formally restored that Union, is clearly divided in two periods. During the first one which lasted to the turn of the fifteenth century, the most prominent among the Metropolitans of Kiev were anxious to remain in communion with the Papacy and the Catholic Church without, however, completely breaking with the Patriarchs of Constantinople who under Ottoman control were unable freely to express their opinions. From the beginning of the sixteenth century, Kiev's relations with Rome ceased almost completely, and while the tradition of the Union of Florence never disappeared, Greek Orthodoxy under the Patriarchate which remained in opposition to the Papacy, seemed to dominate in the Ruthenian lands of Lithuania and Poland exactly as it did under the Grand Princes of Moscow and their separate Metropolitans. If, however, in the later part of that second period the idea of returning to the Union of Florence was making slow but steady progress, it was because the repeated attempts to keep that Union alive, which had been made in the first period, though apparently unsuccessful, had not been entirely vain.

The second of these attempts coming immediately after the fourteen years of Metropolitan Gregory's patient efforts, has left as its only trace just one document [1] which has been even suspected of being spurious. [2]

---

[1] This is the long letter of March 14, 1476, sent by the Ruthenians to Pope Sixtus IV, which is discussed below. The full text is published in *Arkhiv Jugo - Zapadnoi Rossii* (Archives of South-West Russia), Part I, Vol. VII (Kiev 1887), 199-211. The various copies in which that text of the lost original was preserved, have been described by A. S. Petrushevich in *Literaturnyi Sbornik izd. Halitsko-Russkoiu Matitseiu* (Literary collection edited by the Galician-Ruthenian Motherly Organization), Lvov 1863, 223-260. I have examined the copies in two manuscripts of the Vatican Library : 1) *Slav.* 12, fol. 23-54, and 2) *Ms. Borg. P. F. Illirico* 16 (now in the *Fondo Borgiano* of the said library, formerly in the Propaganda Archives A⁰ 175), fol. 1-34, with a Latin translation of the Ruthenian text. There are slight differences in the arrangement of the signatures.

[2] The question of the authenticity of the document, first discovered in 1605 (see the hesitations of K. Chodynicki, *op. cit.*, 66 n. 3 and 622), has been reexamined by

Yet, for the first time prominent partisans of the Union of Florence among the lay leaders of the population were listed, and on no other occasion did the contrast between the religious attitudes of Ruthenians and Muscovites so strikingly come to the open.

In the spring of 1473 the Papal Legate to Russia, Antonio Bonumbre was returning through the Grand Duchy of Lithuania [3] from his mission to Moscow [4] which as so many other similar missions of the following century was a complete failure. Even if the Russian chronicles exaggerate in describing the Legate's defeat when he entered into theological discussions with the Metropolitan of Moscow, it remains certain that the Union of Florence was once more absolutely rejected there, contrary to the expectations which the marriage of Grand Prince Ivan III with Zoë Palaeologus, a niece of the last Emperor of Constantinople, who had been educated in Rome as a Catholic, raised at the Holy See. Bishop Bonumbre's Latin cross shocked Moscow in 1472 no less than that of Cardinal Isidore in 1441, and the Legate who accompanied the papal ward to the residence of her Orthodox husband, could only witness how rapidly Sophia, as the Greek princess now was called, instead of converting Ivan to the Catholic faith, had to conform to the religious beliefs and practices of her new country. Her marriage, first concluded at the Vatican not without misleading assurances and promises of Ivan's representatives, had to be finally celebrated by the Metropolitan of Moscow in his Orthodox Church, and far from contributing to any religious union, was soon to serve as an argument for Moscow's claim to be the third and last Rome.

Though it was impossible for Bonumbre to foresee these far reaching consequences, he must have left Moscow so alarmed and disappointed, that it could not be but a great comfort to him when in Lithuania other representatives of the Eastern Church spontaneously approached him with a solemn declaration in favor of the Union of Florence, which they requested him to bring to Pope Sixtus IV. Unfortunately, that document was to be lost and never reached the addressee possibly because the Legate himself, losing papal favor after his failure in carrying out his main assignment, did not come back to Rome but was sent to Venice. [5]

That lost message had been drafted at a synod of the Ruthenian hierarchy which soon after Gregory's death met in Novogrodek, where the Metropolitan of Kiev frequently resided. It was probably at the same

---

I. Ševčenko, *op. cit.*, n. 74, who added a new argument which led him to the conclusion that the letter is authentic. H. Jablonowski, *op. cit.*, 97 n. 31, considering other arguments, came to the same conclusion.

[3] *Codex diplomaticus ecclesiae Vilnensis*, I, Nr. 280 (April 1, 1473).

[4] Among the many studies of that mission that by P. Pierling, *La Russie et le Saint-Siège*, I, 139-175, remains the best.

[5] See A. M. Ammann, *op. cit.*, 186.

synod that his successor was elected in the person of Misael, Bishop of Smolensk, a native Ruthenian whose family, the Pstruch or Pstrutskis, [6] belonged to the lesser gentry but was related with some more powerful members of the nobility of the Grand Duchy. Very probably, too, most of these outstanding personalities whose names appear on the second letter sent to Sixtus IV when the first remained without answer, had signed already the earlier message. And it is even more certain that the lack of any papal confirmation was the main reason why Bishop Misael was still only Metropolitan-elect, when at a meeting held in Wilno on March 14, 1476, it was decided to send another appeal to Rome, repeating what had been said to the Pope three years before.

While, however, at that earlier date other members of the Ruthenian episcopate must have been present were it only in connection with the election of one of them to the metropolitan see, in 1476 the higher clergy was represented, in addition to Misael himself, only by two abbots who were at the head of the most important monasteries : the old and famous Monastery of the Caves in Kiev and that of Holy Trinity in Wilno. Their signatures were, however, followed by those of no less than thirteen prominent representatives of the nobility whose presence was very significant. Most important was the support of the first of the three princes, Michael Olelkovich, the younger brother of the late Prince Simeon of Kiev, who represented the glorious tradition of that city but at the same time the opposition against his uncle, King Casimir. [7] But immediately after the two other princes, Theodor Bielski and Demetrius Wiazemski, who came from the border region between White Ruthenia and Moscow, followed one of Casimir's most loyal supporters in the Grand Duchy, Ivan Chodkiewicz, [8] whose family was rapidly rising and who himself, though merely a descendant of Kievan boyars, was soon to be the next governor of Kiev.

Among the other nobles from various Ruthenian lands including Polotsk in the north and Volhynia in the south, four brothers, sons of the former Treasurer of Lithuania Alexander Yurievich, deserve special attention. One of them, now Casimir's Court Treasurer, Alexander Soltan whose second name was to become the name of the whole family, occupied an exceptional position among the Ruthenian nobility of his generation. A few years before he had travelled, with the King's recommendation, to almost all western countries, receiving laudatory safe-conducts from the various rulers whom he had visited [9] and studying in particular the religious life of the

---

[6] See about that family J. Wolff, *Kniaziowie litewsko-ruscy* (The Lithuanian-Ruthenian princes), Warszawa 1895, in the appendix on the " pseudo-princes, " p. 669 f., where it is definitely shown that Misael did not belong, as formerly supposed, to the family of the Princes Drutski.

[7] See above, Chapter IV, p. 96.

[8] O. Halecki, *Dzieje Unii*, I, 407, 411, 413, 418.

[9] These safe-conducts, of 1467-1469, issued by King Casimir, Emperor Frederick

peoples of Latin rite. Pope Paul II himself had received him into the Catholic Church of that western rite,[10] and now he was back in his country of origin with the title of Knight of the Holy Sepulcre which he seems to have visited too, and with the Order of the Holy Fleece which he had received at the Burgundian court. Nobody, therefore, could seem better qualified to work at home for religious reunion, and he could do it in cooperation with his youngest brother " kir Ioan " who had just been named Supreme Treasurer of the Grand Duchy and in 1471, in recognition of his devotion to the Roman Church, had received as lord of Poczampov in the diocese of Wilno, special privileges in matters of confession and fasting from the new Pope Sixtus IV.[11] It was only natural that this John or Ivan, was now chosen, along with another signatory of the message, to bring that appeal to the Pope whose favor he enjoyed.

Disappointed not to have received any answer to their first message sent through Antonio Bonumbre and fearing that the Pope had not received it at all, they started their second letter which was at the same time a lengthy theological treatise obviously drafted by a clergyman, perhaps by Metropolitan Misael himself, denying any possible rumors that they were not really true Christians. In evidence of this they included a formal profession of faith, emphasizing that in addition to the first seven oecumenical councils they also recognized the Council of Florence and specifying their belief in the procession of the Holy Spirit from both Father and Son. Furthermore, they not only stressed that the name of the Pope came first in their prayers, but compared him to a common source from which the four other Patriarchs were flowing like so many rivers. Having thus confirmed their loyalty to the Union of Florence and their adherence to those Catholic dogmas which were a matter of controversy with the separated Eastern Churches, they complained that the hierarchy of Latin rite was not fair to them and that attempts were even made to force them to give up the Eastern rite and to be rebaptized. They deeply regretted such unnecessary dissentions within the mystical body of Christ, which were only to the advantage of Turks, Tartars, and other heathens, and urgently requested that two papal delegates, well informed about both the Western and the Eastern Church as well as about the decrees of the Council of

III (who calls him " ritum Grecorum sectans "), Pope Paul II, King Ferdinand of Sicily (who mentioned that Alexander Soltan was travelling all over Europe " ut varios hominum ritus ac varia instituta perdisceret "), Galeazzo M. Sforza of Milan, King Alphonse V of Portugal, Charles the Bold of Burgundy, and King Edward IV of England, have been published in the review *Przegląd poznański*, XXXIII (1862), 66-74. I examined the originals in the private archives of the Soltan family in Warsaw and found them of unquestionable authenticity.

[10] S. Kutrzeba and J. Fijałek, *Kopiarz rzymski Erazma Ciołka* (The Roman copybook of Erasmus Ciołek), Kraków 1923, 75.

[11] *Documenta Pontificum Romanorum Hist. Ukrainae illustr.*, I, Nr. 97.

Florence — possibly one Latin and one Greek — be sent to them. These legates should help both Churches to keep their traditional rites, so that all would be united in the love of Christ. They expected a papal bull in that matter, and also the privilege to participate in the indulgences of the Holy Year which had been proclaimed " in Orthodox Rome. "

Even in such a very brief summary the position of those who assembled in Wilno, in 1476, under the leadership of the new Metropolitan of Kiev, appears clearly enough. It is obvious that they wanted to remain in religious unity with Rome according to the decisions of the Council of Florence, but also that there was a growing suspicion between the followers of both rites, Western and Eastern, who were living together in the same body politic. The signatories of the message were right in their conviction that only an impartial interference of the Holy See could improve the situation, and therefore it is highly regrettable that for the second time they did not receive from Rome the answer for which they urgently asked in the conclusion of the letter. The possibility that even that second appeal did not reach the Vatican cannot be excluded. But it is rather significant that even in the privilege of Sixtus IV for Ivan of Poczampov, of 1471, there was no reference to the Eastern rite and only a specific reservation that any concessions granted to him would lose their validity if he would cease to be in unity with the Roman Church and in obedience to the Pope. On the other hand, one year before the Wilno meeting, on the occasion of the Holy Year of 1475 which was mentioned in the letter of Misael and his followers, a clergyman of the Kiev diocese, Paul, son of Simeon " de Cizuwa, " appeared in Rome and received there a privilege of Sixtus IV [12] who permitted him to chose a Latin priest as confessor although, as the Pope stressed, he was himself a Ruthenian and " hitherto observed the rite of the Greeks. " There were, therefore, at least in individual cases, personal relations between the Ruthenians, both laymen and clergymen, and the Holy See where their eastern rite was recognized, but not without some fear that they might return to the eastern schism, and some encouragement to enter into intimate relations with Latin ecclesiastics.

As usual, however, Rome's attitude toward the Ruthenians which is so insufficiently known and open to diverse conjectures, cannot be isolated from the relations with eastern Christendom in general in which Sixtus IV was very seriously interested. And as usual, too, the purely religious aspect of the problem is inseparable from the Pope's desire to promote the defense against the enemies of Christendom. There were, in particular, the Ottoman Turks whose conquest of Caffa in the Crimea, in 1475, alarmed Sixtus IV and all Catholic powers, strongly urged on that occasion by the

[12] *Ibidem*, Nr. 99.

Holy See to cooperate against the common enemy. [13]   Even in Greek Orthodox Moldavia the tradition of the Union of Florence seemed to revive under
the impression of the growing Turkish danger, and at the request of her
prince, Stephen the Great, the Pope, calling him " a true defender of the
Christian faith, " granted in 1476 the indulgences of the last Holy Year to
all those who were fighting under his command. [14]

Among the Christian nations which would be open to invasion by the
Turks if Moldavia were conquered, there was in the first place the Polish-
Lithuanian federation and particularly its Ruthenian lands.   King Casimir
was indeed deeply concerned with the fall of Caffa which a few years before
had placed itself under his protection, [15] and with the fate of Moldavia
whose princes time and again recognized Polish suzerainty in order to get
assistance against the Turks.   But greater than the danger from the Turks
and even from the Tartars of the Crimea who after the conquest of Caffa
became vassals of the Ottoman Empire, seemed to the Jagellonian another
eastern threat which was coming from Moscow, particularly after the final
conquest of Novgorod by Ivan III, in 1478. [16]   And Sixtus IV, though the
Ottoman onslaught was so much nearer, approaching now Italy and even
Rome, shared that new alarm, especially as the ecclesiastical State of Livonia, always considered to be under the protection of the See of Peter, also
was directly threatened by the absorption of the neighboring Republic of
Novgorod and immediately suffered from Muscovite invasions.

Acting through the Livonian hierarchy which had informed him about
the gravity of the situation, and trying to interest all Catholic rulers in the
defense of that distant outpost of Western Christendom against the Grand
Prince of Moscow and his supporters, the Pope did not hesitate to call the
aggressors " enemies of the Christian name, " [17] exactly as he used to call
the Mohammedan Turks, though this time the danger came from Greek
Orthodox Christians whom only a few years ago he had hoped to reunite
with the Catholic Church.   In spite of the great disappointment in that
respect which had followed Ivan's marriage with the niece of the last Em-

[13] M. Małowist, op. cit., 342 ; in connection with the relations between Caffa where
the Union of Florence continued to be formally recognized, and the Holy See (see
ibidem, 258, 262) the safe-conduct granted by Pope Paul II, on July 16, 1468 to the
envoys of Caffa sent to him in matters regarding the defense of their city (Reg. Vat.
529, fol. 211v-212) deserves attention.

[14] Reg. Vat. 578, fol. 92-93, Jan. 5, 1476 ; see also the bull in favor of the Moldavian Church of April 9 of the same year : A. Theiner, Monumenta Hungariae, II,
Nr. 634, see also Nr. 636.

[15] Małowist, op. cit., 174-179.

[16] Kolankowski, Dzieje, I, 332-334.

[17] See the instructions of Sixtus IV given to the Archbishop of Riga and to the
Bishop of Reval who was to go as papal legate in that matter to Germany, Denmark, and Poland : Vat. Archives, Misc. Arm. II, vol. 129, fol. 221v-225v (see also
vol. 123, fol. 53-54v).

peror of Constantinople, Sixtus IV had quite recently facilitated to her nephew, the unfortunate exile Andreas Palaeologus, a trip from Rome " *ad partes Russiae,* " [18] that is to Moscow, perhaps not without some hope that this visit of a Greek prince whose ancestors he praised as defenders of " the Catholic faith, " would help in propagating that faith in Ivan's growing Empire. Now, when Moscow's power was turning against her Catholic neighbors, the papal bulls denouncing the new " enemies of the Christian name " repeatedly designated them as " *Rutheni* " without distinguishing them from the Ruthenians who were peacefully living under the Catholic Jagellonian king.

This was by no means the only occasion when a rather confusing terminology affected the correct understanding by the West of the involved situation among the Eastern Slavs. But it was the first occasion when Moscow took advantage of the common name of Ruś and of the tradition of dynastic and ecclesiastical unity of all " Russia " in the Kievan period, to claim not only all Great Russian lands — Tver being the next goal after Novgorod — but also the White Ruthenian and Ukrainian territories of the Jagellonian State. [19] Under such conditions the religious problem in these territories, viz., the survival of the Union of Florence in the dioceses which were under the Metropolitan of Kiev, had an important political aspect also, and Misael's efforts in favor of that Union deserved every possible support not only of Rome but also of King Casimir. Unfortunately, two entirely different circumstances were soon to create unforeseen difficulties, and this precisely in the years when the tension in the relations with Moscow assumed the most alarming proportions.

One of these circumstances was the untimely death of Misael [20] of whom it is not even known whether and where he was finally confirmed as Metropolitan of Kiev. Unknown too is the exact date of his death, not later than in 1480. But certain is that it was to last almost twenty years before one of his successors would turn again to Rome with a view to restoring the Union of Florence among the Ruthenians. As to the other metropolitans of these two decades, it is very difficult to find out what their position in the matter of Union really was nor to what an extent the Patriarchs of Constantinople influenced their policies.

One of these Patriarchs, Raphael I who occupied the see of Constantinople from 1474 to 1477, viz., at the time of Metropolitan Misael, tried to oppose him, probably on the order of Sultan Mohammed II himself, another candidate named Spiridon and surnamed Satanas because of

---

[18] *Reg. Vat.* 594, fol. 183-183v ; see P. Pierling, *op. cit.,* I, 231, about his two trips to Moscow, in 1480 and 1490.

[19] Halecki, *Dzieje,* I, 420.

[20] Bučynsky, " Studii, " *Zap. Tov. Ševč.,* vol. 90, 21 f.

the serious troubles he created practically everywhere.[21] King Casimir put him in jail and when he escaped to Moscow, he was hardly better received, perhaps because of his connection with Tver, the rival principality which Ivan III annexed in 1485 ; imprisoned in a Russian monastery, Spiridon died in 1503.

There is no evidence whatever that he found any support in Kiev, among the opposition against Casimir. Different, however, is the question of the Metropolitan whom the new Patriarch Maximos III appointed after Misael's death in 1480. Called Galektion in the Greek sources,[22] he is possibly identical with Gregory Chalecki who according to a later tradition[23] was Metropolitan of Kiev around that time and belonged to a family of. Ruthenian boyars associated with the Olelkovich. This would indicate that he belonged to the circle of Misael, but explain at the same time why in the following year the King put forward another candidate, the Bishop of Polotsk Simeon who after being confirmed by the Patriarch remained in office for about seven years.[24] For in 1481, a conspiracy against Casimir was detected whose main leader was precisely Prince Michael Olelkovich, executed with some of his followers when the rebellion was crushed.[25]

That abortive rebellion which had nothing of a Ruthenian national movement, since purely Lithuanian princes and lords participated in it, did not have any religious implications either. In that respect it could be compared with the tragic fate of Metropolitan Harasim in 1435 when partisans of reunion with Rome had clashed for purely political reasons. One of the King's most loyal supporters in the crisis of 1481 was Ivan Chodkiewicz who had signed Misael's message along with Prince Michael, but whose appointment to the office of Palatine of Kiev was bitterly resented by the Prince, a pretender to the Kievan Duchy of his ancestors. As a descendant of an elder line of the Lithuanian dynasty Michael resented also that a few years before Casimir the Jagellonian, promising that after his death there would be again a separate Grand Duke of Lithuania, had designated one of his sons for that position[26] which Michael's brother once claimed. In that connection the conspiracy was even suspected to be an attempt against the life of not only the King but also his sons.

That under such conditions the repression was severe is understandable,

[21] Golubinsky, *op. cit.*, II 1, 550 f. ; Chodynicki, *op. cit.*, 68.

[22] Bučynsky, *loc. cit.*, 22 ; Ammann, *op. cit.*, 187.

[23] I discussed that tradition which wrongly identified that Metropolitan Chalecki (Halecki) with Isidore's successor, in *Miesięcznik heraldyczny* (Heraldical Monthly), III (1910), 22 f. ; see also *Polski Słownik biograf.* (Polish biographical dictionary), III (1937), 250 and the bibliography.

[24] Chodynicki, *loc. cit.*

[25] That rebellion and its background have been well described by F. Papée, *Polska i Litwa na przełomie wieków średnich* (Poland and Lithuania at the turn of the Middle Ages), Kraków 1903, I, 64-80 ; see now also H. Jablonowski, *op. cit.*, 118-123.

[26] Halecki, *Dzieje*, I, 421 f.

but it had no religious character and had nothing to do with restrictions against the Orthodox Church for which one of these royal sons, the future Saint Casimir, was sometimes held responsible. [27]   Exactly as it had been fifty years before, the internal crisis in the Grand Duchy was of a dynastic character, aggravated by rivalries among the nobility whether of Lithuanian or of Ruthenian origin.   But once more a situation of trouble and suspicion was created which was highly unfavorable to cooperation in the matter of religious Union, and this time the domestic difficulties had grave repercussions in foreign affairs.   For Moscow was no longer, as she then had been, a much weaker neighbor torn by her own civil war, but so powerful and aggressive that just in the year before the conspiracy of the Lithuanian princes King Casimir had planned a joint action against her [28] in the sense recommended by Pope Sixtus IV, in cooperation with Livonia, and possibly also with Sweden and even Emperor Frederick III. [29]

That project which was timed with a last, really dangerous invasion of Moscow by the Golden Horde, failed completely and even any action by Lithuania alone had to be postponed, not only because of the abortive rebellion in 1481 but also for other reasons.   It is true that some leaders of the conspiracy had been in relations with Moscow just as internal opponents of Ivan III, including members of his own family, were looking for Casimir's support.   It is also true that the King, in view of these relations and of the Orthodox faith of many of the opposition leaders, was becoming suspicious of the Orthodox Ruthenians in general. [30]   But except some petty princes in the controversial, ethnically mixed border region on the upper Oka river, [31] whom Ivan's pressure made transfer their allegiance from Wilno to Moscow, there was no separatist movement in the Lithuanian Grand Duchy, and less than anybody else could the supporters of the Union of Florence be suspected to favor the eastern neighbor.   There were, on the contrary, entirely different factors, again of a purely political character, which explain the deterioration of the position of the Jagellonian States, and one of them had at least an indirect connection with the problem of religious reunion between the Western and Eastern Churches.

All these alarming developments were results of the shrewd and skillful diplomacy of Ivan III [32] who avoided to attack Lithuania directly as long

---

[27] See the special studies of J. Fijałek quoted by Chodynicki, op. cit., 79 n. 1.

[28] Kolankowski, op. cit., I, 341-343.

[29] State Archives of Vienna, Russica, fasc. 1a, April 30, 1481.

[30] These suspicions are reflected in J. Długosz, Hist. Pol., V, 698 ; see the comments of Jablonowski, op. cit., 121.

[31] Their position has been studied in detail by J. M. Kuczyński, Ziemie czernihow-sko-siewierskie pod rządami Litwy (The lands of Chernigov and Severia under the rule of Lithuania), Warszawa 1936.

[32] K. V. Bazilevich, Vneshnaia politika russkogo gosudarstva (vtoraia polovina XV veka), Moskva 1952, see partic. Chapter V.

as King Casimir was alive but tried to encircle him and to establish relations with both, the open opponents and the possible supporters of the
Jagellonian.

Among the former the Khan of the Crimea, Mengli Girey, always was
at least a troublesome nuisance. But his invasions of the Ruthenian lands
became a real threat when systematically instigated by Moscow. Such was
in particular the Tartar raid against Kiev in 1482, [33] the year after the
Olelkovich conspiracy, when that city, the nominal see of the Metropolitan,
was completely sacked and its governor, Ivan Chodkiewicz, so active in
matters of religious reunion and of political stabilization, lost his life. Kiev's
situation, always insecure, now became truly desperate, and it is highly
significant that when fifteen years later, in 1497, one of the metropolitans,
the same Macarius who as Archimandrite had signed Misael's letter to Sixtus IV, wanted to visit Kiev, he was murdered by Tartar invaders. [34]

Long before, however, in the eighties, when the Metropolitan was
still Simon whose attitude regarding the Union is completely unknown,
there appeared two other consequences of Ivan's far reaching policies. Decisive for the whole future was the first rapprochement between Moscow and
the Habsburgs [35] who in view of the problem of succession in Bohemia and
Hungary were the main rivals of the Jagellonian dynasty in the West.
The same Frederick III who under the first impression of Ivan's advance
in the western direction had favored a joint action of the Catholic powers
against him, now entered into diplomatic negotiations with him and in
1489, through one of his ambassadors sent to Moscow, offered him even a
royal crown.

The Grand Prince who already started to use the title of Tsar — until
recently given to Moscow's Tartar overlords — and considered himself the
successor of the Emperors of Constantinople, proudly refused such an honor
from the German Emperor. But rumors were spreading that he would be
glad to accept the imperial or royal title from an even higher authority,
from the Pope himself. King Casimir interpreted this news as another
move of Ivan's to obtain a recognition of his claim to control " the whole
Ruthenian nation, " and immediately instructed his envoy in Rome urgently
to request the Pope not to take any decision in that matter before having
consulted the Polish representatives. And the same Sixtus IV who a few
years before had branded the Muscovites as " enemies of the Christian
name, " now, in his reply to Casimir of February 7, 1484, [36] did not reject
at all the whole fantastic project, but only promised the requested consulta-

---

[33] *Ibidem*, 197 f.

[34] See on this Metropolitan, elected in 1495, and duly confirmed by Constantinople, Chodynicki, *op. cit.*, 70 f.

[35] H. Übersberger, *Österreich und Russland*, Wien 1903, I; Bazilevich, *op. cit.*, 263 f.

[36] *Documenta Pontificum Romanorum*, I, Nr. 100.

tion with Casimir's representatives, if the Duke of Muscovy would approach the Holy See in order to obtain such a dignity.

Whether Ivan III ever seriously considered the advisibility of claiming any title from the Pope, is — to say the least — extremely doubtful. It is true that such a recognition by the Holy See would have impressed precisely those Ruthenian subjects of King Casimir who were faithful to the Florentine tradition and, in general, would have weakened the resistance of Moscow's Catholic neighbors. For that very reason the Jagellonian explained to Sixtus IV that such a concession would be in prejudice of himself and of " many others. " But in spite of such prospects and though the conception of Moscow being the Third Rome, definitely replacing the two others, was not yet clearly formulated, any idea of basing his authority on a title granted by the first Rome, was in such a contrast to Ivan's religious and political principles that if it really was propagated in his name and with his knowledge, it was only with a view of creating confusion among Moscow's opponents and of suggesting new illusions to the Holy See. At the very beginning of the pontificate of Sixtus IV Ivan had given him the impression that he favored religious reunion, only to receive in marriage the heiress of Constantinople. Now he wanted again to convince the Pope that he respected him highly and would appreciate any favor received from the Holy See because he was planning to put an end to any projects of Catholic coalitions directed against Moscow's expansion by entering into diplomatic relations not only with the Holy Roman Empire but also with the Vatican.

It was not before 1488 when Sixtus IV who died a few months after his promise to the King of Poland, had already been succeeded for four years by Innocent VIII, that an envoy of " the king of Russia, " as he was called by the papal master of ceremonies, appeared in Rome.[37] He had not, of course, been sent in order to offer to the Pope Ivan's obedience, as the same witness noted not without wishful thinking, nor was any title requested and granted. But in spite of his attacks against Livonia continued, the powerful ruler east of the Jagellonian Union achieved his purpose of being admitted into the community of Christian nations which Innocent VIII, like his predecessors and successors, wanted to unite against the Ottoman onslaught. That Ivan would soon establish friendly diplomatic relations with the Sultan also[38] was hardly anticipated by the Pope who seems, however, not to have entertained any hopes for religious reunion with the Orthodox East. Once more disappointed in that respect by Moscow, the Holy See even with regard to the Ruthenian lands of Poland

---

[37] *Johannis Burckardi Liber Notarum* 1483-1506 (*Rerum Ital. Scriptores*, vol. 32/1), Città di Castello 1906, 245 ; see the note of the editor, E. Celani, and the earlier remarks of P. Pierling, *op. cit.*, I, 203 f.

[38] Bazilevich, *op. cit.*, 421-425.

and Lithuania rather encouraged individual conversions of the schismatics, whether Greeks, Ruthenians, Wallachians or Armenians, to Catholicism of Latin rite, as evidenced in the instructions of June 19, 1487, given by Innocent VIII to the Bernardine Franciscans of the Polish province. [39]

In agreement with the Florentine decrees and earlier decisions of his predecessors the Pope did not request any rebaptism of the converted Ruthenians as did some members of the Latin hierarchy and Catholic theologians in Poland and Lithuania. [40] But even the papal message includes the Ruthenians of these countries among the schismatics as if the Union of Florence had been definitely rejected by them. Formally such an interpretation was correct since none of Misael's successors on the metropolitan see of Kiev seems to have turned towards Rome while all of them were confirmed by the Greek Patriarchs of Constantinople who were neither willing nor able to have any relations with the Holy See. It is equally true that even some of the prominent personalities who had supported Misael's action in favor of the Union of Florence and been in Rome themselves, were looked upon with suspicion by the Latin clergy. It is difficult to find out whether these men including members of the Soltan family, really returned to Orthodoxy or simply were discouraged by such suspicions and even occasional insults. [41] In any case, however, there soon reappeared in the same circles partisans of reunion and at the same time a new chance of returning to the Florentine tradition.

Strange enough, the origin of such a new attempt to restore the Union of 1439 after more than half a century of fluctuations can be traced back to an event which rather seemed to lead the whole Grand Duchy of Lithuania in the opposite direction. The death of King Casimir, in 1492, had been immediately followed by a first open aggression of Ivan III, and having suffered substantial territorial losses, the new ruler of Lithuania, Casimir's son Alexander, decided to appease his dangerous neighbor by not only concluding, in February 1494, an unfavorable peace treaty but marrying on that occasion Ivan's daughter Helen. [42] Moscow requested solemn guarantees that she would remain undisturbed in her Greek Orthodox faith, and her father made it quite clear that he would never permit her to join the Roman Church even if she would so desire herself. The mixed marriage proved quite happy and Helen would later assure her parents that no pressure in religious matters was exercised upon her. But in order to avoid difficulties in the case of the birth of children, Alexander was, of course,

---

[39] *Documenta Pontificum Rom.*, I, Nr. 101.

[40] This problem has been discussed in detail by A. M. Ammann, " Zur Geschichte der Geltung der Florentiner Konzilsentscheidungen in Polen-Litauen, " *Orientalia Christiana Periodica*, VIII (1942), 289 ff., 303 f.

[41] *Ibidem*, 298 f. ; see also my remarks in *Oriens*, I (1933), 8-10.

[42] F. Papée, *Aleksander Jagiellończyk*, Kraków 1949, 12-16.

anxious to remove the difference of faith in his family and possibly also in his country which in spite of his concessions did not cease to be threatened by Moscow. A religious union with Rome respecting the Eastern rite appeared once more as the best solution, and such a project found supporters at Helen's own court.

One of them was her secretary Ivan Sapieha whose family of White Ruthenian origin and Orthodox faith, was rising to prominence from the time when his father had been secretary of Casimir the Jagellonian. [43] After personally submitting to papal authority Sapieha received from Alexander VI the permission to erect in his estates a church where both Latin and Ruthenian clergymen could officiate, it being understood that the latter would be in union with Rome. [44] Even more important was that one of Sapieha's friends and relatives, obviously sharing his views, was Orthodox Bishop of Smolensk and considered the best candidate to the position of Metropolitan when, in May 1497, Metropolitan Macarius was killed by the Tartars. That former signatory of Misael's appeal to Rome does not seem to have been more favorable to reunion than his predecessor Ionas Hlezna who, in 1489, had taken Simeon's place. All three metropolitans of whose activities very little is known, were obviously satisfied with their recognition by the Patriarch of Constantinople and the Lithuanian administration.[45] The new candidate, Joseph, took a different attitude, and even before he was formally appointed, in May 1498, tried to receive from the Patriarch of Constantinople himself an approval of his project to restore the Union of Florence in his ecclesiastical province.

That idea was so significant and could have had so far reaching consequences that it is important to clarify the background of Metropolitan Joseph I. Like some of his predecessors including Misael he came from a noble family of local origin, and in view of the earlier interest of the Soltans in the Union of Florence, he was supposed to be a member of that very family. However, he must be distinguished from Metropolitan Joseph II, who was undoubtedly a Soltan but had no relations with Rome during the years 1507-1525 when he occupied the see of Kiev. [46] As to Joseph I there is some evidence [47] that he rather belonged to the less prominent family

---

[43] See on all matters regarding that family the exhaustive monograph *Sapiehowie*, 3 vol., Petersburg, 1890.

[44] *Documenta Pontificum Rom.*, I, Nr. 103 (April 28, 1501).

[45] Chodynicki, *op. cit.*, 69-70.

[46] It is, however, possible that in earlier years he was considered favorable to the project of Joseph I, since the important diocese of Smolensk near the Muscovite border was soon entrusted to him.

[47] First pointed out by A. W. Byeletsky, *Rodoproiskhodenie zapadnorusskago mitropolita Josifa II Soltana* (The family origin of the Westrussian metropolitan Joseph II Soltan), Vilna 1895, p. 6 (quoting *Arkheograficheski Sbornik*, VI, 8).

of the Bolharynovich, but this is by no means certain, [48] and he might have been identical with the youngest of the four Soltan brothers, listed on Misael's message to Pope Sixtus IV as " kir Joan " who with one of the other signatories was to bring that appeal to Rome : in the bulls of Alexander VI, of 1501, Metropolitan Joseph I is indeed always called " Iohannes Iozeph. " [49]

Why his promising project failed is even more important to explain. It is, first, certain that the main difficulties did not come from Constantinople. On the contrary, in answer to Joseph's inquiry Patriarch Niphon II, though expressing himself for obvious reasons very cautiously, did not oppose at all the idea of following the Florentine tradition. [50] Welcoming Joseph as candidate to the metropolitan see of Kiev, he rather encouraged him to favor there the Union of Florence, as he did it himself in the areas of his Patriarchate which were under Catholic, viz., Venetian rule. He only insisted upon the maintenance of the Eastern rite. And when Niphon II was succeeded in the very year 1498 by Joachim I, the new Patriarch did not hesitate to confirm Joseph as Metropolitan [51] though his attitude favorable to reunion with Rome must have been well known to him. All this gives evidence to the fact that the policies of the Patriarchate were not dictated by any basic hostility to Rome but by reasons of expediency : under Turkish rule no contact with the Holy See was possible, but Eastern Churches in free Catholic countries could make an agreement with the First Rome without necessarily breaking with the Second one which continued to exist as religious center under the Mohammedan Sultans, though in very precarious conditions.

Entirely different was the reaction of Moscow where precisely at the turn of the fifteenth century the theory of the Third Rome was finally formulated. Both as a religious and a political center she now was considered and proclaimed the ultimate successor of both the First Rome which long ago had abandonned Orthodoxy and the Second which for the Union of Florence had been punished by the Turkish conquest. The resulting claim to world domination was a distant dream [52] which hardly was taken seriously by shrewd and realistic politicians like Ivan III, or his son and successor Basil III. But Moscow's new role was another argument which not without strong ideological appeal supported her claim for uniting under

---

[48] F. Papée, *op. cit.*, 32, 53, whose knowledge of the period is outstanding, returned to the earlier opinion that also Joseph I was a Soltan.

[49] *Documenta Pont. Rom.*, I, Nr. 102, 104.

[50] See about the authenticity of that correspondence Chodynicki, *op. cit.*, 71 n. 4, who himself goes too far in his skepticism.

[51] A. M. Ammann, " Zur Geschichte ..., " 305 (particularly n. 4), 306 ; see also C. Giannelli in *Orientalia Christiana Periodica*, IX (1943), 450-459.

[52] As to the mystical, chiliastic character of the " Third Rome " idea see E. Sarkisyanz, *Russland und der Messianismus des Orients*, Tübingen 1955, 95, 186.

her leadership at least "all the Russias" : the lands of Orthodox faith which were the "patrimony" of her dynasty, including, of course, their traditional religious and political center, Kiev.

When, therefore, in the summer of 1499, in another attempt at appeasement a Lithuanian embassy offered even to recognize Ivan's usurped title of "lord of all the Russias" in exchange for a guarantee of the frontiers of the Grand Duchy including Kiev, the proposal was rejected as senseless. And the defense of Orthodoxy against any plans of reunion with Rome was a welcome pretext for breaking the peace treaty of 1494, and launching in the spring of 1500 a general offensive against Lithuania. [53] The invasion was preceded by persuading some more princes of the controversial area on the upper Oka to transfer their allegiance from Lithuania to Moscow, and it is true that some of these deserters, partly of Lithuanian origin, justified their decision by complaining that Alexander, contrary to the practice of his predecessors, wanted to destroy Orthodoxy and to force them to accept the Roman doctrine. But the only fact which the Muscovites themselves could point out in that connection, was the propaganda in favor of reunion which Metropolitan Joseph I, already as Bishop of Smolensk, and the Latin Bishop of Wilno had started in 1499, approaching not only some of the Orthodox princes but even Alexander's wife. [54] There is, however, not the slightest evidence of any pressure or even less of persecution, and the real reason why a few of Alexander's vassals in the most exposed border region, including two refugees from Moscow, abandoned the cause of Lithuania, was the inability of that country to protect them against Ivan. In general, the Orthodox Ruthenians of Lithuania who were not at all anxious to come under Ivan's despotic domination, remained in that political crisis entirely loyal to Alexander whose army was under the command of the most prominent of them, Prince Constantine Ostrogski.

He was defeated on July 14, 1500, at the Vedrosha river and taken a prisoner by the Muscovites along with other magnates of the Grand Duchy, Lithuanian and Ruthenian, Catholic and Orthodox alike. Under the impression of that catastrophe there started immediately negotiations with a view of creating an anti-Muscovite coalition and of securing the support of the other Jagellonian States, particularly of Poland. When Alexander's brother John Albert died unexpectedly and childlessly on June 17, 1501, the Grand Duke of Lithuania was convinced that by succeeding him as King of Poland he would best achieve the full cooperation of both countries. He was indeed unanimously elected by the Poles in the border town of Mielnik where on

---

[53] F. Papée, *op. cit.*, 33, where on the following pages a full account of the whole war is given; see also Basilevich, *op. cit.*, 450 ff.

[54] The source material is quoted and well interpreted by Jablonowski, *op. cit.*, 129-132.

8

the same day, October 3, a new Polish-Lithuanian union was concluded. [55] But even before, only a few days after Ostrogski's defeat, on August 20 of the preceding year, the Metropolitan of Kiev Joseph I signed in Wilno his act of obedience to the Holy See thus renewing the religious union according to the decisions of Florence. [56] And since Alexander's Orthodox wife was now to become Queen of Poland and to be crowned in the Wawel cathedral, such a religious reunion seemed particularly desirable and even urgent. Therefore, in spite of a strong prejudice against " the errors of the Ruthenian rite " which was espressed at the same time by one of the theologians of Cracow University [57] in a violent pamphlet primarily directed against the Muscovites, the royal envoy Erasmus Ciołek, a distinguished Polish humanist and diplomat, who was sent to Rome in the spring of 1501, was instructed to submit the whole project of the reunion of the Ruthenians to Pope Alexander VI and was accompanied on his mission by Ivan Sapieha, now Secretary in King Alexander's own Ruthenian chancery.[58]

The negotiations which he started in Rome early in April, dealing with both the submission of the Metropolitan of Kiev and Alexander's mixed marriage, were continued until well after the Polish election which increased the importance of both problems since now all Ruthenians were united under Alexander and his Orthodox Queen. However, it was already on April 26 [59] and May 7, 1501 [60] that the Pope without writing directly to " Iohannes Iozeph " whom " the peoples of Kiev and Russia recognize and follow as their pastor and director, " answered the letters which he had received on Joseph's behalf from the Bishop of Wilno, Albert Tabor, and from Grand Duke Alexander himself.

The Latin Bishop who had his see in the capital of the Grand Duchy and was equally active in religious and political matters,[61] had not only assured the Pope of his ardent desire to contribute to the reunion with the Roman Church of the whole population of the Grand Duchy and particularly of the metropolitan diocese of Kiev and Russia, but also emphasized that there could not be any better occasion to achieve that result than at the present moment when the Metropolitan himself was ready to offer to the Bishop of Wilno his obedience to the Holy See. In saying so Albert Tabor was entirely right, especially as Joseph I about whom unfortunately so little is known, was according to the information received by the Pope himself, a man of high culture, serious theological knowledge and real prudence,

---

[55] The charters are published in *Akta Unji Polski z Litwą*, Nr. 77-83.

[56] A. Theiner, *Vetera monumenta Poloniae et Lithuaniae*, II, Nr. 296.

[57] That pamphlet by Johannes Sacranus is discussed by Ammann, *op. cit.*, 311-313.

[58] See on that mission Chodynicki, *op. cit.*, 71 f. ; Ammann, *op. cit.*, 307-310.

[59] *Documenta Pontificum Rom.*, I, Nr. 102.

[60] *Ibidem*, I, Nr. 104.

[61] See F. Papée, *op. cit.*, *passim*.

and seemed to be " touched by the divine spirit. " Furthermore, the prominent Metropolitan was not at all isolated in his efforts to restore the Union of Florence among the Ruthenians. Ivan Sapieha, not only his relative but his official representative in the negotiations with the Holy See — *procurator* as the Pope called him — was one of their most influential political leaders and at the same time seemed so sincere in his Catholic convictions that Alexander VI in the very days when he was writing to the Bishop of Wilno and to the Grand Duke granted the privileges which this " beloved son " requested for a church of his foundation. [62] And only a few days later a less known Ruthenian from the Kiev diocese, the son of a priest of the Eastern Church, who was doubtful about the legitimacy of the ecclesiastical orders to which he had been promoted by one of the Ruthenian bishops in the name of the Patriarch of Constantinople, requested in Rome and was permitted to receive a complete new ordination from a Catholic bishop residing at the papal curia. [63]

Furthermore, the action of the Metropolitan, supported as it was by other Ruthenians, both laymen and clergymen, was favored and recommended to the Pope in the strongest terms by the Lithuanian authorities, in particular by the Grand Duke and the head of the Latin hierarchy. When Joseph's " envoy " Sapieha, himself in the service of the court, submitted to the Pope on April 6, [64] the declaration of obedience by the Metropolitan, translated from Ruthenian into Latin, the Grand Ducal Ambassador, Ciołek, then himself a canon of the diocese of Wilno, was present and, in general, participated in Sapieha's negotiations with the Holy See. How deeply he was interested himself in the whole problem of reunion between the Western and Eastern Churches, is best illustrated by a manuscript volume [65] in which he collected a long series of documents related to the history of that reunion beginning with the pontificate of Innocent III and including the Florentine bulls of Eugene IV in the matter of the union with Greeks and Armenians. Some of the documents regarding the negotiations on behalf of Metropolitan Joseph are preserved only thanks to that collection of Ciołek.

There is, however, in the Pope's letter to Alexander the Jagellonian a rather surprising reference to Ciołek's part in these negotiations. Interested by the whole project but fully aware that the normal development of the Union of Florence, though several times attempted, had been interrupted

---

[62] *Documenta Pontif.*, I, Nr. 103 (April 28, 1501).
[63] *Ibidem*, Nr. 105 (May 10, 1501) for " Gregorius de Loszko. "
[64] That date is given on fol. 42 of the manuscript quoted in the following note.
[65] Preserved in the Vatican Archives, *Arm.* 32 vol. 21 ; J. Fijałek and S. Kutrzeba described it and published the most important documents which are copied in the manuscript in *Kopiarz rzymski Erazma Ciołka*, Kraków 1923 (*Archiwum komisji histor.* II, 1, 66-113).

by various obstacles, Alexander VI wanted first to proceed through investigations on the spot and to send to Lithuania a nuncio of sound doctrine
and experience to examine the situation and to deal with the Grand Duke
in the matter of Joseph and the whole Ruthenian people. Such a papal
mission, suggested already in Misael's appeal twenty-five years before, could
have been very helpful indeed and in any case would have clarified and
probably removed some doubts which still remained in the Pope's mind
and, as shown in his letters, influenced his whole policy in the matter of
reunion. But unfortunately Ciołek requested that this papal mission be
postponed until further notice by Alexander of Lithuania whom the Pope
therefore informed that he would wait for such information as to the most
convenient time for sending his nuncio. Even more surprising is the reason
given by Ciołek when he suggested such a delay : the Duke of Muscovy
would consider that mission from Rome a reason for waging war against
Lithuania. [66]

Such a motivation was surprising at the given moment because the war
which Ivan had started a year before, using indeed the plans of reuniting
the Ruthenians with Rome as a welcome pretext, was anyway continuing
unabated and Alexander's efforts to stop the aggressor and to regain the
invaded territories were just reaching their climax in alliance with the
Knights of Livonia and even with the Golden Horde which he opposed to
the Crimean Tartars, Ivan's allies. [67] There was, therefore, no apparent
reason for avoiding to provoke Moscow's anger. In order to discover as
far as possible, the real motives behind Ciołek's opposition against a direct
and immediate interference of papal diplomacy, it must be remembered
that this diplomacy always connected the problem of reunion with Eastern
Christendom and that of anti-Ottoman action. As a matter of fact, Pope
Alexander VI who showed no particular interest in the first of these
problems and was not too familiar with its implications, was no less than
the other Renaissance popes very seriously concerned with the Turkish
advance and precisely in 1501 considered the whole Eastern situation from
that point of view. [68]

Even in his discussion of the project of the Metropolitan of Kiev the
Pope, while never referring himself to the relations with Moscow, did not
fail to point out that it was " the tyrant of the Turks " who controlled
" with violent hand " the Patriarchate of Constantinople. [69] It was against
that Turkish tyrant that a few days after writing to Alexander the Jagellonian

---

[66] " Ne propterea dux Moszkovie belli contra te gerendi aliquid censeretur, " *Documenta Pontif.*, I Nr. 104, p. 180.

[67] F. Papée, *op. cit.*, 36-41.

[68] L. v. Pastor, *Storia dei Papi* (revised and transl. by A. Mercati), III (Roma
1942), 531-545.

[69] *Documenta Pontif.*, I, Nr. 104, p. 181.

about the Ruthenians, on May 13, 1501 he concluded a league with Alexander's brother, Ladislas of Hungary and Bohemia, and with the Republic of Venice. [70]   And when in preparation of such an anti-Ottoman league he sent a few months before Cardinal Peter Isvalich, Archbishop of Reggio, as papal legate to King Ladislas and to his and Alexander's brother, King John Albert of Poland, he suggested in the legate's instructions that the King of Poland, to be enabled freely to turn against the Turks, should make peace or at least a long truce with his other enemies "even the schismatics." [71]

The Jagellonians, too, were well aware of the Turkish danger which threatened particularly their Hungarian kingdom but also — directly or indirectly through the Sultan's Crimean vassals — the Ruthenian borderlands of Poland and Lithuania. But after the failure of John Albert's anti-Turkish expedition of 1497 and the Turkish invasion of the following year, [72] they were even more than after Varna anxious to avoid another conflict with the Ottoman Empire and skeptical as to the projects of an anti-Ottoman league in cooperation with the Western powers. It is true that the alliance which all the Jagellonian States concluded with France and possibly Venice on July 14, 1500, in Buda, [73] was formally directed against the Turks. But as a matter of fact it was a rapprochement with the Western opponents of the Habsburgs in answer to the negotiations between the latter and Moscow. With the Ottoman Empire which at any time could unleash the Tartars of the Crimea against Lithuania and Poland, exactly as Moscow used to do, Poland was negotiating for a truce and had to pay for any delay by other Tartar raids, as it happened in 1500 and was to happen again in 1502 amidst Lithuania's continuing war against Ivan. [74] Under such conditions a papal mission to Alexander shortly after that of the Cardinal of Reggio to his brothers, was not particularly welcome and could provoke the suspicion and anger not only of Ivan but even more of the Sultan.

The indefinite postponement of that mission at the suggestion of Alexander's envoy, who carefully collected the documents regarding the anti-Turkish action of the Holy See, [75] was regrettable from the point of view of the prospects of religious reunion with the Ruthenians; but it did not imply at all a postponement of the whole project of such a reunion. On the contrary, without waiting for the opportunity of sending his nuncio to

---

[70] L. v. Pastor, *op. cit.*, III, 543 note 1.
[71] A. Theiner, *op. cit.*, II, Nr. 297; see Nr. 229 (Ciołek's address of March 31, 1501).
[72] F. Papée, *Jan Olbracht*, Kraków 1936.
[73] Dogiel, *Codex diplomaticus Regni Poloniae*, I, 447-452.
[74] *Ibidem*, I, 449; see also F. Papée, *Aleksander Jag.*, 57 ff.
[75] Vat. Arch., *Arm.* 32, vol. 21, fol. 109-126 (beginning with the Congress of Mantua in 1459).

Lithuania and anxious not to discourage Joseph I, the Pope who did not want to write him directly as long as his metropolitan dignity was not confirmed by the Holy See, entrusted the Grand Duke himself and the Bishop of Wilno with the task of removing any obstacles to that confirmation, fully confident of their sincere intentions in the whole matter. Bishop Tabor was to accept in the name of the Holy See Joseph's obedience and to admit him with all his followers into the Roman Church, thus encouraging also the other people of Kiev and the Ruthenian lands to follow their example. And both the Bishop and the Grand Duke were asked to inform the Pope about the result, so that he might then send his nuncio for the final settlement or forward his bulls in that matter to the Bishop of Wilno.

The main reason why Alexander VI did not consider it possible to settle the problem at once and to accept without any further investigations the obedience of the Metropolitan as submitted to him by Sapieha, was of a strictly legal and formal nature. According to the papal interpretation Joseph was not really Metropolitan of Kiev since the Patriarch of Constantinople who had promoted him to that dignity was " the heretic Joachim " who himself had been placed upon the see of Constantinople by the arbitrary violence of the Turkish " tyrant " and not the legitimate Catholic Patriarch residing in Rome, [76] the successor of the Patriarchs in exile : Isidore and Bessarion. While, however, these two Greeks had been of the Eastern rite, former Metropolitans of Kiev and Nicaea, the present Patriarch of Constantinople, recognized as such by the Pope, was an Italian of the Latin rite, the former Bishop of Orto, Cardinal John Michele [77] whose connection with the Eastern Church was purely theoretical. It was obvious that Alexander VI, notwithstanding this difficulty, was not prepared to tolerate any simultaneous relations of a Metropolitan of Kiev with both the Church of Rome and the schismatic Patriarch in Constantinople, relations such as those which even Metropolitan Gregory, Isidore's disciple and successor in Kiev, and probably also Misael had tried to maintain. But he offered a practical solution of the confused situation : the Bishop of Wilno was authorized to absolve Joseph from any past irregularities, and then the Pope would confirm him in his metropolitan dignity or have him confirmed by the Latin Patriarch of Constantinople.

There were, however, additional difficulties which Alexander VI pointed out more particularly in his letter to Albert Tabor. He had heard *a nonnullis* that the Ruthenians who now offered their obedience to the Holy See did not observe the decrees of the Council of Florence regarding the procession of the Holy Spirit, the administration of the Sacrament of the

---

[76] *Documenta Pontif.*, I, Nr. 104, p. 181.
[77] See the comments of A. M. Ammann, *op. cit.*, 308.

Altar, the doctrine regarding purgatory, and papal primacy. It is impossible to find out from whom the Pope received these critiques or to what an extent they were justified. From the words he used writing to the Bishop of Wilno it might seem that he wanted to go even farther in his requests than the Council of Florence, since he complained that the *Filioque* was not specifically mentioned in the Creed nor in the divine offices, and touched upon details which were rather questions of rite and liturgy. [78] It is also surprising that in the matter of papal authority the lengthy declarations in Metropolitan Joseph's act of obedience, which lacked perhaps theological precision, but were most emphatic and full of good will and even humility, did not fully satisfy him. Nevertheless, the attitude of Alexander VI, though perhaps influenced by conflicting reports and opinions among the Latin hierarchy and clergy both on the papal curia and in Lithuania, was certainly not prejudiced against the Ruthenians nor, in general, the Eastern rite. In his letter to the Grand Duke he made it quite clear that if only the Catholic doctrine were fully accepted, the Ruthenians returning to the unity of faith, would not have to be rebaptized, and they would be permitted to use leavened bread for the Eucharist, to give the Holy Sacrament under both species also to laymen, and to have married priests.

The first of these points was particularly important because in Poland and Lithuania there appeared time and again the opinion, contrary to the decisions of Florence but apparently based upon insufficiently clear expressions in a brief of Nicholas V addressed to the Bishop of Wilno in 1452, [79] that a Ruthenian Orthodox converted to Catholicism had to be baptized again according to Latin rite. Therefore Alexander VI considered it necessary to issue now, a few months after his letters regarding Metropolitan Joseph, a statement [80] which formally and clearly declared that these Ruthenians, if they rejected their earlier errors, ought not to be rebaptized. Contrary to the ordination of priests by schismatic bishops, the sacrament of baptism administered by Greeks or Armenians was recognized as valid, a principle which always had been defended by the Bernardine missionaries in contradistinction to the secular clergy. Bishop Tabor was instructed to make that papal decision known, since he was the highest ranking member of the Latin hierarchy in the Grand Duchy of Lithuania. Shortly before the pamphlet most strongly defending the opposite point of view had been dedicated to him, but there is no evidence that this enlightened prelate who so strongly supported the project of Metropolitan Joseph, had ever opposed himself the validity of the baptism in the Eastern Church. [81]

---

[78] *Documenta Pontif.*, I, Nr. 102, p. 176 : " Accepimus etiam a nonnullis " etc.
[79] Published by Ammann, *op. cit.*, 315 f.
[80] *Documenta Pontif.*, I, Nr. 108 (August 23, 1501).
[81] As implied by Ammann, *op. cit.*, 311, who in other places of his important

In the declaration of Alexander VI only those Ruthenians are mentioned who were living in the Lithuanian State, in particular in the four Latin dioceses of the Grand Duchy : those of Wilno, Kiev, Lutsk and Miedniki, the last of which, in Samogitia, having very few Ruthenian inhabitants. A large number of Ruthenians was, on the contrary, living in the Kingdom of Poland, in the Latin dioceses of Lwów, Chełm, Przemyśl and Kamieniec ; and the Greek dioceses in the first three of these places were exactly as the Ruthenian dioceses of Lithuania under the jurisdiction of the Metropolitan of Kiev. Therefore the earlier efforts to propagate the Union of Florence among the Ruthenians, made by Cardinal Isidore both immediately after the Council of Florence and later, when Kiev was separated from Moscow, had included all Eastern dioceses whether in Lithuania or in Poland. And if Metropolitan Joseph's action had progressed successfully, it would have included too the politically Polish part of his metropolitan province, especially after the election of his protector, Grand Duke Alexander, to the Polish throne.

However, when that election became known in Rome, it only strengthened the Pope's desire to see Alexander's Orthodox wife converted, since she was now to be the Queen of a great Catholic kingdom. Writing, therefore, in that matter on November 26, 1501, to the head of the Catholic hierarchy of Poland, the Cardinal Primate, Archbishop of Gniezno and Bishop of Cracow, who happened to be Alexander's own brother Frederick, the Pope recalling his earlier appeal to the Bishop of Wilno, repeated his stern warning, that if Helen should refuse such a conversion, her husband would have to end his matrimonial life with her. [82] Alexander's VI extreme severity in that matter was hardly in agreement with his expectations of religious reunion with the Ruthenians, if it was not a pressure he wanted to exercise in order to achieve such a reunion. In any case, however, that larger problem was not at all mentioned in the papal warnings against Alexander's living in a mixed marriage, whether they were issued before or after his Polish election. And if the Jagellonian hoped that the restoration of the Union of Florence in his realm would help him in his delicate matrimonial issues, he was to be completely disappointed. For neither did the Holy See ever receive the requested information about the negotiations with the Metropolitan of Kiev nor was anything heard in Lithuania or Poland of Joseph's project after Ciołek's and Sapieha's return from Rome.

It is very difficult to explain why that promising and opportune project, at first so well received, was altogether abandoned. The simplest

---

study discusses the action of Metropolitan Joseph regarding the legal position of the Eastern Church in Lithuania, which as recently pointed out by Jablonowski, *op. cit.*, 51-55, was, however, in general rather satisfactory, in spite of some formal restrictions.

[82] *Documenta Pontif.*, I, Nr. 109.

explanation would be that Joseph died before the final agreement was reached ; very soon indeed, in 1503, a new Metropolitan, Iona II, appeared and remained in office until 1507. He succeeded in 1504 to obtain from King Alexander concessions for the Greek Orthodox, [83] though nothing is known about any inclination he would have shown towards reunion with Rome. It is not impossible that Rome's prerequisite condition of a clear rupture with the schismatic Patriarch of Constantinople seemed contrary to the Kievan tradition and was rejected even by Joseph I who had been in contact with two successive Patriarchs. But there might have been another reason of a political character : the renewed trend towards appeasing Ivan of Moscow.

The war efforts against the invader which were at their height when the project of religious union was submitted in Rome, ended in failure the following year and at the end of 1502 a Hungarian mediator was abroad, trying to obtain from Ivan safe-conducts for the Polish and Lithuanian peace negotiators who in March 1503 arrived in Moscow and after a few weeks of discussion signed there a truce for six years on very unfavorable conditions. [84] In the preliminary proposals of the King of Hungary the papal appeals for cooperation among all Christians against the Turks were used as an argument. [85] It hardly appealed to Ivan who had already established some years before friendly relations with the Sultan and who now, when the chief Polish delegate mentioned the Union of Florence and even suggested a joint Polish-Muscovite mission to Rome, answered that he had no reason for sending to the Pope. [86]

That reference to the Council of 1439 was made in connection with the personal religious problems of Queen Helen who loyal to her husband wrote to her parents in favor of peace and possibly influenced at least her Greek mother shortly before her death. Ivan himself who blamed her for that intervention remained adamant as to his absolute interdiction of Helen's giving up her Orthodox faith even if permitted to retain the Eastern rite. [87] For that very reason even the new Pope's, Julius' II, more conciliatory attitude in the matter of Alexander's marriage was of little help : on August 22, 1505, [88] he wrote to the King, answering a request of his envoys, that he was not insisting upon Helen's conversion since any pressure exercised upon her would provoke a new aggression of Lithuania's stronger neighbor, and that he would be satisfied if the Queen would observe

[83] See A. M. Ammann, *Abriss*, 191.
[84] F. Papée, *op. cit.*, 70.
[85] *Ibidem*, 69.
[86] *Ibidem*, 72.
[87] *Ibidem* ; it is interesting to note that Queen Helen's letters in that matter were written by that same Ivan Sapieha who had been in Rome in the matter of reunion and now acted again as her secretary.
[88] *Documenta Pontif.*, I, Nr. 111.

the decrees of Florence, not show any contempt for the Latin rite and not induce others to join " the Ruthenian sect. "   The first of these conditions was never fulfilled, since the revival of the Union of Florence among the Ruthenians had been given up for the time being and even Ivan's death at the end of the same year did not basically change the situation whether in the political or in the religious field.   There continued indeed the tension between Moscow and Lithuania, but in that Grand Duchy, more and more closely united with Poland, there was no inclination towards the aggressive eastern neighbor, not even among the Ruthenian population of Eastern rite [89].   On the contrary, though their formal relations with Rome remained in suspense, they were living in daily contact with their Catholic fellow citizens, laymen and clergy, having hardly any serious conflicts with them and coming almost imperceptibly under Western influence [90], as did the Orthodox Ruthenians of the kingdom of Poland.

[89] Even the recent study of O. P. Backus on the *Motives of West Russian Nobles in Deserting Lithuania for Moscow 1377-1514*, Lawrence 1957, who greatly overestimates the importance of such individual " desertions ", comes to similar conclusions.

[90] A rich material can be found in the *Codex diplomaticus ecclesiae Vilnensis*, I, 2, Kraków 1939; see, for instance, Nr. 288, 298, 413.

Chapter VI

THE SURVIVAL OF THE FLORENTINE TRADITION
AMONG THE RUTHENIANS

Whatever were the reasons for the failure of Metropolitan Joseph's project of reunion with Rome at the very beginning of the sixteenth century, there followed an interruption in the relations between the Metropolitans of Kiev and the Holy See, which was to last almost to the end of that century. Yet, the tradition of the Union of Florence and of its acceptance by the Ruthenian Church of Poland and Lithuania did not at all disappear during that long interval.

Most significant in that respect were the confirmations of the charter which in 1443, when the Council of Florence was still in session, had been granted to that Church by King Ladislas III, the future hero of Varna, recognizing its equal rights with the Latin Church in view of the union concluded four years before. The first of these confirmations was issued at the Polish Diet which met in Piotrków in 1504 and to whom the Ruthenian Bishop of Chełm, of the Eastern rite, submitted the document of 1443 with the request to include its full text in a new royal charter, because the original had suffered severe deterioration on the occasion of a Tartar raid. This was done on March 6, 1504[1] by King Alexander who solemnly confirmed the privilege of his uncle, as if the Ruthenian Church of his realm had remained faithful to the Union of Florence and thus fulfilled the prerequisite condition for enjoying equal rights with the Polish Church of Latin rite.

There are a few important points which require clarification in connection with that action of Poland's King and Diet taken at a time when the difficulty of restoring the Union in the Ruthenian lands had just been experienced not without serious disappointment. It is true that the initiative of such a restoration had been taken, in 1500-1501, in Lithuania, following the similar steps of Metropolitan Misael in 1473 and 1476, while the charter of 1443 seemed to refer more specifically to the Ruthenian provinces of Poland. But all the dioceses of Eastern rite of both Jagellonian States, now again under one ruler, were under the Metropolitan of Kiev, and it is impossible to discover any difference in their attitude towards the prob-

---

[1] *Acta Regis Alexandri I* (ed. F. Papée), Kraków 1927, Nr. 233.

lem of reunion with Rome. Therefore, though Poland and Lithuania did not yet have any common legislative authority and there remained minor differences in the legal position of the Greek Orthodox in either State [2], the privilege of Ladislas III was usually interpreted as basic bill of rights for all followers of the Eastern rite in the whole Polish-Lithuanian federation. Furthermore, the condition of remaining in union with Rome according to the decisions of the Council of Florence, was frequently disregarded in the course of the sixteenth century, though papal nuncios and representatives of the Latin clergy would sometimes point out that the charter of 1443 could not be invoked by those who had abandonned the Union of Florence. [3]

In 1504, soon after the negotiations between Metropolitan Joseph and Pope Alexander VI, it was particularly difficult to determine whether that Union was still respected by the Ruthenians or not. And soon after the new Polish-Lithuanian Union of 1501, which had been signed on the occasion of the election of Grand Duke Alexander to the throne of Poland and was supposed to be ratified by the Lithuanian Diet, the community of both States which were to have " common councils " [4] in the future, seemed so close, that the relationship of their Ruthenian population with the Holy See could be considered a problem of common interest indeed. The Polish Diet acted first because the charter of 1443 had been issued by a King of Poland who had no real power in Lithuania, and because the original had been in the custody of one of the Ruthenian bishops of Poland. But less than one year later, in February 1505, the Grand Chancellor of the Kingdom of Poland, its future Primate Jan Łaski who took a leading part in all the constitutional developments during Alexander's reign, [5] went to the Lithuanian Diet at Brest, requesting the ratification of the political union of 1501 and submitting in his long speech of February 25 a comprehensive program of Polish-Lithuanian cooperation. In a special point of that program he considered the relations with the Ruthenians [6] including undoubtedly the problem of their religious union with Rome.

It would be extremely interesting to know what Łaski suggested in that matter at the very place where that same problem was to be discussed again in the 'nineties and finally settled in 1596. Unfortunately the address

[2] K. Chodynicki, *Kościół prawosławny*, 76-102.

[3] See my remarks in *Orientalia Christiana periodica*, XIX (1953), 278 f.

[4] See article 3 of the Union charters of 1501, *Akta Unii Polski z Litwą*, Nr. 79 p. 137, Nr. 80 p. 140, Nr. 82 p. 144.

[5] F. Papée, *Aleksander Jagiellończyk*, 54, 76 ; a full bibliography about J. Łaski and information about his background has been given by W. Pociecha, *Królowa Bona 1494-1557* (Queen Bona), II, Kraków 1949, 121 note 221.

[6] *Acta Regis Alexandri I*, Nr. 277, p. 460 : " Qualiter ordinandum, ut nulla in futurum differentia fieret inter Ruthenos et regnicolas et inter Ruthenos et Lithuanos. "

of the Polish Chancellor has been preserved only in a summary which briefly lists his various points without giving the content of his proposals, nor any information on the reaction of the Lithuanian Diet which, as usual, included many Ruthenians. It is well known, however, [7] that the Diet refused to ratify the political agreement of 1501 which was not favored by the dynasty because its clause regarding the common election of the common ruler of both States threatened the hereditary rights of the Jagellonians in Lithuania. The views of the most powerful lords of the Grand Duchy were divided in the whole matter, their division in two main parties having nothing to do with their ethnically Lithuanian or Ruthenian origin nor with their religious opinions and ecclesiastical affiliation. But it is obvious that under such conditions the point regarding the Ruthenian problem raised by Łaski among so many others, did probably not receive any attention at all.

It was not at all for religious, but mostly for political reasons that on the same occasion the Bishop of Wilno, Albert Tabor, who in 1501 had been so interested in the revival of the Union of Florence, lost his influence in the Grand Ducal Council. [8] But it was significant that when precisely at the time of the Diet of Brest Erasmus Ciołek, the main negotiator in the matter of religious union in 1501, returned to Rome, now already as Bishop of Płock and therefore member of the Polish Senate, the numerous problems and requests which he submitted with unusual success to the new Pope, Julius II, [9] did not include this time any reference to the reunion of the Ruthenians. Only the political and military danger which threatened the Ruthenian provinces of both Lithuania and Poland because of the frequent Tartar raids was considered by the Holy See which made financial concessions to King Alexander in view of the badly needed reconstruction of Kamieniec in Podolia and other castles at the frontier. [10] The decrees of the Council of Florence were mentioned when a little later [11] Julius II made concessions to the King of Poland in the matter of his marriage with Helen of Moscow. But that reference only confirms the general impression that even Rome did not have any clear idea as to the religious situation in Eastern Europe, since the Pope seemed to take it for granted that even without being converted to the Catholic faith the queen could be expected to observe the Florentine decrees.

It is hardly necessary to point out that if Queen Helen had been faithful to the Florentine decrees, she would have been a Catholic of East-

---

[7] L. Finkel, *Elekcja Zygmunta I* (The election of Sigismund I), Kraków 1910 103-113.

[8] *Acta Regis Alexandri I*, Nr. 278.

[9] F. Papée, *op. cit.*, 112.

[10] *Documenta Pontificum Romanorum historiam Ukrainae illustrantia*, I, Nr. 110 (May 12, 1505).

[11] *Ibidem*, Nr. 111 (August 22, 1505).

ern rite without any necessity of conversion. Unfortunately this was not so, neither in this personal case of a Muscovite princess, nor in general among the Ruthenians of Poland and Lithuania whose metropolitans, probably discouraged by the failure of Joseph I, did not return to his unsuccessful project. Without any formal break with Rome, all of these Metropolitans of Kiev of the sixteenth century continued to be satisfied with their confirmation by the Orthodox Patriarchs of Constantinople, as well as by the secular authority, the Catholic King of Poland and Grand Duke of Lithuania. Even Metropolitan Joseph II, unquestionably a member of the Soltan family which had been so favorable to religious reunion in the later fifteenth century, was no exception in that respect. [12]

When he succeeded the little known Metropolitan Iona II in 1507, a much more prominent ruler, King Sigismund I, [13] had already replaced a year before Alexander the Jagellonian, starting a long reign — until 1548 — which saw both the climax of Renaissance culture and the beginning of the Protestant Reformation in Poland and Lithuania. Definitely western in his whole education and personal interests, that prominent king, a very devoted Catholic, did not show any concern with the problem of reunion of his Ruthenian peoples who remained undisturbed in their traditional worship. However, time and again the importance of that problem would reappear and receive the attention of some of the king's collaborators, if not as such and in itself, at least in connection with the big political issues of the defense against Moscow and the anti-Ottoman league.

Such was precisely the situation at the Fifth Lateran Council [14] which was in session from 1512 to 1517 and where in June 1513 Jan Łaski, now already Archbishop of Gniezno and Primate of Poland, arrived as representative of King Sigismund I whose declaration of obedience he submitted to the new Pope, Leo X. Doing so at the public consistory of June 12, he described at the same time the twofold danger which threatened Poland and Lithuania, on the one hand from Turks and Tartars, and on the other hand from Moscow. [15] Moved to tears by his address, [16] Leo X designated the Primate of Hungary, Thomas Bakócs with whom Łaski closely cooperated, as legate to Hungary, Bohemia, Poland, and the neighbor countries including " Russia " and "Moscovia" to preach once more a general crusade against the Turks and Tartars. [17] His choice was very natural, since King

---

[12] Chodynicki, op. cit., 130, 146.

[13] W. Pociecha, " Zygmunt I, " The Cambridge History of Poland from the Origin to Sobieski, 300, 321 ; a full biography and survey of [his reign has been given by Z. Wojciechowski, Zygmunt Stary (Sigismund the Old), Warszawa 1946.

[14] L. Finkel, Sprawy Wschodu na soborze lateraneńskim (The eastern problems at the Lateran Council), Lwów 1900.

[15] Ibidem, 7.

[16] L. v. Pastor, Geschichte der Päpste, IV 1, 146 f.

[17] A. Theiner, Monumenta Hungariae, II, Nr. 800. Cardinal Bakócs was not only Archbishop of Esztergom in Hungary, but also titular Patriarch of Constantinople.

Ladislas of Hungary and Bohemia, whom Bakócs represented at the Council, was even more directly threatened by the Ottoman Empire than his younger brother Sigismund of Poland.

It is against that background that must be considered the most interesting report on " the errors of the Ruthenians " [18] which Łaski prepared for the eleventh session of the Council, originally scheduled for April 1514. The session was postponed and there is no evidence that this memorandum was studied in detail. But even so it deserves attention coming from the head of the Catholic Church in Poland, the Kingdom's former Grand Chancellor who remained one of its leading statesmen. Łaski clearly distinguished between the Russia which was under Sigismund I as King of Poland and Grand Duke of Lithuania, and the Russia of the Grand Prince of Moscow, calling the former " Red Russia, " though that name was usually given only to a comparatively small part of it : the region of Lwów in the Polish Kingdom, and using for the latter the ambiguous designation " White Russia " which as a matter of fact was sometimes applied to Muscovy in contemporary western sources, [19] but as a rule designated, as it does today, the lands of the White Ruthenians who then belonged to the Grand Duchy of Lithuania. However, more important than these questions of terminology is the obvious fact that Łaski's distinction was purely political, a fact which becomes even clearer if it is taken into consideration that besides the main two parts of the Eastern Slavs he distinguished a third one, the Ruthenians of Wallachia, or rather Moldavia, merely because these people, not different at all from the Ruthenians of the neighboring Polish provinces, happened to be under another rule.

On the contrary, Łaski made no religious distinction between these three groups, attributing to all Ruthenians — in his terminology the Eastern Slavs in general, including the Great Russians or Muscovites — the same religious errors. Such an approach which seems completely to ignore the impact and tradition of the Union of Florence among the Ruthenians of Poland and Lithuania, and possibly also those of Moldavia, appears particularly surprising in view of the great number of errors — no less than thirty-two — which are listed in the memorandum, and the far reaching accusations which are raised. Łaski stressed, of course, right in his first point the main error of all eastern schismatics : their denial of the Pope's primacy, adding the significant warning that even if they accept that primacy they are merely simulating. It is significant, too, that in one of the following points the Ruthenians are accused of rejecting all universal councils after the seventh : for this would imply the rejection by all of them of the

[18] Raynaldus, *Annales Ecclesiastici*, 1514, Nr. 67-86.
[19] The description of the frequently reproduced picture, illustrating the memoirs of Emperor Maximilian I, where his treaty with Moscow is mentioned, reads : " Der Weissrussen Bund mit Kaiser Max. "

Council of Florence. But Łaski's charges turn into evident exaggerations when he continues by pointing out that the Ruthenians also reject the sacraments of the Catholic Church including even baptism which, as explained a little later, they wrongly administer, sometimes suffocating the child, while confirmation is said to be replaced by a hot bath. Only in a few of the last points real dogmatic differences between the Greek Orthodox and the Catholic Church are recalled, particularly in the matter of the procession of the Holy Ghost and in that of purgatory.

There arises, of course, the question why a high dignitary of the Church, a man of Łaski's unusual intelligence and experience, a politician who only nine years before had shown a genuine interest in the problem of the Ruthenians in Poland and Lithuania, now went so far in his critique of all Eastern Slavs and appeared so prejudiced against them, suspecting them at the same time of strange prejudices against the Catholics. And why did he not mention any earlier attempts at reunion, were it only those of his own life time, nor any future possibilities in that respect, though Pope and Council were just considering such possibilities in their relations with the Maronites of Syria and the Copts of Ethiopia? [20]

The answer to these questions can be found in the alarming turn which the relations between Lithuania and Muscovy were taking in the spring of 1514. [21] After Sigismund's first inconclusive war with Basil III in 1507-1508, and a treaty of " eternal peace " which left to Moscow almost all her earlier conquests, another Muscovite aggression followed in 1512, even before Łaski left for Rome. The invasions of this and the following year failed to take Smolensk, the strategically most important place on the way to Wilno, and it was only now that a third attack against that city and fortress made its fall imminent and the situation critical. But even more alarming was the support which Basil seemed to find in the West thanks to the treaty concluded with an envoy of Emperor Maximilian I who going beyond his instructions promised to Moscow the effective cooperation of the Austrian rival of the Jagellonians. In view of Basil's connections with Albert of Brandenburg, the Grand Master of the Teutonic Order in Prussia, and with the Tartars of the Crimea, the vassals of Hungary's Ottoman foes, the encirclement of the Jagellonian States was so complete that the planned meeting of their rulers with Maximilian on imperial territory could under such conditions only lead to a surrender. And there was a serious danger that even the Pope, under the illusion that Moscow would conclude a religious union with Rome and even join the desired league against the Turks, [22] would be rather favorable to Basil, a ruler less outstanding than

---

[20] Hefele-Leclercq, *Histoire des Conciles*, VII-1, Paris 1917, 503-513.

[21] As to the general political background see E. Zivier, *Neuere Geschichte Polens*, I, Gotha 1915, Chapter IV, 94-154.

[22] P. Pierling, *La Russie et le Saint-Siège*, I, 255 ff.

his successor and predecessor, the two Ivans, but equally shrewd and consistent in his policy of aggrandizement.

Under such conditions it was indeed vital not only for Lithuania but also for Poland and the Jagellonian state system in general to destroy these illusions, and nothing seemed more appropriate in this respect than to show the profound religious opposition between Russian Orthodoxy and Catholicism, to convince the Holy See that the struggle against Muscovite aggression was at the same time a struggle in the defense of the Church of Rome. The Lithuanians who urgently asked for Polish help, even hoped that through Primate Łaski they could obtain from the Holy See the proclamation of a crusade against Moscow and thus gain the support of other Catholic powers, like the Scandinavian kingdoms and Livonia. [23] This was, of course, out of the question, but in any case Łaski's efforts did not remain without success : already on May 10, 1514, Leo X granted indulgences to the Poles attacked by the Russians, [24] and when soon after the unavoidable fall of Smolensk, on September 8 of the same year the Lithuanian army with strong Polish support [25] won the battle of Orsza, that Catholic victory was solemnly celebrated in Rome at the beginning of the next year and welcomed there as an event which would also facilitate the defense of Hungary against the infidels. [26]

Though Łaski's statements regarding the errors of the Russian Orthodox were exaggerated, he was entirely right in stressing Moscow's anti-Catholic attitude which made any religious union with her impossible and contributed to her reluctance to join the struggle against the Ottoman Empire, a struggle which Basil III, following the tradition of his father, was unwilling to undertake even in support of his Greek coreligionists. [27] But the question remains why the memorandum of the Primate of Poland included in the same criticism the Ruthenians of his own kingdom and of the Grand Duchy of Lithuania which largely was under the ecclesiastical jurisdiction of the Archbishopric of Gniezno. And why did he go as far as claiming a reversal of Rome's attitude regarding the validity of the baptism in the Orthodox Church, so that Leo X really cancelled the recent decision of Alexander VI that converted Ruthenians had not to be rebaptized ? [28]

It must be admitted that there was among many Catholic Poles and Lithuanians a suspicion that in view of their common faith all Ruthenians

---

[23] *Acta Tomiciana*, II, Nr. 203.

[24] A. Theiner, *Vetera Monumenta Poloniae*, II, Nr. 376.

[25] O. Halecki, *Dzieje Unii*, I, 64 f.

[26] *Acta Tomiciana*, III p. 7 ; see also Raynaldus, *op. cit.*, Nr. 64.

[27] P. Pierling, *op. cit.*, I, 258 f.

[28] Raynaldus, *op. cit.*, N. 79. However, a few years later, on May 18, 1521, Leo X, confirming the decisions of the Council of Florence, declared himself against the rebaptism of those baptized according to the Greek rite (*Documenta Pontif. Roman.*, I, Nr. 114).

9

were unreliable in the struggle against Moscow. Even the papal nuncio Jacopo Piso who at that critical time went as far as Wilno and hoped to proceed to Moscow as peace mediator, got the impression that the Ruthenians of Lithuania were inclined to side with the enemy and that the opposition between Catholic and Orthodox in the Grand Duchy was a source of trouble and danger, particularly in time of war.[29] Yet, these impressions which Łaski seemed to confirm, were not justified at all. Even the cases of treason which had created real difficulties during the preceding war, had nothing to do with these religious issues, since the leader of the whole movement, Prince Michael Glinski was not of Ruthenian but of Tartar origin, and not an Orthodox but a Catholic of Latin rite who had been in the service of Maximilian I.[30] And in 1514 the Ruthenians of Smolensk, contrary to all suspicions, loyally did their best to defend the city against the Muscovites, encouraged to do so by their Orthodox bishop, and had to surrender only because help was late to come.[31] Furthermore, when the whole province, in spite of the victory of Orsza, had to be given up, many of the local boyars preferred to emigrate to other regions of the Lithuanian Grand Duchy than to come under Moscow's rule.[32] Last, not least, at Orsza the Lithuanian and Polish forces had fought under the supreme command of Prince Constantine Ostrogski, the most prominent Orthodox Ruthenian magnate who in 1514, exactly as in 1500 but more successfully, tried to check the eastern aggressor.

His victory which failed to regain Smolensk, made it easier for the Jagellonians to appease the Habsburgs at the Congress of Vienna, in 1515,[33] and to prevent their actual cooperation with Basil III. But the hope that under such conditions it would be possible to appease Moscow also, to organize a crusade against the Turks and so to save Hungary did not come true. It was in vain that the Lithuanian representative Bohusz Bohowity-nowicz, another Orthodox Ruthenian in the service of Sigismund I, supplied the Emperor with the necessary information for acting as mediator between the King of Poland and the Grand Prince of Moscow.[34] Neither the well known imperial mediation entrusted in the first place to the famous Sigismund von Herberstein, nor the repeated efforts of papal diplomacy[35] had

[29] *Ibidem*, Nr. 59, 60, 65-67. About Piso's abortive mission, see Pierling, *op. cit.*, 260-262.

[30] About Glinski's background see L. Finkel, *op. cit.*; O. Backus, *op. cit.*, 105.

[31] *Acta Tomiciana*, III, Nr. 80.

[32] This list is published in an appendix (II) to Kašprovski, *Borba Vasilija III s Sigismundom I* (The struggle of Basil III against Sigismund I). Nezhin 1899.

[33] On the different interpretations of the results of that Congress see W. Pociecha, *Królowa Bona*, II, 519 note 217.

[34] *Acta Tomiciana*, III, Nr. 559, 591-593, 601.

[35] These efforts of the two Medici Popes are described in detail by P. Pierling, *op. cit.*, Book III; see in particular, on the mission to Moscow of Albrecht's agent Dietrich von Schoenberg, pp. 265-269, and on Ciołek's proposals, pp. 270-272.

any chance of influencing Basil III. Contrary to high expectations which had been raised by an unscrupulous agent of Albrecht of Brandenburg, then Grand Master of the Teutonic Order in Prussia and another enemy of Poland, the Grand Prince had not the slightest intention to conclude a religious union with Rome based upon the decisions of the Council of Florence, nor to participate in any anti-Ottoman league.

Such a league was then so urgently desired by the Jagellonians that through the same Erasmus Ciołek who had worked for the union with the Ruthenian Church in 1501, and in 1518 supported the papal appeal for the common defense against the Turks made at the imperial Diet in Augsburg, the King of Poland himself suggested in Rome to try once more to gain Moscow for both religious union and military cooperation. These suggestions of the Bishop of Płock had no more success than the memoranda on " the power of the Turcs " and an expedition against them under Polish leadership which were submitted to Leo X, in 1514 and 1517, by another member of the Polish hierarchy, Laurentius Międzyleski, Bishop of Kamieniec in the particulary threatened frontier province of Podolia. [36]

That Polish bishop of Latin rite who had to work in a predominantly Orthodox region tried also to intervene with the rivalries among the magnates of the Lithuanian Grand Duchy, [37] which were another obstacle to Sigismund's internal and external policies. Some of these magnates were Lithuanians and Catholics of Latin rite, others were Ruthenians belonging to the Eastern Church. But their disputes were of a purely personal character and dictated by the ambitions of rivalling families, without any nationalistic or religious implications. The most powerful of them, Albert Gasztołd, [38] was opposed at the same time by the Radziwiłłs, Lithuanian Catholics like himself, and by Prince Ostrogski who in spite of his Greek Orthodox faith was so respected for his services in the wars against Muscovites and Tartars, that in 1522 he was appointed to one of the few highest offices in Lithuania proper which were reserved for Catholics only. [39] This is at the same time one of the most significant examples that the legal restrictions from which the Orthodox had to suffer in theory, limited as they were, used to be disregarded in practice and were no serious reason for dissatisfaction. Equally significant is that the same Ruthenian Prince Ostrogski

---

[36] These memoranda are published in *Acta Tomiciana*, III, 168-181, IV, 350-354. On Międzyleski, his background and activities see W. Pociecha, *op. cit.*, 100-106, 505-507 note 196 ; on the discussions at the papal Curia in 1517, and the proposals which were forwarded to all Catholic powers - Pastor, *op. cit.*, IV-1, 152-155. On the Pope's concern with the defense of the Grand Duchy of Lithuania, see *Documenta Pontif.*, I, Nr. 113 (Jan. 15, 1520).

[37] Halecki, *op. cit.*, 75-79.

[38] See his memorandum submitted to Queen Bona in 1525, *Acta Tomiciana*, VII/21, Nr. 36, his biography by M. Kuźmińska in *Ateneum Wileńskie*, VI (1928), and the references in W. Pociecha, *op. cit.*, 593 note 315.

[39] *Acta Tomiciana*, VI, Nr. 36.

was one of the strongest supporters of the political union with Poland [40] where Catholic predominance was much greater than in Lithuania.

It is true that neither Ostrogski nor his old friend Ivan Sapieha who had been so interested in earlier plans of religious union with Rome, but now was involved in various conflicts with both Gasztołd and Międzyleski, [41] did nothing to raise again that difficult issue. But it is equally true that even now, in the twenties of the sixteenth century, the dividing line between Catholic and Orthodox was not very strict in the realm of the Jagellonians where people faithful to either Church were not only living together in peace and daily intercourse, but also concluding very frequently mixed marriages, and where precisely on such occasions the tradition of the Florentine Union was recalled. Typical in that respect was the marriage of Prince George Słucki with Helen Radziwiłł, in 1529. The Prince whose family was no less than the Ostrogskis leading among the Greek Orthodox and had favored the Union of Florence in the fifteenth century, founded already in 1526 a Catholic Church on one of his estates. [42] Now, before marrying the daughter of one of the Lithuanian Catholics, whose party he joined against Gasztołd along with Ostrogski and Sapieha, he wrote to Pope Clement VII asking him to approve that marriage. [43] The King supported his request, explaining that he did it in order to promote " peace and concord among the magnates of his dominions. " [44]

The Pope's decision was delayed for more than two years, but when finally taken [45] constituted an unusually important interpretation of the religious situation among the Ruthenians. He did approve the marriage taking it for granted that between the two consorts there was only a difference of rite. Since Prince Słucki had turned to the Holy See as if he had been a faithful recognizing the Pope's primacy, Clement VII specified that " he was living according to the rite and customs of the Greeks and of the Eastern Church but otherwise professed the Catholic faith. " He therefore granted even the additional request that as far as future children were concerned, sons should follow the Greek rite of the father and only daughters the Roman rite of the mother ; none of them should be forced to pass from one rite to the other. And the Pope quoted in that respect the decisions of the Council of Florence, [46] as if there had been no doubt that the Prince was simply a follower of the Union of 1439 and that Union still in force among the Ruthenians. Stressing the unity of both Churches,

---

[40] Halecki, op. cit., 76.

[41] Ibidem, 79.

[42] Chodynicki, op. cit., 227 n. 2.

[43] A. Theiner, Vetera Monumenta Poloniae, II, Nr. 504 (Jan. 15, 1529).

[44] Documenta Pontif. Rom., I, Nr. 117, p. 210.

[45] Ibidem, Nr. 117 (Nov. 27, 1531), Nr. 118 (to the King, Jan. 3, 1532), Nr. 119 (to Prince George, same date).

[46] Ibidem, p 209

Western and Eastern, he entrusted the Bishop of Wilno and the Abbot of Mogilno in Poland with the carrying out of his decision, and a little later granted to the Princess and to her children of either sex, therefore also to the sons who were supposed to be educated in the Eastern rite, the privilege to chose their confessor and to use a portable altar. [47]

In view of the prominent position which the Dukes of Słuck, a side line of the dynasty, occupied in Lithuania, the Holy See must have been fully informed of all aspects of that important case which therefore can be considered typical of a situation resulting from the continuity of the Florentine tradition in the given region. It was to become apparent only much later that the loyalty of the Słuckis to the Roman Church was rather doubtful : it is true that George's son married a Catholic of the Latin rite, of the purely Polish Tęczyński family, but her mother, a daughter of the Orthodox Bohusz Bohowitynowicz, remained so attached not only to the rite but to the faith of the Greek Church, that through these new family connections Orthodox influence prevailed again at Słuck. [48]

While thus the relations between Orthodox Ruthenians and Catholic Lithuanians and Poles within the limits of the Jagellonian Federation were becoming closer and closer, there were no similar relations at all between these Ruthenians and the Muscovites. A few families which came from Moscow with Princess Helen, the wife of Alexander the Jagellonian, were rapidly assimilated and Helen's own influence in religious matters was rather limited, especially after her husband's death, under Sigismund's rule. [49] Assimilated, too, were the hardly more numerous families which from Lithuania came to Moscow in connection with Glinski's rebellion, [50] and when a third war broke out between Lithuania and Moscow after Basil's III death in 1533, there were no such defections at all. [51] In spite of another armistice which was concluded in 1537 and extended several times in the following years, the tension continued between the two powers, both of the two neighbor countries living their own lives.

This was particularly true in the religious sphere. The ecclesiastical controversies in Muscovy which under Basil III resulted in the victory of the trend towards complete subservience to the State authority, [52] had no repercussions in the Grand Duchy of Lithuania. And Basil's occasional

---

[47] *Ibidem*, Nr 120 (Jan. 10, 1532).

[48] *Monumenta Poloniae Vaticana*, IV (Cracow 1915), Nr. 112, p. 202 n. 7.

[49] That influence of Queen Helen has been greatly overrated by earlier writers ; see Chodynicki, *op. cit.*, 80, 120 n. 1.

[50] It is well known that Michael Glinski's own niece married Grand Prince Basil III himself.

[51] See the detailed history of that war by L. Kolankowski, *Zygmunt August W. Ks. Lit. do r.* 1548 (Sigismund August as Grand Duke of Lithuania to 1548), Kraków 1913.

[52] See Ammann, *Abriss der ostslavischen Kirchengeschichte*, 175-178 ; W. K. Medlin, *Moscow and East Rome*, 80-98.

diplomatic relations with the Holy See, [53] similar to those with the Habsburgs, [54] had nothing to do with any religious problems. They did not even lead to any efficient peace mediation and were considered with a not unjustified suspicion by Sigismund I and his collaborators, especially those in Lithuania who even more than the Poles were alarmed by any rumors that the Grand Prince of Moscow could get a royal crown from the Pope or Emperor. Such fears appeared, for instance, in 1526 [55] and again toward the end of Sigismund's reign, in 1547, [56] when Basil's son and successor Ivan the Terrible, after fourteen years of boyar rule during his minority, assumed the real power and was crowned as Tsar. Exaggerated as they were, these fears and suspicions were a natural consequence of Moscow's persistent effort to gain Western support against her immediate neighbors, and of Western illusions that Moscow could be gained for religious reunion.[57] As a matter of fact, Moscow remained not only basically hostile to the old Rome, but also anxious to stress her independence from that second Rome, from Constantinople, which now was under Ottoman control. Avoiding any political conflict with the Turks, Basil III, in whose time the conception of Moscow's destiny as third and ultimate Rome was fully developed, disappointed those representatives of the Byzantine tradition who like the famous Maxim the Greek [58] hoped to revive that tradition in Russia and had illusions, similar to those of papal Rome, that support against the Ottoman Empire or even liberation from its yoke could come from the growing Orthodox power in Eastern Europe.

Men like Maxim the Greek who studying in Italy had also come in contact with the tradition of the Union of Florence, [59] were disillusioned at the same time as to the possibility of any support from the Catholic West whose projects of crusades or anti-Ottoman leagues never materialized. On the other hand, also Sigismund I, once considered a possible leader of such a league, [60] ceased to be interested in such projects when after the battle of Mohács, in 1526, in which his nephew Louis perished like, in 1444, his uncle at Varna, Hungary was lost to the Jagellonians and involved in an endless civil war in which the anti-Habsburg party, the more sympathetic

[53] See P. Pierling, *op. cit.*, I, 276-315, on the missions of Centurione and the Bishop of Scara 1518-1528.

[54] H. Übersberger, *Österreich und Russland*, I.

[55] O. Halecki, *Dzieje Unii*, I, 78.

[56] P. Pierling, *op. cit.*, I, 324 ff., on the mission of Hans Schlitte, which he rightly calls " une mystification diplomatique. "

[57] Pierling's criticism of the Polish reaction (*ibidem*, 339 ff.) is, therefore, hardly justified.

[58] See the latest discussion of his ideas in that respect by Elie Denissoff, *Maxime le Grec et l'Occident*, Louvain 1943, particularly 340 n. 1, 353-356.

[59] *Ibidem*, 227-260, 276, 320.

[60] See the projects of Międzyleski quoted above, note 36.

to Poland, was supported by Suleyman the Magnificent. [61] Poland tried to remain neutral in that conflict and merely to avoid Moldavian and Tartar invasions, while Lithuania was not interested at all, and therefore the Greek Patriarchs of Constantinople, whether looking for liberation from the Sultans or attempting to appease them through subservience, had no political reasons for developing their relations with Sigismund's dominions. But they did not show any interest either in the religious conditions there nor in the development of the Ruthenian Church which without formally denouncing the Union of Florence and without having any contacts with the Metropolitans of Moscow, continued to recognize the authority of the Patriarchate.

That recognition was, however, limited to the practice that the Metropolitans of Kiev received their formal confirmation and blessing from the Patriarchs of Constantinople. In most cases, particularly of the later sixteenth century, little is known even of these confirmations, [62] even less of occasional relations which, for instance, Orthodox monasteries in Lithuania maintained with Constantinople, [63] and in general the Ruthenian Church of both Lithuania and Poland was completely left alone. Under such conditions it is even more surprising than in the past that the efforts of reuniting that Church with Rome were discontinued for such a comparatively long time.

There is no wonder that no initiative in that direction came from that Church itself, particularly as there was not a single prominent personality among its hierarchy including the metropolitans themselves. This was at the same time one of the main reasons of the poor conditions of religious life and even of its deterioration already in the first half of the sixteenth century. And since the appointments of those metropolitans and bishops were practically decided by the King and his advisers who were only in part members of the Orthodox Church, the Catholic administration under which the Ruthenian lands were placed, was certainly not without serious responsibility for these deplorable conditions. Yet, two other sides of that problem must receive an equally serious consideration.

First, the Jagellonian Kings faithful to the tradition of their predecessors, were not unconscious of their responsibility as supreme " protectors and defenders " of the Orthodox Church of their Ruthenian subjects. [64] The Ruthenian hierarchy, though under a Catholic ruler, was undisturbed in the exercise of its religious authority, much less controlled by the State than in Orthodox Moscow, [65] and on many occasions really protected by the royal

---

[61] E. Zivier, *op. cit.*, I, 327-344 ; see now also W. Pociecha, *op. cit.*, II, 297-377.

[62] K. Chodynicki, *op. cit.*, 121 f.

[63] *Ibidem*, 124.

[64] *Ibidem*, 150-172, where the attitude of Sigismund I and his son and successor Sigismund II Augustus towards the Orthodox Church is very objectively studied in the light of a rich source material.

[65] *Ibidem*, 120, 161 f.

power in the field of jurisdiction and in the maintainance of Church property. Furthermore, in the most important controversial problem which resulted from the coexistence of an Orthodox Ruthenian and a Latin Polish hierarchy in the same places, Sigismund I made an important decision in favor of the former. In the city of Halich which temporarily had been the see of an Orthodox Metropolitan, eventually even the bishopric had been left vacant and administered by representatives of the Metropolitan of Kiev, residing in the not too distant and much larger city of Lwów. But that city continued to be the see of a Catholic Archbishop of Latin rite who started interfering with the appointment of the administrator of the Orthodox bishopric, and that led, of course, to frequent trouble and to an understandable dissatisfaction of the Orthodox Ruthenians. Putting an end to that confused situation, King Sigismund I, in 1539, restored the position of a separate Orthodox Bishop of Halich, residing in Lwów, and confirmed in that office the candidate of the Metropolitan of Kiev. He and his successors remained undisturbed in their authority extending as far as Podolia. [66]

But why was even on such occasions not the slightest attempt made to solve all the difficulties by a return to the union of the two Churches, which were living side by side in one country ? This question leads to the second aspect of the situation which qualifies the impression of neglect of the religious life of the Orthodox in a State under Catholic leadership. If it is true that the Ruthenian hierarchy suffered from royal influence on the choice of its members, it is equally true that the same influence was decisive when the Catholic bishops of Latin rite were chosen and in these cases too many questionable appointments were made in Poland and Lithuania, [67] just like in other countries where the impact of secularized Renaissance culture was experienced. The necessity of ecclesiastical reforms was felt by both Churches, the main difference being that the intellectual level was higher among the Catholic hierarchy and clergy, and that Catholicism had the support of Rome, facilitated by regular free contacts with the Holy See.

There were indeed among the Polish hierarchy of these times of religious crisis outstanding individualities which succeeded in combining their identification with Renaissance culture and their active part in politics with genuine religious zeal. The best example of such a truly excellent prelate was the Bishop of Cracow and Vice-Chancellor of the Kingdom, Peter Tomicki, who until his death in 1535 was for more than twenty years the most influential and at the same time the most respectable dignitary of Poland. [68] More than Primate Łaski with whom he frequently differed in political issues, he

[66] *Ibidem*, 131-134.
[67] *Ibidem*, 127.
[68] See the detailed references of W. Pociecha, *op. cit.*, II, 520 note 220.

always was anxious to be in the friendliest possible relations with the lords, both spiritual and secular, of Lithuania, appeasing their rivalries and working for a closer political union. [69] And there is no indication whatever that he had any prejudice or distrust toward the Orthodox Ruthenians. But neither did he show any interest in religious reunion with them nor was he successful in promoting the consolidation of the Jagellonian federal system.

The loose character of the political ties between the two separate States in which the Ruthenian Church was developing, was an additional reason for the neglect of the problem of religious reunion which required a joint action in both of these States. But even more important was another and final reason : the lack of any initiative in that matter for which both hierarchies and the Catholic King can be blamed, must seem excusable if it is taken into consideration that no initiative nor encouragement in that direction came in these times from Rome herself. However, for that apparent neglect of the Papacy in a matter which had always been and was to be again one of the most serious concerns of papal policy in Eastern Europe, there is an excuse too. The Fifth Lateran Council where all eastern problems had received a great deal of attention, was immediately followed by the outbreak of the Protestant revolt in Germany, a movement which soon was to spread over almost all Western Europe and naturally absorbed the Holy See to such an extent that all other problems had to suffer. This is true even with regard to the most urgent and immediate danger which Christendom had to face in the East when during the long reign of Suleyman the Magnificent the Ottoman onslaught became more violent than ever before. In spite of the fall of Rhodus and Belgrade, the defeat of Mohács, the first siege of Vienna, and the partition of Hungary with most of her territory, including Buda, from 1541 in Turkish hands, the religious crisis in the West combined as it was with the rivalry between the leading Catholic dynasties of Habsburg and Valois, forced the Papacy to postpone all projects of anti-Ottoman leagues, and the only step in that direction which was made in 1538 had very limited and precarious results. [70] It is, therefore, well understandable that the much less acute problem of reunion with the Eastern Churches had to be postponed too, except occasional negotiations with distant Ethiopia. [71] And if there reappeared some vague expectations that relations with Moscow could be resumed, they were so obviously deprived of any chances of success that the most competent experts would regret

[69] Halecki, *op. cit.*, II, 83-92.
[70] L. v. Pastor, *Geschichte der Päpste*, V, 182-184.
[71] They are recalled in a memorandum submitted in that matter to Pope Gregory XIII ; Vatican Library, *Urb. lat.* 854/I, fol. 2-6.

later that instead of these wasted efforts no approach to the Ruthenians of Poland and Lithuania was made for such a long time. [72]

All this being so, it is surprising indeed that among these Ruthenians the Florentine tradition, far from being completely abandonned, still continued to be remembered at the end of the first half of the sixteenth century. Just as it happened soon after the beginning of that period, in 1504, now in 1543, Poland's King, the aging Sigismund I and her Diet, this time meeting in Cracow, solemnly confirmed the charter of King Ladislas III which in view of the Union of Florence granted to the Ruthenian Church the same rights which were enjoyed by the Latin. This time too that confirmation was requested by the Bishop of Chełm " and his Church of Greek or Ruthenian rite, " a bishop whose personality is otherwise almost completely unknown but who was obviously keeping in custody, like his predecessors had done, the earlier charters and complained that the confirmation of 1504 was deteriorating just like the original of 1443. [73]

It is interesting to note that the new charter was issued on March 23, 1543, that is exactly one day after the centenary of Ladislas's grant. But it is, of course, much more important to stress that again it was not made quite clear whether the rights confirmed on that occasion and obviously not limited to the small diocese of the Bishop of Chełm, were valid only in the Kingdom of Poland whose Diet acted alone, or also in the other dominions of the King, that is in the Grand Duchy of Lithuania where most of the other Ruthenian dioceses — all of them except Przemyśl and the recently restored diocese of Halich-Lwów — were situated and where the Metropolitan of the Ruthenian Church continued to reside. In contradistinction to the situation of 1443 when Lithuania had a separate ruler, Sigismund I, like Alexander in 1504, was ruling in Lithuania also, and his son, Sigismund Augustus, was already recognized as successor, elected and crowned in both countries. [74] Furthermore, after a long interruption in the middle of Sigismund's reign, the Polish Diets started in 1539 to claim again a closer unification of the Grand Duchy with the Kingdom, and the Diet of 1543 was no exception in that respect, raising that problem as did the Diet of the following year. [75] But in that year of 1544, the Lithuanian Diet meeting in Brest — the place where the religious union of 1596 was to be concluded — refused any closer political union exactly as it had done at the same place thirty-nine years before when Łaski made his proposals regarding Lithuania and the Ruthenians. The Lithuanian lords considered

---

[72] This opinion was expressed by the famous Jesuit Antonio Possevino in his " De rebus Moscoviticis Commentarius ad Gregorium XIII. Pont. Max., " *Moscovia*, Vilna 1586, part I.

[73] *Acta Regis Alexandri* I, Nr. 233 note 1.

[74] L. Kolankowski, *Zygmunt August*, 11-17.

[75] Halecki, *op. cit.*, II, 98-108.

alliance and friendship sufficient, opposed any common legislature, and as far as ecclesiastical matters were concerned, did not even want the Catholic clergy of Lithuania to be bound by the decisions of the provincial synods of Gniezno regarding the participation in the common defense, though the Latin dioceses of Lithuania belonged from the outset to the Gniezno province. [76]

Under such conditions it was clear that the action taken by the Polish Diet regarding the rights of the Ruthenian Church could not influence the situation in the Grand Duchy nor contribute to a revival of the Florentine tradition there. Furthermore, it was precisely at Brest, in 1544, that Sigismund I entrusted his son with the administration of the Grand Duchy which therefore had once more a separate ruler, though the same person who was to be his father's successor in Poland, a decision which really came into force when the old King died four years later. [77]

In any case, it was obvious that in view of the administrative division of the Ruthenian lands between Poland and Lithuania there was a close connection between the problems of religious and political union, and that the chances of any efficient and constructive action in favor of a revival of the Union of Florence among the Ruthenians depended to some extent on the success of the Polish-Lithuanian negotiations regarding the constitutional ties between both States, negotiations which were to be one of the leading problems during almost the whole reign of the new common ruler, the last of the Jagellonians.

But those chances of religious reunion between Catholic and Orthodox within the boundaries of the federation which was to be finally constituted at Lublin, in 1569, depended even more on the development of the general religious situation in that whole region. And that situation again was to be more and more affected by the spread of anti-Catholic doctrines, Protestant and even Antitrinitarian in the Kingdom of Poland and mainly through Polish intermediacy also in the Grand Duchy of Lithuania. [78] Both countries being open — Poland from her origin, Lithuania from the beginning of the Jagellonian Union — to any western influence, it was only natural that after the Renaissance also the Reformation penetrated there already in the years which followed Luther's break with the Church. But under Sigismund I whose absolute loyalty to the Church was beyond any doubt, the progress of these new, revolutionary doctrines was rather slow and hardly reached the eastern provinces of his two States, where the Orthodox Ruthenians were living. Yet, towards the end of his reign the religious crisis

---

[76] *Ibidem*, 107-108.
[77] *Ibidem*, 106 note 5.
[78] On the early Reformation and the beginnings of Antitrinitarianism in Poland see E. M. Wilbur, *A History of Unitarianism*, Cambridge, Mass. 1945, chapters XIX and XX.

was already conspicuous, and since his son and successor was considered more favorable to these new religious trends, the imminent change on the throne raised high hopes among their partisans.

This was particularly important since in these same years, in consequence of the development of Polish culture under Sigismund I, new highly talented and influential writers started their literary activities, writers who were all involved in the Reformation movement. It so happened that precisely in 1543 appeared the first work of Andrew Frycz Modrzewski [79] who was to propagate ideas of religious union among all Christian creeds, including also the Eastern Churches though his main interest was in the western trends. And it was equally significant that in that same year Stanislas Orzechowski launched his first appeal in favor of a war against the Turks in cooperation with the Habsburgs, [80] while in the following year he started his campaign in favor of reunion with the Ruthenians, a campaign which was inspired by his own experiences in the Polish-Ruthenian borderlands and was to last until the end of the Council of Trent, nineteen years later.

That General Council whose first period started about the same time, following at last the Lateran Council after an interval in which the convocation of such a Council had been requested and suggested time and again, seemed to be an excellent opportunity for religious unification in the Catholic sense, the more so because from the eastern side it was always emphasized that only at such a Council a real union could be achieved. A general union with all Eastern Churches in the spirit of the Union of Florence seemed therefore not impossible. Hence a revived interest in relations with Moscow, now the most powerful center of Orthodoxy, an interest which was stimulated by the amazing successes of Ivan the Terrible in the first period of his reign. [81]

These hopes did not materialize and it was only much later that started the negotiations which led at least to a regional religious union in the Polish-Lithuanian Commonwealth at the end of the century. But the intermediary phase between the interruption of all similar negotiations in its first half and their actual resumption after the Council of Trent is an important link in the chain of developments which were leading from Florence to Brest. And if the Union of Lublin, prepared and concluded during that phase, is considered in all its religious implications, that political union appears as a real turning point on the long way between the two religious unions, the general and the regional.

---

[79] K. E. J. Joergensen, *Ökumenische Bestrebungen unter den polnischen Protestanten*, Copenhagen 1942, 149.

[80] A. Dembińska, *Zygmunt I, 1540-1548*, Poznań 1948, 38, has well explained the whole political background.

[81] *Concilium Tridentinum*, X (Freiburg 1916); see also VIII, *passim*.

PART II.

THE UNION OF LUBLIN AND ITS RELIGIOUS IMPLICATIONS

CHAPTER I

THE RELIGIOUS CRISIS IN POLAND AND LITHUANIA

The reign of Sigismund II Augustus[1] which in Lithuania started in 1544 and in Poland in 1548, and which ended in 1572 with the death of the last Jagellonian, is clearly divided in two parts : before and after 1562. Even in the field of foreign relations where the defense against Ivan the Terrible remained the main issue throughout, there is a great difference between the growing tension before that year and the open warfare which followed and in 1570 was interrupted only by a very precarious truce. But a much more striking change can be observed in the development of the most absorbing internal problems. Here too there is a certain continuity in the Polish claim for " execution of the laws " which sometimes covered and included the desire of rather radical reforms. But during the first phase it was the ecclesiastical reform which raised the most vivid interest in Poland and simultaneously also in Lithuania, while from 1562 the problem of a reform in the constitutional relations between the two countries occupied the first place leading to their closer union in one Commonwealth not without a momentous change in the position of the Ruthenian lands.

The religious concerns which were to reappear after that great political achievement at the very end of the reign, had for a long time distracted the general attention from all other questions. But during the same time when the Lithuanian leaders tried and succeeded to delay the discussions in the matter of political union, the common interest in the great religious

---

[1] See for a brief survey J. Pajewski, " Zygmunt August and the Union of Lublin, " *The Cambridge History of Poland from the Origin to Sobieski*, 348-368, where the importance of the year 1562 is well stressed on pp. 354 f. and 358.

crisis of the mid-century created one more cultural and spiritual link between the Kingdom and the Grand Duchy.[2] The Reformation thus contributed to the assimilation of both nations, including also the Ruthenians on both sides of the administrative border, and did it through an acceleration of the process of westernization in the whole eastern part of the Jagellonian Federation.[3] Avoiding, however, any exaggeration in such an interpretation of the religious crisis, it must be recalled that this process of westernization and cultural assimilation in all spheres of life, including religion, had started more than a century and a half earlier, with the foundation of the Federation by Jagello himself, the conversion of the Lithuanians to Catholicism of Latin rite, and the first projects of reunion with the Ruthenians by the creation, or rather restoration, of a Catholic Ruthenian Church of Greek rite. And just because that whole process was already well advanced, all new western trends including the Protestant movement had a fair chance to penetrate far into the Lithuanian and Ruthenian lands stopping only at the eastern frontier of the Federation with hardly any repercussions in Moscow.[4]

Though western in its origin and of general European character, the religious crisis of the Reformation period had in the Jagellonian States at least two distinctive features. One of them was an unusual tolerance,[5] or rather freedom of religious discussion and worship in a country of old and powerful Catholic tradition and under a Catholic ruler, sincerely attached to the Church of Rome. That Sigismund I had been such a ruler was obvious and unquestionable. But contrary to many misinterpretations by the contemporaries,[6] this was true of Sigismund Augustus also. Misinterpretations were possible and even natural, because the mild and patient methods of that king were in general but more especially in the treatment of religious problems in striking contrast with those employed by practically all other rulers of his time, and also because in some political matters which seemed to have religious implications, his views differed from those of the Holy See, for instance as far as any relations with Moscow were concerned.[7]

---

[2] K. Joergensen, *Ökumenische Bestrebungen*, 237 f.

[3] This is strongly emphasized by S. Kot, *La Réforme dans le Grand Duché de Lithuanie-Facteur d'occidentalisation culturelle*, Bruxelles 1953; see, however, my qualifications in the article " Reformacja czy Unia ? " (Reformation or Union ?), *Wiadomości* (Polish Weekly), London, Aug. 22, 1954.

[4] A. M. Ammann, *Abriss der ostslavischen Kirchengeschichte*, 225.

[5] See the comparative study of K. Völker, *Toleranz und Intoleranz im Zeitalter der Reformation*, Leipzig 1912, and the comments in his *Kirchengeschichte Polens*, Berlin 1930.

[6] O. Halecki, " Rome and Eastern Europe after the Council of Trent, " *Antemurale*, II (1955), 10 f. ; see the repercussions of these misinterpretations in modern historiography, for example, L. v. Pastor, *Geschichte der Päpste*, VI, 555, VII, 387 f., etc. and Ammann, *loc. cit.*

[7] Pierling, *La Russie et le Saint-Siège*, I, 340, 349, 372, etc.

If, however, he permitted all religious doctrines to be freely propagated in his dominions, particularly before the final determination of the Catholic doctrine by the Council of Trent, he contributed to the ultimate failure of the anti-Catholic movement in Poland and Lithuania rather than to its growth, because the unrestricted variety of new denominations and beliefs made impossible the creation of any unified non-Catholic Church. For that very reason the most prominent Protestant leaders in Poland, to mention only Jan Łaski, a nephew of the former Primate of the same name and known abroad as Johannes a Lasco, tried so hard and yet in vain to achieve a religious union of the different Protestant Churches. [8]

He and his followers who continued these efforts after his death in 1560 excluded from any such union all Antitrinitarian groups and hardly showed any interest in including that large body of non-Catholics which long before them had existed in Poland and Lithuania : the Greek Orthodox. Yet, their presence was the other distinctive feature of the Reformation period in that region of Europe where religious unity had not existed even before Luther though the Union of Florence had tried to, and almost succeeded in establishing such a unity. Without even speaking in that connection of minor non-Christian groups like the Jews and a certain number of Mohammedan Tartars, nor of the Eastern Church of the Armenians in Poland who also soon abandonned the Union of Florence, [9] the millions of Orthodox Ruthenians who only vaguely remembered that Union and mostly disregarded it since at least the beginning of the century, contributed more than anybody else to that exceptional religious variety which amazed all foreign observers of the spiritual crisis in that part of Europe. [10] In contradistinction to almost all other lands, the rivalry among Christians had there a three-cornered character, the Protestant movement coming as a new and particularly dynamic addition to the agelong rivalry between Catholic and Orthodox.

This being so, it was only natural that those who took the idea of religious unity most seriously and boldly, would include all three main groups. Completely logical in that respect was the most constructive and at the same time most radical mind among Poland's reformers, both political and religious, of these crucial years, Andrew Frycz Modrzewski, [11] But before that remarkable writer who gradually came under the influence of the most extreme Antitrinitarian ideas, formulated his views on the Eastern

---

[8] K. Joergensen, *op. cit.*, chapter II on J. Łaski's oecumenical ideas.

[9] There final union with Rome was not concluded before the XVII century ; see G. Petrowicz, *L'Unione degli Armeni di Polonia con la Santa Sede 1626-1686*, Roma, 1950.

[10] O. Halecki, *Zgoda sandomierska 1570 r.* (The Agreement of Sandomierz), Warszawa 1915, 22.

[11] K. Joergensen, *op. cit.*, Chapter IV on Modrzewski's oecumenical ideas.

Churches, the versatile Stanislaus Orzechowski who later became a staunch defender of the Roman Church and even of extreme clericalism,[12] was the first to raise as early as in 1544 the question of Eastern Christendom and its appurtenance to the Church universal. And he did it before causing himself to the Church for rather personal reasons the most serious trouble and serving, willingly or not, for several decisive years the Protestant cause.

His approach to the religious problems which in spite of all his qualities of a brilliant propagandist lacked very frequently the necessary consistency and balance, was strongly influenced by the background of the clergyman who called himself " *gente Ruthenus, natione Polonus,* " a formula which has been frequently used and misused ever since. Whatever its original interpretation might have been, he certainly wanted to stress that he was a loyal citizen of Poland but at the same time intimately associated with the Ruthenian people. The latter did not necessarily mean ethnic Ruthenian origin, since the Orzechowski family was originally Polish and only settled in Ruthenian territory when the writer's father in one of the frequent mixed marriages of the period married the daughter of an Orthodox Ruthenian priest. That this influenced his attitude regarding the celibacy of the clergy, is natural, and so is his strong regionalism, his identification with those whom he called in his humanistic terminology the " *Roxolani.* "[13]

But in his first appeal in favor of religious reunion which he addressed in 1544 to a leading member of the Catholic Polish hierarchy, Peter Gamrat, a future Primate but former Bishop of Przemyśl in that very " Roxolania, " Orzechowski did not limit himself to any regional union, but anxious to extend the frontiers of the Church as far as possible in the eastern direction, included not only the Armenians but also the Greek Orthodox of Wallachia and — last not least — of Moscow, and all eastern Patriarchates.[14] Taking as starting point the correct principle that the Ruthenians, and of course in general the eastern Christians, had not to be rebaptized when received into the universal Catholic Church, Orzechowski was in full agreement with papal decisions which after being withdrawn under the influence of Jan Łaski the elder — the Primate — had been reaffirmed in 1520 by a papal legate to Poland.[15] But avoiding Łaski's strange overemphasis of the " errors of the Ruthenians, " Orzechowski went to the opposite extreme, trying to prove in all his writings that these errors which he swore to his bishop not to support, did, as a matter of fact, not exist at all.[16]

---

[12] See the bibliography by K. Chodynicki, *Kościół prawosławny,* 195 note 1; Orzechowski's initiative in the matter of reunion is discussed there, 195-202.

[13] J. Korzeniowski (ed.), *Orichoviana,* Cracoviae 1891, 617.

[14] *Ibidem,* 46, 79.

[15] The title of his appeal is : *Baptismus Ruthenorum. Bulla de non rebaptisandis Ruthenis* ; see *ibidem,* Nr. 6.

[16] *Ibidem,* 89 f., 218.

He was, of course, right in recalling that most of the differences between the Roman and the Eastern Churches, including for instance the much discussed question of using leavened or unleavened bread for the Eucharist, were differences of rite and not of dogma. But even the difference regarding the procession of the Holy Ghost he dismissed as being merely a question of expressing the same belief in different words, [17] and he who always professed his respect for the Pope's supreme authority, strangely underestimated the basic difference between West and East in the matter of papal primacy.[18] It is, of course, only fair to distinguish between the Orzechowski who in the first years of the reign of Sigismund Augustus, having married in spite of being a Catholic priest of Latin rite, became a symbol of resistance against Church discipline and was supported as such by all followers and sympathizers of Protestantism, and the same Orzechowski who a dozen of years later, reconciled with the Church, developed a truly theocratic system of papal supremacy. But he was very slow to realize [19] that in their opposition against the Catholic interpretation of papal authority Greek Orthodox and Protestants came very near to each other, and therefore, in spite of the profound dogmatic differences between them which were indeed much greater than those between Orthodox and Catholics, could easily cooperate against Rome in a matter which had more general appeal than the strictly theological controversies. It was not before 1563 that Orzechowski, getting afraid of such a common front against the Catholic Church which he now wanted to defend, was convinced by the greatest Catholic theologian of Poland, Cardinal Stanislaus Hosius, that his own views in the decisive question of the Pope's place in the Church had not been entirely correct [20] and that no compromise was possible in that question. Furthermore, though Orzechowski was correct, as Hosius himself admitted, in considering possible and even in recommending all the concessions in matters of rite and liturgy which the Eastern Churches requested, he was again insufficiently aware that in these matters too there was an agreement between the Orthodox and the supporters of the new western dissenters which could lead to some kind of cooperation between the two rather than to a reunion of the former with the Roman Church.

Expecially in the early years of the Protestant movement in Poland the most important claims were those of the chalice for laymen, the abolishing of the celibacy of the clergy, and the use of the vernacular in lit-

---

[17] *Ibidem*, 216 f., 561.

[18] *Ibidem*, 564, cf. 505.

[19] As evidenced in his letter to Jan Dziaduski, the Bishop of Przemyśl, who condemned him for his marriage (*ibidem*, 463).

[20] Orzechowski's letters (*ibidem*, 550-574) and the criticism of Hosius (*Opera omnia*, Coloniae 1583, 708-713) have been analyzed in detail by A. Kossowski in the review *Przegląd powszechny*, vol. 177 (1928), 162-186, 327-353.

urgy [21] — all matters which corresponded to the traditional practice of the Eastern Church and in particular of the Orthodox Ruthenians living in the same country. In these matters many of those who favored ecclesiastical reforms without wanting to go as far as a formal break with the Catholic Church, supported the Protestant leaders. Along with the desire of limiting Rome's influence and of increasing lay influence in religious life, all these elements which Orthodoxy and Protestantism had in common were strengthening the forces of religious revolution and leading to a conception of unity of all Christians which was irreconcilable with the Catholic approach to that problem. And this could only discourage the Catholic hierarchy and all those who remained loyal to Rome, from supporting the trends towards reunion with the Ruthenians.

It was, therefore, quite natural that Orzechowski, at least in the first phase of his activity, was supported in that issue rather by those whose loyalty to Rome was very doubtful, for instance, as far as the hierarchy was concerned, by Jan Drohojowski, [22] then Latin Bishop of Chełm where that Polish prelate descending from an old Ruthenian family and a cousin of Orzechowski himself, was of course in contact with the Ruthenian Bishop of the same place. Even if precisely in that diocese of Eastern rite the tradition of the Union of Florence was still remembered in connection with the recently renewed charter of 1443, [23] there was a serious danger that Drohojowski whose Lutheran sympathies were notorious, would come under the influence of the Greek schismatic tradition also. He was indeed suspected of favoring not only the practice of communion under both species but also the Greek doctrine of the procession of the Holy Ghost from the Father alone. [24] Much more important, however, than the occasional support of a bishop without much zeal and theological knowledge who soon was transferred to the see of Cuyavia in northwestern Poland, proved the influence which Orzechowski exercised upon the most outstanding writer of his generation, Modrzewski, chiefly a political thinker and reformer but deeply interested in religious problems also.

To his famous treatise *De Republica emendanda* Modrzewski added a special *Liber de Ecclesia* in which he so openly turned away from the Catholic tradition that it could not be included in the first edition of his work, printed in Cracow in 1551. It was only three years later that the full text appeared in Basel. In one of the first chapters of that section on

---

[21] These were the main concessions which were claimed by the Protestant leaders at the Diet of 1555 and which, in addition to the calling of a national synod, were requested the next year by the King himself from Pope Paul IV; see Pastor, *op. cit.*, VI, 557, and P. Fox, " The Reformation in Poland, " *The Cambridge History of Poland*, 337 f.

[22] About his relations with Orzechowski see Chodynicki, *op. cit.*, 195 f.

[23] See above, pp. 123, 138.

[24] *Acta historica res gestas Poloniae illustrantia*, I, Cracoviae 1878, 483.

ecclesiastical reform [25] he strongly expressed the opinion that in the universal Church and at the general Council which was supposed to reform it, not only the Latin Church should be represented and all Latin, i. e., Western Churches united, but the Eastern Churches as well " which are along with us fighting under the signs of the same Jesus Christ. " And he mentioned on the one hand the Churches of foreign countries : those of the Greeks and — significantly enough — of Ethiopia, and on the other hand, those " which exist in our provinces, " the Churches of the Armenians and the Ruthenians. As to the comparatively small Armenian group Modrzewski quoted the little known writings of a certain Andrzej Lubelczyk and as to the Ruthenians, he highly praised the comments of Orzechowski, who in his opinion had shown the possibility of an agreement regarding the procession of the Holy Ghost, the question in which they seemed to differ most from the Latins.

Modrzewski's information on the Eastern Churches in distant, extra-European lands was rather vague and even influenced by the notorious legends about " peoples in Asia under the rule of the Priest John. " But his concern with his Orthodox fellow citizens was very genuine and he concluded with an appeal to " our Latin Churches " in their favor : " since we agree with them in matters of the State and obey to one monarch, we ought to unite with them and to try to lead them back with us in one sheepfold. " [26]

In saying so he came indeed very near to the Catholic idea of one flock under one pastor, and in support of what had always been claimed and recommended by Rome, he stressed the argument of political community, thus presenting religious reunion as a natural supplement of the Jagellonian supranational political system. In view of Modrzewski's unquestionable erudition and well deserved authority his voice could have been of unusual weight in the whole matter. Greater, however, than his interest in the reconciliation between the Western and Eastern Churches was his interest in reconciling first the conflicting trends in the West, in what he called the Latin Churches including both Roman Catholicism, the new Protestant denominations, and even, as it clearly appeared in his later theological writings, [27] the most extreme Antitrinitarian doctrines which were rejected by Catholics and Protestants alike and had been rejected more than a thousand years ago by Eastern Christendom.

Therefore the problem of religious reunion of West and East practically disappeared in Modrzewski's subsequent discussions and his first appeal in

---

[25] *A. Fricii Modrevii Commentariorum de Republica emendanda libri V* (ed. C. Kumaniecki), Varsoviae 1953, 303.

[26] *Ibidem*, 303.

[27] On his development in the direction of rationalism and his attitude in the Christological controversies, see K. Joergensen, *op. cit.*, 201-204.

that matter, though issued in terms which could seem quite acceptable from the Catholic point of view, not only remained almost unnoticed but could even discredit the idea of religious reunion in the eyes of the Catholics, since it came from a man whose interpretation of unity in one universal Church developed in a direction leading far away from Rome's doctrine. The refutation of such views which could serve only the Protestant cause absorbed the Catholic theologians to such an extent that little time was left for discussions with the Greek Orthodox, and even the great Hosius, concentrating on the dogmatic struggle with the Protestants, was rather reserved when discussing with Orzechowski the ways and prospects of coming to an agreement with Eastern Christendom, an agreement which he considered most desirable but at the same time very difficult because of what he called "the arrogance and pride" and "the light-mindedness and instability" of the Greeks. [28]

The influence of these Greeks, now so deeply humiliated under Ottoman rule, was in those days rather insignificant among the Ruthenians of Poland and Lithuania who, on the contrary, were coming along with the Catholics under the influence of Protestantism. Even more than the Catholics they were attracted first by the moderate claims of the reformers in matters of rite and liturgy, claims which were in agreement with their own traditional practice. And since the poor condition of their Church was deteriorating amidst the growing religious crisis, they were even less prepared than the Catholics to face the next phase of the reform movement which was clearly of a dogmatic character. While the Latin clergy of Poland made a serious effort to oppose the danger by internal improvements at the Synod of Piotrków in 1551, [29] no really important synod of the Ruthenian hierarchy was held after that of Wilno in 1509. [30] And while under the leadership of Hosius the Catholic bishops became more and more conscious of their responsibilities, including even the Primate Uchański whose attitude was open to many suspicions, [31] the Metropolitans of Kiev of the same period were insignificant personalities, chiefly concerned with questions of Church property. Not before the end of the reign of Sigismund Augustus, in 1568, the recently appointed Metropolitan Iona Protasewicz, anxious to improve the situation, submitted to the last separate Lithuanian Diet which met in Grodno, a series of requests which were to give to the Ruthenian hierarchy more authority and prestige. [32] He wanted for its members places in the Grand Ducal Council, similar to those occupied by the bishops of

---

[28] *Opera omnia,* 711,712.
[29] J. Umiński, "The Counter-Reformation in Poland," *The Cambridge History of Poland,* 400.
[30] K. Chodynicki, *op. cit.,* 130, 171.
[31] See his biography by T. Wierzbowski, *Uchansciana,* V. Warszawa 1895.
[32] Chodynicki, *op. cit.,* 128, 135 f.

Latin rite and opposed the practice of Sigismund Augustus to consider ecclesiastical offices as rewards for services rendered to the State and to give them even to lay candidates.

The first of these requests was not granted and even as to the second the last Jagellonian who influenced in a decisive way even the choice of Catholic bishops, made only limited concessions to the Ruthenian Orthodox. If, however, his policy in that important matter made him partly responsible for scandalous rivalries among the candidates for the Ruthenian bishoprics, the Protestant penetration among the Greek Orthodox was at least equally responsible for a growing disintegration of the Ruthenian Church which soon after the death of Sigismund Augustus was to reach its climax. That penetration was mostly the result of the spread of Calvinism which in Lithuania as in Poland proved more popular than Lutheranism and enjoyed the support of some of the leading aristocratic families, especially the Radziwiłłs. Following the example of these purely Lithuanian, formerly Catholic lords, the rivaling families of Ruthenian origin and Orthodox faith, without excepting those who like the Chodkiewicz or the Sapiehas had favored in the past the Union of Florence, now turned Calvinist one after the other. [33] If in the province of Nowogródek, with a predominantly White Ruthenian population, the progress of Calvinism among the Orthodox gentry seemed particularly striking, [34] this was alarming for the very reason that it was in Nowogródek that the Metropolitan of Kiev actually resided, because just like the Catholic bishop of that city — then the notorious Nicholas Pac who showed himself an open inclination to the Calvinist doctrine, [35] — they did not feel safe so near the eastern border of the Grand Duchy.

In some cases Calvinism would lead eventually to Antitrinitarianism, and if in that respect the situation among the Ruthenians was hardly better than that among Poles and Lithuanians, it was to a large extent the result of an energetic propaganda in their own language which was conducted by Simon Budny, [36] a reformer of Polish origin who himself joined one of the most extreme religious groups. That gifted and prolific writer gives at the same time instructive evidence that in those days the Protestant and Antitrinitarian reformers, far from thinking of any religious union with the

---

[33] S. Kot, *La Réforme dans le Grand Duché de Lithuanie*, 15.

[34] See the frequently quoted statement by P. Skarga, *Russkaia istorich. bibl.*, VII 950 f., and also Kot, *op. cit.*, 43.

[35] His attitude was a source of constant alarm for the papal nuncios (see, f. ex., *Vat. Archives, Nunz. di Polonia*, vol. 1 fol. 9, 1567) until he was finally removed from his see.

[36] In addition to his earlier biography by H. Merczyng (*Szymon Budny*, Kraków 1913), see now S. Kot, *op. cit.*, 39, and the same author's recent study on S. Budny in *Studien zur älteren Geschichte Osteuropas I (Festschrift für H. F. Schmid)*, Graz — Köln 1956, 63-118, particularly 83.

Orthodox, a union which most of them, more realistic than Modrzewski, rightly considered impossible, simply wanted to convert them to their own creeds. Budny himself, so active among not only the nobles but also " the common people of Ruthenian tongue, " did not hesitate to express occasionally, in his correspondence with Western reformers, his contempt for these people who, in his opinion, were simply " aping " the Greeks. [37]

These new, revolutionary doctrines, no less than Roman Catholicism, were turning away the Ruthenians from the Greeks to such an extent that in 1561 the Patriarch of Constantinople requested the King of Poland to expel the " Lutherans " from the Ruthenian lands which were under his spiritual jurisdiction. [38] Even, strange enough, some Muscovites who were condemned in their own country for propagating heretical ideas and escaped to Lithuania, found some common ground not only with the Protestants but also with the so-called " Arians " in the White Ruthenian provinces of the Grand Duchy and also of Volhynia. The most prominent political immigrant from Moscow, the famous Prince Andrew Kurbsky, deeply attached as he was to the Greek Orthodox faith, was the first to point out that danger, [39] but rather in vain. And it was easy to foresee that when amidst the frequent changes of beliefs, typical of the general religious crisis, some of the Ruthenian converts to the various new denominations would give them up again and return to traditional grounds, they would not return to their former Orthodoxy which so obviously was in decline, but rather become Catholics and thus remain in the sphere of Western influence.

Nevertheless, the gains which Protestantism and Antitrinitarianism were making, at least for the time being, among the Orthodox Ruthenians could not but alarm the Catholics and convince them that it was not enough to defend themselves against the new doctrines but that the followers of the Eastern Church could not be neglected. The first to realize this were the papal nuncios who were no longer visiting Poland only occasionally and at long intervals but from 1555 were permanent representatives of the Holy See in the Kingdom following one another in uninterrupted succession. [40] But the first among these nuncios to Poland who gave serious attention to the problem of the Ruthenian " schismatics, " and not only to that of the various " heretical " sects, clearly distinguishing between the two, was Giovanni Commendone, and even he not before 1564, the second year of his mission.

---

[37] See his letter to U. Bullinger, of 1563, in Th. Wotschke, *Der Briefwechsel der Schweizer mit den Polen*, Leipzig 1908, Nr. 273.

[38] *Venetianische Depeschen vom Kaiserhofe*, III, Wien 1898, 189 n. 1.

[39] Chodynicki, *op. cit.*, 177 ; see also Halecki, *Zgoda sandomierska*, 23.

[40] See L. Boratyński's introduction to the first volume of the systematic publication of the reports of these nuncios in *Monumenta Poloniae Vaticana*, IV (Cracoviae 1912).

That his predecessors, not only the first of them Luigi Lippomano who, in general, was rather unsuccessful because of his unbalanced harshness, but also Mentovato, whose presence in Poland was rather brief, and even Buongiovanni, practically overlooked the Ruthenian problem, is not too difficult to explain. All of them, less prominent and experienced than Commendone, were completely absorbed by the struggle against the Protestants and their sympathizers in the Polish Diet, a struggle which, in the years from 1555 to 1563, was passing through its most critical phase. [41] Furthermore, the biggest problem which the Holy See and its representatives had to consider in these same years, was the preparation for the third period of the Council of Trent and the work of that last and decisive period until its conclusion in December 1563. And strange enough, while Pius IV made hopeless efforts to invite to the Council Ivan the Terrible of Moscow, creating only alarm in Poland, [42] nothing was done to achieve the participation of the Ruthenians of Poland and Lithuania, which would have been so much easier to obtain. Papal diplomacy limited itself to the task of securing the cooperation of Sigismund Augustus who, far from creating any difficulties, sent to Trent an official representative in the person of Bishop Valentine Herburt, but was not too interested in the work of the Council, since the outbreak of the long delayed war with Ivan the Terrible was then his foremost concern. [43] Not even the Polish Cardinal Hosius, who in the very year 1563 when he was discussing with Orzechowski the possibilities of reunion with the Ruthenians, was one of the papal representatives at Trent,[44] raised there the problem of the Eastern Churches.

It so happened, however, that Nuncio Commendone had to consider the Ruthenian problem at the very moment when he tried to obtain from Sigismund Augustus the official acceptance of the decrees of the Council of Trent and their application in Poland. In one of his reports to the Secretary of State, Cardinal Borromeo, [45] he described in detail the memorable session of the Polish Senate, held at Parczów on August 7, 1564, when after listening to the Nuncio's eloquent address, the King immediately and without any reservations declared through his Vice-Chancellor that he did accept the decisions of the Council. That formal statement which only a few weeks after the final confirmation of these decisions by the Pope him-

---

[41] On the activities of these nuncios see L. v. Pastor, *Geschichte der Päpste*, VI, 555-563, VII, 388 f.

[42] Pierling, *op. cit.*, I, 362-378.

[43] Br. Dembiński, *Rzym i Europa przed rozpoczęciem trzeciego okresu soboru Trydenckiego* (Rome and Europe before the beginning of the third period of the Council of Trent), Kraków 1891, 186-190 f., 232.

[44] Pastor, *op. cit.*, VII, 190, 196.

[45] *Ibidem*, VII, 392 note 2, who quotes that important report along with all other sources; see also M. Malinowski, *Pamiętniki o dawnej Polsce* I, Wilno 1851, 179; *Nuntiaturberichte aus Deutschland*, IV, Wien 1914, 215 f.

self and before any similar declaration of other Catholic rulers was obtained from a king, hitherto considered wavering and weak in his religious convictions, was more than a personal success of Commendone : it was the decisive turning point in the history of the religious crisis in Poland, opening the door to a complete Catholic restoration in that country. [46] Sigismund Augustus also promised he would do his best to have the decrees of the Council put in force in his dominions, and Commendone hoped that some energetic action would be taken in that connection against the enemies of the Church. He was aware that the King, opposed as he was to any violent interference with religious problems, would never proceed to repressions limiting anybody's freedom of worship, but he hoped that at least some royal decrees against the heretics would be issued, and already a month before on July 6, 1564, writing to Cardinal Borromeo from Heilsberg in Warmia, the diocese of Cardinal Hosius with whom he closely cooperated, he pointed out that such a decree would not include the "Ruthenian schismatics." [47] As a matter of fact, the decrees which were published immediately after the acceptance of the Council's decision, were directed only against foreigners who were conducting anti-Catholic propaganda in Poland ; they even could be interpreted as expelling only the most radical Antitrinitarians. [48] But in view of any further action and of determining papal policies it had become indispensable to study more carefully than ever before the position of the followers of the Eastern Churches who without being heretics were nevertheless separated from Rome.

Commendone himself examined their problems in another report to the Secretary of State which one month after the Parczów discussions, on September 9, he sent him from Lwów. [49] It was precisely in that city that he had a first opportunity closely to observe both the Ruthenians and the Armenians. There bishops welcomed him with the Archbishop of Latin rite, and everywhere the Ruthenians "of Greek rite and religion" asked for papal protection against Protestant propaganda from Germany. Therefore, the instruction which in March 1566 was prepared in Rome for the next nuncio, Giulio Ruggieri, included for the first time a paragraph dealing with the Greek hierarchy of Poland and Lithuania. [50]

It is very significant, indeed, that this sentence of the instruction followed immediately after a reference to the Duke of Moscow pointing out that the Pope — already Pius V — knew not only of his great power, but

---

[46] O. Halecki, "Rome and Eastern Europe ..., " *Antemurale*, II, 11.

[47] Vatican Library, *Barber. Lat.* 5798, fol. 351v-353.

[48] E. M. Wilbur, *A History of Unitarianism*, 320 n. 4.

[49] Vatican Library, *loc. cit.*, fol. 371-372 v. ; see also the report of Oct. 7 from Łuck, *ibidem*, fol 372 v - 374.

[50] Vatic. Archives, *Misc. Arm.* II, vol. 82, fol. 195-219, three copies of that instruction. In the last text which seems to be the final, the passage about Moscow is on fol. 217-217v, that about the Ruthenian bishops on fol. 218v.

also of his design to become King of Poland. The nuncio was, therefore, instructed to find out more about his practices in that direction and about his partisans, and also to inquire among these partisans whether that ruler could be expected to be sincerely prepared to ally himself with " the Christians " and to support any enterprise directed against "the Turk, his natural enemy. " That reference seems to be exclusively political without any indication that writing about Ivan's possible cooperation with the West the Holy See was also thinking of religious union. And it is not clear whether passing in the next paragraph to the religious issues among the Ruthenians, the instruction implied that partisans of Moscow could be found among these peoples of the same faith. Furthermore, if the information about Ivan and his intentions was vague and uncertain, the details about the followers of the Greek religion under the rule of Sigismund Augustus were rather inaccurate and incomplete, to such an extent that the instruction, probably aware of this, recommended to Ruggieri to get further advice from Commendone, Hosius and Kromer, the noted historian who was to succeed Hosius in the bishopric of Warmia.

Enumerating the " Greek bishops " which " used to be confirmed by the Patriarch of Constantinople " the instruction said that there were such bishops in the cities of Lwów, Przemyśl — both in Poland — Łuck and Wilno, and also in the city of Polotsk. As to the last three places all of which belonged then to the Grand Duchy of Lithuania, there was indeed a Ruthenian bishop of Łuck, but Wilno which only had a Catholic bishopric, was probably mentioned only because many Orthodox lived there and perhaps also because the Metropolitan of Kiev, the head of the Ruthenian hierarchy, came frequently to the capital of the Grand Duchy ; as to Polotsk, the see of an Orthodox archbishop, it was since 1563 occupied by Ivan the Terrible. The instruction continued saying that among these peoples there were apparently " various ancient condemned and deplorable heresies, " certainly meaning not only the errors of the Greeks but also the doctrines of the Protestants and Antitrinitarians which exercised so much influence among the Ruthenians. In view of that situation Ruggieri was to find out from the Catholic prelates he was asked to consult " how these poor people could be helped in any respect. "

In spite of that brief but excellent recommendation, the new nuncio does not seem to have achieved very much in that direction. While, however, in earlier reports which Rome received about Poland, there was only the vaguest reference to the many people who in Lithuania were living " alla Greca, " and while the lists of the Greek archbishops and bishops in that country, which were available at the Holy See, continued to be strangely inaccurate, [51] Ruggieri made on his return to Rome, in 1568, a com-

---

[51] See, for ex., the notice in Vatic. Library, *Barber. Lat.*, 5146, fol. 2v-3.

prehensive report [52] which included much more detailed and, in general, correct remarks on the Ruthenians and their religious life. He was particularly specific in enumerating the Greek bishoprics of the Kingdom of Poland whose pastors were confirmed by the schismatic Patriarch of Constantinople. Even that information was not considered sufficient, and in the instruction for his successor Vincenzo de Portico, [53] the recommendations regarding the reconciliation between Poland and Moscow in view of their cooperation against the Turks were again followed by a reference to the Ruthenians and the Armenians : the nuncio was briefly advised to get more information about their ways of life and their rites, and to consider what could be done for the salvation of their souls. Furthermore, in one of the letters which three years later, in the fall of 1570, were sent to Portico from Rome, there is some evidence that in connection with the baptism of the Ruthenians the bull of Alexander VI was once more examined. [54]

Yet, such references to the Ruthenians and their religious problems remained rather exceptional in the correspondence of the papal nuncios whose main concern continued to be with the struggle against the Protestants. Even the ecclesiastical organization of the Greek Church in the Jagellonian Federation was insufficiently known in Rome where it was not clearly distinguished which of the eight Ruthenian dioceses were in Poland and which in Lithuania — a question which the shift of the boundary in 1569 made even more confusing — nor which of them were archbishoprics and which bishoprics only. A notice on the religious situation in the Commonwealth which was submitted to the Holy See at the very end of the reign of Sigismund Augustus [55] is typical of the inaccuracies of information about those who in " Russia " and also in Lithuania " observed the Greek rite and recognized as head of their Church the Patriarch of Constantinople. " It was well realized that all the Ruthenians had received their religion from the Greeks at the time of St. Vladimir and had remained loyal to Constantinople ever since, but it did not seem quite clear when they had become schismatics along with the Greeks. Their considerable number was stressed, including the fact that there were whole provinces under the rule of Sigismund Augustus which " had that religion, " but it was a great exaggeration to point out that these Ruthenians were practically all plebeians and " of low condition. " Even conditions in Lwów which the anonymous writer of that report described with most details, were strangely misrepresented, especially as far as the relations with the Metropolitans of Kiev, " Russia and Wallachia " were concerned, and simply phantastic stories were told about

---

[52] Published in a Polish translation by E. Rykaczewski, *Relacje nuncjuszów apos tolskich*, Paris 1864, I.

[53] Vatic. Archives, *Misc. Arm.* II, vol. 34, fol. 40v.

[54] *Ibidem, Nunz. di Polonia* 1, fol. 135 (Nov. 5, 1570) ; see the copy of that bull in Portico's papers, *Misc. Arm.* II, vol. 69, fol. 49v-51v.

[55] *Ibidem, Nunz. di Polonia* 5 B, fol. 56-58.

some Ruthenians in Lwów who divided the year in ten months and the month in six weeks, beginning the year on March 1st. Hardly more accurate were the remarks about the Armenians in that same city whose bishop, obedient to the Patriarch of Armenia, was called an archbishop.

Under such conditions it was not surprising that the method of dealing with that whole problem of the Eastern Churches in Poland and Lithuania was not discussed at all and nothing said about the most important alternative whether individual conversions to Catholicism of Latin rite or a union of Western and Eastern Churches, recognizing the different rite of the latter, would be preferable. In any case, Orzechowski's suggestions in favor of such a union, which Hosius approved in principle but considered difficult to carry out, were not followed, though the difficulties might have been smaller after the conclusion of the Council of Trent ; and even individual conversions of Orthodox Ruthenians seem to have been much rarer than conversions of Protestants which after Trent became more and more frequent. That some of those Protestants, including very prominent personalities, had been originally Orthodox, was a question which hardly received any attention, but the conversion of one of the Chodkiewicz, now so powerful in Lithuania where they could rival with the Radziwiłłs, was typical in that respect. [56]

These conversions resulted not only from the efforts of the papal nuncios, especially Commendone, and of zealous members of the Catholic Polish hierarchy, especially Hosius, but in many cases were achieved by the Polish Jesuits who in the years after 1565 founded their first colleges in the Commonwealth and were greatly encouraged by Hosius himself. [57] And it was precisely these earliest Jesuit preachers, teachers and writers, who were the first to become fully aware of the importance to work not only among the Protestants but also directly among the Orthodox whose number was so much greater, at least in the eastern part of the Commonwealth, whose religious tradition had much deeper roots in the country, and who were represented in all classes of society, including the peasants. That interest of some of the most eminent Polish Jesuits in the Ruthenians started already during the reign of Sigismund Augustus, and the famous Peter Skarga whose work among the followers of the Eastern Church must be traced back to these earlier years, had in that respect a modest but not insignificant precursor in the person of Benedict Herbest. [58]

It is true that this son of a Polish peasant, born around 1530 in the ethnically mixed region of Przemyśl and whose name, before he Latinized

---

[56] See about the origin of that conversion O. Halecki, *Zgoda sandomierska*, 154 n. 5.

[57] The early beginnings of the activities of the Jesuits in Poland are described in detail by St. Załęski, *Jezuici w Polsce*, I, Kraków 1900.

[58] " Predteča Unii " — a precursor of the Union — is the title of a Ukrainian study of Herbest's activities published by A. Suško in *Zapiski Tov. im. Ševčenka*, vol. 53 and 55 (1903). See also Chodynicki, *op. cit.*, 202-204.

it, was Zielewicz, experienced the complex religious aspects of the Ruthenian problem well before he entered the Jesuit Order. Educated in Cracow and first working as a priest in Western Poland, he made in 1562 a trip to his native region which took him as far as Lwów where he had made a first stay from 1550 to 1553. It was only five years later that he described his journey in a short Polish pamphlet, in connection with his discussions with the Calvinists, but what he observed in the Ruthenian lands in the earlier days of the religious crisis, obviously influenced him ever since. Just like Orzechowski, he was impressed by the fact that the differences which separated the Eastern Churches from the Catholic were insignificant if compared with those which separated both of them from the Protestants. He saw no such differences at all as far as the Armenians were concerned, except in matters of rite. But even an agreement with the Ruthenians who still were outside the Catholic Church, did not seem too difficult to Herbest. To get a clearer idea of their religious beliefs, he went to see one of their priests in Lwów who was ready to recognize even the primacy of the Pope though he wanted the whole problem of reunion to be referred to his superiors, the Bishop of Lwów and the Patriarch of Constantinople. Obviously what was considered in such talks was not merely a personal conversion but a real union in which, as Herbest pointed out, far reaching concessions could be made to the Greeks preserving their rite and liturgy, if they only accepted the Catholic doctrine and papal authority.

Writing this in 1567, a few years after the Council of Trent and before his own studies at the Jesuit Novitiate in Rome, [59] Herbest not only quoted Orzechowski whose earlier writings must have influenced him, but stressed the sympathetic interest in the problem of reunion with the Ruthenians which he found among the clergy of both sides. He mentions in particular that same Catholic Bishop of Przemyśl Valentine Herburt, who had been the official representative of Poland at the Council of Trent. Unfortunately, however, nothing is known about any real support which the cause of reunion received either from that Bishop who must have known the local conditions so well, nor from any other member of the hierarchy, and even Herbest's own activity became conspicuous only much later, in rather different conditions which were to influence his attitude. But his influence upon the much greater Peter Skarga appeared already in the very year when he published his pamphlet.

For it was precisely in 1567 that Skarga, as he recalled it ten years later to Prince Constantine Basil Ostrogski, [60] met that son of the great leader of the Orthodox Ruthenians in the days of Sigismund I for the first time at the funeral of the young prince's brother in law John Christopher

---

[59] J. Warszawski, *Polonica z rzymskiego Kodeksu nowicjuszy Tow. Jez.* (1565-1586) (Polonica from the Roman " Codex novitiorum " S. J.), Rome 1955, 102 f.

[60] When dedicating him in 1577 his book on " The Unity of the Church of God, " reprinted in *Russkaia istor. bibl.* VII, 228 f.

Tarnowski at whose court Skarga had passed two years. He impressed on that occasion Ostrogski by a sermon in which he touched the problem of union between the Eastern and the Western Churches. Skarga himself had gotten interested in that problem when as a young priest, born in central Poland, he was sent to the Ruthenian region, chiefly to work in Lwów where he was Chancellor of the Catholic Archbishopric. It was there that he studied not only the Armenians, as he mentioned later, but obviously also the Ruthenians and their religious life, probably met Herbest, as well as Orzechowski, and tried to gain for the Catholic faith both Protestant and Orthodox noblemen. [61]

Nobody could be more important among the latter than Ostrogski who was following the example of his famous father as leader of the Ruthenians being by far the richest and most powerful among them. [62] Having married a daughter of old John Tarnowski, one of the leading Catholic Polish magnates, for many years Commander-in-Chief of the Polish forces, he had the closest possible relations with the Latin world. Skarga's sermon and his approach to the problem of religious reunion interested the Prince so much that he planned to invite him to his home, along with another Polish preacher of the Dominican Order, to discuss with them " questions of salvation." Apparently that visit did not take place, perhaps because Skarga soon left for Rome where he entered the Jesuit Order, [63] but it was there that he was confirmed in his decision to work for the union of the Churches, meeting for the first time the famous Italian Jesuit Antonio Possevino with whom he was to cooperate in that matter later. [64] On his return to Poland he was sent again to Lwów and participated in the foundation of a Jesuit College in nearby Jarosław at the head of which Benedict Herbest was placed and which developed as an important center of Catholic propaganda among the Ruthenians of the whole region and even of Volhynia where Prince Ostrogski had his main estates.

The early contact between Skarga who was to promote so strongly the Union of Brest, and Constantine Ostrogski who after seeming favorable to the union eventually became its greatest opponent, was of unusual significance. But it was significant too that their first discussions took place on the eve of the political union of Lublin which transferred Volhynia and the Kiev province where Ostrogski held the highest office of Palatine, from Lithuania to Poland and established a much closer union with the remaining part of the Grand Duchy in whose capital, Wilno, another, much more important Jesuit College was founded about the same time and soon became the center of Skarga's further activities.

[61] Chodynicki, *op. cit.*, 210 f.
[62] See the genealogy of the Ostrogski family in J. Wolff, *Kniaziowie litewsko-ruscy*, Warszawa 1895.
[63] J. Warszawski, *op. cit.*, 82 ff.
[64] See below, Part III, Chapter I.

CHAPTER II

BEFORE AND AFTER THE DIET OF LUBLIN, 1569

The history of the religious crisis in the middle of the sixteenth century shows better than anything else how difficult it is in the cultural field clearly to distinguish between the Kingdom of Poland and the Grand Duchy of Lithuania even before the Union of Lublin of 1569. Politically these two fully independent States were united before that date only by the person of their common ruler, the tradition and memory, sometimes rather vague and inaccurate, of the union charters of the period from 1385-1501 which were no longer in force, and by an alliance which was unwritten, though close enough to appease any conflicts and to guarantee cooperation in the relations with other countries, in peace and in war. Culturally, however, there was something more : a more and more similar way of life and a common approach, different only in degree, to the problems which were raised by the development of western civilization in the orbit of which, though at its extreme eastern border, Poland and Lithuania including their Ruthenian provinces were developing themselves.

Among these problems the most important were as usual, and at the given moment even more than usually, the religious ones. In the Jagellonian Federation the Catholic Church of the Renaissance needed a reform exactly as it did in the western countries. The revolutionary method to achieve such a reform which was being experienced in most of these countries and gained total or partial victory in some of them, was tried by many intellectual leaders in Poland and Lithuania also. And even when such leaders of either State disagreed in political matters, they favored common action in the struggle against traditional Catholicism. The same Radziwiłłs who were leading the Lithuanian opposition against closer political ties with Poland, encouraged the intimate cooperation of Polish and Lithuanian Calvinists : [1] though not the Diets, the Protestant synods of both countries had to meet in common, in their opinion, as often as possible, just as the Catholic hierarchy and clergy of both, belonging to one ecclesiastical province, was meeting at the same provincial synods. Similar was the situation in the Antitrinitarian camp : the native leaders whom the so-called " Polish

---

[1] O. Halecki, *Zgoda sandomierska*, 64 f. ; J. Jasnowski, *Mikołaj Czarny Radziwiłł*, Warszawa, 1939, 220 f.

Brethren " had in addition to the foreign, mostly Italian initiators of their movement, worked jointly on both sides of the political border between the Kingdom and the Grand Duchy: while, for instance, Simeon Budny, so active in the eastern part of the Grand Duchy, was of Polish origin, Peter of Goniądz, who had a strong influence in Poland, came from the then Lithuanian province of Podlachia. [2]

Yet, in Podlachia the majority of the population was neither Lithuanian nor Polish, but Ruthenian of Orthodox faith, and in Budny's field of action equally Orthodox White Ruthenians predominated. Largely Orthodox Ruthenian too was the population of Poland's second ecclesiastical province, that of Lwów, which then like the first one, the much older province of Gniezno, reached far into the Grand Duchy and precisely into its non-Lithuanian but purely Ruthenian southern provinces, including Kiev. But also the Greek ecclesiastical province under the Ruthenian Metropolitan of Kiev, though it then was mainly within the political boundaries of Lithuania, included three dioceses which were in Poland, one of which, that of Lwów, originally of Halich, had temporarily had its own metropolitan in the past but had given up such claims at least one hundred years ago, precisely at the time when the Union of Florence seemed to have its best chances among the Ruthenians of both Jagellonian States. [3]

Such a rather confusing ecclesiastical situation did hardly correspond to the general principle of both the Roman and the Greek Church that each larger country should have its metropolitan and that ecclesiastical frontiers should coincide with the political. It was, however, possible because the frontier between Poland and Lithuania, though strictly respected in the administrative field, was more and more vanishing in the cultural. This explains, for instance, why Prince Constantine Basil Ostrogski who like his father was still a potentate of the Grand Duchy holding there all his high offices and most of his extensive possessions, got in touch with the Polish Jesuit Skarga when this promoter of religious union was still exclusively working in the territory of the Kingdom. In this case it was Ostrogski's Polish marriage which gave the direct occasion for such a contact, and similar marriages, mixed from both the national and the religious point of view, were becoming more and more frequent, at least among the nobility, and were in addition to ecclesiastical organization one of the most important factors which promoted cultural community in daily life independently of any political consideration. But Ostrogski's case was particularly significant not only in view of his powerful personality and further role in the whole issue of religious reunion, but also because besides Podlachia the Prince's

---

[2] See his biography by J. Jasnowski in *Przegląd historyczny* (Historical Review), XXXI (1935), 1-58.

[3] See above, Part I, Chapter IV, p. 84.

native, much larger province of Volhynia was for obvious geographical and historical reasons the part of the Grand Duchy where already before 1569 Polish influence was strongest. [4]

Nevertheless, the division of the Ruthenian lands and the Orthodox population between the two separate bodies politic of Poland and Lithuania, while no obstacle to religious influence upon individuals whether coming from the Catholic Church or from its opponents, created one more difficulty in working for a religious union with the Ruthenian Orthodox peoples as a whole. On the other hand, any difference in the legal situation of these same peoples in either country was one more obstacle to their political unification. In view of the general principle of freedom of worship in both countries that difference was rather small [5] and only a minor point in the series of differences in their respective constitutions. But when Sigismund Augustus, once determined to prepare the political union of his two States, started the preparatory process of assimilating the Lithuanian constitution to the Polish, even the relatively slight discrepancy in the treatment of the Orthodox citizens had to receive due attention. That process started immediately after the petition for closer and stabler ties with the Poles which the Lithuanian and Ruthenian gentry of the Grand Duchy in agreement with aristocratic opponents of the Radziwiłł faction submitted to the last Jagellonian at the extraordinary assembly of Vitebsk in 1562 [6] and it lasted until the year immediately before the common Diet of Lublin. It is therefore highly significant that the most important charter which Sigismund Augustus issued in favor of the Orthodox in Lithuania, was granted them in 1563 and supplemented in 1568, an undoubted indication that this step was taken in connection with the preparations for the Lublin Union. [7]

That connection is clearly explained in a sentence of the charter of 1563 [8] in which Sigismund Augustus, distinguishing between the two peoples living together within the limits of the Grand Duchy of Lithuania : the Ruthenians and their Lithuanian brethren, pointed out that both of them, the former no less than the latter, were favorable to a closer community, to " the brotherhood of union " with Poland. This statement was indeed in full agreement with the fact that out of the three delegates which the convention of Vitebsk had chosen in the preceding year for submitting to the King the formal petition in the matter of such a union, only one was of purely Lithuanian origin, while the other one was a Ruthenian boyar from Volhynia and the leader of the delegation — one of the Chodkiewicz —

---

[4] A. Dembińska, *Wpływy kultury polskiej na Wołyń* (The influences of Polish culture upon Volhynia), Poznań 1930.

[5] See K. Chodynicki, *Kościół prawosławny*, 92.

[6] See my analysis of that petition in *Przegląd historyczny*, XVIII (1914), 320-352.

[7] This has been definitely shown by Chodynicki, *op. cit.*, 88-90.

[8] *Monumenta Reformationis Polonicae et Lithuanicae*, Wilno 1925, Nr. 4.

a Ruthenian member of that highest aristocracy in which Lithuanian and Ruthenian families were practically amalgamated. [9] The conclusion of Sigismund Augustus resulted no less clearly from that situation : the same privileges ought to be enjoyed by the nobles " of either Christian faith : the Roman faith of the Lithuanians and the Greek faith of the Ruthenians." This sentence was used in the charter of 1568 [10] which specified that the references to the nobility included also the princes, particularly numerous among the Orthodox Ruthenians, but the basic text of 1563 was obviously inspired by the same principle.

What must be explained in some detail is the question which discriminations were removed in both documents with a view of making conditions in Lithuania similar to those in Poland. That question is the more important because in practice the Orthodox Ruthenians, much more numerous in the Grand Duchy than in the Kingdom, certainly had a greater influence in the former country. There remained, however, in the general charters of rights and liberties which had been granted to the Grand Duchy from the early times of its first association with Poland and which Sigismund Augustus had all confirmed once more in 1551, a restriction which originated in 1413, in the privilege which was included in the charter of the Horodło Union [11] and which declared that the offices created on that occasion were to be accessible to Catholics only. This was, of course, a reference to only the four highest offices in Lithuania proper, that nucleus of the Grand Duchy where the Catholic Lithuanians predominated anyway, since it was only to that region that new rights were granted at Horodło. And even there that religious restriction was never strictly observed, as evidenced by the appointment of Prince Constantine Ostrogski (the elder) in 1522. [12] But it had never been made sufficiently clear that such a restriction did not exist at all, not even in legal theory, as far as the predominantly Orthodox Ruthenian lands of the Grand Duchy were concerned, and on the eve of the Union with Poland where they did not exist either, it seemed necessary to cancel them altogether.

It is true that the preparation for that political union was not the only reason for doing so. At a time when so many Protestants occupied the highest dignities in Lithuania as well as in Poland, it was a strange anachronism to create any difficulties in that respect to followers of the so much older Eastern Church. Therefore, while it would be difficult to interpret the charters of 1563 and 1568 as referring to all Christian denomina-

---

[9] O. Halecki, *Dzieje Unii*, II, 155.

[10] *Monumenta Reformationis*, Nr. 5.

[11] *Akta Unii Polski z Litwą*, Nr. 51, p. 66 f., 10.

[12] Well explained by K. Chodynicki in his study of the rights of the Orthodox in the Grand Duchy of Lithuania published in *Przegląd historyczny*, XX (1919-20), particularly in § 5.

tions, including the Protestants, [13] they might have been influenced to a certain extent by the full equality of political rights which even these new religious groups enjoyed in practice. But there was an even more important additional reason for removing everything which could seem unfair to the Orthodox of the Grand Duchy. This was done not only before the final union with Poland but also during another armed conflict with Moscow. And more than ever before the Orthodox Ruthenians of Lithuania deserved an unrestricted recognition for their absolute loyalty and unwavering cooperation in the struggle against Orthodox Moscow. To the cases of treason on the other side, of which that of Prince Kurbsky was the most spectacular, did not correspond any similar defections which would have impaired the defense of the Lithuanian Grand Duchy against Ivan the Terrible. On the contrary, in spite of a community of religious rites and even beliefs, there was not the slightest inclination among the Ruthenians to exchange their free development in Lithuania which their most prominent leaders called " our dear fatherland " or " a wonderful and almost sacred country " [14] against the notorious conditions under Ivan's tyranny.

For them, just like for their Catholic Lithuanian fellow citizens, the urgent desire of getting more Polish support against Moscow, was the strongest argument in favor of consolidating the Polish-Lithuanian Union. And the same is true as far as Sigismund Augustus himself was concerned. The years of preparation for that union were at the same time those of his greatest efforts to bring the war against Moscow to some satisfactory conclusion, either through a military victory which he tried in vain to secure by the abortive plan of a great offensive under his personal leadership,[15] or at least by an acceptable peace treaty or truce. It is, therefore, obvious that in these busy years no time was left for dealing with purely religious problems, the charters of 1563 and 1568 being an exception which simply confirms the importance of their decisions for the political problems absorbing the king.

Even the Polish Diets where religious discussions between Catholics and Protestants including all the controversies between the hierarchy and the laity had taken so much time during the first part of the reign, after having obtained in 1563 the suspension of ecclesiastical jurisdiction, concentrated on the political issues of their reform program and welcomed the opening of negotiations with the Lithuanian Diets and their delegates. [16]

---

[13] See my comments in *Zgoda sandomierska*, 155 n. 4.

[14] In the letter of Prince Roman Sanguszko to the King, of May 21, 1568 (*Archiwum XX. Sanguszków*, VII, Lwów 1910, Nr. 262), which along with many other examples has been quoted by Chodynicki, *Kościół*, 106 f.

[15] K. Piwarski, " Wyprawa radoszkowicka 1568 r. " (The Radoszkowice expedition of 1568), *Ateneum wileńskie*, VI (1928).

[16] O. Halecki, *Dzieje Unii*, II, 159 ff.

And when at last the request for a common Diet, now supported by the Lithuanian gentry and favored by the king, received satisfaction, the long deliberations of that Diet held in the frontier city of Lublin from January 10 to August 12, 1569, [17] were devoted almost exclusively to the problem of the political union between the two States. Not only were religious controversies avoided, but the attitudes of the various political groups and their leaders on either side were hardly influenced by their religious beliefs, whether Catholic, Protestant or Orthodox. [18]

On one occasion, however, the problem of the position of the Greek Orthodox was raised in connection with one of the most important political changes which were decided in Lublin. [19] During the long interruption of the negotiations concerning the relations between the Kingdom and the Grand Duchy whose representatives had left the city at the beginning of March, the King promised to the Poles already in the course of that same month that the provinces of Podlachia and Volhynia, objects of long Polish-Lithuanian disputes, would be incorporated with the Kingdom of Poland, and by the end of May that decision was carried out with a view to extending that incorporation also to the province of Kiev. That territorial transfer was not only to exercise a pressure upon the Lithuanian opposition, but also to secure a better defense of the Commonwealth as a whole against Moscow and the Tartars along a frontier which henceforth would be the eastern boundary of both federated States. The King and the Diet wanted, however, to get in that matter the agreement of the nobility of the interested provinces, [20] and the attitude of the powerful Volhynian aristocracy was particularly important. Before giving their consent and swearing a formal oath of allegiance to the Crown of Poland on May 24, four of the most prominent Volhynian magnates requested guarantees in two matters. [21]

---

[17] *Ibidem*, II, 256 ff., see 251 n. 1 on the editions of the diaries of that Diet.

[18] On the religious tensions between Catholics and Protestants during the Diet, which, however, remained in the background, see my remarks in *Zgoda sandomierska*, 146 ff.

[19] Discussed in detail in my book *Przyłączenie Podlasia, Wołynia i Kijowszczyzny do Korony Polskiej* (The incorporation of Podlachia, Volynia and Kiev with the Crown of Poland), Kraków 1915 ; many documents which I quoted there from manuscript sources are now published, along with some additional material, in *Akta Unii*, Nr. 96-147.

[20] See the long lists of those who swore allegiance to the Crown of Poland, in *Akta Unii*, Nr. 131, 132, 135, 137, 139, 140, 142, etc. Particularly interesting is the document of June 16, 1569 (Nr. 141), which put on record that the Archimandrite (Abbot) of the famous Orthodox monastery of Żydyczyn wanted to swear such an oath, though the king had not requested it from him.

[21] See these speeches in the diary of the Diet (*Dnevnik lublinskago seima*, 382 (only the title of the edition of the Polish text is in Russian, since it was published with a Russian translation in 1869 in St. Petersburg, by the Russian historian M. O. Koialovich ; W. E. D. Allen, *The Ukraine — A History*, Cambridge 1940, wrongly assumed that the diary itself was in Russian.

Since all of them, including Constantine Ostrogski, were princes — a title which did not exist in Poland — they demanded first that their families be conserved in their dignity and permitted to use their titles. Furthermore, since all of them, even those who originally came from Lithuania proper and, like the Czartoryskis, were side lines of the Jagellonian dynasty, professed the Orthodox faith, they wanted the equal rights of their Church to be once more recognized. That demand could seem surprising, since no such restrictions as those which were quite recently removed in the Grand Duchy, had ever existed in the Kingdom. But in practice very few Greek Orthodox were holding any higher offices in Poland, because in the comparatively small Ruthenian lands which before 1569 belonged to the Kingdom, most of the leading families had become Catholics of Latin rite long ago.

Both guarantees were granted without difficulty and included in the royal charter of May 27 [22] which restored the land of Volhynia along with Bracław (eastern Podolia) to the Kingdom of Poland : besides a general promise of participation in all Polish liberties, of the continued use of the Lithuanian code and of the Ruthenian language in all official documents — except those concerning the mainly Polish cities — that document confirmed not only " the ancient honor and dignity " of the princes, but also the equal rights of the Greek Orthodox. The same was said, without any further discussion, in the similar charter [23] which on June 6 incorporated the province of Kiev, Ostrogski having sworn another oath of loyalty to the Crown, this time as Palatine of Kiev. [24]

In consequence of these incorporations, the Kingdom of Poland included now practically all lands which were Ruthenian in the strict sense of that name, viz., Ukrainian in modern terminology, while the Grand Duchy of Lithuania kept the White Ruthenian provinces. It is true that the province of Brest was also left to Lithuania, though some of its nobles were inclined to join the Kingdom, [25] and that its population must be considered rather Ukrainian than White Ruthenian ; but in most of that region of transition, especially in the wide Pripet marshes, there was no well defined national consciousness at all, and in general, the differentiation of the Ukrainians and White Ruthenians of today started after the Union of Lublin and played no part at all at the time of its conclusion.

What was a rather strange consequence of the shift of the States frontier, was the division of one of the Greek dioceses, that of Brest and Volo-

---

[22] *Akta Unii*, Nr. 136 ; the repeated reference to the equal rights of the " Roman " and the " Greek " religion is in § 8, p. 305 f.

[23] *Ibidem*, Nr. 138 ; the same reference is on p. 316.

[24] *Dnevnik lublinskago seima*, 407.

[25] O. Halecki, *Dzieje Unii*, II, 306, 311.

dymir, since the former city remained in the Grand Duchy, while the latter went with the whole of Volhynia to the Kingdom, as did the other Volhynian diocese, that of Łuck and Ostrog. And though the metropolitan see of Kiev was now in the Kingdom also, the actual residence of the metropolitans continued to be in Lithuanian Nowogródek. In order to understand, however, that such facts did not involve any serious inconveniences, the terms and general character of the Polish-Lithuanian Union which on July 1 followed the transfer of some of the Ruthenian provinces, must be considered in turn.

That final union [26] was a compromise between the extreme claims of some Poles who wanted an incorporation of the whole Grand Duchy, and the desire of a small, but powerful aristocratic Lithuanian group which was opposed to the creation of a common Diet. The agreement — mainly the result of the King's patient persuasions — corresponded to the ideas of the Polish Senate and to the desire of the Lithuanian and Ruthenian gentry as expressed in the Vitebsk petition of 1562. Though the Kingdom and the Grand Duchy were proclaimed one body politic, a Commonwealth in which " two States and nations were united in one people, " Lithuania continued to be an equal partner with her own title, administration, army, treasury, and code of law. Since, however, in the structure and constitution of the Commonwealth the legislative power, that is the common Diet, was supreme, the community was now, in general, much closer than before, and the clause regarding the common election of the ruler guaranteed the permanence of that community even after the expected childless death of the last Jagellonian. Furthermore, all restrictions which in the past had forbidden the Poles to acquire land property in Lithuania were removed, and it was permitted to citizens of either country to own such property in the other.

Under such conditions the internal frontier between Poland and Lithuania lost much of its former significance, and the fact that the followers of the Eastern Church remained divided between the two, though they now were much more numerous in Poland than before, became much less important too. That in a Commonwealth under one legislature there could not be any longer any difference in the situation of the same religious group in either country, had been realized by Sigismund Augustus already on the eve of the Union when he abolished some exceptional restrictions in Lithuania, and made him abolish soon after the Union local restrictions of a different character which were directed against Orthodox Ruthenians, this time not nobles but burghers, in one of the cities of the Kingdom, in Lwów. [27]

---

[26] See the charters in *Akta Unii*, Nr. 148, 149, 151 (confirmation by the King on July 4).

[27] See K. Chodynicki, *op. cit.*, 101 f.

The royal decree in that matter, [28] though dealing with a strictly local problem, was issued, on May 20, 1572, at the Diet of Warsaw, the second of the common Diets which followed that of Lublin, and was signed by the Polish and Lithuanian senators beginning with the Primate and all Catholic bishops. Confirming the full equality of rights of both the burghers of " Greek or Ruthenian rite and faith " and those of them who were Catholic Poles " of Roman obedience, " the King did it " in view of the laudable act of union between the Kingdom of Poland and the Grand Duchy of Lithuania " concluded at the preceding Diet of Lublin. Since according to its decisions all the dignitaries, senators and other officials, spiritual as well as secular, of the Grand Duchy and of the lands of Volhynia and Podlachia, including those of " Greek rite and Ruthenian faith, " had been joined to the magnates of the Kingdom of Poland in full equality, Sigismund Augustus declared it even more necessary that there should be a similar equality among " men of minor and inferior condition. "

It would seem that such a general principle should apply also to the clergy, but it is important to note that in contradistinction to the earlier charters which had been granted to the Ruthenian clergy and confirmed by King and Diet as late as 1543, no reference was made any longer to the religious Union of Florence, but only to the political Union of Lublin. Whether dealing with the burghers of Lwów or, a few years earlier, with the nobles and princes of Lithuania, the King spoke not only of peoples of different rite but also of different, though of course Christian faith, Greek or Ruthenian in opposition to the Roman. That difference was taken for granted just as were other differences in legal and administrative practice which even after Lublin continued to exist among the two parts of the Commonwealth and even some of its autonomous provinces.

It is true that at the very end of the Diet of Lublin on August 12, 1569, Sigismund Augustus in a speech [29] pointing out the problems which in spite of the successful conclusion of the political union remained open, mentioned also, besides minor political issues, " the diversity in the worship of God. " He referred to it with obvious regret, and though he made it quite clear that faithful to his principle of non interference with religious matters, he would not enforce any unity of worship, just as he had not used any force and violence in promoting the political union, he declared that he wanted to see " the holy Christian faith in one and the same Christian Church " — words which were rightly interpreted as an appeal to religious union. But to what kind of such a union ? Certainly not to a union on any non-Catholic basis, as some partisans of Protestantism were

---

[28] *Monumenta Confraternitatis Stauropigianae Leopoliensis* (ed. W. Milkowicz), I, Leopoli 1895, Nr. 53 ; see particularly p. 58 f.

[29] *Dnevnik lublinskago seima*, 634 f.

inclined to believe. [30] The papal nuncio, Portico, who reported that statement to the Holy See, [31] was certainly right in welcoming it, issued as it was by a monarch who five years before had officially accepted the decrees of the Council of Trent. But on the one hand, he was too optimistic when expressing the hope that the King would take some action in favor of religious union interpreting his appeal as a formal request that everybody should give up erroneous opinions contrary to the Catholic faith. And on the other hand, even he seems to have thought on that occasion only of those whom the Protestant revolt had recently separated from the Roman Church. In that connection he added with satisfaction that nothing had been said at Lublin either about the King's marriage which he wanted to be dissolved — a problem which once more raised some hopes among the Protestants — or about the establishment of any *fidicula nova*, a new, obviously Protestant faith.

Whether Sigismund Augustus himself, making his rather general declaration, was thinking of the Greek Orthodox also and recommending a religious union with them which would make the recent political union "last for ever," is not easy to determine. [32] He must have been aware that for the Commonwealth as a whole the old project of union with the Eastern Church which had appeared immediately after the first start of the Polish-Lithuanian federation, was of even greater importance than for each of the two States taken separately. And it was no less evident that the closer relations between these two States made cultural cooperation in general and a joint approach to that common religious problem much easier than before. It was not by mere chance that precisely in 1569, at the time of the Diet of Lublin, the plan of extending to the Grand Duchy the activities of the Jesuit Society materialized through the foundation of a College of the Society in Wilno, a city where Catholic propaganda among Protestants and Antitrinitarians could not be separated from that among the Orthodox Ruthenians who in that region were much more numerous and influential than in Poland where the Jesuits had faced that task first.

The initiative of that important foundation came from the active and zealous Bishop of Wilno Valerian Protasewicz who had played an important part in the negotiations regarding the political union with Poland, and though his illness prevented him from attending the Diet of Lublin, contributed to the final agreement and loyally supported it later. [33] It was he who invited the Polish Jesuits to come to Wilno where Skarga himself was

---

[30] O. Halecki, *Zgoda sandomierska*, 170.

[31] In his letter to Commendone, August 17, 1569; Vatican Archives, *Nunz. di Polonia*, vol. 6, fol. 31-31v. See also his letter to Cardinal Morone, of August 18, published in a Polish translation by Rykaczewski, *Relacje nuncjuszów*, I, 218 f.

[32] See my comments in *Zgoda sandomierska*, 174 f.

[33] O. Halecki, *Dzieje Unii*, II, 213, 256, 294, 343.

called in 1573 and where even before, right in 1569, some of them realized that a college and even an academy was badly needed in the city to defend the Catholic doctrine not only against the new heresies including even Arianism and Anabaptism, but also " against the Schismatics who could be led again to obedience towards the Church. " [34]

These expectations as to the future role of the Wilno Academy in the work of reunion with the Ruthenians of the Grand Duchy were to come true to a large extent. But the hopes of some Jesuits, especially the foreigners among them, the Provincial Maggio, an Italian, and his substitute and later successor Sunyer, a Spaniard, went even farther. Writing in 1569 and 1570 to the General of their Society in Rome, [35] they called the foundation of their college in the capital of Lithuania the " opening of a wide gate to Moscow, " adding even that through Moscow a penetration as far as " Tartaria " and distant China would be possible. While the references to the Asiatic Far East were indeed mere speculations, the opinion that the regaining of the Ruthenians of the Commonwealth for the Catholic Church would be a first step leading to religious union with Muscovite Russia was neither new nor peculiar to the Jesuits only. It was a return to the original conception of the Union of Florence and to repeated efforts of the Holy See throughout the more than one hundred years which had elapsed since, efforts which even the regular disappointments in that whole period had by no means discouraged. And at the given moment, right before and after the Union of Lublin, Rome and her representatives in Eastern Europe were particularly anxious to enter into relations with Moscow, [36] not because the prospects of religious union had improved but because that rising power, Christian though still separated from Rome, was considered a most desirable partner in the planned league against the Turks.

All this was, of course, well known to Sigismund Augustus who like his predecessors on similar occasions and as he had done it himself in the early years of his reign, watched most carefully the relations of his dangerous eastern neighbor with the West. His kingdom was recognized by the Holy See as an indispensable link between the Empire and Moscow, since all the neighbors of the Turks were supposed to join in the struggle against them on land, supplementing the efforts of the naval powers, Venice and Spain, and leading to the liberation of the Christian populations in the Balkans. After the successful achievement of the Union of Lublin which had been closely observed by imperial, papal, and Muscovite diplomats

---

[34] See the letter of Father B. Hostovinus to the General of his Order, of October 10, 1569, published by St. Bednarski and quoted by Chodynicki, *op. cit.*, 207.

[35] *Ibidem*, 207 n. 1.

[36] P. Pierling, *La Russie et le Saint Siège*, I, 372-397.

present at the Diet, [37] the cooperation of Sigismund Augustus seemed particularly desirable.

The King was, however, rather alarmed by the political and military aspect of the whole project and highly skeptical as to its religious implications. He considered Moscow, and in particular its present ruler Ivan the Terrible, the most dangerous enemy of the Commonwealth which the last Jagellonian had so painstakingly erected. It is true that at the same Diet of Lublin the King rejected a Turkish proposal to cooperate against Moscow, [38] but simply because he did not want to join nor to support either of his two aggressive and imperialistic neighbors against the other. And while at least formally in peace with the Ottoman Empire in spite of occasional entanglements in the Moldavian troubles — a peace confirmed as recently as 1568 — Sigismund Augustus continued to be in open war with Moscow, a war which he wanted to end or at least to interrupt by diplomatic negotiations, now to be conducted jointly by Lithuania and Poland, [39] but without hoping to remove the basic opposition between the two powers.

Rejecting the Turkish offer, the King did not hesitate to declare that he did not want to shed Christian blood fighting a country which other Christian powers were recommending to him. [40] And to Pius V he declared that he desired a conversion of Moscow to Catholicism in the interest of both religion and peace. But he did not hesitate either to warn the Pope at the same time that there was no real chance of such a conversion and that there was not the slightest evidence of any inclination of Ivan the Terrible towards the Catholic religion. [41] Writing a little earlier to his own representative in Rome, Cardinal Hosius, [42] Sigismund Augustus, expressing the same views and stressing how well he knew that barbarian ruler " hostile to the Latin and Roman name, " added that any approaches coming from the Holy See made him even wilder in his ambitions. And he added also a general comment that the conversion of a Greek or a Ruthenian was more difficult than that of a Hebrew : what should we think, therefore, asked the King in conclusion, of the idea of bringing back all the Greek or Ruthenian peoples to the Catholic religion ?

---

[37] Particularly rich in information are the reports of the Austrian diplomats published by A. Przeździecki, *Jagiellonki polskie*, V.

[38] J. Pajewski, " Projekt przymierza polsko-tureckiego za Zygmunta Augusta " (A project of a Polish-Turkish alliance at the time of Sigismund Augustus), *Księga ku czci O. Haleckiego*, Warszawa 1935, 185-202.

[39] O. Halecki, *Dzieje Unii*, II, 348.

[40] In an unpublished letter to the Sultan, summarized by Pajewski, *op. cit.*, 198.

[41] *Akta podkanclerskie F. Krasińskiego* (The acts of Vice-Chancellor F. Krasiński), III, Warszawa 1871, Nr. 126 (September 3, 1571).

[42] *Ibidem*, Nr. 38 (May 23, 1571).

That skepticism which Sigismund Augustus expressed in the matter of religious reunion with any followers of the Eastern Church, apparently including even his own Ruthenian subjects, was obviously dictated by his long experiences in the relations with Moscow and by his awareness of the danger threatening from this new center of Orthodoxy. Such an attitude was similar to that which more than half a century before appeared in Primate Łaski's memorandum on the errors of the Ruthenians, [43] written during an earlier, no less critical phase of the conflict between the Jagellonian Federation and its eastern neighbor. It is true that Sigismund Augustus, avoiding to enter into any theological questions, did not go so far as Łaski in emphasizing the religious differences between West and East. But in any case, even the casual remark which he made in that respect near the end of his life, two years after the Union of Lublin, explains why, in spite of his genuine desire for religious unity, he did not attempt to supplement the political union of 1569 which gave so much attention to various problems of his Ruthenian lands, by a religious union with their Greek Orthodox population to whom he always was prepared to grant full equality of rights independently of their religious beliefs.

Sigismund Augustus, in his relations with the Holy See, wanted to distinguish between the religious and the political side of what might be called the Eastern question of his time. They were, however, inseparable and, strange enough, it was in Rome that the political necessities resulting from the Ottoman danger were put first. On the other hand, Poland which in the early part of the century, when the Jagellonians still hoped to defend Hungary, was particularly anxious herself to see an effective cooperation of all Christian powers against the Turks, now was much more alarmed by the Muscovite danger, and this was even more true of Lithuania. This situation was to complicate the problem of religious reunion for a long time, at least for the lifetime of the next generation, and to delay the restoration of the Union of Florence even within the limits of the Commonwealth.

But the situation was made still more complex and involved for two additional reasons, one of them purely political, the other purely religious. No anti-Ottoman league, as contemplated in the eastern policy of the Holy See and as always tied up with the relationship between Rome and Eastern Christendom, was possible without the participation of the House of. Austria. But Poland's relations with that neighboring Catholic power, though better than those between these same Habsburgs and France whose hostility was the main difficulty of papal policy in the West, were passing once more through a serious crisis in view of the desire of the Austrian dynasty to gain after the Bohemian and Hungarian also the Polish and Lithuanian suc-

---

[43] See above, part I, Chapter VI, p. 127 f.

cession after the Jagellonians.   That policy of the Habsburgs seemed particularly alarming because of their repeated attempts to cooperate in that succession problem with Ivan the Terrible who had similar ambitions.   And such a cooperation between the two neighbors of the Commonwealth could eventually lead to its partition, Austria gaining the Polish and Moscow the Lithuanian succession. [44]   Therefore, the support which the Holy See gave in that matter to the Habsburgs, both at the end of the reign of Sigismund Augustus and in all three elections which followed the extinction of the Jagellonians, disturbed Poland's relations with Rome and affected their joint action in the Eastern question.

On the other hand, the approaching disappearance of the Jagellonian dynasty which especially in the person of its last representative had proved so anxious to avoid any religious wars and persecutions, but nevertheless — or rather precisely in result of such a policy — had kept Poland and Lithuania loyal to their Catholic tradition and to the Holy See, raised serious fears among the still quite numerous Protestants of the Commonwealth.   Having failed to gain the control of the country, they now were in danger of loosing even their freedom of worship under less tolerant rulers. Hence, their last minute efforts to create immediately after the Union of Lublin some religious unity among themselves or at least a united anti-Catholic front, and their desire to influence the forthcoming elections of the king's successors, to have religious freedom guaranteed by them and possibly to cooperate in that matter with the Greek Orthodox.   Such a cooperation was to be a basic obstacle to any reunion of the latter with the Catholic Church, a danger which appeared very clearly when at last the problem of such a reunion was seriously taken up and led to the Union of Brest.

The situation at the time of that Union, as well as its origin and background would, therefore, be impossible to understand without a study of the last years of Sigismund Augustus when the papal plans of an anti-Ottoman league in cooperation with Moscow and the Habsburgs, and the Protestant plans of anti-Catholic action for the first time simultaneously troubled the prospects of religious reunion with the Orthodox Ruthenians.

---

[44] See. H. Übersberger, *Österreich und Russland*, I.   I have added some new material regarding the role of the Lithuanian magnates in *Mitteilungen des Instituts für Österreichische Geschichtsforschung*, XXXVI (1915).

Chapter III

PIUS V, SIGISMUND AUGUSTUS, AND THE EASTERN QUESTION

It was only natural that after the successful conclusion of the Council of Trent the Papacy would turn again to the vital issues which the Catholic Church had to face in the East and which had been necessarily somewhat neglected as much as the long delayed reform of the Church and the reaction against the Protestant Revolution absorbed the Holy See. Since it had become obvious that in spite of these efforts Catholicism had suffered irreparable losses in the West, it could seem that Rome would look at once for compensation in the East resuming the projects of religious reunion which once had resulted in the Union of Florence. But even more urgent seemed a solution of the other eastern problem which always had been inseparable from that of reunion with the Eastern Churches, that of opposing the advance of Islam which had destroyed any chance of maintaining the Florentine tradition in southeastern Europe, placed all Christians of that region under Ottoman domination, and threatened the Christian powers of central and northeastern Europe whether they were Catholic or Greek Orthodox. This was definitely the opinion of Pius V, the saintly Pope who from the beginning of his pontificate, in 1565, soon after the Council of Trent, started his tireless efforts to organize an anti-Ottoman league and was confirmed in his determination by the fall of Sziget in Hungary, in 1566.[1]

The idea of including in such a league not only the Catholic Polish-Lithuanian Commonwealth but also the Orthodox Moscow of Ivan the Terrible was soon to reappear in that connection. In spite of so many earlier disappointments particularly at the time of Ivan's father, Basil III,[2] such projects were now suggested with even more insistence and concreteness, having at least three different sources, two of them purely political, the third influenced by religious considerations also.

The first of these sources was the impression which the military successes of Ivan the Terrible in the first part of his reign, when he was

---

[1] See for the general background and many details connected with this chapter my essay on " Rome and Eastern Europe after the Council of Trent, " *Antemurale*, II (1955), 8-35.

[2] See above Part I, Chapter VI, p. 133 f.

conquering more and more Tartar territory, produced in the West, and particularly in Italy. Typical in that respect was the report on Moscow which one of the Tiepolos, a family very prominent in Venetian diplomacy, drafted in or about 1560 for the authorities of the Republic, [3] raising much interest in other parts of Italy including Rome. Though admitting at the end, that it was difficult to collect information on such a distant land, the author, without having visited it himself but having obviously met persons who had fought under Ivan, emphasized that this young ruler, now thirty years old, was a valliant military leader : he wrote about his conquest of Kazan and Astrakhan a few years before, his expedition against the Crimea and his victory over the Nogay Tartars, who after invading Muscovy were pushed back as far as Siberia. Tiepolo added, it is true, that at present Ivan was involved in a war in Livonia which had placed herself under the protection of the King of Poland, and therefore fighting against Catholics. Furthermore, the general introduction to the report did not fail to mention that the Muscovites professed the Christian faith " *alla Greca,* " but did not go into any further details regarding that religious difference, merely distinguishing, as Łaski had done before, between " *Russia bianca* " which was under Moscow and " *Russia rossa* " which Lithuanians and Poles had liberated from Tartar rule. Tiepolo did not give any clear idea of the strong tension, both religious and political, between Ivan the Terrible and Sigismund Augustus, nor did he make any reference to the former's despotic methods of government which had not yet developed into the ruthless terror of the subsequent years. His report, therefore, greatly contributed to the impression that Ivan was a most desirable ally in the struggle against Islam and that the religious difficulty in cooperating with Moscow as well as her hostility against her western, Catholic neighbors were negligible.

The Venetians were confirmed in that impression when ten years later, in 1570, the year of the outbreak of the long avoided war with Turkey over the possession of Cyprus, Emperor Maximilian II suggested to their envoy who wanted to gain him for the planned anti-Ottoman league, that such a league should and could " easily " include not only the Empire, but also Poland, Moscow, and even Persia. [4] The old idea of using against the Turks their eastern neighbors in Asia, Muslims like themselves but different in their interpretation of Islam and political rivals, reappeared time and again in Venetian as well as in papal diplomacy, but always proved a very remote possibility. There remained, however, the new conception of some kind of a triple alliance uniting against the Turks, the

---

[3] P. Romanin, *Storia documentata di Venezia*, VI, Venice 1914 (reprint), 505-521. See about the Mss. and the other editions of that report my remarks in " Rome and Eastern Europe ..., " **33** n. 72.

[4] L. v. Pastor, *Gesch. der Päpste*, VIII, 556 ; see also State Archives of Venice, *Annali* (Misc. Cod. No. 100), fol. 30.

Habsburgs, the Polish-Lithuanian Commonwealth and the Muscovite Tsardom, and supplementing by such a joined action of these land powers the naval cooperation of the Mediterranean countries. That idea appealed not only to Venice in her temporary distress but even more to the Holy See to whom it was duly reported by the Nuncio to Venice [5] and recommended with equal optimism by the Venetian Ambassador to the Holy See. [6] Their comments that it would be easy to make Ivan move against the Turks, since having troubles with them, he was their natural enemy and very ambitious, and that the opposition of the King of Poland against western intercourse with " the Muscovite " was equally easy to overcome, could only confirm the Holy See in similar opinions which in the preceding years had made headway among the papal nuncios to Poland.

Turning to that third source of the whole project, it must, of course, be pointed out that there was a basic difference between the approach of Rome and that of either Venice or Vienna. For the Venetians who favored the papal idea of an anti-Ottoman league only when they were directly attacked by the Turks and in need of allies, it was exclusively a matter of temporary political expediency. Merely political too was the approach of the Emperor who having made peace quite recently, in 1568, with Sultan Selim II, had no intention to re-enter the war against him, but wanted to impress the Venetians by stressing his good relations with both Poland and Moscow. [7] On the contrary, the Holy See always considered political negotiations with the latter a useful preparation for an agreement in religious matters which remained the ultimate objective. So urgent seemed, however, at the given moment Ivan's military cooperation against the enemy of Christendom, that far from making religious reunion a prerequisite condition, even Rome was putting the political league first and was anxious to facilitate such a league by trying to mediate once more between Poland and Moscow.

The first nuncio who was sent to Poland by Pius V, Giulio Ruggieri, received when leaving Rome in 1566 only vague instructions in that respect, [8] being merely expected to find out whether Ivan really had partisans in Poland who would favor his succession after Sigismund Augustus and whether there was any hope that he would sincerely ally himself with the Catholic powers and support any enterprise against the Turk " his natural enemy. " As to the chances of Ivan becoming King of Poland, it was easy to discover that they were null, and that question did not reappear for a long time in the instructions or reports of the papal nuncios. But

---

[5] Vatican Archives, *Nunz. di Venezia* 10, fol. 63v-64 (Aug. 2, 1570).

[6] State Archives of Venice, *loc. cit.*, fol. 39v-40 (instructions for the Ambassador in Rome, March 10, 1570).

[7] *Venetianische Depeschen vom Kaiserhof*, III, Nr. 196, 197.

[8] Vatican Archives, *Misc. Arm.*, II, vol. 82, fol. 217-218v. See above, 152 f.

the other one, though far from being clarified, remained a serious concern of the Holy See.

Ruggieri did not answer that question directly when after his recall in 1568 he made a detailed report on the situation in Poland and her relations with the neighbor countries. [9] Stressing that there was no chance of peace between Poland and Moscow, he simply pointed out the main difficulty of the whole project. But on the other hand, he was more optimistic as far as the religious aspect of the problem was concerned : he did not hesitate to express the hope that Ivan, being hostile to Protestantism, would perhaps rather accept a union with Rome, if the principles of such a union were clearly explained to him.

Nevertheless, there was no reference to such a hope in the instructions given to Ruggieri's successor, Vincenzo de Portico, [10] while it was strongly recommended to him to persuade Sigismund Augustus to make an agreement with Moscow so that both would turn their forces jointly with the other Christian rulers against the infidels, " our common enemies. " And he was to offer the good offices of the Holy See for the conclusion of such an agreement, declaring that, if necessary, the Pope would send to Moscow a special ambassador.

It was only later, when such negotiations with Moscow in the matter of the anti-Ottoman league were suggested by Venice and Vienna, and when it appeared that even Poland's participation in that league was not easy to obtain, that the former nuncio Ruggieri, now residing in Rome as Apostolic Protonotary, was again consulted in the whole matter. The first part of his comprehensive memorandum [11] was very realistic. Explaining the reasons why Sigismund Augustus, opposed to any war, was hesitating to join the struggle against the Turks, Ruggieri mentioned not only the king's strained relations with the Habsburgs, but even more the danger which continued to threaten him from Moscow in spite of the precarious three years truce which had been concluded in 1570. He also mentioned the dangerous Tartar and Wallachian neighbors, but was particularly outspoken as to Moscow's " barbaria " and inveterate hostility.

Yet, when making suggestions how the obstacles to Poland's participation in the league might be removed, Ruggieri, in addition to some very constructive proposals, recommended precisely the inclusion in the league of Poland's most dangerous neighbors, not only the Tartars who after all were indifferent in matters of the religion, and Wallachia where, as the Holy See knew from other sources, [12] the prospects of Catholic propaganda were

---

[9] *Relacje nuncjuszów*, I, 203, 208. See the original Italian text in Vatican Archives, *Fondo Pio* vol. 26, fol. 137-182.

[10] Vatican Archives, *Misc. Arm.* II, vol. 34, fol. 40.

[11] Vatican Library, *Urbin. lat.* 855, fol. 326-348v. See *Antemurale* II, 33 n. 74.

[12] See, f. ex. Portico's report of Aug. 29, 1571 ; A. Theiner, *Vetera Monumenta Poloniae*, II, N. 813, p. 773.

rather doubtful, but first of all Moscow, a Christian nation anxious to fight the Turks, as he now assured the Pope. It is difficult to explain how he could outline simply fantastic prospects of Muscovite contributions to the planned war : mobilizing no less than 150,000 horsemen, Ivan the Terrible would launch an attack from Podolia — a Polish province — and after crossing the Dniester and the Danube, reach in eight more days Constantinople, march at the same time through the Crimea against Caffa, and cooperate with the Persians ! But even more fantastic was his conclusion that both " to the Wallachian and to the Muscovite " the Holy See ought to promise a royal crown, if only they would abandon their schismatic errors and recognize the spiritual supremacy of the Pope. For, as he added, with such a condition attached, such a papal promise made to Poland's enemies could not " reasonably irritate " Sigismund Augustus whom, on the contrary, such an extension of the league would best persuade to join it " with public profit. "

As a matter of fact, nothing could more alienate the King of Poland than the offer of a royal crown to the ruler of Moscow, a possibility which like his predecessors Sigismund Augustus had suspected and feared from the very beginning of his reign, [13] deeply convinced that it would increase the prestige of an already too ambitious neighbor and encourage his hopes for western support against an encircled Polish-Lithuanian Commonwealth. In his report on the conditions in Poland which Ruggieri had submitted in 1568, he had pointed out himself how strongly that country was opposed to the desire of the Duke of Muscovy to be crowned as " King of Russia " with the consent of the Emperor and of the Pope. It is even more difficult to understand how Ruggieri could now believe that in order to get a royal crown which already Ivan's grandfather had proudly refused when it was offered to him by the Habsburgs and which he himself needed even less after his coronation as Tsar in 1547, that ruler would accept the condition of a religious union under papal authority. [14] Fortunately, however, Pius V was soon to receive from Ruggieri's successor, Nuncio Portico, much more reliable information on Ivan the Terrible's real attitude and intentions, information partly collected in Poland where he discussed at length the prospects of the anti-Ottoman league, partly obtained through contacts with peoples who had been in Moscow where Portico himself sent his emissaries.

He did all this in view of additional instructions which he had received in September 1570, [15] after the outbreak of the Turkish-Venetian war, when Pius V considered Moscow's cooperation so urgent and — perhaps under the influence of Ruggieri's arguments — so easy to obtain that he wanted the

[13] See Pierling, *La Russie et le Saint-Siège*, I, 340 f.
[14] Pierling, *op. cit.*, I, 212 ; Übersberger, *Österreich und Russland*, I, 11.
[15] Pierling, *Rome et Moscow 1547-1597*, Paris, 1883, App. V, 140-144.

Nuncio to procede there in person, carrying a papal letter to the Tsar, written already in August.[16] Vaguely recalling earlier relations with Moscow at the time of Paul III and Julius III, though these relations had remained without any practical result, Pius V touched both the religious and the political side of the problem. But he insisted primarily on Ivan's participation in the war against the Turks, referring to the alliance between Rome, Venice, and Spain which was being negotiated and hoping that the Tsar would attack the common enemy in the following year along with the Emperor and the King of Poland. Entering into the details of that military action, Portico's new instruction advised him to touch the religious issue, that is reunion with the Holy See, only very cautiously, if Ivan did not raise that point himself, interested as he was in theological questions. In cipher, however, a paragraph was added to the instruction, saying that the Pope had heard of " the Muscovite's " desire not only to receive the royal title but also to welcome in Moscow, besides " certain artists, " priests who would " instruct his peoples in the ceremonies of Rome. " It therefore seems that there were expectations that Ivan would even accept the Latin rite, though Portico was supposed to ascertain these " and other things. "

The nuncio to Poland must have been familiar with the spectacular developments in the neighbor country where the Tsar's system of despotism and terror was just reaching its climax in the brutal repression of a suspected revolt in Novgorod and in the execution of the Metropolitan who had dared to criticize the most shocking acts of cruelty.[17] Dealing so ruthlessly with the head of his own Orthodox Church, Ivan could certainly not be expected to recognize papal supremacy. Furthermore, Portico, being in regular contact with the Venetian diplomatic agents who were forwarding from Poland the most important news on the political situation in eastern Europe,[18] must have also known that the Turkish invasion of Russia in the preceding year had ended in failure, because the Sultan's forces were not permitted to pass through Polish territory and received no loyal support from the Crimean Tartars, so that Ivan succeeded in re-establishing peace through his ambassador sent to Constantinople and was no longer interested in any cooperation with the western enemies of the Ottoman Empire.[19]

It was, therefore, not only the reluctance of Sigismund Augustus to permit any western representatives, whether Venetian or papal, to cross the frontier between the Commonwealth and Moscow,[20] which prevented Portico

---

[16] See Pastor, *op. cit.*, VIII, 557 n. 4.
[17] Pierling, *La Russie*, I, 388 ; Ammann, *Abriss*, 228 ; Medlin, *Moscow and East Rome*, 122.
[18] See the sources in the State Archives of Venice, quoted in *Antemurale*, II, 16.
[19] Halil Inalcik, *The Origin of the Ottoman-Russian rivalry and the Don-Volga Canal* (1569), Ankara 1947.
[20] See, f. ex., *Akta podkanclerskie Fr. Krasińskiego*, III, Nr. 274, 277, 282, 284.

12

from going there: as a matter of fact, he was not at all anxious himself to undertake that mission, not because he had come too much under Polish influence [21] but because he rightly considered it hopeless.

Among the many reports to Rome in which he justified the delay in carrying out his orders, his dispatch of August 15, 1571, [22] is particularly significant. He would have gravely troubled his conscience — so he answered the Vatican — if seeing any readiness of the Muscovite to make himself a Catholic, he would lose courage and not trust "that God would give him strength and help in such a Catholic and pious action." And he also assured that in such a case the King of Poland "would not be so impious to deny him the passage." But in full agreement with Sigismund Augustus with whom he had spoken about the whole matter so frequently, Portico declared in a carefully worded understatement that "it seemed difficult that such a project — viz. Ivan's conversion — would succeed."

Without being, however, satisfied with impressions received in Poland, the Nuncio, before taking any final decision, sent to Ivan, after consulting the Russian ambassador to Poland and obviously with Polish permission — one or two preliminary emissaries, including a priest, and was waiting for their report, [23] particularly on the question "whether the Muscovite desired to embrace the Catholic religion." One of these emissaries was even to go to the distant region of Byelozero where the Tsar had sought refuge during the Tartar raid against Moscow, but most probably he never reached him, and Portico hoped in vain that after a few weeks he would hear "the truth" from his agent. In the meantime, he did not hesitate to make expensive preparations for his own possible journey to Moscow, setting aside the necessary money even for reimbursing the travelling expenses of his emissaries, buying books which were to be sent to Moscow probably for purposes of religious propaganda, and paying for a translation of the theological discussion between Ivan and "a heretical minister." [24] That minister was one of the leaders of the Czech brethren, Jan Rokyta, who had accompanied to Moscow the Polish-Lithuanian embassy of 1570 and tried on that occasion to convert the Tsar to Protestantism, [25] another hopeless undertaking but not without alarm for the Catholics.

At the same time, however, the tireless Nuncio had also translated into Latin some entirely different material which was to illustrate the real intentions and proceedings of the enigmatic ruler of Moscow. These included not only an account how badly he had treated the ambassadors of Sigismund Augustus before he concluded with them a three years truce, but

[21] As suggested by Pierling, *op. cit.*, I, 391.
[22] Vatican Archives, *Nunz. di Polonia* vol. 1, fol. 165.
[23] A. Theiner, *op. cit.*, II, Nr. 813, p. 772-774.
[24] *Ibidem*, 774.
[25] O. Halecki, *Zgoda sandomierska*, 311-313.

also even more shocking accounts of other nationals, including a German nobleman, who had experienced as prisoner in Moscow "the mores and cruel government of the tyrant." Collecting and filing all that evidence for the use of the Vatican, Portico did not fail to include a copy of the peace proposals which Ivan had sent to Constantinople and which were to lead to a "permanent peace" with the Sultan. [26]

That material convinced Pius V that a conversion of the Tsar was entirely out of the question and that it was useless to make any efforts in order to gain his cooperation against the Turks. Furthermore, he was so shocked by what he had heard about Ivan's life, that in reply to Portico's reports he wrote to the Nuncio to give up the idea to go to Moscow, even if the King of Poland would approve and favor that mission. And he added : " We do not want to enter into relations with a nation so cruel and barbarian. " [27]

That papal decision was taken even before there arrived in Rome the long letter of September 3, 1571, [28] in which Sigismund Augustus clearly and sincerely explained to Pius V why he had refused to grant free passage to Moscow to any papal envoy other than Portico and why, in general, he had serious doubts regarding the advisibility of such a mission. The conditions which he formulated were in full agreement not only with the secret instructions he had given a few months before to his own representative in Rome, Cardinal Hosius, [29] but also with the conclusions to which Portico arrived after a most careful study of the matter. The King of Poland whom the Pope finally notified on November 21 of the same year, that he had " completely renounced the Muscovite affair " in view of the information received about the Tsar, [30] was therefore not only right in his objections but not at all responsible for the failure of a project which was so obviously based upon misleading illusions. These illusions were particularly baseless as far as the religious side of the affair was concerned, and the facts about Moscow's real attitude towards Catholicism could only discourage those who were interested in the general problem of reunion with Eastern Christendom. Since, however, even in Rome the main interest was at the given moment in the defense of Christendom against the Turks, it was a comfort that the disappointment as to Moscow's possible assistance came after the great victory of Lepanto which western forces alone had gained over the infidels.

Even after that decisive naval victory the Pope, in agreement with

---

[26] The whole material collected by Portico is preserved in the Vatican Archives, *Misc. Arm.* II vol. 69 ; the peace proposals made by Ivan to Turkey are on fol. 57.
[27] Pierling, *op. cit.*, I, 395, and the sources quoted there on p. 396 n. 1.
[28] *Akta podkanclerskie*, III, Nr. 126.
[29] *Ibidem*, Nr. 38 (May 23, 1571).
[30] Pierling, *loc. cit.*

the other western powers, especially the Italians, [31] considered it necessary to combine the planned continuation of the joint action in the Mediterranean with a parallel attack of the Ottoman Empire on land, if not by Moscow, at least by the Emperor and the King of Poland. It was, therefore, to both of them that the most experienced and successful of the former nuncios to Poland, Commendone, now already a Cardinal, was sent as papal legate, an appointment which he had already received a few months before Lepanto, immediately after the conclusion of the alliance between the Holy See, Venice and Spain. [32] There was, however, little hope that Maximilian II would join that alliance and facilitate the prosecution of the war by a diversion in Hungary, and therefore Commendone who like the Pope and the Doge of Venice was warmly congratulated by Sigismund Augustus on the victory of Lepanto, [33] hurried to Warsaw in order to second Portico's efforts to gain at least Poland's participation in the anti-Ottoman league.

The expectations of the Holy See in that matter were shared by Venice, since some time before the King of Poland had said to one of the agents of the Republic that after a first success of the western powers it would be easier for him to make a decision. [34] And Portico who knew the King so well and enjoyed his confidence, had time and again received the impression, that the Jagellonian, while excluding any cooperation with Moscow, was ready to enter an anti-Ottoman league with the Habsburgs. [35] Why, then, was Commendone's second mission to Sigismund Augustus a failure ?

It would be impossible to explain it by some misunderstandings and rivalries between the Legate and the present Nuncio. And there is ample evidence that the skillful diplomat who was Commendone, assisted by his devoted secretary Antonio Maria Gratiani, [36] did his best to persuade not only the King but also the Polish Senate to enter the alliance of Catholic powers against the Turks. The official answer which he received on May 31, 1572, during the Diet of Warsaw and which was drafted by the able Vice-Chancellor of the Kingdom, Francis Krasiński, [37] who three years before had drafted the charter of the Union of Lublin, gave indeed the most important political reasons why the proposal was rejected. It was first pointed out that the King could not break the treaty of peace which was still in force between Poland and the Ottoman Empire, since engagements had to be kept and respected also in the relations with infidels. But the

---

[31] *Antemurale*, II, 25.

[32] *Ibidem*, 23.

[33] *Ibidem*, 25.

[34] On the reports of G. Vancimuglio see *ibidem*, 16, 19, and particularly note 48.

[35] F. ex. in his report of Oct. 17, 1570, discussed below (see note 39).

[36] His biography of the Cardinal (*Vita card. Commendoni*, published in Paris, 1669) is an important source of information, but has to be used rather carefully.

[37] *Akta podkanclerskie*, III, Nr. 358; see also *Ms.* 3 of the Polish Library in Paris, p. 8-20.

strongest argument, besides all the other difficulties of Poland's position which even Ruggieri's memorandum had admitted, was the attitude of the Emperor who obviously had not the slightest intention to move against the Turks himself, so that any action of Sigismund Augustus would have been completely isolated, since even the naval powers were practically doing nothing to take advantage of the victory of Lepanto.

Already in his letter of congratulation to Pius V after that victory, Sigismund Augustus in answer to the papal appeal for cooperation had made a significant reference which must be considered in connection with his reply to Commendone. Promising to the Pope to do what would be possible he added: " as far as my intention would not be retarded by preposterous efforts of other princes. "[38] That reservation could only refer to the efforts of the Emperor who was less anxious to fight the Turks than to secure for his dynasty the succession after Sigismund Augustus. To that project the King was definitely opposed, and precisely because he knew of all the intrigues which were going on in that matter, he was hardly more inclined to an alliance with the Emperor than to cooperation with Moscow. But he also knew that papal diplomacy favored the plan of Habsburg succession in Poland, and this was the only matter, purely political indeed, in which he really disagreed with the aims of that diplomacy and did not reveal his intentions neither to Commendone nor even to Portico. When the latter in his report of October 17, 1570[39] accompanying an autographic but rather vague letter of Sigismund Augustus to Pius V, tried to interpret what the King had told him for the Pope's information, he was correct in stressing that the last Jagellonian wanted a Catholic successor. But he was wrong in believing that the King was inclined not only to ally himself with the house of Austria against the Turks but also to chose as successor a member of the Habsburg dynasty. On the contrary, hoping to influence in advance the election after his death, Sigismund Augustus was already negotiating for several years in the strictest secrecy with the French court, favoring a Valois candidate,[40] a plan which was perhaps even more favorable to the Catholic restoration in Poland, but anticipated an entirely different diplomatic alignment.

Since Commendone was even more active than Portico in working for the Habsburg succession which seemed to facilitate a Polish-Austrian understanding against the Turks, he was looked upon with suspicion by the King whom he hurt at the same time in a delicate, personal matter. His severe admonitions that Sigismund Augustus should give up any idea of divorce

---

[38] *Ibidem*, III, N. 204 (Dec. 11, 1571).
[39] Vatican Archives, *Nunz. di Polonia*, vol. 1, fol. 100 ; see my comments in *Antemurale*, II, 34 n. 87.
[40] See, for instance, E. Charrière, *Négociations de la France dans le Levant*, III, Paris 1853, note on pp. 73-78, also the later references pp. 169 and 300.

were unnecessary because the King had already written to the Pope that, in spite of his desire to have annulled his third marriage with the Emperor's sister, he was decided to leave that matter to the authority of the Holy See. [41] Furthermore, when the Legate discussed that matter in Warsaw on March 3, 1572, the Queen had already died three days before in Linz, and the King was too ill to remarry, though his desperate desire to leave a successor of his own blood troubled the last months of his life and caused the most extravagant rumors. [42]

The rapidly deteriorating health and eventually the death of this pious Catholic ruler [43] on July 7, 1572, two months after the death of the Pope, made it impossible to reach any last minute coordination of their eastern policy. The extinction of the Jagellonian dynasty, only three years after its greatest achievement : the Union of Lublin, produced a profound impression in Poland and abroad, and Commendone realized very well that the forthcoming election in the midst of the unsettled conditions of the interregnum would be of great important for all Christendom. And though he was busy with organizing and supporting the pro-Habsburg party among the Polish and Lithuanian aristocracy, whether Catholic or not, he must have been aware as well as Portico, that the interregnum and its outcome would be a decisive test not only for the political unity of the Commonwealth, but also for the religious situation within its limits and for the direction in which the trend towards religious unity would develop. It is true, however, that clear indications in that respect could be discovered already in the last years of the reign of Sigismund Augustus.

---

[41] *Akta podkanclerskie*, III, Nr. 179 (Oct. 24, 1571 ; see *Antemurale* II, 31 n. 31, and 32.)

[42] See Pastor, *op. cit.*, VIII, 509 f., where, however, these rumors receive too much credit ; how unreliable some of these accounts were, has been pointed out by Übersberger, *Österreich und Russland*, I, 372 n. 1.

[43] On the pious death of Sigismund Augustus see the contemporary reports which I quoted in *Zgoda sandomierska*, 419, and *Antemurale*, II, 34 n. 91.

CHAPTER IV

FROM THE SYNOD OF SANDOMIERZ TO THE CONFEDERATION OF WARSAW

The Diet of Lublin, that great political convention which consolidated the political structure of the Commonwealth, was followed the next year by a religious assembly which wanted to achieve religious unification by adopting a " Polish " confession. But that synod held in April 1570 in the Polish city of Sandomierz without any notable Lithuanian or Ruthenian participation [1] was not at all the " national " synod which the Protestants had claimed when their movement was strongest and which even many Catholics had favored as a chance of religious reconciliation and as a substitute for the general Council which had been so long delayed and twice interrupted. [2] When, however, the Council of Trent completed its task and when its decisions were accepted by the King who in the past had seemed interested in a national council, it was obvious that there could convene in Poland only one more of the regular provincial synods of the Catholic hierarchy or an assembly of non-Catholics only, similar to the synods which the various new denominations had quite frequently organized during the preceding years. These synods had on some occasions consolidated the Protestant movement, as for instance when in 1555 at Koźminek the Calvinists and the Czech Brethren concluded a religious union, [3] but on other occasions they would evidence the conflicting tendencies of the reformers, particularly when ten years later, in Piotrków the break between Calvinists and Antitrinitarians became final. [4] Now at the synod of Sandomierz, in 1570, all Antitrinitarians were excluded in advance, but in addition to the Calvinists and Czech Brethren their Lutheran rivals participated also and were expected to accept with the others a slightly revised Polish

---

[1] O. Halecki, *Zgoda sandomierska*, 195, 204-206 (see also the supplementary note at the end of the book, where the scarce information on preparatory discussions in Lithuania and messages sent to Sandomierz by Prince Andrew Wiśniowiecki, Castellane of Volhynia, and a few nobles of the Chełm and Bełz regions is discussed in detail.)

[2] O. Fox, " The Reformation in Poland, " *The Cambridge History of Poland*, 337 f.

[3] O. Halecki, *op. cit.*, 20 f.

[4] E. M. Wilbur, *A History of Unitarianism*, 322-325.

translation of the Confession of the Swiss Reformed Church which was to unite all Polish Protestants in one common creed opposed to that of the Catholic Church.

Even that strictly limited project of Protestant unification did not succeed because the Lutherans could not be persuaded to approve the Calvinist doctrine in the most controversial matter of the Eucharist. The result was, therefore, a mere juxtaposition of two conflicting interpretations and what might be called an agreement to disagree in that matter. [5] The " Polish " confession, though printed with a dedication to the King and privately submitted to him after the synod, was neither approved by the Lutherans nor even less by Sigismund Augustus himself. [6]

Nevertheless, the very fact that he had permitted at least tacitly, the holding of such a synod, was criticized in Rome both by the Vatican and by Cardinal Hosius, and the dedication of the Confession was considered "destructive" [7], though the King writing to the Cardinal strongly denied the rumors of his approval and even signed a formal protest against that dedication. [8] Portico, too, was alarmed and not only sent to Rome copies of the Confession and of the so-called " Consensus, " that is, the agreement signed at Sandomierz, as well as the list of those present, [9] but had printed at his expense a refutation of the Confession and of its various articles. [10]

It is highly significant how he explained the necessity of such a publication : he wanted to send it, along with other propaganda material, to Moscow because he was informed that the " heretic Minister " who tried to convert Ivan the Terrible, [11] intended to present to him the Sandomierz Confession as being a profession of " Catholic faith. " This is a clear evidence that, in spite of the absence of any Greek Orthodox representation at the Synod of 1570 which had not even considered their invitation nor any relations with them, at least the Czech Brethren, faithful also in that respect to the Hussite tradition, were interested in such relations and in the possible extension of the Sandomierz agreement to followers of the Eastern Church. The main spokesman of the " *Unitas Fratrum* " — as the Czech group used to be called — at the Synod, Simeon Turnovsky, who described his journey to Sandomierz in a valuable report, [12] was to be at the end of

---

[5] O. Halecki, *op. cit.*, 264 ff. ; see the comments of K. Joergensen, *Ökumenische Bestrebungen*, 252 ff., 268, 271.

[6] *Ibidem*, 274.

[7] Vatican Archives, *Nunz. di Polonia*, vol. 1, fol. 80v, 134 (letters of Cardinal Rusticucci to Portico, May 13 and Nov. 4, 1570).

[8] On May 8, 1570 ; see Halecki, *op. cit.*, 322 n. 1, and *Antemurale*, II, 31 n. 27.

[9] Vatican Archives, *Misc. Arm.* II vol. 69, fol. 59 f., 112 f, 146-149, 160 f, 166-169, 212-214.

[10] A. Theiner, *Vetera Monum. Poloniae*, II, Nr. 873, p. 774 ; see also Portico's report in *Nunz. di Polonia* vol. 1, fol. 146.

[11] See above, Chapter III, p. 178.

[12] See K. Joergensen, *op. cit.*, 261.

the century, when he similarly described his journey to the Synod of Wilno in 1599,[13] the strongest advocate of a religious union with those Ruthenians who rejected the Union of Brest.

It was to appear on all similar occasions and certainly was realized in 1570 by the followers of the " Polish " Confession of Calvinist inspiration, that a dogmatic agreement was even more difficult with the Greek Orthodox than with the Lutherans. While, however, the " *Confessio Sendomiriensis* " remained the creed of the Calvinists and Czech Brethren only, the much shorter " *Consensus Sendomiriensis* ", that is, the pledge to struggle in common against the Antitrinitarians on one side and the Roman Catholics on the other, was to become the frequently confirmed basis of an anti-Catholic alliance [14] which did not want to have anything in common with the left-wing extremists, the abhorred " Arians, " but could easily be extended to the followers of the Eastern Church.

There is no evidence that anything in that direction was attempted when at the last Diets under Sigismund Augustus, which met in Warsaw in 1570 and 1572, the Protestants raised again their voice and after failing to get the King's approval for the Sandomierz Confession, tried at least to put in practice for the first time the " *Consensus* " in order to get an official recognition of their freedom of worship in full equality with the Catholics. [15] At these first common, Polish-Lithuanian Diets the number of non-Catholic senators and deputies, though already decreasing because of so many individual returns to the Church of Rome, was at the same time increased by the comparatively numerous representatives of the Grand Duchy and of the incorporated Ruthenian provinces who were either Protestant or Orthodox. Nevertheless, at neither of these Diets of which especially the second one is very little known, did the Protestants succeed in realizing their objective. In the interval between the two Diets, on August 22, 1571,[16] Portico could report with satisfaction that their further action based upon the decision of the Synod of the preceding year, had no support from the King who declared to the Nuncio orally and in writing that he had prevented it. On the eve of the death of Sigismund Augustus they planned, therefore, as Commendone reported,[17] to hold another of their synods, this time at Radom, but that last minute effort to prepare for the imminent interregnum could not materialize either.

---

[13] See K. Chodynicki, *Kościół prawosławny*, 349 n. 1 ; on the synod of 1599 see D. Oljančyn, " Zur Frage der Generalkonföderation in Wilna, " *Kyrios* I, 1936.

[14] K. Joergensen, *op. cit.*, 272 ff.

[15] O. Halecki, *op. cit.*, Chapter V. According to a frequently quoted Austrian report there were then 60 non-Catholic (including two Greek Orthodox) members of the Senate against 70 Catholics.

[16] Vatican Archives, *Nunz. di Polonia*, vol. 1, fol. 172 (" Negotii di Varsavia ").

[17] *Ibidem*, vol. 2, fol. 50 (July 9, 1572).

[18] *Ibidem*, vol. 2, fol. 31v (June 5, 1572).

A little earlier, at the very end of the Diet of 1572, [18] Commendone expressed some fear that the Protestants, having failed to enforce any " agreement in the matter of religion " at that Diet, would try it again at the next. Since, however, the King died one month later, they had to do it at the extraordinary conventions which preceded the election of his successor, and they succeeded indeed to a certain extent at the so-called Convocation held in Warsaw, in January 1572. In order to understand the background and significance of the article on religious peace which was included in the text of the " Confederation of Warsaw " [19] and so frequently quoted in all the subsequent religious discussions, particularly at the time of the Union of Brest, the general situation of the Commonwealth during the Interregnum must be briefly considered.

Already on July 9, 1572, [20] when Sigismund Augustus' death on the 7th was not yet known to him, Commendone, in a ciphered memorandum which he sent to Rome, warned of the threatening election of a " heretic " in view of the political divisions among the Catholics. In doing so he under-estimated the progress of the Catholic restoration which had been achieved under the last Jagellonian, largely because of his wise moderation, and as a matter of fact, he could not point out any serious Protestant candidate to the throne. There had been some suspicion in Rome that Sigismund Augustus himself favored his nephew, Prince John Sigismund Zápolya of Transylvania, who was considered " a heretic and ally of the Turks. " [21] But that prince died shortly before his uncle who did not like him at all, and his successor Stefan Báthory who, hardly mentioned during the first interregnum, was to be elected during the second, professed already in 1572 his Catholic convictions. [22] Also the idea of electing a Swedish candi-date which was to triumph in the third interregnum leading to the election of a decidedly Catholic king, Sigismund III — another nephew of Sigismund Augustus — and which in 1572 could alarm the Catholics, since then young Sigismund's Protestant father, John III of Sweden, was the only possible choice, had little chances of success. There remained, therefore, only the danger of the election of an Orthodox neighbor, of course not of the power-less Prince of Moldavia, Bogdan, whose apparent inclination towards the Catholic faith had even raised the hope of a conversion of his country, [23] but strange enough, of Ivan the Terrible himself.

The Tsar had indeed the ambition of gaining the crown of Poland or,

---

[19] An English translation of that article (3) of the Confederation of Warsaw, of January 28, 1573, has been given by E. M. Wilbur, *A History of Unitarianism*, 363 f.

[20] Vatican Archives, *Nunz. di Polonia*, vol. 2, fol. 51-53.

[21] *Ibidem*, vol. 1, fol. 58-59, 68 (Oct. 1, Nov. 11, Dec. 13, 1567).

[22] *Ibidem*, vol. 2, fol. 30 (autogr. letter of St. Báthory to the Archbishop of Kalocsa, March 21, 1572).

[23] A. Theiner, *op. cit.*, II, Nr. 809, p. 762 (Aug. 8, 1571).

at least, that of the Grand Duchy of Lithuania for himself or for his son, and while the hopes of some misinformed Poles that such an election could lead to a political union with Moscow just as Jagello's election had led to the union with Lithuania, [24] could hardly be taken seriously, there was some danger that in Lithuania the desire to escape the endless troubles with Moscow would suggest a final appeasement of that aggressive neighbor by accepting Ivan's succession to the throne. If, during the peace negotiations with him, one or two Lithuanian representatives mentioned such a possibility, [25] they were most probably not sincere and only trying to get better terms. But immediately after the death of Sigismund Augustus, Ivan tried to exercise even military pressure in order to influence the election by moving his armed forces in the direction of Vitebsk. [26] Furthermore, there was an additional danger of disagreements between Poland and Lithuania, since some of the magnates of the Grand Duchy reclaimed its southern, Ruthenian provinces lost in 1569, a request which even Commendone recommended to the Emperor. [27] He was, however, well aware of the factional divisions among the Lithuanian and Ruthenian aristocracy which he wanted to gain for the Habsburgs, whether these powerful magnates were Catholic, Protestant, or Orthodox.

In that connection the Legate, [28] welcoming the reconciliation of the Radziwiłł and Chodkiewicz families, regretted that Prince Constantine Ostrogski, another supporter of the Austrian candidature, was at the same time a supporter of Prince George Słucki in the latter's rivalry with the Radziwiłł and Chodkiewicz. And he was even afraid that the " Duke of Słuck, " as he called him, being " of Greek rite, " would make himself the leader of all followers of that rite whom he suspected in general to " have intelligence with the Muscovite. " He knew very well that the Słuckis were not of Ruthenian but of Lithuanian origin and even of Jagellonian blood, claiming in view of their descent a hereditary seat in the Senate. [29] But he failed to realize that this claim was practically the only reason of their dispute with the other magnates, which had no religious implications whatsoever, no more than the attitude of Ostrogski who was not only a member of the Eastern Church but of Ruthenian origin indeed.

It was certainly significant that the two leading families of wealthy princes which remained attached to their religious tradition, were playing

---

[24] J. Czubek (ed.), *Pisma polityczne z czasów bezkrólewia* (Political pamphlets of the time of the Interregnum), Kraków 1906, where such comparisons can be found.

[25] H. Übersberger, *Österreich und Russland*, I, 402.

[26] Vatican Archives, *Nunz. di Polonia*, vol. 2, fol. 57 (Portico's report of July 23, 1572).

[27] Übersberger, *op. cit.*, I, 388.

[28] In his report of Jan. 14, 1573, Vatican Archives, *Nunz. di Polonia*, vol. 3, foli 26.

[29] *Ibidem*, fol. 134 (April 22, 1573) ; *Akta Unii Polski z Litwą*, Nr. 170 (April 20, 1572), see also Nr. 172, 173.

once more an important part in the policies of the aristocracy of the Commonwealth, and that the papal legate stressed their " Greek rite, " without however speaking of a different faith.   But once more the differences of rite or even faith among the magnates had nothing to do with their alignement in the basic political issues, this time in the support of one candidate to the throne or another.   That neither of these princes favored the election of Ivan the Terrible, so hostile to the aristocracy of his own Muscovy, is beyond any doubt, and if they finally disappointed Commendone as did the Catholic lords, it was because they all accepted the choice of the French candidate, Henri de Valois.   So did even those who were Protestant and Orthodox, and even among the lesser gentry of Orthodox faith there was no serious action in favor of Ivan the Terrible whose pressure, reduced by another Tartar invasion of Muscovy, [30] was exercised in vain.

Protestant and Orthodox leaders, including the Ruthenian Prince Proński, were even among the Polish-Lithuanian delegates who after the election were sent to Paris [31] in order to conclude there the negotiations with Henri and to accompany him on his way to Cracow.   However, the non-Catholics among these delegates took advantage of that visit in France not only to interfere in favor of the Huguenots in the name of the Polish Calvinists [32], but also to claim at once from the future King a confirmation by oath of the conditions under which he had been elected and in particular of the guarantee of religious freedom which had been included in the Warsaw Confederation. [33]

That guarantee had been given in the form of a pledge that those who differed from each other in religious matters would nevertheless live in peace.   That promise of peace " *inter dissidentes de religione* " — this was the Latin formula inserted in the Polish text — was, of course, a recognition that religious unity was impossible to achieve and, as a matter of fact, a substitute for such unity, which was agreed upon and supposed to be confirmed by the King and his successors in the interest of public order in the Commonwealth.   That religious peace proclaimed in Warsaw was to be general and all inclusive, in contradistinction to similar agreements in other countries which recognized only certain denominations.   The term " dissidents " which later was used to designate only the dissenters from the Catholic faith — what might be called the religious minorities of the Common-

---

[30] *Ibidem*, fol. 358 (July 15, 1573).

[31] See my remarks about their background and coats of arms in *Miesięcznik heraldyczny* (Heraldic Monthly), V (1912), 116-120, 166-169.

[32] That whole problem has been discussed at length by W. Sobieski, *Polska a hugenoci po nocy Św. Bartłomieja* (Poland and the Huguenots after St. Bartholemy's Night), Kraków, 1910.

[33] See Sobieski's article, " Si non iurabis — non regnabis, " in the review *Reformacja w Polsce* (The Reformation in Poland), II (1922), 54-70, and the English translation of the final text of the royal oath by E. M. Wilbur, *op. cit.*, 364.

wealth — in 1573 included even the Catholics themselves, and there was quite a number of them [34] among the signatories of the Confederation, including even one of the bishops, the experienced Vice-Chancellor, and since the end of the reign of Sigismund Augustus also Bishop of Cracow, Francis Krasiński, a prelate of undoubted zeal who had signed at Commendone's headquarters a profession of faith according to the decrees of the Council of Trent. [35] And though the intention of all the signatories was primarily to appease the relations between Catholics and Protestants, the Confederation and its royal confirmation were at the same time a guarantee that also the peaceful relations with the followers of the Eastern Church would continue undisturbed.

That the situation of the Orthodox was seriously considered at the Convocation of 1573 clearly results from an amendment to the Confederation which was proposed by the deputies of the province of Sandomierz and accepted by the Election Diet in May of the same year : this was an additional guarantee that ecclesiastical offices which would be granted by the King, as far as they concerned " Greek churches, " would be reserved exclusively for candidates " of that same Greek faith. " [36] Since there were no Orthodox in the Sandomierz region, its deputies acted obviously on the initiative and in support of their colleagues from other provinces, and there is a contemporary testimony that the request was made by Orthodox nobles from Volhynia, two of whom signed the final text of the Confederation to which the amendment had been added. [37] The whole action, therefore, can be considered a first evidence of cooperation between Protestants and Orthodox who in the future so often were to invoke jointly the Confederation of Warsaw, whenever their religious rights and liberties seemed threatened.

Of course, such a cooperation was thinkable only as long as the " Greek Church " was, like the various Protestant denominations, separated from Rome and really a " faith " different from the Catholic. Therefore, the Ruthenians were interested in a joint action with the Protestants from whom they differed in their beliefs much more than from the Catholics, only as long as the Union of Florence was obliterated and their Church of Eastern rite opposed to the Latin. The question, therefore, arises once more whether Rome, alarmed as she was by the Confederation of Warsaw which seemed to perpetuate the religious division in Poland — that " bulwark against the most powerful infidels and schismatics " [38] — was not considering

---

[34] 41 out of 98 ; see Wilbur, *loc. cit.*

[35] Original in the Vatican Archives, *Nunz. di Polonia*, vol. 2, fol. 34 (June 12, 1572), received in Rome on July 12 (*ibidem*, fol. 16).

[36] Chodynicki, *op. cit.*, 346 f.

[37] *Ibidem*, 357 n. 4.

[38] That expression frequently appears in the reports of the nuncios.

in these critical years the possibility of religious reunion with those who within the boundaries of the Commonwealth were " of Greek faith, " and whether the papal nuncios were not interested in that important problem.

Strange enough, even Portico who was so concerned with the Eastern question as a whole and while rightly skeptical as to any religious union with Moscow studied its possibilities in Moldavia, [39] did not mention that problem when leaving Poland in 1574, after five years and eight months of activity there, he outlined detailed suggestions for his successor. [40] He interpreted even the will of Sigismund Augustus and his appeal that Poles and Lithuanians should remain faithful to their political union as an appeal for " unity of Christian faith " also. But he was speaking all the time only of the relations between Catholics and " heretics, " and when he recommended that the new king should replace at last the Catholic Bishop of Kiev what the late Jagellonian had failed to do, he stressed that point only because of the notorious Calvinist leanings of that bishop, the Lithuanian Nicholas Pac, and not in any connection with the position of the numerous Orthodox Ruthenians of his diocese, who were not mentioned at all, though even the 70-80 thousand Jews, particularly in Lithuania, received attention. Even emphasizing the importance of the Jesuit colleges, the former nuncio did not write about the work of the Jesuit Society among the schismatics.

Equally surprising is that Portico, in spite of his disappointing experiences in the attempted relations with Moscow at the time of Pius V and Sigismund Augustus, writing his memorandum for the new Pope, Gregory XIII, and recommending what the new King, so recently elected, should do, pointed out the excellent occasion for raising once more the question of an " eternal " peace with Moscow, since the truce with that country was to expire soon. In his opinion, it would be in the interest of all Christendom if Henri de Valois could be persuaded to act in that sense at the next Diet. And suggesting the arguments which could be used, he mentioned not only the economies which the King would achieve through such a peace having promised to contribute to the war expenses out of his own fund, but also the inspiring idea that " through such a union with the power of the Muscovite, he would be able to think of some most glorious undertaking. " The union which was considered so desirable was, of course, merely political, the religious difference not being mentioned at all, and the undertaking which was to be made possible, was obviously nothing else but the old project of an anti-Ottoman league with the support of Orthodox Moscow.

---

[39] Theiner, op. cit., II, Nr. 809 p. 762 ; cf. however, Nr. 831 p. 773.
[40] Vatican Archives, Misc. Arm. 64, vol. 29, fol. 92-100. The passages quoted in the text are on fol. 97v and 98v-99.

There was, however, not the slightest chance that the French Prince who had been elected King of Poland in opposition to the Austrian candidate and with the support of the Sultan, would be more favorable than Sigismund Augustus to an alliance with the Habsburgs and Moscow against the Turks. And in any, case all speculations about his possible " glorious undertakings " in Eastern Europe proved entirely vain when after only a few months spent in Cracow he abandonned his Polish throne in order to return to France as heir and successor of his brother Charles IX. [41] After that French interlude the question of the Polish succession was therefore reopened and in that second interregnum problems similar to those of the first were to reappear immediately.

Once more the Holy See anxious to see elected an undoubtedly Catholic candidate, supported the Austrian, this time Emperor Maximilian II himself, and the new nuncio, Vincent Laureo, worked again very hard in that sense. [42] Again the whole issue was to be a test, not only of the Catholic forces in the Commonwealth, but also of the Union of Lublin, and this for two reasons. First, what remained of the Lithuanian opposition against that Union, now almost exclusively the Radziwiłł family, was particularly favorable to the election of a Habsburg, even independently of the Poles. [43] And secondly, Ivan the Terrible in secret negotiations with Vienna, tried once more to gain at least the Grand Duchy of Lithuania leaving the Kingdom of Poland to the House of Austria. The Emperor rejected both proposals, [44] and must have realized that those of the Tsar, if seriously considered, would have alienated his Lithuanian partisans who were at the same time violently opposed to Moscow. As to the Holy See, it was completely unaware of these intrigues, though Laureo had strange illusions that Ivan's election could favor his conversion to Catholicism and his cooperation against Constantinople. [45] But even when Maximilian's rival in the competition for the Polish crown, the Prince of Transylvania, Stefan Báthory, was definitely in control of Poland and started there his brilliant reign, the Pope and his Nuncio, not yet fully convinced of Báthory's unwavering loyalty to the Catholic Church, hesitated whom of the two elected kings of Poland Rome should recognize.

One of the arguments in that respect which the Emperor used still in

---

[41] F. Nowak, " The Interregna and Stephen Batory, " *The Cambridge History of Poland*, 374.

[42] His reports have been published by T. Wierzbowski, *Vincent Laureo*, Varsovie 1887.

[43] O. Halecki, " Die Beziehungen der Habsburger zum litauischen Hochadel, " *Mitteilungen des Instituts für österreichische Geschichtsforschung*, XXXVI (1915) ; see my additional remarks in *Kwartalnik histor.*, Vol. 50 (1937),

[44] H. Übersberger, *op. cit.*, I, 408-411, 437 f.

[45] Wierzbowski, *op. cit.*, 257.

the summer of 1576 negotiating with Cardinal Morone, [46] was connected
with the attitude of Ivan the Terrible : he pointed out that Moscow, his
ally, was so hostile to Báthory that in case of his recognition Ivan could
threaten not only Poland but also the other Catholic countries, while the
Prince of Transylvania would try to appease the Turks. Such an argument
could indeed influence the Cardinal whose mission to Germany included
again the plan of an anti-Ottoman league and the establishment of friendly
relations with Moscow : he wanted even the Emperor to send there, along
with Ivan's envoys returning from the imperial court, a rather obscure
diplomatic agent, Rudolph Clenck, who pretended to be in a position to
gain Ivan for the whole plan. [47] In his reply of July 15, 1576, [48] Maximilian
II expressed the opinion that it would be a mistake to send " the said
Clenck or anybody else " to Moscow immediately, since the plan of the
Legate had not yet been discussed with the Muscovite envoys and since
a solemn embassy was to be dispatched to Ivan, not only by the Empire
but also by the kings of Spain and Denmark.

That comprehensive diplomatic action did not take place at all, Clenck
disappeared in obscurity, and it soon became evident that the Tsar, far
from thinking of any cooperation with the West against the Ottoman Empire, was merely preparing another aggression against the Polish-Lithuanian
Commonwealth. Therefore, Cardinal Morone himself who at first had fully
shared the high hopes of the Vatican, [49] became rather doubtful about the
advisibility of entering into negotiations with Ivan : on September 14, 1576,
he wrote to the Cardinal Secretary of State [50] that by doing so the Holy
See could raise Báthory's suspicion that it encouraged Moscow's policy, and
without gaining the Orthodox Muscovites alienate the Catholic Poles. The
whole project was indeed given up for the time being and could be dismissed as just one more illusionary and abortive attempt of obtaining Moscow's assistance in the defense of Christendom, if even more fantastic illusions and projects regarding her ecclesiastical position had not reappeared
on that occasion.

Already in Morone's instruction to the Diet of Ratisbon, [51] of April 26,

---

[46] The rich material regarding these negotiations in the Vatican Archives, particularly *Misc. Arm.* 64, vol. 29, where the statement quoted in the text is on fol.
318v-319, has been used and partly published by Karl Schellhass, " Zur Legation
des Kardinals Morone, " *Quellen und Forschungen aus italienischen Archiven*, XIII
(1910), 272-355.

[47] The first to discuss his projects was Pierling, *La Russie et le Saint-Siège*, I,
410-413 ; see also his earlier study *Rome et Moscou 1547-1597*, Paris 1883, where some
of the documents are printed as appendices.

[48] Pierling, *Rome et Moscou*, appendix 12, p. 155.

[49] See his proposals made in April 1576, published by Schellhass, *op. cit.*, appendix
2, p. 319.

[50] *Ibidem*, appendix 15, p. 353 ; see also the editor's comments on pp. 309 f.

[51] *Nuntiaturberichte aus Deutschland*, III Abt., II, 25 f.

1576, the Pope expressed his readiness to send " his own man " to Moscow in order to gain Ivan " entirely for a union with the Roman Church, " and wanted the Emperor to be convinced that this would also help " temporal interests and particularly the league against the Turks. " And later, on August 25, the Secretary of State wrote to the Cardinal Legate [52] that Ivan seemed very devoted to Rome and that there was a chance that a " Patriarch " of Moscow would recognize the authority of the Pope, just as the Coptic Church of Ethiopia would do it at the request of the King of Portugal.

That comparison indicates one of the sources of these new optimistic expectations regarding Moscow's and Ivan's conversion and of the amazing idea to elevate the Metropolitan of Moscow to the dignity of a Patriarch on the initiative of the Holy See. For in those very years a project was discussed at the Vatican [53] which primarily dealt with the prospects of religious union with the Coptic Patriarchate of Alexandria and with the King of Ethiopia, but for the first time established an analogy between that distant African problem and the relations of Rome with the Greek Church, suggesting a parallel treatment of both problems as it really happened at the time of the Union of Brest, though in entirely different circumstances. This time it was suggested that since both the Coptic Patriarch of Alexandria and the Greek Patriarch of Constantinople were completely under the control of the Sultan, Rome should approach directly the independent rulers who professed their faith, the King of Ethiopia and the Duke of Moscow, in order to gain them for religious reunion. Their example would then be followed by the Patriarchs and Ottoman power would be much easier to destroy.

Though that memorandum was much more detailed in dealing with the case of Ethiopia, it added that in the case of Moscow whose ruler was not yet a king, the royal crown ought to be offered him first, granting him what his predecessors had requested in vain, because of the opposition of the Kings of Poland. Furthermore, papal ambassadors should be sent to Moscow promising that Rome would send there also a Patriarch chosen by the Holy See who would crown the Duke and make Moscow his permanent residence. Such a Patriarch would be independent of the Turks who then would be attacked from all sides, including Ivan the Terrible who was already " fighting continuously " with them.

Extravagant as they were the ideas of the anonymous writer of this " discourse " seemed to be confirmed by a much more serious source : the

---

[52] Schellhass, *op. cit.*, appendix 7 ; see also Pierling, *op. cit.*, appendix 10.
[53] The full text is preserved in the Vatican Library, *Urbin lat.* 854/I, fol. 1-21 ; see my comments in the essay " Rome, Constantinople et Moscou au temps de l'Union de Brest, " 1054-1954 : *L'Eglise et les Eglises*, Chevetogne 1954, I, 445-447.

13

— 194 —

report of one of the Austrian ambassadors to Moscow, Hans von Kobenzl, [54]
who after describing the " greatness " of her ruler, emphasized that he had
never before shown so much " reverence and obedience " toward the Holy
See. The " confidence " which at last had been established between him
and the House of Austria, was one more reason why the Pope should seize
the opportunity to encourage him through some " private person " to conclude the union with Rome where he would not fail to send an embassy.
And using the same comparison with Ethiopia, it was recalled that a similar
method had been used by King John of Portugal resulting in the obedience
offered by the King of Ethiopia to Pope Clement VII, in 1533, and in a
joint attack against the Turks. It also was pointed out how inconvenient
it was that such a great Christian ruler as was the Grand Prince of Moscow
should have a Metropolitan subject to the Patriarch of Constantinople who
himself was subject to the Sultan.

To this report which was carefully studied in Rome [55] additional material was added which on the one hand praised the Muscovites for being
hostile to the " heretics " even more than to the Turks, while they were
not at all unfriendly to the Holy See and to Union with Rome, and on the
other hand recommended that their Metropolitan whom they venerated
like the Catholics the Pope and who, as a matter of fact, had " little correspondence " with the Patriarch of Constantinople, should be elevated
himself to the rank of a Patriarch. In connection with that rather misleading and confusing information it was suggested in a special memorandum [56]
that even if the Muscovite " would obstinately persist in schism, " a special
Patriarch should be created by the Holy See for the whole State and
nation of Moscow. Such an offer could not possibly be rejected, because
of the obvious advantages of such an appointment for " the Muscovite. "
These advantages were summarized in seven points, including even the prob-
ability that " the whole Greek Church " would soon come under the obedience of that new Patriarch because of the " identity of customs and rites, "

---

[54] See on this famous report and its editions Pierling, *La Russie et le Saint Siège*,
I, 404-406 ; Uebersberger, *op. cit.*, I, 461 n. 1 ; Schellhass, *op. cit.*, 300 n. 1, app. 1 and
4 (another optimistic report of Kobenzl, sent from Łowicz in Poland on May 27,
1576.)

[55] See the copy in the Vatican Archives, *Misc. Arm.* 2, vol. 117, fol. 58-62v, and
the additional material on fol. 32-55v (particularly fol. 48 f.).

[56] *Ibidem*, fol. 53-53v (see my comments in " Rome, Constantinople ..., " 447-448).
Schellhass who published that memorandum, *op. cit.*, appendix 5, p. 326/7 (see also
his comments on p. 303) could not identify the " unbekannte gelehrte Hand " which
crossed out the last paragraph of the proposal and added a critical comment. That
addition which is difficult to read indeed and full of corrections, he interpreted differently and expressed the opinion — without, however, any convincing argument —
that it was Kobenzl who pointed out the problem of the Ruthenians in Lithuania
and Poland. Whether the memorandum was written by one of the Cardinals, in August 1576, is also uncertain.

thus increasing also Moscow's political power. Last not least, Ivan's prestige would grow both among his own people and among the foreigners who would think that he had the support of the Holy See and of all Christian princes.

How the Holy See could appoint a Patriarch, even if Moscow would remain schismatic and what advantages the Catholic Church would gain through such an arrangement, this was not explained in the memorandum. Its identification with the exclusive interests of Moscow was so obvious that the last paragraph of the original was crossed out by another hand which added a few very critical remarks : the whole project was called " almost incredible, quite abominable and intolerable, " and it was recalled that besides the Orthodox Muscovites also the numerous Ruthenians of Lithuania and various Polish provinces ought to be taken into consideration. In case of any conflict with Muscovy their situation would be rather delicate if the Patriarch of the Greek Church would reside in Moscow where he would have much more power and influence than in Constantinople. The conclusion was, therefore, that instead of planning such new, extravagant solutions, it would be much wiser to encourage the return of the Ruthenians to the Union of Florence according to their own earlier promises.

It is not difficult to discover that these critical comments were written by the famous Jesuit Antonio Possevino, but probably several years later, after his disappointing experiences with Ivan the Terrible, when in his report about his unsuccessful attempts to convert the Tsar he did not hesitate to express the regret that so many Popes had wasted time and effort in trying to establish relations with Moscow instead of putting first things first and concentrating on the much easier task of restoring the Union of Florence among the Ruthenians of the Polish-Lithuanian Commonwealth. [57] But even before Possevino could give such a sound advice, immediately after Cardinal Morone's unsuccessful mission to Germany which convinced him that the Emperor himself did not take the projects of co-operation with Moscow too seriously and that it was much more urgent to settle the relations with Báthory, the Holy See gave up his initiative in that matter : the optimistic or rather utopian memoranda on the religious situation in Moscow were put on file in the Vatican archives and no step was made to approach Ivan the Terrible before 1579 when in entirely different circumstances, Gregory XIII consulted in that matter the new King of Poland. [58]

In the meantime that same Stefan Báthory whose position seemed so uncertain in 1576, had not only established himself solidly on the Polish throne while his imperial rival died before the end of the year, but succeed-

---

[57] See his statement quoted above, 138 n. 72.
[58] Pierling, *op. cit.*, I, 419 ff.

ed in the following years to check Ivan's aggression against the Commonwealth, starting precisely in 1579 the first of his three brilliant campaigns.[59]
But the King of Poland succeeded also in convincing the Pope that his Catholic convictions and his loyalty to the Holy See were absolutely sincere
and that he was decided to complete the work of Catholic restoration in the
Commonwealth continuing to use the methods of wise moderation which
Sigismund Augustus had applied. He too, like Henri de Valois before him,
had to swear to maintain religious peace and he respected indeed the Confederation of Warsaw. But it was under his reign that at last, in 1577,
the decrees of the Council of Trent were formally accepted at a provincial
Synod of the Catholic hierarchy, and in encouraging the peaceful conversion
of non-Catholics he cooperated both with the Jesuit Society and with the
papal nuncios as soon as Laureo who had so openly favored the Habsburg
candidate was replaced by Caligari, in 1578. [60]

In these same years, 1577 and 1578, important steps were taken to
include in the program of Catholic restoration in Poland and Lithuania the
conversion not only of the Protestants but also of the Greek Orthodox,
and as to the latter to revive the tradition of the Union of Florence. And
that initiative in the vast region which the Union of Lublin had consolidated,
happened to be simultaneous with an initiative of Gregory XIII which was
taken in the very spirit of the Council of Florence and considered this time
not the hopeless situation in Moscow, but the Greeks themselves as well
as all peoples including the Ruthenians who had been for centuries under
their ecclesiastical leadership. Decisive in that respect was the foundation,
by a papal bull issued on January 13, 1577, of the Greek College in Rome [61]
which became immediately a center of Catholic education for young men
from all eastern countries and of Catholic propaganda in these countries
themselves where a Greek translation of the Roman Catechism was distributed in thousands of copies, while the decisions of the Council of Florence
and earlier Greek writings in favor of that Council were reprinted at the
same time. [62] But the origin of all these activities can be traced back to
the earlier years of the pontificate of Gregory XIII, at least to 1573 when
the Greek Congregation was founded on the initiative of Cardinal Santori, [63]
the official protector of the Eastern Christians in Rome, and to 1575 when

---

[59] F. Nowak, *op. cit.*, 378-383.

[60] See the chapter on the religious situation in the collective work *Etienne Batory,
Roi de Pologne, Prince de Transylvanie*, jointly published in 1935 by the Polish and
Hungarian Academies.

[61] Pastor, *op. cit.*, IX, 179 f.

[62] *Ibidem*, IX, 737 ; Chodynicki, *op. cit.*, 204 f.

[63] *Ibidem*, IX, 42 n. 6 ; see J. Cugnoni (ed.), *Autobiografia di Mons. G. A. Santori*,
2 vols., Rome 1889-1890.

a Catholic mission was sent to Constantinople to establish the first contacts with Patriarch Jeremiah II and to oppose Protestant influence at his court. [64]

Similarly to these initiatives of the Holy See which were to prove so important at the time of the Union of Brest, also the events of 1577-78 which inaugurated in the Commonwealth the patient preparations for that Union, had been prepared themselves for several years, at least from 1573 when Father Skarga was transferred by the Polish Provincial Maggio to Wilno. [65] It was there that he found new opportunities to work among the numerous Greek Orthodox population, to participate in the elevation of the local Jesuit college to the rank of a University of which he was to be the first Rector, and last not least to write at the Provincial's order a Polish book on the whole problem of the Greek schism. That book was already written in 1574, but Skarga was not yet decided to publish. This happened only in 1577, again at the order of his superiors and already in March of that year the book could be sent to the General of the Society in Rome. [66]

The very title of that outstanding publication: " On the Unity of the Church of God under one Pastor " shows the close connection of Skarga's achievement with the desire for religious unity which eight years before Sigismund Augustus had expressed at that end of the Diet of Lublin. And it was the political union concluded at the Diet which explains why a Polish Jesuit, one of the glories of Polish literature and oratory, published in the capital of the Grand Duchy of Lithuania an appeal for religious union which was directed to the Ruthenians of both the Kingdom and the Grand Duchy. Based as it was on the Florentine tradition, that appeal was the best evidence that this tradition was still alive in that region of Europe, and that this regional initiative was well coordinated with that which the Pope himself — the " one Pastor " — developed at the same time regarding all Eastern Christendom.

---

[64] Chodynicki, *op. cit.*, 205/6.

[65] *Ibidem*, 212.

[66] See his letter to General Mercuriano, of March 12, 1577, published by J. Sygański, *Listy ks. Piotra Skargi* (the letters of Father Peter Skarga), Kraków 1912, 85.

PART III

THE ORIGINS OF THE UNION OF BREST

CHAPTER I

SKARGA AND POSSEVINO, 1577-1587

In the whole history of the Union of Brest, from its origins and from the preparatory negotiations to the heated polemics which followed its conclusion, theological writings by partisans and opponents of reunion with Rome played a very important part.[1] They all not only contributed to the development of intellectual life and literary activities in the Ruthenian lands, which never before had been so intense, and definitely put an end to the stagnation of the preceding century, but also influenced to a large extent the actual events and the attitude of both camps. But no other single publication can be compared in all these respects with Skarga's masterpiece whose two editions, of 1577 and 1590,[2] might be considered introductions to the two consecutive phases of the preparations for the successful conclusion of the Union.

Since the first of these phases, which developed in the decade from 1577 to 1587, ended in apparent failure and disappointment, while in the second the most important negotiations were for several years conducted in secret, it could seem that the preparation for the momentous decisions of 1595 and 1596 was rather inadequate and that the interval between the last serious attempts to restore the union of Florence among the Ruthenians and its real revival through the Union of Brest lasted almost to the very eve of the latter. However, Skarga's book which first appeared nineteen years before the Synod of Brest, having been written three years earlier

---

[1] See A. Brückner, " Spory o Unię w dawnej literaturze " (Disputes about the Union in ancient literature), " *Kwartalnik histor.* X (1896) ; a new study of that polemical literature is now being prepared by M. Wojciechowski who reported on the progress of his work in 1956 to the Polish Historical Institute in Rome (*Relationes Instituti polonici Romae*, Nr. 24.)

and planned probably since the author's first meeting with Prince Ostrog-ski[2], ten years before the edition of 1577 dedicated to that same prince — a book which had been prepared itself by the earlier writings of the less prominent Jesuit Herbest and the discussions between Orzechowski and Hosius — is the best evidence that the project of reunion did not emerge suddenly or accidentally. It shows, first, that the idea of regaining the Ruthenians for religious unity with Rome was growing out of the religious crisis of the mid-century through the lifetime of an entire generation, and secondly, that it was nothing but a natural return to the unforgotten tra- dition of the Union of Florence, encouraged by both the positive and the negative results of the recent Council of Trent.

That long Council had, on the one hand, strengthened the Catholic Church by an internal, comprehensive reform and clarified the dogmatic foundations on which religious reunion with any separated Church was possible, while on the other hand the deliberations at Trent had led to the conviction that for the time being no such reunion was possible with the Protestants. [4] That in the relations with them only individual con- versions could be achieved, in the Polish-Lithuanian Commonwealth like elsewhere, this was experienced in particular by men like Skarga, [5] who was instrumental in many such conversions of Protestant leaders to the Catholic faith of their fathers and continued to promote through such methods the Catholic restoration in his country. At the same time he became convinced that something more ought to be tried in the relations with the Greek Orthodox who were much more numerous and had been separated from Rome for a much longer time, but without such profound dogmatic differences as in the case of the Protestants and not without a historic precedent of agreement such as the decision of the Council of Florence. He therefore decided to make an appeal to all his Ruthenian fellow-citizens, not by encouraging once more individual conversions to Catholicism of the Latin rite — conversions for which he and the other Polish Jesuits never ceased to work — but recommending, independently of any such conversions, a return of the whole Ruthenian Church of Poland and Lithuania to full religious community with Rome in one Church of God, united as it had been at its origin and again according to the Flor- entine decrees.

---

[2] Reprinted in *Russkaia istor. bibl.*, VII, col. 223-580.

[3] See above, p. 156 f.

[4] See L. Cristiani, *L'Eglise à l'époque du Concile de Trente*, Paris, 1948, particu- larly p. 131 f., on the negotiations with the Protestants, and 223 f., on the general significance of the Council.

[5] The basic study on Skarga's role in the history of the Union of Brest remains J. Tretiak, *Skarga w dziejach i literaturze Unii brzeskiej*, Kraków 1912; his French biography by P. Berga, *Pierre Skarga — Etude sur la Pologne du XVIe siècle et le protestantisme*, Paris 1926, gives more attention to his struggle against the Protestants.

In making such an appeal the patriot Skarga was, of course, working for religious unity in the Commonwealth which had been politically united at the Diet of Lublin, a religious unity which was indeed endangered by so many Protestant and Antitrinitarian denominations, but for that very reason was particularly desirable at least among Catholics and Orthodox. Since, however, such a compensation for the irreparable losses which the Church had suffered through the Protestant revolt was desirable not only in the Polish case but in general, the appeal of the most prominent Polish Jesuit was made on the instruction and with the encouragement of his superiors in Rome, as part of the action of the Holy See which wanted to use the tradition of the Union of Florence in order to regain all the eastern Churches. [6]   That all these Churches had been originally united under papal authority and had accepted the Union of Florence, following the Emperor and the Patriarch of Constantinople, this was one of Skarga's main arguments when addressing the Ruthenians who continued to look with respect and loyalty towards Constantinople whence their ancestors had received the Christian faith.   Skarga could point out in his detailed historic developments [7] that this had happened before the Eastern Schism which the Greeks themselves had given up at the Council of Florence.   And as to the present situation, he explained the attitude of the Greek Patriarchs who were again separated from Rome, by emphasizing their complete dependence on the Turks.

That humiliating dependence of the once glorious Patriarchate was to remain another of Skarga's favorite arguments whenever he tried to convince the Ruthenians how preferable it was for them to submit to the Pope rather than to a Patriarch who was not free himself but under Muslim control.   But it was equally obvious that in such a situation no general return to the Florentine tradition, no reunion with all Eastern Churches was possible, and therefore Skarga was writing only in favor of a regional religious union within the limits of the Commonwealth whose Catholic leadership would naturally facilitate such a decision.   That conception differed from the universal one, as considered by the Holy See and by the non-Polish Jesuits, [8] not only in view of the hopeless condition of those Eastern Churches which were under Ottoman domination, but also as far as Moscow was concerned, a large Orthodox country which having not yet its own Patriarch was ecclesiastically still under that of Constantinople though politically free from Turkish control and influence.   There reappeared, therefore, the old alternative whether or not simultaneous efforts ought to be

---

[6] See above in the preceding chapter, p. 196 f.

[7] They constitute the whole second part of his book, *loc. cit.*, 337-463; about the situation of the Patriarchate of Constantinople 496.

[8] See Chodynicki, *Kościół*, 219, in conclusion of a detailed analysis of Skarga's book.

made to include in the project of reunion, in spite of so many earlier disappointments, the powerful neighbor country which had rejected the Union of Florence and all projects of its revival, but continued to be of special interest to the Papacy. At the time when the first edition of Skarga's book appeared, Ivan the Terrible was attacking once more the Commonwealth and King Stefan Batory preparing for his campaigns against that most dangerous enemy. Any cooperation even in religious matters was therefore out of the question and the conflict with an Orthodox power seemed to create one more obstacle in dealing with Orthodox people anywhere, were it even at home. But the desire and hope of gaining also Moscow for religious reunion or at least for cooperation against the Turks, [9] not only continued in Rome but was to influence a little later even that leading Orthodox magnate of the Commonwealth to whom Skarga dedicated in moving terms the first edition of his work : Prince Constantine Ostrogski. [10]

At the given moment that dedication was highly significant for two different reasons. First, it indicated that even a man perfectly familiar with local conditions shared then the optimistic expectations which Rome would never give up entirely, that precisely this ambitious magnate whose influence among the Ruthenians was indeed tremendous, could be gained for the Union, possibly as its main supporter. The interest which Ostrogski was showing in that matter, at least since his first contact with Skarga in 1567, could justify such an approach and there was not yet any reason for doubting whether his repeated statements, apparently favorable to the project, were genuine and sincere. Furthermore, dedicating his work to a layman who belonged to one of the leading aristocratic families of dynastic origin, Skarga was obviously sharing the opinion that in view of the strong lay influence in the Eastern Church and of the authority which the ducal families enjoyed among the Ruthenians, it was advisable to start the whole campaign in favor of religious reunion by trying to win the support of one or two of these most powerful leaders. Since there was no Orthodox ruler who in the given region could play the part, if not of the Byzantine Emperor in mediaeval Constantinople, at least of the Grand Princes of Kiev in the early days of the Ruthenian Church, and since the present hierarchy of that Church was so obviously inadequate, Ostrogski who was considered a direct descendent of Rurik and even now occupied the highest state offices

---

[9] About the papal suggestions made in that respect to Batory in 1579 and 1580, though without any success, see Pierling, *La Russie et le Saint-Siège*, I, 419-430 ; see now also L. Boratyński, *Stefan Batory i plan ligi przeciw Turkom* (St. B. and the plan of an anti-Ottoman league), Kraków 1903, 228-248 (partic. 237, n. 3, 4).

[10] The whole attitude of the prince toward the Union of Brest has been studied in detail by K. Lewicki, *Ks. Konstanty Ostrogski a Unia brzeska 1596 r.*, Lwów 1933, who tried to vindicate Ostrogski's policy.

in the Ruthenian lands as Palatine of Kiev and Marshal of Volhynia, was undoubtedly the first choice.

This was not only Skarga's personal opinion : during the whole earlier phase of the preparatory negotiations such views prevailed among those who propagated the idea of religious reunion, starting on the regional level, and in particular of those to whom Gregory XIII had entrusted that responsibility in the Commonwealth. One of them was naturally his Nuncio to the King of Poland who in that matter, as in all others, had to approach Stefan Batory himself, fully aware of the leading role which such an unusually brilliant and energetic ruler as the successful rival of Maximillian II soon proved to be, could play in the whole northeastern part of Europe, in a loyal cooperation with the Holy Sea to which he was fully prepared. When, therefore, Monsignor Caligari [11] arrived in Poland in that capacity, he was to give more attention than his predecessors to the problem of the Greek Orthodox in general and more particularly to the possibility of reviving the Union of Florence among the Ruthenians of the Commonwealth pending a similar action beyond its limits. Already in his first audience with the King on November 1, 1578, [12] he touched in connection with the problem of the anti-Ottoman league also that of reunion with the Eastern Churches, presenting to Batory a beautiful Greek volume about the Union of Florence. He noted on that occasion that the King seemed well informed and interested in the matter, promising to show the volume to a prominent Ruthenian of Greek faith. And exploring further possibilities to promote the cause of reunion, Caligari soon started to cooperate with a man who though a simple Jesuit monk like Skarga was to become something like an extraordinary agent of the Holy See in both the North and the East, combining purely religious and diplomatic activities. [13]

Father Antonio Possevino's role was throughout the first phase of the preparation for the Union of Brest equally important as that of Skarga, even in Poland which was only part of his field of action. Less spectacular than his missions to Sweden and to Moscow both of which ended in failure as far as Catholic restoration or religious reunion were concerned, his propaganda in the Commonwealth was equally tireless, full of enthusiasm and versatility. And while he not always agreed with the papal nuncios, and himself changed his views or at least his methods, his experiences proved invaluable with regard to precisely the two big issues which had to be decid-

---

[11] L. Boratyński has published the whole source material regarding Caligari's mission in *Monumenta Poloniae Vaticana*, IV, Kraków 1915, and discussed his personality in the introduction, pp. XXIV-LXXI.

[12] *Ibidem*, Nr. 47, p. 68 ; see also appendix, Nr. 1.

[13] The latest biography of Antonio Possevino is by J. Ledit in *Dictionnaire de théologie catholique*, XXI-2, Paris 1935, col. 2647-2657 (with bibliography) ; an exhaustive work about the famous Jesuit is being prepared by Mario Scaduto, of the Jesuit Historical Institute in Rome.

ed in the matter of religious reunion, viz., whether the return of the Ruthenians to the Catholic Church was of primary importance in itself or merely in connection with the much desired conversion of Moscow, and whether that return had to include the adoption of the Latin rite or was to follow the precedent created in Florence which so happily combined unity in faith with diversity in rite and liturgy.

When the two Jesuits, the Pole and the Italian, started cooperating in that matter with both the new King and the new Nuncio, the prestige and possibilities of action of their Order and of Skarga personally were considerably increased thanks to an important royal decision. In 1578 the Jesuit College of Wilno which had been founded immediately after the Union of Lublin, was elevated to the rank of an Academy with Skarga as its first Rector. [14] A first center of higher education thus came into existence in the area east of the old Catholic University of Cracow and the new Protestant University of Königsberg, and it was at the same time the first University in a country with partly Orthodox population, an institution which from the outset was considered " a gate " for spreading Catholicism as far as Moscow and even the Tartar world and China. [15] The importance of Wilno and of its Academy as a center of Catholic restoration and as a bulwark against heresies spreading from Germany and schism spreading from Moscow, was fully realized by all contemporaries and particularly by the Bishop of Wilno, Valerian Protasewicz, on whose initiative the University came into existence, [16] by the King who signed its charter on July 7, 1578,[17] and by Pope Gregory XIII who confirmed its foundation on October 29, 1579. [18] When that bull was issued, the King himself who staying in Wilno in the spring of that year had witnessed the reception into the Catholic Church of 82 Protestants and 40 Greek Orthodox, [19] was already engaged in the first of his three campaigns which were to stop the aggressions of Ivan the Terrible, and had retaken from him the city of Polotsk, lost by Sigismund Augustus sixteen years before. And it is highly significant that the following year he founded in that old center of White Ruthenian culture another Jesuit college and put Skarga in charge of that extreme outpost

---

[14] The origin of that Academy has been studied by St. Bednarski in the *Księga pamiątkowa* (Memorial Volume) published in Wilno in 1919, on the occasion of the 350th anniversary of the foundation of the University, vol. I.

[15] See *ibidem*, 13 n. 1 and 14 n. 1, the letters written by the Jesuit provincials in 1569 and 1570.

[16] His requests addressed to the Pope in that matter, on June 25, 1576, and July 8, 1577 preserved in the Vatican Archives (*Vescovi* vol. 10, f. 104 and 293) have been published by A. Theiner, *Annales ecclesiastici*, II, Rome 1856.

[17] Published by J. Bieliński, *Uniwersytet wileński*, I, 48.

[18] *Bullarium Roman. Pontif.*, VIII (Naples 1882), 560.

[19] L. v. Pastor, *Geschichte der Päpste*, IX, 673,

of Catholicism and Western civilization, where he was friendly received by the local Orthodox Archbishop. [20]

As to Gregory XIII whom Nuncio Caligari kept informed on all these promising developments, he took already on November 1, 1578, [21] an initiative which clearly indicates how deeply he was interested in promoting the religious reunion with the Orthodox Ruthenians of the Commonwealth. It indicates at the same time that he was in full agreement with the idea of first approaching in that matter a few of the most prominent laymen belonging to the leading families of dynastic origin. But it is rather surprising that on this occasion he did not write, as he and his successors were so often to do later, to Prince Ostrogski to whom Skarga had dedicated his book a year before. Unfortunately, Ostrogski's reaction had not been favorable, and though the reply to Skarga's appeal, written on the Prince's instruction and rejecting most decidedly the Jesuit's suggestions, was published only a few years later, [22] it seemed advisable to look for another Orthodox magnate as prospective leader of the movement in favor of reunion.

The name of Prince George Słucki was obviously suggested to Gregory XIII by his representatives in Poland, the Nuncio as well as Possevino, certainly in agreement with Skarga who had sent a copy of his book to that Prince and knew of Słucki's opinion that nobody was able to answer it. [23] On the other hand, it is quite possible that it was remembered in Rome how respectfully Prince Słucki's father had asked Clement VII in 1529 to sanction his first marriage with a Catholic of Latin rite [24] and how his influential position in the Grand Duchy of Lithuania had impressed Cardinal Commendone during the interregnum after Sigismund Augustus. [25] The Słuckis were not descendents of Rurik like the Ostrogskis, but were of Lithuanian origin, a sideline of the Jagellonian dynasty. This was precisely the reason why, hardly caring for appointments to high offices, they rather claimed, though in vain, the exceptional privilege of a hereditary seat in the Senate, and why Gregory XIII referred in his letter to the

---

[20] In addition to the sources quoted by Chodynicki, *op. cit.*, 230 n. 6 and 7, see the King's letter written from Polotsk on Sept. 4, 1579, in the Roman Archives of the Jesuit Order, *Epistolae selectae* VII, 650, Nr. 455, and the account in *Annuae Litterae Societatis Jesu Anni* 1583, Romae 1585, 66-112.

[21] *Monumenta Poloniae Vaticana*, IV, Nr. 46 ; see the comments of Chodynicki, *op. cit.*, 227 n. 5, where the background of the Pope's letter to Prince George Słucki is well explained.

[22] In 1588, reprinted in *Russk. istor. bibl.*, VII, 601-938 ; that the author, a certain Basil of Ostrog, was influenced also by the exile from Moscow, Prince Kurbsky, has been pointed out by J. Tretiak, *op. cit.*, 115-116.

[23] *Mon. Pol. Vat.*, IV, Nr. 112, p. 119 (see n. 4), 202.

[24] See above, p. 132.

[25] See above, p. 187.

Catholic kings of Poland as "ancestors" of Prince George. [26] However, his direct ancestors had been autonomous rulers of Kiev under the suzerainty of their brothers or cousins, the Grand Dukes of Lithuania, and from their early conversion to Greek Orthodoxy had been most closely associated with the traditions, both political and religious, of that historic center of the Ruthenian lands, including the tradition of close relations with the Patriarchate of Constantinople. It is in agreement with Constantinople that Prince George's grandfather had once accepted the Union of Florence which also his father seemed to favor at least temporarily. [27] And though Kiev had been taken away long ago from that family, the Duchy of Słuck which was left to them and from which they took their modern name — the last autonomous principality within the limits of the Grand Duchy of Lithuania — was not without importance. Skarga would report after his visit there [28] that it was 40 miles long and wide, not too far from Kiev and connected with that city through "navigation" on the rivers, and, while remote from Moscow, had trade relations with Constantinople. The great majority of the population was Greek Orthodox, though there also were a few Catholics, having a Catholic Church in the city of Słuck and four or five parishes outside.

The Pope and his advisers hoped that the conversion to Catholicism of Prince George and of his whole duchy would have far reaching repercussions among all Ruthenians of the Commonwealth, no less than a similar conversion of Ostrogski, and Słucki's case seemed more hopeful, since, as Gregory XIII stated in his letter, George was showing much "humanity" towards the Catholics and a strong "hatred of the heretics," i. e., of the Protestants whose influence upon Ostrogski was well known and proved so decisive later. Unfortunately Słucki died at the beginning of 1579 before receiving the papal message. Skarga who on Possevino's instruction was supposed to bring it to the Prince, could only visit in May his widow and hand over to her a similar brief of Gregory XIII which like the other had been drafted by Possevino himself. [29]

In both of them the Pope, in agreement with Possevino's original approach to the problem of reunion, was writing of "a complete removal of the diversity of rites," [30] making it quite clear that what he expected was not simply a return to the Union of Florence but the observance of the Latin rite. This would have created an additional difficulty in the negotiations with the old Prince himself, but could seem appropriate in the case of his widow who was born a Catholic of Latin rite, being the daughter

---

[26] *Mon. Pol. Vat.*, IV, Nr. 46 : "maiores tui Poloniae reges."
[27] See above, pp. 60, 132.
[28] *Mon. Pol. Vat.*, IV, Nr. 112, p. 208.
[29] *Ibidem*, Nr. 46 n. 1 and 2.
[30] "Omni rituum diversitate remota" ; *ibidem*, p. 65.

of a Pole, the Palatine of Cracow, Tęczyński. However, her mother and maternal grandmother had been Ruthenians deeply attached to the Greek rite, and Skarga was soon to discover that Catherine herself, especially after her long intercourse with schismatics, had come to the conviction, later expressed by Ostrogski, that the Ruthenian and the Roman Churches were equally good. She even became accustomed to receive Holy Communion " *sub utraque specie,* " a situation which was indeed typical of many families in the Commonwealth thanks to frequent intermarriage between persons of different religions, rites, and ethnic origins.

Nevertheless, the report on his mission to Słuck [31] which Skarga wrote in June at the request of Possevino and which through the latter was sent to the Cardinal Secretary of State, was rather optimistic. The Duchess was obviously flattered by his congratulations that she had kept her faith " amidst so many temptations by schismatics and heretics " (a compliment which Possevino had suggested), and by his comparing her with queens of the past and the present : Dąbrówka of Poland, Clotilde of France, and Catherine of Sweden, who had contributed to the conversion of their husbands and peoples. Skarga having pointed out that she was now in control of the whole duchy as its *gubernatrix* and responsible for the education of her three sons whom she ought to send to papal colleges, she assured him in her answer that she was anxious to contribute to " the unity of the Church. " Her main excuse for not having converted her late husband was his determination " in keeping his rite, though he felt very friendly toward the Holy Roman Church. " When he begged her before writing his will " not to turn away their sons from the Greek Church, " she promised — as she now explained at length to Skarga — not to use any persuasion in that matter, though they might join the Roman Church inspired by the Holy Spirit and by their experience in the countries where they were supposed to study, just like Prince Ostrogski's oldest son had done it. In her presence the old Prince had threatened to curse his sons if they would abandon " the rite and Church of their father " and authorized her to disinherit them if they would do so. Therefore she felt unable to urge them as Skarga wanted her to do, but she would send them to Italy where perhaps they could be " moved towards the unity of the Church. " She also promised to send other young men — Skarga had spoken not only of Ruthenians but also of Muscovites and even Tartars — to Jesuit colleges, such as Brunsberg (in Polish Prussia) and Wilno.

In further conversation with Skarga, the Duchess repeated that she could not violate her husband's will nor irritate her eldest son who was a decided defender of the Eastern Church, but pointed out that the two youngers felt differently : especially the second had already declared openly

---

[31] *Ibidem,* Nr. 112, p. 199-202.

that he would be a Catholic after his father's death, did not want to receive Communion " according to the Greek rite, " and did not like the Orthodox priests. She admitted herself that she was aware of " absurd errors of the Greeks " and that even her husband had " blamed many things among his own people and had a high opinion about the Roman Church. " Among, the various inconsistencies which were apparent in Catherine's statements as recorded by Skarga, her hesitations regarding the best way of receiving Holy Communion were particularly significant : she promised not to receive any more under both species, having heard from a monk who escaped from Moscow and was sympathetic to the Roman Church that even " Ruthenians following the Greek tradition received *sub una specie*. " In any case that problem appeared of special interest and importance in the whole matter, probably convineing Skarga that in agreement with the decisions of the Council of Florence religious reunion had to be achieved with due respect to the Eastern rite.

It was only three years later that Possevino who was particularly anxious to see the young princes educated in Jesuit institutions, could report to the Secretary of State [32] that their mother " who is the most important person of Russia " (as he always called the Ruthenian provinces of the Commonwealth in contradistinction to Muscovy) had finally decided to give up the *utraque species*, to make her confession to a Jesuit father and to endow the new Jesuit college in Lublin. But, though she remained in relations with the Jesuit Order, [33] it was a great disappointment to the new Nuncio Bolognetti and to Rome where he sent that information in December of the same year 1582, [34] that just when the Duchess seemed definitely gained for the Catholic cause she remarried with Prince Christopher Radziwiłł, a leader of the Lithuanian Calvinists who was to be later a strong supporter of those Orthodox Ruthenians who remained opposed to the Union of Brest. At the time of that Union, all three Princes Słucki who were expected to lead the movement in its favor were already dead and, therefore, their conversion to Catholicism which two of them accepted in the Latin and the third in the Greek rite, did not have the far reaching consequences which were expected. [35]

Nevertheless, the lengthy negotiations with that family proved highly instructive and contributed to convince the Catholic side that in order to arrive at a real and general religious union with the Ruthenians, it was not enough to gain some of their powerful magnates individually. In the same letter to Cardinal Galli in which Possevino emphasized the importance of the favorable attitude of the Duchess of Słuck, he expressed his hope

---

[32] *Ibidem*, V, Nr. 340, p. 358 f. (May 27, 1582).
[33] *Ibidem*, V, Nr. 359 n. 25.
[34] *Ibidem*, V, Nr. 506, p. 601.
[35] See the sources quoted by Chodynicki, *op. cit.*, 243 f.

that the papal briefs which were to be sent to the Ruthenian bishops of the Commonwealth and which Possevino was to receive from the Cardinal, would help to promote the cause of reunion with the assistance of " that lady " and of the Chancellor, [36] the great statesman, Jan Zamoyski, whose name was first connected on that occasion with the problem of union with the Ruthenians and whose support was to prove indeed of much greater importance at the time of decision. As to the briefs which Gregory XIII was to address to the Ruthenian hierarchy, Possevino could really expect that they would arrive soon, since already on February 17, 1582, [37] the Cardinal Secretary of State had written him that these letters would be prepared in the form suggested by the Jesuit and dispatched as soon as ready. This step would have been so significant that the questions arise why, on the one hand, Possevino had conceived such a project of a direct papal appeal to the Ruthenian bishops and why, on the other hand, the whole idea, though originally approved at the Vatican, was never carried out.

In order to answer the first of these questions, it must be remembered that in the preceding year Possevino had lived through one of the most exciting experiences of his eventful life : his mission to Ivan the Terrible. [38] When in, February 1581, the Tsar made his surprising request for papal mediation in his war against the King of Poland, he did not even mention the problem of religious reunion : [39] the only promises he made in case he would obtain peace through the mediation of the Pope's representative, were to open his country to trade relations with the West and to join Gregory XIII and the other Christian powers in their struggle against the Turks. While the first of these perspectives could raise special interest in Venice where Ivan's envoys stopped on their way to Rome and on their return, [40] the second was, of course, welcomed by the Holy See. Like so many of his predecessors Gregory XIII who, already at the very beginning of the war between Batory and Ivan, in 1579, had tried in vain to persuade the King of Poland to end that war and to turn together with Moscow against the Turks, [41] now was convinced that his diplomatic media-

---

[36] *Mon. Pol. Vat.* V, Nr. 359.

[37] *Ibidem*, V, Nr. 216, p. 227.

[38] That mission has been studied in several works of P. Pierling and finally described in detail in his *La Russie et le Saint-Siège*, II, Paris 1897, 1-181 ; see now also St. Polčin, *La mission religieuse du P. Antoine Possevin S. J. en Moscovie (Orientalia Christiana Analecta Nr. 150)*, Rome 1957.

[39] *Mon. Pol. Vat.*, IV, Nr. 318, p. 573 (Card. Galli to Caligari, March 4, 1581).

[40] The State Archives in Venice contain a rich material in that matter which has been used by Pierling only in part ; see the sections *Relazioni Senato III Secreta F. 25* (where there is a special file *Negocio Possevino — Moscovia*), *Esposizioni Principi (Secreta)*, vol. 4, fol. 120v-125v, vol. 5, fol. 22v-27v, and *Cerimoniali*, vol. 1, fol. 83v, 85, vol. 2, vol. 68v, 70v (see also vol. 1, fol. 93v-94, on Possevino's stay in Venice on his return from Moscow in August 1582).

[41] See above, p. 195.

14

tion would serve not only the cause of the struggle against the Ottoman onslaught but also that of religious reunion.

Possevino, to whom the Pope entrusted the requested mediation, did not return to the fantastic project of establishing a Patriarchate in Moscow, even if for the time being it would remain schismatic. [42] On the contrary, there seems to have been, in 1581, some hope at the Vatican that Ivan would give up even " his schismatic rite. " [43] And in any case, in the letter of Gregory XIII which Possevino brought to the Tsar in August 1581, [44] it was made quite clear that political cooperation, were it even against the Turks, was impossible without a real religious union as established at the Council of Florence. Ivan who was asked to study with his theologians the decisions of that Council including the recognition of papal primacy by the Greeks, postponed any negotiations in religious matters until the conclusion of peace with Poland. But even when Possevino succeeded in his mediation and after the signing of a ten years truce on January 15, 1582, returned to the Tsar, the latter evaded any commitments even in the matter of an anti-Ottoman league, and when Possevino, in the lengthy discussions of February 21 and 23, returned to the problem of religious union, simply insulted the Pope and brutally threatened his representative. A few days later, Ivan changed his tactics and, in addition to the Greek text of the Florentine decrees which Possevino had presented to him along with precious gifts of the Pope, asked for a special memorandum on the religious differences which separated Greeks and Russians from Rome. On the same occasion the courageous and tireless Jesuit also drafted a paper replying to the anti-Roman arguments of the English merchants present in Moscow. [45] But in spite of a continuation of negotiations between Ivan the Terrible and Gregory XIII until the end of 1582, Possevino himself, though participating in these negotiations was completely disillusioned: in his famous *Commentarii* [46] on Moscow, submitted to the Pope immediately on his return (the first was written already on September 29, 1581 after the initial discussions with the Tsar), though not printed before 1586, he came to the conclusion that the conversion of Muscovy would require long, systematic, and patient missionary activities. And he strongly advised to concentrate first

---

[42] See above, Part II, Chap. IV 194.

[43] *Mon. Pol. Vat., loc. cit.*, p. 575.

[44] The text is included in Possevino's *Moscovia* (ed. Coloniae 1587), 58.

[45] In Possevino's *Moscovia* (first printed in Vilna " apud Ioannem Velicensem " in 1586) his report on the " colloquia " with Ivan constitutes the third part ; it is followed by the " capita " on the religious differences separating Greeks and Russians from the Catholics, which he submitted to Ivan on March 3, and by his reply to the English merchants.

[46] They constitute the first two parts of his *Moscovia*, reprinted in *Supplementum ad Historica Russiae Monumenta*, Petropoli 1848, Nr. 11, pp. 22-41.

on the reestablishment of religious union with the Ruthenians under the King of Poland.

Considering that such a regional union within the limits of the Commonwealth would be much easier to achieve and at the same time would facilitate the subsequent union with Moscow, Possevino did not hesitate to express the regret that the Popes of the fifteenth and sixteenth century had wasted so much time and effort in hopeless negotiations with the rulers of Moscow, instead of promoting the reunion with the Ruthenians. [47] And it was precisely on that occasion that he recommended, [48] in addition to approaching their aristocratic leaders, especially the ducal families of the Ostrogskis and Słuckis, to turn to their hierarchy which though practically separated from Rome, were it only because of the traditional dependence on the schismatic Patriarchs of Constantinople, continued to invoke as legal basis of their position in the Commonwealth, the royal charter of 1443, confirmed in 1504 and 1543, which was granted to their predecessors in view of their acceptance of the Union of Florence.

Possevino's suggestion that the Pope himself should write to these Ruthenian bishops must have been made even before his unsuccessful discussions with Ivan the Terrible and he must have sent the draft of such letters from Russia to Rome. Why, then, had they not yet arrived when on his way back he was again in Poland, in the spring of 1582, and why were they never dispatched in spite of the promises of the Cardinal Secretary of State ? [49] In order to answer that second question, both the situation in the Commonwealth and that in distant Constantinople, must be taken into consideration.

In Poland and in Lithuania, the opinion seems to have prevailed and a little later, on December 7, 1583, [50] was reported to Cardinal Galli by the new, experienced and active Nuncio Bolognetti, [51] that first of all the question of the validity of the charter of 1443 ought to be clarified. Both the Archbishop of Lwów, John Demetrius Solikowski, and the Bishop of Wilno, George Radziwiłł, equally interested in the problem of reunion with the numerous Greek Orthodox population of their respective dioceses, [52]

---

[47] *Supplementum*, 34.
[48] *Ibidem*, 38.
[49] *Mon. Pol. Vat.*, V, Nr. 216, p. 227 (Card. Galli to Possevino, Rome, Feb. 17, 1582).
[50] *Ibidem*, VI, Nr. 394, p. 633 ; see also VII, Nr. 79, p. 113 (Galli to Bolognetti March 3, 1584).
[51] L. Boratyński who in 1907 published his " Studies " on the Polish mission of Bolognetti in the Proceedings (*Rozprawy*) of the Polish Academy in Cracow, started the comprehensive edition of the whole source material relating to that mission, which was completed by Cz. Nanke and E. Kuntze : *Mon. Pol. Vat.*, V-VII, 1923-1950.
[52] A memorandum on the conditions in the diocese of Wilno was submitted to Bishop Radziwiłł by Possevino on his way to Moscow, in July 1581 ; *Mon. Pol. Vat.*

after studying that charter realized that its concessions were " totally based upon the agreement between Greeks and Latins achieved at the Council of Florence. " In full agreement with Possevino [53], they convinced the Nuncio and tried to convince the King, that these privileges had ceased to be valid since the Ruthenians had turned away from the Florentine Union. The King was opposed to any such pressure, pointing out that the Ruthenians had enjoyed the said privileges " even after apostasy, " but it seemed that even the possibility of their cancellation would make many of them " abandon the schism ". Under such conditions the papal appeal to their hierarchy could seem premature, especially as their most prominent lay leader, Prince Constantine Ostrogski, in his discussions with Bolognetti and Possevino, allegedly conducted with the knowledge of the King and of the Ruthenian clergy, seemed rather conciliatory and even favorable to the fantastic project of a Greek exile, Dionysius Palaeologus, to establish in his city of Ostrog a Catholic Patriarchate of Greek rite. [54]

There was, however, another, much more serious reason why the Holy See may have decided to limit its action in Poland to such individual negotiations without, for the time being, approaching the local hierarchy, and otherwise simply to wait for the results of the literary propaganda and of the educational efforts in which Possevino himself was particularly interested. [55] Even he, who sometimes would consider, just like the Nuncio, that the particular rites of the Ruthenians should be tolerated only temporarily, was thinking not only of the gradual acceptance of the Latin rite, but also of a return to the " ancient and legitimate " rites of the Greeks. [56] And this was possibly connected with the renewed hope of the Papacy to achieve through direct negotiations with the Greeks themselves not any regional union, but a general union with the whole Greek Orthodox Church, in agreement with the original character of the Union of Florence. To have that Union accepted by Moscow had once more proved impossible. But would it not have been an even greater success to gain for reunion the traditional head of the Eastern Church, the Patriarch of Constantinople

---

IV, Appendix 20 (see particularly the reference to the Orthodox population whose conversion could have repercussions as far as Moscow, on p. 842.)

[53] He would return to this problem in his *Bibliotheca Selecta*, Coloniae, 1607, Lib. VI, pp. 243 f., writing " de ratione agendi cum Graecis et Rutenis, " especially those living in Lithuania.

[54] See Chodynicki, *op. cit.*, 246ff., but also, in addition to the sources quoted there, later references to the rather ambiguous role of Dionysius Palaeologus : *Mon. Pol. Vat.*, VI, Nr. 295, and VII, Nr. 206.

[55] *Ibidem*, 235 f. ; particularly important was the foundation in Wilno, besides the Jesuit University, of a special college or rather seminary for " iuvenes scholares Rutheni et Moschovitae " — see the papal bull of Feb. 2, 1582, *Documenta Pontif. Rom.* I, Nr. 123, where (Nr. 124-128) also the papal letters sent in 1583 to the Princes Ostrogski and Słucki have been published.

[56] *Supplementum ad Hist. Russ. Mon.*, 39.

himself who would be followed by both the Muscovites and the Ruthenians of the Commonwealth ?

Such a hope could seem an even greater illusion than that of gaining Moscow through direct negotiations with her Orthodox ruler. For under Ottoman rule the Patriarchs of Constantinople, entirely dependent on the Sultans, were supposed to avoid any contact with the Papacy, the main enemy of the Ottoman Empire, and to remain in absolute opposition against the Union of Florence and its possible revival. Less obnoxious from the Turkish point of view were, on the contrary, relations between the Patriarchate and the Protestants, the Western opponents of the Vatican. And even before a common front of Protestants and Orthodox against Catholicism and its plans of reunion with the Ruthenians was established in the Polish-Lithuanian Commonwealth, Protestant theologians of the German Universities of Wittenberg and Tübingen tried to gain the Greek Patriarch of Constantinople for some kind of religious union or at least cooperation against the Papacy. [57] However, these negotiations which started in 1576, during the first period of the rule of Patriarch Jeremiah II (1572-1579), ended in failure in 1581, when that Patriarch, one of the most prominent,[58] having been restored to his position after a brief interruption, definitely rejected these proposals.

That " censure " of Protestantism by the Eastern Church was first published in a Latin translation in Cracow as early as 1582 by the Polish theologian Stanislaus Sokołowski, [59] a former preacher at Batory's, court who had received the Greek original from a canon of Cracow of Dalmatian origin. But already in 1578, Sokołowski had met in Lwów with a Greek emissary of the Patriarch, Archimandrite Theoleptus (possibly the future Patriarch in the years 1585-1586), who told him about the polemics with the Protestants and later sent him from Constantinople the first answer of Jeremiah II. Even before being printed in Poland and reprinted in Germany and France, Sokołowski's manuscript with his autographic annotations was sent to the Vatican where that evidence of agreement between Latins and Greeks in their opposition against Protestantism was, of course, welcomed and seemed to confirm an earlier report on Jeremiah's friendly attitude toward Catholicism, brought to Rome by another Dalmatian, the Bishop of Nona Peter Cedulini who had been received by the Patriarch in March

---

[57] See about the whole background E. Benz, *Die Ostkirche im Lichte der protestantischen Geschichtsschreibung*. Freiburg, München 1952, 9-38.

[58] A brief but excellent biography of Jeremiah Tranos was published by L. Petit in *Dictionnaire de théologie catholique*, VIII-1 (Paris 1934), col. 886-894 ; see col. 886-889 about his relations with the Protestants.

[59] See H. Cichowski, *Ks. Stanisław Sokołowski a Kościół Wschodni* (Rev. St. S. and the Eastern Church), Lwów 1929.

1580, when visiting on the instruction of Gregory XIII the Catholic Chur-ches in Turkey. [60]

All this encouraged the Pope to send in the spring of 1582 a represent-ative to Constantinople, the Venetian Livius Cellini, [61] who joined an embassy of the Republic of Venice to the Sultan, but was received by the Patriarch on May 28 and had an opportunity to tell him about the friendly attitude towards the Greeks of the Pope himself and of his main collaborator in matters related to the Eastern Church, Cardinal Sirleto. However, Cellini's chief assignment was to gain Jeremiah II for the reform of the calendar which Gregory XIII had recently announced and which was to remain associated with his name. The Pope was rightly proud of that scholarly achievement and it seemed that an agreement in that purely scientific matter would be comparatively easy and open the door to an understanding between Greeks and Latins in more important and difficult religious matters. Unfortunately, what really happened, was just the contrary : it was to appear very soon that the Eastern Churches would reject the proposed change in the calendar, justified as it was from a scientific point of view, simply because it was introduced by the Pope — a reason which they shared with the Protestants — and also because of their conservatism which was shocked by any innovations affecting religious customs, including in that case the date of celebrating the Easter feast. [62] A new object of heated controversy was thus introduced into the relations between Catholics and Orthodox wherever they were living together, and more than any other dispute it was to affect their daily intercourse, as it was to be experienced particularly in the Polish-Lithuanian Commonwealth at the time of the Union of Brest.[63]

That the matter was much more delicate than expected, this was discovered already by Cellini : the Patriarch resented that the reform had been decided upon in advance without consulting him, and only when the papal representative pointed out that the bull regarding the reformed calen-dar was to come in force only a few months later, did he make rather vague oral promises of agreement and wrote in the matter to his own representative in Venice [64] which also had both Catholic and Orthodox subjects and therefore was interested in a solution of the problem. Neverthe-less, Gregory XIII, encouraged by Cellini's rather optimistic reports, [65] not only sent another mission to Jeremiah II in February 1583, chosing this time two highly educated Greeks, but in his letter which they brought

[60] On Cedulini's mission see Pastor, *Gesch. d. Päpste*, IX, 738-740.

[61] On this and the following missions of Gregory XIII to Constantinople see G. Hofmann, *Griechische Patriarchen und römische Päpste*, II 4. *Patriarch Jeremias II*, in *Orientalia Christiana*, XXV-2 (1932), 228 ff.

[62] Pastor, *op. cit.*, IX, 205-215.

[63] Chodynicki, *op. cit.*, 188-192.

[64] Published by G. Hofmann, *op. cit.*, doc. Nr. 4.

[65] *Ibidem*, doc. Nr. 1-3.

to Constantinople added again to his words of appreciation for the negative answer given to the German Protestants, an appeal to accept the calendar reform. While, however, the first part of the papal message was well received by the Patriarch who once more declared his opposition against Protestantism, he was evasive as far as the calendar was concerned asking for another delay of two years which would enable him to get in touch with the followers of the Greek Church scattered in other countries, mentioning in particular Wallachia, Moldavia, Poland and Russia. [66]

Writing at the same time in August 1583 to the Pope and to Cardinal Sirleto, [67] Jeremiah II praised their attitude towards the Greeks and went so far as to express his pleasure because of the foundation, by Gregory XIII, of the Greek College in Rome, that center of Catholic propaganda. He also thanked the Cardinal for sending him his memorandum on the calendar reform, though, as a matter of fact, he had already taken a negative decision in that matter: as early as July 9 of the same year Prince Constantine Ostrogski received in far away Volhynia a message of the Patriarch of Constantinople with whom he was in close contact and who, after consulting with the Patriarch of Alexandria, advised him not to accept the new calendar. [68] Though the Prince requested and received from Possevino material in defense of the reform and though, therefore, Rome was soon informed about these disappointing developments, [69] Gregory XIII in March 1584 decided to send again to Constantinople one of the Greeks who had negotiated on his behalf with the Patriarch a year before, raising once more the calendar problem. [70]

Unfortunately, however, before the papal representative could reach the Patriarch, Jeremiah II was arbitrarily deposed by the Turks and emprisoned on the island of Rhodus, while his rival Pachomius, the Archbishop of Cesarea, who had intrigued against him, was made Patriarch. [71] It is highly significant that the victim was accused of having been in some kind of secret agreement with the Pope, and though in Rome this was declared entirely false, since the negotiations had been limited to the calendar issue and remained inconclusive anyway, Gregory XIII was in sympathy with the " doct and pious " Patriarch who now suffered persecution, considering

---

[66] *Ibidem*, doc. Nr. 6, p. 243.

[67] *Ibidem*, doc. Nr. 7 and 8.

[68] About this and other letters of the Patriarch sent to the Ruthenians in that matter see Chodynicki, *op. cit.*, 246.

[69] *Mon. Pol. Vat.*, VII (Cracoviae 1939-1950), Nr. 8 (Possevino to Galli, Jan. 1 1584) and Nr. 53 (reply of Feb. 11).

[70] Hofmann, *op. cit.*, 230.

[71] For this and the following see my remarks in " Rome, Constantinople et Moscou au temps de l'Union de Brest, " 448 ff., where also the reports of the papal nuncio in Venice (Vat. Archives, *Nunziatura di Venezia*, vol. 25, vol. 106v-107, 341) are used.

his successor " an ignorant man of bad character whom the whole Greek nation hated. " Furthermore, the Holy See decided to use the opportunity of that ecclesiastical conflict in Constantinople in order to promote the cause of religious reunion with part at least of Eastern Christendom and to combine the support of Jeremiah II with the old projects regarding the Orthodox peoples of the Ruthenian lands and possibly even of Muscovy by transferring the deposed Patriarch after his liberation " somewhere to Russia. " [72]

It was only natural that the Cardinal Secretary of State turned for advice in that delicate matter to Poland where Sokołowski's publication of Jeremiah's discussion with the Protestants had made the Patriarch highly appreciated among all those who realized the importance of reunion with the many Orthodox of the Commonwealth. [73] Both Nuncio Bolognetti and Father Possevino were consulted as best experts and instructed to approach in that matter the King himself. In view of the changed situation, another mission of Possevino to Moscow where Ivan the Terrible had died a few months before, was even considered. For in spite of the disappointing experiences with the late Tsar, the Holy See hoped once more, by bringing the deposed legitimate Patriarch to a place in Muscovy but near to Poland, to influence at the same time the Ruthenians of the Commonwealth and the Muscovites both of whom were, after all, " of the same rite " and were supposed duly to appreciate the advantage of having no longer to depend on Turkish controlled Constantinople. [74]

Stefan Batory was indeed less optimistic, not only with regard to the expected reunion with Rome of all followers of Jeremiah, but even more as to a common attitude in that matter of Ruthenians and Muscovites who, as he pointed out to Bolognetti, [75] being strongly opposed to each other, were likely to take different stands. Strange enough, Possevino was even more sceptical : [76] being rather doubtful as to Jeremiah's own intentions, he advised to bring him first of all to Rome and in any case not to send him to Muscovy where, if favorable to the union with the Latins, he would share the experience of Cardinal Isidore after the Council of Florence or those, more recent, of Maxim the Greek, imprisoned under Basil III and Ivan the Terrible. The new Tsar, Fedor, seemed to follow the religious policies of his father and grandfather and would, according to the well-informed Jesuit, prove as suspicious as they had been of both Latin influ-

---

[72] *Mon. Pol. Vat.*, VII, Nr. 141, 142 (letters of Card. Galli to Bolognetti and Possevino, of April 27, 1584).

[73] H. Cichowski, *op. cit.*, 139 f., where in the footnotes a letter of Sokołowski to his Dalmatian friend, written in 1583, is published.

[74] *Mon. Pol. Vat.*, VII, Nr. 142, p. 206.

[75] *Ibidem*, Nr. 206, p. 307-309 (Bolognetti's report of June 18, 1584).

[76] *Ibidem*, Nr. 258 (Possevino to Bolognetti, August 2, 1584) and 261 (Bolognetti's report of August 6).

ence and intrigues of the Turks to whom he might even extradite the Patriarch at any request.

Possevino came to the conclusion that Jeremiah ought to reside among the Ruthenians of Poland, preferably in Kiev, their age old religious center which was equally respected by the Muscovites whose own metropolitans had once resided there. And entering with his usual zeal into the details of carrying out that promising project, he recalled his recent, but rather neglected suggestion of sending an appeal to the Ruthenian hierarchy. [77] Never indeed would there have been a better occasion for sending them at last the delayed papal messages. Constructive, too, was Bolognetti's amendment to Possevino's scheme: since Kiev was so dangerously near to the Tartar and Muscovite border that neither the Ruthenian metropolitan nor the Catholic bishop of Latin rite really resided there any longer, he proposed to send the Patriarch rather to Lwów or Wilno [78] where he would be much more under Catholic influence. Last not least, there appeared a third alternative which before the end of August 1584 — the month of that exciting correspondence — both representatives of the Holy See duly stressed in their reports: [79] Prince Constantine Ostrogski whom both of them still hoped to gain for the cause of reunion, was so attached to Jeremiah that he seemed very anxious to receive him on his own estates. But sharing the opinion that the Patriarch's alleged negotiations with Rome in the matter of reunion were the real reason of his present misfortune, Ostrogski himself seemed to indicate in advance that, wishing to be of service to Jeremiah, he would hardly encourage his sympathies towards Rome. There reappeared in any case Prince Constantine's ambitious interest in the possible establishment of a Greek Patriarch at Ostrog.

Before, however, receiving such reports from Poland, the Holy See heard from Constantinople [80] that under the pressure of Greek public opinion the Turks themselves were reconsidering the case of the deposed Patriarch. It therefore seemed advisable not to interfere with his chances and instead of trying to liberate him, not without serious risks, through outside interference, wait for his release from prison and possible restitution, hoping that he would continue anyway to be well disposed towards the Catholics. The difficult plan of bringing him to either Poland or Muscovy was therefore dropped, and if Catholic influence contributed to Jeremiah's liberation by the Turks, it was that, purely political, of the ambassador to Constantinople of King Henri III of France with whom Jeremiah had entered into friendly

---

[77] *Ibidem*, Nr. 258, p. 386.

[78] *Ibidem*, Nr. 261, p. 392.

[79] *Ibidem*, Nr. 272 (Bolognetti's report of August 24) and 281 (Possevino's report of August 29).

[80] *Ibidem*, Nr. 269 (Galli to Bolognetti, August 18, 1584); see also Nr. 295 (September 29).

relations before, in connection with the French support for the Patriarch's candidate to the Principality of Wallachia. [81]   Whether religious relations with the Papacy would be possible for Jeremiah after his liberation, was of course very doubtful in advance, and though they deposed his rival, the Turks prohibited for several years his formal re-election to the patriarchal See.

In addition to that confused situation in Constantinople and to the precarious situation of Jeremiah on whom Rome had placed so high hopes in connection with the prospects for reunion in the Commonwealth, there were a few other reasons why even there these prospects were again delayed during the following years.   Nuncio Bolognetti who had so frequently discussed the problem of religious union with the King, died on his way to Rome in March 1585, and one month later the Pope himself who had been so deeply interested in the problem of reunion with all the Eastern Churches, died also.   His successor Sixtus V soon appointed another Nuncio to Poland, Girolamo de' Buoi, but his brief mission left little traces in the religious life of that country [82] and ended even before the death of King Stefan Batory, on December 12, 1586, which changed the situation altogether and in Rome was rightly considered a great loss not only for the Commonwealth but also for the Catholic Church.

The shock of Sixtus V who expressed his grief in moving terms [83] was particularly deep because the protracted negotiations of the Holy See with the King of Poland regarding an anti-Ottoman league seemed at last to lead to concrete results.   Batory who, were it only in view of his Hungarian origin, had always been anxious to fight the Turks, had felt obliged to delay any such action as long as he was threatened by Ivan the Terrible.   After the Tsar's death he conceived the bold plan first to get control of Moscow and then to lead the joint forces of all Eastern Europe against the Ottoman Empire.   He succeeded in convincing the Holy See of the practicability of such a scheme through the same Possevino who once had tried to reach the same goal by reconciling Batory and Ivan, and who continued to be considered in Rome the best expert on all Eastern European problems. [84]

---

[81] See Jeremiah's letter to Henri III, of 1583, published by G. Hofmann, *op. cit.*, doc. Nr. 9; see also N. Iorga, *Histoire des Roumains, V*, Bucarest 1940, 256.

[82] His reports to the Secretariate of State, from April 16, 1585, to January 13, 1586, are to be found in the Vatican Archives, *Nunz. di Polonia*, vol. 22, fol. 4-91 (see also in vol. 27A some papers relating to his mission); he regretted the untimely death of his predecessor (fol. 25v), reported on the death of the " heretical " Bishop of Kiev, Nicholas Pac (fol. 23), and recommended to the Holy See the brothers of George Radziwiłł (fol. 19, 25), then Bishop of Wilno, who later was to be a strong supporter of the Union of Brest.

[83] At the secret Consistory of January 7, 1587; Vatican Library, *Barb. lat.* 2886, fol. 225v, 2871, fol. 530.

[84] Pierling, *op. cit.*, II, 287-314 ; see now also L. Boratyński's monograph quoted

And as usually, the idea of a league in defense of Christendom against Islam, in whatever form it was expected to materialize, was connected with the hope of regaining the Eastern Churches for religious unity with Catholicism.

It was precisely in that connection that the King of Poland whom many of the Balkan Christians already considered their future liberator, recommended to Sixtus V, as before to Gregory XIII, exiles from the countries under Ottoman rule who were at the same time religious leaders, for instance, in 1586, the Archbishop of Ochrida Gabriel, who claimed to be a Patriarch and also a legate and vicar general of the Patriarch of Constantinople. [85] At the same time a rather enigmatic Greek metropolitan, after visiting Moscow where he found much "ignorance" and a young though very pious Tsar, passed through Lithuania and Poland on his way to the imperial court and seemed interested both in the liberation of the Greeks from Turkish rule and in their religious union with Rome. He assured that his people favored such a union which only the fear of the Turks hindered them to proclaim openly, and that the Patriarch of Constantinople himself was sending to the Pope two bishops with a declaration of obedience. Which of the rivaling Patriarchs had such intentions and whether such reports could be taken seriously was, of course, difficult to find out, though particularly Possevino was deeply interested. [86]

There is, however, no evidence that these prospects, whether the diplomatic action of the King in preparation of the league, which obviously had to remain secret, or the arrival of Greek emissaries who were or seemed to be favorable to reunion, promoted the cause of such a reunion among the Ruthenians of the Commonwealth. On the contrary, toward the end of the reign of Batory, who was himself seriously interested in whatever could favor the Catholic restoration but remained cautious and reserved in the matter of reunion with the Orthodox, [87] the chances of such a union seemed rather poor. It is true that Bolognetti when leaving Poland was hopeful as to the conversion of the Ostrogski family, convinced as he was that sooner or later the old Prince Constantine would follow the example of two of his sons. [88] But that powerful leader of the Orthodox, though

---

above in footnote 9 (up to the year 1584), and, for the last years of the reign, the article of St. Załęski in *Przegląd powszechny*, III (1884).

[85] A. Theiner, *Vetera monumenta Poloniae*, III, Nr. 2 ; see my comments in " Rome, Constantinople et Moscou, " 453 f.

[86] He received a detailed report in that matter, dated June 4, 1586, from the Jesuits of Wilno (Vat. Archives, *Nunz. di Polonia*, Add 2, fol. 124v ; Roman Archives of the Society of Jesus, *Opp.* NN 331, fol. 121) ; see my comments, *loc. cit.*, 452 f.

[87] Chodynicki, *op. cit.*, 261 n. 4, where the conflicting opinions in that matter are discussed in detail.

[88] *Mon. Pol. Vat.*, VII, Nr. 429, p. 665 (Bolognetti to Constantine Ostrogski jun., March 3, 1585) ; see also Nr. 396, p. 588 (about Ostrogski's eldest son, Janusz, already a zealous Catholic, who was named Palatine of Volhynia).

maintaining friendly relations with the Nuncio and showing his pleasure
and even respect when receiving letters and presents from the Pope, did
not hesitate to make it quite clear when discussing on such occasions with
Possevino [89] that, in spite of his interest in reunion, he considered both
religions, the Catholic and his own, equally good. Furthermore, all such
discussions were made more difficult than ever before because of the serious
troubles which were raised in Poland by the calendar reform which in agreement with the King's orders, the Latin Archbishop of Lwów, Solikowski,
tried to enforce. He was so violently opposed by the Orthodox Bishop
of that same city, Gregory Bałaban, that a compromise had to be negotiated which permitted the temporary use of both calendars. [90] The king
approved that agreement, but Possevino who in contradistinction to other
Jesuits attached much importance to that issue blamed the influence of
" heretics and politicians " in that matter, resented the exaggerated charges
against the Archbishop, and turned for the time being to some equally
exaggerated pessimism regarding the attitude of the Ruthenian hierarchy
and clergy. [91]

Even before Batory's death, a somewhat similar pessimism made a
Polish Jesuit, the same Benedict Herbest who had been the first to work
among the Ruthenians, criticize their " errors " so violently in a widely
distributed pamphlet, that not only the Orthodox were shocked but also
his superiors duly alarmed. [92] How Possevino himself, the most ardent partisan of reunion with the Eastern Church, now felt in that matter, was
expressed in a memorandum [93] which he drafted during the interregnum
after Batory, when he was consulted by a Polish prelate, Stanislaus Gomoliński, [94] as to the best candidates to the vacant throne, and strongly
warned against the possible election of Tsar Fedor. He was entirely right in
pointing out the danger of such a choice both for Poland's political independence and for the Catholic religion in that country, and it is well understandable that after his own experiences in Moscow he dismissed any illusions

[89] See *ibidem*, VII, Nr. 281, p. 434 f., Possevino's letter to Cardinal Galli, of Aug.
9, 1584.

[90] *Monumenta Confraternitatis Stauropigianae Leopol.* (ed. W. Milkowicz), I, Lwów
1895, Nr. 76 (Feb. 15, 1585) ; among the many references to that conflict in Bolognetti's reports those of August 24 and 29, 1584 (*Mon. Pol. Vat.*, VII, Nr. 272, p. 405
and Nr. 280, p. 427 f.) are particularly interesting.

[91] See my article " Possevino's last statement on Polish-Russian relations, " *Orientalia Christiana Periodica*, XIX (1953) ; the statement is published on pp. 298-302.
On the different attitude of other Jesuits as to the importance of the enforcement
of the revised calendar, see my comments on p. 285 and the sources quoted there
in n. 1.

[92] See *ibidem*, 286 n. 1. Herbest's pamphlet is reprinted in *Russkaia istor. bibl.*,
VII, col. 581-600 ; the shocking conclusions are on col. 597.

[93] This is the statement quoted above, note 91.

[94] As to the origin and purpose of that consultation see my comments, *ibidem*,
261 ff.

as to a possible conversion of the Tsar if and when he would be made King of Poland. But it is rather surprising that, on that same occasion and without any apparent necessity, Possevino made far reaching charges against the Ruthenian *Vladicae ac Poppi*, calling those bishops and priests " violent enemies of the Catholics " and suspecting them even of possible attempts against the lives of the Catholic bishops. [95] Though he could point out the abandonment of the Union of Florence even " *in Russia Poloniae subiecta* " and the pressure which the Ruthenians exercised upon the royal administration in order to enjoy nevertheless the rights granted to them in view of that Union, the passage on these internal conditions in the Commonwealth, which Possevino inserted in his memorandum, is so obviously biased, that it is not easy to explain his exaggerations so different from his usual approach to the problem.

Probably he used the severe criticism of the Orthodox inside Poland as one more argument against the possible election of an Orthodox King. Furthermore, he was, in general, in a rather pessimistic mood, regretting Batory's untimely death, resenting the recent orders to interrupt all his political activities, and realizing that he would have to leave Poland where he was never permitted to work again. [96] It is true that his recall had nothing to do with the problem of reunion between the Western and the Eastern Churches, but resulted from the papal decision to support the Austrian candidate to the Polish throne, while Possevino was known to favor the Swedish Vasa. However, that purely political division among Catholics and, in particular, the complete absorption of the new nuncio in Poland, Hannibal of Capua, by his diplomatic action in the interest of Austria, [97] was at the same time another important reason why, in the critical year of 1587, the relations with the Orthodox Ruthenians ceased to receive that careful attention which the representatives of the Holy See had given them throughout Batory's reign.

When the Nuncio's commitment on the side of Archduke Maximilian became a source of embarrassment to the Vatican and when Pope Sixtus V turned to the more appropriate scheme of mediation between the two rivals, both equally good Catholics, the victorious Sigismund III and the Habsburg, taken a prisoner by Jan Zamoyski, that delicate mission was entrusted to a special papal Legate, Cardinal Ippolito Aldobrandini. [98] After long negotiations he succeeded in having a treaty signed in Będzin on March 9, 1589, but had, of course, to concentrate on that assignment without much

---

[95] *Ibidem*, 299 f. and the comments, 278 f.

[96] *Ibidem*, 265 f.

[97] Described in detail by Cz. Nanke, *Z dziejów polityki Kurii rzymskiej wobec Polski* 1587-1589 (The Policy of the Papal Curia toward Poland), Lwów 1921.

[98] The diary of his mission and the papers regarding the negotiations in Będzin have been published in Polish transl. by E. Rykaczewski, *Relacje nuncjuszów*, II.

time left for any other problems. Nevertheless, when a few years later, he was elected Pope as Clement VIII, in 1592, the unusual experience of his earlier mission to Poland was to prove of great importance for the Union of Brest which was even called a fruit of that mission. [99]

This was true, to a certain extent, for at least two reasons. His visit to a distant part of Europe where no other Pope before him had ever been, made him acquainted with and interested in the Slavic peoples. Furthermore, as legate to Poland, Cardinal Aldobrandini had made many friends among the Polish magnates and bishops, including those who were to be instrumental in the preparation of the Union with the Ruthenians. Nevertheless, it was precisely during his mission in 1588 that he, too, failed to seize an extraordinary opportunity to promote not only such a union, but an agreement with the Patriarch of Constantinople himself, in the line of the earlier projects of Skarga and Possevino.

[99] G. Hofmann, " Wiedervereinigung der Ruthenen mit Rom, " *Orientalia Christiana*, III-2, (1925), 167 ; see below, Part IV.

CHAPTER II

A PATRIARCH OF CONSTANTINOPLE IN THE COMMONWEALTH, 1588-1589

The visit of Patriarch Jeremiah II in the Ruthenian lands of Poland and Lithuania, in 1588 and 1589, was an entirely exceptional event. On several earlier occasions representatives of the Patriarchate of Constantinople including Patriarchs of the other oriental Sees, [1] had appeared there, and such appearances were to occur also later, under the most diverse circumstances. Similarly, prominent Greek laymen, favorable to Catholicism and suffering persecution from the Turks, would time and again pass through Poland. Even Nuncio Hannibal of Capua, otherwise scarcely concerned with any eastern problems, issued in the critical summer of 1587, waiting in Warsaw for the result of the Polish election, a warm letter of recommendation for one of them, [2] a descendant of the imperial Phocas family, who had approached Popes Gregory XIII and Sixtus V. But never before nor afterwards did the Greek Patriarch himself come to far away northeastern Europe with a view of interfering personally with the religious situation among the eastern Slavs.

The hopes that Jeremiah II, when deposed by the Turks, could be brought there after liberation and perhaps persuaded to make an agreement with the Holy See, had soon been given up at the time of Batory's reign. [3] But after hardly four years, when Sigismund III was consolidating his rule in Poland, that same Patriarch, free from Turkish jail, visited that country on his own initiative and seemed to favor a reunion of the Greek and Latin Churches. Further events were to prove that he was far from being definitely decided to take such a step, and at the given moment he had not yet regained his authority in Constantinople, where after Pachomius no less than three Patriarchs succeeded one another within a few years. [4] Yet, that initiative and favorable disposition of the prominent man who, in spite of all the fluctuations in the attitude of the Turks, could be considered

---

[1] Most recently, in 1586, the Patriarch of Antioch Joachim ; see *Monumenta Confraternitatis Stauropig.*, I, Nr. 80 and 82 a (in Arabic).

[2] Vatican Archives, *Arch. Nunz. Vars.* vol. 158, fol. 56 (July 24, 1587).

[3] See above, in the preceding chapter, p 217.

[4] *Dictionnaire de théologie catholique*, VIII-1, col. 886, where L. Petit pointed out that the last two of these Patriarchs were themselves partisans of Jeremiah II.

the only legitimate Patriarch, seemed so promising that it was taken very seriously by the highest Polish authorities, both secular and spiritual.

Particularly significant in that respect was the interest in that extraordinary opportunity which was manifested by the Grand Chancellor, Jan Zamoyski himself who, in spite of the opposition he had to face during the interregnum after his close friend King Stefan Batory, continued to be the most powerful and influential personality in Poland. [5] If that statesman who, in spite of his very sincere Catholic convictions, was first of all a realistic politician and at the given moment was kept busy with the struggle against Archduke Maximilian and his partisans, carefully studied the proposals of Patriarch Jeremiah and in a long letter [6] brought them to the attention of the papal Legate, the matter must have been in his opinion an important development with concrete chances of success. He even saw a possibility of returning to the project of transferring the see of the Greek Patriarchate to Kiev, a project which only four years before had raised so much interest in Rome and which now seemed so much easier to carry through, since Jeremiah himself was discussing the issue with the Grand Chancellor visiting him at Zamość.

When Cardinal Aldobrandini received that letter dated October 5, he had already more detailed information on all the religious implications of the Patriarch's visit to Poland, because the Nuncio had communicated to him at once a letter written as early as August 23 by the Latin Bishop of Łuck, Bernard Maciejowski, [7] full of hope regarding the prospects of reunion with the Eastern Church and including concrete proposals as to the procedure to follow. That letter deserved special attention were it only because of the personality of the writer who in Poland's religious life was as outstanding as was Zamoyski in politics. While in a recent past, in connection with the religious crisis of the mid-century, some of the Latin Bishops in the eastern borderland had been hardly more reliable than the Greek — to mention only the notorious Nicolaus Pac, practically a Calvinist, who nevertheless continued to consider himself Bishop of Kiev until his death in these very years [8] — there was now a definite change to the better, and in particular Maciejowski, though only recently ordained as priest and almost immediately elevated to the bishopric of Łuck, was known to the Nuncio as a

---

[5] K. Lepszy, *Walka stronnictw w pierwszych latach panowania Zygmunta III* (The Struggle of Parties in the first years of the reign of Sigismund III), Kraków, 1929, describes the whole political background.

[6] *Archiwum Jana Zamoyskiego* (The Archives of J. Z., ed. K. Lepszy), IV (Kraków 1950), Nr. 1329, p. 249.

[7] A. Theiner, *Vetera Monumenta Pol.*, III, Nr. 46, p. 41 f.

[8] Rumors about the death of this deposed " intruder " to the bishopric of Kiev (see also *Mon. Pol. Vat.*, VII, Nr. 273, p. 412) were already heard in 1585 (Vatican Archives, *Nunz. di Pol.*, vol. 22, fol. 23), but actually he did not die before 1589 ; see the list of bishops in *Sacrum Poloniae Millennium*, I, Rome 1954, 529.

man of extraordinary piety and virtue. [9] And no other bishop of Latin rite was to prove more interested in religious reunion with the Ruthenians for whom he had the greatest possible sympathy and who constituted the great majority of the population in his diocese, Łuck being at the same time the see of a Greek bishopric.

The project which Maciejowski now submitted to the representatives of the Holy See had been considered already before the arrival of Patriarch Jeremiah. And most important, it had been suggested first by one of the Ruthenians themselves, a prominent nobleman though not belonging to the most powerful aristocratic families like the Ostrogskis, the Judge of Brest, Adam Pociej, [10] recently reconverted from Calvinism to Orthodoxy and even more recently elevated to the senatorial office of Castellane of Brest. There appeared thus for the first time the man who, more than anybody else was to contribute to the Union, concluded eight years later in that very city. The Jesuits whom Bishop Maciejowski had invited to send from their college of Jarosław — in the Lwów region — a mission to Volhynia, were the first to know [11] that a movement in favor of reunion was developing in the Brest district, in the neighborhood of Volhynia though in the limits of the Grand Duchy of Lithuania, and that Pociej, though still fluctuating in his mind, was more and more inclined to Catholicism. In the presence of one of these Jesuits, he spoke with Maciejowski early in 1588 about the possibility of a religious union of the Ruthenians with Rome " precisely at the time when the Byzantine Patriarch would be present " ; for it was already known that coming to Poland, he would hold in Wilno a synod with his bishops of eastern rite.

A little later the Jesuits of Nieśwież — in the very center of the White Ruthenian part of the Grand Duchy, where Prince Nicholaus Christopher Radziwiłł, another prominent magnate who was to promote the Union of Brest, had recently founded a Jesuit College which in that rather small and isolated place developed unexpectedly well, [12] also reported to Rome [13] that the Orthodox clergy of that region was getting interested in religious reunion but that the decision had been postponed to a convention soon to

---

[9] *Nunz. di Pol.* vol. 28, fol. 52v (letter of March 26, 1587, to the Chapter of Łuck) ; see his biographical data in *Sacrum Pol. Mill.* I, 508.

[10] See his detailed biography up to 1599 by I. Savicky in *Jubilejna Kniha v 300-litni rokovini smerti Mitropolita Jpatiya Potiya* (Memorial volume on the occasion of the 300th anniversary of the death of Metropolitan I. P.), Lviv 1914, 1-133.

[11] *Annuae Litterae Societatis Jesu* 1588, Romae 1590, 115 (in the report of the " Missio Voliniensis ").

[12] Among the many reports on the development of that college, the letter of Cardinal George Radziwiłł, a brother of the founder, to Cardinal Montalto, sent from Nieśwież on Sept. 15, 1589, deserves special attention (*Nunz. di Polonia*, vol. 31, fol. 77).

[13] *Annuae Litterae Soc. Jesu* 1589, Romae 1591, 136.

15

be gathered in Wilno where Patriarch Jeremiah was to be present on his arrival from Turkey.

The movement was, therefore, already widespread but when the Patriarch really established contacts with those interested in the matter, it was decided to hold the synod of the Orthodox hierarchy not in Wilno but in Brest where the other high officials though Protestants, seemed sympathetic, [14] not without influence of Maciejowski and the Jesuits, and where a discussion of all dogmatic issues was to take place, resulting — as Maciejowski and his collaborators earnestly hoped — in a formal proposal of religious reunion. This was the promising prospect which the Bishop of Łuck, full of enthusiasm, outlined to the Nuncio and which seemed to be fully confirmed by Zamoyski's letter, written a few weeks later to the Legate after his talks with the Patriarch himself.

Cardinal Aldobrandini realized at once the importance of the matter and, under the impression of Maciejowski's communication, reported already on September 6 [15] — one day after the Nuncio [16] — to the Secretary of State Cardinal Montalto on the possibility that Catholic bishops and even Archbishops would meet the representatives of the Greek hierarchy somewhere in Poland in a " disputation " which would even " determine questions of dogmatic character. " But precisely in that interpretation, the project seemed to him rather too ambitious, since, as he pointed out, this was not a matter to be settled at a provincial Council and since the general Council of Florence had already determined the conditions of reunion between the Greek and the Latin Churches. The Legate therefore concluded that, in a so serious problem, he would not take any decision "without special orders from His Holiness. "

If, when writing this, Cardinal Aldobrandini had already been in possession of Zamoyski's additional information, he would have been perhaps more optimistic, but even more convinced that the project, connected as it was to be with the transfer of the residence of the Greek Patriarch, was aiming not at any regional union but, like in Florence, at a general union with the whole Greek East. It also was understandable that the idea of deciding such an issue of universal significance in some obscure place in the Ruthenian provinces of Poland or Lithuania, seemed rather surprising. And nobody, of course, remembered that a somewhat similar idea had appeared as early as 1396 when soon after the original political union of Poland and Lithuania a Council was supposed to meet somewhere in their Ruthenian lands with a view of preparing a general religious union between East and West. [17] Then the Patriarch residing in a still unconquered though

---

[14] *Ibidem* 1588, 116.
[15] Theiner, *op. cit.*, III, Nr. 61, p. 72.
[16] *Ibidem*, Nr. 60, p. 61.
[17] See above, Introduction, p. 25.

already seriously threatened Constantinople had no intention of coming there
and the Papacy suffered from the Great Western Schism. Now the Holy
See, so much stronger after the Council of Trent, was still looking for
evidence that the Patriarch who for unknown purposes had travelled so
far, was really considering a return to the Union of Florence. This was probably the reason why the decision of Sixtus V, sent to the Nuncio in Poland
already on October 1,[18] almost immediately after receiving his report of
September 5 and before Zamoyski's letter was even written, was so unusually
brief and completely negative. After saying that Hannibal's last reports
did not require any detailed answer, Cardinal Montalto simply wrote : " The
advice of the Bishop of Łuck to reunite the Latin Church with the Greek
is a Greek vanity and therefore does not deserve any basic consideration. "

If Cardinal Aldobrandini received any special answer which is unknown,
it was certainly quite similar, and occupied with his diplomatic negotiations,
he did not insist, having been rather doubtful himself. Dismissing the project as a " Greek vanity, " the Vatican clearly indicated that its distrust
was directed against the Patriarch of Constantinople and not against Maciejowski who continued to enjoy full confidence in Rome where he was soon
to appear in person.[19] He also was to increase there the interest in the
Ruthenian problem, an interest which, after the disappointing experiences
of the last years, was obviously much smaller than that in the more limited
project of promoting religious reunion in nearby Moldavia. For in the
same years, from 1583 through 1589,[20] strenuous efforts were made to win
for Catholicism the frequently changing princes of that land which always
had close relations with Poland, and possibly even those of Wallachia.
According to the well informed Polish Jesuits[21] who participated in that
action, the Orthodox peoples of these Danubian principalities, especially of
Moldavia, were not at all anxious to recognize the authority of the Patriarchs
of Constantinople who so obviously depended on the Turks, and this might
have contributed to Rome's more optimistic approach, and also to the
interest shown in that matter by the Latin Archbishop of Lwów, J. D.
Solikowski. As a matter of fact, before Solikowski took an active part in
the reunion of the Ruthenians with whom he had much trouble in his
diocese, he made tireless efforts in promoting the negotiations with Moldavia,
a question which was specifically entrusted to him by the Holy See[22] and

[18] Vat. Arch., *Nunz. di Polonia*, vol. 23, fol. 262, partly quoted by E. Šmurlo,
Russia i Italia (Russia and Italy), II-1, St. Petersburg 1911, 152.

[19] See below, Chapter III, p. 237, 246.

[20] The references to that Moldavian project, which are very frequent in the papers
of the papal missions to Poland, have been collected by Šmurlo, *op. cit.*, II-2, Appendix
X, 425-505. See also Chodynicki, *op. cit.*, 252-255 and N. Iorga, *Histoire des Roumains*,
V, 284.

[21] See, for example, the report on the " Missio Moldavica " and its historical
background in *Annuae Litterae S. J.* 1588, 100-104.

[22] Theiner, *op. cit.*, III, Nr. 87, p. 111.

precisely in 1588 seemed to develop very satisfactorily. For at the very time when the possibility of negotiating with Patriarch Jeremiah on the occasion of his visit to Poland was considered in vain, two envoys of Prince Aaron of Moldavia, Jeremiah Movila, later his successor and particularly friendly to Poland, and the Albanian Bartholomeus Brutti, arrived there and made before Cardinal Aldobrandini a declaration of obedience to the Holy See, calling also at the Grand Chancellor in Zamość. [23]

All this, desirable as it was from both the Catholic and the Polish point of view, could, however, not compare in importance with the perspectives of a general union of the Latin and Greek Churches nor even with that of a regional union with the Ruthenians. Furthermore, it soon became apparent that even in the Danubian principalities which themselves depended so much on the attitude of the Ottoman Empire, the influence of the Patriarchate of Constantinople was not at all negligible. On the other hand, it was not only the Vatican and its representatives who had little confidence in Patriarch Jeremiah and the chances of an agreement with him. Such was also the attitude of the majority of the Polish hierarchy which meeting on October 2, 1589, at their provincial synod in Piotrków, expressed their concern with the presence in the kingdom of " a certain alleged Patriarch " who along with the Ruthenian bishops was creating trouble for the Catholics. The King was requested to keep them within the limits of their own jurisdiction and the acceptance by the Ruthenians of the Gregorian Calendar was once more to be enforced. [24]

Whether these complaints were justified or not, it was highly significant and seemed to confirm the suspicions of the Latin side that, even before Rome's negative reaction, Patriarch Jeremiah had left for Moscow where, after passing in June through Smolensk, he arrived on July 11, 1588. [25] Most probably he had planned in advance to visit both the Ruthenian lands of the Polish-Lithuanian Commonwealth and the Orthodox power east of it where a little earlier, in 1585-86, along with the Patriarch of Antioch two Greek emissaries from Constantinople had tried to obtain, as usual, financial subsidies for the Eastern Church under Turkish rule. [26] It is true that these two bishops had been sent to Moscow by one of Jeremiah's rivals, Theoleptus II whom the Turks had placed on the patriarchal see ; but for the man who all the time considered himself the only legitimate Patriarch, this was just one more reason to do what none of his predecessors had ever undertaken : to go to Moscow in person looking for her support not only in the continuous financial plight of his Church, but also

---

[23] *Ibidem*, Nr. 52, 54, 55; see also Nr. 16, 38, 49, 50, 65, 79.

[24] *Ibidem*, Nr. 91, p. 118.

[25] See in his biography in *Dictionnaire de théologie cathol.*, VIII-1, col. 892-894, the chapter on the foundation of the Patriarchate in Moscow.

[26] A. M. Ammann, *Abriss der ostslavischen Kirchengeschichte*, 231 f.

in his own troubles. When still in Poland, Jeremiah met there at Zamoyski's residence one of these Greek bishops, Arsonius of Elasson, who on his way back from Moscow stopped in Lwów and being obviously not too anxious to return to Constantinople, accepted there a position as teacher of Greek in the school of the newly formed Orthodox Brotherhood. And he must have heard from him what Moscow most urgently wanted in return for her assistance : the elevation of her Metropolitan to the rank of a Patriarch.

It is well known that this was granted by Jeremiah during his visit at the court of Tsar Fedor, but not before January 26, 1589, when the formal installation of Metropolitan Job of Moscow as Patriarch took place at a synod of the Muscovite hierarchy. And it was not before May of that year that the Patriarch of Constantinople issued in Moscow a solemn charter, confirming that elevation and the reorganization of the Orthodox Church within the limits of the Tsardom. All these delays can be explained to a large extent by the protracted negotiations regarding the final recognition of the full autonomy of the Muscovite Church under the Tsar and the rank which the new Patriarch of Moscow would occupy among the other Patriarchs of Eastern Christendom. But as to the first of these questions, Jeremiah was ready from the outset to recognize a situation which *de facto* existed from the middle of the fifteenth century, and as to the second, it could not be finally settled in Moscow, but had to be left to a synod in Constantinople where the other eastern Patriarchates would be represented. There was, however, another issue which had to be decided first, and probably not without some difficulty.

In view of the uncertainty of his own position in Constantinople, Jeremiah seems to have been seriously interested in the project of transferring his residence to a country free from Ottoman control. Zamoyski's impression that he could be persuaded to remain in Kiev or, in general, in the Ruthenian lands of the Commonwealth was certainly more than wishful thinking. But since such a solution could easily lead to Latin influence upon the Patriarch, replacing the Turkish, and to a restoration of the Union of Florence for which Jeremiah was hardly prepared. it is no wonder that from such a solution for which the Latin side was not ready either, Jeremiah turned to another alternative. Just like Bishop Arsonius of Elasson who accompanied him to Moscow, the Patriarch was inclined to remain there himself. [27] Whether this was to be a transfer of the residence of the Patriarch of Constantinople, the head of the Eastern Church, or an acceptance by Jeremiah of the new position of Patriarch of Moscow, is impossible to find out, the negotiations being of course secret. What seems certain is

---

[27] About the different attitude of his other Greek companion, Hierotheus of Monembasia, see *Dictionnaire de théol. cath., loc. cit.*

that neither of these possibilities satisfied the Tsar and his adviser, Boris Godunov, who wanted Moscow itself to be recognized as the Third Rome, with a Muscovite, chosen by the Tsar, appointed as Patriarch of the " Great Russian Tsardom " and serving as a tool of its autocrat. That is precisely what Jeremiah approved and stressed himself in so many words when answering the Tsar's address on the occasion of Job's ordination. [28]

Whether the Patriarch who had to leave for Constantinople without having gained anything in return, was satisfied with such a solution, is of course another question. Nor were the other eastern Patriarchs who assigned to the new Patriarch of Moscow the fifth and last place, a decision which, as a matter of fact, was only natural, but during the following years caused a great deal of dissatisfaction in Moscow which requested in vain the third place, and a serious tension between the Tsardom and the Patriarch under Ottoman rule. [29] But in addition to this question of prestige, there was another reason why Moscow was disappointed and the apparent triumph of her diplomacy incomplete. In her interpretation, just like the Tsar had taken the place of the Orthodox Emperors of Constantinople, so the Muscovite Patriarchate was to replace the Greek and exercize its authority wherever Orthodox peoples were free from Muslim rule. Such an interpretation of the momentous decision of 1589 was included in the instructions of an embassy which in 1591 was sent from Moscow to the King of Poland. [30] The implication was clear enough : the new Patriarch of Moscow wanted to have over the Orthodox Ruthenians of the Commonwealth the same authority which was exercised hitherto by the Patriarch of Constantinople. Thus the result of the ecclesiastical separation of the metropolitan see of Kiev from that of Moscow, in 1458, was to be annulled and Moscow to obtain another juridical claim for interfering with the religious life in the Commonwealth. This serious political threat to the latter was at the same time a disappointment for the Papacy which in the past had considered the possibility that under a separate Patriarch, independent of Constantinople, Moscow could be more easily gained for religious reunion with Rome : [31] what happened was just the contrary, since in the same instruction, though addressed to a Catholic King, it was pointed out that the Popes had separated themselves from the true Greek faith. But Moscow's claim to control Kiev and all the eastern dioceses of Lithuania and Poland was also unacceptable to the Patriarch of Constantinople and therefore Jeremiah, in spite of the poor results of his first visit to the Commonwealth on his way to

[28] See the summary and interpretation of his speech by M. K. Medlin, *Moscow and East Rome*, 117.

[29] Ammann, *op. cit.*, 234.

[30] See Chodynicki, *op. cit.*, 259 f. and the references in notes 2 and 3.

[31] See above, p. 194.

Moscow, decided to stop there once more on his way back and to settle himself the religious problems of its Greek Orthodox population.

This time the problem of their religious reunion with Rome did not seem to be considered by anybody. No action was taken by those who during Jeremiah's first visit had expressed serious hopes in that connection, viz., Bishop Maciejowski and Chancellor Zamoyski. Rome did not interfere at all, Cardinal Aldobrandini having already returned from Poland and Hannibal of Capua nearing the end of his mission as Nuncio. And as to King Sigismund III, he merely acted as traditional protector of the Orthodox Church in the Commonwealth, as the Jagellonians had done before, and on July 15, 1589, issued a charter authorizing not only Jeremiah's sojourn in his realm, but any action he would take in religious matters. [32]

That action was unusually energetic and could be considered a last minute effort of the Patriarchate of Constantinople to reform the Ruthenian Church [33] on the ground of the Orthodox doctrine, in defense against Catholic propaganda, Protestant penetration, and internal disintegration, without caring for any possible interference, were it even in that same sense, which would come from the new Patriarchate of Moscow. The encouragement of the Brotherhoods where the opposition against Catholicism and reunion was strongest, was, on the one hand, an evidence that Jeremiah if he ever had any leanings towards Rome had given up any such projects, fully aware that they would impede his return to the patriarchal see to which he was at last formally restored by the Turks on July 4, 1589. On the other hand, the rights he granted to the Brotherhoods were seriously limiting the power of the bishops, and since such a policy could only increase the conflicts within the Ruthenian Church, it must be explained by Jeremiah's lack of confidence in the Ruthenian hierarchy. The same critical attitude is indicated by the changes he made in the composition of that hierarchy which were justified indeed by the poor qualifications of its members. This was particularly true with regard to the Metropolitan himself: Onesifor Dziewoczka who occupied the highest position in the Ruthenian Church from 1579, was even more unworthy of it than any of his predecessors in the sixteenth century. [34] A layman until his elevation to the see of Kiev, he neglected his ecclesiastical duties to such an extent that already in 1585 the Orthodox nobility wrote him a letter full of complaints. It is true that in that same year he obtained from the King a guarantee against any interference of the administration with his jurisdiction and the property of the Church. But he did not respect the ecclesiastical law himself and having remarried, tolerated second and third marriages among the clergy. This

---

[32] *Russk. istor. bibl.*, VII, col. 1117-1121, where that royal charter is reprinted in connection with the later polemics against the Union of Brest.

[33] See the interpretation by Chodynicki, *op. cit.*, 124-126.

[34] See *ibidem*, 128-130.

was the main reason why Patriarch Jeremiah, a few days after receiving the royal authorization to punish even the highest dignitaries of the Orthodox Church, on July 21, deposed the Metropolitan and replaced him by Michael Rahoza.[35] Six days later King Sigismund III confirmed that decision at the request, as he declared, of the whole Ruthenian nobility, it being understood that the new candidate would be duly consecrated by the Patriarch.[36]

Even more exceptional were the decisions taken by Jeremiah when, in August, he moved from Wilno to Brest : he gathered there a provincial synod of the Ruthenian hierarchy, instructed the new Metropolitan to hold such synods every year, and appointed at once an Exarch who after his return to Constantinople would be his personal representative in the Ruthenian lands.[37] This extraordinary assignment was given to the Bishop of Łuck, Cyril Terlecki, who was indeed considered a much more zealous pastor than the others. At the same time the Patriarch declared that the charges made against Terlecki by the Bishop of Lwów, Gedeon Bałaban, had proved completely unjustified. But the elevation of the Bishop of Łuck to the rank of an Exarch was a disappointment not only to his personal enemy, a notorious troublemaker in conflict with the Brotherhood of Lwów,[38] but also to the hardly chosen Metropolitan whose authority was thus limited from the outset and who along with all the other members of the hierarchy was supposed to be under the control of Jeremiah's man of confidence. Another step in the same direction, resented not only by Bałaban but by all bishops and to a certain extent by the whole local clergy, was a far reaching privilege granted by the Patriarch to the Brotherhoods of Lwów and Wilno : though mainly composed of laymen, they were freed from episcopal jurisdiction and placed directly under the Patriarch to whom they could report on the whole religious situation. This, too, was confirmed by the King[39] who must have particularly welcomed Jeremiah's decision that no other foreign dignitaries of the Eastern Church, whether legitimate or usurpers, should exercise any power among the Orthodox of the Commonwealth[40] as they had tried to do on earlier occasions.

Along with other decrees which wanted to raise the moral standard of the Ruthenian clergy, the whole reform program of the first and last Patriarch of Constantinople ever to appear in these regions, could seem constructive and salutary amidst the religious crisis of his time. And his most important request to hold annual synods which would assure the continuity

---

[35] *Akty zapadnoi Rossii*, III, Nr. 149.
[36] *Ibidem*, IV, Nr. 19.
[37] *Ibidem*, IV, Nr. 21; see Iv. Franko in *Kwart. hist.*, IX (1895) 8-9.
[38] See his biography by Chodynicki in *Polski Słownik biograficzny*, I (1935), 249 f.
[39] *Akty zap. Rossii*, IV, Nr. 18.
[40] *Ibidem*, Nr. 20.

of these efforts, was strictly followed during the next years. The Patriarch had hardly left the Commonwealth in November 1589 when early in 1590 [41] a meeting of the Ruthenian Bishops took place in Bełz, obviously in preparation for the regular synod which in June was convoked in Brest where Jeremiah had started the whole movement. But the Patriarch had certainly not anticipated that that movement, far from strengthening the authority of Constantinople in the Ruthenian lands, would turn away the Orthodox of these lands from the Patriarchate and within a few years lead them back to religious union with Rome, to be finally ratified in that same city of Brest. [42]

Particularly surprising is that the first serious initiative in that respect was taken by the same Bishop Terlecki whom Jeremiah had chosen as his official representative and man of confidence, and who under such conditions had no personal reasons whatever for opposing the Patriarch. The question therefore arises whether Jeremiah who during his first visit in the Commonwealth, in 1588, had experienced the growing interest in the problem of reunion with the Catholic Church, had not noticed during his second visit any such trends which were to appear so soon after his departure. In particular, it is difficult to understand that he left the supreme control of the Ruthenian hierarchy and clergy precisely to the bishop who obviously already then must have had some leanings towards Rome.

There are indeed only two possible interpretations of Jeremiah's policy : either he was very badly informed on the real situation and on the progress which the movement towards reunion with the Catholic Church was making among the Ruthenians including some of their most prominent ecclesiastical leaders, or he was himself not too strongly opposed to such a reunion in a country where the political situation was so much more favorable to such a step than it was in Constantinople. Such a possibility cannot be excluded in view of the Patriarch's own relations with Rome in earlier years, [43] his decided opposition to Protestant propaganda which he might have considered the greatest danger for the Ruthenians, and the impression which he created at the time of his first visit in the Commonwealth, in 1588, before he went to Moscow. If so, it was regrettable from the Catholic point of view that, in spite of Zamoyski's and Maciejowski's suggestions, no advantage had been taken of Jeremiah's favorable dispositions on that earlier

---

[41] The exact date of that preparatory meeting is not known, since there is only a brief reference to it in the decisions taken in Brest on June 20 (*ibidem*, IV, Nr. 25, p. 85).

[42] For all that follows until the end of this chapter, see *Appendix I* to the present edition.

[43] After studying these relations, J. Hofmann came, however, to the conclusion that Jeremiah, though strongly opposed to any union with the Protestants, could not decide either for any serious efforts in favor of a union with the Roman Church in spite of his acceptance of almost all its doctrines (*Orientalia Christiana*, XXV-2 (1932), 232).

occasion. Now, after his turn towards Moscow and on the eve of his final return to Constantinople, he obviously could not show openly even the slightest inclination towards Rome, though by strengthening in a last minute effort his own direct control of the Ruthenian Church, he was opposing not only Roman but Protestant and Muscovite influence as well, particularly any possible claims of the recently established Patriarchate of Moscow to authority over Kiev.

It is true that by strengthening at the same time the position of the Orthodox Brotherhoods, he seemed to favor those elements among the Ruthenians which were most hostile to reunion with Rome. [44] But that very step proved a stimulus to work for such a reunion, at least as far as the opponents of the growing influence of these Brotherhoods were concerned. This was naturally the case of Bishop Gedeon Bałaban, and it was recalled later when Bałaban greatly disappointed the sincere partisans of Rome, that it was precisely that bishop who first approached the Catholic hierarchy of Latin rite in the person of the Archbishop of Lwów with the request of liberate himself from the " slavery " under the Patriarch of Constantinople, giving as main reason the Patriarchs' support of the local Brotherhood and promising to be obedient to the Roman Pope. [45]

The exact date and circumstances of that incident remain unknown and certain is only that Bałaban was hardly motivated by any sincere religious conviction but rather by his personal interests. Therefore Archbishop Solikowski, though deeply interested in the problem of reunion with the Orthodox as he was showing it in his relations with Moldavia, did not take too seriously the proposal of the Ruthenian bishop of his own city with whom he had had until recently so many troubles, but simply referred him to the much more reliable Bishop of Łuck, Cyril Terlecki. That Bałaban followed this advice seems to result from the fact that he was one of the three bishops who joined Terlecki at the meeting in Bełz, on the eve of the Synod of Brest, in 1590, and who at the synod itself signed under Terlecki's inspiration a formal declaration in favor of reunion with Rome. [46]

That these important developments which were to lead to the Union of Brest, started in secrecy and as a personal initiative of a few bishops only, can be explained by the general confusion and the individual rivalries which the two visits of Patriarch Jeremiah had left behind in the Ruthenian lands of the Commonwealth. In that body politic which was in majority Catholic, under a Catholic King and a predominantly Catholic administration, the head of the Greek Orthodox Church had acted on two occasions in full liberty, without being exposed to any pressure as he always was in

---

[44] See about the origin and character of these Brotherhoods Chodynicki, *op. cit.*, 177-186.

[45] *Russk. istor. bibl.*, XIX, 617 f.

[46] See below, in the next chapter, p. 237.

Constantinople and to a large extent even in Moscow, and his decisions were sanctioned and confirmed by royal authority. But thanks to his own wavering, undecided attitude and perhaps also because of his insufficient understanding of the local conditions, he missed that last opportunity for successfully reorganizing the Ruthenian Church under the traditional leadership of the Greek Patriarchate. And perhaps the Catholic Church did miss at the same time a last opportunity to come to an understanding with a Patriarch of Constantinople who harassed by his Ottoman masters had come to Catholic lands, apparently ready for discussions which could have made the planned regional religious union a basis for some larger agreement. Only Moscow seized the unique opportunity offered to her by the Patriarch's visit, thus increasing her prestige with regard to both the Polish-Lithuanian Commonwealth and the Ottoman Empire.

CHAPTER III

THE INITIATIVE OF 1590 AND ITS CONSEQUENCES

The year 1590 and, in particular, the month of June of that year must be considered the decisive turning point in the history of the immediate preparations for the Union of Brest. Furthermore, it is evident that among the various events which made that year and that month so significant in the history of the Ruthenian Church, by far the most important occurred on the memorable day of June 24, the very day which almost at the same time was fixed as regular date of the annual synods to be held according to the instructions of Patriarch Jeremiah, the city of Brest being chosen as place of these meetings, following the precedent created by the Patriarch himself in August 1589. It was indeed on June 24, 1590, four days after the formal conclusion of the first of these synods that four bishops who had taken part in its deliberations issued a declaration of obedience to the Pope and determined the conditions on which they were ready to place their dioceses under his authority. [1] No similar initiative had been taken since 1500 when the Metropolitan Joseph II conceived his plan of restoring the Union of Florence in the Ruthenian lands.

There was, however, one notable difference : this time the initiative came not from the Metropolitan, the recently named Michael Rahoza who signed the other decisions of the synod on June 20, but not the declaration of June 24. The same is true of the local pastor : the Bishop of Brest and Volodymir in Volhynia. Only part of the hierarchy was already decided to return to the Florentine tradition. Therefore, the persons of these initiators of 1590 ought to be considered first.

The foremost of them was the Bishop of Łuck, Cyril Terlecki, and his support was of special value since he was the Exarch of the Patriarch of Constantinople, elevated to that exceptional position less than one year before by Jeremiah himself. It is easy to point out that this clever and energetic man was not free from personal ambition, [2] but morally and intellectually he was much superior to the average members of the contemporary Ruthenian hierarchy, and when King Stefan Batory confirmed his election a few years before, that decision was certainly in the interest of the Church.

---

[1] *Russk. istor. bibl.*, XIX, 55-57 ; as to the date see Chodynicki, *op. cit.*, 206 n. 1.
[2] About the various opinions regarding Terlecki see Chodynicki, 269 n. 2.

There is no evidence of any initial anti-Latin attitude of Terlecki, were it only in the matter of the Gregorian calendar,[3] but he was not under any Latin influence either, being not even familiar with the Latin language.[4] He could have rather been under the influence of Prince Constantine Ostrogski, the city of Ostrog being the second center of his diocese which included the main part of the rich province of Volhynia with its comparatively dense and almost exclusively Greek Orthodox population. On the other hand, it must be remembered that Łuck itself was the see of a Latin bishopric also, occupied for already more than two years by the zealous Bernard Maciejowski, though that Polish bishop who had shown so much interest in the reunion with the Ruthenians during Jeremiah's first visit, was in 1590 absent on a mission to Rome.[5] In any case, a man like Terlecki must have made his momentous decision of that year in full consciousness of his responsibility, and since he remained faithful to his first declaration throughout all the difficulties of the following years, it is only fair to consider it an expression of serious religious conviction.

For all these reasons, Terlecki hardly needed any spuring from Bałaban, the last of the signatories of the declaration, whose earlier record was so entirely different and who later, under the pressure of Prince Ostrogski, though rather distant from the Prince's main sphere of action and as Bishop of Lwów particularly subject to Latin and Polish influence, completely reversed his attitude. It is quite possible that in 1590 he joined Terlecki's initiative following the advice of the Latin Archbishop of Lwów to cooperate with the Bishop of Łuck.[6] But since Bałaban when turning to that Archbishop with his first pro-Roman statements, had admitted himself that he was chiefly prompted by his conflict with the Orthodox Brotherhood of Lwów, it is not unfair to suppose that this remained the basic reason of his temporary inclination toward reunion.

As to the two other signatories of the declaration of June 24, 1590, very little is known about Leontine Pełczycki, Bishop of Pinsk and Turov whose diocese, situated in the sparcely populated and backward region of the Pripet marshes, was the least important. Nevertheless, his participation deserved attention, not only because Latin influence was obviously weakest in that region, but also because his diocese was within the limits of the Grand Duchy of Lithuania, so that in view of his participation the initiative of 1590 was not limited to the Ruthenian lands of the Kingdom of Poland.

---

[3] See my remarks in *Orientalia Christiana Periodica*, XIX (1953), 285 n. 3.

[4] As evidenced at the conclusion of the Union in Rome, in Dec. 1595; see below, p. 329.

[5] As to the dates of his absence, from April 1590 to May or June 1591, E. Likowski, *Unia brzeska* (The Union of Brest), Warszawa 1907, 97 n. 2. See also Vat. Arch., *Nunz. di Polonia*, vol. 26, fol. 360.

[6] See above, in the preceding chapter, p. 234.

Pełczycki died shortly before the Union of Brest was finally concluded with the active participation of his successor. [7]

Both the declaration of 1590 and the Union of 1596, as well as the pro-Roman statements of the years between these two dates, were signed by Dionyse Zbirujski, Bishop of Chełm. Though he, too, is little known personally, his part is highly significant for two reasons. First, a statement he made later, on July 7, 1595, [8] confirmed clearly that, five years before, he and his three colleagues decided to place themselves under Rome's authority, because they did not want to be involved any longer in the disorderly conditions of the Orthodox Church. Secondly, it were the Bishops of Chełm, another diocese which had a Latin bishop besides the Greek and was close to Western influence, who preserved the famous charter of 1443 which had been granted to the Ruthenian Church in view of the Union of Florence and confirmed at the request of Zbirujski's predecessors at the Polish Diets of 1504 and 1543 [9] though that Union was no longer respected. In the declaration of 1590 the four bishops asked that all rights and liberties granted to the Ruthenian Church by the Kings of Poland be safeguarded and confirmed once more. And it was precisely in Bełz, the second center of Zbirujski's diocese, that a few bishops met before the June synod in Brest, probably inspecting the privilege of 1443, when discussing the conditions for reunion with Rome.

Unfortunately, nothing is known about these discussions, and the very fact of that preparatory meeting of part only of the hierarchy would be unkown if not a brief reference in one of the resolutions of the Synod of Brest, adopted by the Metropolitan and five bishops on June 20, 1590. [10] That resolution confirmed the decisions taken at the earlier meeting at Bełz where " some " bishops had been present, but did not give the names of these bishops nor the content of their decisions. Since a few days later, on June 24, Terlecki, Pełczycki, Bałaban, and Zbirujski acting without the others, issued their statement in favor of reunion with Rome, it is probable that it was the same group which, before the Synod of Brest, had met in Bełz; and that the decisions taken there had been in the same direction. There is, however, no certainty in that respect and it must be pointed out that, if this really was so, it would seem obvious that also the two other members of the hierarchy, viz., Metropolitan Rahoza and the Bishop of Volodymir and Brest, Meletius Chreptowicz, who signed only the resolutions of June 20 but implicitly sanctioned the Bełz decisions also, were already then equally in agreement with the project of reunion. Such an

---

[7] *Documenta Pontif. Rom. hist. Ukrainae illustr.*, I, Nr. 132, p. 237.
[8] *Akty izd. Vilenskoi Archeogr. Kommisseiu*, XIX (Vilna 1865), Nr. 21, p. 365 f.
[9] See above, Part I, Chap. VI, p. 123, 138.
[10] *Akty Zap. Rossii*, IV, Nr. 25, p. 35 ; see Chodynicki, *op. cit.*, 264 n. 3.

interpretation is supported by a later tradition [11] according to which at the Synod of 1590 Metropolitan Rahoza, angered by the Patriarchate's requests for financial contributions, raised the question which of the Patriarchs should be obeyed : Jeremiah who had been wandering around in Russia, or his rivals in Constantinople. And the conclusion was that the Ruthenians, tired of the perpetual interferences of the Muscovites, should place themselves under the protection of Rome.

In any case, the project of turning toward Rome, even if discussed not only in Bełz but also in Brest, was not yet made public, and the official resolutions adopted at the synod by all those present [12] were dealing exclusively with questions of administration and discipline regarding the Ruthenian Church which, as openly admitted, was in chaotic conditions of disorder and disagreement to the detriment of religious worship. With a view of improving that situation and implementing the recommendation which Patriarch Jeremiah himself had made a year before, it was decided that a synod should be held every year at Brest on June 24. Those bishops who would not attend that annual synod were to be fined and in case of repeated, unjustified absence even deposed. This threat was directed against the two who were not present in 1590 : the Archbishop of Polotsk, at the same time Bishop of Vitebsk and Mohylev — Athanasius Terlecki (possibly a relative of the Bishop of Łuck) who in rank came next after the Metropolitan, and the Bishop of Przemyśl, Michael Kopysteński. As to the former, whose see was far away from the place of the meeting, he was in 1590 engaged in a dispute with the city of Mohylev which may have kept him busy at home, and was to die two years later. [13] As to the Bishop of Przemyśl, a city which was at the same time the see of a Latin bishopric and had a mixed population, he was to take nevertheless a wavering attitude in the matter of reunion and, in general, did not enjoy a favorable reputation. [14]

In addition to these disciplinary resolutions, it was decided on June 20, 1590, that all monasteries should be under the exclusive control of the clergy and not of laymen, and that the jurisdiction of each parish should be respected without interference of the neighboring one. And last not least, all documents concerning the privileges and liberties of the Orthodox Church were to be brought to the next synod, in 1591, in order to secure the confirmation and respect of these rights. Since the charter of 1443 was always considered the most important, and since in case of a strict inter-

---

[11] In a memorandum on the history of the Union of Brest, submitted in 1741 to the Congregation of the Propagation of Faith (Roman Archives of the Society of Jesus, *Pol.* 67, at the very beginning of the MS).

[12] *Akty Zap. Rossii*, IV, Nr. 25, pp. 34-36.

[13] *Ibidem*, Nr. 23 ; Chodynicki, *op. cit.*, 160 f., 271.

[14] See my remarks in *Sacrum Poloniae Millennium*, I (1954), 97.

pretation its validity depended on the respect of the Union of Florence, it was almost inavoidable to consider in that connection the whole problem of reunion. And this was precisely done in the declaration which four days later, on June 24, 1590, was drafted by four of the assembled bishops. [15]

Considering it their duty to care for their own salvation as well as for that of their flock entrusted to them by God, and also to lead them to concord and unity, the four bishops declared themselves ready to recognize the Pope of Rome, the successor of Saint Peter, as their supreme Head and to place themselves along with their Churches under the Pope's obedience and blessing, not to be troubled any longer in their conscience. In doing so, they only requested that all ceremonies and liturgical rites of the Eastern Church be maintained by the Pope without any changes or alterations. And they also asked for a confirmation of all privileges granted to that Church by the Kings of Poland. That brief declaration which did not touch any doctrinal questions, since the unreserved recognition of the Pope's authority seemed sufficient in that respect, was signed and sealed by the four and left in the hands of Bishop Cyril Terlecki for further action including presentation to the King.

Before answering the question when that momentous declaration was really submitted to Sigismund III and why he did not answer it until March 18, 1592, it must be pointed out that at the very time when the Ruthenian bishops were deliberating in Bełz and in Brest, the King was approached in the same matter by the Polish Jesuit who had been working in that sense for the last twenty odd years, Father Peter Skarga. It was indeed on June 1, 1590, that he signed in Warsaw the long letter in which he dedicated to Sigismund III the second edition of his already famous book "On the Unity of the Church of God under One Pastor," [16] first published in 1577.

The first edition had been dedicated to Prince Constantine Ostrogski, recalling Skarga's earliest meeting with the Palatine of Kiev ten years before and expressing the hope that the example of the Prince would help to gain the Ruthenian peoples for reunion with Rome. [17] That hope had been disappointed in the course of the following ten years : on the contrary, Ostrogski's equivocal attitude largely contributed to the failure of all efforts which Skarga and Possevino along with the papal nuncios made throughout these years in order to prepare such a reunion with the support of the most prominent members of the Orthodox aristocracy. Skarga could not know that already then Ostrogski favored Calvinism rather than Catholicism, [18]

---

[15] *Russk. istor. bibl.*, XIX, 55-57.

[16] *Ibidem*, VII, 527-534.

[17] *Ibidem*, VII, 228-230.

[18] See his letter to Janusz Radziwiłł, of April 14, 1575, published by S. Golubev, *Kievskii Mitropolit Petr Mogila*, I (Kiev 1883), Doc. Nr. 6, p. 27.

but he must have suspected that it was at the order of the Prince that an obscure Orthodox clergyman from his city of Ostrog, called Basil, published in 1588 the most violent attack against Skarga's thesis under the significant title " On the One True Orthodox Faith, " [19] definitely rejecting that same Union of Florence which the Jesuit writer had so vigorously defended and recommended as basis for the return of the Ruthenians to unity with Rome. Furthermore, it was of Prince Ostrogski that Skarga was thinking in the first place when he complained in the preface to the new edition [20] that " wealthy Ruthenians " had bought out and burned so many copies of the first edition that it was almost impossible still to find any and that he was urgently asked to republish his book.

The new edition was considerably enlarged including more arguments both theological and historical in favor of the unity of the Church under the Pope. But particularly important was Skarga's decision to replace the appeal to Prince Ostrogski, which had been made in vain, by an introductory letter to the new King who deeply impressed the Jesuit by his profound piety when they first met at his coronation[21], and who was universally recognized since the Pacification Diet of 1589. It is true that in that same year Sigismund III showed some inclination to return to his Swedish country of origin, and turning more and more towards cooperation with the House of Austria, raised even the suspicion that he was ready to abandon the Polish crown to the Habsburgs, a suspicion which was to lead to a great humiliation of the King by the opposition at the so-called Inquisition Diet of 1592. [22] But it was precisely in the interval between these two Diets, in 1590 that the royal authority seemed to be growing and — most important for Skarga — his strong Catholic convictions were already quite obvious, in spite of the fact that he continued to appoint non-Catholics to high offices [23] and that equally good Catholics were among his partisans and his opponents, the latter being led by Grand Chancellor Jan Zamoyski, so highly regarded in Rome.

It was to Sigismund's religious zeal as well as to his " love for his subjects " that Skarga now appealed : dedicating to him the new edition of his work, he asked him to dedicate himself to the cause of religious

---

[19] *Russk. istor. bibl.*, VII, 601-938 ; see above, Chapt. I, p. 205. Another answer to Skarga's book which on Ostrogski's instruction was written by an Antitrinitarian has not been preserved ; see Chodynicki, *op. cit.*, 222 n. 1.

[20] *Ibidem*, VII, 529.

[21] See Skarga's letter to Bishop George Radziwiłł of Jan. 13, 1588 (Polish Library in Paris, *Ms.* 11, nr. 3).

[22] About the whole political background see K. Lepszy, *Rzeczpospolita polska w dobie sejmu inkwizycyjnego* 1589-1592 (The Polish Commonwealth at the time of the Inquisition Diet), Kraków 1939.

[23] See the list of nominations given by E. Barwiński, " Zygmunt III i dyssydenci," *Reformacja w Polsce*, I (1923) ; also *Nunz. di Polonia*, Vol. 30, fol. 82.

16

union and to help to achieve it. Stressing the importance of ecclesiastical unity for the political unity of the Commonwealth, he expressed the opinion that the conversion of the Ruthenians was more difficult than that of the "heretics," viz., the Protestants whose number was rapidly decreasing. For the errors of the former were much older and therefore difficult to heal. How this should be done, Skarga did not specify, but simply pointed out that at present many Ruthenians were realizing their mistakes, just as the Greeks had done on earlier occasions — a clear reference to the Union of Florence, and therefore all that was needed was more zeal of both, the clergy and the secular authority. As to the role of the latter, he recalled that in the past the Kings of Poland, following the ancient laws, had admitted to their councils only those who were united with the Church, while now the "heretics" who wanted to confirm their own errors by those of the Ruthenians, had opened to both of them the access to the highest offices. [24]

Laws which prohibited the appointment of non-Catholics to some of these highest offices had existed only in the Grand Duchy of Lithuania and even there had been cancelled on the eve of the Union of Lublin. Therefore Skarga's suggestion could only influence the King's choice in the selection of candidates. It can be explained by his disappointment in the attitude of the dignitaries whom he had tried in vain to persuade, and here again the case of Prince Ostrogski must have been foremost in his mind. But such a pressure which the King would exercise in the future upon ambitious magnates was not only of doubtful value from the religious point of view, but had nothing to do with the issue which was proving decisive : the attitude of the Ruthenian hierarchy. Skarga was, however, entirely right in pointing out the danger of Protestant and Orthodox cooperation against Catholicism, a cooperation which so strongly influenced Ostrogski himself ; and in general, this first appeal which Sigismund III received in the whole matter, was of great importance were it only because it made him interested in a problem, vital for the Commonwealth, but hitherto quite unknown to the Swedish born ruler. The work of the learned Jesuit made it much easier for him to get acquainted with an intricate situation which he had hardly studied at all during the first difficult years of his reign in Poland.

He was thus much better prepared to grasp the significance of the declaration of no less than half of the Ruthenian bishops, recognizing the supreme authority of the Pope. But there is no evidence that Terlecki who was supposed to act in the name of the other three, approached Sigismund III before the next Orthodox synod which in due course met in Brest the following year, 1591, though not on June 24, but only in October.

---

[24] *Russk. istor. bibl.*, VII, 533 f.

However, this time no further action in the matter of reunion was taken by the four initiators who only joined once more with the Metropolitan and the Bishop of Brest and Volodymir in trying to improve the conditions of the Ruthenian Church, again in the absence of the Archbishop of Polotsk and the Bishop of Przemyśl, but in the presence of other members of the Orthodox clergy and many nobles of their faith, including Prince Ostrogski and Adam Pociej.

Entering into much more details than in the preceding year and acting in the same spirit, the Synod of 1591 adopted on October 26 a whole program of constructive reforms. [25] Very important was the decision that, in case of the death of the Metropolitan or any other bishop, the successor should be appointed by the King from among four candidates elected in Brest by the assembly of the hierarchy. The power of the bishops was strengthened by placing the Brotherhoods of Lwów and Wilno under their control. This was contrary to the decision of Patriarch Jeremiah and could only please Bishop Bałaban of Lwów who had so many troubles with the local Brotherhood. Bishop Terlecki who in 1590 had been along with Bałaban the main initiator of the declaration in favor of Rome, was now instructed to " correct, " with the assistance of two clergymen, the theological books which were to be published at the expense of the episcopate and printed by the Brotherhoods. The confidence shown in that delicate matter to the bishops whose pro-Roman attitude must have been known to the Synod, clearly indicates that there was no dissatisfaction with, nor opposition against that attitude, even if there still was some hesitation among, other members of the hierarchy. Last not least, the decision to place all Orthodox schools under strict ecclesiastical control might be interpreted as evidence that the Synod was well aware of the penetration of Protestant influence into some of these schools including the most important which Prince Constantine had founded in Ostrog, a penetration which was one of the main obstacles to any agreement with the Catholic Church.

In conclusion, it can be said that at the Synod of 1591 which made so serious an effort to reform and to strengthen the Ruthenian Church internally, the general atmosphere was certainly not unfavorable to the plans of reunion, though these plans were not openly discussed nor even mentioned. That silence is easy to explain in view of the delay of the King's answer to the declaration made by four of the bishops more than a year before. Whatever the reasons of that delay may have been, probably nothing else but the difficult political issues which at the same time absorbed the attention of Sigismund III, possibly also the tension in religious matters created by the Protestant synod of 1591 — there is not the

---

[25] Summarized by Chodynicki, *op. cit.*, 267 f., who used the new material discovered by the Russian historian P. Zhukovich.

slightest evidence that the King did not trust Terlecki.[26]   On the other hand, he must have been impressed by the activities of the October Synod of 1591.   For already on January 2 of the following year, he issued a decree forbidding the secular authorities to interfere with the internal affairs of the Ruthenian Church,[27] a decision which was in full agreement with the ideas expressed at Brest.

It is quite possible that Sigismund III had expected also some action of the Synod in favor of reunion, or even a general, open adherence to the declaration of four of the bishops in that matter.   But since nothing was done in that sense and the next Synod was not to meet before June 1593, the King without waiting so long decided at last to give his support and encouragement to the signatories of that declaration.   This he did in an official statement, signed and sealed in Cracow on March 18, 1592,[28] which is the first pronouncement of the secular power of the Commonwealth regarding the religious reunion of the Ruthenians with Rome.

Sigismund III made public the decision of four of their bishops whose sees were duly enumerated, to recognize the authority of the Pope retaining however their rite and liturgy.   After such a brief summary of the declaration of 1590, the King " accepted it from them with gratitude, " considering their action " necessary for salutary matters. "   In addition to that approval, he wanted to assure them of his royal benevolence, by solemnly promising to the said bishops " and to the whole clergy of the Oriental Church of Greek religion " in his own name and in the name of his successors, the future Kings of Poland, that he would protect these bishops and their clergy against the consequences of any reprisals and excommunications by " patriarchs and metropolitans, " whatever reasons might be given.   He promised them in particular that, notwithstanding any such accusations and excommunications, their episcopal sees would not be taken from them but remain in their safe possession until the end of their lives.   Furthermore, he guaranteed them " and to everybody who would join that unity and order, " the same liberties which were enjoyed by " the Roman clergy. "   There was even at the end a reference to other privileges which might be granted them in the future.

This was even more than what the four bishops had requested when referring in their declaration to the earlier privileges of the Polish kings which they wanted to be safeguarded and confirmed.   There also was in the careful wording of Sigismund's statement an interpretation of these earlier charters which recalled that union with Rome was the prerequisite condition for enjoying equal rights with the Latin clergy.   This was, how-

---

[26] See *ibidem*, 269 n. 1.

[27] *Akty Zap. Rossii*, IV, Nr. 31.

[28] *Russk. istor. bibl.*, VII, col. 1133-1137.   About the date of that document and its other editions see Chodynicki, *op. cit.*, 269 n. 2.

ever, the only pressure which, at least implicitly and in full agreement with the original sense of these charters, was exercised by the King who far from interfering with the further discussions and negotiations in the matter of reunion left the matter in the hands of the Ruthenian bishops themselves. Even when appointing in that same year of 1592 a new Archbishop of Polotsk after the death of Athanasius Terlecki, Sigismund III who continued to be absorbed by political problems, did not seem to be particularly interested in entrusting that important see to a partisan of religious union with Rome : an otherwise entirely unknown Bohusz Sielicki received the archbishopric as a reward for military services in the defense of the Ukraine, and though made a monk under the name of Naphanael, neglected to attend the synods of the hierarchy, just as his predecessor had done. [29] It was only later, on the eve of the Union of Brest, when the see of Polotsk was again vacant, that a more appropriate candidate was chosen.

Another appointment, however, which the King made at the beginning of 1593, before leaving for Sweden, was to prove of decisive importance for the cause of reunion and for the ultimate success of the initiative taken by some bishops three years earlier. On January 13 of that year died the Bishop of Brest and Volodymir, Meletius Chreptowicz, whose role at the synods of 1590 and 1951 seems to have been rather passive, and on March 20 Sigismund III informed Metropolitan Rahoza that he had given that see to Pociej, [30] formerly when still a layman, called Adam but recently made a Basilian monk and named Hypatius.

That appointment was not yet made in agreement with the procedure which had been requested at the Synod of 1591, but since the next synod was not to be held before June 1593 and eventually had to be postponed for another year because of the King's absence from the country, it would have been in any case unadvisable to wait so long. But making his choice, the King had taken into consideration the desires and recommendations of the most prominent Orthodox Ruthenians, including Prince Constantine Ostrogski, Pociej's friend who was present when the candidate received the religious orders. An important letter which Ostrogski sent to the new Bishop three months after his appointment by the King, [31] clearly shows that the Prince was well aware of Pociej's interest in the problem of reunion and that he hoped to influence him in that matter according to his own conceptions and desires. But it is equally evident that Pociej's inclinations were also known to those who had been positively working for union with Rome during the preceding years, as well as to those Orthodox who were definitely opposed to any such idea.

---

[29] Chodynicki, *op. cit.*, 271.
[30] *Akty Zap. Rossii*, IV, Nr. 44.
[31] *Ibidem*, IV, Nr. 45 (June 21, 1593) ; see also *Russk. istor. bibl.*, XIX, 575 ff.

That opposition was led by the Brotherhoods, especially by that of Lwów which in September 1592, writing to Patriarch Jeremiah about the confused situation in the Ruthenian Church, [32] warned him that negotiations with Rome had already started, that many Orthodox had decided to recognize the authority of the Pope and that a papal representative had appeared celebrating mass in the Ruthenian churches according to the Latin rite. These alarming news were greatly exaggerated : there is no trace of any negotiations with Rome in the reports of the papal nuncio before the fall of 1594, and the only propagandist who had already arrived from Rome to work for reunion among the Ruthenians, was a Catholic priest of Greek origin, faithful to the eastern rite who was anxious to convince them that their rite would not suffer any alteration after that reunion. This was Peter Arcudius, a native of the island of Corfu and pupil of the Greek College founded in Rome by Gregory XIII, the first to receive there the degree of doctor in theology. [33]

His first mission to the Ruthenian lands of the Commonwealth had been entrusted to him during the brief pontificate of Gregory XIV whom the Latin Bishop of Łuck, Bernard Maciejowski, sent to Rome with the declaration of obedience of Sigismund III, [34] had asked in December 1590 for some alumni of the Greek College who would work in his diocese as well as in those of oriental rite. Arcudius was chosen by the Pope after consulting Cardinal Santori [35] who was in charge of the relations with the eastern Churches, and soon came to Łuck when Maciejowski returned there after his embassy to the Vatican. He must have met at once the Ruthenian Bishop of Łuck, Cyril Terlecki, the main initiator of the project of reunion conceived in the spring of 1590 and obviously confirmed him in his pro-Roman attitude. Since, however, Terlecki's initiative had been taken before the arrival of Arcudius and in Maciejowski's absence, there was no need for any pressure. If Terlecki in these years had troubles with the Starosta of Łuck, Alexander Siemaszko, a nobleman of Ruthenian origin but of Catholic faith, they had nothing to do with any religious issues nor with any interference of Maciejowski ; and the whole conflict in which Terlecki looked in vain for Prince Ostrogski's support, ended in the agreement of June 18, 1592. [36] At that time Arcudius was already busy discussing the problem of religious union not with Terlecki who favored it

[32] *Ibidem*, IV, Nr. 33, p. 46.

[33] See about Arcudius E. Legrand, *Bibliographie hellénique du XVIIe siècle*, III (Paris 1895), 209-232 ; D. Placide de Meester, *Le Collège pontifical grec de Rome*, Rome 1910, 52-54 ; L. Petit in *Dictionnaire de théologie catholique*, I-2 (Paris 1932), col. 1771-1773 ; K. Chodynicki, in *Polski Słownik biograficzny*, I (1935), 158 f. ; and my remarks in *Sacrum Poloniae Millennium*, I, 75 f.

[34] A. Theiner, *Vetera Monumenta Pol.*, III, Nr. 120.

[35] Vatican Archives, *Arm.* 52, vol. 19, fol. 421 v.

[36] Chodynicki, *op. cit.*, 270 (second paragraph of footnote).

anyway, but with the Prince and with Pociej whom he must have visited in Brest.

The learned Greek's discussions with Ostrogski were to be unsuccessful, and the reason for this failure, given by his biographers with reference to his own account, is highly significant : Ostrogski's leanings toward reunion could not materialize, because the Calvinists, numerous at his court, incited him to " hatred against Rome. "[37] The case of Pociej was entirely different : that Ruthenian magnate, less powerful indeed and also less ambitious than Prince Constantine, but son of a prominent member of the royal court and chancery under Sigismund I, had been himself a Calvinist in his early youth but returned to the Orthodox faith of his ancestors. Already as judge of the district of Brest he had shown serious interest in the earlier phase of discussions about a possible reunion with Rome,[38] and now he was so anxious to contribute to the progress of the Ruthenian Church that he gave up his senatorial office of Castellane of Brest and, as a widower, accepted his nomination to the see of Brest and Volodymir.

He did it on Ostrogski's advice but most probably also on that of Maciejowski, another old friend, and of Arcudius who soon became convinced that as a member of the Ruthenian hierarchy Pociej would join the group working for reunion and do it out of the most sincere religious convictions, his earlier hesitations having been overcome by the arguments of the Greek theologian.[39] It was, however, obvious that the details of the plan which Terlecki cautiously propagated since 1590 and which since 1592 had the King's basic approval, had to be worked out, taking into consideration the whole religious and political situation, and nobody among the Ruthenian hierarchy was better qualified to contribute to such a solution than its most recent but at the same time most experienced and zealous member : Hypatius Pociej. For that very reason Prince Ostrogski did not wait long before forwarding to him his own scheme.[40]

Recalling his persistent interest in a thorough reorganization of the Ruthenian Church and his earlier discussions with Possevino and other Catholics — without, however naming either Skarga or Arcudius — the Prince, on the one hand, mentioned the possibility that travelling to Italy for reasons of health he might see the Pope himself and, on the other hand, encouraged Pociej to study with the other Ruthenian bishops all that was needed in order to promote the concord between the western and eastern Churches. Many of Ostrogski's concrete suggestions in that matter were

---

[37] E. Legrand, op. cit., III, 215.
[38] See above, Chap. II, p. 225.
[39] E. Legrand, op. cit., III, 214.
[40] See in his letter, quoted above (note 31), the " articles " in which he summarized his conditions for reunion : Russk. istor. bibl., XIX, 586 ff.

practically uncontroversial and in full agreement with both, the reform program of the latest synods and the conditions for reunion which were already formulated in the statement of Cyril Terlecki and his first associates. There was no doubt indeed as to the necessity of guaranteeing to the Eastern Church its traditional rite and to the eastern hierarchy the same privileges which the Latin clergy enjoyed, including — as Ostrogski specified for the first time — places in the Senate of the Commonwealth for the Ruthenian metropolitan and bishops. Obvious, too, was the need of working at the same time for internal improvements in the Ruthenian Church, particularly by founding new schools and raising the intellectual standard of the clergy. And Ostrogski's concern with the danger of Latinization and any kind of pressure coming from the Latin side, for instance in the case of mixed marriages like his own, was well understandable and shared by many other Orthodox.

There was, however, in the statement of the Prince one almost casual remark which must have revealed to Pociej a rather strange and unexpected state of mind of the writer who pretended to speak in the name of the Orthodox laity. Referring to the need of internal reforms in the Ruthenian Church, Ostrogski mentioned, just as an example, the sacraments " and other human inventions. " [41] For Pociej, a former Calvinist himself, the implication was clear, and never indeed did the impact of Protestant doctrine upon the Prince appear more strikingly than in these brief words, which could only raise a well justified doubt as to the seriousness of his intention to promote religious union with Rome. Furthermore, there was another fundamental difference between his approach to the problem of reunion and the practical possibilities which were under consideration in connection with the initiative of 1590 : that initiative was aiming at a regional union limited to the Ruthenian dioceses of the Commonwealth, possibly even to some of them only, and in any case independently of the Patriarchate of Constantinople, while Ostrogski was thinking of a union with the whole Eastern Church.

Two of the conditions, which he enumerated to Pociej, clearly indicate such a desire. He requested an understanding with all Eastern Patriarchs and in particular with Wallachia and Muscovy. To the former country he suggested to send the Archbishop of Lwów, while Pociej himself, after consulting with the Metropolitan and the other Ruthenian bishops and obtaining the King's permission, was to go to Moscow [42] to discuss there with the Grand Prince and the clergy the religious problems of the Eastern Church in the Commonwealth.

---

[41] *Ibidem*, XIX, 588.
[42] *Ibidem*, XIX, 582.

It was that last point which raised the strongest objections of Pociej who was not at all anxious to undertake such a mission : he even expressed the fear that in Moscow he would simply get a good beating, if coming there with any project of union with Rome. [43] It was indeed easy to anticipate that now, after the recent elevation of the metropolitan see of Moscow to the rank of a Patriarchate, such a project would be rejected even more definitely than at the time of Possevino's mission. Furthermore, it was more than doubtful whether a similar mission, to be undertaken by one of the Ruthenian bishops and opening the door to Muscovite intervention with the situation of the Ruthenian Church of the Commonwealth, would receive the approval of the local hierarchy and of the King.

More acceptable was, of course, the idea to connect the project of a reunion of the Ruthenians with similar attempts which Solikowski, the Latin Archbishop of Lwów, was making for a number of years with regard to the Orthodox of Moldavia [44] — in Poland frequently called Wallachia — and which could be extended even to Wallachia proper if the political situation would permit. That situation, however, depended on the relations with the Ottoman Empire whose influence opposed that of the Commonwealth in both principalities. And Turkish influence, or rather direct Turkish control, was also the main obstacle to any negotiations with the Patriarch of Constantinople and even more with the distant Patriarchates in Asia and Africa.

Among these Patriarchates that of Alexandria in Egypt was then of special importance and in particularly close relations with that of Constantinople, thanks to the outstanding personality of Meletius Pigas, [45] who after acting as vicar was made precisely in 1593 Patriarch of Alexandria himself. That Greek from Crete, the island which after the loss of Cyprus twenty years before remained for another century the strongest outpost of Venetian power in the Levant, started already there to oppose any Catholic influence among the Orthodox population. And though thanks to his studies at the University of Padua he was himself familiar with Western culture, he continued throughout his life a relentless struggle against Rome, mobilizing the forces of all countries of Greek faith, including Wallachia and Moscow where he established contacts as early as 1588. Even before he sent his younger relative, Cyril Lucaris, another Greek from Crete educated in Padua, to teach at the school which Prince Constantine had

---

[43] See his answer to Ostrogski's letter, *ibidem*, XIX, 590.
[44] See above, Chap. II, p. 227 f.
[45] The basic work on Patriarch Pigas or Pegas still remains I. Malishevsky, *Aleksandriiskii Patriarch Meletii Pigas i iego uchastvie v dielakh russkoi tserkvi* (The Patriarch of Alexandria M. P. and his part in the affairs of the Russian Church), 2 vols., Kiev 1872 (with many documents published in vol. II) ; see now also Chodynicki, *op. cit.*, 287 f. and n. 2, and my remarks in " Rome, Constantinople et Moscou ... , " 459, and *Sacrum Poloniae Millennium*, I, 79 f.

founded in Ostrog, [46] and in 1592 Pigas himself entered in correspondence with the Brotherhood of Lwów. The cooperation of these two Greeks in opposing the Union of the Ruthenian Church with Rome began as soon as a final decision in that matter was imminent, viz., in the spring of 1594. But already the year before the Patriarch of Alexandria was to come to Poland in order to explore the situation, probably sent there from Constantinople where he had a stronger influence than the old Patriarch Jeremiah himself, remaining always in good relations with the Ottoman authorities.

Whether Meletius Pigas really came in person to Poland in the summer of 1593 or preferred as usual to act through one of his emissaries, is rather irrelevant. [47] In any case, the information that the Greek Patriarch of Alexandria had arrived there, reached the papal nuncio Germanico Malaspina who had arrived himself exactly one year earlier, [48] in the middle of July [49] and raised his alarm so that he asked the King to have the Greek's activities strictly observed by the Grand Chancellor Jan Zamoyski and to make him leave the country as soon as possible. It is, however, interesting to note that when reporting to Rome on that unwelcome visit, the Nuncio did not describe it as an obstacle to religious reunion between Ruthenians and Latins. Only several years later when leaving Poland after the Union of Brest, Malaspina in his final survey of his mission [50] gave such an interpretation of the visits to the Commonwealth by Greek Patriarchs from Constantinople and Alexandria. In 1593, he was not yet thinking of any such union but only stressed that the Greek visiter would try to keep divided as much as possible the Schismatics and the Catholics. He also expressed the fear that taking advantage of the King's imminent departure for Sweden where the Nuncio was to follow him, the Patriarch would act as Turkish spy.

That political aspect of the problem which Malaspina pointed out in connection with the danger of Muscovite propaganda, particularly alarmed the papal Secretariate of State which about the same time had been warned by the Archbishop of Lwów that in Constantinople preparations were being made against Poland. Though the Vatican did not consider such an attack probable at the time when the Turks were concentrating all their forces

---

[46] Chodynicki, *op. cit.*, 187 and 288 n. 6.
[47] See K. Lewicki, *Ks. Konstanty Ostrogski a Unia brzeska*, 101 f.
[48] Vatican Archives, *Nunz. di Polonia*, vol. 35, fol. 15v and *Borgh.* III 96 D, fol. 19 ; on the papers relating to Malaspina's mission see *Sacrum Poloniae Millennium*, I, 71 f. and notes 5-8.
[49] *Nunz. di Polonia*, vol. 35, f. 334v (July 21, 1593 ; original in *Borgh.* III cd, fol. 286).
[50] *Relacje nuncjuszów*, II, 90 f. (Polish transl. ; orig. text in Vat. Library, *Urbin. lat.* 837, fol. 503).

in Hungary, the answer to Malaspina's report [51] admitted that the presence in Poland of " the Greek who called himself Patriarch of Alexandria " was undesirable and that the King should make him go before his own journey to Sweden. The religious implications of the Greek visit were not considered at all in that instruction to the Nuncio.

Yet, while it is quite possible that that visit was to serve the political aims of the Ottoman Empire also and at least to find out whether there were any chances that Poland would join the planned league against the Turks, it is certain that the main interest of Pigas and of the Eastern Church, in general, was in the initiative of some of the Ruthenian bishops to break away from that Church and to place themselves under papal authority. But, strange enough, neither the Vatican nor its nuncio in Poland seemed to know anything about such an initiative though it was being discussed for the last three years. Only more than one year later, when the initiative of 1590 had led to a formal decision, was that matter, so important for the Catholic Church, mentioned for the first time in one of Malaspina's reports [52] and even then remained rather secondary among the other problems which were discussed in his correspondence with Rome. [53] The main concern of the Vatican's Polish policy in these years was and remained the participation of the Commonwealth in the political union of the Christian powers against the Ottoman Empire, and this was part of a larger problem : the planned participation of all East European countries in the war against Turkey which for the time being Emperor Rudolf II was conducting practically alone.

It is true that in the eastern policy of the Papacy the problems of fighting the infidels and of reuniting Eastern Christendom with Rome were always inseparable. But there always was the alternative which of the two should receive priority at the given moment. And it so happened that, in view of the obvious impossibility even to approach the eastern Patriarchates and of the recent disappointments in the religious discussions first with Ivan the Terrible and then with the Orthodox leaders of the Commonwealth, the skeptical attitude regarding the immediate chances of religious reunion, so evident at the time of Patriarch Jeremiah's trip to Eastern Europe, still prevailed in the early nine'ties. On the contrary, the fact that at least Austria was opposing not without success the Ottoman on-slaught in Hungary [54] raised once more the hope that perhaps that onslaught could be broken and even the Christians of the Balkans liberated, if other Christian powers, particularly those east of the Hungarian battlefields, would enter the war. It seemed, furthermore, that the participation of

---

[51] Vatican Archives, *Borgh.* III 18 c., fol. 103v (Aug. 28, 1593).
[52] *Ibidem, Borgh.* III 91 ab., fol. 226 (Oct. 15, 1594) ; see below, Chap. V, p. 269 f.
[53] See *Sacrum Poloniae Millennium*, I, 74.
[54] L. v. Pastor, *Geschichte der Päpste*, XI, Chap. V.

Orthodox countries in such a political union with Catholics could create the most favorable conditions for resuming eventually the negotiations in the matter of religious reunion.   Towards the end of 1593 these far reaching schemes found full expression in one of the most extraordinary missions ever sent from Rome to Eastern Europe, a mission which, therefore, overshadowed for some time any other, more limited prospects of Catholic advance in that region, especially as the project of restoring through Sigismund III Catholicism in Sweden proved hopeless. [55]

Chapter IV

THE MISSION OF ALEXANDER KOMULOVICH

When after the three brief pontificates of Urban VII, Gregory XIV, and Innocent IX, which followed in rapid succession after that of Sixtus V, on January 30, 1592, Cardinal Ippolito Aldobrandini was elected Pope as Clement VIII, he received unusually numerous and enthusiastic letters of congratulation from Poland.[1] Among the prominent members of the hierarchy and the secular dignitaries who gratefully recalled on that occasion his successful legation to that Kingdom in 1589 when they had met him for the first time, there were many of those who were particularly interested in the religious union with the Ruthenians and only a few years later most strongly supported the Union of Brest. One of them, Archbishop Solikowski of Lwów,[2] immediately recommended to the new Pope the Ruthenian lands as well as nearby Moldavia where already Sixtus V had entrusted him the task of promoting reunion with Rome.

But only two months later, on May 15, 1592, a particularly long and interesting letter of congratulations was sent to Clement VIII by the Bishop of Nona in Dalmatia, Peter Cedulini,[3] a Croat in spite of his Italianized name, who also started by recalling the Pope's recent legation to Poland. He did it, however, in order to stress that on that occasion the then Cardinal Aldobrandini had familiarized himself with both the amplitude and the calamities of all " kingdoms and provinces of the Illyric language, " using that ancient name as a designation of the Slavs. Pointing out that he belonged himself to that " Illyric people and language, " he expressed in the name of all of them the special pleasure with which they welcomed his election, and the fond hope that as Pope he would unite that large region of Europe, next to Italy, which in part was occupied by the Turks and in part separated from the Catholic Church. In Cedulini's interpretation, the mission of 1589 through which, as legate of Sixtus V, the present Pope had settled the conflict between the rulers of Poland and Austria, was a

---

[1] Vatican Archives, *Vescovi*, vol. 2, fol. 128, 132, 142, (letter of Bishop Bernard Maciejowski, from Łuck " in his remotissimis partibus, " March 8, 1592) ; *Principi*, vol. 51, fol. 140, 177, 223 (letter of J. Zamoyski), 247, 251.

[2] *Ibidem*, fol. 152 (March 17, 1592 ; see fol. 107 his similar letter to Pope Gregory XIV, of March 28, 1591).

[3] *Ibidem*, fol. 174-175 ; published by A. Theiner, *Monum. Slavorum meridion.*, II, Nr. 89.

first step in that direction because, in the following enumeration of thirteen kingdoms or provinces of Illyric tongue, he included besides, the Balkan countries, Poland, and Russia, also the various Slavic lands under Habsburg rule and even " all Noricum which now is called Austria " between the Alps and the Adriatic Sea, on the shores of which his native Dalmatia was situated.

The Croat bishop's " panslavism " or Slavic " nationalism " appeared not only in the extension he gave to his impressive list, covering even areas which were no longer really " Illyric, " but also in his request that " Illyric " churches should not be placed under foreigners but under men of Slavic origin and language, and that such men should also be included in the College of Cardinals which according to the decrees of the Council of Trent should be composed of representatives of all nations. Only at the end of this comprehensive memorandum did Cedulini turn to the local problems of his own diocese and to his personal, mainly financial difficulties after thirty-two years of loyal service to the See of Peter, referring in particular to his " visitation of Constantinople " under Pope Gregory XIII.

That visitation of the Latin churches which still remained in Constantinople and its environs — the first such inspection after the Union of Florence and the Turkish conquest — had lasted from the fall of 1580 to the spring of 1581, [4] and had been accompanied and followed by inquiries into the religious situation of almost all Balkan countries through visits of Cedulini himself or of his emissaries which he sent even to the Crimea. [5] He was alarmed by Lutheran propaganda among the Orthodox population, [6] and though he was well received by Patriarch Jeremiah, there is no evidence of any negotiations in the matter of reunion. But in his final report to Gregory XIII made on his return in 1583, he wished him an opportunity to liberate all these Christian peoples " from the tyranny of those rabid wolves which are devouring them. " [7]

That same desire inspired Cedulini when he addressed Clement VIII, and having received information that the new Pope, so fully aware of the plight of the Balkan Slavs, had started his pontificate by inviting the free Slavs and their prospective allies to join in a league, obviously directed against the Ottoman Empire, he sent to Rome in January 1593 a " discourse on the defense against the Turk. " [8] The old bishop was, however,

---

[4] Vatican Archives, *Fondo Pio*, vol. 107, (see about the " Visite delle Chiese di Constantinopoli " in this volume the remarks of A. Mercati in *Orientalia Christiana Periodica*, XVIII (1952), 379), fol. 8-57.

[5] *Ibidem*, fol. 58-117.

[6] *Ibidem*, fol. 19 (about a Lutheran church and school in the house of an Englishman at Constantinople).

[7] *Ibidem*, fol. 5-7v.

[8] See about the manuscripts in which this discourse has been preserved, Pastor, *Gesch. der Päpste*, XI, 198 n. 8 and 648 n. 2 (of the Italian transl.)

not the first Croat nor the only one in these critical years who proudly stressed the solidarity of the Slavic peoples and suggested to the Holy See the organization of a league for liberating those of them who were under Muslim domination. A precursor of the movement which was to effect so deeply the policies of Clement VIII had been another Dalmatian, Vincent Pribojevich, who during the pontificate of Clement VII wrote in 1525 and published seven years later in Venice a treatise " on the origin and success- es of the Slavs, " [9] praising in particular King Sigismund I of Poland for his victories not only over the Tartars and Wallachians supported by the Turks but also over the Slavic Muscovites. [10] When his work was printed in an Italian translation in 1595, his and even more Cedulini's ideas had already been taken up and considerably enlarged, with special emphasis on Muscovite cooperation, by a Dalmatian priest educated at the Croatian College of St. Hieronymus in Rome, Alexander Komulovich. [11]

He too had started his activities as apostolic visitator in the Balkans where he was sent by Gregory XIII, along with the Italian Jesuit Tom- maso Raggio, soon after Cedulini's return, in 1584. [12] Already his first report, forwarded from Sofia in Bulgaria in November of that year, [13] evi- denced his optimism, emphasizing how many people were living as good Catholics in Macedonia, Serbia, and Greater Bulgaria. But even more optimistic, or rather greatly exaggerated, were his final conclusions [14] as to the number of Christians of either rite suffering under Muslim oppression and ready to rise in cooperation with liberators from the free countries. Already then he was particularly interested in the Albanians, most of them of Latin rite, but he gave even more impressive figures, going into hundreds of thousands, of Slavs and Greeks in the other Balkan countries, as well as in the Turkish controlled parts of Croatia and the Black See region, all of them to be used in the struggle against the Ottoman Empire.

---

[9] This extremely rare publication has been reprinted from the copy preserved in the Marciana Library in Venice by G. Novak under the title : *Vincentius Priboevius — De origine successibusque Slavorum*, Zagrebiae 1951, with a biographical introduction and a detailed commentary.

[10] *Ibidem*, 76 f.

[11] The first to study the role of Komulovich in the relations between the Holy See and Moscow was P. Pierling, particularly in the chapter " Un nonce slave à Moscou " in vol. II, 329-360, of the work *La Russie et le Saint Siège*, where the author's earlier contributions are quoted. See now also M. Vanino, *Aleksander Komu- lović (1548-1608)*, Sarajevo 1935 (reprinted from the Calendar *Napredak*), and the references in M. Kombol, *Poviest Hrvatske Književnosti do preporoda* (History of Croa- tian Literature until its Revival), Zagreb 1945, 206. I am indebted for valuable bibliographical information in this matter to Rev. Josif Burić, of the Croatian College in Rome, and to Mr. A. Nisiteo. The most important sources have been published by P. Pierling, F. Rački, and E. Fermendžin in the series *Starine* of the Yugoslav Academy in Zagreb, vol. 14 (1882), 16 (1884), and 36 (1918).

[12] *Starine*, vol. 16, Nr. 1, 2. See also Pastor, *op. cit.*, IX, 736.

[13] *Ibidem*, vol. 16, Nr. 3.

[14] *Ibidem*, vol. 14, Nr. 1.

Promoted to higher ecclesiastical offices, including the position of an abbot in Cedulini's Nona, Komulovich immediately joined his bishop in taking advantage of Clement VIII's special interest in the Slavs and of the new Pope's desire to unite in a powerful anti-Ottoman league both western and eastern Christendom. In the course of 1593, the problem was becoming more and more urgent since the hostilities between the Turks and Austria, which had begun soon after the Pope's election, in June 1592, [15] led, in July of the following year, to a defeat of the Pasha of Bosnia before Sissek — specifically mentioned in the correspondence between the Secretariate of State and the Nuncio in Poland. [16] War was now formally declared and Grand Vizir Sinan Pasha invaded imperial Hungary. At that very time when Clement VIII tried his best to encourage the resistance of Rudolf II and to get him assistance from Spain and the Italian States, especially Venice, Komulovich, referring to his experience as visitator in the Balkans under Gregory XIII, submitted to the Holy See a detailed project of a general attack on the Turks. [17]

It was here that he developed in great detail his favorite idea of combining the advance from the West with a simultaneous offensive on a long eastern front running from Transylvania and the Danubian principalities to the Muscovite border. Remembering the role which King Stefan Báthory of Poland had been expected to play in such an action, he suggested that his nephew Andrew Báthory, made a Cardinal by Gregory XIII and as Bishop of Warmia, a Senator of the Kingdom of Poland, be placed at the head of the forces of his native Transylvania and also of Moldavia and Wallachia. He would be assisted by the Cossacks of the Polish Ukraine, and also by Moscow if that power were invited by the Holy See, and Grand Chancellor Jan Zamoyski would join that action as Commander-in-Chief of the Polish forces. And in his vivid imagination Komulovich already anticipated that all these eastern forces would join those which another Cardinal Legate, Francesco Sforza, would lead from Albania through the Balkans — to Constantinople, where all Christian armies would meet.

Strange enough, that fantastic project, conceived by a zealous prelate and Croat patriot who had, however, only a superficial knowledge of the conditions in the Balkans and no knowledge at all of the problems of

---

[15] On the war in Hungary see L. F. Mathäus Voltelini, "Die Beteiligung des Papstes Clemens VIII an der Bekämpfung der Türken," *Römische Quartalschrift*, XV (1901), where, however, the short references to the mission of Komulovich (p. 320-322) are based exclusively on Pierling's studies, and K. Horvat, *Vojne ekspedicije Klementa VIII v Ugarsku i Hrvatsku* (The military expeditions of Clement VIII to Hungary and Croatia), Zagreb 1910, with a few general remarks about Cedulini (p. 18, where the Croat form of his name is given as Čedomil) and Komulovich (6, 28, 37 f.)

[16] Vatican Archives, *Borgh.* III 18 c, fol. 103v (Aug. 28, 1593).

[17] Published by K. Horvat, "Monumenta historica nova historiam Bosnae et vicinarum provinciarum illustrantia," *Glasnik zemaljskog Muzeja v Bosni i Herzegovini*, XXI (Sarajevo 1909), Nr. 20, pp. 14-16.

northeastern Europe, appealed to the papal Chancery and served as a basis for two complementary instructions which he received as extraordinary nuncio to all countries included in his scheme. According to the first of these instructions of November 10, 1593,[18] he was to go as papal representative "to various princes and potentates of the northern regions," a vague formula which included the princes of Transylvania, Moldavia, and Wallachia, the Cossack leaders and, last not least, the King of Poland. The second instruction of January 27, 1594,[19] outlined his additional negotiations with Fedor, Grand Prince of Muscovy.

In both of these lengthy documents Komulovich was instructed to gain all the rulers he was to visit for cooperation against the Turks. To all of them, including Fedor,[20] Clement VIII wrote letters of recommendation for his representative praising him highly and always adding to his name the designation *Illyricus*. Such letters were also addressed to those dignitaries of Poland, both ecclesiastical and secular,[21] whom Komulovich was advised to see besides the King himself, their names having probably been chosen in the light of the information received from Nuncio Malaspina. One of them was Cardinal Radziwiłł, Bishop of Cracow,[22] who enjoyed special confidence of the Holy See, and it is highly significant that it was to him that Komulovich was to turn for advice how to reach Moscow and where to cross the eastern border of the Commonwealth. For it was stressed in his second instruction, dealing with his mission to Fedor, that without such help the Poles would not let him pass. As usual on such occasions, the Vatican must have been aware that in the Commonwealth the inclusion of Moscow in these diplomatic negotiations would not be too favorably considered, but probably it was not sufficiently realized in Rome that the role assigned to the Muscovites in the planned league, as outlined in the second instruction of Komulovich, would have been totally unacceptable to the Poles.

It was indeed anticipated that Moscow would send armed forces to Podolia and use that Polish province as a basis for penetrating into Moldavia and making acquisitions in the Black Sea region, thus entering the sphere of influence of the Commonwealth. Furthermore, Komulovich was

---

[18] Best edition (by E. Fermendžin) in *Starine*, XXXVI, 8-22.

[19] *Ibidem*, 22-28; see my remarks about the earliest edition by Count D. Tolstoy (1863) in *Orientalia Christiana Periodica*, XIX (1953), 296 n. 4.

[20] On January 22, 1594; published by A. Theiner, *Monumenta Slavorum merid.*, II, Nr. 93, p. 86 f.

[21] Vatican Archives, *Arm.* 44, vol. 39 (briefs of Clement VIII, from Nov. 5, 1593, to Dec. 31, 1594), fol. 17-21, 30v-31, 33v-34, 37v-42. These briefs, all of Nov. 8, 1593, are listed and partly edited by A. Theiner, *Vetera Monum. Poloniae*, III, Nr. 164, who is, however, not correct when saying (at the bottom of p. 210), that they are all identical.

[22] *Ibidem*, fol. 20-21.

to open to the Grand Prince encouraging perspectives that Moscow could extend " her Empire in those regions of milder and happier climate, " eventually gaining even Constantinople, " according to the old pretentions of the Muscovites who think that this Empire belongs to them for hereditary reasons. " In that connection reappeared the old question of granting to the Grand Prince, whose title of Tsar was not yet recognized abroad, the royal or imperial title which was always opposed by the Commonwealth.

But even more surprising than such an acknowledgement of Moscow's far reaching political claims and ambitions was the approach of Komulovich's instruction to the religious problem. It is true that also in dealing with the princes of Moldavia and Wallachia as well as with the Cossack leaders — all of them Greek Orthodox — the documents of the papal Chancery which the nuncio received, were ignoring any religious differences, writing to all of them as if they had been Catholics loyal to the Roman Church and to the Roman Pontiff. But even in the case of Moscow, no reference was made to the existing schism nor to any expected reunion when speaking of the " defense of the common religion " ; and the fact that the Christian populations, which were to be liberated from Turkish domination, " observed the Greek rite, " was simply considered one more circumstance which would facilitate Moscow's " progresses " in that direction.

Another such circumstance was the fact that " the oppressed nations are of the same Muscovite language or a little different, " so that they would be glad to receive help from " their own relatives. " Here the influence of Komulovich on the drafting of his instruction is particularly evident, reflecting the ideas of Slavic community which this precursor of George Krizhanich had in common with such Croat contemporaries like Cedulini. At the end of the same instruction the " religious differences " separating Moscow from Rome were at last briefly touched, but only to contrast the free position of the Pope with the dependence of the Patriarch of Constantinople on Ottoman power. Such an approach was quite similar to the treatment of the same problem by Pius V when a quarter of a century before Clement VIII he made strenuous efforts to obtain Moscow's cooperation against the Turks. And in general, the appeal of Komulovich's whole project, when submitted to the Vatican, can be explained by an already old tradition of similar plans which, in spite of many disappointments were time and again resumed with the expectation that Moscow, joining a league of Catholic powers, were it even for political motives, would not only contribute to victory over Islam, but be prepared, at least indirectly, also for religious union. However, in the given case, the official support which the Croat priest received in Rome for his ambitious undertaking, must have been to a large extent the fruit of his own persuasiveness and of an unusual ability in making friends which, with a few exceptions, was to appear in the different places he visited on his trip, including Poland.

Typical for his method in convincing the Vatican that the time was ripe for resuming the conception of a joint anti-Ottoman action not only of Poland but also of Moscow along with the Emperor, a conception which Komulovich fully shared with Cedulini, was his attempt to show through documentary evidence that this conception was shared also by the populations of the Balkans, encouraging them in their resistance against the Turks. Already in earlier years, appeals from these populations were coming to Rome, particularly from Albania which was nearest and where the resistance movement was strongest. [23] But it was just a few months before Komulovich was entrusted with his mission, on June 1, 1593, that " the elders of Albania " sent to Clement VIII a message which most faithfully corresponds to the suggestions of the priest-diplomat. They wrote in the name of " Catholic Albania of Roman faith, " invoking the memory of George Skanderbeg, the fifteenth century hero supported by the Papacy, and expressing the conviction that " all the other Albanians of Greek faith " would join them. " And when His Holiness would move against the said Turk, the Emperor as well as the King of Poland, as well as that of Muscovy with their forces, we would get out of these our lands with a good army in the direction of Constantinople and make also the other Christian peoples rise in great number. "

This rather strange document, [24] without any individual signatures and just one hardly recognizable seal, vaguely dated " from Albania " where nobody had clear ideas about the distant Kings of Poland and Muscovy, could not inspire much confidence. However, it seemed to confirm so obviously all that Komulovich was saying in his own memoranda and conversations that it may have been considered one more argument in favor of his project. It was only a little later, when the nuncio to all northeastern Europe had already left Rome on his way to these lands, that the Secretariate of State received an alarming warning and an expression of serious doubt as to Komulovich's reliability from the first place which he visited on his journey and where he started his propaganda in favor of the military action against the Ottoman Empire — from Venice.

Though Clement VIII, following the example of his predecessors, never ceased in his efforts to persuade the Republic to join that action, this task was not included in the instructions of the Dalmatian prelate, a Venetian

---

[23] See, for instance, in the Vatican Archives, *Arm.* I-XVIII, Nr. 1745-1748 (in the years 1577-1582). It is significant that sometimes the Albanians would claim the restoration of the Greek rite (*Arm.* 52, vol. 29, fol. 16 ; note of Cardinal Santori, of Feb. 26, 1586). About Komulovich's continued contact with them see *ibidem*, fol. 135 (March 12, 1587).

[24] Vatican Archives, *Borgh.* IV 278, fol. 47 (the address is on f. 48v).

subject himself and hardly in a position to negotiate with the Doge Pasquale Cicogna. That task, difficult and delicate in view of the usual reluctance of the Republic to get involved in a Turkish war without immediate necessity and good chances of success, and also in view of the strained relations with the House of Austria, was entrusted to the papal nuncio in Venice, the Bishop of Lodi, Lodovico Taverna. In his reports [25] he never failed to stress the cautious attitude of the Venetians who were alarmed by rumors spread in Constantinople that they had already joined an anti-Ottoman league. [26] But he also reported in detail about any real or planned struggles against the Turks in various regions of eastern Europe [27] on which it was easier to get information in Venice than anywhere else.

Strange enough, Nuncio Taverna had not been informed by the Vatican about the mission of Komulovich about which, on the contrary, the Venetian authorities had been notified by their ambassador in Rome, the outstanding diplomat Paolo Paruta. [28] But soon after the departure of the papal emissary from Venice where he remained only for a short time without establishing any official contacts, the Bishop of Lodi heard a truly sensational story about what happened there to " the Slavonic priest Alexander sent by His Holiness to the land of the Turks to make some peoples rise against them." That story he tried to explain as well as he could in his reports of February 5, 19, and 24, 1594. [29] Knowing very well that there were in Venice Albanian exiles, anxious to organize such an insurrection against the Turks and even offering their cooperation to the Holy See, the Nuncio was not surprised to hear that " Don Alessandro Comoli " had entered into close relation with them, especially with their leader, a certain " Cavaliero Pelissa " whose name frequently appears in connection with the whole matter,[30] and that Komulovich even lived with one of these Albanians in the same room during his stay in Venice. It was, however, surprising if not shocking that after the papal representative had left the city, his occasional roommate discovered, hidden in his bed and obviously forgotten, three letters *in lingua Serviana*, apparently written to the Pope, the Secretary of State and Komulovich himself by " peoples from Albania, " but most probably drafted by the latter addressee and provided with seals which seemed to

---

[25] *Ibidem, Nunz. di Venezia*, vol. 30, 31, 32, covering the years 1592-1596 ; the ciphered reports of the same period are (deciphered) in vol. 40.

[26] *Ibidem*, vol. 30, fol. 70 (March 27, 1593) ; see also f. 291v and 300v (Oct. 21 and Nov. 4, 1594), about the reluctance of the Venetians to join the league.

[27] See, for example, *ibidem*, vol. 30, fol. 255, 283, about the events in far away Georgia.

[28] His reports (1592-1595) are published in *Monumenti storici pubbl. dalla R. Deputazione Veneta di storia patria*, IV, Misc. I-III, Venezia 1887; see II, 40.

[29] *Nunz. di Venezia*, vol. 41, fol. 34v-36, and vol. 30, fol. 148-149v ; published in *Glasnik* (see above, note 17), Nr. 21, p. 17, and Nr. 23, p. 28 f.

[30] In many reports of the Nuncio, most of whom are published in *Glasnik*, see there particularly Nr. 26-34 (the name is usually spelled " Pelesa ").

be false. These letters were appeals to the Holy See to help the Albanians to rise in large number against the Turks on the occasion of the Hungarian war and to send them — obviously as leader of the whole undertaking — the said Komulovich whose high authority they stressed. When these letters were brought to the Doge, the general impression was that they had been fabricated by Komulovich " without any foundation, " in order to get the Pope involved in an undertaking which in the opinion of the Venetians could only be dangerous for the Christian populations of the Ottoman Empire and had to be carefully watched by the Venetian authorities in Dalmatia.

Collecting this information and conveying it to the Vatican, the Nuncio did not utter any definite opinion about the charges against Komulovich, admitting that he did not know whether they were true or dictated by some personal hostility ; he simply noted all rumors in the matter and all possible interpretations, leaving the final judgment to the Secretariate of State. Such a judgment was never formulated, Komulovich was not recalled, and during his whole mission seemed to have the continued support of the Holy See and its representatives in various countries, particularly in Poland. It seems to be the safest interpretation of the whole incident that in his desire to see something done in order to liberate the Balkan Christians and to check the Ottoman onslaught, he would sometimes draft appeals by peoples who otherwise would have hardly known how to write to Rome and whose requests he formulated not without some wishful thinking but probably in agreement with their basic aspirations. It is, however, evident how dangerous such a method was, how easily the propagator of rather fantastic plans could mislead both sides even if his intentions in bringing them together were entirely honest and sincere. In any case, he was hardly qualified for a highly confidential [31] mission in the name of the Pope himself, the difficulties of which were to increase when he moved to even more distant and unknown countries.

For contrary to the supposition expressed in one of the reports of Nuncio Taverna, Komulovich did not go back to Rome after noticing that he had forgotten and lost important papers, but continued his journey, which brought him first to the Danubian region where the war against the Turks was already in full course. When his rather painful Venetian experience was discussed by the professional diplomats of the Holy See, he had already passed through Vienna and arrived at Alba Julia, [32] the residence of the Prince of Transylvania. If on his way he entered into relations with the Imperial Court, he must have been rather well received, because

---

[31] See the introduction to his first instruction, quoted above, note 18.
[32] He reported from Alba Julia to Rome on Feb. 16, 17 and 23, 1594, *Starine* XIV, Nr. 3-5.

any extension of the anti-Ottoman action was in Austria's obvious interest. Nor did his difficulties openly start in Transylvania, then ruled by Sigismund Báthory, a devout Catholic who was soon to enter into a formal alliance with Rudolf II whose cousin he married. But even if Komulovich contributed to that decision and to Sigismund's active participation in the war during the following years, [33] this could not help him in his further activities : not only was the Prince of Transylvania in bad relations with those of Moldavia and Wallachia where his interests clashed with the Polish, but that nephew of the late King of Poland was also in conflict with the other Báthory's : only a few months later, the " Transylvanian tragedy " as it was called in Poland, [34] led to the execution of Sigismund's cousin Balthasar and to the natural alienation of the remaining members of the family, including Cardinal Andrew Báthory whom Komulovich had hoped to see at the head of the anti-Turkish forces in that part of Europe. [35]

After his not unsuccessful but undecisive visit to Transylvania, where the largely Rumanian, Greek Orthodox population was free from Ottoman control but ruled by Catholic Hungarians, Komulovich proceeded to the Danubian principalities where the Rumanians had their own native rulers but under the Sultan's suzerainty. The trend towards a union of all Rumanian lands which occupied such a crucial position between the Ottoman Empire, the possessions of the Habsburgs, and Poland, was becoming more and more apparent in the last decade of the sixteenth century, and particularly influenced the policy of the new Prince of Wallachia, Michael the Brave, who had ascended the throne a year before the arrival of Komulovich in that region. [36] But the papal emissary did not reach at all Wallachia where Catholic propaganda hardly penetrated, Turkish influence was strongest, and Michael's desire to liberate himself from that influence had not yet led to any open break and proved very difficult to coordinate with the anti-Ottoman action of his neighbors. Therefore, Komulovich limited himself to a visit in Moldavia.

Even that visit was very brief in view of the unexpected difficulties which resulted from a recent change on the Moldavian throne. In 1591 Emanuel Aaron, significantly called the Tyrant, had seized the power and after the appearance of two other pretenders — one of them Michael's predecessor in Wallachia — in 1592, was now definitely established on the

---

[33] See Pastor, op. cit., XI, 202 ff. ; about the role of Komulovich in Transylvania : Monum. Vaticana Hungariae, II-3, 42-69.

[34] Scriptores rerum Polonicarum, VII (1881 ; Diary of the Jesuit Monastery in Cracow 1579-1599), 193 ; see also the reports in the Roman Archives of the Society of Jesus, Epistolae Germaniae 173, fol. 142, 179, 189-194.

[35] It was not before 1597 that the Báthory's were reconciled through Nuncio Malaspina : see the original statement of the Cardinal and his brother Stephen, of January 7, in the Vatican Archives, Borgh. III 124 b, fol. 116.

[36] See N. Iorga, Histoire des Roumains, V, 342, also 327-329.

throne. Though Clement VIII in his letter of recommendation for Komulovich was writing to Aaron, [37] his " beloved son, " as if he had been a
Catholic and praised his " greatness of mind, " the religious attitude of the
new prince was entirely different from that of his predecessor Peter Schio-
pul [38] who under the influence of the Archbishop of Lwów and of the Polish
Jesuit Stanislaus Warszewicki, very well received in Moldavia, had been in
good relations with the Holy See and through his main advisors, the Albanian Bartholomeus Bruti and Jeremiah Movila, a brother of the Moldavian
Metropolitan and leader of the pro-Polish party, had made a declaration of
obedience to Sixtus V. That former Prince, so favorable to religious reunion, and his Metropolitan were now in exile, while Aaron who had taken
his place with the support of the English envoy in Constantinople, under
the influence of the emissaries of that envoy who suggested a cooperation
of Orthodox and Protestants against the Catholics, forced the Jesuits to
leave Moldavia and abandoned any idea of union with Rome. He was
equally unwilling to take any action against the Turks who had so recently
recognized him as prince, and under such conditions the two secret audiences which he granted to Komulovich, could hardly lead to any positive
results.

From Jassy, Aaron's residence, the Croat prelate could easily cross
the Dniester river into Polish Podolia, appearing in its main city, Kamieniec, at the end of March 1594, [39] and four weeks later he was already in
Lwów, [40] starting in both places his lengthy negotiations with Polish dignitaries, which in October were to lead him to Cracow. [41] These negotiations
were dealing exclusively with the planned anti-Ottoman league, and therefore
it is rather surprising that Komulovich did not go at all to the headquarters
of the Ukrainian Cossacks whose participation in that league had seemed
so important to Clement VIII that he had given to his envoy, on November 8, 1593, two letters of recommendation or rather credentials, [42] addressed
to the *capitaneus generalis* and to the *milites* of the Cossacks. These
letters were drafted with so much optimism not only as to the services
which that *illustris Cosachiorum militia* was ready to render to the common
cause of Christendom but also as to their loyalty towards the Holy See
and the Catholic Church, that once more the influence of Komulovich's
expectations and interpretations seems highly probable. In that case, however, it is equally possible that the Vatican was relying upon information

---

[37] A. Theiner, *Vetera Monumenta Poloniae*, III, 210.

[38] Well explained by Octavianus Barlea, *De confessione orthodoxa Petri Mohilae*,
Frankfurt 1948, 44 f.

[39] *Starine*, XIV, Nr. 6 (March 31, 1594).

[40] *Ibidem*, Nr. 7 (April 27, 1594).

[41] *Ibidem*, Nr. 8 (Oct. 14, 1594) — 15 (Nov. 17, 1594) ; see also Malaspina's reports
of the same period (Oct. 10-Dec. 2), *ibidem*, XVI, Nr. 5-11.

[42] *Documenta Pontificia historiam Ukrainae illustrantia*, I, Nr. 129, 130.

coming from at least two other sources : from the Imperial Court which already a year before had started negotiations with a view to gaining Cossack cooperation in the war against the Turks, [43] and from Venice where the papal nuncio carefully noted all news received there about the continuous local struggles of the Cossacks " of Poland " against Turks and Tartars. [44] Their traditional opponents were indeed the latter, but since Sinan Pasha hoped that Tartar reinforcements would join him in Hungary, it was encouraging to hear that the Cossacks, in cooperation with Transylvanian forces, were blocking their passage. [45]

All these news were rather vague and included rumors not only of Polish but even of Muscovite cooperation, which were as unreliable as Komulovich's own version of the matter. Writing to the leader of the Cossacks, the papal Chancery did not even know his name, and it is equally uncertain in whose name the Cossack *senior* Stanislaus Chłopicki, whose name sounds Polish, was negotiating about the same time in Prague with Emperor Rudolf II. [46] In any case the " hetman " Christopher Kosiński, probably another Pole who had led the Cossack rebellion of 1592, mainly directed against Prince Ostrogski, was no longer in power, and his successor, Severian Nalevayko, who was to cause so much trouble in the following years, was still in a secondary position. [47] And before undertaking the long and perilous journey to the Cossack headquarters on the lower Dnieper, Komulovich must have found it advisable to collect more precise information about these prospective allies in the Ruthenian lands of Podolia and Lwów which he reached first.

In his instruction [48] old Prince Constantine Ostrogski had been mentioned to him as well informed about the Cossacks, and so was his son, Prince Janusz, Castellane of Cracow who had helped the Emperor to get in touch with them. They must have warned the papal emissary how difficult it was to direct and to control the courageous but undisciplined activities of the Cossacks, and rather discouraged him to approach them in person. [49] As to the general plan of an anti-Ottoman league, Prince Con-

[43] M. Hrushevsky, *Istoria Ukrainy*, VII, 196 ff. (see the bibliography, 579 ff.).

[44] Vatican Archives, *Nunz. di Venezia*, vol. 30, fol. 151 (news from Poland, Feb. 26, 1594).

[45] *Ibidem*, fol. 172-172v (April 23, 1594) ; see also fol. 189, 191v, 201v, 213v, 223, 234v-235 (Aug. 23, 1594).

[46] He is mentioned by the Emperor in his letter to Prince Aaron of Moldavia, of March 7, 1594 (*Documente privitore la istoria românilor*, III-1 (1880), Nr. 179, p. 187), as being in the Emperor's service to fight the Turks; see *ibid*. XII (1903), Nr. 54.

[47] According to the editor's note (150) in *Documenta Pontif.*, I, 23, a certain Mykošynskyj may have been the leader of the Cossacks at the time of Komulovich's mission.

[48] *Starine*, XVI, 226 f ; see also Theiner, *op. cit.*, III, Nr. 164.

[49] See Malaspina's reports about Ostrogski's troubles with the Cossacks : Vatican Archives, *Nunz. di Polonia*, vol. 35, fol. 197v, 219, 221 (Feb. 18 and 28, 1593).

stantine seemed at first quite favorable and ready to play a leading part, [50] an attitude which was understandable were it only in view of the relations of the Ostrogskis with the Austrian court whose favors they wanted to obtain through papal intermediary [51] having themselves estates in the Habsburg lands. But eventually there developed some misunderstanding between the Prince and Komulovich, and there is not the slightest indication that the discussions with the Croat prelate had anything to do with Ostrogski's desire to include Wallachians and Muscovites in the plan of religious reunion which he discussed with Bishop Pociej a year before. [52] That plan was certainly not touched at all in the talks with Komulovich whose interest was exclusively in the struggle against the Turks, to such an extent that when Prince Constantine gave up his earlier plans of an expedition into Moldavia and Wallachia, and Grand Chancellor Zamoyski received his proposals with skepticism and even suspicion, he turned to one of the latter's strongest opponents, Nicholas Jazłowiecki. On August 31, 1594, [53] Komulovich received the formal promise of that nobleman that within three months he would invade the lands of the Tartars or attack those of them who were returning from Hungary, and he paid him in return most of the subsidy which he was to bring to the Cossacks. That strange agreement with an individual Pole who was holding only the rather modest position of Starosta of Śniatyń and whose private enterprises, though undertaken in cooperation with some of the Cossacks, were to prove of limited significance, was the only result of Komulovich's efforts to propagandize in the Commonwealth his vast plan of anti-Ottoman action.

There were indeed in Poland a few other magnates, partisans of the Habsburgs, who, like Palatine Albert Łaski, were even interested in a possible cooperation with Moscow against the Turks and discussed such ideas with Nuncio Malaspina [54] at the very time of the arrival of Komulovich. But in spite of his restless versatility, he does not seem to have met them, though his whole action quite obviously had the full support of the much more balanced and experienced Nuncio to Poland [55] who after returning with the King from Sweden, concentrated more than ever before on his task to bring Poland into an anti-Ottoman league along with the Emperor. The patient negotiations which Malaspina conducted in that

[50] See *ibidem*, *Borgh*. III, 18 d, fol. 149 (June 25, 1594).

[51] *Ibidem*, *Borgh*. III 66 CD, f. 230v (also *Nunz. di Polonia*, vol. 35, fol. 293v-294; June 8, 1593).

[52] Such a supposition has been made by Chodynicki, *op. cit.*, 276 f.

[53] *Starine*, XIV, 102; French translation of that agreement in Pierling, *op. cit.*, II, 347 f.

[54] Vatican Archives, *Borgh*. III 91 AB, fol. 93 (April 22, 1594).

[55] See Malaspina's letters of recommendation for Komulovich, addressed to the imperial envoy and to various personalities in Poland and Lithuania, at the end of November 1594 (Bibl. Vallicelliana, *Ms.* L 18, fol. 120-122v, also fol. 127).

respect, rightly stressing that only papal initiative could persuade the Poles to join such a league, [56] were continuing without much prospect of speedy success, when Komulovich, after spending the fall of 1594 in Cracow, decided to proceed from Poland to Moscow. But even this most delicate part of his mission does not seem to have been taken too seriously in the Commonwealth, and probably he did not even need the advice or support of Cardinal Radziwiłł in order to be able to cross the eastern frontier.

There is little evidence regarding the discussions of Komulovich with the Polish hierarchy, though according to his instruction he was to see at least the Archbishop of Lwów and the Bishop of Łuck. As to the latter, he had been seriously ill and even wanted to go to Italy for reasons of health, but was kept busy in his diocese " in the midst of Schismatic people, " as he wrote to the Nuncio. [57] A meeting with Maciejowski would have perhaps familiarized Komulovich with the problem of reunion with the Ruthenians, and made him aware of the importance of that problem and of the better chances of achieving such a reunion in the Commonwealth rather than in Moscow. But his political activities obviously did not leave him time enough for dealing with these religious issues during his first sojourn in Poland, and this is one more reason why he hardly could have influenced Prince Ostrogski in the matter of including Moscow in the project of reunion.

It is not even known whether Komulovich met the Ruthenian bishops favorable to that project, though Malaspina recommended him to those bishops shortly before his departure for Moscow[58], having received for the first time some information on their initiative which he found important enough to report in detail to Rome. [59] He did it independently of any considerations regarding Moscow, though he wrote in that same report of October 15, 1594, about the political relations of the Commonwealth with its eastern neighbor. [60] There seemed to be some prospect of replacing the precarious truce between the two powers by an " eternal peace " which would include also Sweden and improve the chances of an anti-Ottoman league. Already on December 8, 1593, [61] the Nuncio, when still in Stockholm with Sigismund III, had reported on such possibilities in which the Holy See was so interested. He had expressed the hope that the Grand Prince of Moscow would join such a league, if " the liberation of Greece from Turkish tyranny " were proposed to him and peace with Poland and Sweden guaranteed, pointing out that only in case of an understanding

---

[56] *Borgh*. III 91 AB, fol. 81v (that reference in his report of April 6, 1594, is underlined in the original).

[57] *Borgh*. III 66 B, fol. 107-108 (Feb. 27, 1594).

[58] Bibl. Vallicelliana, *Ms*. L. 18, fol. 123-123v (Dec. 4, 1594).

[59] *Borgh*. III 91 AB, fol. 226.

[60] *Ibidem*, fol. 226v.

[61] *Borgh*. III 66 CD, fol. 429.

with Poland Moscow could participate in an action through Wallachia while otherwise she could attack the Turks only in the Don and Azov region. Now, in the fall of 1594, Malaspina again took up that matter getting in touch with the imperial ambassador sent to Moscow who, as usual, was very much in favor of including that power in the league. [62] But though the instructions of Komulovich considered it advisable that he, too, should act in Moscow jointly with Austrian diplomacy, his part in all these negotiations remains rather obscure. The exceptionally " splendid " reception of the papal envoy at the Muscovite frontier [63] seemed to confirm the high hopes with which he went there. But after his discussions with the Tsar, he had to report that there was little hope that Moscow would move against the Turks, so that in spite of a rather vague letter received from Fedor, the Vatican eventually came to the conclusion that at the given moment no " glorious enterprise " could be expected from the *barbaria* of these people and from " the incapacity of the prince whom they serve. " [64] Komulovich himself returned to the Commonwealth in the spring of 1595 without any concrete results[65] and remained there for the next two years.

During his absence, the cause of religious reunion with the Ruthenians had made much more progress than that of the anti-Ottoman league, but only in the sense of a regional union within the frontiers of the Commonwealth. And it became more and more apparent that in contradistinction to wide and ambitious schemes as expressed in Komulovich's instructions, that limited but concrete achievement would be the most important and lasting result of Rome's eastern policy in the pontificate of Clement VIII. His nuncio to Poland, who at first seemed to consider that problem rather secondary, would gradually give more and more attention to it, and also the interest of the Secretariate of State would steadily increase. The first evidence of that was precisely Malaspina's report of October 15, 1594, where he started discussing the news about the pro-Roman initiative of the Ruthenian bishops which had developed since 1590, but only now reached the Nuncio and through him the Pope himself.

[62] See the reference in his report of Oct. 15, as quoted above note 60.

[63] *Borgh.* III 89 b, fol. 69 (Malaspina's report of April 14, 1595).

[64] *Borgh.* III 18 c, fol. 236 (in the instruction sent to Malaspina on August 12, 1595).

[65] See his rather vague letter sent to Leo Sapieha from Smoleńsk (May 25); *Archiwum Sapiehów,* I, Nr. 141.

Chapter V

THE YEAR OF DECISION

In 1594 the annual synod of the Ruthenian hierarchy, which was supposed to take place at Brest in the month of June, could not be formally held, because the King had not yet returned from Sweden and in his absence no public assemblies were permitted. This was recalled to the Ruthenian bishops by the Primate of Poland, the old Archbishop of Gniezno, Stanislaus Karnkowski, who in contradistinction to Solikowski and Maciejowski rather neglected the first news about the project of religious reunion. However, one of the Jesuits, who was particularly interested in that project, Father Caspar Nahaj (of Tartar origin), went to Brest where Metropolitan Rahoza, Pociej and Terlecki met at the usual time.[1] They apparently limited themselves to a re-examination of the endless conflict between the Bishop of Lwów, Gedeon Bałaban, and the Orthodox Brotherhood of that city, and the Metropolitan decided to excommunicate the bishop in view of his disobedience to the decisions of the preceding synods.[2]

Terlecki did not consider that step expedient because Bałaban still seemed to be favorable to reunion with Rome to which the brotherhoods were so strongly opposed. And he did not hesitate to continue the cooperation with Bałaban, though he also continued to enjoy the confidence of Rahoza who gave him full powers to negotiate with Zamoyski.[3]

Similar to the private meeting of four bishops at Bełz which had preceded the Brest Synod of June 1590 and taken a first initiative in favor of reunion, a meeting composed again of four bishops and again under Terlecki's leadership had taken place three months before the abortive assembly at Brest, in the little town of Sokal, not far from Bełz, and renewed the pro-Roman decision which had been taken there four years earlier. Again Terlecki and Bałaban were joined by the Bishop of Chełm, Zbirujski, in whose diocese both meetings were held. This time, however, the fourth bishop was not Pełczycki of Pińsk, who died not much later and probably was already ill, but the Bishop of Przemyśl, Michael Kopys-

---

[1] *Listy Żolkiewskiego* (Letters of St. Żółkiewski, ed. by Lubomirski), Nr. 33.

[2] *Akty Zap. Rossii*, IV, Nr. 50 (July, 1 1594).

[3] On July 2; that unpublished document is quoted by K. Lewicki, *Ks. K. Ostrogski*, 108 n. 2.

teński, the same who finally was to turn against the Union along with Bałaban. [4]

Terlecki can be hardly blamed for not having foreseen the change in the attitude of these two collaborators and was perhaps particularly anxious to secure the adherence of these unreliable colleagues. In any case, he soon started collecting the signatures of the other members of the Ruthenian hierarchy under the statement drafted at Sokal. [5] In this he was rather successful, because within a few months he was in possession of a document sealed and signed by all Ruthenian bishops of Poland and Lithuania, with the exception of only one, and could submit it, accompanied by one of them, to the foremost statesman of the kingdom, Grand Chancellor John Zamoyski. [6] All the bishops, except the one who had not yet signed the statement, were unanimous to recognize the Pope as Vicar of Christ, to live in future according to the prescriptions of the Holy See and to reform the Greek Church in that sense. They also asked Zamoyski to protect them if the " schismatic " Prince Ostrogski would molest them because of their Union with Rome, to advise them what to do in order to carry out their plan, and to support with all his authority their request that after reunion all Ruthenian bishops or at least one of them should receive a seat in the Senate of the Commonwealth. The fear of Ostrogski's hostility to the whole project and the desire to be admitted to the Senate, like the bishops of Latin rite, appear for the first time in that important statement.

Unfortunately, its text has not been preserved and the summary included in Nuncio Malaspina's report does not give the names of either the bishop who went with Terlecki to the Grand Chancellor, or the one whose signature had not yet been obtained. There is no evidence that it was precisely the ambitious Bałaban whom Terlecki had taken as companion on that memorable occasion, but it was undoubtedly under Terlecki's influence that Zamoyski rejected the simultaneous request of Metropolitan Rahoza that Bałaban's excommunication be confirmed by royal decree. [7] In connection with this, it seems highly probable that the missing signature

---

[4] About the probable date (March 27) and the composition of the Sokal meeting, see Chodynicki, *Kościół prawosławny*, 279 n. 4, 280 n. 1 and 2.

[5] Chodynicki's arguments (*ibidem*, 280 n. 3) in defense of the authenticity of these signatures are confirmed by Malaspina's report which is discussed and quoted (see the following note) below.

[6] This and all the following details regarding the negotiations of the two Ruthenian bishops with Zamoyski are taken from Malaspina's report of Oct. 15, 1594, Vatican Archives, *Borgh.* III 91 ab, fol. 226. K. Lewicki, *Ks. Konstanty Ostrogski*, 109 ff. who used a copy of that report in the collections of the Polish Academy and translated it into Polish (p. 111 n. 1), gives a different interpretation of the whole situation. Also A. M. Ammann, *Abriss*, 209, blames the apparent secrecy of Terlecki's action and supposes that it was Bałaban who accompanied him on his visit to Zamoyski.

[7] *Akty Zap. Rossii*, IV, Nr. 51 (Sept. 28, 1594).

was Rahoza's, though it is possible too that it was Pociej's, [8] since the latter, whose adherence was rightly considered of greatest importance by the King and the Chancellor, was informed only a few months later of the details of an action which was so fully in agreement with his own intentions. In any case, the secrecy, with which Terlecki proceeded in that early phase of his negotiations and which later was held against him, is understandable in view of Ostrogski's threatening position. For that same reason, Pociej was not kept fully informed of all initial steps, since his close relations with the Prince were generally known, while their disagreement as to the conditions of reunion had not yet appeared except in their private correspondence. [9]

Even before Zamoyski interfered with these personal matters and immediately after receiving the statement of the Ruthenian bishops, the Chancellor did exactly what he had done in 1588, when an earlier possibility of religious reunion between Latins and Greeks appeared in connection with the visit of Patriarch Jeremiah in the Commonwealth : [10] he referred that whole religious issue to the representative of the Holy See with a view of bringing it to the knowledge of the Pope himself. On that earlier occasion, the attitude of both, the Nuncio and the papal Legate then in Poland, had been very cautious and reserved, and Rome's reaction purely negative. And now again much depended on the position which would be taken by Nuncio Malaspina and by Pope Clement VIII who was precisely the former Cardinal Aldobrandini, Legate to Poland in 1588.

Just like the papal representatives in that earlier period, Malaspina was absorbed by entirely different problems. Though he had accompanied Sigismund III on his trip to Sweden, his attempts to contribute to the restoration of Catholicism in that Kingdom were obviously unsuccessful. [11] But what remained his main concern, in agreement with the instructions received from Rome, was to obtain Poland's participation in the anti-Ottoman league in cooperation with the Emperor. And the only case in which hitherto he had shown some interest in the problem of the Eastern Church, getting alarmed about a possible visit of the Patriarch of Alexandria in the Kingdom, was in close relation with the struggle against the Ottoman Empire and all those who were serving its interests. [12] Nevertheless, as soon as Zamoyski placed before him the project of religious union with

---

[8] His signature appears indeed only on a text which has a later date ; see *ibidem*, Nr. 55 ; he admitted himself in the course of the polemics after the Union of Brest (*Russk. istor. bibl.*, XIX, 590 ff.) that he had not sealed the copy which had been originally handed over to Terlecki.

[9] See above, p. 248 f.

[10] See above, p. 224.

[11] During his absence he kept in touch with the foremost senators of the Commonwealth, but exclusively in matters regarding Sweden and the anti-Ottoman league ; see the rich material in the Vatican Archives, particularly *Borgh*. III 66 B.

[12] See above, Chap. III, p. 250, about his report of July 21, 1593.

the Ruthenians, a project suggested not by any Greek visitor of dubious intentions but by their own native ecclesiastical leaders, Malaspina fully realized the significance of such an opportunity. He stressed in his report sent to Rome on October 15, 1594 that " if it would please the Lord to touch the hearts of these people of Russia and Lithuania, a million of souls would be gained and the Moldavians and Wallachians would easily follow. " He was aware, too, that the King was favorable, both for religious reasons " and for some respects concerning the advantage and security of the Kingdom. " Therefore, he wrote at once to the Chancellor asking him to make the two bishops who acted as spokesmen of the Ruthenian hierarchy visit the Nuncio as soon as possible.

Significant, however, is the reason given by Malaspina for receiving these rather surprising news with confidence. He gave them " some credit, " because the eldest son of Prince Ostrogski, Janusz, a convert to Catholicism of Latin rite and, as Castellane of Cracow, the highest lay dignitary of the realm, had told him that a few weeks before his father had established contact with " a Catholic Patriarch " in Venice in order to " reform his estate and himself. " These rather obscure and enigmatic rumors sufficed to make Malaspina believe that the same Prince Constantine whose opposition the initiators of the project of reunion so rightly feared, would at last make true his own earlier statements in favor of that reunion and thus increase the chances of success of the whole movement.

Similar illusions were shared for a long time also by others, but in the case of the Nuncio, who was to keep them until almost the last minute, they were based upon a specific reason connected with his activities in favor of the struggle against the Turks. While Alexander Komulovich, working for the same cause, did not succeed to convince the old prince of the seriousness of his projects, Malaspina, who from the beginning of his mission to Poland had very close and friendly relations with the whole Ostrogski family, [13] considered Prince Constantine one of the main supporters of the idea of Poland's participation in the anti-Ottoman league. Reporting in that matter to Rome during the months which preceded his involvement in the problem of union with the Ruthenians, the Nuncio emphasized [14] that Ostrogski was only waiting for the King's permission to interfere with the troubled situation in Moldavia and Wallachia, opposing there Turkish influence. And it was obvious that in contradistinction to his political opponent Zamoyski who was planning in that same region an independent Polish action, Prince Constantine seemed ready for cooperation with the Emperor, hoping that the papal curia, following Malaspina's recommendations, would

---

[13] See, for instance, his report of February 2, 1593 (*Borgh.* III 66 CD, fol. 48 ; copy in *Nunz. di Polonia*, vol. 35, fol. 211v) on the promotions of old Prince Constantine's sons to high senatorial offices.

[14] *Borgh.* III 91 AB, fol. 103 (April 9, 1594).

in turn support at the imperial court the private interests of the Ostrogskis.[15]

All such reports were studied at the Vatican with special interest, and in the instructions, which Malaspina received in reply, it was emphasized time again that the planned anti-Ottoman league would serve the interests of Poland even more than those of Hungary and Germany.[16] For the Pope wanted Moldavia and Wallachia to be united with Poland which would regain full access to the Black Sea, possibly as far as Varna, and if also the whole of Prussia would be united with her, extend from the Black to the Baltic Sea, to the advantage of all Christendom.[17] But precisely in view of these vast perspectives, the limited action envisaged by Prince Ostrogski seemed inadequate and the cooperation of Zamoyski indispensable, and the Chancellor, in spite of his well known opposition to the House of Austria, received on behalf of the Pope high praise for his wisdom and devotion to his country as well as to Christendom.[18]

For Clement VIII who "loved Poland as if she were his own country" and desired nothing more than "the greatness and happiness of her King and the Kingdom,"[19] it was, therefore very welcome news that Zamoyski, acting on that occasion in full agreement with Sigismund III, supported and recommended a project of purely religious character, which was another particularly striking example of Rome's and Poland's community of interests. Replying at once on November 12, 1594,[20] to the Nuncio's report on the initiative of the Ruthenian bishops, Cardinal Passeri Aldobrandini, the Pope's nephew who in the Secretariate of State was in charge of Central and Eastern European affairs, without entering into any discussions as to the real intentions of Prince Ostrogski in that matter, and far from showing any scepticism similar to that of 1588, fully agreed with Malaspina that if these bishops, about whom the Grand Chancellor had written, would come to see the Nuncio and show themselves ready to recognize the primacy of the Holy See, this would be "in itself most useful and salutary for an infinite number of souls." Furthermore, this would be, as he wrote, an evidence that Divine Providence, touching the hearts of men, would also prove "more propitious to the started undertakings." Most probably he was so referring to that other "undertaking," the anti-Ottoman league, which was making so little progress and yet remained the basic concern of the Vatican. In any case, he wanted to receive from the Nuncio "certainty and more light in the whole matter."

---

[15] This was indeed promised by the Pope ; see *Nunz. di Polonia*, vol. 35, fol. 341 (August 5, 1593).

[16] *Borgh*. III 18 e, fol. 204 (instruction of May 6, 1595).

[17] *Ibidem*, fol. 204v and 214 (instruction of June 10, 1595).

[18] *Ibidem*, fol. 216v.

[19] *Ibidem*, fol. 204.

[20] *Ibidem*, fol. 179v.

Even before these words of encouragement could reach Malaspina on November 25, 1594,[21] he returned in one of his reports, in which the Turkish problem continued to receive most of his attention, to the question of reunion with the Ruthenians. He did not connect it with any political issues, not even with Poland's relations with Moscow which already in his first report of October 15, he had treated separately, but he simply stressed Zamoyski's desire to see that religious matter handled by the Nuncio rather than by himself and the authorities of the Commonwealth. The Chancellor had written him " that he could not attend to the settlement of the question raised by these Ruthenian and Lithuanian bishops, being far away from them and busy with the Tartars, but would call them as soon as possible and try to persuade them to turn to me " (the Nuncio). Zamoyski's desire to avoid any direct State interference with the problem of religious reunion and to settle it in full agreement with the competent ecclesiastical authority appears very clearly in that statement.

It is true, however, that the Chancellor wanted the leaders of the Ruthenian hierarchy also to get in touch with the King, as soon as all of them would have arrived at an unanimous agreement and at a detailed formulation of their aims and purposes. This was indeed accomplished before Terlecki or any of his colleagues followed Zamoyski's suggestion directly to approach the Nuncio in whose correspondence with Rome the Ruthenian problem did not reappear before the spring of the following year. For the further discussions among the bishops of Eastern rite themselves took more time than originally expected, so that their decisive declaration was not drafted before December 1594. And this was achieved thanks to the helpful cooperation of one of the Polish bishops of Latin rite, that same Bernard Maciejowski who from the very day he had been named Catholic bishop of Łuck showed so much sympathetic interest in the project of religious union with the Ruthenians and was in the best position to second and to promote the initiative of the Orthodox bishop of the same place, Cyril Terlecki.

It was in Maciejowski's residence at Torczyn, not far from Łuck, that in the first days of December, from the 2nd to the 4th, a small but decisive meeting took place and removed the last difficulties, thus opening the door to further negotiations with both papal and royal authorities and preparing the ground for the next synod of the Ruthenian hierarchy. From among the latter only Terlecki and Pociej were present at Torczyn, but in their persons the most sincere, reliable, and active leaders of the whole movement had at last been put forward and brought to a full understanding. Maciejowski himself who most probably acted in agreement with Zamoyski, has,

---

[21] *Borgh.* III 91 ab, fol. 321v.

18

briefly put on record, in an autographic notice, [22] the origin of the memorable document which they drafted in common and which replaced all earlier statements in favor of reunion. The text written by Terlecki in two copies, both in the Ruthenian language and both considered authentic originals, was ready already on the first day of the meeting, December 2, and signed and sealed at once by Terlecki and Pociej who were to collect the signatures and seals of all other members of the hierarchy. And on the last day, December 4 after mass, Pociej handed to Maciejowski a Polish translation, written by himself, which both Ruthenian bishops signed while their Polish colleague added his explanatory note.

Longer and more comprehensive than any earlier statements the originals of which were not preserved and obviously lost their significance, the Torczyn document [23] was drafted as a joint declaration of all who would ultimately give their adherence. From the outset it was made quite clear that the main reason which made religious union so urgent " in these our most unhappy times " was the dissemination of numerous and various heresies " which made so many abandon the Orthodox Christian faith and separate themselves from the Church of God and His true worship in Trinity. " Pociej's own experience, who born a Greek Orthodox had for some time joined the Calvinists, and the awareness of the penetration of even Antitrinitarian doctrines into the churches and schools of the Ruthenians, dictated that argument. And it was admitted that the real cause of such a dangerous situation was " our disagreement with the Romans " which made mutual assistance impossible, and that " we had never seriously cared " for reunion with them, " merely waiting until " our superiors would do something about it.

These " superiors " were, of course, the Patriarchs of Constantinople, but there was no longer any hope that reunion could be achieved through them, simply because " oppressed by the yoke of the pagans, they could not do anything, even if, perhaps, they were willing. " Realizing, therefore, that under such conditions it was their own responsibility to return to that original unity under a single superior, the Roman Pope, which once had made the dissemination of heresies most difficult, the Ruthenian bishops

---

[22] Published by G. Hofmann in appendix I, p. 136 (Latin translation of the Polish original in n. 1), of his study " Wiedervereinigung der Ruthenen mit Rom, " *Orientalia Christiana*, III-2 (1925), from the original in the Vatican Archives, *AA* I-XVIII, 1731, Nr. 3, fol. 4v.

[23] The file in the Vatican Archives, *loc. cit.*, contains one of the Ruthenian originals (Nr. 5-6, fol. 7-8), the Polish text written by Pociej (Nr. 3, fol. 3-4), a later copy of that text (Nr. 4, fol. 5-6) and a contemporary Latin translation (Nr. 7, fol. 9-10). Hofmann has published (*op. cit.*, 137-139) that translation whose earlier editions were inaccurate, and (on plate 1) a photographic reproduction of the Ruthenian original with the seals (except the last one which is on fol. 8 v).

expressed their firm decision to put an end to a schism which in their time permitted the heretics to become so strong.

There was, strange enough, in their statement no reference to the Union of Florence, but speaking about similar efforts of their predecessors who had given much thought to the problem, they could only mean the earlier attempts to assure the survival of that Union in the Ruthenian lands. Regretting that these attempts had been interrupted, as they had been indeed throughout most of the sixteenth century, the bishops devoted the whole remaining part of their declaration to a mutual pledge to follow up that urgent matter in order to be able to worship God " with our dearest brethren the Romans, remaining under the same visible pastor of God's Church, to whom such a pre-eminence had always been due. " They also decided to bring to such a union and concord with the Roman Church " our ecclesiastical brethren and the common people, " the clergy and laity of the Ruthenians.

A close examination of the original of that solemn script shows very clearly [24] that after the date, in the narrow space left between the text and the place for seals and signatures, a brief reservation was added that the ceremonies and rites, including the administration of the holy sacraments should be " fully preserved ... according to the use of the Oriental Church, after correcting only those articles which hindered the union itself, so that everything should be done following the old custom, as it had been once when the union lasted. "

If this was only a last minute addition, merely recalling the principle, it was certainly not because it was considered of secondary importance, but because that general principle which had already been stressed in the earliest statements in favor of reunion, beginning with that of 1590, was to be developed in detail, in a long series of " articles, " as soon as another synod of the Ruthenian hierarchy would meet and formally confirm what had been decided at Torczyn.

It now was the first task of the two leaders, who had drafted the declaration of December 2, 1594, in consultation with Maciejowski, to collect even before such a synod due in June of the following year, the signatures of all their colleagues, as it had been done in the cases of all similar earlier declarations, but this time, if possible, without a single exception left. In order to find out to what an extent they succeeded, it is necessary to study both originals which, in addition to the Polish copy given to Maciejowski with the signatures of Pociej and Terlecki only, were prepared in Torczyn for the use of either of the two initiators. One of these originals, undoubtedly Pociej's, was preserved in the archives of the Metropolitans of

---

[24] As pointed out by Chodynicki, *op. cit.*, 283 n. 2, though he could only examine the photograph.

the Ruthenian Church united with Rome, [25] but was never signed nor sealed by anybody except the two initiators themselves who had done so at once, at Torczyn. It therefore appears that it was once more Terlecki who, like on similar occasions in the preceding years, actually collected all further adhesions, while Pociej limited himself to persuasions in writing. And it must be Terlecki's copy which is preserved in the Vatican Archives, signed and sealed by five more members of the Ruthenian hierarchy.

There are on that document traces of eight seals, of which, however, only five are preserved and only two clearly recognizable, viz., the second of which is Pociej's with his well known coat of arms, and the sixth with the coat of arms of Kościesza belonging to Bishop Zbirujski of Chełm. The first seal is obviously that of Metropolitan Rahoza whose signature appears besides that seal, while all other signatures follow under the two rows of seals. [26] The first two signatures are those of Pociej of Volodymir and Brest, with the title " protothronius " indicating his first rank among the bishops, and of Terlecki of Łuck and Ostrog with the title of exarch, i. e., representative of the Patriarch of Constantinople as granted to him by Jeremiah II in 1589. Then came the signatures of Gregory, Archbishop-elect of Polotsk and Vitebsk, Dionysius Zbirujski, Bishop of Chełm and Bełz, and Leontius Pełczycki, Bishop of Pinsk and Turov. Finally, added on another folio, there are two more signatures, not of the two remaining bishops, but of Ionas Hohol, who signed twice : first as Archimandrite (Abbot) of the Church of the Holy Savior in Kobryn, a city belonging to the diocese of Pinsk-Turov, and then as Bishop-elect of that diocese ; he had been obviously designated as successor of the sick Pełczycki, and specified that he was signing " that agreement of my brethren. "

Out of these " brethren, " i. e., the eight full members of the Ruthenian hierarchy, two are missing, and strange enough, these are precisely the two who later joined the opposition against the union of Brest : Bałaban of Lwów and Kopysteński of Przemyśl. But since both of them had signed with Terlecki the Sokal declaration in favor of reunion a few months before, it is hard to suppose that they refused to sign the similar statement which he now submitted to all bishops, especially as precisely Bałaban was the first to proclaim the Union with Rome in his own diocese, a few weeks after the Torczyn meeting. [27] In any case, however, Pociej and Terlecki's effort to have their draft accepted by the whole Ruthenian hierarchy and

---

[25] Along with other material taken from the archives of these Metropolitans of whom Pociej himself was to be the second, that document is published in *Akty Zap. Rossii*, IV, Nr. 53.

[26] Chodynicki's careful examination of the photograph (*loc. cit.*) made him suppose that Rahoza signed last which is quite probable indeed, but there is no evidence on the original that Pociej and Terlecki signed when the other bishops had already affixed their seals, which would be difficult to explain.

[27] *Akty Zap. Rossii*, IV, Nr. 58 (January 28, 1595) ; see below p. 278.

to coordinate the activities of all its members was not without meeting some difficulties, and best known are the apparent hesitations of the Metropolitan himself whose agreement was, of course, the most important and seems to have been made a prerequisite condition of official support by the King and Zamoyski, who even wanted to see him personally. Rahoza's correspondence in the months between the Torczyn meeting and the following synod, a correspondence conducted at the same time with Pociej and with one of the most prominent Orthodox magnates, Theodor Skumin Tyszkiewicz, as well as some of his letters written after the synod, could even give the impression that the Metropolitan did not sincerely support the movement in favor of reunion with Rome. [28] His attitude can, however, be well explained without accepting such an interpretation.

Pociej did not approach him before January 26, 1595, [29] several weeks after the Torczyn meeting, and while recommending him the cause of reunion in the warmest and most convincing terms, was showing himself, as in the earlier years of his discussions with Maciejowski and the Greek Arcudius, some hesitation in going ahead too rapidly. It is true that he became impatient [30] when the Metropolitan whose cooperation he rightly considered indispensable, delayed his answer, and that both Pociej and the particularly active Terlecki were disappointed, when as late as May 17 Rahoza failed to appear at a planned conference in Kobryn not far from Brest. But nevertheless, after receiving from both of them a renewed appeal, [31] he duly convoked for June 12 a formal synod of the whole Ruthenian hierarchy in Brest. That synod was to confirm the Torczyn decisions which the Metropolitan must have signed in the meantime, probably participating also in the drafting of the final conditions for reunion with Rome on June 1.

If before taking his decision Rahoza asked for the advice of Tyszkiewicz, [32] he acted very wisely. In view of the opposition of Prince Constantine Ostrogski, the Palatine of Kiev who was the uncontested lay leader of the Orthodox in the Kingdom of Poland, it was indeed of the highest importance to act in full understanding with at least another member of the aristocracy who still belonged to the Eastern Church, was second in influence only to Ostrogski himself and to none as far as the Grand Duchy of Lithuania was concerned. It was precisely in the limits of the Grand Duchy, in Brest, that the Ruthenian synods were meeting, and Theodor Tyszkiewicz, a scion of a powerful family whose other members had already

---

[28] This is the opinion of practically all historians who underestimated the statement which through Terlecki he submitted to Zamoyski (*Akty Zap. Rossii, IV, Nr* 54).

[29] *Akty Zap. Ross.*, IV, Nr. 56.

[30] See his letter of Feb. 11, 1595, *ibidem*, Nr. 59.

[31] *Ibidem*, Nr. 66 (May 20, 1595).

[32] *Ibidem*, Nr. 57.

turned Catholic or Protestant as most of the other princes and lords, [33] happened to be Palatine of Nowogródek, a province where Protestant penetration seemed particularly threatening and where, on the other hand, the Orthodox metropolitans used to reside rather than in the frontier city of Kiev. For all these reasons, it was advisable not to give Tyszkiewicz the impression that the hierarchy, and in particular Rahoza, were deciding the whole matter of reunion without caring for his opinion. That opinion, as first evidenced in his answer delayed until May 10, [34] was rather reserved, but in any case the Palatine concluded that if the Union was desired by God, it would be vain to oppose it ; and he was correct in pointing out the two main sources of trouble : the policies of the Patriarchs of Constantinople who created division within the Church — a remark in full agreement with the Torczyn declaration, and the inconsiderate actions of Bałaban in conflict with the Lwów Brotherhood.

Premature was indeed the decision of the Ruthenian Bishop of Lwów to convoke there already on January 28, in the midst of all these discussions, a rather well attended diocesan synod where he pledged in public to turn away from the Patriarch of Constantinople and to recognize the authority of the Pope. [35] This was precisely what all the signatories of the Torczyn declaration had promised to do, but jointly and without any advance publicity. And Bałaban was certainly not qualified to call upon the Metropolitan and the other bishops to follow his example, since it was not before March that Rahoza, following Zamoyski's advice, released him from excommunication. [36] That the Metropolitan himself proceeded more slowly, step by step, was not only much more appropriate but also had two additional reasons.

He was deeply attached to the Eastern rite and liturgy, and when he continued to deny that he was abandoning the Eastern Church, this was not a repudiation of the union with the Latin Church, but, as he stressed himself on some later occasion, [37] a pledge to defend the traditional ceremonies, dear to the Ruthenians, to all of whom he recommended a similar attitude. It is quite possible that the reservation regarding the Eastern rite which was added to the Torczyn pledge in the matter of reunion, was squeezed between the text as originally drafted and the place left for seals and signatures, at the request of Rahoza before he signed himself. And he was still waiting for the elaborate statement of all guarantees of the

---

[33] On the list of these princes and lords who abandonned Orthodoxy already before the Union of Brest, given by the contemporaneous theologian Meletius Smotrycki and very frequently quoted (see, f. i., H. Likowski, *Unia brzeska*, 53), the Tyszkiewicz are among the first lords to be mentioned.

[34] *Akty Zap. Rossii*, IV, Nr. 65.

[35] *Ibidem*, Nr. 58.

[36] *Ibidem*, Nr. 61.

[37] *Ibidem*, Nr. 69 ; see below p. 296.

preservation of Eastern customs and ceremonies, which was to be worked out on the eve of the synod which he was asked to convoke.

Furthermore, the Metropolitan was a rather old man, too old for having been educated in Jesuit schools so that the suspicion that he acted under Jesuit pressure has proved entirely wrong. But the well informed Jesuits of Lwów were among the first to point out [38] that already in the critical year of 1594-95 Rahoza was known by the Ruthenians to think of a union with Rome, and they added that he was "a honest, modest, and pious man, though already elderly." They made at the same time an interesting distinction between those Ruthenians who simply considered themselves loyal followers of the Patriarchs of Constantinople, and those who followed the Patriarch of Alexandria, that Meletius Pigas who was the most violent opponent of the Union of Brest among the Greeks. Rahoza obviously belonged to the former, faithful to Kiev's old tradition, and in addition to his desire to preserve as much as possible of that tradition, his old age made him differ in method of action from the versatile and dynamic Terlecki and even from Pociej who after making his decision was to fight so hard for the cause of reunion.

That, however, also the Metropolitan greatly contributed to that cause, is evidenced not only by his attitude when the union was to be finally confirmed in 1596, but also by some important aspects of a last problem which has to be considered in connection with the signatures on the Torczyn document. These signatures include in addition to the names of bishops who had been active already in earlier years, and to the Archimandrite Hohol as Bishop-elect of Pinsk, another newcomer who at the given moment was only nominated to a vacant see: Gregory, Archbishop-elect of Polotsk and Vitebsk. He is much less known than the others, sometimes called Herman Ivanovich, and his last name, Zahorski, is rarely given, though according to his seal he belonged to a noble family using the coat of arms Gozdawa. What is well known, on the contrary, is the great importance of his see, the only one besides Kiev which from the early fifteenth century was an archbishopric, the only large diocese, or rather archdiocese, which, besides the much smaller and scarcely populated bishopric of Turov remained after the Union of Lublin entirely within the limits of the Grand Duchy of Lithuania and included almost all of its White Ruthenian population. The city of Polotsk itself was situated, along with Vitebsk and Mstislav which also appear in the full title of the archbishop, near to the Muscovite frontier and was even occupied by Ivan the Terrible from 1563

---

[38] See the ms. comments to their report printed in *Litterae Societatis Iesu duorum annorum* 1594 *et* 1595, Neapoli 1605), in the Roman Archives of the Society of Jesus, *Fondo Gesuitico*, Nr. 1537, Busta Nr. 160/9, p. 13. Rahoza himself pointed out that he was to old to learn Latin (*Akty Zap. Rossii*, IV, Nr. 80.)

to 1579. Immediately after its liberation in the first campaign of Stefan Báthory, a Jesuit college was founded there but encountered unusual difficulties in a remote region where the hostility of the Orthodox was stiffened by the rather numerous Calvinists and even Antitrinitarians some of whom occupied the highest offices in the administration. [39]

Under such conditions, it was of the highest importance who would be the successor of the insignificant Archbishop Anastasius Sielicki, deceased amidst the earlier preparations for the union with Rome but without having participated in the movement. When Gregory was elected as candidate of Rahoza in whose service he had been, probably as head of the Metropolitan chancery, King Sigismund III first named him only auxiliary bishop, [40] and delayed his nomination to the archbishopric until September of the following year. [41] Even then he granted it only provisionally, on the condition that Gregory would transfer his obedience from the Patriarch of Constantinople to the Roman Pontiff, in agreement with the charter of King Władysław III which made loyalty to the Union of Florence a condition of the recognition of the rights of the Ruthenian clergy. Following on that exceptionally important occasion Skarga's advice to insist upon a strict interpretation of that charter, the King must have had some doubts whether the Archbishop would remain faithful to the Torczyn pledge which he had signed. That, however, these doubts were completely unjustified, is proved not only by the outstanding role of Gregory in supporting the Union of Brest, but particularly [42] by an earlier statement of Prince Constantine Ostrogski [43] who blamed Rahoza for having elevated to the see of Polotsk his former "servant," in reward, as he added, for having persuaded his master to betray Orthodoxy. This is indeed a clear testimony that both the Metropolitan of Kiev and the Archbishop of Polotsk were definitely and sincerely, though at the beginning not quite openly, in favor of the Union.

In the light of all these facts it is fully understandable that the optimistic Terlecki, after approaching his colleagues in execution of the Torczyn decisions, at once took the next step and went to see the Nuncio according

---

[39] Among the many reports about the difficult situation in Polotsk, which can be found in the (printed) *Annuae Litterae S. J.* (see f. i. the year 1597, Neapoli 1607, p. 62) and the references in the unpublished letters in the Roman Archives of the Society of Jesus, see *Epistolae Germaniae* 170, fol. 101, a report of L. Maselli to General Aquaviva, sent from Wilno, on Nov. 25, 1592.

[40] *Akty Zap. Rossii*, IV, Nr. 64 (May 5, 1595).

[41] A contemporary copy of that nomination, probably forwarded to Rome by Nuncio Malaspina, is preserved in the Vatican Archives, *Borgh.* III 91 B, fol. 206v. The figure indicating the day is difficult to read; the late Monsignor A. Mercati kindly expressed the opinion that it indicates the tenth of September.

[42] See also the Archbishop's own letter to Prince Radziwiłł, of Aug. 30, 1595, and Skarga's opinion of Sept. 27, 1595, both quoted by Chodynicki, *op. cit.*, 282 f (n. 2).

[43] In a letter of July 2, 1595, published by K. Lewicki, *Ks. Konstanty Ostrogski*, 133 f. (Note 4), which will be discussed below.

to Malaspina's own desire and to the suggestions of the King and the Chancellor with whom he conferred in Cracow in February 1595. Already on the tenth of that month [44] the Nuncio could report to Cardinal Aldobrandini that " the Ruthenian and Lithuanian bishops have sent to me one of them, the Bishop of Łuck, with a document drafted by them and confirmed with their seals, which shows that they desire to unite with the Catholic Church, requesting to be admitted to the Senate and preserved in their religion, though reformed according to the pleasure of the Supreme Pontiff. " This is indeed a brief but accurate summary of the Torczyn declaration which already then must have been accepted by all bishops, though only in secret. Secret, too, were Terlecki's negotiations with the King, as Malaspina added in his report, explaining that such secrecy was motivated by Terlecki's fear of Prince Ostrogski.

The Nuncio himself, while making the Bishop of Łuck feel how welcome his action was to the Holy See and to its representative in Poland, found it necessary " to procede cautiously. " What he mainly feared was the reaction of the " heretics " and in particular their satisfaction if he would prove too credulous in his dealings with the Ruthenian bishops. He therefore decided to send to Terlecki the Latin Archbishop of Lwów, J. D. Solikowski, who had so much experience in relations with the Orthodox of Poland and Moldavia, in order to find out his real intentions and to receive a reliable report including the opinion of Solikowski himself.

A week later, [45] Malaspina included in one of his own reports in which he described chiefly the situation in Sweden, a few additional remarks about the task entrusted to the Archbishop of Lwów. The King, after his discussions with Terlecki, had instructed the Latin Bishop of Łuck, Maciejowski, who was indeed particularly qualified, and the Grand Chancellor of Lithuania, Leo Sapieha, the prominent statesman who a few years ago had been converted from Calvinism to Catholicism [46] and now started his outstanding contribution to the Union of Brest, to join Solikowski and carefully to study with him " the writings sent by the Ruthenian bishops, " obviously the Torczyn declaration, in order to come to a definite conclusion whether the one who was present, viz., Terlecki, as well as those absent, were entirely sincere or not. All the information thus collected was to be referred later to the Nuncio who then hoped to be able to write with certainty about their conversion. At once, however, he concluded praying to God that he might be permitted " to seal " his mission to Poland by three achievements : the reduction of the Ruthenians to unity with Rome, the conclu-

---

[44] The relevant passage of that report (*Borgh.* III, 89 b, fol. 38) has been published by G. Hofmann, *op. cit.*, 134 n. 1.

[45] *Borgh.* III 89 b, fol. 42 (Feb. 17, 1595).

[46] See about that conversion, in 1586, the article of K. Tyszkowski in *Reformacja w Polsce*, II (1922).

sion of an offensive league against the Turks, and the regaining of Sweden for the Catholic Church. All this, he added, had been prepared by the present Pope at the time of his own legation to Poland, and he, Malaspina, would not fear even death if only he could complete these initiatives.

With regard to the anti-Ottoman league and to the Catholic restoration in Sweden the zealous and tireless nuncio proved indeed much too optimistic. And so he was, when two months later, [47] reporting on the peace negotiations with Moscow in which Sweden participated also, he forwarded to Rome the news received from Komulovich who pretended to have been received at the Muscovite border with so much splendor, that no ambassador of any prince had ever received a similar treatment from the Grand Duke. Amidst all the disappointments which unfortunately not only in the case of the Komulovich mission but also in practically all the other issues of East European policies awaited Clement VIII, the success in the matter of reunion with the Ruthenians was to prove the only concrete and long lasting compensation. And though, in general, that problem continued to occupy a rather secondary place in the correspondence between Malaspina and the Secretariate of State, he was duly encouraged in the instructions coming from Rome to give to that question all his attention and diligence. For, as Cardinal Aldobrandini wrote on March 11 [48] in reply to Malaspina's dispatch of February 17, " if the project started by these Ruthenian bishops should serve the intention of divine worship and salvation of souls, we would feel the greatest consolation in seeing it materialize in the sense most desired for the unity of the Church. " As a matter of fact, in no other undertaking, which the Holy See decided to sponsor in that part of Europe, was the purely religious factor and concern so obviously if not exclusively predominant.

That same aspect of the problem was emphasized by the King of Poland when the day after Malaspina's report of February 17, he wrote to Pociej [49] whom, as a former senator, he knew best and rightly considered the most reliable and experienced among the Ruthenian bishops. Praising him for what he had already done in favor of reunion and encouraging him to continue his efforts until a successful conclusion, he stressed that this was in the genuine interest of the Ruthenian Church. He also recalled that the ancestors of the Ruthenian people had been in earlier centuries in religious union with Rome, as evidenced in their own liturgical books. That historical argument, whether referring to the early origin of Christianity in Kiev before the repercussions of the Cerularian schism or to the temporary

[47] *Borgh.* III 89 b, fol. 69 (April 14, 1595) ; see above, p. 267.

[48] *Borgh.* III 18 f., fol. 328.

[49] *Akty Zap. Rossii* IV, Nr. 60. There is no evidence of any " rivalry " between Pociej and Terlecki, as supposed by Chodynicki, *op. cit.*, 299 n. 2, who did not know the correspondence of the Nuncio relating to Terlecki's negotiations in Cracow.

acceptance of the Union of Florence, or to both, was probably taken from Skarga's book, dedicated to Sigismund III in its recent re-edition. It could appeal to all Ruthenians, so attached to the traditions of the past, and particularly to a highly educated man like Pociej who was to use that same argument himself in defending later the Union of Brest.

The King was, however, at the same time fully aware, even more than the Nuncio, of the political implications of the problem and especially of the danger which was to result from Prince Ostrogski's opposition. This was probably one of the reasons why he associated with the project Leo Sapieha, another magnate of Ruthenian — specifically White Ruthenian — origin, a descendant of an Orthodox family, which in a not too distant past had proved favorable to a revival of the Union of Florence, familiar with the problem of relations with Moscow in which Ostrogski was so interested, [50] and not at all a political opponent of the old prince, as was the Chancellor of the Kingdom, Zamoyski. But even closer and friendlier had been until recently, the relations between Ostrogski and Pociej who seemed best, qualified to appease the Prince in the sense desired by Sigismund III.

As a matter of fact, soon after the King's letter Pociej received another one, written on March 9 by Ostrogski [51] who, in spite of the secrecy of the negotiations in the matter of reunion and of Terlecki's visit at the royal court and with the Nuncio, must have heard at least vague rumors of what was going on. He therefore asked the Bishop of Brest and Volodymir about the whereabouts and activities of his colleague, the Bishop of Łuck, and Pociej's quick answer, [52] though evasive as to the details of Terlecki's trip to Cracow, was one more urgent invitation to join a movement which was so obviously in the interest of both nations, Poles and Ruthenians, politically united in one Commonwealth.

Ostrogski too replied at once on March 21, [53] but with bitter criticism and disregard for the Ruthenian bishops and unfair insinuations regarding the intentions of his former friend. He must have heard, among others, about the document on which Terlecki collected the signatures of the other bishops, but for Pociej who had so actively participated in the drafting of the Torczyn declaration, it was easy to answer, only four days later, [54] that the Prince was entirely wrong in believing that he had given to Terlecki blank papers with only his signature affixed. He resented, of course, Ostrogski's suspicion that he was acting out of personal ambition, and

---

[50] K. Tyszkowski, *Poselstwo Lwa Sapiehy w Moskwie* (L. Sapieha's mission to Moscow), Lwów 1927.

[51] *Russk. istor. bibl.*, XIX, 593-596.

[52] *Ibidem*, 597-598.

[53] *Ibidem*, 599-601.

[54] *Ibidem*, 601-612.

recalling that he had accepted his bishopric at the Prince's own request, he denied any desire of being made a Cardinal or Metropolitan.

But he was particularly alarmed seeing that Ostrogski's growing hostility to the idea of reunion with Rome, which he once had pretended to favor, at least on certain conditions, was dictated not only by his pride and disappointment that the project was making progress without his participation, but even more by the growing influence which not only Calvinists but also Antitrinitarians and Anabaptists were exercising upon the aging magnate. Disregarding Pociej's conclusion that the whole matter had to be submitted to a synod, the Prince wrote with open contempt of the synods of the Ruthenian hierarchy, opposing them to the synods of the Anabaptists. Deeply shocked by the praise given to the most radical sects, the Bishop of Brest expressed his concern with Ostrogski's own soul in view of his ever closer association with all kinds of heretics. Nevertheless, he suggested a personal interview, but it was obviously too late for such a meeting of the two former friends before the June synod which was already being prepared.

In the meantime, Malaspina received the report of the Archbishop of Lwów and his colleagues on their inquiry, where it was suggested for the first time that Terlecki with another member of the Ruthenian hierarchy should go to Rome to submit their obedience to the Pope, a suggestion which was discussed at once in the Nuncio's correspondence with the Secretariate of State. In a letter sent to him on March 18,[55] Cardinal Aldobrandini once more expressed the pleasure which the favorable prospects of reunion with the numerous Ruthenian peoples had given to the Pope, recommended again that great cause to the solicitude of the Nuncio and advised him to move the King by the consideration of how much glory such an achievement would bring to his reign. And he added : " If the Vladica (Ruthenian bishop) of Łuck would come to Rome for that purpose, we would not fail to treat him here with every possible charity and humanity. " Malaspina was therefore instructed to encourage Terlecki to make that journey, describing to him and to his colleagues with how much courtesy the Vatican had just received the Bishop of Wenden (in Livonia), because he was contributing to the Catholic restoration in that province of the Commonwealth. And the interest of the Holy See in the whole problem was growing so rapidly that one month later [56] the Nuncio was even slightly criticized for not having sent more information on the negotiations concerning the reunion of the Ruthenians with Rome and requested " to warm up " that matter as soon as his basic preoccupation with the anti-Ottoman league would permit.

---

[55] *Borgh*. III 18 f., fol. 335v, probably written after receiving Sokolikowski's report of Feb. 17 (*Fondo Aldobrandini*, vol. 7).

[56] *Ibidem*, fol. 343 (April 15, 1595).

Malaspina, therefore, treated the Ruthenian problem at length in his report of May 12 [57] and started by saying that it would be very easy for him to sent to Rome the bishops of Greek rite which had come to see him a few months ago, meaning of course Terlecki and possibly also Pociej. Yet, he insisted even then upon the necessity to avoid any undue hurry and any suspicion that he believed too easily the representatives of a people who was "reputed to be rather lighthearted." He still wanted to wait for guarantees, as those expected from the royal commission under Solikowski, that not only the bishops he had already met, but "the whole rest of the clergy" were determined in their purpose. Moreover, he wanted to be sure that the whole matter of reunion of that clergy with Rome would not disturb the peace of the Kingdom and that such possible troubles would not be attributed to the Pope's representative. Therefore, in agreement with the royal delegates, he concluded that the Ruthenian bishops should first return to their respective residences, then get together again with all the others — that is hold their usual synod — and, only after having reached a full agreement, come back to Cracow with a sufficient mandate. He added that Terlecki had been there again a week ago, assuring both the King and the Nuncio that there already was a unanimous agreement of hierarchy and clergy in the matter of reunion and that the opposition came exclusively from Prince Constantine Ostrogski about whose threats and acts of violence against the clergy he bitterly complained. The King who according to Malaspina "has taken to heart that reunion more than all the others of us", again promised full protection against any persecution by the Prince, so that Terlecki left "satisfied and with the assurance that within six or seven weeks the ambassadors (of the Ruthenian hierarchy) to Rome would be elected with all the necessary power for such a sacred cause."

These news were well received in Rome, where the cautious Nuncio to Poland enjoyed full confidence though he was reminded time and again to use every possible diligence to accelerate the matter. [58] An additional reason why the Holy See was so anxious to see the Union concluded with the Ruthenians was the apparent connection of the project with similar possibilities in Moldavia and Wallachia, which in turn seemed connected with the preparation for the anti-Ottoman league. That connection had already been lightly touched in the instructions sent to Malaspina on April 15; [59] on June 24 [60] he was informed that, according to news received from the Nuncio to Transylvania, the schismatics of Moldavia and Wallachia were ready to unite with Rome after liberation from the Turks. Both nuncios

[57] *Ibidem*, III 89 b, fol. 109v.
[58] *Ibidem*, III 18 f, fol. 328, and particularly III 18 c, fol. 217v (June 10, 1595).
[59] *Ibidem*, III 18 f, fol. 343.
[60] *Ibidem*, III 18 e, fol. 221; published in *Mon. Vat. Hung.*, II-3, Nr. 301, but wrongly referred to 1596.

were supposed to communicate in that matter, and the hope was expressed that at the same time when the Ruthenians would sent their representatives to the Holy See, the others, viz., the Orthodox of the Danubian principalities, would do the same, and these parallel negotiations be conducted jointly " for the greater glory of God and the salvation of more souls."

Events were soon to prove that the situation in Moldavia was so confused and that in Wallachia so hopeless, that such an extension of the planned religious union within the limits of the Commonwealth to neighboring Orthodox populations had no chances whatever. Zamoyski was particularly aware of these difficulties as well as of those which hindered the conclusion of an anti-Ottoman league as desired by the Holy See, but continued to support without reservation the union with the Ruthenians ; while Ostrogski, who was so much more favorable to the idea of a league with the Habsburgs, created to that limited union the greatest possible obstacles. Neither the Vatican nor even the well informed Malaspina fully realized these implications which made it so difficult to coordinate all papal initiatives. But in the meantime at least the Ruthenian problem made a decisive progress thanks precisely to the synod of Brest, in June 1595, which already in the preceding weeks had appeared with ever clearer evidence to be the next indispensable step in carrying out the Torczyn decisions of December 1594. As Malaspina rightly anticipated, only after that synod could the idea of sending a delegation of that hierarchy to Rome materialize successfully. What he did not anticipate were new obstacles raised by Prince Ostrogski in cooperation with the Protestants of the Commonwealth.

PART IV.

THE UNION OF BREST

Chapter I

AT BREST, TORUŃ AND CRACOW

In the history of the Union of Brest, which can be dated 1595 as well as 1596, the Synod held at Brest in June of the former year proved second in importance only to the Synod assembled in that same city in October of the following year. To a certain extent the first of these two meetings, though only preliminary, was even more successful than the second, the final. For in June 1595 the Ruthenian hierarchy was unanimous in fulfilling the Torczyn pledge of December 1594 and in authorizing its representatives to go to Rome where, as a matter of fact, the promised reunion was solemnly concluded at the end of the year; while in October 1596 only a majority of that same hierarchy ratified that agreement, two of its members having passed to the opposition.

The opposition had become so strong and powerful because already in August 1595 another synod, neither Catholic nor Orthodox, but Protestant, held in the city of Toruń, had prepared a common anti-Catholic front in which Protestant support encouraged the resistance of the anti-Roman part of the Orthodox laity against their pro-Roman bishops. Conferences held in Cracow soon after the Toruń Synod tried hard to avoid that danger : they succeeded indeed in making possible the Ruthenian mission to Rome, but not in guaranteeing the unanimous acceptance of what was decided there. Hence the last minute split in 1596, and hence, too, the importance of all that happened in the eventful summer of 1595.

The June Synod of that year was very brief : convoked by Metropolitan Rahoza for the twelfth of that month — June 22 according to the Gregorian calendar — it approved already on that same day the messages which were addressed to the Pope and to the King of Poland. However, not only these general statements, but also the detailed " articles pertaining to the union with the Roman Church " which accompanied them, were of course prepared before, the latter being even dated June 1 (11 new style), so that the discussions must have started at least eleven days before the formal opening of the synod.

The original text of the articles of June 1st, preserved along with the address to Clement VIII of June 12, in the Vatican Archives, [1] shows only five signatures : in addition to Rahoza, Pociej, and Terlecki, obviously the main initiators responsible for the draft, only the old Bishop of Pinsk and Turov, Pełczycki, and his successor-elect Hohol signing this time only as Archimandrite of Our Savior's Church at Kobryn, were present. They resided indeed nearer to Brest than the other bishops. The seals attached to the same document were eight in number, and among the three added to those of the five signatories, the seals of Bałaban and Zbirujski, the Bishops of Lwów and Chełm, whose sees were not too far either, are recognizable. If not all signatures were collected and one of the bishops did not even affix his seal, it probably was because this was not considered so important in view of the fact that all eight members of the hierarchy signed and sealed the decisions of June 12, of which the articles were only an explanatory appendix. Whether all of them were present in person at the final session, or were approached later as it happened after the Torczyn meeting, is difficult to ascertain and rather irrelevant : in any case the statements of the synod already had their formal approval when on July 17 [2] they were submitted by their elected delegates, Pociej and Terlecki, to Sigismund III and Malaspina, in Cracow.

The message to the Pope which was written in Ruthenian, but had, of course, to be translated into Latin, was a formal notification that the Ruthenian hierarchy had decided to return to the Union " which formerly existed between the eastern and the western Church, and was established at the Council of Florence by our predecessors. " This was precisely what had been promised half a year before in the Torczyn declaration which also was forwarded to the Pope, the explicit reference to the Union of Florence thus restored being very appropriately added. A general reference to the well remembered unity of the Church " which our ancestors maintained under the obedience and direction of the sacred apostolic Roman See " was made also at the very beginning of the address where, just like at Torczyn

---

[1] The articles of June 1 are preserved in the Vatican Archives, A. A. Arm. I-XVIII, 1858, fol. 1-5 (Latin text), and 1859, fol. 1-7 (Polish text), best edition of both texts by G. Hofmann, " Wiedervereinigung der Ruthenen, " *Orientalia Christiana*, III (1925), append. III, 142-158 ; the letter to the Pope of June 12 in A. A. Arm. I-XVIII, 1732, fol. 2 (end on fol. 6, Latin text) and fol. 3 (Ruthenian original). G. Hofmann, *op. cit.*, gives the best edition of the Latin translation, append. II, 139-142, and a photograph of the original on plate II.

[2] *Scriptores rerum Pol.* VII, 203, see below, p. 300 f.

but this time without mentioning the danger from the contemporary heresies, the regret was expressed that "the superiors and pastors" of the Oriental Church had failed to restore that unity "suffering under the heaviest yoke of servitude of a cruel, non-Christian tyrant." To that servitude they opposed the freedom which they enjoyed in their own country under Sigismund III, King of Poland and Sweden, Grand Duke of Lithuania, who had shown such "a special and most pious zeal in that matter" of reunion, and they concluded that with his knowledge and approval they were sending to the Pope the Bishops Pociej and Terlecki, who had the mandate to offer him due obedience in the name of all other archbishops and bishops, of "our whole ecclesiastical order and the folk entrusted to us," that is in the name of the whole Ruthenian Church, clergy and laity.

However, to that unequivocal declaration of obedience there was attached, again in agreement with the Torczyn pledge or rather the addition to it, an equally unequivocal condition : Pociej and Terlecki were to declare that obedience, if His Holiness "would preserve and confirm to us the administration of the sacraments, rites, and all ceremonies of the Eastern Church without any violation and in the same way in which we had used them at the time of union," granting that confirmation also in the name of his successors "who would never innovate anything in that respect." Only if they would obtain all that was so requested, would they, the Ruthenian hierarchy and their successors, remain under the authority of His Holiness and his successors.

As to the place where that document was issued, they did not mention the city of Brest but in general the Kingdom of Poland and the Grand Duchy of Lithuania, thus emphasizing the character of the union limited to the regions which belonged to the Catholic Commonwealth but including all of them. That close connection of the religious union with the political situation appeared also in the simultaneous message to the King,[3] which repeated the main points of the earlier declarations in favor of reunion, including the requests which had been addressed to him from the start of the movement in 1590. But it was in the articles of June 1st where all the concessions which both Pope and King were expected to grant, were systematically listed as "guarantees which we need from the Romans before we join the union with the Roman Church."

It is significant that this long statement which more than any other gives evidence of the attachment of the Ruthenians to all their traditional, particular customs and of their reluctance to be "Latinized" in any way, was drafted in Polish, not in Ruthenian, therefore in Latin characters, with even a few Latin expressions interwoven, as it frequently happened in Poland where not before the middle of the sixteenth century Latin had

---

[3] *Akty Zap. Rossii*, IV, Nr. 78 (the King's reply of July 30).

been replaced by Polish as official language. In particular, in order to distinguish those concessions which were requested not from the Pope but from the King, the word *Regia* was placed before thirteen of the thirty-two articles. [4]

Beginning with the most important difference between the Roman and the Greek doctrine concerning the procession of the Holy Spirit, the Ruthenians, without quoting the decision of the Council of Florence, wanted to make it sure that they would not be forced to go beyond that decision which did not require the Greeks to add the *filioque* to the Apostolic Creed, admitted their interpretation that the Holy Spirit procedeed from only one, and not two principles, and was satisfied with the formula *ex patre per filium* used by the Greek fathers of the Church.

In the only other dogmatic question in which there seemed to be a difference between West and East, that of purgatory, the Ruthenians followed again, without quoting it, the Florentine precedent : without arguing about it, they declared in article five to be ready for being instructed in that matter by the Holy Church.

The second article was the first of those which insisted upon the permission to keep all the rites, prayers and liturgies of the Oriental Church which, as it was added, were used also in Rome *sub obedientia Summi Pontificis*. Particularly important was the addition that all these ceremonies and forms of worship should be *idiomate nostro*, meaning the Ruthenian vernacular or rather the customary Old Slavonic.

There followed the request to be permitted to receive, as before, the Holy Eucharist *sub utraque specie panis et vini*, a permission which was to be granted forever. And second only in importance was the brief article nine about the marriage of the priests which should be permitted too, *exceptis bigamis*. But even minor differences in liturgy and traditional customs, not mentioned at all at the Council of Florence, some of them specifically Ruthenian, were listed in a long series of articles (4, 7, 8, 22, 23, 24), insisting that all this should remain unchanged without any addition or restriction.

A new matter of controversy which had arisen long after the Union of Florence, was the reformed Gregorian calendar. In article six the Ruthenians accepted it, " if necessary, " but not without restrictions regarding the dates of Easter and certain other feasts — a formula which made foresee further difficulties in that matter.

Articles ten and eleven dealt with the election and confirmation of the Ruthenian bishops including the Metropolitan. The King was requested

---

[4] That word is missing in the Latin translation of the whole document, as quoted above (note 1) ; in another Latin translation, included in Malaspina's register (*Borgh.* III 67 A, fol. 94-97), the order of the articles is changed (see Hofmann, *op. cit.*, 149).

not to give these ecclesiastical offices to anybody who would not be of Ruthenian or Greek origin and religion nor to any layman who would not receive the holy orders within three months, as promised already by King Sigismund Augustus. [5] In the case of any vacancy, four candidates should be freely elected by the clergy and one of them chosen by the King who otherwise could not select the most qualified man, "not being of this religion." That motivation of an otherwise well justified and sound suggestion (*sacra enim Regia Maiestas alterius religionis cum sit* — as it was translated into Latin) was rather surprising in view of the religious unity which otherwise was so strongly emphasized in the whole project. It probably echoed resentments of the past, and was part of a well understandable trend of combining the Union with a long overdue reform of the Ruthenian Church and its relations with the secular authorities of the Commonwealth, different if not in religion at least in rite and tradition. At the same time the Pope was asked that the Ruthenian bishops thus appointed be dispensed from waiting for papal approval but consecrated at once by their Metropolitan as in the past. Only the Metropolitan, before being consecrated by at least two of the bishops, if he had not been a bishop himself, would have to send to Rome for letters of *sacra*, or if already consecrated before as bishop, declare his obedience to the Holy See before the Archbishop of Gniezno as Primate of the realm.

Turning again to the King, article twelve renewed the request for seats in the Senate which should be granted to the Metropolitan and the bishops of Eastern rite, not only because their dignity was identical with that of the "Roman" bishops, but also, as it was significantly added, for a reason of expediency : their oath as senators could include an oath of obedience to the Supreme Pontiff, and thus there could be avoided what happened after the death of Metropolitan Isidore, when the Ruthenian bishops, being not bound by any oath and residing in far away places, abandoned the Union of Florence. This was certainly an oversimplification of the causes why the survival of that Union among the Ruthenians was not uninterrupted, and in general, the information about the time and fate of Cardinal Isidore was no longer quite accurate. But the point was good in itself and one more evidence of a growing interest in the tradition of the Council of Florence and its aftermath.

This would necessarily lead to an interest in a reunion with Rome which would be again not regional but universal, including the remaining part of the Eastern Church, "our brethren of Greek nationality and religion." The relations with the Greeks were touched in the following two articles (13 and 14) which, strange enough, were repeated with slight alte-

---

[5] See about similar requests submitted to that King and partly granted by him, Chodynicki, *Kościół prawosławny*, 136 f.

rations at the end of the list (31 and 32). In the first of these articles
the hope was expressed that in case of such a general union the Ruthenians
should not be blamed for having, with good reason, preceded the others
in the movement towards reunion, nor excluded from any improvements
in the Greek Church. On the other hand, as long as " Greece " was not
united with Rome, the Ruthenians, as they stressed in the second article
of these two similar groups, wanted royal protection against any Greek
interference with their ecclesiastical life and administration. For, as they
rightly warned, the union would be vain, if those who still opposed it,
could receive from Greece any encouragement, decrees of excommunication
against the partisans of reunion, confirmation in their positions, contrary
to the authority of their local superiors, etc. In order to make such contacts
or the arrival of foreigners who would act as ecclesiastical dignitaries, impossible in the interest of public order, the King was asked in the final draft
of that article (32) to close the frontiers of the realm by giving the necessary instruction to his officials. How necessary such measures really were,
was to become apparent in a near future and in particular at the time of
the Synod of 1596.

However, anxious as they were to be free from any undue Greek
influence, the Ruthenians, as evidenced in their following two articles (15
and 16), wanted to retain the identity and autonomy of their Church,
even after reunion, also in their relation with " the Romans. " Nobody of
them should be permitted to join the Latin rite disregarding the Eastern,
since both would be in one Church and under one Pope, and for the same
reason marriages between " Romans " and Ruthenians should be " free "
without any pressure to change the " religion " as the rite was once more
inaccurately called.

Among the remaining articles two more (26 and 27) deserve special
attention in view of the general background of the religious situation on
the eve of the Union of Brest. A sound compromise was suggested in the
matter of the Brotherhoods, instituted by the Patriarchs and approved by
the King, as those of Lwów, Brest, and Wilno : they were recognized as
very useful for the Church and should be maintained, but only if they
would accept the Union and the control of the Metropolitan or the Bishops
of their respective dioceses. Recognized, too, was the utility of schools
and seminaries with Greek or Slavonic language of instruction and with
their printing offices : therefore their foundation should be freely permitted,
but they should be, like the Brotherhoods, under the control of the hierarchy and print nothing without episcopal permission lest heresies be disseminated. This was, in the whole text, the only reference to the danger
of Protestant penetration, undoubtedly dictated by the experience of the
most important of these schools : the Academy of Ostrog.

All the other articles, mostly addressed to the King as were these two, were supposed to protect the Ruthenian Church against any abuses and discriminations contrary to the charter of equality with the Latin clergy, granted by King Władysław III and now invoked with full justification, since the Union of Florence was to be restored in a form adapted to new conditions. In particular, the authority of the bishops was to be strengthened through new guarantees against any arbitrary interference of secular power, but also in their relations with their own clergy, including the powerful monasteries, and with the laity irrespective of rite.

In a long concluding paragraph, Pociej and Terlecki, as delegates of the hierarchy, were instructed to ask " our most Holy Father the Pope " as well as the King for an approval of all these articles, so that the bishops might accede with good conscience " to that holy union with the holy Roman Church. " But in the last sentence an additional reason was given for first putting forward such conditions : it had to be done so that " also the others who still are hesitating, might follow us the more rapidly to that sacred unity, seeing that we have preserved all that is ours. "

The question, therefore, immediately arises to what an extent such a painstaking solicitude to keep unaltered the ecclesiastical tradition of the Ruthenian Church and even to improve its legal position in the Commonwealth would not only appease the consciences and remove the last doubts of the signatories themselves, but also gain them the adherence and support of the Ruthenian people and its political leaders. In that respect, the June Synod which followed the drafting of the thirty-two articles, short as it was, seemed quite promising. For even before Pociej and Terlecki arrived in Cracow, it was known there, that these two bishops had been unanimously elected as delegates to the Pope, and Malaspina did not hesitate [6] to compare their mission with that of Metropolitan Isidore to the Council of Florence more than one hundred and fifty years ago, expressing the hope that after such a long interruption in the direct relations of the Holy See with the Ruthenians, that new attempt towards reunion would, with God's grace prove more successful than Isidore's. Furthermore, the King was informed, and in turn informed the Nuncio, [7] that the Synod of Brest had been attended by many lords of distinction, Catholic, Protestant, and Orthodox, and that at least one of the most prominent, Nicholas Sapieha, Palatine of Vitebsk, a relative of Grand Chancellor Leo, after listening to the discussions, decided to abandon Calvinism and to return to the " Ruthenian religion, because the union with the Apostolic See led it to perfection and the Ruthenians had recognized the Roman Pontiff as Vicar of Christ " ; if another decision had been taken, he would have made himself, as he openly declared, a Catholic of Latin rite. That spectacular

---

[6] In his report of July 1, *Fondo Aldobrandini*, vol. XI.

[7] See Malaspina's report of July 7, 1595, *Borgh*. III 89 ab, fol. 183 v.

conversion of another member of the powerful and influential Sapieha family was highly welcomed not only by Malaspina but also in Rome [8] where it was considered " a good start " of the movement towards reunion, a reunion which would make " totally Catholic " the Palatine of Vitebsk who ought to be encouraged in his determination by special favors of the King. However, as the Nuncio immediately added, the case of Nicholas Sapieha made both " heretics and schismatics " even more angry with " these poor bishops and with the Ruthenian laymen who promote the union. "

In order to describe the violence of that resentment, Malaspina used on that occasion the same expression *strident dentibus* which he had used already a few weeks before, [9] adding to his usual optimistic remarks about the intentions of the Ruthenian bishops and even about the prospects of Catholicism in Sweden, a serious warning against the Protestants " who much prefer the schism of the Ruthenians to our religion and now, seeing that these Greeks themselves condemn that schism, cannot suffer this at all. " It was precisely that awareness of Protestant cooperation with the opponents to the Union which confirmed the Nuncio in his conviction that he ought to continue to proceed with mature circumspection, quietly, and avoiding any unnecessary risk, basing the agreement with the Ruthenians on solid foundations of canon law, without being satisfied with vain appearances of success. [10] This explains his cautious attitude and constant reference to Rome before sending there the two delegates of the Ruthenian hierarchy whose statements he forwarded in advance to the Vatican for careful study. But it also leads directly to the main problem which worried all promoters of the Union even after the successful June synod : to the unabated opposition of Constantine Ostrogski.

Nobody was more alarmed by that opposition than Bishop Pociej who knew so well the Prince and his tremendous influence. Having failed to come to an understanding with him nor even to meet him before the Synod, he after its adjournment, already on June 16, [11] a month before going to Cracow with Terlecki to submit the decisions of the hierarchy to the King and the Nuncio, wrote to Ostrogski another letter enclosing the articles with the specific conditions for reunion. He thus hoped to convince him that these conditions went even further than those which the Prince had formulated in 1593, except the secondary matter of the calendar and the inclusion of the Patriarchate of Constantinople which was hopeless in view of its subjection to the Turks. Being at last in a position to inform Ostrog-

[8] See the letter of the Secretary of State, *Borgh.* III 18 e, fol. 234 (July 29, 1595).

[9] In his report of May 27, 1595, *Borgh.* III 89 b, fol. 131.

[10] See his report of July 1, quoted above, note 6.

[11] *Akty Zap. Rossii*, IV, Nr. 70.

ski of the final agreement of all bishops including the Metropolitan, he begged him for his support and an occasion to meet him.

Prince Constantine in his harsh reply of June 24 [12] simply protested against the planned union and at the same time sent an appeal to the clergy, nobility, and common people of the Ruthenians [13] in which, disregarding Pociej's arguments, he accused the bishops of having betrayed the Church of Christ, and abandoned the Orthodox faith and their superiors, the eastern Patriarchs, by going over to the western. And since he, Ostrogski, was considered their leader by most of the Orthodox in the country — though he considered himself only an equal brother — he publicly promised to oppose with them " these enemies of our salvation. "

Even then Pociej did not give up and meeting the prince at last in Lublin, [14] on his way to Cracow, through the intermediary of the Palatine of Podlachia, Prince Janusz Zasławski, a descendent of a sideline of the Ostrogskis already converted to Catholicism, he told him again the full story of the union movement since 1590, showed him all the documents sealed and signed by the bishops, and kneeling before the proud magnate implored him amidst tears not to oppose but rather to support a pious undertaking which once he had suggested himself. And he was very happy when Ostrogski finally declared that if the King would call together another synod of the Ruthenian hierarchy, he would participate and work at that synod for a union which would be useful to the Church. The idea of holding another synod almost immediately after the one which had formally decided the whole matter was rather extravagant, but Pociej, after arriving at Cracow with Terlecki on July 17, and informing Sigismund III and the Catholic senators of all that happened at the Synod of Brest, [15] persuaded the reluctant King to consider Ostrogski's condition. Therefore, Sigismund III on July 28 [16] sent to the Prince the same Zasławski who had proved helpful at Lublin, along with another senator, recalling the Council of Florence, expressing the hope that the Palatine of Kiev would cooperate with the bishops in the matter of reunion, and asking for his opinion regarding the convocation of an additional synod before Pociej's and Terlecki's departure for Rome. The King himself thought, however, such a synod unnecessary, since the bishops had already settled the matter at Brest, and since, as he added on the basis of inaccurate information

---

[12] *Russk. istor. bibl.*, XIX, 632 f.

[13] *Akty. Zap. Rossii*, Nr. 71.

[14] Pociej described himself that dramatic meeting in one of his later writings (*Russk. istor. bibl.*, XIX, 634 f).

[15] This and Skarga's support is noted in the diary of the Cracow Jesuits (*Scriptores rerum Pol.*, VII, 203.)

[16] The King's letter of that day (*Akty Zap. Rossii*, IV, Nr. 76) is discussed in detail by K. Lewicki, *Ks. Konstanty Ostrogski*, 137 f.

received from Rome, the Patriarch of Alexandria and the Bishops of Wallachia, Serbia and Bulgaria had returned to religious unity with the Holy
See. [17] For Ostrogski's answer Sigismund III was to wait only four weeks,
and he invited the two delegates of the hierarchy who returned to their
respective dioceses, to come again to Cracow if during that period the new
synod should not gather with Ostrogski's approval and participation.

Pociej, still hopeful, wrote during these weeks two more letters to
Prince Constantine, [18] fully endorsing the project of such a synod and even
admitting that he would prefer not to go to Rome until such an assembly
had approved the whole project once more. And there met indeed a synod
before the delay of four weeks was over, not, however, a synod of the
Ruthenians to sanction the union of their Church with Rome, but a synod
of the various Protestant denominations to which Ostrogski turned for joint
action against the Catholics and the partisans of union with them.

That he was not sincere when discussing with Pociej and only wanted
to gain time, became obvious already at the beginning of July, because it
was under his unquestionable influence and in his presence that on the
first of that month, Bałaban, the versatile Bishop of Lwów who had first
initiated the pro-Roman movement and first proclaimed the Union in his
diocese, filed at the court of Volodymir in Volhynia a protest against
everything that had been decided at the June Synod in Brest, [19] pretending
that he had signed only a blank paper on which Terlecki was supposed to
list complaints against the oppression of the Ruthenian Church. A little
later, [20] also Bishop Kopysteński of Przemyśl was persuaded by Ostrogski
to withdraw from the joint action of his colleagues. Though their change
of mind became definite only at the last moment, Prince Constantine could
be sure of having on his side at least two members of the hierarchy who
only quite recently had signed with the others the statements in favor of
reunion.

Much depended, of course, on the attitude of the Metropolitan himself,
and again his correspondence with Theodor Tyszkiewicz, which continued
after the June Synod, could raise some doubts as to his sincerity and
loyalty to the engagements he had signed and to the decisions made at
the Synod under his own presidency. For his assurances that he would
never sacrifice the Eastern rite and that he was unwilling to do anything

[17] This information was probably based upon the fact that in January 1595 delegates of the Patriarch of Alexandria — not, however, the Greek but the Coptic — had
arrived in Rome to conclude a religious union ; see below, p. 326.

[18] *Russk. istor. bibl.*, XIX, 638-640.

[19] *Archiv Yugo-Zap. Rossii*, I-1, Nr. 109 ; see Chodynicki, *op. cit.*, 297, who points
out that Bałaban's statements were entirely false and quotes the similar opinion of
Metropolitan Macarius, the official historian of the Russian Orthodox Church.

[20] About his protest of August 18, 1595, see A. Prochaska in *Kwartalnik
hist.*, X (1896), 569.

without the agreement of his friend, the Palatine, were combined with surprising denials of his role in the negotiations and even of any intention to put himself under the authority of the Pope. [21]   Such utterances of Rahoza, repeated as late as August 19, [22] but contradicted the following day in a letter to the Catholic Prince Nicholas Christopher Radziwiłł [23], to whom he wrote about his desire to unite " with the Holy Catholic Church, " seem to have been dictated merely by his fear to alienate the Orthodox dignitary who could counterbalance to a certain extent the influence of Ostrogski. The latter was fully aware of the real feelings of the Metropolitan whom he considered a traitor to Orthodoxy just like the other bishops and therefore called " a scoundrel, " in a most revealing private letter to a Protestant member of the Radziwiłł family, written already on July 2, [24] in the midst of his misleading negotiations with Pociej.

That letter, the same in which he declared Rahoza responsible for appointing a promoter of the Union to the see of Polotsk, is the best key to an understanding of Ostrogski's policy. Not only does he use the most violent terms in denouncing the whole project of reunion with Rome and in particular the mission of Pociej and Terlecki, identifying obedience to " the Father Pope " with obedience to " the Devil himself, " but he already then, while still pretending to favor another synod of the Orthodox Ruthenians, entered into the closest cooperation with one of the Calvinist leaders who were preparing for the end of August a Protestant synod at Toruń. For, in contradistinction to the Catholic line of the Radziwiłłs, the addressee of Ostrogski's letter, his son-in-law Prince Christopher " the Thunderbolt, " Palatine of Wilno, was the main supporter of all religious dissenters in the Grand Duchy, and hoping to arrive at Toruń to a full understanding with all similar trends in the Kingdom of Poland, he was particularly interested in " the troubles among the Ruthenians. " [25]

The Toruń meeting of 1595 [26] was indeed one of the synods which following that of Sandomierz, in 1570, were to revive the anti-Catholic agreement which had been concluded there a quarter of a century before. It was expected that the differences between Calvinists and Lutherans which had been so evident at Sandomierz, could now be overcome and that perhaps even the Antitrinitarians could be included in the anti-Catholic

---

[21] *Akty Zap. Rossii*, IV, Nr. 69 (June 14, 1595 ; with the answer of Tyszkiewicz).
[22] *Ibidem*, Nr. 80.
[23] S. Golubev, *Mitropolit Petr Mogila*, I, 44 (appendix 13).
[24] Published by K. Lewicki, *op. cit.*, 133 f (note 4).
[25] See his letter of July 22, 1595, to Jan Abramowicz, Palatine of Minsk, another Calvinist leader married to an Orthodox, whose role is discussed by Chodynicki, *op. cit.*, 305, and Lewicki, *op. cit.*, 137.
[26] About that synod see also J. Bidlo, *Jednota bratrska v prvnim vyhnanstvi* (The Unity of Czech Brethren in its first exile), IV, Prahu 1932, 139-209, and K. E. J. Joergensen, *Ökumenische Bestrebungen*, 314-317.

front which, in view of the progressing Catholic restoration, seemed more necessary than ever before. It was with a view of including the Orthodox in that same front and of gaining Protestant support in the struggle against reunion with Rome that Ostrogski, following up his earlier contacts with the Palatine of Wilno, sent on August 12 to the Synod of Toruń a certain Łuszkowski, a nobleman in his service, with a letter [27] which went even farther than the private message to Radziwiłł six weeks before.

That letter was a formal invitation that the Protestants, united at their Toruń Synod, should participate in the Orthodox Synod which the King had promised to convoke before the mission of the Ruthenian bishops to Rome, and join there the opposition against the Union and in general the struggle of the Eastern Church against the Catholics. Recalling that he had always been friendly to the " Evangelical " Church and concerned with the wrongs which it had to suffer, and emphasizing that in their " ceremonies " — he avoided to speak about doctrine — the Orthodox were nearer to the Protestants than to the " Romans, " he asked in return for their cooperation in the present plight of the Eastern Church. If the King should try to enforce the Union without the general agreement of another Ruthenian Synod, Ostrogski would not hesitate to use violence, threatening to mobilize himself at least fifteen thousand, if not twenty thousand men, and suggesting that the Protestants, so numerous precisely in the Grand Duchy of Lithuania where the new Synod would take place, add their forces to those of the Orthodox. Ironical remarks about the celibacy of the Roman clergy who could only mobilize their cooks, were added to that appeal to open revolt, and forwarding to the Protestants assembled at Toruń the articles of the June Synod which he had received from Pociej, Ostrogski claimed that by drafting them insidiously and in secret, the Ruthenian bishops " were leading us to the enemy of the Son of God, subordinating us to the antichrist, and separating from the Christ our Lord. "

This letter, possibly intercepted, or rather its copy, was already in the hands of Sigismund III when he received from Ostrogski, in reply to his message of July 28, a formal request for another Orthodox Synod, as suggested in his discussion with Pociej. [28] The King was of course deeply shocked : having never authorized the meeting of the Protestants in Toruń and therefore considering it illegal, he particularly resented that the Palatine of Kiev to whom he had shown much favor in the past, as well as to his whole family, had made to those assembled there " seditious " proposals

---

[27] The text was published a few years later in the polemics following the Union of Brest (*Russk. istor. bibl.*, XIX, 642-654) and has been discussed in detail by Chodynicki in *Rocznik Wołyński* (Volhynian Annual), V (1936).

[28] About the role of Leo Sapieha who in that matter acted as an intermediary between Ostrogski and the King, see *Archiwum domu Sapiehów*, I (1892), Nr. 144.

which went far beyond their own program. Though he later accepted Ostrogski's apologies, he never believed that the Prince, as he pretended, was not really responsible for Łuszkowski's message, such an excuse being contrary to the information received in Cracow from Catholics who had been present in Toruń. [29] In any case, Sigismund III now definitely gave up the plan of organizing another synod of the Ruthenian hierarchy with Ostrogski's participation, [30] a plan which never had appealed to him and after such an experience proved meaningless and even dangerous.

As to the Nuncio, it seems that he never took that plan seriously, and he did not even mention it in his reports sent to Rome. However, he wrote in these reports [31] extensively about the synod of Toruń which had alarmed him in advance. He was convinced that it had been the original purpose of the " heretics " to induce their ministers " to approve all sects of the world and to receive them into their community " in order to oppose Catholicism, and that, taking advantage of Ostrogski's offer of cooperation, they proceeded " to unite with the Greeks, to turn them from schism to Arianism, and thus not only to impede the incorporation of these schismatics with the Holy See but also to draw them into that condemned sect. " Even if these rumors were exaggerated, they reflected the widely spread opinion that Prince Constantine was inclined not only to Calvinist but even to Antitrinitarian doctrines. [32] But, as Malaspina continued, the scheme did not succeed : even the Lutherans and the Calvinists, who were to be reconciled first, could not agree, as usually, when they started discussing the dogma of the Eucharist ; and both of them " conspired " against the Arians and the Anabaptists, and decided once more to anathemize these sects. Under such conditions the Synod of Toruń where only the Czech Brethren showed, as usual, a genuine interest in an agreement with the Eastern Church, [33] simply welcomed Ostrogski's address, but without following his suggestions, and decided to negotiate with him in view of a possible meeting of Protestant and Orthodox theologians in Wilno. [34] These were rather vague prospects for the future which were to materialize only a few years after the Union of Brest, [35] but the very fact that at Toruń Prince Constantine had offered through his emissary to mobilize " from ele-

---

[29] All this is taken from the King's last appeal to Ostrogski, in June 1596, which will be discussed below, Chap. III, p. 348 f.

[30] Pociej considered Ostrogski's message to the Synod of Toruń the main obstacle which made such a synod impossible (*Russk. istor. bibl.*, XIX, 654).

[31] Particularly in that of Sept. 21, 1595, *Borgh.* III 91 d, fol. 15 ; see also *Borgh.* III 89 b, fol. 213 (Sept. 8, 1595).

[32] As a matter of fact, he warned in his letter the Protestant Synod not to repel any " other sects " in the present difficult situation.

[33] J. Bidlo, *op. cit.*, 159-161, 172-174.

[34] Chodynicki, *op. cit.*, 307.

[35] *Ibidem*, 349.

ven to twenty thousand horsemen not against the Tartars but against the Catholics, " disillusioned for the time being the Nuncio as to the magnate whom he had hoped to gain for the anti-Ottoman league. In spite of some remaining hope to influence him through his Catholic son, the Castellane of Cracow, Malaspina considered the old but unbalanced man so dangerous, that he found it necessary " to humiliate and castigate him. " [36]

If the Nuncio, always in favor of moderation and mild methods of action, felt so strongly in that case, it was because he realized that Ostrogski's " objective was to hinder the Ruthenian union " and in particular Pociej's and Terlecki's mission to Rome, by severely persecuting these *poverelli*. There were even rumors that he had sent ten thousand florins to Austria and to Italy to have them assassinated on their way. [37] In any case, the question now arose whether it was wise to let the two bishops go to Rome, since not only the approval of their mission by a synod with Ostrogski's participation was now excluded, but the situation had seriously deteriorated thanks to the obvious duplicity and openly revealed hostility of the powerful Prince who was even looking for and receiving support from foreign lands. He had written to the Patriarchate of Constantinople suggesting that the pro-Roman bishops be deprived of their positions, [38] and there arrived a message from the Orthodox bishops of Moldavia, assembled at Jassy, [39] who afraid that the movement towards reunion might spread to that country admonished the Ruthenian clergy and people not to follow their apostate bishops but to remain faithful to the Patriarchs of Constantinople.

The preparations for the mission of Pociej and Terlecki who were expected to leave for Rome at the beginning of September [40] were, however, already well advanced, because immediately after their arrival in Cracow on July 17 without waiting for the results of the negotiations with Prince Ostrogski, both the Nuncio and the King started with their advisers to study the conditions for reunion submitted by the Ruthenian hierarchy. Both arrived at favorable conclusions and were already providing for the travelling expenses of the two bishops. [41] This was the first result of the " congregations " held in Cracow during a summer which was already very

---

[36] *Borgh.* III 91 d, fol. 15v.

[37] See one of the later reports of the Nuncio, published in part by G. Hofmann, *op. cit.*, 134, n. 2, and discussed below.

[38] *Ibidem.*

[39] *Monumenta Confraternitatis Stauropigianae*, I, Nr. 382 (August 17, 1595).

[40] See Malaspina's report of July 28, 1595, *Fondo Aldobrandini*, vol. XI, where he suggested for the first time that the Holy See should instruct the Bishop of Padua and the other Italian bishops to receive most cordially the Ruthenian delegates, and expressed the hope that delegates from Wallachia would arrive in Rome at the same time.

[41] See Malaspina's report of August 4, 1595, *Borgh.* III 91 d, fol. 4v.

busy for the Polish authorities and the Papal representative in view of the simultaneous deliberations in the matter of the planned anti-Ottoman league in cooperation with the Emperor. Both matters were kept separate, but their connection was to appear later, in Poland as well as in Rome, and from the outset some of the most prominent senators of the Commonwealth were dealing with both of them, serving on the Diet's Commission which studied the project of the league [42] and participating in the " congregations " which considered the chances of the religious union.

Malaspina's answer to the articles of the Ruthenian bishops was given already on August 1 and enclosed with the report he sent to Rome three days later, [43] where he explained that he had acted on advice of the lords who had assisted him in the " congregations. " These lords certainly included the two Grand Chancellors, Zamoyski of Poland and Sapieha of Lithuania, and the Latin Bishop of Łuck Maciejowski, who were in charge of the negotiations with the two Ruthenian bishops, probably also the Latin Archbishop of Lwów Solikowski who had been the first to investigate in the whole matter, [44] and possibly those who along with Leo Sapieha participated in the " congregations " of September : [45] Cardinal George Radziwiłł, Bishop of Cracow, who was in all matters one of the Nuncio's closest confidents, the Latin Bishop of Przemyśl Goślicki, and one or two theologians, in particular Father Peter Skarga who at last saw the results of his long and tireless efforts in favor of reunion with the Ruthenians.

The answer of the Nuncio, [46] without going in detail through all the thirty-two articles, distinguished the requests addressed to the Pope from those whose acceptance depended on the King, and among the former, those " pertaining to divine dogmas " and those " regarding human law. " As to the dogmatic questions, he recognized that all that was requested was in agreement with the Catholic faith and divine revelation, had been proposed as such to the whole Church by the oecumenical Council of Florence, and therefore would be " without any doubt approved and accepted by the Supreme Pontiff. " It now appeared how well inspired the Ruthenian bishops had been when basing their approach to these most important issues, particularly the procession of the Holy Spirit, on the Florentine

---

[42] Rich material on these deliberations is published in *Scriptores rerum Polonicarum*, XX, Kraków 1907.

[43] See above, note 41.

[44] See above, Part III, Chap. V, p. 281, 285.

[45] See the report quoted above, note 37.

[46] Published by G. Hofmann, *op. cit.*, append, IV, 158 f., from the copy in *Borgh.* III 67 A, where on fol. 97v there is a notice that the " articles and conditions " were submitted by Cardinal Aldobrandini to the Consistory of August 30. At the end of the volume, fol. 163-165 (published in *Analecta Ordinis S. Basilii Magni*, Seria II, I (1950), 368), follows a Latin memorandum on the importance of the Union with the Ruthenians and its historical background including the Council of Florence, probably forwarded by Malaspina along with the articles and his answer.

decisions, and how vital the tradition of the Union of Florence was for the success of the Union of Brest.

As to the other concessions which were asked from the Pope, the Nuncio admitted that he could not simply guarantee that they would be granted, since he had no specific instructions as to these points, but he did not hesitate to express his conviction that His Holiness would gladly give his consent. Since all the requests were rather reasonable and depended only on the Pope's pleasure, there was no doubt that " as pious and clement father " who desired nothing more than the salvation of the souls entrusted to him by Christ, he would show his favor " to his most beloved sons who approached him with their supplications. "

But Malaspina went even farther in trying to prove to the Ruthenian bishops the sympathy and understanding of the Holy See and of its representative in Poland. Turning to the requests which they had addressed to the King, he formally promised to make all possible efforts that their proposals be granted " in the interest of Christian Union and in a liberal spirit, as it is worthy and just. " And realizing that some of these requests, especially the most important one : the admission of the bishops of Eastern rite to the Senate, went beyond the constitutional powers of the King himself, he wisely added that he would approach in these matters both the King and the authorities of the Polish-Lithuanian Commonwealth. Finally, he promised to beg the Pope to intercede with his own authority through letters of recommendation, and his conviction that Clement VIII would be very glad to do so, was to prove entirely justified.

Even before any papal interference, in agreement with the Nuncio's desire and the views of his advisers, the King, one day only after Malaspina answered the articles of the Brest Synod in a charter, [47] which specifically approved all those which depended on his authority, beginning with a confirmation of the Charter of his predecessor Władysław III, of 1443, and thus stressing again the continuity of the Florentine tradition, but including also the new issues of the present time. Only with regard to the seats in the Senate, he had to make it clear that though he was personally ready to grant them, he would have to submit that matter first to the Diet. As a matter of fact, according to the basic constitution *Nihil novi* of 1505, such an innovation, enlarging the composition of the Diet's Upper House, required the approval not only of the King but of both houses.

A few days earlier, on July 28, the date of his appeal to Prince Ostrogski, Sigismund III wrote a special letter to the Metropolitan Rahoza, [48]

---

[47] *Akty Zap. Rossii*, IV, Nr. 79 (August 2, 1595); see also Nr. 78 (July 30, 1595).

[48] *Ibidem*, Nr. 77.

thanking him for his decision to separate the Ruthenian Church from Constantinople where at the given moment four candidates were rivalling for the Patriarchate, and for his readiness to submit that Church to the Holy See. He also promised him all necessary protection, so that he had nothing to fear, and encouraged him to go ahead, expressing only some doubts whether the Metropolitan's candidate to the Archbishopric of Polotsk deserved full confidence.

It is not easy to find out whether that message was dictated by any similar doubts as to Rahoza's own determination and loyalty. Malaspina reported in September [49] that even Pociej and Terlecki were tested after their arrival as to their "intention and consistence." The result of that examination was indeed favorable, and the Nuncio could add that only one of all the eight Ruthenian bishops of the Commonwealth who had signed the June decision, Bałaban of Lwów, had "committed apostasy," Kopysteński's similar change of attitude being not yet known. But a little later, [50] realizing the danger of Ostrogski's pressure, he suggested that the two members of the hierarchy, who were only elected to their vacant see but not yet confirmed by the King, be named only administrators of these dioceses pending the final conclusion of the Union. This was decided by the "congregation" in spite of some doubts whether it was in agreement with the procedure of nominating new bishops, requested by the hierarchy and approved by the King. In one of those two cases, that of the Archbishop-elect of Polotsk whose provisional confirmation by Sigismund III, of September 10, was drafted exactly in the terms suggested by the Nuncio, [51] such a precaution was hardly necessary, because in addition to ample earlier evidence of Gregory's sincere dedications to the cause of reunion, there followed the testimony of Father Skarga himself, that he fully shared the views of Pociej and Terlecki and was "already in his soul united with the Church." [52] His final nomination was, therefore, signed by the King on September 22. [53] The other case was that of Ionas Hohol which became of similar importance when Bishop Pełczycki of Pinsk died soon after signing the Brest statements of June; but he too was to remain faithful to what he had promised as designated successor.

But what about the Metropolitan himself? Skarga who summarizing to the General of the Jesuit Society the antecedents of the project of reunion [54] seemed to consider Rahoza one of its first initiators, remained obviously

---

[49] In his report quoted above, note 37.

[50] In his report of September 21, *Borgh.* III 91 d, fol. 15v.

[51] See above, part III, Chap. 5, p. 280 and note 41.

[52] J. Sygański, *Listy Ks. Piotra Skargi* 1566-1620 (The Letters of P. S.), Kraków 1912, 260 (Sept. 27, 1595).

[53] *Akty Zap. Rossii*, IV, Nr. 86.

[54] In the letter quoted above, note 52.

convinced of his integrity. And when on the same occasion he wrote about " two schismatic Palatines who are very favorable to the Union, " he was obviously referring not only to Nicholas Sapieha, the Palatine of Vitebsk, whose attitude at the June Synod was so encouraging, but also to the Palatine of Nowogródek, Theodore Tyszkiewicz with whom the Metropolitan had such a strange correspondence after that Synod. It may be that just the cautious approach which Rahoza used in his relations with that magnate, giving him the impression that any final decision was left to him, was the most appropriate and efficient making Tyszkiewicz a real partisan and later even defender of the Union. Justified too seems the similar caution which the Metropolitan used in his pastoral letter of September 1, [55] in which without arguing about the Union itself, he simply tried to dispel all fears that he would give up the Eastern rite and introduce innovations in the Church.

More objectionable could seem Rahoza's letter to Ostrogski, of September 28. [56] Knowing only too well how the Prince felt about him, accusing him publicly of betraying the Church, he expressed his sorrow and denied once more that he was " selling the Church into Roman slavery. " But in his opinion the project of reunion, accompanied as it was by so many conditions guaranteeing the tradition and autonomy of the Ruthenian Church, was indeed something entirely different. And he was simply evasive when in answer to Ostrogski's suggestion of convoking another synod, he asked the Prince to do so himself and to bring to such a synod a protest against the Union signed by at least two hundred Ruthenian noblemen. He was, of course, fully aware that even the Palatine of Kiev, influential as he was, could not respond to such a challenge. When the Metropolitan finally, on October 28, [57] convoked a synod which was to meet at Nowogródek on January 25, 1596, he did it conditionally, pending the King's permission which was never granted. [58]

It is quite possible that Rahoza, as he pointed out in his letter and in that abortive convocation, was of the opinion that it was not wise for Pociej and Terlecki to go to Rome as long as the danger threatening from Prince Constantine was not removed one way or another. But this was precisely the same opinion which after the Synod of Toruń prevailed in the " congregations " which continued to deliberate in Cracow under the joint auspices of King and Nuncio. Both of them as well as their advisers were so alarmed by the prospects of seditious movements that it was decided to postpone the journey of the two bishops pending a clarification of

[55] *Akty Zap. Rossii*, IV Nr. 83.
[56] *Ibidem*, Nr. 87.
[57] *Ibidem*, Nr. 89.
[58] See K. Lewicki, *op. cit.*, 147 ; the informal character of the meeting which nevertheless took place in Nowogródek, is explained below, Chap. III, p. 344.

Ostrogski's intentions and full assurance of their security. Even when it became known that in the meantime Pociej and Terlecki had already left their residences and were on their way to Cracow, Malaspina anticipated [59] that on their arrival in the capital the problem of their mission to Rome would be reconsidered in order to find out whether it would be more expedient to let them continue their journey or rather to keep them safely under the shadow of His Majesty. For obviously — as the Nuncio added — the spirit of evil disliked the planned Union so much, that all his followers tried to oppose it.

On September 9, [60] a " congregation " was held in the Nuncio's residence and with the participation of the senators present in Cracow, who in connection with the problems raised by the Synod of Toruń, discussed the situation of the Ruthenian bishops whom Prince Constantine " and all the heretics " persecuted so violently. But after the arrival of Pociej and Terlecki on September 16, [61] everybody agreed [62] that the two Ruthenian bishops were proceeding in full agreement with canon law and the decisions of the Council of Florence. General was also the agreement that at least some of the Bishops ought to be admitted to the Senate, in view of Pociej's and Terlecki's argument that because after the Union of Florence even the Metropolitan, Cardinal Isidore, did not receive the dignity of a Senator, he was not held in sufficient esteem and finally expelled. But the most urgent issue how to remedy the dangers which threatened all these bishops and in particular their delegates to Rome, was postponed for discussion at the next meeting which was to consider both " the utility and the harm that reasonably might result from their mission. "

It was not before September 22 that this decisive session took place, [63] and even then no answers had been received from the senators whom the King had consulted through letters nor was it known whether the Castellane of Kamieniec, Jacob Pretwicz, who had been sent to Ostrogski, had obtained anything from the old Prince. In view of that uncertainty opinions were divided as to the advisability of Pociej's and Terlecki's departure for Rome. When Malaspina reported the same day to Cardinal Aldobrandini,

---

[59] In his report of September 21, 1595, quoted above, note 50.

[60] As announced by Malaspina in his report of the preceding day, *Borgh.* III, 89 b, fol. 213.

[61] The date is given in the diary of the Cracow Jesuits, *Scriptores rerum Polon.*, VII, 205.

[62] As pointed out in Malaspina's undated report published by G. Hofmann, *loc. cit.* (see above, note 37), who supposed that it was written at the beginning of September. In the Vatican Archives this document, with the notice " *Mandata dal Nunzio in Polonia,* " is indeed attached to the report of Sept. 8, but since it was written after the arrival of Pociej and Terlecki, it must have been written between Sept. 16 and 22.

[63] Described in detail in Malaspina's report of the same day, published by G. Hofmann, *op. cit.*, append. V, 159-164.

20

he summarized in detail these conflicting opinions without, however, pointing out who expressed either of them. Even the full list of those present and participating in the long discussion is unfortunately not known. From among those who, according to the Nuncio's earlier report, had been chosen by the King for a special investigation of the problem, the Latin Bishop of Przemyśl Goślicki may have been one of the consultants who concluded in a negative sense, since he is the only one of them who did not take any part in further negotiations and since the Ruthenian Bishop of the same city whom he must have known particularly well, proved indeed one of the two " apostates " and was to be excommunicated by Goślicki. [64]

The arguments of those opposed to Pociej's and Terlecki's trip were quite serious and, as a matter of fact, concerned not only that mission but the implementation of the whole project of reunion in general. They started by admitting that in the Ruthenian lands of both Poland and Lithuania the Greek religion was older than the Catholic and had old privileges confirmed by the King and his predecessors which had to be respected. They insisted that first of all the Ruthenian nobility and common people who were "exasperated" had to be "mollified" and in particular Prince Ostrogski gained by all means. Furthermore, they argued that any action of the pastors was vain without the support of the people, and that in turn the attitude of the people depended on that of the Brotherhoods which were showing such a growing hostility that they had just published a script full of invectives against the Holy See. They feared that while Pociej and Terlecki would make in Rome their act of obedience, a " schism " might originate in the country with equally dangerous political and religious consequences : the Patriarch of Constantinople would undoubtedly depose the Metropolitan and the other bishops, as some Ruthenians had already asked him to do, and thus, the people being left without any hierarchy, the Union would be " interrupted " anyway. As to Ostrogski, the opponents referred not only to the exciting appeals he had disseminated in print, but also to rumors that he had chased Pociej and Terlecki on their way to Cracow through 150 horsemen who were instructed to kill them and whom they hardly escaped. The conclusion was that in view of all these troubles and the danger " to the peace and concord which the Kingdom at present enjoyed, the Union ought to be preceded, as suggested before, by another synod of the Ruthenians or, if this seemed hopeless, by a general synod of the Latin hierarchy of the Commonwealth which would incorporate the Ruthenian episcopate and clergy. "

That last suggestion was entirely new and could hardly be made without the knowledge and possibly even the advice of the Primate of Poland, the Archbishop of Gniezno Stanislaus Karnkowski. He was to make a some-

---

[64] See A. Prochaska's study in *Kwartalnik histor.*, X (1896), 546-551.

what similar proposal soon after the Union of Brest, [65] when planning a national synod which would stabilize the union with the Ruthenians and possibly even hear those who were not yet united with Rome. However, having his own archdiocese in purely Catholic Western Poland, he was originally less interested in the negotiations with the Eastern Church and might have been afraid of the difficulties and even risks of the project, before finally giving his approval, under the impression of Pociej's and Terlecki's achievements in Rome. [66] The misunderstandings which the Primate had with Malaspina, though primarily arising from political suspicions, might also have contributed to his rather reserved attitude regarding even the purely religious project in which the representative of the Holy See was so deeply interested and which Karnkowski preferred to discuss with Prince Ostrogski to the dissatisfaction of the Nuncio. [67]

Closest to Malaspina from the very beginning of his mission to Poland [68] was the other leading member of the Latin hierarchy, George Radziwiłł, who as Bishop of Cracow was second in rank only to the Primate himself and as Cardinal even outranked him. Though transferred by the King from the see of Wilno to that of Cracow, not without some Polish opposition, [69] Cardinal Radziwiłł belonged to the leading family of Lithuania, a family of purely Lithuanian origin but necessarily in close relation with the Ruthenians of the Grand Duchy and therefore seriously concerned with their religious problems. Furthermore, George was a brother of Nicholas Christopher called " the Orphan, " Grand Marshal of Lithuania and Palatine of Troki, whose two duchies, Nieśwież and Ołyka, were situated in Ruthenian regions, the former in the White-Ruthenian section of the Grand Duchy, the latter in Volhynia, not far from Prince Constantine's Ostrog. The Duke *de Olica*, as he was called in Rome, was no less than his ecclesiastic brother, a devoted Catholic, [70] contrary to their own father and to the other line of the Radziwiłłs, including the Palatine of Wilno, which remained Calvinist from the early days of the Reformation. How strongly " the Orphan " favored the union of the Ruthenians with Rome, in which his brother started to be interested when still Bishop of Wilno with its large Orthodox

---

[65] In his letter to Malaspina of Dec. 13, 1597, *Borgh.* III 91 c, fol. 158-159, which will be discussed below, Chap. V, p. 418, in connection with a slightly different project of the King.

[66] See below, Chap. II, p. 339.

[67] Malaspina complained about it to Rome in his report of October 20, 1595 (Borgh. III 89 b, f. 357), pointing out that he would not use similar methods in reacting against the Primate.

[68] See Malaspina's letters to Cardinal Radziwiłł and the frequent references to him in the papers relating to the first year of his mission : *Nunz. di Polonia*, vol. 35, fol. 14v-16, 16v, 151, 204v etc.

[69] *Ibidem*, fol. 22v (decipher in *Borgh.* III 96 d, fol. 57 ; August 15, 1592).

[70] *Ibidem*, fol. 105, where Malaspina, in his report of Oct. 22, 1592, highly praised the brother of the Cardinal for his strong Catholic convictions.

population, this is best evidenced by the letter which during the deliberations in Cracow he wrote from distant Nieśwież directly to the Pope, [71]
expressing his great pleasure and satisfaction with Pociej's and Terlecki's
going to Rome, particularly praising the former, his old friend whom he
called " the leader and author of that union. " For all these reasons it is
safe to assume that at the " congregation " of September 22, held at his
new episcopal see, Cardinal Radziwiłł was one of those who defended the
optimistic point of view, and since Skarga in his report written five days
later, [72] when a positive decision was finally taken, mentioned only him,
besides the Nuncio, as participant in the discussions, it is probable that he
even was the main supporter of the idea of going ahead with the mission
to Rome of the two Ruthenian bishops.

The more optimistic group agreed with the other that the issue to be
decided was one of the major ones which for many years had involved the
Commonwealth. Nevertheless they estimated that the Catholics should not
let pass such a grand opportunity. Their starting point was a comparison
with the Council of Florence which did not disregard the sole Ruthenian
bishop then present : it welcomed him and the Popes honored him with
the Cardinalate and entrusted him with the most important missions. So
why should now the whole body of their bishops be treated with neglect ?
Since in the future the King would name only bishops who accepted the
Union, there would be time enough for the pastors gradually to lead the
people to the true faith. As to another synod, an assembly with the participation of " all sects of the Kingdom, " as Ostrogski seemed to suggest,
was undesirable and unacceptable, while waiting for a general synod of the
whole Catholic clergy would mean missing the present occasion. The Prince
and his partisans could not disturb the peaceful condition of the Commonwealth, since the authority of the King and the Catholics had not declined
to such an extent : far from inflicting violence to anybody, they could use
the very " shield of the heretics and schismatics, " viz., liberty of conscience,
because if everybody was supposed to be free to join any sect, why should
the Ruthenian clergy be forbidden to unite with the Catholic Church ?
That last point was leading to an answer to the initial argument of the
other side regarding the necessity of respecting the privileges of the Greek
Church : the King was no longer bound by these privileges, since precisely
those to whom they had been granted, were asking him on their own
initiative to change the former situation.

In view of such a diversity of opinion, the " congregation " turned to
Malaspina, as representative of the Holy See, to reconcile the two viewpoints and to draw a conclusion. He asked, however, to be excused even

---

[71] *Fondo Aldobrandini*, vol. 83, Sept. 14, 1595 a few days later he received from
Malaspina a full report on the situation, *Bibl. Vallicelliana* L 18, fol. 167-167v.

[72] Quoted above, note 52.

from expressing his own view, and his wisely reserved attitude was in full agreement with his usual cautious way of procedure, dictated by his conviction that it was precisely because he represented the Papacy, he had to avoid any interference with the internal problems of the Commonwealth and any responsibility for the consequences of a decision with possible political implications.

Fortunately, the senators discovered another solution of the apparent deadlock. They agreed to invite Pociej and Terlecki to join the meeting and asked them a few questions of such decisive importance that the main responsibility was turned over to those who took the initiative in the matter. Answering these questions, the two Ruthenian bishops briefly and firmly declared, first, that they were " sure of the Metropolitan and the other bishops, " probably under the impression of another declaration in favor of the Union in which on August 27 [73] even Bałaban and Kopysteński, in spite of their earlier protests, had joined Terlecki himself at Łuck ; secondly, that the clergy, at least in their own dioceses, had been gained for the union and would influence in turn the people, though they admitted that its authority was lesser than that of the Latin clergy ; thirdly, that many nobles and, in general, laymen would have already signed the declaration in favor of reunion along with the bishops if, feeling obliged to promote the matter secretly, the bishops themselves had not abstained from inviting them. Referring to that necessary secrecy, they admitted, of course, that there was a real danger threatening from the opposition led by Ostrogski, but obviously even Pociej, after his latest experience with the Prince, was now determined not to care any longer for his attitude.

That determination appeared even more clearly in the considerations which both bishops on their own account added to the requested information. If they now would return home, their adversaries would proclaim that they had been rebuffed and treated with contempt by the Romans, and then the whole cause of reunion would be lost with them. They did not deny that they faced serious dangers, particularly the deposition of all of them, including the Metropolitan, by the Patriarch of Constantinople, which would make the Ruthenians believe that not their real pastors, but private and condemned individuals had made the union. But for that very reason it seemed safer to go to Rome at once before such a deposition. In any case, unable to remain " without head, " they had only two alternatives : either to recognize again the Patriarch of Constantinople — and they would rather die than ever return to that " state of damnation " — or to unite with the Latin Church under the Roman Pontiff.

Particularly moving was their conclusion : no ambition nor human respect had led them to that Union, but indeed " heavenly grace and

---

[73] *Akty Zap. Rossii*, IV, Nr. 82.

light which led them out of darkness." Therefore, they asked to be received into, and incorporated with " the ecclesiastical order of the Kingdom, " a decision which would remove all difficulties. And returning to the comparison with the Union of Florence they recalled : " Isidore was alone, we are many ; there was then no King of similar zeal and piety, nor a Supreme Pontiff so in love with Poland and so anxious for the salvation of souls in that Kingdom. "

Deeply impressed, the members of the " congregation, " after asking Pociej and Terlecki to retire, decided unanimously not to abandon them, and instead of speculating about what might happen in the future, to leave the whole cause to divine Providence which had made the two bishops arrive before receiving the letters cancelling their invitation. At the same time it was agreed that the King should issue a decree declaring that the Union conformed to ancient tradition, to the sacred Councils, and to earlier desires of the Ruthenians, and that, therefore, he was taking their hierarchy and clergy under his protection, since their action had his full approval. Furthermore, taking up the idea of a formal incorporation of the Ruthenian clergy with the Latin, as suggested by the more cautions members of the meeting, and requested by Pociej and Terlecki, it was recommended that without waiting for any general synod and proceeding with the Union, such an incorporation be made by the Pope immediately after that union. With all these guarantees, it seemed reasonable to expect that the ultimate success would be better than after the Council of Florence, and it was rightly observed that, after all, in spite of Isidore's failure who was wrongly believed to have been killed after returning to the Ruthenians, and in spite of the lack of implementation of the Florentine decrees, the Union of 1439 and the testimony of its decisions had remained very useful for the defense of the faith against schismatics and heretics. Thus the intimate connection between the two unions, the universal and the regional, was once more emphasized on a particularly solemn occasion.

CHAPTER II

THE UNION OF ROME, 1595

The momentous decision taken in Cracow on September 22, 1595 had to be implemented at once in two respects. First, the preparations for Pociej's and Terlecki's mission to Rome had to be completed; and secondly, the partisans of reunion among the Ruthenians had to receive the promised encouragement and protection, while the opponents had to be appeased as far as possible, so that there would be a good chance for acceptance in the country, after the return of the two bishops, of the agreement which they were expected to conclude in Rome.

In the interpretation of the Holy See, that agreement, or rather the reception of the Ruthenians into the Catholic Church by the Supreme Pontiff, was, as a matter of fact, the real Union, though ratification of the declaration made by two bishops in the name of all others was considered most desirable and required indeed the convocation of another synod on their return. Because of the place of that synod, which could not meet before October 1596, history speaks usually of a Union of Brest, finally concluded in that year; but in the tradition of the Papacy the great event is connected with the solemn ceremony held at the Vatican on December 23, 1595, so that the designation of that ceremony as Union of Rome is certainly not inappropriate.

This is, however, not the only reason why describing separately the developments concerning Pociej's and Terlecki's trip[1] and what happened in the Commonwealth during their absence, the first of these problems must be treated with special attention. It was in Rome rather than in the Ruthenian lands or even at the royal court that there appeared in the fall and winter of 1595-96 the usual connection between the idea of the Union of the Churches and that of the Crusade or anti-Ottoman league, and also the connection between the concrete project of a regional union and the possibilities of a universal union with all eastern Christendom which the Papacy never ceased to consider. The whole eastern policy of Clement VIII, a Pope so particularly interested in all these connected issues, was,

---

[1] A special study of that trip, which proved very helpful for the present re-examination of that problem has been made by A. M. Ammann, " Der Aufenthalt der ruthenischen Bischöfe Hypathius Pociej und Cyrillus Terlecki in Rom im Dezember und Januar 1595-96, " *Orientalia Christiana Periodica*, XI (1945), 103-140.

therefore, involved, and his Nuncio to Poland was fully aware of these implications.

Already at the end of his long report on the discussions of September 22,[2] expressing the hope that the two Ruthenian bishops would leave for Rome within four or five days and recalling that provisions had to be made for their trip both ways, he was thinking not only of their travelling expenses but also of the question who should accompany them to Italy where neither of them had ever been before, Terlecki knowing not even the Latin language. A few weeks before Malaspina had written in that matter to a person who seemed to him particularly qualified to conduct them to Rome and who was nobody else but the versatile Monsignor Alexander Komulovich : he had failed both in his endeavors to propagandize the anti-Turkish action in Poland and in his mission to Moscow, but continued to be considered an expert in East European problems, was a Slav himself deeply interested in all Slavic peoples and their relations with Rome, and, after all, had established already in 1594 some contacts in the Ruthenian lands. The Nuncio who wanted him to come to Cracow before the end of September, had not yet received any answer and therefore was already considering his replacement by a man recommended by the Latin Bishop of Łuck, Maciejowski, but the final decision was to be made in Rome.

Without waiting for the settlement of that question, Malaspina, on September 27,[3] wrote a letter to the Pope himself which confirms the impression that thinking of Komulovich he was thinking at the same time of the two projects which the Croat priest-diplomat was supposed to promote. For the first time the Nuncio, pointing out the repercussions which the decision of the Ruthenians of Poland and their favorable reception by Clement VIII could have in other Orthodox countries, referred not only to the Moldavians and Wallachians but in the first place to the Muscovites : he hoped that all these peoples would be moved to turn " from darkness to light. " And toward the end of the same letter he spoke of the hope of the Ruthenians themselves, that the Pope would love them more particularly as " a bulwark of the rest of Christendom against the Turks and the Tartars, " and that God who had defended them against these " barbarians " even when they were living in schism, would lead them to victories and triumphs as soon as through Clement VIII they would be made members of His Church.

Anticipating the conversion of all Orthodox of Eastern Europe including Moscow and the development of the defensive war against the Muslims into a victorious advance, all this in consequence of the reunion of the

---

[2] *Orientalia Christiana*, III-2 (1925), 164.
[3] *Ibidem*, 164-167 (appendix VI).

Ruthenians, Malaspina, usually so restrained, was sharing the illusions which men like Komulovich were propagating at the Vatican and was to be disappointed as he was in his expectations regarding the chances of Catholicism in Sweden. Otherwise, however, the enthusiasm of his letter, which he wanted the Pope to share, was quite understandable and a natural consequence of the strong arguments in favor of the Ruthenian project which obviously had impressed him so much during the last " congregation" in Cracow. Echoing those arguments, the comparisons with the Union of Florence, and the praise of the present King of Poland and the present Pope whose earlier legation to Poland as efficient peacemaker was now bearing its fruits, Malaspina did not fail to recommend already on that occasion two of the requests of the Ruthenian hierarchy which he considered essential for the success of their project. It was not quite accurate to say that the failure of Cardinal Isidore to stabilize the Union of Florence in Poland resulted chiefly from the fact that he was neither a senator of the realm nor " incorporated with the ecclesiastical order " of the country. But the Nuncio was perfectly right in emphasizing that if these two privileges were granted to the present Ruthenian bishops — all native noblemen, as he recalled, and therefore better qualified for dignities in the Kingdom than the Greek Isidore had been — their position would be greatly strengthened in front of their adversaries, both schismatics and heretics. Unfortunately he did not realize that precisely the joint votes of Orthodox and Protestant members of the Diet could prevent the admission into the Senate of all or part of the bishops of Eastern rite even after their incorporation with the Latin clergy by the Pope.

In any case, Malaspina's various suggestions and recommendations received all due attention at the Vatican where " the most minute reports " on the progress of the negotiations with the Ruthenians were expected from the Nuncio, including full information on the reasons why in the past similar efforts of Cardinal Isidore had failed. [4] From the outset, however, the Secretariate of State, equally interested in the mission of Monsignor Komulovich but disappointed with his reports about the poor chances of Moscow's cooperation against the Turks, was rather skeptical as to the idea of sending him to Rome with Pociej and Terlecki. For, on the one hand, in spite of the impression that little could be expected from the " barbarian " Muscovites and their incapable ruler, [5] the Vatican was already considering the possibility of sending Komulovich back to Moscow in connection with the diplomatic relations between the Tsar and Emperor Rudolf

---

[4] See in the long instruction sent to Malaspina on August 12, 1595 (*Borgh.* III 18 cf, fol. 236-237) the passage on fol. 237.

[5] That phrase about Moscow's " barbaria " which was used in the instruction just quoted (fol. 236), was to reappear in that of Dec. 2, 1595 (*ibidem*, fol. 276).

II ; [6] while on the other hand, the Vatican was rightly pleased with the new activity which the tireless Croat had started in the meantime in the Commonwealth. The bishopric of Wilno being vacant because the Lithuanians opposed the nomination of the Pole Maciejowski whom the King wanted to be transferred there from Łuck, Komulovich had been made administrator *pro tempore* of that large diocese. [7] There is no evidence of his participation in any preparations for the reunion with the Ruthenians, so numerous in that region, but in general his achievements there were quite remarkable and made him much more appreciated by Poles and Lithuanians alike than his vast and rather fantastic political projects. It was, however, obviously impossible for him to deal at the same time with Pociej's and Terlecki's mission to Rome, [8] and even less to accompany them there. Malaspina eventually agreed with these objections, and it was a Canon of Wilno, Monsignor Eustachius Wołłowicz, probably the candidate of Maciejowski, who conducted the two bishops to the Vatican, and being of Ruthenian origin himself and familiar with their language, was to prove very useful even as interpreter. [9]

They left Cracow where they spent only ten days, on September 26, [10] with the letter of recommendation to the Pope which the King had given them the day before, [11] while Skarga recommended them in a letter of the following day [12] to the General of the Jesuit Society, Father Aquaviva, giving him on that occasion a full account of the background of their mission. Both the King and the Nuncio provided them with the financial means necessary for their journey and for a dignified appearance at the Vatican, [13] since even their financial situation had suffered from the treatment inflicted upon them by Prince Ostrogski, though nothing is known about any direct interference with their trip by that dangerous enemy.

Unjustified, too, proved other fears which arose in Rome in connection with their expected passage through Venice. They were raised by the same Catholic Greek Arcudius who, during his earlier visit in the Ruthenian

---

[6] *Ibidem*, fol. 240v (August 19) and 256 (Oct. 2, 1595).

[7] His report on the situation in that diocese, of Dec. 12, 1595, has been published by J. Kurczewski, *Kościół zamkowy wileński* (The Cathedral of Wilno), II, 97-99 ; see the comments of Chodynicki, *op. cit.*, 276.

[8] This was pointed out in Malaspina's instruction of August 19, 1595, quoted above, note 6 ; see also the praise of Komulovich's activity in Wilno (*Borgh.* III 18 ef, fol. 260v, Nov. 4, 1595).

[9] See below, p. 328.

[10] *Scriptores rerum Polon.*, VII, 205.

[11] Copies of that letter are in *Borgh.* III 89 b, fol. 238 (*ibidem*, fol. 239, the original of a similar letter to Cardinal Aldobrandini, of Sept. 28), and *Borgh.* III 91 d, fol. 43.

[12] J. Sygański, *Listy Ks. P. Skargi*, Nr. 124, pp. 259-261.

[13] See A. M. Ammann, *op. cit.*, 119, where their own financial efforts are pointed out. The contribution made by the Nuncio was reimbursed to him by papal order of Nov. 15, 1595 (*Docum. Pontif. Historiam Ucrainae illustr.*, I, Nr. 131.)

lands, had so successfully contributed to the preparations for reunion with Rome, particularly thanks to his relations with Pociej, and now, working in Rome at the Greek Church of Saint Athanasius, heard with pleasure that his friend was to arrive, along with Terlecki, in order to implement the projects and promises of the past. But for that very reason he was afraid of any possible last minute obstacles and became very alarmed by news received from Venice that the Greek colony of that city, mostly Orthodox and in close relations with the Patriarchate of Constantinople, was trying to get information on the expected arrival of the two Ruthenian bishops on their way to Rome. He suspected that these Greeks would try to meet their delegates and to persuade them to give up their intention to submit to the Holy See. [14]

Under the influence of Arcudius who was rightly considered a reliable expert in all these matters, the Vatican became alarmed too, remembering that a few years ago, in 1588, the permanent representative of the Patriarch of Constantinople in Venice, the Greek Archbishop of Philadelphia, had been suspected by the authorities of the Republic of being a Turkish spy and of forwarding to Constantinople information suggesting a possible attack of the Ottoman Empire against the Venetian possessions. [15] These suspicions proved rather doubtful, and it was through private individuals knowing that Archbishop well, that the Secretariate of State and the papal Nuncio in Venice tried to find out what the Greeks there really wanted to do on the occasion of the visit of Pociej and Terlecki. [16] It so happened, however, perhaps because they themselves wanted to avoid any possible troubles, that they did not pass at all through Venice on their way to Rome, but visited only the nearby city of Padua and its famous University where so many Poles used to study and where they signed their names in the register of the " Polish Nation. " [17] The bishop of that city had been instructed well in advance by the Secretariate of State to receive them most friendly, and similar instructions were sent to the bishops of other Italian dioceses to make their first impressions as pleasant as possible. [18] It was, therefore, after an undisturbed and rather uneventful trip that they safely arrived in Rome on November 15, 1595. [19]

The Pope and the Secretariate of State expected them eagerly, having been convinced by Malaspina's reports, particularly those about the last

---

[14] All this is described in a letter of Peter Nores, a member of Cardinal Aldobrandini's household, to G. V. Pinelli in Padua, of Sept. 23, 1595 (Vatican Library, *Ottob. lat.* 1088, fol. 123-125, 274-275), first indicated by A. M. Ammann, *loc. cit.*

[15] *Nunz. di Venezia*, vol. 26, fol. 388, 392 (reports of Oct. 29 and Nov. 12, 1588).

[16] *Ibidem*, vol. 31, fol. 148v-149, 163v. (reports of Sept. 30 and Nov. 4, 1595).

[17] *Archiwum do dziejów literatury i oświaty w Polsce*, VI/1, 28.

[18] *Borgh.* III 18 cf., fol. 240v (August 19, 1595).

[19] Vatican Library, *Urbin. lat.* 1603 (Avvisi di Roma, 1595), fol. 874v; already on Nov. 11 they were expected in Rome " d'hora in hora " (*ibidem*, fol. 865).

discussions in Cracow, that really " the hand of God was guiding the whole matter according to His most Holy Providence " so that all the machinations of the adversaries, though supported by the heretics would end in failure. [20] Praising the Nuncio for his friendliness in all relations with the Ruthenian bishops, the Roman authorities were decided to treat them the same way " with all charity and convenient zeal, " and as soon as the Bishop of Padua notified their arrival in Italy, preparations were made at the Vatican for a most favorable reception, so that they might return home " with fullest satisfaction. " [21] There were, however, two entirely different problems which had to be carefully considered before such a completely satisfactory solution of the unusually important issue which Pociej and Terlecki were to submit to the Holy See.

One of these problems, of a purely religious character, concerned the conditions for reunion which were contained in the thirty-two articles of June 1 and through Malaspina were forwarded to Rome where the Secretary of State submitted them to the Pope at the Consistory of August 30. [22] In full agreement with the Nuncio's expectation, as expressed in his answer of August 1, that the Pope would consider these requests most favorably, Cardinal Aldobrandini assured him already on September 16 [23] that with regard to these articles everything would be done that would serve the glory of God, the salvation of souls, and also " the consolation of those who were coming there and expected with desire. " But he had to write at the same time that these articles were being examined by the Congregation of the Holy Office which had not yet arrived at any conclusion in the matter. And before that report was completed, there appeared another problem which, though definitely political, affected the attitude of the Holy See in all matters concerning the Commonwealth and just before the arrival of Pociej and Terlecki provoked at the Vatican much more excitement than the theological subtleties of the agreement with the Ruthenian bishops.

Their arrival almost coincided with that of a Polish bishop of Latin rite, Adalbert Baranowski, [24] whose diocese, that of Płock in Masovia, was purely Catholic and Polish, so that he did not show any special interest in the union with the Ruthenians, and he does not seem to have travelled together with their delegates. Yet, when it became known in Rome that he too would appear there at the same time, it was expected[25] that, as a bishop and senator of the Commonwealth, he would contribute to the

---

[20] *Borgh.* III 18 ef, fol. 253v (Oct. 2, 1595).

[21] *Ibidem,* fol. 260v (Nov. 4, 1595).

[22] *Borgh.* III 67 A, fol. 94-97 ; see above, Chap. I, p. 302, n. 46.

[23] *Borgh.* III 18 ef, fol. 249v.

[24] *Urbin. lat.* 1603, fol. 872, where his arrival and reception a few days before is described in detail.

[25] *Borgh.* III 18 ef, fol. 253 (Oct. 7, 1595).

" conversion of the Ruthenians " and also to the punishment of those who at the Synod of Toruń, so frequently mentioned in Malaspina's reports, had threatened even to disturb the public order with a view of thus opposing that reunion. But Baranowski, a prominent member of the hierarchy, considered even a candidate to the cardinalate, and at the same time an experienced diplomat, was sent to Rome for an entirely different purpose. Though the object of his mission was clouded in secrecy, and even the impression created that he was on a private trip, it soon became apparent [26] that he was instructed to clarify some rather serious misunderstandings which were arising between the Polish government, in particular Grand Chancellor Zamoyski, and the Secretariate of State in the delicate matter of Poland's participation in the anti-Ottoman action. Bishop Baranowski whose obvious piety and virtue at once favorably impressed the Vatican, seemed well qualified to restore the confidence which hitherto had characterized the relations between Poland and Clement VIII, and which was a prerequisite condition for the success of the mission of the Ruthenian bishops also, though they were concerned with an entirely different problem.

The event which threatened to trouble that confidence had occurred in the middle of October, when they still were on their long way to Italy, in far away Moldavia. Polish forces under Zamoyski who was not only Grand Chancellor but also Grand Hetman of the Crown, i. e. commander-in-chief of the Polish army, and as such carefully watching all that was going on at Poland's border and particularly the movements of the Crimean Tartars, had entered that neighboring principality after hearing that a large number of Tartars, estimated at seventy thousand, were moving through Moldavia in order to join the Turkish forces in Hungary. After several days of fighting, from October 18 to 21, the Poles succeeded in repressing and stopping the Tartars, whom Sinan Pasha, the Turkish commander in Hungary, therefore expected in vain so that he had to recross the Danube, harassed during his retreat by the Prince of Transylvania, Sigismund Báthory. [27]

This Polish success could seem, therefore, to the advantage of the Christian forces fighting in Hungary, both the Austrians and their Transylvanian ally, and a useful contribution which Poland, without formally joining the anti-Ottoman league, made to the defense of Hungary against them. For nothing was more feared in the course of that difficult struggle than a penetration of the Sultan's Crimean vassal through the Danubian principalities and across the Carpathian mountains. However, after frustrating the Tartar invasion of Hungary, Zamoyski made an agreement with

---

[26] *Urbin. lat.* 1603, fol. 884 (Nov. 18, 1595).

[27] See the diary of the Cracow Jesuits, *Scriptores rerum Pol.*, VII, 209 and the interpretations by J. Sas in *Przegląd powszechny*, vol. 50 (1897), 74-89, and N. Iorga, *Histoire des Roumains*, V (1940) 375-381

their Turkish overlords, [28] according to which the Prince of Moldavia, Rozvan, who recently had replaced the tyrannical Aaron, but was unable to defend the country, was replaced in turn by Jeremiah Movila who already on August 27 had paid homage to the Kingdom of Poland and, though he continued to pay the usual tribute to the Turks, practically brought the principality under Polish control. This, too, could seem rather welcome from the Catholic point of view, since the Movilas also belonged to the partisans of religious union with Rome. But on the other hand, the deposed prince had been placed on his throne by the Prince of Transylvania, who deeply resented the removal of his partisan, always hoped to control Moldavia himself through such a convenient puppet, and in full agreement with the Habsburgs did not want Moldavia to come definitely under Polish influence.

While, therefore, in Cracow these developments were celebrated through a solemn *Te Deum*, almost the same day when the Ruthenian bishops soon after Baranowski entered Rome, [29] indignant reports which arrived not only from Transylvania [30] but also from the imperial court, [31] created at the Vatican a serious alarm and the painful impression that Poland instead of helping those who were really fighting the Turks, was creating for them new difficulties and supporting the infidels by setting up in the crucial region of Moldavia an " intruder, " in agreement with Turks and Tartars. [32] The violent anti-Polish propaganda which reached all those interested in the eastern question, did not mislead the Venetians [33] who besides the biased reports from Prague [34] where Emperor Rudolf II resided, regularly received full information from Constantinople [35] and quite frequently also

---

[28] See the comments about that agreement in the " avvisi " received in Rome (*Urbin. lat.*1603, fol. 787v, 790v, etc.) and including also news about a simultaneous, advantageous agreement with the Tartars (fol. 941). Jeremiah's homage to Poland is published in *Documente privitore la istoria Românilor*, III/1, Nr. 48.

[29] On November 17 ; see *Scriptores rerum Pol.*, *loc. cit.*

[30] The reports of the Nuncio in Transylvania are published in *Monumenta Vaticana historiam Regni Hungariae illustrantia*, II/3, Budapest 1909.

[31] *Urbin. lat.* 1603, f. 814, 820 (Oct. 28, 1595).

[32] See the letter of Peter Nores to Malaspina, Nov. 18, 1595 (*Ottob. lat.* 1088, f. 104v-116, partic. fol. 108v) and the comments of A. M. Ammann, *loc. cit.*, 122.

[33] Already on Oct. 7, 1595, their Ambassador to the Holy See, Paolo Paruta, short by before his recall from Rome sent to Venice a highly objective report on the whole background of the situation (*La Legazione di Roma di P. Paruta*, III, Nr. 429), and his successor, Giovanni Dolfino, reported about rather optimistic interpretations of the Polish action by the Pope himself (State Archives of Venice, *Dispacci Roma*, vol. 36, fol. 159v, 168; Nov. 18 and 25, 1595) after his discussions with Baranowski.

[34] State Archives of Venice, *Dispacci Germania*, vol. 24 (without pagination), reports of Oct. 17, Oct. 31 (giving also the Polish interpretation), Nov. 11, etc.

[35] *Ibidem, Dispacci Costantinopoli*, vol. 42, containing an extremely rich material, of which only a small part is published in *Documente privitore la istoria românilor*, III/1 (Bucarest 1880), appendix ; see particularly Nr. 56, 57 (Dec. 2 and 14, 1595).

from Poland. [36]   In Rome, however, the partisans of the House of Austria and of an anti-Ottoman league under Habsburg leadership, were seriously moved, and the Pope himself was deeply hurt, were it only by the complaints that because of his " particular and extraordinary affection " for Poland, known to the whole world, he was " closing his eyes " at her " invasion " of Moldavia without any previous information of either the Emperor or the Prince of Transylvania. [37]

What made the whole situation particularly involved was the connection, stressed in some at least of the anti-Polish statements, of the rather local Moldavian question with the big issue of Moscow's possible part in the struggle against the Muslims.   Those who wanted to answer Zamoyski's argument that Rozvan had to be replaced because he proved unable to defend Moldavia against the Tartars, pretended that there was no real danger of Tartar penetration into that country, in view of Muscovite action against the Crimea. [38]   Even Cardinal Aldobrandini himself who was less excited about the " dishonorable " action of Zamoyski and the Poles, and about the displeasure of the Prince of Transylvania, than were minor agents of the Vatican who pretended to write in his name, [39] preceded his comments on that matter, made in one of his frequent letters to Malaspina, [40] by wondering whether after all Alexander Komulovich would not really have to go to Moscow again, since the Emperor who was sending there his ambassador wanted " our man " to go with him.

The Nuncio to Poland, who by some was blamed himself for having created hopes that no unilateral Polish action was to be expected in Moldavia, [41] did his best to supply the Vatican with reliable information on what had really happened there, including the battle which the Poles had fought against Turks and Tartars.   He forwarded to Rome a letter received from Zamoyski [42] and seconded his interpretation of the necessity of entering Moldavia which the prince appointed by Sigismund Báthory could not defend.   At the same time, explaining Poland's difficult position, he reported about troubles with the Cossacks who had raided, among others, the estates of the Castellane of Cracow, the Catholic member of the Ostrogski family,

---

[36] Vatican Archives, *Nunz. di Venezia*, vol. 31, fol. 148, where the Nuncio in one of his numerous reports in that matter quotes news received from Lublin.   See also *Urbin. lat.* 1603, fol. 823v, 869v, 965 etc.

[37] From the letter quoted above (note 32), fol. 107 ; see also the Pope's letters sent to Poland, *Documente privitore*, XII (1904), Nr. 234-236 (Nov. 8, 1595), and Zamoyski's answer, Vatican Library, *Capponiano* 164, fol. 92-95 (Jan. 1, 1596).

[38] See in the letter quoted above (note 32), fol. 110-110v.

[39] Nores stressed that he wrote in the name of the Cardinal" of S. Giorgio. "

[40] *Borgh.* III 18 ef, fol. 256 (Oct. 2, 1595).

[41] See in the letter of P. Nores the criticism on fol. 105v-106.

[42] *Capponiano* 164, fol. 1-7 (Malaspina's report of Nov. 11, 1595) ; Zamoyski's letter in *Docum. priv.*, XII, Nr. 177.

and about the danger threatening from the Muscovites who, contrary to the treaties, were building a fortress near the border and making " thousand insolences " in Livonia. The latter of these significant details indicated once more the impossibility of uniting in a joint anti-Turkish undertaking both the Muscovites and the Poles who continued to regard with suspicion any diplomatic relations of the West with their eastern neighbor. [43] The former point was to gain its full importance only later when the real background of the growing Cossack dissatisfaction appeared on the eve of the Union of Brest though without any direct connection with it.

There was no direct connection either between the mission of Baranowski and that of the two Ruthenian bishops who seem to have negotiated in Rome quite separately. [44] Obviously, however, the delicate task of the Bishop of Płock was facilitated by the fact that at the same time the other delegates from Poland brought to the Pope so welcome news. And on the other hand, their offer must have been considered particularly important at a moment when the policies of the Commonwealth raised so much interest and conflicting interpretations. In any case Baranowski as well as Pociej and Terlecki were received with the greatest possible consideration and courtesy.

As to the Bishop of Płock, he first prayed at St. Peter's in company of a large number of distinguished Polish noblemen present in Rome, and then was received in audience for more than three hours by Clement VIII, who remembered how splendidly Baranowski had received him at the time of his legation to Poland and knew about the bishop's great influence at the royal court. The Pope also instructed his two nephews who directed the Secretariate of State, to show the same " infinite kindness " to the Polish guest when he called upon them immediately after the papal audience. [45] And when he fell ill a little later, though only for a short time, the special solicitude of Clement VIII was generally noted. [46] It is true that during the lengthy negotiations which he had to conduct, it became apparent that he was not too favorable to the project of an all-inclusive anti-Ottoman league as conceived by the Holy See, but the news and suggestions which the Vatican continued to receive in that whole matter and in particular about the Moldavian situation, not only from Malaspina but also from special agents sent to Poland before Baranowski's arrival, were

---

[43] See about these negotiations H. Übersberger, *Österreich und Russland*, I. Many additional details are given in *Dispacci Germania* of the State Archives of Venice, vol. 24, Jan. 1 and 9, 1596, etc.

[44] However, both missions are described jointly by the Venetian Ambassador ; see *Dispacci Roma*, vol. 36, fol. 159v.

[45] See the news of Nov. 15, 1595, in *Urbin. lat.* 1603, fol. 872.

[46] *Ibidem*, fol. 932v (Dec. 6, 1595).

so conflicting and confusing [47] that for the time being no decision could be reached anyway. At least with regard to any Muscovite cooperation against the Turks [48] the Holy See, perhaps under the influence of the Bishop of Płock, became more and more skeptical and convinced that if the Grand Prince of Moscow asked for recognition of his imperial title by the West — a point which always alarmed the Poles — it was merely a matter of vanity, and that nothing constructive could be expected " from these barbarians, " a situation which was considered regrettable " in view of the inclination of the Greeks because of the similitude of their faith. " [49]

In that connection it is significant that when the two Ruthenian bishops arrived in Rome, some otherwise well informed people there seriously believed that they were " schismatics coming from Muscovy " [50] in order to unite with the Catholic Church and to recognize the supreme authority of the Pope. These rumors were soon corrected and it was generally realized that they arrived with such a purpose not from Moscow, but from " White Russia, a province under the rule of the Kingdom of Poland. " [51] On the contrary, the widely spread information, was correct [52] that Clement VIII who was, of course, fully aware of their origin and identity, highly pleased anyway with their mission, immediately took care of all details regarding their accommodation and all living facilities in the Holy City, and received them in audience on the very evening of the day of their arrival. And great was the impression in Rome when it became generally known that they had mandates from at least five other bishops whose dioceses were said to include twenty thousand parishes — a tremendous acquisition for the Church. [53]

The decision to unite with Rome which according to the statement submitted by Pociej and Terlecki, had been taken by the Metropolitan and the other bishops of the province, was highly praised at their first audience [54] by the Pope himself, when the two Ruthenians, both " men of beautiful appearance and very circumspect in negotiating, " were introduced to him by Cardinal Aldobrandini. Clement VIII did not fail to recognize the special effort the two had made undertaking the long and exhaustive journey

---

[47] *Urbin. lat.* 1603, fol. 823v, 832, 842v, 853v, 865v 881v-882, 904, 920v, 938, 950, 965, 966v. See also Theiner, *Momum. Pol.*, III, Nr. 186.

[48] See *ibidem*, f. 938v (Dec. 12) : News about the deliberation of the congregation " de Ungheria " which considered such a cooperation desirable.

[49] *Borgh.* III 18 ef, fol. 276 (Dec. 2, 1595) ; see the earlier reference to that problem, *ibidem*, fol. 253 (also Vatican Library, *Barb. lat.* 846, fol. 348 ; Oct. 7).

[50] *Urbin. lat.* 1603, fol. 874v (Nov. 15, 1595).

[51] *Ibidem*, fol. 879 (Nov. 18).

[52] See both reports quoted in the two preceding notes.

[53] *Ibidem*, fol. 884 (in another report of Nov. 18).

[54] That audience of Nov. 17 is described in the news of the next day (*ibidem*, fol. 879) and in a letter of P. Nores to Pinelli, of Dec. 2, 1595 (*Ottob. lat.* 1088, fol. 125v-127, 275v-276v.)

21

to Rome, and answering their request for a favorable reception, he assured them at once in general terms that he was receiving them " as beloved sons with all fatherly love. " However, not keeping them longer not to delay their rest, he referred the whole matter to the Cardinal in charge of East European affairs, and it took well over a month before the planned general congregation of all Cardinals at which they were to be solemnly and publicly received into the Church, could be held at the Vatican. In the meantime, they were merely kept informed of all the news which arrived from Poland through their friend, the Nuncio, in the matters which concerned their mission, including the measures which in their absence were taken by the King in view of protecting the partisans of reunion and appeasing Prince Ostrogski. [55] During those same days Pociej and Terlecki had in Rome various private talks in which they explained the origin of their decision, tracing it back to the encouragement received from another bishop (meaning a Polish bishop of Latin rite, probably Maciejowski who had been in Rome before), and pointing out that they were submitting to the Holy See no less than eight thousand parishes in their respective dioceses. They added that two other bishops of their province, with eight thousand more parishes, wanted to do the same (probably a reference to the still hesitating Bałaban and Kopysteński), but were waiting for a report about the result of the negotiations with the Pope. [56]

The delay in these negotiations and in concluding what might be called the Union of Rome, had nothing to do either with the news from Poland nor with the complexities of the general political situation. What remained to be settled were the difficulties of purely religious and ecclesiastical nature which resulted from the long series of conditions submitted by the Ruthenian hierarchy. The document where these requests were listed, was formally presented by Pociej and Terlecki, though the copy forwarded by Malaspina had been received much earlier and continued to be under careful scrutiny by the Holy Office. Before making a final decision, a special commission of Cardinals who studied the matter, holding on November 28 a congregation at the residence of Cardinal Santori, took the rather unusual step to ask for the opinion of a few prominent theologians, hoping to receive their advice within a week. [57]

The first of these opinions was submitted by a *doctus vir*, probably of the Carmelite Order, [58] whose name is unknown and who explained

---

[55] *Borgh.* III 18 ef, fol. 271-271v (Nov. 18, with another reference to the audience of the preceding day), and 273v (Nov. 28, 1595).

[56] *Urbin. lat.* 1603, fol. 895 (news of Nov. 22).

[57] *Ibidem*, 1603, fol. 917 (news of Dec. 2 about the congregation held on the preceding Tuesday).

[58] Published later by the Spanish Carmelitan Thomas a Jesu and summarized by A. M. Ammann, *op. cit.*, 124 f.

at length why the Ruthenians should accept the Latin formula *ex Patre Filioque* rather than the expression *ex Patre per Filium*, and expressed some reservations regarding their conditions for accepting the Gregorian Calendar. However, the most elaborate criticism of all articles which were to be granted by the Pope, came from the Spanish Dominican Juan Saragoza di Heredia, assistant to the Master of the Sacred Palace. [59] His memorandum did not at all represent an unqualified approval of the long petition. On the contrary, Father Saragoza admitted that from the outset some expressions used in its very title had troubled him and made him go through the rest with some rigor. His basic objection was that the articles were called " conditions " that had to be granted before the reunion with the Catholic Church. In contradistinction to that approach he stressed that entering the Church was necessary for anybody's salvation and could not depend on any outside considerations. As to the articles themselves, of which he omitted those which were addressed to the King, he distinguished three categories : in his opinion only a certain number could be granted without restriction, others were to be " totally refused, " and the remaining had to be " clarified and limited. "

Most interesting are, of course, his strong objections to four of the articles though not all of these were equally important. As to the first article regarding the procession of the Holy Spirit, which was the most important indeed, Father Saragoza like the other theologian was not satisfied with the carefully worded formula of the Ruthenian bishops who referred to the Greek fathers of the Church, though in basic agreement with the Florentine decree. He wanted them to conform to the decisions of " the Latin Church " not only in their content but also " in the form of the expressions " lest there could arise " some alterations in the essence of faith. " Without saying it in so many words, he too seemed to desire the acceptance of the addition *Filioque* to the Apostolic Creed, rather than the formula *per Filium*.

Quite outspoken and more surprising was Father Saragoza's insistence upon an unconditional acceptance of the Gregorian calendar which, after all, had nothing to do with faith and doctrine. However, he considered it essential that Easter be celebrated by the Ruthenians " at the proper time " and not simultaneously with the Jews. His fear of any apparent agreement with the " heretics who have the benedictions in horror, " was the reason for rejecting article eight which, without specifically mentioning benedictions, requested a guarantee against the enforcement of any new

---

[59] A very detailed summary was given in a letter of Nores to Pinelli of Dec. 16, 1595, (*Ottobon. lat.* 1088 fol. 130-139 = 278v-283v), where it is preceded on fol. 127-130 = 276v-278v by a summary of the twenty articles which Saragoza discussed See the comments of Ammann, *op. cit.*, 126 ff.

ceremonies. Last not least, Father Saragoza opposed article thirty (the eighteenth on his list) which wanted any excommunication by the bishops of Eastern rite to be recognized by the Church of Rome. He objected that the Pope could absolve those excommunicated by the Ruthenians : otherwise — he argued — the papal primacy would not be recognized by them ; and most probably he raised that point in connection with one of the last articles, because he missed in the whole draft any direct reference to the crucial problem of the Pope's supreme authority. He also missed a clear adherence to the Catholic doctrine on purgatory, and since the Ruthenians asked to be taught that doctrine, he gave them at once a detailed instruction on that matter, referring in particular to canon 66 of the last session of the Council of Florence.

Father Saragoza's reservations to seven more articles of the Ruthenian bishops were partly dictated by his fear that, objecting to Catholic practices, they could follow the example of the Protestants, for instance in the matter of the Corpus Christi procession, partly by his desire to emphasize Papal authority, in his opinion the best guarantee against any schism or heresy, and partly also by his impatience with Eastern conservatism which refused any new customs even when they were an improvement. He finally wanted on at least two occasions regarding matrimony clear references to the decisions of the Councils, including the recent Council of Trent which for the first time had to be taken into consideration in negotiating with the Ruthenians.

The learned comments of Father Saragoza did not fail to produce a serious impression at the Vatican. The belief was even expressed [60] that they would definitely influence the concessions to be made by the Pope, and that Pociej and Terlecki would have to submit another " script " with the appropriate changes. This would have been extremely difficult for them since they were merely mandatories of the other bishops who had signed the articles, and as a matter of fact, there is no trace of such a revised statement. But fortunately there remained another alternative, viz., neither to approve nor to reject any of the articles, avoiding at the same time the interpretation that they really were " conditions " of the conversion of the Ruthenians, a kind of bargain in a matter of principles — and to follow instead another procedure for which there was a recent and very instructive precedent.

For it so happened and was, of course, well remembered in Rome that, at the beginning of that same year of 1595, on January 15, a solemn ceremony had taken place at the Vatican which was just another regional union with part of Eastern Christendom, a union based exactly like that with the Ruthenians on the tradition of the Council of Florence, and con-

---

[60] At the end of the letter quoted in the preceding note.

cluded, like the present, with a limited number of delegates representing their Church. The analogy was indeed so striking than even Polish chronicles did not fail to note that earlier event, [61] though it concerned a remote African community in which the Poles could hardly be interested. Much more important, if not decisive was that analogy for the Holy See which always considered the problem of reunion a universal one, regretting that there was in the given situation no serious chance for any universal solution, and yet hoping all the time that any regional union, welcome even as such, would set an encouraging example for others. Dealing with the Ruthenians, Rome was, of course, usually thinking of their Orthodox neighbors in the Danubian principalities and particularly in Muscovy, possibly also of the Orthodox populations, Slavic, Albanian or Greek, under Ottoman rule and of the Greek Patriarchate in Constantinople itself. But the problem was also considered inseparable from any projects of reunion with other Churches of the East, separated from both Rome and Constantinople long before the Cerularian or even the Photian schism, Churches which all had seemed to be united with Rome at the Council of Florence. One of them was the Jacobite Church of the Copts in Egypt and Ethiopia with which, in spite of the disappointing failure of their union concluded at Florence, further negotiations had been conducted, though not without long interruptions, throughout the sixteenth century. [62]

In that case, too, Clement VIII was more successful than his predecessor had been, but already at the time of Gregory XIII, equally interested in the relations with all Eastern Christendom, rather unexpected comparisons were made between the relations with the Copts and those with the Greeks and their followers among the Slavs. [63] One of the arguments for dealing with Moscow rather than directly with Constantinople controlled by the Turks was the analogy with independent Ethiopia where the Copts were not under Ottoman rule as was their Patriarch in Alexandria. It is true that the high hopes connected with either Moscow or Ethiopia, hopes which seemed to justify even political concessions in favor of their schismatic but independent rulers, proved nothing but illusions. However, in both cases there appeared alternative solutions which materialized at the time of Clement VIII, though in entirely different forms. In the case of the Greek Orthodox of Eastern Europe, negotiations with Moscow, as hopeless as those with Constantinople, were at last replaced by a concrete pro-

---

[61] See the reference in Paul Piasecki, *Chronica gestorum in Europa singularium*, Cracow 1648, 138 f.

[62] See the exhaustive study of V. Buri, "L'Unione della Chiesa Copta con Roma sotto Clemente VIII, " *Orientalia Christiana*, XXIII/2 (1931), including the aftermath under Paul V.

[63] See the memorandum in *Urbin. lat.* 854 I, fol. 1-12, discussed above, Part II, p. 193.

ject limited to the Orthodox Ruthenians of a body politic under Catholic leadership. In the case of the Jacobite Copts of North Africa, it appeared, after all, easier to come to an agreement with Alexandria than with far away Ethiopia, for Turkish control was less direct and strict in Egypt than in the Balkans. Furthermore, the importance of Alexandria proved particularly great and — strange enough — connected with the situation in the Ruthenian lands, because there were in that city two different dissident Patriarchates side by side : the Jacobite which seemed favorable to religious union with Rome, and the Greek which at the given moment was occupied by the famous Meletius Pigas, particularly hostile to Rome, influential in Constantinople more than the local Patriarchs so frequently changing under Turkish pressure, and last not least profoundly concerned with the defense of Orthodoxy against Catholic penetration even among the distant Ruthenians. That interest which had appeared and alarmed the papal Nuncio already in 1593, was to prove a real danger to the Union of Brest right before and after the Synod of 1596 and already at the time of Pociej's and Terlecki's mission to Rome. [64]

For all these reasons, including the direct repercussions on the result of that mission, it is instructive to study that other " Union of Rome " which ten months before their arrival had been celebrated in a ceremony and according to methods, similar to those which were to be applied, with minor changes, in the case of the two Ruthenian bishops, and which are recorded in analogous documents partly written by the same hand. The Copts of Egypt did not have a Jacobite hierarchy as numerous as was the Greek hierarchy of the Ruthenians. It was only their Patriarch Gabriel who already on November 22, 1593 had written to Pope Clement VIII about his readiness to recognize his primacy and to unite his Church with the Roman, [65] and on the same day instructed two members of his clergy, Joseph and Abdel Messia, to go to Rome as his envoys and plenipotentiaries with a declaration of obedience. [66] In addition to them, the Patriarchate's first " co-bishop, " [67] John Commos, sent to the Holy See his own representative, Barsum, Archdeacon of St. Marc's Church in Alexandria, with a similar instruction. On their arrival in Rome after a long voyage, all three were received on Sunday January 15, 1595 at the Vatican in a ceremony which raised a great deal of interest and to which the Pope had invited twenty-five cardinals. [68]

---

[64] See below, Chapter III, p. 356 f.
[65] Vatican Archives, *AA. Arm.* I-XVIII, 1841 ; see also the different Latin translations published by Buri, *op. cit.*, N. 16 (dated Nov. 23).
[66] *Ibidem*, 1842.
[67] So called in Mucante's diary, quoted below. In his declaration which along with that of the two others is published by Buri, *op. cit.*, Nr. 20, 21, Barsum calle him " Patriarch. "
[68] In addition to the official account by Anselmo Dandini, notary public (*A. A.*

The representatives of the Egyptian clergy were introduced by the Latin Bishop of Sidon and by the papal Master of Ceremonies, Silvio Antoniani, surrounded by alumni of the Roman College of Jerusalem and Maronite Dominicans, emphasizing the importance of the event for the whole Christian East including the Holy Land. First, the letter of Patriarch Gabriel was read to the congregation, both in the Arabic original by the Bishop of Sidon and in a Latin translation by Monsignor Antoniani. Then each of the three delegates read in Arabic, again with a translation into Latin, a profession of faith, [69] renouncing all heresies and errors of the Jacobites which were contrary to the decisions of the Council of Florence, once accepted by their Church. Finally each of them signed, in Latin, his statement, kissed the Pope's feet as on their arrival, and after receiving his blessing they all retired to prepare for their way back via Naples and Malta. A papal bull describing the whole ceremony was addressed to their Patriarch who was expected to ratify the union thus concluded at a local synod.

It was in a similar, though even more solemn way, that Pociej and Terlecki, as representatives of the whole Ruthenian hierarchy were received into the Catholic Church. All controversial questions which resulted from the articles they had submitted, could be thus settled either in the text of their profession of faith or in the papal bull which was issued simultaneously and followed later by a few others. Little is known about the discussions which preceded the ceremonies of reunion. There was, however, on December 5, exactly a week after the first meeting, another congregation of several Cardinals and " many " theologians, again at Cardinal Santori's residence, where most probably the observations of Father Saragoza and other experts were considered, the final decision being left to Cardinal Sfondrato. [70] It was he who most probably suggested to Clement VIII to follow the procedure which had been applied in the case of the Copts, and the solemn consistory in which the Ruthenian bishops were to be received into the Catholic Church, was already planned for the following week : a last delay resulted from the poor health of the Pope who on Wednesday night, December 13, had such a violent attack of arthritis, that the next morning he had to receive in bed the members of the Congregation of the Holy Office and to postpone the consistory for another week. [71] For in spite of his continuous pains, frequently mentioned by all witnesses,

---

Arm. I-XVIII 1846 ; see the comments of Buri, op. cit., Nr. 19), the ceremony is described in the diaries of the Papal Masters of Ceremonies Alaleone (Buri, *op. cit.*, Nr. 18), and Mucante (*Barb. lat.* 2808, fol. 3) and in three " avvisi " from Rome, Jan 18, and 21, 1595 (*Urbin. lat.* 1603, fol. 26, 29, 39 only the first being published by Buri Nr. 17.)

[69] *A. A. Arm.* I-XVIII, 1843, 1844, and 1845. See the contemporary comments published by Buri, *op. cit.*, Nr. 22.

[70] *Urbin. lat.* 1603, fol. 935, 967 (news of Dec. 6, 1595).

[71] *Ibidem,* fol. 955 (news of Dec. 16).

he wanted to be present at the ceremony which was to convince the two Ruthenian representatives that, putting aside all formal difficulties, he was not going to refuse them anything of real importance, so that their mandatories would be fully satisfied with the result of their mission.

It was the day before Christmas Eve, Saturday, December 23, 1595, late in the evening that the great event of the reception of the Ruthenians into the Catholic Church to which their ancestors had belonged, took place in the beautiful Constantine Hall of the Vatican. Since eleven months before there had been some criticism that on the occasion of the reception of the Egyptians only a certain number of Cardinals had been invited, this time a " general congregation " of all Cardinals was held which really almost all of them attended. A semi-official contemporary description [72] enumerates the most important of them, including, of course, Cardinal Sfondrato, the old Cardinal of Como, Ptolomeo Galli, former Secretary of State and " protector " of Poland, the Cardinal of San Severino, Santori, who continued to be in charge of all relations with the Eastern Churches, and, in addition to a few others, the Pope's nephew Cardinal Aldobrandini, so deeply concerned with all Polish problems.

When Pociej and Terlecki were introduced into the crowded hall where Clement VIII was sitting, as usual, on the *sedes gestatoria* under a baldachin, the two Ruthenian bishops, dressed according to their Greek rite, knelt down and before kissing the Pope's feet, three times kissed the soil, following their local custom, a tribute which even the Copts had not paid. Their interpreter, Canon Wołłowicz of Wilno, briefly explained that they had arrived " for union and obedience, " and Pociej handed to Clement VIII the two declarations of the Ruthenian hierarchy in that matter, which they had brought with them. Then both of them were conducted to an opening of the benches where the Cardinals were sitting and listened to the reading of the documents, first in the Ruthenian original by Wołłowicz and then in the Latin translation by the same Monsignor Antoniani who had performed the same function at the reception of the Egyptians, and this time also delivered in answer an address on behalf of the Pope. The two documents were, first the Torczyn declaration of December 2, 1594, the decisive importance of which thus appeared once more, and the letter to the Pope, signed at Brest on July 12, 1595, announcing Pociej's and

---

[72] In the diary of Mucante (*Barb. lat.* 2802, fol. 154-160). Briefer is the description in the diary of Alaleone (*Barb. Lat.* 2815, fol. 420-420v.) The official account by the same Dandini who acted as notary public at the Union of Copts (*A. A. Arm.* I-XVIII, 1735) has been published by A. Theiner, *Monum. Pol.*, I, Nr. 185 F.; about other references see A. M. Ammann, *op. cit.*, 131. A brief account of the ceremony is given also in the report of the Venetian Ambassador of Dec. 30 (State Archives of Venice, *Dispacci Roma*, vol. 36, fol. 281), who stressed the extreme exhaustion of the Pope after the congregation and the violent pains he suffered during the following days.

Terlecki's mission to Rome and serving as their credentials. Both had been, of course, known before and therefore the attention was concentrated on Antoniani's speech. [73] Though rather brief and not containing anything new, it produced a profound impression and was highly praised by many of those present. Moving were indeed the cordial words in which the spokesman of the Vatican welcomed the Ruthenians who after one hundred and fifty years of separation, i. e., from the time when the Union of Florence fell into oblivion (its renewal in 1458 seemed to be disregarded, since it lasted only a short time), under the inspiration of Divine grace returned to the rock upon which Christ had built his Church. Paying a tribute to the Metropolitan and the other bishops for having sent Pociej and Terlecki to Rome with a declaration of obedience to the successor of St. Peter and Vicar of Christ, and with a view to accept the pure, unaltered Catholic faith, he invited in conclusion the two delegates to make their profession of faith, since the Pope was ready to receive them, with the Ruthenian hierarchy and people, into the unity of the Church under one pastor.

There followed indeed, the solemn reading of the requested profession of faith [74] first by Pociej in Latin, then by Terlecki in Ruthenian, since he did not know Latin, and this was, as in the case of the Union with the Copts, the climax of the whole ceremony, both Ruthenian bishops kneeling before the Pope and swearing on the Gospel. A Latin translation of Terlecki's profession was also read, although it was, of course, identical with Pociej's, so that this seemed superfluous to some assistants. It was, however, one more evidence of the importance attached to that statement which was so carefully drafted that it gave satisfaction to both the basic desires of the Ruthenian hierarchy as expressed in their articles of June 1, and to the objections which these " conditions " had raised among some Roman theologians.

In the introduction each of the two representatives *nationis Russorum seu Ruthenorum*, stressing his agreement with the other and enumerating all six absent members of their hierarchy without exception — Kopysteński and Bałaban were mentioned with the others — declared that he was submitting his obedience to the Pope in the name of all of them and of their flock, and making his profession of faith " according to the formula pre-

---

[73] Included in Dandini's account and preserved in numerous copies. One of them was forwarded by Nores to Pinelli, as an appendix to his letter of Dec. 30, 1595 (*Ottobon. lat.* 1088, fol. 139-144v = 283v-287v), in which he refers to his description of the ceremony of Dec. 23 in his preceding letter, unfortunately not included in the manuscript.

[74] The Ruthenian originals and Latin translations of both professions of faith, preserved in *A. A. Arm.* I-XVIII, 1733 and 1744, have been published several times ; see also G. Hofmann, " Wiedervereinigung der Ruthenen, " 128 n. 2 and the photographs of the signatures, on pl. 6 and 7.

scribed for the Greeks returning to the unity of the Roman Church, '' [75] also in the name of all members of the hierarchy who would in due course ratify everything and forward to the Holy See similar professions of faith, signed and sealed by each of them.

Inserted was then the full text of the Creed, " as used by the Roman Church, " hence with the addition of the controversial word *filioque*. This was the clearest possible confirmation that the signatories considered that addition licit and in agreement with the Orthodox, traditional doctrine. But it did not mean that the Ruthenian Church would be obliged to use that same addition in its own liturgy. For there followed a long passage which, after accepting all the decisions of the Council of Florence about the union of the Western and the Eastern Church, defined in particular the doctrine regarding the procession of the Holy Spirit in terms even more detailed than those used in the Florentine decree and very similar, though more specific, than those used in the first article of the Ruthenian petition. For it was admitted that the Holy Spirit, though proceeding from both Father and Son, still proceeded *ex uno principio et unica spiratione*, and that the expression *per filium*, favored by the Greeks, expressed the same that the word *filioque* really meant. It was for that reason that the addition of the word to the Nicaean Creed, explaining the truth in view of an urgent necessity at the given time, was licit and reasonable. In a similar spirit the next paragraph recognized that leavened bread could be used for the Holy Eucharist, but again without requesting the Ruthenians to adopt that Latin custom, sanctioning on the contrary both the Western and the Eastern liturgy in that matter.

The Ruthenians could not object that in another lengthy paragraph the whole doctrine of the Church regarding purgatory was explained in the profession of faith, since in one of their own articles they had expressed the desire to be instructed in that matter. Nor was it surprising that the primacy of the Pope which they had recognized in all their statements was defined more clearly, repeating the very terms which had been approved by both sides at the Council of Florence.

Unforeseen in their earlier discussions was the last part of the profession of faith which to their renewed adherence to the Florentine decrees added a similar acceptance of the most important dogmatic decisions of the recent Council of Trent. This was, however, easy for them to include since in all these matters the Eastern Church had always been in agreement with the Western : the ecclesiastical tradition, the interpretation of the Holy Scriptures by the Church alone, the seven sacraments and their administration by the Church, the character of the Mass, Christ's real presence

---

[75] That this was the formula prescribed for the Greeks by Gregory XIII, is explained by A. M. Ammann, *op. cit.*, 131.

in the Eucharist including the transubstantiation, the veneration of the Saints and of their images including those of Christ Himself and of His Virgin Mother — all this was questioned only by the Protestants and those Orthodox who had come under their influence. To that influence the Ruthenian hierarchy and in particular the bishops who had been working for reunion with Rome, had always been strongly opposed, pointing out that influence as one of the main reasons for that reunion and being in their earlier statements even more outspoken about the danger of Protestant penetration than was the profession of faith submitted to them in Rome which at its end merely rejected " any schism and heresies condemned by the Church. " Nor was it difficult for the Ruthenian bishops to adhere to the decisions of Trent which clarified the doctrine of the Church regarding original sin, justification, and indulgences, in answer to the Protestant interpretations which were alien to the Eastern as well as to the Western tradition.

When after the reading of that long profession of faith Pociej and Terlecki, at the Pope's invitation, approached his throne and once more kissed his feet, Clement VIII spoke to them himself in a low voice, of course, in Latin which at least Pociej perfectly understood, repeating in words full of paternal affection what Antoniani had said about the pleasure which the reunion of the Ruthenians, after one hundred and fifty years gave to the Holy See, and recommending to them, as main Christian virtues, " humility and charity. " At their request, though suffering from arthritis all the time, the Pope permitted also their companions who had come with them from the Ruthenian lands to kiss his feet and gave his benediction to these humble and unknown men in the service of the two bishops. However, his formal and exhaustive answer to their declaration was given, not in any verbal form, but in a long bull which, obviously prepared before, was issued on that same memorable day of December 23 and supplemented all that the Ruthenians could have missed otherwise as far as their requests or " conditions " for reunion were concerned.

That famous bull *Magnus Dominus et laudabilis nimis*, [76] as it is called after its first words, started praising the reunion of the Ruthenians as an evidence of God's goodness towards Clement VIII and as a compensation for the many calamities and painful experiences of his pontificate. There followed a description of the origin of that reunion, summarizing the statements of December 2, 1594, and June 12, 1595, and carefully enumerating their signatories, with a special reference to Leontius Pełczycki, Bishop of Pinsk, who had died soon after and was replaced by Ionas Hohol. Speaking further in detail about Pociej's and Terlecki's mission and the way they

---

[76] Published many times, most recently in *Documenta Pontificia historiam Ucrainae illustr.*, I, Nr. 132, pp. 236-243.

had carried it out, the bull stressed two important points concerning the negotiations and discussions which preceded the ceremony of reunion. On the one hand, it was clearly stated that the two Ruthenian bishops had requested the preservation of " their rites and ceremonies in the divine offices and the administration of the sacraments, and otherwise, according to the Union between the Western and the Eastern Greek Church celebrated at the Council of Florence. " On the other hand, it was confirmed that their " petitions and offers had been, at the Pope's order, carefully studied and examined by the Cardinals of the Congregation of the Inquisition. " That the result of that examination was a general approval of the articles of reunion submitted by the Ruthenian hierarchy, without any reservations except those which resulted from the profession of faith requested by the Holy See, is best evidenced by one of the most important sections of the bull, which followed after the description of the ceremony of December 23 including the text of the said profession of faith. Proclaiming the reception into the Catholic Church of the Ruthenian hierarchy, clergy, and nation which was under the temporal authority of the King of Poland, Clement VIII not only liberated them all, whether present or absent, from any censures and other consequences of their earlier schism, confirming the ecclesiastics in their dignities and offices, but added the momentous sentence :

" In greater evidence of our love for them, we permit, concede, and grant to the said Ruthenian bishops and clergy, out of our Apostolic benevolence, all sacred rites and ceremonies which they use according to the institutions of the sacred Greek fathers, in the divine offices, the sacrifice of Holy Mass, the administration of all sacraments, and any other sacred functions, as far as those are not in opposition to the truth and doctrine of the Catholic faith and do not exclude the communion with the Roman Church. "

The basic principle of unity in doctrine and variety in rite, which was so typical of the Union of Florence, was thus reaffirmed once more, in full agreement with what the Ruthenian initiators of the regional restoration of that Union had declared and expected from the very beginning. Some specific applications of that principle, as requested by the Ruthenian Church in connection with local conditions of the given moment, were left to subsequent decisions of Clement VIII, and all carried out during the following months of Pociej's and Terlecki's presence in Rome.

Most of them, including the Pope's appeal to the Polish authorities regarding such requests which were addressed to them, had to be delayed until the month of February, because further discussions and preparation of the various papal documents were needed. But the general atmosphere of friendliness and sympathy which the two Ruthenian bishops had enjoyed from the very beginning of their stay in Rome, became even more evident after the decisive congregation of December 23, which was commemorated at once by a medal with the inscription *Ruthenis receptis*, showing Pociej and Terlecki before Clement VIII and immediately distributed to them and their companions.

The regular ceremonies of the Christmas season were an appropriate occasion for giving evidence of that incorporation of the Ruthenian hierarchy with the ecclesiastical order of the Catholic Church, which Malaspina after the Cracow discussions had so strongly recommended. One of the Cardinals wanted to go too far in the direction of assimilation, or rather of Latinization, criticizing the guests from the East for coming to Roman services in their ordinary vestments which they had used on the day of their reception : he wanted them to conform in everything, even in their dress, to the Latin Church. But he was told by one of the masters of ceremonies [77] that Pociej and Terlecki simply did not have all the requested vestments and had to come in those which were used in their country. In any case the Pope who, not yet very strong on his feet, still conducted the vesper service on Christmas eve, did not mind at all that the two Ruthenian bishops were dressed according to the Greek custom : on the contrary, after they had taken their seats among the other bishops behind the bench of the Cardinals, Clement VIII ordered them to be conducted to the places of those bishops who were assistants to the papal throne and to be accommodated in the very center, right before his own face. [78] The same honor was bestowed upon them at the vesper service of December 31, which the Pope attended in better health ; [79] at the offices of New Year's day, when the envoys of Venice and Savoy joined Clement VIII in his chapel ; [80] on the eve and on the feast of Epiphany ; [81] and a little later, at the ceremonies of February 2, including the blessing of the candles by the Pope. [82] On all these occasions they occupied the honorary places assigned to them on December 24, always in the same traditional vestments of the Eastern Church which continued to raise the interest of the masters of ceremonies, but no objection on their part, and were explained to one of them by the one of the Ruthenian bishops who spoke Latin, i. e., Pociej. [83]

In the general atmosphere of genuine satisfaction which prevailed at the Vatican in the days and weeks following the reunion with the Ruthenians of Poland, the whole situation in that country was interpreted very optimistically, including even the prospects of Polish participation in the anti-

[77] See Mucante's diary, *Barb. lat.* 2808, fol. 168-170.
[78] *Ibidem*, fol. 163, 167-168 ; see also the diary of Alaleone who conducted them to their place, *Barb. lat.* 2815, fol. 421.
[79] *Barb. lat.* 2808, fol. 180-181 ; *Barb. lat.* 2815, fol. 422.
[80] *Barb. lat.* 2808, fol. 184-185 ; *Barb. lat.* 2815, fol. 423.
[81] *Barb. lat.* 2208, fol. 192-193 ; *Barb. lat.* 2815, *loc. cit.*
[82] *Barb. lat.* 2208, fol. 197-198 ; *Barb. lat.* 2815, fol. 425.

— 334 —

Ottoman league. Immediately after Christmas, news was received from Cracow and recorded by the same observers who were impressed by the success in the matter of the Ruthenians, [84] that the Poles themselves were now convinced that the suggested league would guarantee them forever against any Turkish danger and, God helping, send them next year as far as Constantinople. A contribution of fifty thousand horsemen was expected from the Polish cavalry. Only the news concerning the troubled situation in Moldavia [85] continued to be confusing, and the chances for a papal mediation between Poland and Transylvania uncertain, even after the return of one of the papal emissaries sent to Sigismund III. Nevertheless, the sending to Poland of the Bishop of Caserta who possibly would replace Malaspina — too conciliatory according to some — or even of a papal legate, was postponed time again, pending the arrival of a royal secretary who was to clarify all issues. [86]

But even before, not later than January 20, [87] it became known at the Vatican, thanks to a report of Malaspina himself dated through a strange coincidence from the very day of the Ruthenian reunion, what really had happened in Moldavia in the middle of December. Encouraged and supported by the Prince of Transylvania, his old candidate to the Moldavian throne, Rozvan, had tried in vain to regain his position by expelling Jeremiah Movila, who with Polish support, sent by Zamoyski himself, first defeated him in battle on December 12 and later, when he was captured, cruelly put him to death. [88]

There started immediately, exactly as it had happened on the eve of Pociej's and Terlecki's arrival in Rome after Zamoyski's penetration into Moldavia, another violent campaign of anti-Polish propaganda, making the Poles and especially the Grand Chancellor responsible for all that had happened, and for hindering any joint action of all Christian powers against the Turks with whom they were suspected to be in some kind of connivance. Particularly upset was, of course, Prince Sigismund of Transylvania, suspecting also his own cousins, the pro-Polish Báthory's, of fomenting troubles in his principality and deploring the severe losses which Rozvan's Transylvanian auxiliaries had suffered. But it was not only from the Nuncio at Sigismund's court [89] that interpretations highly critical of Polish

---

[83] *Ibidem*, fol. 181.

[84] *Urbin. lat.* 1603, fol. 987 (Dec. 27, 1595).

[85] *Ibidem*, fol. 990v-994v (Dec. 30).

[86] *Urbin. lat.* 1604, fol. 14v (Jan. 10, 1596), f. 19v (Jan. 11).

[87] *Ibidem*, fol. 27, where also the reports of Nuncio Visconti are quoted : see also fol. 29.

[88] Among the many contemporary accounts, that in the diary of the Cracow Jesuits (*Scriptores rerum Polon.*, VII, 210) is again one of the most reliable; see also *Docum. privit.*, XII, Nr. 303, 309, 350.

[89] *Monum. Vaticana historiam regni Hungariae illustr.*, II-3, *passim*.

policy reached the Vatican : hardly less indignant was the Emperor, influenced by his Transylvanian ally and brother-in-law and by his desire to explain his own failures in the Turkish war by the faults of the Poles. [90] It is true that the Pope received at the same time much more objective information from the Venetians who, as usual were fully informed themselves on all developments in the East by their diplomatic agents in Constantinople, [91] and whose ambassador in Rome, Dolfino, like his predecessor Paruta at the time of the crisis in the fall of 1595, well explained to Clement VIII the intricacies of a situation in which even French and English diplomacy, as well as Moscow were involved. [92] But the King of Poland considered it necessary to supplement the mission of the Bishop of Płock, still present in Rome, by dispatching there another extraordinary envoy to supply the Holy See with a full report and to remove all doubts which could arise in the Pope's mind. [93]

He chose for that delicate task a comparatively young prelate who on the joint recommendation of Cardinal Radziwiłł and Grand Chancellor Zamoyski had been recently placed at the head of the Chancery of the Kingdom, the future Primate of Poland, Laurentius Gembicki. [94] This time again, like in Baranowski's case, that other Polish mission had no direct connection with Pociej's and Terlecki's activities in Rome. But again the result of these religious activities, so welcome to the Pope, could only make him better disposed toward Poland even in political matters, especially as, besides the King himself, the same Polish statesmen, spiritual and secular, stood behind both undertakings. And at the same time the presence of another, very able Polish diplomat who brought the latest news from the Commonwealth, must have been helpful for the two Ruthenian bishops in a phase of their negotiations where the relations with the Polish authorities were involved.

Gembicki's mission was eminently successful, though the negotiations which he conducted in strict secrecy, lasted almost two weeks, delayed as they were, among others, by the poor health of the Pope, who however, soon after his arrival on January 16, received him in a first brief audience. [95]

---

[90] State Archives of Venice, *Dispacci Germania*, vol. 24, where to the report of Feb. 6, 1596, a copy of the Emperor's letter to the King of Poland, of January 15, is attached. See also in vol. 25, the reports of March 13 and 26 and April 9 on the situation in Transylvania.

[91] An excellent example is the second report from Constantinople of March 9 (State Archives of Venice, *Dispacci Costantinopoli*, vol. 43) to which copies of the diplomatic correspondence between Poland and Turkey in January 1596 are attached.

[92] On Jan. 13, 1596, he reported on an audience in which he communicated to the highly interested Pope the news received from Constantinople (*Dispacci Roma*, vol. 36, fol. 328); see about the Pope's doubts J. Sas in *Przegląd powsz.*, 1897, 88 f.

[93] See the King's letter to the Pope of Dec. 12, 1595 (*Borgh.* III 89 b, fol. 240).

[94] See his biography in *Polski Słownik biograficzny*, VII (1948), 382-384.

[95] *Urbin. lat.* 1604, fol. 33v-34 (news of Jan. 24, 1596) ; see also *Dispacci Roma*, vol. 36, fol. 345v.

When he left for Poland on February 17 [96] to be home in time for the Diet which was to consider once more the project of an anti-Ottoman league, he had convinced Clement VIII with whom, as well as with the Cardinals, he had frequent discussions, that the Polish interference with the affairs of Moldavia was well justified ; that the negotiations which the Commonwealth conducted in Constantinople, did not mean at all that a peace treaty was to be concluded with the Turks ; that the Emperor himself, who as the Pope knew from other sources was inclined to conclude such a peace, did not insist upon Polish participation in an anti-Ottoman league ; and last not least, that even the Prince of Transylvania, in spite of his claims to Moldavia, would eventually be reconciled with Poland's control of that principality, if only the passage of the Tartars was thus made impossible.

All these arguments of the Polish diplomat were supported by the regular reports of Nuncio Malaspina who continued to enjoy the Pope's confidence, though in order to strengthen his position and in full agreement with the King's desire, expressed through Gembicki, it was decided that after the less formal mission of the Bishop of Caserta, [97] a legate of the Holy See would soon be sent to Poland, and eventually, on April 3, 1596, that legation was entrusted to Cardinal Caetani. [98] Though the main purpose of that legation was to be political : the creation of the long planned anti-Ottoman league through a conciliation of both the Austrian and the Polish viewpoint, it was obvious that the legate would have to deal with the problem of the Ruthenian union also. Furthermore, the growing evidence that one of the main obstacles to the league was Poland's alarm as to the intentions of Moscow and the real purpose of the Emperor's negotiations with the dangerous Orthodox neighbor of the Commonwealth, was one more reason why the two problems were intimately connected, [99] though not even Malaspina was fully aware of it.

All this was to appear more clearly after Pociej's and Terlecki's return to Poland, but already during the last stay in Rome, as well as in the following months, Clement VIII was writing to the King of Poland and his main advisers at the same time, though separately, about the anti-Ottoman league and the implementation of the Union with the Ruthenians. [100] That implementation required, on the one hand, the convocation of another synod of the Ruthenian hierarchy which would ratify the Union of Rome and had to be convoked with the King's permission, and on the other hand,

---

[96] *Ibidem,* fol. 91 ; see the detailed information about his activities in Rome in the news of Jan. 27 and 31 and Feb. 17 and 24 (*ibidem,* fol. 38, 44, 52v, 98, 108v).

[97] See his instruction of January 7, 1596, in Pastor, *Storia dei Papi,* XI, 215 n. 2.

[98] See the sources quoted by Pastor, *loc. cit.,* note 4.

[99] See Caetani's instruction of April 13 (*Borgh.* IV 269, fol. 144-157) which will be discussed below, p. 353 f.

[100] A. Theiner, *Vetera Monumenta Poloniae et Lithuaniae,* III, Nr. 186-192.

the granting by Sigismund III and the authorities of the Commonwealth of those Ruthenian requests which were addressed to them but which the Pope, as recommended by Malaspina, was decided to support. The connection of these issues is best explained in the long letter which Clement VIII wrote to Metropolitan Rahoza and to the five bishops, who were not present in Rome on February 7, 1596, [101] in the midst of his discussions with Gembicki.

In that document which must be considered a supplement to the bull of December 23 of the preceding year, the decisive ceremony of that day and the reception of the Ruthenians into the Roman Church, similar to that of their ancestors at the Council of Florence, are described once more in shorter terms but with particularly enthusiastic expressions of the Pope's great satisfaction. Described is also Pociej's and Terlecki's participation, as " our domestic prelates and assistants " in the religious services of the following weeks, with specific reference to the Pope's private intercourse with them. And recalled is the fact that Clement VIII granted all their requests, permitting them to keep their rites and ceremonies in the same way as the Council of Florence had done it. What is, however, new and particularly important in the letter of February 7, is, first, a reference to the Pope's letter of recommendations to the King of Poland, including the request that the Ruthenian bishops should be admitted into the Senate of the Commonwealth, and secondly, the formal order that a " provincial synod " be convoked by the Metropolitan on behalf of the Pope where the whole Ruthenian hierarchy would confirm and ratify what their two representatives had done in Rome, and following their example, make a public confession of faith and promise of obedience to the Holy See. At that synod which was instructed to send to the Pope a written statement in these matters, three Polish bishops of Latin rite were to be present, so that " this union among brethren might have even deeper roots of charity and even stronger coalesce in the Lord. "

These three members of the Latin Polish hierarchy whom the Pope also instructed to represent him at the future synod, wisely avoiding to delegate there any foreigners, were very well chosen : they included of course the two who in the past had most efficiently promoted the reunion with the Ruthenians, viz., Solikowski and Maciejowski, the latter receiving special thanks for his outstanding contribution to that cause, and to these Latin pastors of Lwów and Łuck Clement VIII added the Latin bishop of another diocese with mixed population, Stanislaus Gomoliński of Chełm. [102] On the

---

[101] Best edition by G. Hofmann, " Wiedervereinigung, " *Orientalia Christ.* III-2, appendix 7 ; see now also *Documenta Pontif. historiam Ucrainae illustr.*, I, Nr. 145.

[102] *Documenta Pontificia*, I, Nr. 146, 147 (the appreciation of Maciejowski's " special zeal " is on p. 262), 149.

same day of February 7, the Pope, as mentioned in his message to the
Ruthenian hierarchy, strongly recommended them also to a dozen of other
Polish senators, besides the King himself, [103] emphasizing in all these letters
the advisability of admitting the bishops of Eastern rite to the Senate in
the interest not only of the Union but also of the Commonwealth. Among
the addressees were a few more members of the Latin hierarchy, not only
Cardinal Radziwiłł, [104] so deeply concerned with the whole matter and the
Bishop of Przemyśl Goślicki [105] who had participated in the preliminary
negotiations in Cracow, but also the Bishop of Cuyavia, Hieronymus Roz-
drażewski, [106] well known in Rome as a zealous prelate and able diplomat,
though in view of the situation of his diocese less interested in the Ruthenian problem, and — what was particularly urgent — the even more active
and influential Primate of Poland, Stanislaus Karnkowski, [107] who as Archbishop of Gniezno was the first senator of the realm. As to the lay dignitaries, letters were sent, of course, to the two Grand Chancellors, Zamoyski
of Poland and Sapieha of Lithuania, [108] who had so actively participated
in the preparations for the Union, and the two Vice-Chancellors ; [109] Prince
Janusz Ostrogski was considered doubly important, as highest ranking
secular member of the Senate and as eldest son of Prince Constantine, the
leader of the opposition against the Union, [110] and similar letters were sent
to the Palatine of Cracow, Nicholas Firlej, [111] and last not least to the Duke
of Ołyka, Nicholas Christopher Radziwiłł, [112] brother of the Cardinal and
more than any other interested in the matter.

All those briefs of the Pope himself were only part of the messages
which, before and after February 7, were sent from Rome to various personalities in the Commonwealth whose assistance was expected in making
the Union a success. Thus for instance already on December 12, 1595,
Cardinal Santori had sent an autographic letter to Prince Nicholas Christopher Radziwiłł : [113] highly praising Pociej's and Terlecki's piety and hoping
for a reunion " with the whole Greek nation living in Russia, " in which he
stressed that he was fully aware of Radziwiłł's interest in them. As to the two

[103] *Ibidem*, Nr. 135 ; already on Dec. 30, 1595 (*ibidem*, Nr. 133) the Pope had
briefly informed the King about the conclusion of the Union on Dec. 23.
[104] *Ibidem*, Nr. 136.
[105] *Ibidem*, Nr. 148.
[106] *Ibidem*, Nr. 150 ; the Vatican Archives are particularly rich in documents
regarding that bishop.
[107] *Ibidem*, Nr. 137.
[108] *Ibidem*, Nr. 139, 141.
[109] *Ibidem*, Nr. 140, 142.
[110] *Ibidem*, Nr. 144.
[111] *Ibidem*, Nr. 143.
[112] *Ibidem*, Nr. 138.
[113] Published (with photographic reproduction) by A. Staerk in *Kwartalnik litew-
ski*, I-3 (1910), 4-5.

Ruthenian delegates themselves, they wrote not only to their enigmatic colleague Bałaban,[114] describing the ceremony of December 23 and stressing the presence of many Polish and Lithuanian lords and many distinguished foreigners including the envoys of the King of France, but also to Primate Karnkowski,[115] thus joining the papal efforts to use his influence upon the King. They wanted him in particular to persuade Sigismund III to inform officially the Ruthenian people that after the Union there would be no change in their rites nor in their old calendar. That last detail is of special significance, because it confirms that the question of accepting the Gregorian calendar was not only omitted in all statements connected with the act of December 23, but eventually dropped by a wise decision of the Holy See which realized how unpopular that reform of secondary importance continued to be. Pociej himself tried to clarify the issue in a memorandum which along with Terlecki he submitted to the Pope, and he even had prepared new calendar tables in Ruthenian which, in spite of the difficulties in securing the necessary types, were printed during his stay in Rome and, at least in part, brought to Wilno.[116] But he must have been glad that Clement VIII whose coat of arms appeared on the title page, did not insist upon the introduction of the planned changes in the practice of religious life.

Equally interested were the two Ruthenian bishops in other matters raised in their memorandum which Cardinal Santori, whom they frequently visited, handed over to the Pope already on January 11 with their request for an audience.[117] That audience for which Pociej and Terlecki asked again, not without insistence, two weeks later,[118] was delayed not only because' of the health of Clement VIII, but also in view of the political problems regarding Poland which kept him busy, and of the time which was needed for preparing all the papal documents in favor of the Ruthenian hierarchy. Waiting for these final decisions, the two bishops visited Rome with special interest for all traces of Slavic culture,[119] and were preparing for their return home, wishing to arrive in Poland before the spring Diet where they expected to see their problems discussed.[120]

In Rome these problems were examined once more at a congregation held on February 1,[121] and after consulting through correspondence with

[114] Archiv. Yugo-Zapadnoi Rossii, I-1, Nr. 116 (December 29, 1595).

[115] J. Niemcewicz, Dzieje panowania Zygmunta III (History of the Reign of Sigismund III), Kraków 1860, 274-277.

[116] See A. M. Ammann, op. cit., 140, where the interesting notice in the diary of audiences of Cardinal Santori (Vatican Archives, Arm. 52, vol. 21, fol. 146v), of February 6, 1596, is quoted.

[117] Arm. 52, vol. 21, f. 138, 139v-140.

[118] Ibidem, fol. 142v (Jan. 25, 1595).

[119] See A. M. Ammann, op. cit., 135.

[120] Borgh. III 18 g, fol. 357v (The Secretary of State to Malaspina, Jan. 27, 1596).

[121] Arm. 52, vol. 21, fol. 144.

Nuncio Malaspina, [122] everything was finally settled at the end of the month. For Pociej and Terlecki it was a matter of great personal satisfaction that on February 26, [123] after a very careful drafting of the documents in a matter which was not familiar to the papal Chancery, [124] they were granted the right to use special liturgical vestments, described in detail, which in the past had been reserved for the Metropolitan only. But Rahoza himself was not forgotten by his delegates who convinced the Holy See of the precarious financial situation of even the leading members of the Ruthenian hierarchy. While Pociej obtained the attribution of the Basilian Monastery of the Savior to his own bishopric to be used by the school he had founded, [125] the famous Monastery of the Caves in Kiev was united with the metropolitan see in order to increase its limited income. [126] And a few days earlier [127] a much more important document was issued granting one of the requests of the Ruthenian hierarchy, which was particularly desired by the Metropolitan, but not included in the general confirmation of their traditional customs. The whole procedure for electing and consecrating the Ruthenian bishops, as described in their articles of December 2, 1594, was formally approved, including the right of the Metropolitan to confirm and consecrate new bishops in the name of the Pope himself, without any obligation for them to apply to Rome. A newly elected Metropolitan would have to ask the Holy See for a letter of confirmation which, however, would be made out free of cost.

Independently of these concessions of lasting value, Pociej and Terlecki continued to receive many personal proofs of the Pope's benevolence. And when, at the beginning of March, after taking leave from their Roman friends, they were granted a last audience by Clement VIII, he not only contributed to their expected travelling expenses [128] and presented them with beautiful liturgical vestments, medals, [129] etc., but also made a substantial contribution to the foundation of a college or seminary for the instruction of the Ruthenians in the Catholic faith — all this moving them to tears. [130]

---

[122] See in particular, the instructions sent to him on February 3, 1596, *Borgh.* III 18 g, fol. 358.

[123] *Documenta Pontificia*, I, Nr. 153 (for Pociej) and 154 (for Terlecki).

[124] See the various preliminary drafts which were revised several times, in the Vatican Archives, *Secr. Brev.*, vol. 372, fol. 71-90.

[125] *Documenta Pontificia*, I, Nr. 155 (March 1, 1596).

[126] *Ibidem*, I, Nr. 156 (March 4, 1596).

[127] *Ibidem*, I, Nr. 152 (February 23, 1596).

[128] The first orders of the Pope in that matter were given already on February 7 (*ibidem*, I, Nr. 134). See also *Borgh.* III 18 g, fol. 359v (Feb. 10).

[129] The payments for the vestments were made on February 13 (*ibidem*, I, Nr. 151), and the medals blessed by the Pope "in camera" already before (*Urbin. lat.* 1604, fol. 57, news of February 3).

[130] *Urbin. lat.* 1604, fol. 126v, 132 (news of March 2). The project of the Semi-

In the project of a new Ruthenian seminary, the two bishops, and particularly Pociej, were interested both personally and under the influence of their closest old friend, the Greek Arcudius who had so eagerly and anxiously awaited their arrival in Rome and now was to accompany them home, along with his countryman Moschetti.[131] Though Arcudius would have preferred now to work for religious reunion in his own country, the Pope himself decided that he should go again to the Ruthenian lands[132] where he had worked so successfully in earlier years and where he could explain better than anybody else that the Union concluded in Rome did not mean any break with the Greek tradition.

Before at last leaving Rome on March 9,[133] anxious to return with the highly satisfactory results of their mission, Pociej and Terlecki informed the Venetian Ambassador Dolfino that they wanted to visit Venice on their way back, having missed that opportunity when arriving. There was no longer any fear that the Greeks of that city would make them change their mind, but a letter of recommendation seemed desirable, both to assure their friendly reception by the authorities of the Republic, and to guarantee them against being molested by the Greeks because of their conversion. An autographic letter of Dolfino to the Doge, of March 7,[134] settled the matter, and the return trip of the two bishops seems to have been as undisturbed and probably even more pleasant than their journey from Poland. There, however, very difficult tasks and even serious troubles fomented in their absence by the opponents of the Union, were awaiting the tireless promotors of a great cause.

---

nary is already discussed in the instructions for Malaspina, of February 3 (*Borgh*. III 18 g. fol. 358).

[131] The papal order for paying their travelling expenses is dated March 5, 1596. (*Documenta Pontificia*, I, Nr. 157). See the payment for an interpreter used by the two bishops, of March 7 (*ibidem*, Nr. 158).

[132] *Arm*. 52, vol. 21, fol. 144 (Feb. 1, 1596); see the reminiscences in a letter of Arcudius written from Łuck on Sept. 25, 1597 (G. Hofmann, *op. cit.*, 132 note 2).

[133] *Urbin lat*. 1604, fol. 151 (News of March 9, where all what the Pope had done for the two bishops is recalled once more).

[134] *Dispacci Roma*, vol. 37, fol. 17.

Chapter III

THE OPPOSITION AGAINST THE UNION

During all the time — about three months and a half — they spent in Rome, Pociej and Terlecki were kept well informed about the developments at home, were it only because Nuncio Malaspina, forwarding his reports and enclosing various important documents, always requested that such news be communicated to the two Ruthenian bishops. And this was done in due course at the Vatican.

Two days before their departure from Cracow on September 24, the King had issued, in agreement with one of the suggestions of the congregation of September 22, a manifesto to the Ruthenian people, [1] expressing his desire for religious unity among his subjects and announcing the mission to Rome of the two delegates of their hierarchy. A few days later, Malaspina, referring to news received from the Bishop of Chełm Gomoliński, reported that the Ruthenian people had well understood and favorably received the decision of the hierarchy : only Prince Ostrogski " with a few others showed himself opposed with all his might. " [2] Therefore, when forwarding to Rome on October 14, [3] a copy of the royal manifesto and asking that it be shown to the two Ruthenian bishops, the Nuncio added for their information, that Sigismund III had summoned Ostrogski to appear before the next Diet and to justify his action taken at the time of the Synod of Toruń. Whether such a summons was really made public is, however, doubtful, [4] and on October 27, [5] the Nuncio could send to Rome a copy of the proposals which the old Prince had finally made through the Castellane of Kamieniec who was very hopeful as to final agreement. Ostrogski repeated his demand that another synod of the Orthodox be held at once, but since this would have been, as a matter of fact, a synod of " schismatics " who opposed the Union under his leadership, a meeting held in Cracow to study his " articles " decided not to grant that request, but instead to send a delegation to Ostrogski with a view of appeasing his " proud and vain mind. " The persons entrusted with that delicate mission were the Bishop of Łuck Maciejowski, the Palatine of Podlachia Prince

---

[1] *Monumenta Confraternitatis Stauropigianae*, I, Nr. 390.

[2] Vatican Archives, *Borgh*. III 91 d - fol. 57v (Sept. 30, 1595).

[3] *Ibidem*, fol. 50v.

[4] See K. Lewicki, *Ks. Konstanty Ostrogski*, 153 n. 5.

[5] *Borgh*. III 91 d, fol. 55v. see also the information he sent to a companion of the two bishops on Oct. 21, *Bibl. Vallicelliana*, L. 18, fol. 170-171.

Zasławski who had already negotiated with his cousin before, the Lithuanian Grand Chancellor Sapieha and Father Peter Skarga, as theologian. This was indeed a well selected and impressive group which Malaspina himself was ready to join, if necessary, in order to invite Ostrogski in the name of the Pope.

Hearing this, everybody in Rome was hopeful and the Nuncio received high praise for his zeal. [6] A few weeks later the delegates, of whom Maciejowski kept himself in touch with Malaspina, actually met Prince Constantine, and the result of their intervention seemed at first quite satisfactory. Ostrogski finally decided to follow in the matter of reunion with the Catholic Church the advice of his sons whom, as the Nuncio reported on December 14, [7] he was to meet within a few days in the presence of Maciejowski and the other delegates. Since his eldest son Janusz, the Castellane of Cracow, was already a good Catholic, and the other one Alexander, Palatine of Volhynia, seemed " much inclined to our faith, " Malaspina hoped that they would eventually induce their father to sign the Union, and then — he added — a convention of theologians could be permitted, who would persuade also the Ruthenian laity to send a message to the Pope in favor of that union. Cautiously, however, the Nuncio suggested to keep these prospects secret for the time being : " matters have been started quite well, yet those, with whom they are being treated, are inconsistent and lighthearted. "

In any case, even one month later Malaspina was rather optimistic and, forwarding on January 12 [8] another letter of Maciejowski and copies of the letters which Ostrogski himself had written to the King, he pointed out that both the Secretariate of State and the two Ruthenian bishops present in Rome could see from that correspondence that there was real hope to " draw Prince Constantine to the Union. " Strange enough, however, he never gave in his subsequent reports, chiefly dealing with the problem of the anti-Ottoman league, the promised detailed account of further developments in the matter of Ostrogski's attitude. He only mentioned on January 26 [9] that the King, very pleased with the papal brief he had received after the Union of Rome, immediately sent a copy of it to the Prince. And he also suggested [10] that Pociej and Terlecki should return as soon as convenient, since it would be easier to promote the union with their assistance.

Both bishops were only too anxious themselves to be back on time to

[6] *Borgh.* III 18 ef, fol. 273v (Nov. 28, 1595).

[7] *Borgh.* III 91 d, fol. 88v ; see also fol. 95, at the end of the report of Dec. 17, 1595, and his letter to Prince Janusz of Dec. 10, *Bibl. Vallic.* L 18, fol. 177.

[8] *Ibidem*, fol. 201v = Borgh. III, 89 c, fol. 3-3v.

[9] *Borgh.* III 89 c, fol. 18.

[10] *Ibidem*, fol. 17 (January 29, 1596).

be present during the forthcoming Diet and to secure seats for themselves in the following ones. And they were, of course "extremely jubilant" when they heard that Prince Constantine was to approve the Union they had concluded and to support it with his authority. Sharing that optimistic impression, the Secretariate of State insisted [11] that as a final guarantee of success, their request for seats in the Senate be granted, and that the Nuncio should collect information as to the best procedure for founding a seminary for the Ruthenians which the Pope was ready to support financially. The discussion of that project Malaspina wanted to postpone until Pociej's and Terlecki's arrival, [12] but otherwise he remained silent on what both of them, as well as the Holy See, wanted to know most : the concrete results of the much more urgent discussions with Ostrogski.

That silence can be explained not only by Malaspina's growing concern with political problems which were at best indirectly connected with that of the Ruthenian Union — a connection which anyway continued to escape his attention —, but also by an extremely confused situation which developed in that matter and made it really impossible to evaluate the chances of appeasing the opposition against the Union. It seems obvious that the stubborn old Prince, even when he met the royal delegates and possibly his own sons, avoided any definite commitment. And instead of a conference with Catholic theologians there was, after all, held in January, in the Lithuanian city of Nowogródek, another Ruthenian synod, as convoked by Metropolitan Rahoza already on October 28, [13] though nothing is known about any royal permission and only very few members of the hierarchy and clergy were present. [14] Again, however, Rahoza can hardly be blamed for yielding in that question to the pressure of Ostrogski whom the most sincere promoters of the Union wanted so much to conciliate. And the little that is known about that synod seems rather to indicate that the Metropolitan, far from satisfying Prince Constantine's expectation that at such a convention in Pociej's and Terlecki's absence their mission to Rome would be repudiated by at least some of the other bishops, took a rather important step in silencing or at least officially condemning the most vociferous criticism which had been raised against reunion with Rome among part of the Orthodox clergy.

That criticism did not yet openly come from the two bishops, those of Lwów and Przemyśl, who were particularly subject to Ostrogski's influ-

[11] In the instructions of February 3, 1596, *Borgh.* III 18, fol. 358 ; see also those of January 27, *ibidem*, fol. 357v, and the comments given above, in the preceding Chapter, p. 338.

[12] *Borgh.* III 89 c, fol. 83 (March 1, 1596).

[13] *Akty Zap. Rossii*, IV, Nr. 89 ; see above, Chap. I, p. 304.

[14] *Ibidem*, IV, Nr. 91.

ence, not even from Bałaban whom Rahoza, after excommunicating him in 1594 because of his persistent conflict with the Brotherhood of Lwów, had readmitted into the Church the following year making possible his participation in the joint action of the hierarchy,[15] and who now was present at Nowogródek. Before that meeting the Metropolitan himself and all those who cooperated with him were attacked by the Brotherhoods, especially that of Wilno whose influence was greatest, and branded as traitors of the Orthodox Church because they were turning towards Rome.[16] Besides two otherwise unknown monks who were connected with that Brotherhood, one of the teachers in its school Stefan significantly surnamed Zizania, was leading that attack and shortly before Pociej's and Terlecki's mission to Rome published a pamphlet against " the Antichrist " as he called the Pope.[17] Not only that designation, but many other statements in his writings and sermons gave evidence of the Protestant influence which he followed, opposing the doctrine of both the Catholic and the Greek Orthodox Churches and raising heated polemics. In view of these Protestant leanings, so typical of many Ruthenian opponents of the Union, it was easy for Rahoza to have Zizania and his two companions excommunicated at the Synod of Nowogródek[18] as heretics and to exclude them from teaching and preaching in the Churches.

That decision was disregarded by all three who continued to appear in the Holy Trinity Church of Wilno and to call upon all Orthodox to turn against the bishops who had betrayed them. Finally, the King himself had to act against the troublemakers and on May 28[19] banished them from the country in view of their disobedience against their own ecclesiastical superiors. Their appeal was received by the Lithuanian Supreme Court which even summoned Rahoza, and though the King blamed that court for interfering with ecclesiastical matters,[20] troubles continued in Wilno for quite a time.

This would have been hardly possible if the three revolted clerics had not had behind them powerful protectors, and one of them, besides the Calvinist Palatine of Wilno, Christopher Radziwiłł, was of course his friend and relative, Constantine Ostrogski himself. But the Prince's role behind the scene of that shocking dispute was after all, much less dangerous than the political action which he started before that same Diet which Pociej and

---

[15] See above, Chap. I, p. 278.

[16] See the appeal of the Orthodox clergy of Wilno to the Palatine of Nowogródek, Theodore Tyszkiewicz, made already in November 1595 (*Akty Zap. Rossii*, IV, Nr. 90).

[17] That pamphlet which was an answer to one of Pociej's writings (*Russk. istor. bibl.*, VII, 111-168), has not been preserved; see Chodynicki, *op. cit.*, 317 f.

[18] *Akty Zap. Rossii*, IV, Nr. 91 (January 27, 1596).

[19] *Ibidem*, Nr. 94, 95; about the King's friendly attitude towards Rahoza, see K. Lewicki, *op. cit.*, 159.

[20] *Monumenta Confraternitatis Stauropig.*, I, p. 714.

Terlecki wanted to attend and which opened in Warsaw at the end of March. Even in Italy, where alarming news were received [21] about the resistance of " many people " in the Ruthenian lands against Pociej's and Terlecki's plans, it was fully realized that the real danger came from Ostrogski and the troubles he would create. It was indeed under the influence of Ostrogski, Palatine of Kiev and Marshal of Volhynia, that at the Dietines of these two provinces, as well as at some Dietines in the Grand Duchy of Lithuania, where the Palatine of Wilno was the highest dignitary, protests were raised against all what Pociej and Terlecki had done in Rome, viz., against the Union which by now had become universally known ; the deputies which these Dietines elected as representatives to the Diet were even instructed to request there that the two Ruthenian bishops be deposed and the Union concluded in Rome annulled. [22]

This was to be the ominous beginning of a long lasting struggle against the Union which even after the Synod of Brest, five months later, was to continue at so many Diets of the Commonwealth for many years to come. [23] Those who conducted that attack were, in 1596 as well as later, only a small minority among the senators and the deputies, but in view of the unanimity rule they made it impossible to move with any chances of success the admission to the Senate of the Ruthenian bishops, united with Rome, a request to which they rightly attached special importance and which was so strongly supported by the Holy See. Under such conditions Pociej and Terlecki who having stopped in Cracow and then visited their dioceses, reached Warsaw only towards the end of the Diet, had to be satisfied with a most cordial reception by Sigismund III and his advisors, particularly Bishop Maciejowski, [24] and with a royal decree dated May 21 [25] which confirmed them on their episcopal sees, contrary to the claims of their opponents that they should be deposed.

On the other hand, in view not only of the same unanimity rule but also of the ever growing Catholic majority in both Houses of the Diet, these opponents, too, had no chance whatever of having these or any other claims accepted. Unfortunately no diary of the Diet of 1596 has been

---

[21] *Urbin. lat.* 1604, fol. 25 (news from Venice, January 17, 1596).

[22] See about that Diet where on May 6 Ostrogski made a strong protest (*Archiv Yugo-Zap. Rossii*, I-1, 533-536 ; *Russk. istor. bibl.*, VII, 1123-1129), Chodynicki, *op. cit.*, 321 ; and K. Lewicki, *op. cit.*, 160.

[23] See P. Zhukovich, *Seimovaia borba pravoslavnago zapadnorusskago dvorianstva s tserkovnoi uniei do* 1609 *g.* (The struggle of the Orthodox West-Russian nobility against the Union of the Churches at the Diets before 1609), Petersburg 1901, based upon a rich, partly unpublished source material; on the Diet of 1596, p. 204.

[24] See the letter of P. Arcudius of June 20, 1596, published in *Sacrum Poloniae Millennium*, I (1954), 105. About their visit in Cracow and the friendly reception there see the news received in Venice on March 30 (*Urbin. lat.* 1604, fol. 283).

[25] *Arkhiv Yugo-Zapadnoi Rossii*, I-1, Nr. 119.

preserved, but it is known from other sources [26] that the opposition leaders, having obtained nothing from the King, had to limit themselves to violent speeches on the last day of the deliberations, declaring that they would not recognize any longer those bishops who arbitrarily, without the consent of the Eastern Patriarchs and of their own people, had placed themselves under the authority of the Pope. Strange enough, however, Prince Ostrogski, who joined in these protests and even spoke of religious persecution, took an entirely different attitude in his talks with the King, [27] raising again the hope that eventually he would change his mind. For not only did he renew his request for another Orthodox Synod where the whole controversial matter would be reconsidered, but he did not hesitate to say, or at least to give the impression, especially when taking leave from Sigismund III, that he was ready for the Union and even would lead others towards that goal.

The request for another Synod, which was in agreement with what the Pope himself was demanding and expecting and which now could be held with the participation of Pociej and Terlecki, was indeed granted without hesitation. On May 12, [28] the King wrote to the Metropolitan authorizing him to convoke such a Synod in view of the return from Rome of the two delegates of the hierarchy, adding that it should be held at Brest, the usual place, and soon after St. Michael's day, September 29, but suggesting that place and date should not be made public at once, probably in order not to encourage the opposition to prepare for a showdown. The necessity of adequate preparation by the supporters of the Union was a well justified reason for a delay of more than four months, another reason being the negotiations with the Emperor and the Holy See regarding the anti-Ottoman league, which the Diet had entrusted to a special commission [29] and which were to absorb the most prominent senators, both spiritual and secular, including those whose presence seemed necessary at the Synod of Brest, keeping them busy all summer. In conclusion, the King expressed the hope that Rahoza would energetically promote the Union, the ratification of which was to be the main if not the only objective of the Synod.

This was, however, not at all Ostrogski's interpretation. And while Sigismund III was not disappointed in his expectations concerning the Metropolitan who did not show any longer his apparent or real hesitations

---

[26] Quoted in the books which are mentioned above (notes 22 and 23); see also the protest of Prince Drucki-Horski, made simultanously with Ostrogski's.

[27] Who recalled it in his appeal to the Prince, quoted below, note 32.

[28] *Opisanie dokumentov zapadnorusskikh uniatskikh mitropolitov* (Description of the documents of the West-Russian Uniate Metropolitans), I, Petersburg 1897, Nr. 169.

[29] The proceedings of that Commission are published in *Scriptores rerum Polonicarum*, XX, 240-322.

of the preceding years, the old Prince deeply shocked the King by a behavior exactly contrary to what he had promised him at the Diet. It was probably only later, in a last minute effort, that he even tried to bribe Rahoza by offering him the possession of no less than twenty villages if he would turn against the Union, [30] an offer which could seem tempting for an old man who neither as Archbishop of Kiev nor as a nobleman of rather modest origin had any substantial income, but now rejected that proposal of the powerful magnate whom he had tried so long to appease. Ostrogski himself, however, organized immediately after the Diet a systematic action with a view of making the Union impossible. In addition to vehement protests which under his obvious inspiration were circulated by some of the Deputies in their respective districts and filed with the district courts, the Prince issued a manifesto to the Ruthenian people in which he gave a detailed picture of the situation in a sense most hostile to the Union, calling for general opposition. [31]

This was precisely what the King most deeply resented both as a challenge to his own authority and in view of the obvious distortions of the whole story, including the part of the King himself. Sigismund III therefore decided, some time during the earlier part of June, to send to Ostrogski once more a royal delegate with a strong expression of his dissatisfaction and with a last appeal, if not to join the Union, at least not to oppose it nor to incite others to do so. The name of the delegate is unfortunately unknown, but the full text of the message he had to convey has been preserved [32] and greatly contributes to a better understanding of the situation, especially of the policies of King and Government in the matter of reunion.

Recalling on the one hand the unusual favors he had always shown to the Prince, to his whole family and even to his servants, and on the other hand Ostrogski's ingratitude and contempt of all obligations towards the Crown, Sigismund III returned to the Prince's seditious appeal to the Protestant Synod of Toruń, in 1595, having never been convinced by his apologies. But the main charge was that the Palatine of Kiev, a high ranking senator, was now resuming a similar policy, apparently directed only against the two Ruthenian bishops whom he openly threatened and persecuted, but as a matter of fact, against the King himself whose duty it was to protect them. Point after point the royal message corrected the untrue statements and unconfirmed rumors contained in Ostrogski's mani-

---

[30] Mentioned in the letter of Arcudius of Nov. 10, 1596, published in *Sacrum Poloniae Millennium*, I, 108.

[31] See the King's appeal quoted in the following note.

[32] In the Vallicelliana Library in Rome, Ms. 35, fol. 129-132v ; the full text with my detailed comment is published *Sacrum Poloniae Millennium*, IV (1957) 117-139.

festo which as such was an illegal action and particularly angered the King because it branded his convocation of a Synod — requested by the Prince himself — as nothing but a " fraud. " And Sigismund III blamed his senator not only for intruding into the field of royal authority, but also for usurping, though a layman, decisive powers in ecclesiastical matters. It was here that the basic issue between the supporters and the partisans of the Union of Brest appeared most clearly, since the former considered only the ecclesiastical authorities — in the given case the Ruthenian hierarchy — competent in such matters, while the latter, under the influence of both the Byzantine tradition and the Protestant idea of the Church, wanted the laity and its secular leaders to have the decisive voice. The King proclaimed it his duty, as a Catholic ruler, to protect and assist those who wanted to reunite the Ruthenian Church with Rome, recalling the deplorable consequences of the Eastern Schism for the whole Christian Republic and also the charter of his predecessor, Władysław III, who after the Union of Florence had granted equal rights to the clergy of either rite. He stressed, however, time and again, particularly in his conclusion, that he did not want to force anybody, and in particular Ostrogski, to join the Union, but likewise would not permit the Prince to exercise violence against those who " spontaneously endeavored to accede to that sacred unity. " [33]

These truly noble words, inspired by a genuine respect of religious freedom, explained at the same time the King's foremost and urgent request that the injuries which Pociej and Terlecki were suffering from the Prince be discontinued and repaired. In that connection an appendix to the memorandum pointed out, first, that Ostrogski whose father had received from Sigismund I the Duchy of Turov, had usurped property and rights of a third Ruthenian bishop too, namely that of Pinsk and Turov, Hohol, who like his recently deceased predecessor Pełczycki was another, though less conspicuous supporter of the Union. And secondly, it was made quite clear that Prince Constantine was also responsible for the injuries which the most active of these supporters, the Bishop of Łuck and Ostrog, Terlecki, had suffered, not directly from the lord of Ostrog, but from an entirely different side : from the revolting Ukrainian Cossacks and from their main leader, Nalevayko.

The significance of that last point goes far beyond the interpretation of Ostrogski's personal role. A particularly heavy charge, indeed, was involved against the outstanding dignitary of the Commonwealth, a charge or at least a suspicion of clandestine connivance with a notorious rebel of obscure origin who, in cooperation with another Cossack leader Loboda, was responsible for a real civil war in the Ukraine [34] and for cruel devastations

---

[33] *Ibidem*, fol. 132.
[34] Described in detail by M. Hrushevsky, *Istoria Ukrainy*, VII, 210 ff.

which reached far into Volhynia and the southern part of Lithuania. Ostrogski himself would occasionally call Nalevayko " a scoundrel " with whom he had nothing in common. [35] Yet, the man who later, after his military defeat in which Loboda perished first, was tried as a public enemy and executed, had originally been a serf on the estates of Prince Constantine who continued to use the services of his brother, to pay a stipend to Nalevayko himself and was supposed to determine to a certain extent the choice of his victims. [36] It was said that those whom he did not want to suffer from the Cossack invasion were really spared, while the possessions of the Prince's enemies, and especially those of Bishop Terlecki, were most thoroughly plundered.

All this leads to the important question whether the Cossack movement under Nalevayko turned so violently against Terlecki only because of Ostrogski's instigation and because the bishop's estates were on its way and poorly defended, or because the revolt of 1596 was at least partly directed against the Union of the Churches, as were the Cossack rebellions of the seventeenth century — in other words : whether that Union was not one of the causes of a growing danger which almost ruined the Commonwealth about fifty years later. It is true that already in the year of the Union of Brest that danger was much more serious than four years before when the first Cossack revolt under Kosiński had the character of an exclusively social issue and of a personal feud mainly directed against Ostrogski himself. [37] But there is in the contemporary sources not the slightest indication of any Cossack interest in the religious problem, an interest which did not start before 1620, under the influence of both Constantinople and Moscow. [38] What, then, was the real reason why the rebellion of Loboda and Nalevayko was more than a social revolution of Cossack masses which included so many former peasants afraid to be again reduced to serfdom and ready to plunder the estates of rich landlords, though this time the richest of them, Ostrogski, was not touched at all ?

In the reports of Nuncio Malaspina who observed the development of these troubles very closely, without even considering the possibility of their connection with the religious problem of reunion, there are two most significant indications regarding their real character and background. Most surprising are his references to the participation in the movement of one of the bishops of Latin rite, the Pole Wereszczyński who as Bishop of Kiev could have substantially contributed to the Union, but instead joined the Cossacks, was even wrongly believed to have been made their head and

---

[35] See K. Lewicki, *op. cit.*, 163.
[36] See at the end of the King's appeal, fol. 132v.
[37] M. Hrushevsky, *op. cit.*, VII, 181 f.
[38] K. Chodynicki, *op. cit.*, 419 ff.

in any case behaved so strangely that his episcopal authority was seriously harmed to the Nuncio's understandable concern. [39] But it was precisely that bishop who was deeply interested in the struggle against the Ottoman Empire, as were the Holy See and its representatives in Poland, and in his writings [40] suggested far reaching schemes for organizing the defense of the Ukraine against Turks and Tartars with the participation of the Cossacks.

On the other hand, when the rebels of 1596 suffered defeats from the Polish army and the Bishop of Kiev hardly escaped while his brother was made a prisoner, the victors discovered that the Cossacks used banners which they had received from both the Emperor and the Prince of Transylvania. That fact, confirmed by other sources, [41] particularly alarmed the Nuncio, [42] because obviously it was to make the Poles even more reluctant to enter the planned anti-Ottoman league jointly with those Catholic rulers who so clearly supported a dangerous revolt against the authorities of the Commonwealth. [43] It is, however, equally obvious that the Cossacks could not be encouraged by these rulers in an undertaking which even in part would have been directed against a religious union with Rome. It was, on the contrary, well known, were it only thanks to the mission of Alexander Komulovich in 1594, [44] that the cooperation of the Ukrainian Cossacks was desired against the Turks; and since, in view of the hesitation of most Poles to enter into an anti-Ottoman league along with Austria and Transylvania, no large scale military action of the Commonwealth was contemplated for the time being, the warlike Cossacks, disappointed as they were to be later in similar occasions including the crisis of 1648, turned against the Polish authorities and landlords. Prince Ostrogski, who was in favor of cooperating with the Habsburgs, could have in such a situation better relations with the rebels than other Polish dignitaries had and divert their movement against persons whom, like Bishop Terlecki, he wanted to embarrass and to punish for reasons in which the Cossacks were not interested at all. And if not the Emperor himself, at least his ally Sigismund Báthory could be suspected not without reason to encourage the Cossack rebellion, both in order to have a revenge for the troubles which the pro-Polish line of the Báthory's had apparently provoked in Transylvania, [45]

---

[39] See his reports of February 9 and May 27, 1596 (*Borgh.* III 91 d, fol. 114v and 131) and the reactions of the Secretary of State in the instructions of March 2 and June 22 (*Borgh.* III 18 g, fol. 361, 385 ; see also 18 h, fol. 416v).

[40] Re-edited by J. Turowski, *Pisma polityczne J. Wereszczyńskiego*, Kraków 1858. About his strange ideas that only Moscow could finally defeat the Turks see a letter of P. Tylicki to Malaspina, of Jan. 5, 1594 (*Borgh.* III 66 B, fol. 162v).

[41] *Urbin. lat.* 1604, fol. 480 (news received in Rome from Cracow, August 3, 1596).

[42] See his report of April 21, 1596 (*Borgh.* III 89 c, fol. 125)

[43] About the escape of the Bishop of Kiev see also *Borgh.* III, 91 d, fol. 134, April 18.

[44] See above, Part III, p. 264 f.

[45] *Urbin. lat.* 1604, fol. 114v (news of Feb. 24), fol. 203 (news of March 30) ;

and to divert the Cossacks from any participation in the Moldavian policy of Zamoyski, the main opponent of the planned league and of Sigismund's influence in the Danubian principalities.

In that intricate situation of which men like Nalevayko could hardly be fully aware, serving perhaps unwittingly as tools of foreign interests, Nuncio Malaspina, realizing that in the matter of the anti-Ottoman league he had to proceed very carefully, rather wanted to obtain at least a limited cooperation of Zamoyski in order to stop the Tartar invasions, equally dangerous for Poland, Moldavia, Wallachia, Transylvania, and even Hungary. Therefore, as he noted in the same report of May 27, 1596, [46] in which he complained about the role of Bishop Wereszczyński among the Cossacks, he asked the King whose personal relations with Zamoyski were always rather cool and strained, to dispatch to the Chancellor, in agreement with the Senate, a qualified person to find out what could be expected from Zamoyski during the summer. And he was glad when Sigismund III entrusted that delicate task to the Grand Treasurer of Lithuania Demetrius Chalecki, an able, non-partisan negotiator with whom the Nuncio had friendly contacts almost from the beginning of his mission and who was soon to play an important part at the Synod of Brest.

The problem of the religious union which was to be settled at that synod, was not entirely forgotten by Malaspina amidst all those political troubles. It was even mentioned in that same important report [47] but, strange enough, not in connection with the Ruthenians of the Commonwealth but on the occasion of Monsignor Komulovich's second mission to Moscow. That mission, which was to be combined with another effort of Austrian diplomacy to gain that Orthodox power for cooperation against the Muslims, and which, when still undecided, had frustrated the Nuncio's project of using Komulovich in the negotiations of the Ruthenian bishops with Rome, [48] was now materializing and Malaspina suggested to the papal agent four points for discussion at Moscow, including, besides the political issues, a proposal to speak there " about the Ruthenian union with the Apostolic See. " Returning to his earlier idea of connecting that union with the old hopes of the Vatican to gain Moscow for a similar agreement, the Nuncio made a mistake which is, to a certain extent, surprising, because he was quite well informed about Moscow's hostile attitude against the Commonwealth, which the restoration of the Union of Florence within its limits could only increase, raising new suspicions. And if Komulovich, for whom Malaspina even obtained from Sigismund III not only a passport

---

Dispacci Germania, vol. 25, reports of March 26, and April 9, 1596 ; *Dispacci Roma*, vol. 37, fol. 75 (March 30).

[46] *Borgh.* III 91 d, fol. 130 ; see *Borgh.* III 66 B, fol. 138 (Feb. 9, 1594).
[47] *Ibidem*, fol. 129-129v.
[48] See above, Chap. I, p. 313 f.

but also a letter of recommendation to the Tsar, [49] really mentioned to the latter that union concluded by the Ruthenian bishops with whom, in spite of the Nuncio's efforts, he never established any contact, this could only contribute to the failure of his new mission which was to be even greater than that of the first. [50]

All these issues and connections were getting particularly important, since Clement VIII, not fully satisfied with the reports of his Nuncio nor with the results of the recent extraordinary mission to Poland of the Bishop of Caserta, [51] decided at last, in agreement with the King's own desire, to send to that country a Cardinal Legate, [52] just as he himself had several years before supplemented there as Legate of Sixtus V the activities of the nuncio. And again it was the problem of improving Polish-Austrian relations, this time not in connection with the Polish succession but with the much desired anti-Ottoman league, which was to be the main task of the well chosen papal diplomat, Cardinal Caetani, as clearly evidenced in his long instructions of April 13, 1596. [53]

That document which directed the intense activity of the Legate from his arrival in Cracow two months later to his departure in the spring of the following year, included, however, a few direct or indirect references to the Ruthenian Union which was to be ratified in the middle of that period. Anticipating with some optimism that the League, if happily concluded, would result in the acquisition of parts of the Ottoman Empire by Poland as well as by the other allies and that the ecclesiastical organization would be restored there, the Pope added that if there should be in those territories " peoples of Greek rite, there ought to be no hesitation in leaving them the use of the said rite, as it has been done with the Ruthenian bishops. " [54] There was also, though at the very end of the instructions, [55] a special article dealing with these bishops two of whom had so recently been in Rome. Clement VIII not only recommended to his legate to support the claim of these bishops to get seats in the Senate along with those of Latin rite, a concession on which " the certain perpetuation " of the whole achievement was supposed to depend, but in general to give them any possible proof that the Holy See was anxious to protect them and to embrace them in charity in spite of the long distance, and in particular to receive " with all expressions of love and charity " any of those bishops

---

[49] A copy of that letter was forwarded to Rome by Malaspina (*Borgh.* III 91 c, fol. 132).

[50] See M. Vanino, *Komulović*, Sarajevo 1935, 54, also Pierling, *op. cit.*, II, 366.

[51] Interesting information about that mission can be found in *Dispacci Germania*, reports of June 11 and 25, 1596.

[52] See above, Chap. II, p. 336.

[53] *Borgh.* IV, vol. 269, fol. 144-157.

[54] *Ibidem*, fol. 153.

[55] *Ibidem*, fol. 156-156v.

who would appear before him. Cardinal Caetani was to conform strictly to that wise advice, in cooperation with Malaspina, though on other occasions that cooperation between the legate and the Nuncio would, as usually in such cases, raise some difficulties.

Equally wise was a reference which in the main part of the instructions [56] was made on the mission of Alexander Komulovich. Sending him again to Moscow together with the imperial ambassadors, the Pope decided that the Croat Monsignor would have to obey the legate sent to Poland who in turn was advised to consider in that delicate matter the desires of the King and the senators. For Clement VIII was fully aware that the Poles were not the only ones to blame for the little progress made hitherto in the negotiations about the anti-Ottoman league ; on the contrary, rightly discouraged by extravagant claims of the imperial court, they considered with not unjustified suspicion the simultaneous diplomatic negotiations between the Habsburgs and Moscow, which throughout the last century had time and again threatened the Commonwealth with an Austro-Russian encirclement. Therefore he referred in Cardinal Caetani's instruction briefly but pointedly to the opinion of some well informed people that those Polish fears were at the root of all the trouble and difficulties his legate would have to face in the matter of the league. He added that he was going to write himself to the Emperor, especially as the Poles were at the given moment particularly alarmed by the concentration of Muscovite forces at the Livonian border.

This had been reported to the Vatican by Nuncio Malaspina [57] who forwarded also, as early as in February, [58] again in connection with the projects of an anti-Turkish action, news received from Moscow that those who, amidst the internal tension in that country, had gained the strongest influence upon the weak Tsar Fedor, were stimulating him to start a war against the Poles. These were indeed only rumors but the general picture was accurate and confirmed to Clement VIII by his Nuncio in Venice [59] who was also working for a general anti-Ottoman league with the participation of the Republic, but encountered similar difficulties in view of its inveterate distrust of the Habsburgs. And the Venetians, who in agreement with the Holy See considered Poland's participation in the league absolutely indispensable and a prerequisite condition for their own adhesion, knew as well as the best observers in Cracow that the Poles were hesitating chiefly because of their fear that the cooperation between their western and eastern neighbor could turn against them. [60]

---

[56] *Ibidem*, fol. 153v.

[57] *Borgh.* III 89 c, fol. 106 (March 23, 1596).

[58] *Ibidem*, fol. 54v (February 16, 1596).

[59] *Nunz. di Venezia*, vol. 32, fol. 260, 286. See also *Dispacci Germania*, vol. 25, third report of March 12, 1596, and first report of April 30.

[60] *Ibidem*, vol. 41, fol. 56-59v (a particularly interesting retrospective report of

It is true, however, that for the time being these fears were exaggerated in view of precisely those internal problems of Muscovite Russia which resulted from Ivan the Terrible's disastrous reign and were soon to lead to a particularly critical time of trouble. And this was also the reason why there is no trace of any Muscovite support received by the opposition against the Union of Brest, which was mobilizing all forces on the eve of the decisive synod. There is, on the contrary, ample evidence that such an encouragement of these forces for opposition was coming from and through the much smaller Orthodox neighbor country of Moldavia where, on the one hand, Rome expected some favorable repercussion of the reunion of the Ruthenians, and which on the other hand, Ostrogski had always wanted to include in any negotiations with the Holy See, as well as Moscow.

The situation in that principality where the influences coming from Constantinople, both from the Sultan and from the Greek Patriarch, though still weaker than in Wallachia, were rivalling with those of Poland and Transylvania, continued to be extremely confused and constituted another source of Austro-Polish controversies and of difficulties for Cardinal Caetani's mediation. [61] Soon absorbed by that political task, neither he nor Malaspina were fully aware of the religious aspects of that Moldavian problem nor of their connection with the struggle for and against the Ruthenian Union. However, already in December 1595, soon after Jeremiah Movila's establishment as Prince of Moldavia by Zamoyski and his victory over the candidate supported by Transylvania which had caused so much alarm in Rome, there appeared in one of the Nuncio's ciphered reports [62] a brief reference to the emprisonment by Movila " of that man who formerly has been Patriarch of Constantinople and was sent by Sinan to Zamoyski with the offer of Wallachia and Moldavia. "

The surprising facts given in this almost casual notice are really a key to a better understanding of the most important further developments, and confirmed by other sources. Inaccurate is only the comment that the man in question had been before Patriarch of Constantinople, but even this mistake is easy to explain. For the enigmatic Greek whose name, Nicephorus, was to become known to the Nuncio only later, was basing his whole action including his leading part in the struggle against the Union of Rome and Brest on a document [63] apparently issued in November 1592 by Patri-

Dec. 21, 1596). See also *Urbin. lat.* 1604, fol. 265v-266, 296, 330, 332, 396 (very important news of April 27, May 11, 15, and 25, June 22).

[61] *Ibidem*, vol. 31, fol. 198, 212v, 223 ; vol. 32, fol. 286. See also *Dispacci Germania*, vol. 24, first report of February 27, 1596 ; vol. 25, second report of May 21, 1596. *Dispacci Roma*, vol. 37, fol. 241. *Urbin. lat.* 1604, fol. 213, 238.

[62] *Borgh.* III 91 d, fol. 86 (December 14, 1595).

[63] *Russk. istor. bibl.*, VII, col. 1319-1323, one of the many documents — some of them otherwise unknown — which are inserted in " Apokrisis, " a treatise written by an opponent of the Union of Brest ; the date : November 7701 (ind. VI) corresponds to the year 1592.

arch Jeremiah, in which that former Patriarch of Constantinople, in the presence of Meletius, Patriarch of Alexandria, named Nicephorus not only a " protosyncellus, " i. e. a vicar of the Patriarch, but gave him so extraordinary powers in all ecclesiastical matters that he could be considered acting Patriarch indeed, in any case superior in authority to all the other members of the hierarchy of the Greek Orthodox Church, including even the Metropolitans.

That document, which has not been preserved in its original, seems to have had, contrary to serious doubts expressed, at least appearances of authenticity, [64] and it is quite possible that the shrewd, unscrupulous, and ambitious Nicephorus obtained it really from the old, weak, and vaccillating Jeremiah who after his repeated depositions and temporary re-establishments never again felt secure in his patriarchal see and easily could be exposed to Turkish pressure. But even so, the almost unbelievable privileges granted to a cleric who was not even ordained as priest, were dated 1592, had no connection with the project of the Ruthenian Union — then discussed only in secret — and had lost their validity with Jeremiah's death at the end of 1595. [65] In the meantime the occupants of the Patriarchate had already changed twice, and it is well known through the confidential reports of the Venetian bailos in Constantinople, [66] that these successors of Jeremiah were, during their short tenures, exclusively concerned with their financial difficulties. None of them confirmed the exceptional rights of Nicephorus who claimed at Brest that in September 1595 Jeremiah had written him to go to the Ruthenian lands in view of the troubles which had arisen there. However, he could not produce any document other than that of 1592, and in any case at the time of the Synod the see of Constantinople was vacant after the death of Patriarch Gabriel in August 1596. [67]

But during all these critical years the real power in ecclesiastical matters, still left to the Greek Patriarchs, was exercised even in Constantinople by another Patriarch of the Ottoman East, that of Alexandria in Egypt. And that see, much more important than the dissident Coptic Patriarchate of the same city which was renewing his union with Rome, was occupied

---

[64] As pointed out by Arcudius who examined it in 1597 at the time of Nicephorus' trial ; see his letter of March 20, 1597, *Sacrum Poloniae Millennium*, I, 111.

[65] About the date A. Papadopulos-Kerameus in *Bessarione*, 1905, 286 ff.

[66] *Dispacci Costantinopoli*, vol. 42, report of Feb. 24, 1596 ; vol. 43, report of July 20 ; and vol. 44, report of October 20 (that volume is in so bad condition, that only the contemporary summary (Rubr. 6, fol. 98v) can be used). These important reports confirm the statement in " Apokrisis " (*Russk. istor. bibl.*, VII, 498) about the rapid changes in the see of Constantinople.

[67] See *Bessarione*, 295, and the comments of Zhukovich, *op. cit.* 182 n. 385, 216 n. 476 on the statements in *Russ. ist. bibl.*, XIX, 341, 500, 544. Not before November 24, 1596, could the Venetian bailos report (*Dispacci Costantinopoli*, vol. 44, rubr. 6, fol. 111). that the new Patriarch had arrived in Constantinople.

by Meletius Pigas whose unusually great and always anti-Catholic influence had reached as far as the Ruthenian land when the project of such a union was first conceived there. [68] Now during all the successive vacancies of the Patriarchate of Constantinople, he was the most serious candidate to that see which he accepted, however, only a few months after the Synod of Brest, [69] and even then only as administrator, preferring to remain Patriarch of Alexandria. This did not mean at all that he wanted to remain more independent from the Turkish authorities. On the contrary, as he quite sincerely explained to his Venetian friends, [70] he considered it advisable to collaborate with a regime which, though already disintegrating, seemed too strong to be reversed even by a joint, highly improbable action of all Christendom. He therefore did not hesitate to serve the Sultan's interests even when Orthodox countries like Wallachia were concerned, where he persuaded Michael the Brave to appease the Turks, [71] and particularly in the relations with Catholic powers, like the Polish-Lithuanian Commonwealth, which could be dangerous to the Ottoman Empire and where interests of the Greek Orthodox Church could be protected at the same time.

Meletius was careful enough not to appear personally in any such countries in the double role of a high dignitary of that Church and of a secret agent of the Turks. He would rather use other, less conspicuous Greeks, [72] and one of them, though, as a matter of fact, not even the most distinguished, was precisely Nicephorus, who like Meletius came from the island of Crete, a Venetian possession, had studied, like the other, at the University of Padua, and started his ecclesiastical activity in Venice, where, as he admitted later, he was administering sacraments, including confession and ordination, without being ordained himself. [73] Better than his theological training seems to have been his experience in the art of diplomacy which he gained there and which the Turkish government, undoubtedly at the suggestion and through the intermediary of Meletius, let him try first

---

[68] See above, Part III, Chap. III, p. 249 f.

[69] See the Venetian report of April 12, 1597, in *Dispacci Costantinopoli*, vol. 45, summarized at length in Rubr. 6, fol. 150v.

[70] See the reports of March 27 and Dec. 31, 1597, in the same volume, which have been copied by XIX century archivists when the volume was still readable. I discussed them, as well as the reports quoted above, in my essay " Rome, Constantinople et Moscou au temps de l'Union de Brest," *L'Eglise et les Eglises* 1054-1954, 460-463.

[71] See the appendices to the Venetian reports — copies of the correspondence between Meletius and Michael the Brave, published in *Documente privitore la istoria romanilor*, III-1, pp. 518-522 (app. Nr. 75, 76, 79).

[72] So he did when asked by the Turks to go to Wallachia in May 1597 (*Dispacci Costantinopoli*, Rubr. 6, fol. 157v).

[73] See the letter of Arcudius, quoted above in note 64, and my comments (*loc. cit.*, 86), where other sources are indicated also.

in that crucial region of Moldavia where Turkish, Polish, and so many other influences clashed all the time.

His main and most astonishing assignment was, as the Nuncio to Poland rightly stressed, to approach Zamoyski, probably through the Chancellor's man of confidence in Moldavia, and to find out whether Sinan Pasha, the commander of the Turkish forces in the Hungarian war, could not induce the Polish leader, not only to continue his policy hostile to any league with the Emperor, but to cease to block for the Tartars the much needed passage through the Danubian principalities, if the control of these principalities were spontaneously offered to him by the Ottoman Empire. This was, however, a hopeless scheme, since Zamoyski, suspicious of the Habsburgs and of their Transylvanian ally, was for good reasons even more suspicious of Turks and Tartars, and without strictly following the line of papal policy in the controversial matter of the league, was too good a Catholic and too concerned with Poland's honor as a Catholic power for practically siding with the enemies of Christendom, were it even for a tempting price which could prove of precarious value anyway. [74]

The great statesman who wanted Poland's policy to be independent of any other power, hoped to control at least Moldavia, not by the grace of the Sultan but through the cooperation of the native Movilas. It was, therefore, against Prince Jeremiah that Nicephorus, when his mission to Zamoyski failed, started intriguing to such an extent that he was put in jail, as a Turkish spy, in the fortress of Hotin near the Polish border. He succeeded, however, in escaping across that border and found " a haven at the court of Prince Constantine Ostrogski " [75] who certainly was as much as Zamoyski against any collaboration with the Turks and rather favorable to the idea of joining the league against them, but quite willing to protect a man now hostile to his main rival in Poland and representing a most precious tool in the struggle against the Union of the Ruthenians with Rome.

For the troubles in Moldavia had a religious aspect also, and while the Movilas continued to be interested in a similar union and Prince Jeremiah himself was expected to work in the same direction, there was among the Orthodox clergy of that country a party as strongly opposed to any

---

[74] The proposals of Sinan Pasha were known to Malaspina who wrote about them, not without alarm, still on March 2, 1597 (*Borgh.* III 91 d, fol. 178v-179). But even the proposals of Michael the Brave to place Wallachia under Polish control like Moldavia were rejected in order not to trouble (*intorbidare*) the plans of an anti-Turkish league (*Dispacci Germania*, vol. 25, report of July 16, 1596). About the real intentions of the Poles see also the news from Cracow, Aug 24 and 31, received in Venice and Rome (*Urbin. lat.*, 1604, fol. 588-592v, 601).

[75] The whole Moldavian background of that incident is described by O. Barlea, *De confessione orthodoxa Petri Mohilae*, 45-46, where the earlier publications of the Rumanian historians are quoted. See also Chodynicki, *op. cit.*, 325.

such Union as was Ostrogski, the same party which already on August 17, 1595 had sent from the synod of Jassy to the Ruthenians a message warning them not to follow their pro-Roman bishops. [76] Nicephorus had closely cooperated with them during his stay in Moldavia, producing already there that same document of the late Patriarch Jeremiah which now served him as the best introduction to the opponents of the Union in Poland.

There was still another reason why he was so well received at Ostrog. His own protector, Meletius Pigas, in addition to his earlier messages to the Ruthenians who, though outside the jurisdiction of the Patriarch of Alexandria, were impressed by his growing authority in the whole Eastern Church, sent to Ostrogski not only another long letter, [77] condemning those who had abandoned the Patriarch of Constantinople and encouraging the Prince to oppose them, but also a personal representative, the same Cyril Lucaris who had already taught before at the Orthodox Academy of Ostrog and now was instructed to stay there and to participate in the struggle against the Union. [78] As a theologian of real distinction he was better qualified to do so than Nicephorus, but already then under a strong Calvinist influence which many years later, when he was several times Patriarch of Constantinople, was to cause his fall and tragic death, while it proved a valuable asset at the time of the Union of Brest.   For Ostrogski himself was precisely under the same influence, and the crypto-Calvinism of one of his Greek collaborators facilitated that joint action with the Protestants of Poland and Lithuania which made the opposition against the Union so dangerous. Yet, on that occasion Lucaris remained rather in the background, leaving the official direction of the opposition to that other Greek, Nicephorus, who pretended to be the formal representative of the Patriarchate to which the Ruthenian Church belonged.

How he planned to take advantage of his alleged position became first evident on September 13, 1596, [79] when calling himself exarch and protosyncellus of the Patriarch of Constantinople he wrote to Metropolitan Rahoza, as if he were his superior, asking him whether it was true that he had ceased to mention that Patriarch in the liturgy.   That letter received no answer, since Rahoza was decided not to recognize Nicephorus' authority. It was, however, a first warning what the opposition would try to do at the synod which was to take place the following month.   For Prince Constantine had obviously already assigned to his Greek guests a leading part at that synod.

---

[76] See above, Chap. I, p. 300.
[77] *Monumenta Confraternitatis Stauropig.*, I, Nr. 423, (August 30, 1596).
[78] About the role of Lucaris, see Chodynicki, *op. cit.*, 288 (particularly note 6) and 322, and my remarks in *Sacrum Poloniae Millennium*, I, 78.
[79] *Russk. istor. bibl.*, XIX, 341 f.

The close cooperation of both those Greeks started soon after the message of Nicephorus to Rahoza : three days later he wrote from Dubno in Volhynia to Lucaris, " vicar of the Patriarch of Alexandria ", a long and most revealing letter [80]. He first claimed that Jeremiah Movila and his Moldavians, whom Rome expected in vain to follow the example of the Ruthenian bishops [81], had asked him to act as mediator in their relations with Sinan Pasha. Pretending that he was accompanied by more than one hundred Greeks, but failing to mention the sad outcome of his activities in Moldavia, he continued asking Lucaris to join him now in his struggle against the " apostate " Ruthenian bishops and the Jesuits, suggesting that they both should meet at Ostrogski's court. The emissary of Meletius Pigas was already present there, of course, not " by chance " as the opponents of the Union later tried to explain [82], but because he continued to be in close contact with the old Prince in ecclesiastical matters, writing to him in terms of highest respect and finally settling in Ostrog, [83] after exercising throughout the critical summer of 1596 a probably decisive influence on the Palatine of Kiev, who was preparing for the final struggle.

In his reply to the King's message, the text of which has unfortunately not been preserved but seems to have been rather evasive, he no longer called the planned synod a fraud but preferred to distort in advance the whole project, by putting forward four conditions which were submitted to Sigismund III by a delegation composed of two Volhynian nobles. [84] He asked the King, first, to guarantee full security and freedom to the participants in the Synod, by not permitting anybody to bring with him armed forces ; secondly, to permit the participation of the Protestants and thirdly, that of the Greek Nicephorus ; and lastly, to admit an appeal to the Diet, if the Synod would not lead to a full agreement.

It was obvious that Sigismund III would grant the first of these requests, which were reasonable and corresponded to his own desires, but reject the three others. As a matter of fact, he had already taken position in the next two questions when on June 14 [85] he issued a manifesto to the Ruthenian clergy and people, informing them that the Metropolitan, as he had asked him to do a month before, would convoke a synod in Brest, to ratify the Union which Pociej and Terlecki had concluded in Rome. He specified already on that occasion that only the hierarchy and clergy, as well as

[80] E. Legrand, *Bibliographie hellénique du XVII-e siècle*, IV (Paris 1896), Nr. 51, 221-225.

[81] *Monumenta Vaticana Hung.*, II-3, Nr. 119 (March 23, 1596).

[82] *Russ. istor. bibl.*, XIX, 333.

[83] Legrand, *op. cit.*, 219-221 (undated letters of Lucaris).

[84] Recalled in the discussions between Ostrogski and the royal representatives at the Synod of Brest (*ibidem*, VII, 944 f) ; see below in the next chapter.

[85] *Akty Zap. Rossii*, IV, Nr. 97; as to the date see Chodynicki, *op. cit.*, 323 note 1.

Ruthenian laymen interested in the Union would be permitted to attend, but neither foreigners — this excluded Nicephorus and any other Greeks — nor people of other faith, meaning of course the Protestants.

The date of October 8 which Rahoza later changed to October 6 — a minor point which was, however, to cause some inconvenience — was given according to the old calendar which was used by the Ruthenians and eventually left unchanged in spite of their reunion with Rome. It was indeed October 18, or 16, according to the Gregorian calendar generally accepted in the Commonwealth, and in any case meant another delay in the convocation of the Synod which originally was to meet on St. Michael's day or soon after. But it is equally clear that the Metropolitan who did no longer show any sign of hesitation, was not responsible for that delay, which resulted rather from the King's desire to see the important assembly prepared as well as possible, and perhaps even the opposition appeased.

As far as the preparations of the promoters of the Union were concerned, Bishop Pociej whose son, following the footsteps of his father — once a lay senator and now exclusively dedicated to this religious cause — had recently been admitted by the Pope to the Greek College at Rome, [86] proved particularly active and successful. He had been well received in his diocese, except by the Brotherhood of Brest which he once had favored and protected, but which now, like the other brotherhoods, was so adamant in its opposition, that the Bishop felt obliged to prohibit clandestine gatherings in cooperation with the " heretics " [87]. On the other hand, he succeeded in organizing in that same city a meeting of the clergy of that part of his diocese, attended by more than one hundred priests. He convinced them that all rumors spread by Ostrogski were wrong, whether they concerned the attitude of the King or the alleged changes in the liturgy which were supposed to result from the Union. Celebrating with them the holy offices, he called upon Peter Arcudius who accompanied him, to testify as a Greek priest himself, that all traditional rites remained unaltered. Teaching his clergy about the Catholic faith, he tried at the same time to make them well disposed towards the Synod which was to meet precisely in Brest. But he also went to the other part of his diocese, to Volodymir in Volhynia, where assisted again by Arcudius, he worked in the same sense. [88]

Much more difficult was the situation of the other Ruthenian bishop in Volhynia, Pociej's companion Terlecki, whose diocese of Łuck and Ostrog was closest to Prince Constantine Ostrogski and included the Monastery of Żydyczyn, where its abbot, Gregory Bałaban, a relative of the Bishop of Lwów, was equally opposed to the Union. [89] Furthermore, Terlecki had

[86] *Urbin. lat.* 1604, fol. 245 (news of April 17, 1596).
[87] *Russk. istor. bibl.*, VII, 1775-1777.
[88] Arcudius' letter of June 20, 1596 (*Sacrum Poloniae Millennium*, I, 106).
[89] *Akty Zap. Rossii*, IV, Nr. 109.

been so terribly looted by the Cossacks, that he had first of all to repair the losses of his diocese, [90] and Nalevayko's final defeat, in August, though reestaplishing peace and order in the Ruthenian borderlands, could not help those who had already suffered from his devastations.

However, this victory over a rebellion which had nothing to do with the problem of religious Union, but could be easily misused, as it apparently happened in the conflict between Ostrogski and Terlecki, by the opponents of that Union, left the King and his advisers freer to deal with other issues, including the religious. That Sigismund III soon afterwards did himself his best to create favorable conditions for the approaching synod, is best evidenced by a letter which he wrote from Warsaw on September 6 [91] to the Archbishop of Polotsk and Vitebsk, that same Herman Ivanovich whom first he had confirmed in his high ecclesiastical position only conditionally, but who by now had proved to be a sincere supporter of the Union. He urged him not to fail to attend both the Synod of Brest itself, as convoked by the Metropolitan, and a preliminary conference of all Ruthenian bishops which was to take place one week earlier in a small nearby town, Kamieniec in Lithuania. That little known preparatory meeting, suggested by the King,[92] was successful chiefly thanks to Bernard Maciejowski to whose Latin diocese of Łuck that place belonged, and who once more, as he had done at Torczyn in December 1594, greatly assisted and encouraged the Ruthenian initiators of the Union discussing with them all relevant problems with his usual zeal, prudence and kindness. It was thanks to him that already there the individual professions of faith of those bishops who had not been in Rome were signed and sealed, later to be forwarded to the Pope, and that they agreed to be absolved from their earlier schism by Pociej, acting on behalf of the Pope himself. Arcudius who seems to have been present again, was impressed by the constancy, sincerity and good spirit of all bishops who attended, notwithstanding the " great danger " which continued to threaten them from some laymen, especially from their leader, Prince Ostrogski.

That very real danger worried more and more all those interested in the Union, as the date of the Synod was approaching. How it worried the King who sent to Ostrogski an official warning that the Metropolitan was not under the jurisdiction of the Palatine of Kiev, [93] is best explained in the reports of the Cardinal Legate who precisely in that critical period became particularly interested in the matter, perhaps even more

---

[90] The references of Arcudius and of the King (see notes 88 and 32) are confirmed by many other sources; see Zhukovich, *op. cit.*, 207 n. 453.

[91] *Opisanie dokumentov arkhiva zapadnorusskikh uniatskikh mitropolitov*, I, Nr. 19.

[92] Described by Arcudius in his letter of November 10, 1596 (*Sacrum Pol. Mill.*, I, 207 f.).

[93] *Akty zap. Rossii*, IV, Nr. 99 (August 19, 1596).

than the Nuncio who, after working so hard for the Union through the two preceding years, now hardly mentioned it when writing to Rome about so many other problems, in particular the anti-Ottoman league. Caetani, too, was absorbed by that primary objective of his mission, and it was from that point of view that he considered [94] not without alarm the case of Nalevayko who, closely examined in prison, might reveal something harmful to the negotiations in that delicate political matter. In the same connection the Legate studied the chances of the mission to Moscow of Alexander Komulovich [95] whose achievements as administrator of the diocese of Wilno had impressed him favorably and who now sent him valuable furs which were a present of the Muscovite ruler for the Pope. Caetani interpreted this as an evidence that " even the Muscovite respected and recognized by his gifts the Monarch of the world. " It was not before the end of September, [96] that Caetani got in touch with " those Ruthenian bishops " united with the Latin Church who had been recommended to him, and promised them his " help and patronage. "

He discussed at length their problems with Sigismund III at the beginning of October, [97] apparently the same day, October 4, when the King appointed his own representatives at the Synod of Brest, in addition to his confessor, Father Skarga, whom he also wanted to be present, and to Bishop Maciejowski, the one of the papal representatives whom the King too instructed to serve on that occasion the cause with which he was so deeply concerned. The three royal delegates who were not to participate in any religious debates, but only to assure peace and order, [98] were chosen among the senators of Lithuania, since the Synod was to meet in the territory of the Grand Duchy : they were the Grand Marshal, recently also appointed Palatine of Troki, Prince Nicholas Christopher Radziwiłł, Duke of Nieśwież and Ołyka, well known in Rome for his great piety ; the Grand Chancellor Leo Sapieha who had already participated in the earlier negotiations in the matter; and the Grand Treasurer Demetrius Chalecki, originally an Orthodox himself, but of a family with earlier traditions of favoring the Union of Florence, now known as " a great Catholic " like the two others, and at the same time as being opposed to any violence against non-Catholics and experienced in conciliatory politics. [99]

---

[94] In his report of September 26, 1596 (Vatican Archives, *Fondo Pio*, vol. 114, fol. 97 ; the same reports of Caetani which are quoted in this and the following notes, can be found also in *Bibl. Casanatense*, vol. 1563).

[95] In his report of September 6, 1596 (*ibidem*, fol. 87v).

[96] See the report quoted in note 94.

[97] See his report of October 5, 1596 (*ibidem*, fol. 109-110).

[98] This is stressed in the King's letter to them, of October 4 (*Opisanie dokumentov*, I, Nr. 200).

[99] See his biography in *Polski Słownik biograficzny*, III (1937), 230, and my comments on all three delegates in *Sacrum Pol. Mill.*, I, 99.

Since Chalecki was, among others, also Starosta of Brest, he was *ex officio* responsible for maintaining in that city and district lawful conditions and representing there royal authority. But it was Sapieha who left the court first, already the day following their appointment, and was instructed in cooperation with Maciejowski, carefully to study the whole situation and, if necessary, even to postpone the whole matter to gain time for considering what to do. That possibility of a last minute adjournment of the Synod, in order to avoid a break " in such a useful and saintly work " was considered, as the papal Legate easily discovered, [100] out of fear of some violent action by the Palatine of Kiev, and father of the Castellane of Cracow, Prince Ostrogski. Calling him a "rabid, perfidious, and most obstinate schismatic, " Caetani pointed out, [101] having obviously been told so at the royal court, that he could at any time mobilize more than six thousand horsemen from among the nobles under his control being the lord of more than seventy cities and a thousand villages in Russia, Volhynia, Podolia, and Poland proper.

These current talks about Ostrogski's personal power and dangerous intentions not only impressed the papal Legate, but through various channels of information reached faraway Italy, [102] where it became known that along with Grand Chancellor Sapieha another of the principal lords of Lithuania, obviously Grand Treasurer Chalecki, left the royal court for the Grand Duchy in order to appease the differences among the Ruthenian bishops which had arisen after the return of two of them from Rome, where they had reconciled Greek and Latin rites. The third royal representative, Prince Radziwiłł, whose influence was to counteract that of the Calvinist line of his family — the most powerful in Lithuania — was delayed by a very special reason, revealed by the Jesuits [103] with whom the founder of their Nieśwież College had so close relations. His dearly beloved wife, a former Protestant whom he had converted to the Catholic faith, was dying and he did not want to leave her : but she herself, while giving the instructions for her funeral which she ordered to be as modest as possible, begged him not to neglect his duty, deeply convinced that his mission to Brest was more useful and important than her life. All three delegates were decided to oppose, if necessary, any acts of violence by what was considered a " furious, tumultuous and insolent " opposition, but, according to the King's own desire, not by any violent counteraction, but, as the

---

[100] See his report quoted in note 97.

[101] This is added in the text of his report copied in *Bibl. Casanatense*, vol. 1563, fol. 251.

[102] *Urbin. lat.* 1604, fol. 767v (news from Rome, Nov. 23, based upon a letter sent from Warsaw on Oct. 26).

[103] *Annuae Litterae S. J. anni* 1596, Neapoli 1605, 43 (in the report of the Nieśwież College).

Greek Arcudius would point out later, [104] by their "Christian zeal and kindness," relying more upon prestige than upon force.

Persuasion instead of force was also the method which advocated the Jesuits when the achievement they had helped to prepare for so many years, was at last to materialize. In addition to the already famous Skarga, three more Fathers were sent to Brest as expert theologians, Justin Rab, Martin Laterna — a former preacher at the court of King Stephan Báthory, and one of the most active, Caspar called Nahay because of his Tartar origin. [105] For the last two months he had been with Bishop Maciejowski in Łuck helping to prepare the synod and working, as usual, for individual conversions of both Orthodox and Protestants. It was there, during these months of preparation, that Pociej and Terlecki who even in Rome had made their confessions only to one of their own Ruthenian priests, made general confessions to the distinguished Jesuit whose Society they had in great esteem. Then one of them celebrated a solemn Ruthenian, i. e., in the Eastern rite, Mass in a Latin Church, Father Nahay preaching in Polish, while the following mass, sung according to the Latin rite, was accompanied by a sermon in Ruthenian.

It was, furthermore, at a Jesuit College, that of Wilno, [106] that Metropolitan Rahoza himself, accompanied by his friend, the Archbishop of Polotsk, whose cooperation the King considered so important, stopped on his way to Brest, asking for the advice of the Fathers in the most important problems, of course those of the Union, and for prayers for the success of the Synod. Praying for that success was also Cardinal Caetani in Warsaw, hoping that the final Union would be another triumph in the happy pontificate of Clement VIII. [107] Anxious to make himself some contribution, he, too, had given to the Ruthenian bishops written advice in special matters they had submitted to him, particularly that of the planned Ruthenian seminary, a truly important educational problem which at the same time also Arcudius [108] studied with special care, including the question of the most convenient place. The constructive optimism of all those who were looking forward to the Synod, inspired by purely religious motives, was to prove justified to a large extent, though not without serious difficulties, as ancitipated at the royal court where even the expediency of a last minute postponement was taken into consideration.

---

[104] In his letter of Nov. 10, 1596 (*Sacrum Pol. Mill.*, I, 108).

[105] It is from Nahay's letter to General Aquaviva of January 20, 1597, that the following information is taken (Roman Archives of the Soc. od Jesus, *Epist. Germ.*, vol. 177, fol. 58).

[106] *Annuae Litterae S. J. anni* 1596, 14 (in the report of the Wilno College).

[107] This, too, and the following information is taken from his report of October 5,

[108] See his letter of June 20 (*Sacrum Pol. Mill.*, I, 106 f.).

CHAPTER IV

THE SYNOD OF BREST, 1596

Among the various synods of the Ruthenian Church which met in the city of Brest in Lithuania, the one which was opened on October 16, 1596, and concluded its activities on October 20, was by far the most important and remained of truly historical significance, because it was there that on the memorable day of October 19, the Union of Rome was formally ratified and made final. Since the old Calendar continued to be used by the Ruthenians even after the Union and, of course, also in the charter of that day, usually the dates of October 6, 9 and 10 are given.

More important than any other, the October Synod of 1596 is by far the best known in all details. Thanks to endless polemics[1] which started immediately between the supporters and the opponents of the Union, the brief story of that great event has been recorded day by day, if not hour by hour. Both sides agree as to the basic facts but differ as to their interpretation and evaluation, most controversial being the question which of the two assemblies deliberating at Brest simultaneously, was the real, legal Synod. For the opposition, conforming to Ostrogski's final approach, far from opposing the convocation of the Synod as such, stressing on the contrary[2] that it was on the request of their leaders, viz., in the first place

---

[1] The most important and earliest of these writings are : a) an Orthodox account entitled *Ekthesis*, published in Cracow in 1597, b) Skarga's history of the synod, published the same year, c) a refutation published the same year under the title *Apokrisis*, probably written by a Protestant, Martin Broniewski, d) a defense of Skarga's work published in 1600 under the title *Antirrisis*, probably written by Pociej in cooperation with Arcudius — all four reprinted in *Russk. istor. bibl.*, VII, 939-1820, and XIX, 183-376, 477-982. Other sources which have been used in modern historiography are quoted by Chodynicki, *Kościół prawosławny*, 328 n. 1. Repeating here only briefly what has been written before on the basis of that material, I am trying to supplement that information by two accounts of eyewitnesses, both Greeks, but one of them, Peter Arcudius, a Catholic favorable to the Union, the other one, an anonymous companion of Nicephorus, hostile to the Union.   I published these new sources, with my comments in *Sacrum Poloniae Millennium*, I, 70-136 ; using them here, I am quoting the letters of Arcudius to Claudius Aquaviva, General of the Jesuit Order (Roman Archives of the Society of Jesus, *Epist. Germ.* vol. 176, fol. 184-185 and 259-b-259d, vol. 177, fol. 142 and 203-204) as A 1-4 (the second letter, written from Brest on Nov. 10 being the most important), and the report of Nicephorus' friend ((Περὶ τῶν 'Ρυτένων, Vatican Library, *Borg. lat.* 450-490), as N, indicating where it seemed advisable the folios of the manuscript which are noted in my printed edition.

[2] N, fol. 476v.

Prince Constantine, that the King had duly ordered the Synod to be assembled, denied only the right of the " apostate " Metropolitan to preside over its sessions, claiming that right for the alleged representative of the Patriarch of Constantinople, the Greek Nicephorus, who contrary to the King's interdiction came to Brest to assume that role.

He was not at all the only foreigner who attended in agreement with Ostrogski's request and disregarded the refusal of Sigismund III. There was, first of all, that other, much more famous Greek, Cyril Lucaris, the emissary of Meletius Pigas, and with both of these leaders came a few minor members of the Greek clergy whose names are not even known but who participated in the activities which one of them described in a semi-official report based upon the proceedings or minutes of the various sessions held under Nicephorus' presidency.[3] Even an otherwise unknown Metropolitan of Belgrade, called Lucas, another subject of the Ottoman Empire, is mentioned[4] among those present but did not play any important part.

Disregarding also another interdiction of the King, Ostrogski had decided in advance to secure the support of the Calvinist leaders, for, as he wrote on August 15, 1596, to the Palatine of Wilno, Radziwiłł " the Thunderbolt, "[5] in case of such a cooperation " not only those scoundrels, the Vladicas (meaning the Ruthenian bishops and adding with special reference to Pociej and Terlecki), the two little fellows, but even the Pope could achieve nothing. " Neither Christopher Radziwiłł, whom he informed on September 29 that he himself would arrive at Brest on October 13, three days before the opening of the assembly, nor the Palatine of Minsk, John Abramowicz, who was Ostrogski's second choice, like the year before at the time of the Synod of Toruń,[6] appeared in person at the Synod of the Ruthenians. But Prince Constantine was accompanied there by a large number[7] of Protestants and even of Antitrinitarians with whom he had been in contact for years ; he even chose as his headquarters at Brest the house of one of these, a notorious " Arian ". Furthermore, the Prince was accompanied by quite a few Orthodox laymen who were supposed to represent various Ruthenian provinces of both, the Kingdom of Poland and the Grand Duchy of Lithuania, and the most important cities, particularly the Brotherhoods in some of them. The list of these delegates[8] who hardly could have been formally elected except those of the Brotherhoods, is, however, not very impressive. As given by the Orthodox side, that list includes

---

[3] N, fol. 489v-490.
[4] *Russk. istor. bibl.*, XIX, 338, 373.
[5] This letter and a few others, including that of Sept. 29, are quoted by K. Lewicki, *Ks. Konstanty Ostrogski*, 168 (notes 1, 3 and 4) and 173, from manuscript sources.
[6] See above, Part IV, Chap. I, note 25.
[7] Arcudius writes about " *una massa di heretici* " (A, 2).
[8] *Russk. istor. bibl.*, XIX, 357 f.

in the first group, viz., noblemen from various districts, only 22 persons, ten of them from Volhynia where Ostrogski's influence was greatest and not more than three from his Palatinate of Kiev, and in the second group — 35 persons from 16 cities and towns, including 10 from Wilno (8 from the Brotherhood) and 7 from Lwów (4 from the Brotherhood); an unnamed man represented the burghers of Brest itself. It proved even more difficult, in spite of Ostrogski's pressure, to get any substantial representation of the Orthodox clergy, since, as admitted in the Greek, strongly anti-unionist report on the Synod, [9] that clergy almost in its totality followed the bishops whom they considered their legitimate pastors cooperating with them and thus " misleading " the people. For that very reason it was indeed Prince Constantine's greatest asset that the two bishops whom he had persuaded to abandon the project of reunion, Bałaban of Lwów, one of its earliest initiators and Kopysteński of Przemyśl, followed him faithfully and joined the opposition in Brest. [10] Important, too, was the support of some archimandrites who were at the head of the traditionally influential Orthodox monasteries : in particular the archimandrite of the oldest and most famous of them, the Monastery of the Caves in Kiev which the Pope wanted to place under the Metropolitan's direct authority, a monk of the name of Nicephorus Tur, was to be, besides the two bishops, the most conspicuous partisan of Ostrogski.

All of them, however, had to face one initial difficulty which resulted from the very choice of the place where, according to the rule established in 1589 by Patriarch Jeremiah himself, the Synod was convoked. Brest, where Pociej when still a layman had been first Judge and then Castellane — a senatorial office — and enjoyed, as well as his family, a considerable prestige, was now his episcopal see. The most devoted supporter of the Union which he had so efficiently propagandized before the Synod among the clergy and people of his diocese, was now the host of the assembly and in control of the only convenient and dignified place where its session could be held : his own cathedral. [11] Only through an act of open violence could the opposition occupy that church. Ostrogski was indeed in a position to try it, since, contrary to the King's decision which was even in agreement with one of his own requests, he had introduced into the city, to supplement the rather small group of qualified representatives of the opposition, a much larger number of armed followers : the number which in the various reports is given very differently, between two hundred [12] and

---

[9] N, fol. 475v-476 ; the decree of the anti-synod is signed by 11 archimandrites and 25 other members of the clergy ; the account adds that more than 200 were present (*Russk. istor. bibl.*, XIX, 373-376).

[10] See, for instance, N., fol. 477.

[11] According to N, fol. 477v, also all the other churches of the city were in the hands of the " apostates, " and controlled by " dirty heretics " (viz. Catholics).

[12] Lewicki, *op. cit.*, 177, accepts that minimum figure.

three thousand, [13] was in any case smaller than the Prince's boasting promises made to the Protestant Synod of Toruń, in 1595, and the pessimistic expectations of the Catholic side. However, even if he disposed only of a few hundred men, this would have been quite sufficient to terrorize the partisans of the Union and to create those violent troubles which the King so rightly wanted to avoid. Yet, even on the first day of the Synod, when the royal delegates, including the local Starosta Chalecki, had not yet arrived with their own limited number of followers, the old Prince did not proceed to any violent action, feeling that otherwise he would have completely discredited and compromised his cause. Instead of trying to penetrate into the Cathedral where the Metropolitan inaugurated the Synod, he gathered the opposition at his own headquarters, the private home of a Antitrinitarian layman.

He pretended, however, that in spite of such an inappropriate place the sessions which started there were precisely the legitimate Synod, because presided over by the representative of the Patriarch of Constantinople. And while neither side conducted any discussions on the religious aspects of the problem, one of them having arrived long ago to a decision in favor of the Union and the other one being irreductibly opposed to it, practically all the time was taken by the formal controversy which of the two gatherings was really the Synod of Brest and had the right, and even the obligation, to request the members of the other group to join it and to submit to its authority.

However, quite independently of the meeting place, there cannot be the slightest doubt that such a claim could be seriously made only by the assembly presided over by Metropolitan Rahoza. He and nobody else had been authorized and even requested by the King whose decisive power in the matter Ostrogski and even Nicephorus [14] always recognized, to convoke and direct the Synod according to the agelong tradition of the Ruthenian Church. Even on the unique occasion of 1589 when the Patriarch of Constantinople, present in person, wanted to interfere with the problems of that Church, he had to obtain the King's authorization. To Nicephorus, who was considered in Poland like in Moldavia, a Turkish agent if not spy, such an authorization was never given and the charter which he had received four years before from the deceased Patriarch, was to raise serious doubts even among the opposition gathered at Brest. Terlecki who could also claim to have been made a personal representative of that same Patriarch and therefore continued to use the title of exarch, belonged to that

---

[13] That figure given by Arcudius (A, 2), appears also in the report of Cardinal Caetani of October 26 (Bibl. Casanatense, *MS* 1563, fol. 276v; " ottomille " in another copy of the same report, *Fondo Pio*, 114, fol. 120, seems to be an error, instead of " tremille ").

[14] See N, 476v.

great majority of the Ruthenian hierarchy including the only archbishop besides the Metropolitan himself, who was in full agreement with the latter, had even prompted him to turn towards Rome, and now under his official leadership was ready to ratify the Union which their two plenipotentiaries had concluded there.

Unfortunately, the exact number of those who joined them at the Synod under the lawful Metropolitan, is not known. Only the three archimandrites of Bracław, Ławryszów and Minsk — a counterpart to those who led by Tur sided with the opposition — are specifically mentioned. [15] The number of the secular clergy which in the various dioceses followed their bishops, seems to have been rather large, certainly larger than on the other side which had to admit this. [16] On the other hand, there is no indication of the presence of any laymen ; even the Palatine of Nowogródek Tyszkiewicz who after the Synod was to defend the Union very definitely, waited for final information from the Metropolitan about the decisions taken and the results achieved. That absence must be explained partly by lack of interest in the matter and partly by the view which was consistently held by the pro-Roman side that the Union was a matter to be decided not by the laity but by the hierarchy and clergy.

In any case, there was from the outset no trace of hesitation or disagreement among the members of the legitimate Synod to whom Pociej and Terlecki reported in detail about the friendly treatment they had experienced in Rome. [17] The only problem was from the beginning to the end of the deliberations in the Cathedral of Brest, where on Wednesday, October 16, Rahoza inaugurated the Synod by a solemn service in the presence of the three Latin bishops representing the Pope, how to deal with the opposition and to persuade all or at least part of them to give up their negative attitude and to approve the ratification of the Union or at least not to oppose it. Since, however, it was well known that all depended on Ostrogski and that nobody had any chance of convincing and influencing him except his fellow senators who were to represent at Brest the King, it was decided to wait until their arrival and not to take any further steps on that first day.

A different method was followed by the other side, [18] perhaps with a view of creating accomplished facts before the arrival of the royal delegates. Both noblemen and clergymen met already on that first day at Ostrogski's residence and decided to send a message to the Metropolitan and to

---

[15] They signed with the bishops the charter of October 9 ; see below, p. 386.
[16] See above, note 9.
[17] This is stressed in news from Rome, Nov. 27, 1596 (*Urbin. lat.* 1604, fol. 776).
[18] Described by N, fol. 477 ; see *Russk. istor. bibl.*, 356, XIX, XX4 f (Ekthesis) were also a message of Nicephorus and Lucaris to Rahoza sent the day before is recorded (338, 342 f).

" the apostates who were with him " asking them whether they still were faithful to the dogmas of the Orthodox religion, and inviting them in that case to join Nicephorus, as representative of the Patriarch, and the other Orthodox bishops, viz., those of Lwów and Przemyśl, as well as " the whole holy Synod. " That invitation, along with a letter from Nicephorus to Rahoza, was immediately brought to the latter by seven delegates of the opposition. It is irrelevant whether these delegates really met the Metropolitan in person, or — as it seems to result from some accounts — not having found him at his residence handed over their message to the Bishop of Pinsk. In any case, Rahoza was fully aware that the very invitation to join the meeting presided over by Nicephorus, was a challenge to his own authority as well as to that of the real Synod. Furthermore, the opposition did not hesitate to ask him, under the appearances of a " brotherly " call to participate in their discussion, to justify himself before the representative of the Patriarch for having convoked the synod and assumed its presidency. [19]

The answer of the Metropolitan, formerly so reluctant to commit himself, was, therefore, very outspoken. He claimed that even exarchs sent by the Patriarch, when coming to his own ecclesiastical province, had to recognize him as superior and, instead of expecting him to come to them, rather to join him, his door always being open to everybody. But, in the given case, he did not hesitate to question whether Nicephorus, " called a protosyncellus, " was such an exarch of the Patriarch at all, and to express his belief that the man, suspected by everybody, was rather " a spy and impostor. "

Thus started an exchange of harsh statements between the two ecclesiastical leaders, which formally seemed to make the rivalry between the Synod and what might be called the countersynod a duel between the Metropolitan whom the records of the opposition present as the villain of the story, and the enigmatic Greek who pretended to represent Constantinople, supported already on that first day, at the preparatory meeting of the opposition, by the other Greek Cyril Lucaris representing the Patriarch of Alexandria, and by Gedeon Bałaban, the only Ruthenian bishop who played an active role on their side. Everybody knew, however, that behind these members of the clergy, there was Prince Ostrogski with all his power and prestige, pretending to play the traditional role of the secular authority in all religious discussions of the Eastern Church with the Western, a role which, indeed, nobody else could play in the given situation where the real secular authority was in the hands of a Catholic king.

Taking advantage of the fact that the representatives of that King were not yet present, he tried to organize a real religious debate under his

---

[19] *Ibidem*, fol. 477 v. ; see also Russk. ist. bibl. VII, 1035 f. (*Apokrisis*).

auspices, with a Greek theologian on either side. For it is true that on the side of the promoters of the Union, where even the Holy See was represented by Polish bishops to avoid any impression of foreign interference, there were two Greeks who, however, modestly kept in the background : one of them, Arcudius, [20] was well known to Prince Constantine from his earlier visit in the Ruthenian lands, and while the other, also an alumnus of the Greek College in Rome, George Moschetti, was known only to one of Ostrogski's assistants, the former seemed to the Prince important enough to serve as opponent of Nicephorus in a discussion of the main dogmatic problem separating East and West : the procession of the Holy Spirit. He hoped, of course, that the guest from Constantinople, so highly recommended by a former Patriarch, well known among the Ruthenians, would easily defeat his countryman who in Rome had turned away from the genuine Orthodox tradition. But Nicephorus himself, also educated in Italy but without serious theological training, obviously evaded the dangerous debate with a priest who was not holding nor pretending to hold any high ecclesiastical office but, as first doctor graduating from the college founded by Gregory XIII, had brilliantly defended his thesis on the procession of the Holy Spirit according to St. Thomas Aquinas. [21]

Instead of such a theological contest between two Greek clergymen, which never took place, there started the next day, Thursday, October 17 (7 old style), the long discussions between Ostrogski and the three royal delegates, which were to be the decisive feature of the divided convention. Radziwiłł, Sapieha, and Chalecki arrived in Brest on the morning of that second day of the Synod, accompanied by their own armed force but obviously decided not to use it, except in case of absolute necessity.[22] This point leads to the puzzling question why all three arrived one day late, though at least two of them had left Warsaw twelve days before and could have easily reached Brest on time. Though it is quite possible that there was some confusion in view of the original opening date of the Synod, October 18 (8), first announced by the King, their delay seems to have been intentional: in agreement with the royal instructions,[23] his representatives wanted, on the one hand, to avoid the impression of immediate State interference with the original organization of an ecclesiastical assembly and, on the other hand, not to begin their own activity before having some evidence whether there was any chance of orderly debates and successful mediation. If not, they would have been obliged merely to suggest an adjournment.

---

[20] He described the whole incident in his letter of Nov. 20 (A, 2).

[21] The text of his diploma, of Jan. 24, 1591, is published by E. Legrand, *Bibliographie hellénique du XVIIe siècle*, III, 210-211.

[22] Arcudius (*loc. cit.*), writes that they arrived " *con molta gente, ma molto più con auttorità.* "

[23] See above, in the preceding chapter, p. 363.

Since, however, it appeared that Ostrogski, too, had not the intention of using his armed forces in a disgraceful showdown, the three Lithuanian senators [24] immediately proceeded to their colleague, the Palatine of Kiev, in a first attempt to persuade him to give up his opposition and to make sure that he would not act through open violence. They only blamed him for having disobeyed the King by bringing to the Synod armed forces at all, as well as persons " of other faith, " viz., neither Catholic nor Orthodox, and in particular foreigners who were suspected of hostility against the country, a clear allusion to Nicephorus. The Prince, evasive as usually on similar occasions, declared himself ready for peaceful negotiations, asking only for " a quiet synod. " [25] Since this was precisely what the King and his representatives wanted, the situation could seem quite hopeful.

But Ostrogski must have been fully informed of what his partisans had done and decided in the meantime. They had started the day [26] by first organizing formally and definitely their own synod or rather counter-synod, and since they had found out that " the apostates " controlled all the churches of the city, deliberating in the Cathedral together with " the papal bishops, " they themselves continued to meet in the large building where Prince Constantine had his headquarters and which, according to the other side, was a usual meeting place, if not a temple of the Protestants. After thus finally dividing the Synod in two hostile camps, they furthermore divided their own assembly, as if it had been a political convention, in two " circles " or houses, each of which elected its " marshal " — this was in Poland and later in the whole Commonwealth the title of the Speakers of the Diets and leaders of the so-called confederations of the nobility for political purposes. One of them was to preside over the group of laymen and was a nobleman from Volhynia, Damian Hulewicz — according to the Catholics a Protestant if not Anabaptist. The other group was composed of members of the clergy with two Orthodox priests, one of them from Ostrog, as leaders, though it was Nicephorus who really directed all deliberations and immediately after these elections, in one of his formal addresses, suggested to invite once more the Metropolitan and the bishops who were on his side, to join them and " not to despise the honor to participate in the Synod. "

This time twelve delegates, six noblemen and six clergymen led by three Archimandrites were sent to the real Synod with that second invitation and with a first threat that if Rahoza and his followers would not comply nor explain their connection with the " Latins, " the representative of the

---

[24] According to an anonymous notice (*Akty Zap. Rossii*, IV, nr. 106) Radziwill arrived before the two others and had a first talk with Ostrogski.

[25] *Russk. istor. bibl.*, VII, 941.

[26] N, fol. 478 ; other accounts state (*Russk. ist. bibl.*, XIX, 334.) that the two " circles " were organized already on the first day, October 16.

Patriarch would deprive them of the episcopal dignities. In the name of the Synod the Metropolitan answered briefly that, if necessary, they would go to meet them, though it was rather for the opposition to join him, the head which the members of the body had to follow.[27] Though he stressed that their convention was not really a synod, and therefore acted illegally, his answer was made in a conciliatory spirit, since obviously the Metropolitan did not want to create difficulties for the mediation of the royal delegates. Coming to the Synod right from their first meeting with Ostrogski, they were present when the delegates of the opposition performed their mission, and surprised and shocked by their threats, they returned at once to the Prince, fully aware that his position would prove decisive.

As a matter of fact, while the countersynod, after receiving Rahoza's answer, was wondering through the rest of the day until evening what to do with the "apostates," but could only listen to another speech of Nicephorus full of generalities about peace and order in the Church, Ostrogski had to listen to the reproaches of the Senators who considered that the message to the Metropolitan which — as the Prince admitted — had been sent with his knowledge and approval, was contrary to his recent promise. They could now point out that in religious matters a procedure, similar to that of political assemblies with "circles" and marshals was contrary to the laws, and that, though a layman himself, Ostrogski pretended to conduct the synod, what the King himself would not dare to do. Once more the Prince, avoiding openly to challenge the royal authority, seemed ready for peaceful cooperation and for a debate between the representatives of both sides.[28]

Such a debate, this time not conceived as a specific theological controversy, but supposed to cover the whole problem, really took place the following day and made Friday, October 18 (8) the decisive turning point of the whole Synod. In any case, that private conference at Ostrogski's residence proved much more important and revealing than the rather awkward repetition of the exchange of formal messages between Rahoza and Nicephorus, which was so obviously leading nowhere.

Neither of the two ecclesiastical leaders was present at the long meeting[29]. While the royal delegates brought with them, as theological experts, only Father Skarga and another Jesuit, Rab, probably to avoid a clash between the Prince and those Ruthenian bishops with whom he had broken, Ostrogski was accompanied at their own request by the two bishops who were completely under his control, viz. Bałaban and Kopysteński, and apparently also by

---

[27] *Ibidem,* fol. 478v.

[28] *Russk. istor. bibl.,* VII, 942 f.

[29] This is probably the reason why that meeting is not mentioned at all in N where only the last conference of the royal delegates with Ostrogski is described; in A, 2, there is only a brief summary of all these conferences.

a few Protestants. But theological questions were not touched at all, and the whole conference turned into a discussion between the three senators who favored the Union and the one who opposed it.[30]

The representatives of the King first expressed his pleasure that all Ruthenian bishops including Bałaban and Kopysteński, as evidenced by their signatures, had decided for that Union, without having been persuaded and even less forced to do so by the King. They further recalled that Ostrogski himself had worked for the Union through Possevino at the time of Pope Gregory XIII, and they clearly explained why Sigismund III could not grant three requests which the Prince had made in connection with the present Synod : neither Protestants nor the Greek Nicephorus could be admitted, the former because only the relations between Orthodox and Catholics were on the agenda, the latter as a notorious enemy of the country who quite recently escaped from his Moldavian prison ; and no appeal from the decisions of the Synod to the Diet could be permitted, since Parliament had no competence in religious matters. The conclusion was a warning that although the Prince, contrary to his own request and the King's order had brought to the Synod armed forces and from the outset split the Synod in two, the senators would not tolerate any violent disturbance of the deliberations of the bishops who had decided for the Union.

Turning to the two recalcitrant bishops and to the nobles who surrounded Ostrogski, the royal delegates complained about the methods used by the opposition which instead of looking for an understanding with them had organized some kind of separate dietine with the participation of heretics and under the leadership of an apparent spy and was usurping the power to depose their own pastors. The complete dependence of the Patriarchs of Constantinople on the authority of the Turkish Sultan was most emphatically stressed, and finally an appeal in favor of reunion with Rome was made in the name of the King [31].

There was no immediate answer, and instead of entering in the expected discussion which Ostrogski had suggested himself, he and his companions left the conference and went to the countersynod which, probably in the same building, was continuing its separate deliberations from the morning of that critical day. After long debates, Nicephorus, creating again appearances of a conciliatory spirit, proposed to send for the third time a delegation to the Metropolitan and his supporters, inviting them to come to " our Synod ; " and he added : " May be they will change their minds and after conversion will be healed by the Church " which is always ready to forgive repenting sinners. [32]

---

[30] *Russk. istor. bibl.*, VII, 943-952.
[31] See also Russk. istor. bibl., VII, 1043 (*Apokrisis*).
[32] N, fol. 479.

It seems, however, that simultaneously with such an invitation the answer of both groups of the opposition, the nobles and the clergy, to the admonitions of the royal representatives was sent to them, of course, after consultation with Ostrogski. That answer started with an expression of thanks for the King's solicitude in the matter of religious unity, but recalled the failure of earlier attempts in the same direction and therefore claimed that this time the union should be based on more lasting foundations. The obvious conclusion was a request that the whole matter, at present entrusted to " suspect " bishops, be postponed until all differences in doctrine and rite between the Western and the Eastern Church were settled, not at the present Synod where this was impossible, but with the agreement of the whole Eastern Church and particularly the Patriarchs. In support of that statement, Archimandrite Tur, after giving a survey of the background of the negotiations, quoted instructions received from the Orthodox nobility of various provinces. [33]

It is easy to recognize in these demands the condition which Ostrogski had already three years ago put forward in his correspondence with Pociej, considering impossible any regional Union, before a universal one with all Eastern Patriarchates could be concluded, a scheme which was obviously impracticable and out of the question. In other words, it was a proposal to postpone any union indefinitely. Taking that position, the counter-synod pledged to remain faithful for the time being to the Eastern faith and tradition, recognized by earlier royal charters, and not to admit the slightest change, a special reference being made to the old calendar though the acceptance of the new one was not requested anyway in the Union of Rome.

All this was emphatically recommended by Nicephorus in a long speech which he delivered while the opposition was waiting for the Metropolitan's reply to their invitation. And a similar address was delivered on that occasion by Cyril Lucaris, the representative of the Patriarch of Alexandria, who used the Latin language which even to the Orthodox noblemen was much more familiar than the Greek. [34] They had not yet finished when the expected answer was brought by the emissaries sent to Rahoza. According to an account hostile to the Union, [35] he would have said : " Rightly or wrongly we have surrendered to the Western Church " — a strange statement indeed which would give the impression that he still was not fully convinced of having taken the correct decision. However, the semiofficial report of one of Nicephorus' collaborators [36] quotes an entirely different reply : the Metropolitan simply confirmed his answer given to the earlier

[33] Russk. istor. bibl. VII, 9 52, XIX, 354-359 ; *Arkhiv Yugo-Zap. Rossii, I-I* Nr. 121.
[34] N, fol. 479v.
[35] *Russk. istor. bibl.*, XIX, 346.
[36] N, fol. 479-480.

invitation, pointing out that he wanted to study well the whole problem with the other members of the Synod, in particular the chief representative of the Holy See, Archbishop Solikowski, and the other Ruthenian bishops, in order to find out whether it was necessary to come to see the members of the opposition.

Obviously he still wanted and hoped to avoid a final break, and the same attitude was taken by the royal delegates who throughout the whole day, as they had done the day before, tried everything possible to make Ostrogski change his mind and accept the Union, being fully aware that all depended, as a matter of fact, on the old Prince. Each of the three senators had private talks with him [37] in which they explained in particular that Nicephorus whom he so strongly supported, not only had no authority whatever to speak in the matter of reunion, but having been involved in the Moldavian troubles and having escaped from prison, ought to be surrendered to the King for investigation by Ostrogski who otherwise would be suspected himself of conspiracy and rebellion. In that connection they blamed the Palatine of Kiev, as the King had done before the Synod in his message, for his ingratitude towards Sigismund III and his inconsistency, so that the Prince really seemed impressed and worried about his own situation even more than about the Synod.

Particularly important was a last minute effort made later in the day when Ostrogski in the midst of the deliberations of the antisynod was called once more to such a private meeting with the King's representatives, [38] which lasted so long that Nicephorus became seriously alarmed. The Palatine of Kiev was accompanied on that occasion by his younger son Alexander, Palatine of Volhynia, who was not yet a convert to Catholicism like his elder brother the Castellane of Cracow, but in any case was considered less adamant and opposed to the Union than his father. On the other hand, the three Lithuanian senators had again brought with them Father Skarga who implemented their arguments, this time chiefly religious and concerning the primacy of the Vicar of Christ as well as the whole doctrine of the Roman Church, by delivering an address which, according to the other side, lasted three or four hours and was full of " blasphemies " against Orthodoxy. But the only two concrete matters which were singled out in these critiques as especially shocking, were not at all of a doctrinal character and could really influence the two Princes. First, the eloquent Jesuit recalled once more the humiliating dependence of the Greek Patriarchs on the Turkish " tyrant " whom they had to appease by regular payments, being thus unable, if not unwilling, to help the Ruthenian Church. Further-

---

[37] These talks are summarized by Arcudius (A, 2).

[38] Described in detail N, fol. 484-485v. In Skarga's brief account (*Russk. istor. bibl.*, VII, 952) not his own speech but the arguments of the royal delegates receive special attention.

more, he opposed their neglect to the loving care of the Pope for the poor
and destitute Ruthenians, announcing the foundation of a seminary for
them which Clement VIII had promised to endow through the intermediary
of their bishops sent to Rome ; he even gave concrete figures in order to
illustrate the Pope's solicitude for the education of the Ruthenians, a question which always had seriously interested Constantine Ostrogski.

But neither he, nor even his son, nor even less Bałaban and Kopysteński who also participated in some at least of these talks, were convinced
and instead of influencing their followers in the sense suggested by the
royal delegates and by Skarga, they returned to them and continued to
participate in their deliberations which were going on all the time. However, even at the antisynod [39] there were many, particularly among the
nobles, who, though opposed to the Union, were not fully convinced of
Nicephorus' ecclesiastical authority, and when it was openly proposed to
remove the bishops who were favorable to the Union, from their sees and
no longer to recognize them as pastors in view of their unforgivable " blasphemies against the Holy Spirit, " the rather unknown foreigner who pretended to represent the Patriarch, was specifically asked whether he really
had the power to depose members of the hierarchy. It was then that
Nicephorus submitted the document he had received a few years before by
Patriarch Jeremiah and which included indeed, among many others, the
right to depose even the highest dignitaries of the Church. And though
serious doubts in that matter were to reappear even the next day, there
started at once a strong pressure to carry out that radical decision. Yet,
Nicephorus was wise enough not to proceed with any undue hurry and
suggested himself to send once more an urgent invitation to the Metropolitan
and his supporters to join the opposition under the formal threat of deposition. This time the answer for which the emissaries of the antisynod
had to wait several hours, was an unequivocal refusal and a clear declaration that the Union would not be given up. Nevertheless, the invitation
was repeated [40] by more than twenty members of the Orthodox clergy and
laity who tried in vain to find Rahoza at his headquarters and were not
received by him. Therefore another delegation brought him a little later
the act of deposition which had been drafted in the meantime. But the
Metropolitan and the other bishops refused to recognize that decision, protested against the unprecedented attempt to remove the legitimate pastors

---

[39] See the account of that session N., fol. 480-481v.

[40] According to N, fol. 481v, this happened in the morning of the following day,
but here the chronology of the report is obviously confused ; see Chodynicki, op.
cit., 332, who based his presentation upon the text of the reply of the antisynod
to the proposals of the royal delegates, published in " Apokrisis " (Russk. istor. bibl.,
VII, 1043 f.).

through an undisciplined action of the flocks, and appealed to those who had sent the message, warning them against such a rebellion. [41]

The pressure to go ahead with the deposition continued, and the delegates from the various communities whom Ostrogski had brought to Brest, produced their " instructions, " [42] pledging them not to give up their Orthodox faith, not to join the " apostates " who were introducing innovations, whether great or small, but on the contrary to request their expulsion. Therefore, when the Prince returned from his last conference with the royal delegates, all those present at the antisynod, according to the official record, [43] asked Nicephorus to proceed with the excommunication of those who had given up the religion of their fathers and conspired against the authority of the Church. But even then, the astute Greek who was receiving at the same time serious warnings from the other side decided to delay the solemn proclamation of the deposition of almost the whole Ruthenian hierarchy until the morning of the next day, Saturday, October 19 (9 old style).

When that day started, [44] it clearly appeared that Nicephorus had to face not only threats from the Catholic side, but the continued suspicion of many of the Orthodox. For once more was he asked by their own leaders whether he was entitled to depose the Metropolitan and so many bishops. He therefore made another speech in which he had to concede publicly that he was generally suspected to be a spy — of course of the Turks — and to conspire against the authorities of the realm. Showing again the document of the late Patriarch, which was read to all on that occasion, he succeeded to convince the Ruthenian lords and the whole assembly that far from being a spy and " preparing ambushes, " he was a " teacher of the Church " and an exarch of the Patriarchate and therefore authorized to proclaim the planned deposition according to canon law. Furthermore, it was decided that before that solemn procedure, the final act of deposition which had been rejected the day before by those concerned, should be brought by twelve prominent noblemen to the cathedral where the Synod was in session.

This was indeed a critical moment, because the representatives of the opposition obviously wanted to read that act before all those who were just engaged in the final deliberations regarding the ratification of the Union. Even the most enthusiastic supporters of that Union were rightly afraid that such a humiliation of the pro-Roman hierarchy before all the

---

[41] N, fol. 483.

[42] That word " *Instructiones* " appears in Latin in the Greek text of the report (fol. 483v).

[43] N, fol. 485v-486.

[44] See the account of that session N, fol. 486-486v.

people assembled in church would have caused a great deal of trouble [45] and at least interrupted the work of the Synod. It was, therefore, quite natural that on that occasion the armed forces of the public authorities made their only interference with the growing conflict of the two rivaling assemblies. At the order of the royal delegates and in particular of the one of them, Demetrius Chalecki, who was the local Starosta, these soldiers who never disturbed the activities of the opposition did not permit that opposition either to disturb the legitimate synod : they stopped its twelve delegates at the door of the Cathedral which they had surrounded and did not allow anybody to enter.

The nobles opposed to the Union, that is Ostrogski and his followers, were of course indignant, [46] but their anger was mainly directed against the " apostates " who had " fooled " them and were now in position to disregard the Patriarch or rather his doubtful representative. Even Nicephorus himself who now delivered a lengthy and pathetic address, [47] did not blame the King, stressing on the contrary that the Synod had gathered at his order and identifying as usual his own group with the Synod ; he turned exclusively against " Michael, " viz., Metropolitan Rahoza and the bishops on his side. Recalling that they had been invited three or four times to come and to justify themselves, he summed up all the charges against them, made them responsible for the consequences, that is their deposition, and then proceeded to the well prepared ceremony of public condemnation.

Amidst the silent assembly before two candlelights with the Holy Gospel between them, he started reading in Greek the document, which could not be read in the Cathedral, in the presence of the condemned and of their adherents. But even limited to the opposition, the captive audience was not only " weeping bitterly, " but, as the official record noted, [48] was " stunned by such a terrible and alarming event, because they had never seen anything similar. " It was, indeed, for the first time in history that a Metropolitan of Kiev and five prominent members of the hierarchy were removed from their sees, which some of them had occupied for years, by a representative of Constantinople of a highly doubtful character. Nevertheless, Nicephorus now disregarded a last minute warning not to dare such an intervention which was brought to him in the name of the royal delegates. An otherwise unknown protonotary, Nestorius, read after him the verdict in the Ruthenian language, and Nicephorus concluded

---

[45] This is pointed out by Arcudius (A, 2) at the beginning of his account.
[46] N, fol. 486v.
[47] *Ibidem*, fol. 487-488 ; see also *Russk. istor. bibl.*, XIX, 371 ff.
[48] *Ibidem*, fol. 488v ; the act of excommunication has been published (*Akty Zap. Rossii*, IV, Nr. 104) but according to Chodynicki (*loc. cit.*, note 2) not in its final form.

the ceremony, calling upon both, the clergy and the faithful, not to obey any longer the deposed bishops, but " to despise them as they had despised God and his Church. "

It so happened, however, that when he still was talking the bells of all churches started ringing and a great movement in the city attracted the attention of the people, confusing those who were present at the anti-synod. For in the meantime the real synod had successfully ended its deliberations and was going to celebrate the happy conclusion of the Union. [49] Having lost any hope to appease Prince Ostrogski, the royal representatives decided to do without him and called upon the Metropolitan and his supporters not to delay any longer the solemn proclamation and celebration of the great event, the charter of ratification being already written, signed and sealed. It was hardly necessary that in another measure of precaution armed forces took position in the gateways of the city and around both the Latin and Greek churches to protect the procession which now started against any possible act of violence : as a matter of fact, even the most hostile witnesses had to recognize the impressive and dignified character of what was going on with the participation of a large crowd of people, clergy and laymen, and after seeing this, they could only quietly go home. Bearing the Holy Sacrament and singing aloud the *Te Deum*, the Ruthenian bishops who had remained faithful to their decision and were surrounded by the papal and royal representatives, proceeded through the streets of Brest and went first to the Ruthenian St. Nicholas' Church, all being dressed in their pontifical vestments either Greek or Latin. The Metropolitan celebrated Holy Mass and then the Archbishop of Polotsk read first the papal bull addressed to the Ruthenian hierarchy and then their reply, the final act of ratification which was to be sent to Rome. After singing there the *Te Deum* in Ruthenian, the procession moved in turn to the Latin Church of St. Mary's where in a symbolic gesture they placed the Holy Sacrament brought from the Greek Church and where after singing again the same hymn of triumph, the bishops of either rite embraced one another exchanging " the *osculum pacis* with such solemnity and pleasure that no similar act had taken place after that of the Council of Florence. " That comment, emphasizing the continuity of tradition leading from Florence to Brest, was made by the Catholic Greek Arcudius who witnessed the memorable event.

Finally, a step was taken which was to counteract the decree of deposition issued by Nicephorus and, as the opposition complained, " to turn into ridicule " their decision. For the real Synod issued in turn a decree

<hr />

[49] The accounts of Arcudius and of the companion of Nicephorus (A, 2, and N, fol. 488v-489), though representing two entirely different viewpoints, perfectly supplement one another and are in agreement as to all facts. It is, therefore, on these sources that the following description is based.

deposing Bałaban and Kopysteński, the only two Ruthenian bishops who had dissociated themselves from the others and participated in the anti-synod whose members, including Archimandrite Tur, were now excommunicated by the Metropolitan. [50] That verdict was duly forwarded to them.

October 19 (or 9) must, therefore, be considered the historical date of the Union of Brest, or the ratification of the Union of Rome — that regional revival of the Union of Florence among the Ruthenians of the Polish-Lithuanian Commonwealth. But the Synod was not concluded before the following day, Sunday, October 20 (or 10), and this is equally true of the antisynod.

As to the legitimate Synod, [51] its members, including the Latin prelates, attended Holy Mass at the Ruthenian Church of St. Nicholas, where in the presence again of the papal and royal delegates, and before a numerous congregation, Father Skarga delivered a sermon on the unity of the Church of God. This had been the title and theme of his famous book first published nineteen years before, and nobody was better qualified to praise the blessings of the Union, than the learned Jesuit who through the changing conditions of the whole lifetime of the last generation had worked so patiently and successfully for the great cause which he now saw achieved. On that same day Metropolitan Rahoza, whose contribution came later and not without some apparent hesitation, but was nevertheless decisive were it only because of his office, issued a pastoral letter [52] in which he informed the faithful of the whole ecclesiastical province, the Ruthenian clergy and people of the concluded Union and also of the deposition of the bishops of Lwów and Przemyśl, threatening with excommunication, similar to that cast upon the members of the antisynod, all those who would still recognize them.

No less active was on that Sunday the other side. There were first meetings of the nobles at Ostrogski's residence and of the clergy under the presidency of Nicephorus. The members of both groups signed and sealed the verdict condemning the Metropolitan and the bishops who supported him, [53] the final text of that document being probably established only now. [54] Motivating the depositions, it was pointed out that accepting the Union, these bishops acted not only against the Patriarch of Constantinople, their superior, but also against the decrees of the second, fourth and sixth oecumenical councils, because they turned to another Patriarch who according to these councils was nothing but an equal of that of Constantinople, and admitted everything in which the Western Church differed from the

[50] *Akty Zap. Rossii*, IV, Nr. 107-108.
[51] See the brief accounts of Arcudius (A. 2) and Skarga, *Russk. ist. bibl.*, VII, 957.
[52] *Akty Zap. Rossii*, IV, Nr. 109.
[53] N, fol. 489-489v.
[54] *Russk. istor. bibl.*, XIX, 371-376.

Eastern. In addition to an arbitrary interpretation of the decisions of the earlier councils where at least the honorary primacy of the Pope had been recognized, there appeared once more the basic difference between the two camps, one of which based its whole action upon the decision of the Council of Florence while the other simply ignored that Council of 1439.

Once more, too, the opposition tried to reach Rahoza and to hand him personally their verdict. This time it was Tur, the Archimandrite of the Kiev Monastery, who was entrusted with that mission and succeeded in meeting the Metropolitan at the residence of the local bishop, Pociej. While they were arguing about the signatures and the authority of the antisynod, the three royal delegates joined them and protested against Tur's message, calling it an open act of disobedience against the King. Knowing, however, very well who was really responsible for it, they decided to take another step in dealing directly with Ostrogski. But they did not repeat their personal interventions which had proved useless to the obvious detriment of the King's authority : they sent to the Prince three noblemen of minor rank, one of whom, the Castellane of Kamieniec Pretwicz, had already been used before in the endless negotiations with the Palatine of Kiev. They had to recall to him that in the presence of representatives of the King nobody had the right to issue any statement without submitting it in advance to their approval. The decree of the meeting which opposed the Union was, therefore, null and void, and offensive to the royal delegates.

Ostrogski in reply to that communication merely expressed his astonishment that these delegates could feel offended in view of what he himself and his party suffered from those who had abandoned the Eastern Church and from their supporters meaning, of course, the three senators themselves. He failed, however, to specify what these alleged sufferings were and simply stressed that in any case he would not change his attitude. Hulewicz who was present as Speaker of the lay section of the antisynod, added that the verdict was sent to the Metropolitan not only in the name of the Prince, but on behalf of all of them who were ready to send it to the royal delegates also. Their three spokesmen refused to talk with him at all, calling him an Anabaptist and stressing once more that members of other denominations had nothing to say in the discussions between Catholic and Orthodox. Nevertheless, the antisynod elected four delegates to approach directly the three senators and to ask them what the King really wanted. The answer was that he wanted all followers of the Eastern Church to unite with the Church of Rome. At the same time they were told that Nicephorus, too, had no right to interfere with the Ruthenian Church and was, according to reports received from the Prince of Moldavia, a Turkish spy. [55]

---

[55] These last discussions with the royal delegates are described in fragmentary notes of a representative of the opposition, published in *Akty Zap. Rossii*, IV, Nr. 106, p. 145.

— 384 —

After all these exchanges of messages and replies, which remained as
fruitless as the direct contacts of the responsible leaders in the preceding
days, the opposition which after Sunday Mass had also listened to a sermon
praising them for tirelessly defending their faith, decided to appeal to Sigismund III himself, [56] choosing as their delegates two Orthodox noblemen
from Volhynia, the same partisans of Ostrogski whom the Prince had used
in a similar mission shortly before the Synod. [57] The Prince and his followers
also sent appeals to the dietines of the Ruthenian provinces of Poland
and Lithuania, calling upon them to instruct their deputies to the next
Diet to support the protests against the Union of Brest. [58] The next day,
October 21, Ostrogski left Brest with all his followers, disappointed indeed
because after spending so much effort, time, and money, he had not succeeded in preventing the Union, but decided to repay his own " very great
confusion, " [59] by creating confusion in the whole country. With the same
purpose in mind, Nicephorus, on that same Monday, imitating the Metropolitan's action in issuing the pastoral letter of October 20, sent out an
appeal to the same Ruthenian clergy, [60] warning them in the name of the
Patriarch — though the see of Constantinople continued to be vacant — not
to follow the deposed members of the hierarchy, and requesting them to
elect another Metropolitan and other bishops, loyal to the Patriarchate.

It was, therefore, obvious that the division which, without delaying the
Union any longer and without leading to any disturbance of the public
order, had so painfully appeared during the Synod of Brest, would continue
unabated, the scene of the conflict being merely transferred, contrary to
the King's desire, to the Diet which was to convene in Warsaw in the
spring of 1597 and where also the political aspect of Nicephorus' case was
to be considered. However, in order to realize the chances of both the
Union and the protests against it, the texts of the documents which were
drafted in Brest in that matter and were the concrete result of the synod,
must be carefully studied.

Most memorable was indeed the Charter of Union itself, [61] written in

---

[56] N, 489v.
[57] See above, in the preceding chapter, p. 360. They were M. Maliński and W.
Drzewiński, of whom the latter actively participated in the struggle against the
Union at the subsequent Diets ; see Chodynicki, op. cit., 323 et passim.
[58] Russk. istor. bibl., XIX, 1049.
[59] A, 2.
[60] Akty Zap. Rossii, IV, Nr. 111 ; pending the establishment of a new Patriarch,
he recommended to mention in all prayers the deceased Patriarch Gabriel.
[61] The Ruthenian original and a contemporary Latin translation, slightly different
from that published by A. Theiner, Vetera Monum. Pol., III, Nr. 195, are preserved
in the Vatican Archives, A. A. Arm. I-XVIII, 1847. See G. Hofmann, " Wiedervereinigung, " Orientalia Christiana, III-2, 131 note 3. Of the nine seals only seven
are preserved, and the original is now so pale that it can hardly be read, as can be
seen from the photographic reproduction in Hr. Lushnytskyi, Ukrainska cerkva mizh

Ruthenian and read at the impressive ceremony of October 9, that old style date appearing on the document itself. Comparatively brief and not returning to all the problems decided by the Union of Rome of which this was the requested and promised ratification, the document was nothing but a historical survey of the whole story of the schism and of the reunion. The signatories recalled first, the original unity of the Church which Christ himself had founded on the rock of Peter and which had lasted under one authority from Apostolic times throughout all centuries. It was strongly emphasized that the supreme authority of Peter's successor, the Roman Pope, was recognized by all patriarchs in matters of faith and jurisdiction, as evidenced by the Councils, canon law, and the Fathers of the Church, and in particular by " our Slavic scriptures long ago translated from the Greek. " This was recognized — so the text continued — in agreement with the Fathers of the Eastern Church, by the Patriarchs of Constantinople also, " from whom this Ruthenian land had taken its faith " and who for a long time were under the authority of the See of Rome.

After so stressing that at the time of the conversion of St. Vladimir Constantinople had been in Union with Rome, it was indeed admitted that its Patriarchs " many times " abandoned that union, but also returned to it again. And after that brief reference to the vicissitudes in the relations between both Sees, the Council of Florence received special attention : in 1439 Constantinople through Patriarch Joseph, whose death shortly before the conclusion of the Union was disregarded, and Emperor John Palaeologus, returned to the obedience of the Roman Pope and recognized him as the head of all Christendom and rightful successor of St. Peter ; the expressions which were used in that connection were to indicate clearly that the primacy of Rome, then recognized, was one of authority and jurisdiction, and not merely of honor, though the text of 1439 was not quoted verbatim, nor the formula of Pociej's and Terlecki's profession of faith repeated. There followed a reference to " our " Metropolitan Isidore who brought that Union of the Patriarchate of Constantinople " and of all Churches which belonged to it " to the Ruthenian lands and established there the supremacy of the Roman Church. It was for that reason that the Kings of Poland, and in particular Władysław III of Poland and Hungary, granted privileges to the clergy of Greek rite and conceded to that clergy at the Diets the liberties of the Catholic Church. This was indeed the only correct interpretation of the Charter of 1443 and of its confirmation at the Diets of 1504 and 1543. It was, however, omitted that the same Charter remained in force and other privileges were granted to the Ruthenian Church even though that Church no longer observed the decrees

---

skhodom i zakhodom (The Ukrainian Church between East and West), Philadelphia 1954, 268.

25

of the Council of Florence and continued to be under Patriarchs of Constantinople separated from Rome. It only was pointed out that these Patriarchs were punished for their return to schism and for disrupting the Union by coming under the " pagan " yoke of the Turks. And this again led to a great neglect of the ecclesiastical control of the Ruthenian lands, where " heresies spread and dominated almost all Ruś, devastating the churches and corrupting the worship of God. "

The connection between the consequences of the Greek schism and the danger of Protestant penetration among the Ruthenians was again emphasized, when the following section of the charter briefly described Pociej's and Terlecki's mission to Rome " with the knowledge, permission, and support of King Sigismund III, " and the Union concluded there a year before, when Pope Clement VIII liberated the Ruthenian Church from the control of the Patriarchs of Constantinople and accepted its obedience " conserving the rites and ceremonies of the Eastern Greek Churches and not making any changes in our Churches, " again a proclamation of the unaltered, traditional continuity of religious life which the Union respected and guaranteed.

Even briefer was the reference to what had happened in Brest : the Pope had ordered that a Synod be convoked by the Ruthenian hierarchy, where they would all make their profession of faith and declaration of obedience to the Roman See, to Clement VIII and his successors. " This we did today at the present Synod, " handing over the signed and sealed document to the three representatives of the Pope, in the presence of the three delegates of the King " and of many other clergymen and laymen. " The names of the Polish bishops and of the Lithuanian senators who witnessed the Union, were followed by the signatures of Metropolitan Rahoza, of the five other members of the hierarchy, and — replacing in a certain sense the two bishops who had changed their minds — of three Archimandrites who joined the Union.

The reaction and conflicting interpretation of those opposed to the Union were first expressed in a short protest which was drafted immediately after the proclamation of that Union and dated, like the act of the hierarchy, October 9 (old style). [62] It was issued on behalf of all those who attended the convention at Ostrogski's headquarters, which they claimed to be the real synod. But, strange enough, the laymen : " senators, dignitaries, officials, and knights " of Greek Oriental religion are mentioned first, the words " also the clergymen " coming afterwards. And while it was natural not to use the name of Nicephorus, nor of any other foreigner, it is surprising not to find in the text any reference to the two bishops who refused to join the Union. That Union is called " some kind of agreement

[62] *Arkhiv Yugo-Zap. Rossii*, I-1, 530 f.

concerning the Greek and Roman Churches, " of which " we received certain notice today, " confirmed by the royal envoys to the Synod. Without entering into any further details about the negotiations between the two assemblies, the protest simply said that the agreement was concluded and proclaimed by the Metropolitan and a few bishops, apostates of the Greek Church, who the day before had been deposed and deprived of their ecclesiastical offices. There followed an emphatic declaration, that protesting against such a " wrong deed, " the signatories would oppose it, God helping, with all their power, and in particular through requests addressed to the King. This protest, as added at the end, was being sent to the court of Brest to be inserted in its records. Once more, however, it appeared how important it was that one of the royal representatives at the Synod, Grand Treasurer Chalecki, was holding at the same time the office of Starosta of Brest. As such he was in control of the local court and did not permit to file a protest which, in his opinion, was a misrepresentation of what had happened at the Synod and an expression of contempt for the Union and the Ruthenian hierarchy. Therefore, the signatories had to approach the court of another district, that of Volodymir in Volhynia, where it was accepted but could not have the same significance. [63]

In any case, much more important than such a protest drafted in general terms and without any specific arguments and suggestions, were the instructions given the same day to the two delegates of the opposition,[64] who were to turn directly to Sigismund III since the last negotiations with his envoys proved of no avail. As a matter of fact, the protest itself indicated such an appeal to the King as the starting point of the planned action. And it was only natural that the instruction given to Maliński and Drzewiński faithfully reflected the opinions which the leader of the opposition, Prince Ostrogski, had expressed before and during the Synod.

Following his usual approach to the problem, the lords, dignitaries, and nobles of Greek religion, both in the Kingdom of Poland and the Grand Duchy of Lithuania — only the noble laymen without any reference to the clergy and the people at large — started by thanking Sigismund III for his " fatherly " endeavors to unite the Eastern and the Western Church, assuring that they desired such a union themselves. But since they knew from history, how often similar attempts had failed, they did not want to join something that could not possibly endure. And they gave, as Ostrogski had done before, the reasons why, in their opinion, such were precisely the prospects of the Union of Brest.

The first and basic objection was its merely regional character, an objection which reappeared so many times in the history of the various efforts

---

[63] *Ibidem*, 531 f ; a contemporary copy is in the Polish Library in Paris, *Ms.* 11, *Nr.* 38.

[64] *Ibidem*, 510-517.

to heal the Eastern Schism step by step, through special agreements with individual Eastern Churches of individual countries. As to the Ruthenian Church, the instruction pointed out that it was only part of the Eastern Church as a whole and had been for six hundred years under the Patriarchs of Constantinople, so that it was inappropriate to abandon them and to accept the Union without their permission at a local, particular synod. That six hundred years ago the Patriarchs themselves had been in union with Rome, and that at the given moment the Patriarchate was vacant and its representative of highly dubious character, this was, of course, not taken into consideration.

Purely personal and dictated by Ostrogski's animosity against the supporters of the Union of Brest, including his former friend Pociej with whom he had discussed the same points at the beginning of the negotiations, was the second reason for rejecting that Union: the bishops to whom its conclusion had been entrusted, did not deserve confidence. No arguments were given in support of such a charge which would have been much more justified with regard to one at least of the bishops opposing the Union in its final phase along with Ostrogski: Gedeon Bałaban.

The real motives of the opposition appeared in the third point which, however, was directed not only against a regional union, but against any union with Rome as such. They refused to accept a union with the Western Church which recognizes the Pope as head of the Church of Christ, while the Eastern Church sees only Christ himself as its head. Furthermore, the papal Church was different from the Eastern in many matters of doctrine and rite. The differences of doctrine were not specified, and it was disregarded that the Union of Brest, similar to that of Florence, admitted the traditional differences of rite. Significant was, however, that the instruction, returning to its first objection specifically directed against the Union of Brest, added that such differences could not be removed at a particular synod, as if the oecumenical Synod of Florence, never even mentioned by the opposition, had not clarified these controversial issues long ago, and as if another oecumenical synod would have been possible at the given moment. Even more significant was the conclusion, the only concrete, positive request submitted to the King: he was asked to remove from their offices the Metropolitan and the bishops who remained on his side, and to entrust those offices, viz., the six sees in question, to other candidates. Quoting in that connection the constitutions of 1575, 1576, and 1589, the opposition recognized that the final decision as to the appointments of the Orthodox bishops was reserved to the King, and that the depositions made by Nicephorus at the Synod of Brest needed the confirmation of Sigismund III.

For similar reasons, the supporters of the Union who had excommunicated and deposed Bałaban and Kopysteński, had been wondering, before the Synod adjourned, how their sentence would be carried out. [65] In the case of the former, the Ruthenian Bishop of Lwów, who already on an earlier occasion had been excommunicated by Rahoza, doubts were raised as to the validity of his appointment, and it was planned to cancel it through common agreement of all the other bishops of Eastern rite, including the Metropolitan, and also of the Latin Archbishop of the same city. As to the Ruthenian Bishop of Przemyśl, it was pointed out as an additional argument against him that having been married at the time of his appointment, he continued to live with his wife. These considerations seemed to indicate that the opposition against the Union was not considered a fully sufficient reason for deposing these bishops. And here again the final decision seemed to rest with the King.

This was in particular the opinion of the Greek promoter of the Union of Brest, Peter Arcudius who, in general, was surprised to find so much freedom in Poland [66] and always was ready to rely upon the King's *bracchium saeculare*. He did it even in the matter of the calendar [67] which was raised again at the Synod of Brest, though Rome did not insist upon the acceptance of the revised Gregorian Calendar by the reunited Ruthenians. In the course of these deliberations, it was suggested that each of their bishops should determine the date when the new calendar should be introduced in his diocese, and that the King, taking into consideration the local differences, should instruct the various Palatines and Starostas to support these decisions. It was, however, realized that this was an issue which could cause, as in the past, serious disturbances among the people, and following the wise example of the Holy See, the whole idea of enforcing the reformed calendar, desirable as it would have been for practical reasons, was soon completely abandoned in order not to strengthen the opposition against the Union which indeed did not require such a unification in a non-religious matter.

Another, much more important problem which was touched during the Synod of Brest, though with so many others it was overshadowed by the efforts to appease the opposition, was that of the seminary for the Ruthenians. Mentioned by Skarga in the debates with Ostrogski, it was the main concern of Arcudius [68] who was to be in charge of that badly needed educational center, worrying about the financial difficulties, but happy to see that in agreement with his earlier suggestions, the majority of the hierarchy, with the exception of Pociej who continued to want the seminary in his own Brest, considered Wilno the most appropriate place for that

---

[65] Both cases are discussed by Arcudius in his letter of Nov. 10 (A, 2).

[66] At the beginning of that same letter he writes about " *la libertà che comporta questo Regno* " and its possible consequences.

[67] *Ibidem*, in the paragraph following the reference to the two deposed bishops.

[68] See his letters of both June 20, at the end, and Nov. 10 (A, 1, 2).

foundation which was to supplement there the Jesuit university and the seminary for the clergy of Latin rite.

This was to be one of the many problems of the future resulting from the Synod of Brest where only preparatory discussions in the matter could take place. There was, on the contrary, much immediate interest in the question of ascertaining that no change would have to be made in the old ceremonies of the Eastern Church. It was in particular the Metropolitan himself who continued to be concerned with that issue which he had always stressed in his earlier statements and private letters and which seems to have been the only motive of his initial wavering. Nobody was better qualified to appease Rahoza's apprehensions than Arcudius [69] who remaining modestly in the background as far as the work of the Synod itself was concerned, could again testify as *Romano Greco* as he called himself, that the Church of Rome did not require any change in the Greek rite. This had been one of his strongest arguments when he worked for the reunion of the Ruthenians during his first visit in their country a few years earlier. Now he celebrated Holy Mass at Brest in the presence of the old Metropolitan who was at last fully convinced and satisfied to see that the Pope had approved the maintenance of all the ceremonies to which he, with so many other Ruthenians, was deeply attached, and in spite of his age he manifested the desire to see Rome himself.

There occurred, however, a strange incident at that Mass of Arcudius : at Holy Communion he suddenly noticed that instead of wine water had been offered to him, and therefore he had to repeat the Consecration after requesting some wine, thus giving an example to Catholic Ruthenian priests how to proceed under such circumstances. Strange enough, even that incident served as an argument to some opponents of the Union who did not hesitate to pretend that God, in order to show that He did not like that Union, miraculously changed the wine into water. The shrewd Greek was quick to answer that, if so, God would have completed the miracle by changing the bread into stone, but this would have been the contrary of what He did at Cana and refused to do in the desert when tempted by the devil.

A more serious problem was the displeasure of Rahoza when he heard that Pociej and Terlecki had received in Rome a papal privilege [70] permitting them to use liturgical vestments which hitherto only the Metropolitan could bear when celebrating according to the custom of the Patriarch of Constantinople himself. But that difficulty too was satisfactorily settled

---

[69] All the following details are taken from the last part of his long letter of Nov. 20.

[70] See in the preceding chapter, p. 340.

when the two bishops promised not to take advantage of their new right when celebrating together with the Metropolitan.

Such details were giving evidence of minor troubles which would appear in the organization of the Ruthenian Church, now united with Rome, but opposed to even the slightest modification of traditional customs. But approached as they were at Brest in a true spirit of Christian charity which impressed an unprejudiced foreign observer, they were insignificant if compared with the basic difficulty which resulted from the unsettled disagreement with a well organized opposition, obviously in minority at the Synod but decided to fight against its great achievement. The decisive issue was whether in spite of that opposition it would prove possible gradually to gain all the Ruthenians for the Union of Brest, or whether that Union endangered by the split among the Ruthenians would vanish soon after the Synod just like once the Union of Florence had practically vanished not only as a universal reconciliation between Western and Eastern Christendom but even when restored in 1458 within the political boundaries of the Ruthenian lands of Poland and Lithuania. Additional but no less important were questions of the future: whether the regional Union of Brest could be extended beyond the limits of the Commonwealth, and whether its whole internal situation would not be affected by the struggle for and against that Union.

CHAPTER V

PROSPECTS FOR THE FUTURE

"The Ruthenian Synod has passed well". These few words are the only reference to the Union of Brest in Nuncio Malaspina's report of October 27, 1596,[1] which otherwise deals mainly with the problem of the anti-Ottoman league, similar in that respect to the following ones where the Union is not mentioned at all. The conclusion is clear: the Nuncio's impression after receiving the first news about the Synod, was fully optimistic, and considering the matter happily settled, he felt free to concentrate again on the big political objective of his mission. And he knew that the papal Legate, Cardinal Caetani, with whom he was in close contact, shared that optimistic opinion about the results of the Synod of Brest and the general situation.

However, what the Cardinal himself wrote to Rome the day before, October 26,[2] was much more specific and detailed as far as the Synod of the Ruthenians was concerned. Recalling the constructive contribution of the three royal delegates, of Father Skarga who received special praise, and of the three papal representatives, he explained that with the grace of God, the King's favor, and the skill of the said prelates, the Synod could treat and terminate his task much more quietly than it was expected in view of the hostility of Prince Ostrogski and the presence of his armed forces. Stressing that "almost all" had accepted and ratified what Pociej and Terlecki had brought from Rome, and that both Latins and Greeks had participated with joy and comfort in the same religious ceremonies, the Legate expressed the hope that soon the few who remained opposed would all join the Union, so piously and prudently established, especially if the old Palatine of Kiev, the supporter of all schismatics, should die. The general result would be the suppression of all heresies and errors in the Kingdom, a notable progress of the Catholic religion and of the authority of the Holy See in these remote regions — a statement which well expressed the significance of the Union of Brest as part of the Catholic restoration which Orthodox and Protestant opposed in common.

---

[1] Vatican Archives, *Borgh.* III 89 c, fol. 194.
[2] *Fondo Pio* 114, fol. 119v-120, also Bibl. Casanatense, *MS* 1563, fol. 275v-277v.

— 393 —

In an autographic postscript to that report,[3], Caetani, not without referring again to the Palatine of Kiev who, after all, seemed now to leave alone the Ruthenian bishops, added that these bishops had just arrived in Warsaw after the conclusion of the synod and would come to see the next day the papal Legate who was jubilating with them without end about the Union and was decided to recommend them to both the King and the Pope.

It was indeed in that atmosphere of exultation and optimism, that on October 27, immediately after his audience with Sigismund III, the Cardinal received the visit of these bishops or rather of their delegation composed of four of them : the Metropolitan, the Archbishop of Polotsk, the Bishop of Pinsk, and the Bishop of Łuck, while Terlecki's companion during the mission to Rome, the equally tireless and enthusiastic Pociej obviously considered it necessary to remain at his see of Brest after the Synod. That visit which greatly interested and impressed Caetani and his Italian assistants, has been described in detail by one of them, the papal Master of Ceremonies Mucante, in his diary of the Legate's mission to Poland. [4] He preceded that description by a few general remarks about the Ruthenian Church in that country and its recent synod, noting, among others, that in Poland there were sometimes bishops of Greek and of Latin rite in the same cities, the authority of the latter being greater because they were senators — one more indication that the Roman curia was well aware of the advisability to admit to the Senate the Ruthenian bishops also. As to the Synod of Brest which interested Mucante particularly since he had witnessed and described in another part of his diaries the Union of Rome which was ratified at that Synod, [5] he added to the information well known from other sources, that the Lithuanian Grand Chancellor Sapieha had been of special assistance to the papal representatives in achieving the desired result, in spite of Ostrogski's violent opposition and the defection of two of the Ruthenian bishops under the Prince's pressure.

The four who called upon Cardinal Caetani to report to him about the work of the synod, were dressed exactly as Pociej and Terlecki had been at the ceremonies in Rome. Since in contradistinction to the former — now absent — neither of the four spoke Italian or Latin, their Ruthenian address was translated by the same alumnus of the Greek College of Rome, Moschetti, who had been present with Arcudius at the Synod [6] and now served as guide to its delegates. Their report on " the happy success " of

---

[3] *Ibidem*, fol. 122v, also Bibl. Casanat., *loc. cit.*, fol. 282v-283.

[4] Vatican Archives, *Misc. Arm.* I, vol. 82, fol. 107v-110v, also in Vatican Library, *Ottobon. lat.* 2633, fol. 177v-182. Parts of that Diary have been published in Polish translation, as early as 1822, by J. Niemcewicz, *Zbiór pamiętników*, II.

[5] See above, Chap. II, p. 328.

[6] See above, Chap. IV, p. 372.

the Synod which achieved what the Pope desired, admitted that the two sides clashing at Brest had excommunicated each other, and that the two bishops who opposed the Union did it at Ostrogski's instigation. From him and in general from " the schismatics and Lutherans " the bishops loyal to Rome expected " grave persecution " and therefore asked the Legate to recommend them both to the King and to the Pope to whom this information should be forwarded.

In his reply Caetani could point out that even before the arrival of the delegates he had recommended their cause to Sigismund III and would do so again, having no doubt as to the King's favorable attitude, since he was very happy about the Union. He also promised to report to the Pope and expressed the hope that through God's mercy also the two bishops who had refused at Brest to ratify the Union would be attracted to it and to the true religion thanks to the example of the others. Finally, he stressed, as he had done writing to Rome, that Ostrogski was old and certainly would not live much longer, and then their persecution would cease, since the son of the Prince, the Castellane of Cracow, was a good Catholic.

There followed a conversation on many other questions which the four Ruthenian bishops discussed in Polish, a language which Moschetti did not understand, so that a Pole had to act as interpreter. Terlecki complained in particular that after being so well treated on his trip to Italy, he found his church at Łuck pillaged and looted by the Cossack leader Nalevayko " on the initiative and instigation " of Ostrogski. The losses suffered exceeded one hundred thousand florins, affecting both the Church and Terlecki himself. But since Nalevayko was already in prison, the Legate could ask the King that these losses be returned at least in part. In this matter, too, Caetani who had watched the struggle against Nalevayko very carefully and was aware of its political, non-religious background, promised nevertheless his support, and then accompanied his guests to the door of the reception hall and to the staircase. [7]

He was to see them again in the next three days, because similarly to the experience of Pociej and Terlecki at the papal Curia, the delegates of the Ruthenian hierarchy were honored on any convenient occasion at the royal court. Thus on October 28, [8] at a solemn Mass in St. John's Cathedral next to the royal castle of Warsaw, they were invited by the King to sit together with the prelates accompanying the Cardinal Legate whom Sigismund III informed that after Mass *Te Deum* would be sung to thank God for the conclusion of the Union. There came, however, an unexpected objection from Caetani : on the preceding evening the pleasure,

[7] How they appreciated his kindness was noted in news sent to Rome ; see *Urbin, lat.* 1605 I, fol. 5 v.

[8] Recorded in the two copies of the Diary, as quoted above in note 4, fol. 110v-111v, and fol. 182v-184.

which the Union had given him, was troubled by bad news from Hungary where the important fortress of Agria had been taken by the Turks. It was not easy to foresee what kind of repercussion that disaster, which shocked all Christendom, would have upon the attitude of the Poles towards the anti-Ottoman league. The Legate's main concern was would it make them aware that the Turkish advance was nearing Cracow or rather confirm them in their reluctance to get involved in the Emperor's unsuccessful war. [9] In any case, there appeared again some strange connection between the problems of military league and religious union : the Cardinal who otherwise would have welcomed the King's intention, feared that under such circumstances thanksgiving could be misinterpreted and observed that, after all, a *Te Deum* of thanks for the Union had already been sung at Brest.

The King agreed but the following day, October 29,[10] he gave the Ruthenian bishops another mark of esteem in the Legate's presence, on the memorable occasion of the funeral of the last member of the Jagellonian dynasty, old Queen Ann, the sister of Sigismund Augustus, widow of Stefan Báthory, and aunt of Sigismund III. The four delegates of the Synod of Brest marched in the procession, again dressed as they had been at the ceremonies at the Vatican, preceded by twelve Ruthenian musicians and followed by four Ruthenian monks. Their presence was indeed symbolic of the Ruthenian part of the Jagellonian tradition which included both the idea of a Commonwealth of federated nations and of religious unity among all of them.

Particularly instructive for the Italian Cardinal was the conversation at the dinner of October 30 [11] to which he invited the three most prominent Ruthenian bishops — the fourth, the Bishop of Pinsk having already left Warsaw — after accepting from the Archbishop of Polotsk, who continued to be particularly active in the matter, the act of ratification of the Union, which the said Archbishop had solemnly read at the Synod of Brest and which he now asked the Legate to send at once to Clement VIII. After the translation of his Polish speech, Caetani promised to do so and then continued the talks at table, the three bishops being accompanied by the four monks of their party and all of them strictly observing fast and abstinence, since it was a Wednesday. Speaking again in Polish, the bishops who probably knew very well that at Rome the reunion with the Ruthenians was sometimes considered a mere stepping stone — a " machinery " as Possevino once had written [12] — towards a similar agreement with Mos-

---

[9] See the news received in Rome about these repercussions : *Urbin. lat.* 1604, fol. 767v, 773, 782, 797, 799, 816.

[10] Recorded in the *Diary*, fol. 113, and fol. 186v.

[11] *Ibidem*, fol. 114-115, and fol. 188v-190.

[12] See above, Part III, Chap. I, p. 211.

cow and that the various " Russias " were not always clearly distinguished, seized that opportunity to submit to the Legate their own views in that controversial and confusing matter. They admitted that Muscovy, / in Poland's neighborhood and under her own Grand Duke — they did not cal him Tsar — was a very large country — impressive figures were given in Italian miles — and that the peoples living there were observing the same rite as the Ruthenians " but they are schismatics, and do not want by any means to unite themselves with the Holy See nor to recognize the Pope as head of the whole Church. Furthermore, they abhor the Catholics and hold that only theirs is the true Christian faith and that we and all the others are in error. " They also said — continued Mucante's diary — " that those Muscovites have many rites and abuses repugnant to the Catholic faith, and practically hold St. Nicholas in greater veneration and reverence than Christ our Lord, the True God and Savior of the World. " Although that last charge, if correctly recorded, was an obvious exaggeration and hardly taken seriously, the general picture of the religious situation in Moscow, which the Legate received not from Latin Poles nor from political leaders but from Ruthenians profoundly attached to the Eastern rite and prominent members of their hierarchy, was a most valuable piece of information which could dissipate many illusions in that matter.

Obviously Caetani's guests returned on that occasion to their own worries also, and admitted that they were rather afraid of " persecutions from the people in their cities who adhering to the Palatine of Kiev " resented that they had ratified the Union with the Holy See. Speaking in particular about the cities, the bishops were probably thinking chiefly of the Brotherhoods in the major urban centers, which were indeed most opposed to the Union and had sent their representatives to the antisynod at Brest, [13] under Ostrogski's influence. But Rahoza did not feel certain either of the support of the Orthodox aristocracy which was connected with the old Prince through so many intimate ties. It was precisely for that reason that the Metropolitan before leaving Brest for Warsaw, had written in addition to his pastoral message a private letter [14] to that same Palatine of Nowogródek, Theodor Tyszkiewicz, whose advice he had requested more than once during the preliminary negotiations and to whom he now apologized for not having personally invited him to attend the Synod. He fully informed him now about the Union, as proclaimed on October 9, assuring, as usual, that nothing had been changed in the ceremonies of the Ruthenian Church, not even the old calendar : that Church would only cease to recognize the Patriarch who deprived the bishops of their power giving it to the Brotherhoods. Rahoza, therefore, asked Tyszkiewicz to support the Union,

[13] See above, in the preceding chapter, p. 368.
[14] *Akty Zap. Rossii*, IV, Nr. 110.

expressing only the regret that the unity was not complete, since Ostrogski and his partisans could not be persuaded by any means to join the agreement.

It was to appear soon that this appeal to the Palatine of Nowogródek was not made in vain, but the danger threatening the Union from the more powerful Palatine of Kiev remained so great that it was not astonishing at all, if the supporters of the Union returned to that disturbing issue time and again. And even the papal Legate could only repeat, concluding the talks at his dinner table, that they would certainly be protected by the King to whom he promised once more to recommend their cause, as well as to the Pope.

The Charter of Brest, as might be called the document of October 9, which the Archbishop of Polotsk had left with the Cardinal at their last meeting, was so precious, including as it did the ratification of the Union and the declaration of obedience to the Supreme Pontiff, and constituted such a voluminous object, with the nine seals attached to the parchment in wooden boxes, that Cardinal Caetani hesitated to forward it " through the ordinary way, " that is along with one of his regular reports, fearing that it could be lost. Finally, as he wrote to Rome two months later, on December 21, 1596, [15] he decided to keep it for the time being, with " some ambition, " as he admitted, to present it in person to Clement VIII on his return to Italy. The only thing he did at once in the matter of the Union, was to take care of the Greek Arcudius who continued to assist the Ruthenian bishops and was badly in need of money for his own support : already on October 31, [16] the Legate, though busy with so many other problems, reported to the Vatican on the conditions of life of that valuable collaborator and on the detailed arrangements which he suggested regarding the payments to be made to the Greek Catholic priest.

The delay in deposing the formal charter of the Union with the Ruthenians at the Vatican, where it was to be preserved for centuries to come, was of no harm, since, after all, its text, difficult to read anyway by Italians, did not contain anything new nor unexpected, and since the information on what happened in Brest, which reached Rome within a few weeks through Caetani's letters and also through other channels, was comprehensive enough to convey to the Holy See not only the basic facts but also their optimistic interpretation by the representatives of the Holy See and by the Catholic side in general. It is true that the Synod of Brest, held in a distant land, did not produce in Italy the same strong impression as the Union of Rome which naturally was considered the decisive climax

---

[15] *Fondo Pio* 114, fol. 145, also Bibl. Casanat., *Ms.* 1563, fol. 447-447v.
[16] *Ibidem*, fol. 126-127, also Bibl. Casanat., *loc. cit.*, fol. 286-287.

of the whole story. But at the Vatican itself, the satisfaction was great [17] when the reports of Caetani and Malaspina were confirmed by both the papal and royal delegates to the Synod. To all of them, to the three Latin bishops who had in their hands the individual professions of faith of their colleagues of Eastern rite, and to the three Senators whose co-operation guaranteed the support of the public authorities, Clement VIII expressed on January 18, 1597, [18] obviously after careful consideration of the whole matter, his pleasure to hear that the act which a year before was celebrated in Rome, was now ratified. Thanking them all for their contribution, the Pope on the same day sent a special brief to Archbishop Solikowski [19] who on his return from Brest where he had signed the joint report of the six, wrote from his residence in Lwów his own letter to Rome, probably with supplementary information. In his answer the Pope emphasized once more how glad he was about all what had happened in Brest " to the glory of God and to the advantage of so many souls " and praised the Lord that thanks to the Catholic leaders, and Solikowski in particular " the machinations of the ancient enemy, through which he tried to impede such a pious work, had been annihilated. " Furthermore, he requested the Latin Archbishop to continue his protection and support of the Ruthenian hierarchy, favoring their " honest desires, " so that those already united with Rome, as well as their whole nation, might be confirmed in their determination, and the others who had not yet accepted the Union, invited to " the light of Catholic truth. "

Even before these papal messages, which so strongly recommended the Union to the spiritual and secular authorities of the Commonwealth, Sigismund III took a decisive step in the same direction, making it clear that after consultation with the Ruthenian bishops and his own delegates to the Synod, he had arrived at the conclusion that the decisions taken in Brest were sound and final, and deserved his full approval and support. On December 15, 1596, [20] he issued in Warsaw an appeal to all his subjects of " Greek Ruthenian faith, " whether of higher or lower condition, clergymen or laymen, which was so strictly based upon the charter of October 19 (9), ratifying the Union, that it must have been drafted in close cooperation with those who had acted in Brest.

The King started by recognizing his obligation to promote the glory of God and the salvation of souls, especially of those of his subjects, and then gave a survey of the original unity of the Church, of the Eastern

---

[17] See a report from Rome, Nov. 27, 1596 (*Urbin. lat.* 1604, fol. 776) where the " provincial synod " of the Ruthenians is briefly, but accurately described.

[18] *Documenta Pontificia Historiam Ukrainae illustr.*, I, Nr. 161. Malaspina received a copy of that papal brief (*Borgh.* III 18 f, fol. 493v).

[19] *Ibidem*, Nr. 160.

[20] *Akty Zap. Rossii*, IV, Nr. 114.

Schism, of the Union of Florence including the participation of Metropolitan Isidore, of the destinies of that union in the Ruthenian lands, and of its recent renewal there through Pociej's and Terlecki's mission to Rome, — a survey which repeated, sometimes in almost identical words though in longer phrases, the whole historical argumentation of the Charter of Brest. There followed an account of the Synod held there which in particular blamed Kopysteński and Bałaban for joining rather Anabaptists, Arians, and other heretics " hostile to the Orthodox Ruthenian faith, " then the legitimate Synod. Recalling that these two bishops had first voluntarily acceded to the Union, notifying their agreement to the King, he pointed out that they had deserted the others " persuaded by obstinate men. " This was, of course, a reference to Ostrogski who, however, was not mentioned, while Sigismund III did not hesitate to condemn the cooperation with Nicephorus and other Greeks, with foreign people whom he called " spies and traitors. " The King had indeed ordered soon after the Synod the arrest of Nicephorus as " disturber of public order and Turkish spy, " but liberated him at the request of Ostrogski who considered him still a high dignitary of the Orthodox Church, on the condition that the Prince would bring the Greek to the next Diet for public trial. [21] Without entering into these political matters, the royal message of December 15, before describing the proclamation of the Union by the Synod of Brest, raised another charge against the opposition, namely, that the signatures on its protests against the Union were not valid, since many people who did not belong at all to the Synod, had been induced or even forced to sign in blank the papers on which these protests were written later, to be circulated all over the country.

Warning his Ruthenian subjects " not to listen to, nor to accept and trust, any stories and writings from obstinate and silly apostates, " the King called upon them to respect and to obey their spiritual superiors, the Metropolitan and the Bishops, not to rebel against them nor to permit " juniors " to do so. And since the Metropolitan with the whole Synod had excommunicated and deposed Kopysteński and Bałaban, nobody was to consider them any longer as bishops but avoid any contact with them. Finally, all public officials, from the Palatines and Starostas to the city councils, were summoned not to oppose in anything the decisions of the Synod of Brest and to punish those who would do so.

That solemn royal edict seemed to give full satisfaction to the supporters of the Union, including the use of the *bracchium regale* against the deposed bishops — though not ordering their removal as, for instance, Arcudius had expected it [22] — and to meet in advance the papal recommenda-

---

[21] See K. Lewicki, *Ks. Konstanty Ostrogski*, 185.
[22] See his letter of Nov. 10, 1596 (A, 2).

tions. It is true that one of these recommendations, which endorsed one of the main requests of the Ruthenian bishops, did not receive satisfaction and was not considered at all in the long text of December 15 : nothing was said there about their admission to the Senate. This was, however, definitely beyond the King's constitutional power and could not be settled by royal decree, but only by a unanimous decision of the Diet, and therefore had to wait for the unavoidable showdown at the next session of the legislature.

Even more important was another question, that of the enforcement of the whole decree in practice, and this, too, depended on the further development of the situation, since Sigismund III himself had wisely decided from the outset to avoid any violence and any danger of internal troubles in the realm. The text of his appeal, including the apparently stern and severe conclusion, did not make it clear for what the public authorities should punish those opposing the decisions of the Synod, and in view of the constitutional guarantees of religious freedom, this could not refer to religious beliefs and practices, matters in which the King could only make a solemn appeal to his subjects, explaining to them which of the two assemblies held in Brest was really the legitimate Synod of the Ruthenian Church.

The sound principle that "treating matters of religion, one should proceed with all suavity," was basic for the Commonwealth and in agreement with the promise of not permitting acts of violence against anybody, which the King had made in his earlier personal message to Ostrogski, on the eve of the Synod [23]. But these very words were used also by the papal Nuncio Malaspina when about the same time, the end of the fateful year 1596, he had to admit in one of his reports sent to Rome, [24] that the situation was not quite as favorable as he had expected immediately after the Synod of Brest. "The Greek bishops — he wrote — are being vexed by a thousand artifices and impostures by Prince Constantine, and though from our side strong obstacles are made to his petulance, yet, since he is more powerful than considerate," he can do a great deal of harm. The Nuncio, therefore, suggested that the papal Secretariate of State approach his son, the Catholic Castellane of Cracow, advising him seriously to warn his father not to abuse without limits the patience of the King who had good reasons for taking action against the old Prince.

All the implications of the situation, of which Ostrogski himself was probably not quite aware, were revealed to the Papal Legate when his secretary and close collaborator, Boniface Vannozzi, during that same second half of December visited Prince Constantine's political opponent, Jan Zamoy-

---

[23] See above, Part IV, Chapter III, p. 349.
[24] *Borgh.* III 89 c, fol. 232v ; also *Borgh.* III 91 c, fol. 287v (Dec. 28, 1596).

ski, [25] in his city of Zamość where the Grand Chancellor had recently founded, with papal approval, a private university [26] as outpost of Western
culture in that region of Chełm whose Latin and Greek bishops loyally
supported the Union of Brest. That religious Union was not directly involved in Vannozzi's mission who already for the second time was instructed
to approach Zamoyski in the matter of the anti-Ottoman league which
King Báthory's intimate adviser and friend saw from a different viewpoint than the Habsburgs, keeping therefore aloof from the Polish-Austrian
negotiations promoted by Caetani. Yet, in the course of these political
discussions the Grand Chancellor who, in spite of such differences of opinion,
was highly regarded at the papal curia as a good Catholic, explained some
surprising connections between the two matters.

" Those few Ruthenians — he said [27] — who did not want to join the
Union with the Catholic Church, have established contacts with the Hussites
(meaning the Czech Brethren expelled from Bohemia and settled in Poland)
and with the Calvinists in order to come to an understanding with the
heretics of Germany who are in understanding with the Turks. " This
was already an indirect reference to Ostrogski's plan of cooperation with
the various Protestant denominations and of a common, Orthodox-Protestant
front against the Union of Brest, a plan first submitted to the Synod of
Toruń in 1595 and later to be fully developed at the Synod of Wilno in
1599. It was a hint that Prince Constantine, a partisan of the Habsburgs
and apparently more favorable to the anti-Ottoman league than was Zamoyski, was conspiring with all anti-Catholic forces to the advantage of the
Turks. And the Chancellor continued saying that one of the Ruthenian
bishops in union with Rome — this was, of course, Terlecki — being menaced
by the Palatine of Kiew (now specifically mentioned) had turned to Zamoyski
for help and received it, since the Chancellor was ready to help all partisans of the Union with the Catholic Church.

Speaking in that same connection about the recent Cossack rebellion
under Nalevayko, Zamoyski did not, however, connect it at all with the
opposition against that Union, but, as Caetani and Malaspina had rightly
feared, [28] with the anti-Polish intrigues of the Habsburgs and their partisans.
Nalevayko himself, he said, had for a long time negotiated in Hungary
with Archduke Maximilian, the pretender to the Polish throne whom Za-

---

[25] The diary of Vannozzi's two missions to Zamoyski, to whom he was sent for
the second time on Dec. 12, 1596, and copies of the related documents, can be found
both at the Vatican Archives, *Fondo Pio*, vol. 156, and the Biblioteca Casanatense,
Ms. 1564. See also *Docum. priv. la istoria românilor*, XII, app. B.

[26] J. K. Kochanowski, *Dzieje Akademii Zamojskiej* (History of the Academy of
Zamość), Kraków 1899-1900, 23 f.

[27] *Fondo Pio* 156, fol. 60-62 ; also *Bibl. Casanat.*, Ms. 1564, fol. 117-121.

[28] See above, Part IV, Chap. III, p. 351.

moyski had defeated in 1588 and whom he still suspected not to have given up his claims in spite of the mediation of the present Pope when sent as legate to Poland by Sixtus V. The result of these intrigues, continued the Grand Chancellor, was very harmful to the Kingdom, as evidenced by the confessions of some of Nalevayko's Cossacks who after defeat at their trial admitted their understanding with the Emperor, the Archduke, and the Prince of Transylvania, to the prejudice of Poland.

Finally, Zamoyski disclosed to Vannozzi that he was in possession of the intercepted letters " of that Greek who today is kept by Prince Ostrogski " — this was of course the notorious Nicephorus, so conspicuous and troublesome at Brest — letters in which that alleged representative of the Patriarchate of Constantinople invited the Turks to invade Poland. And the Chancellor added in significant words which the Legate's emissary quoted in Latin in his Italian diary : " These letters will be produced, they will be produced indeed, if necessary. "

This evidence, compromising for Nicephorus but also for Ostrogski as the Greek's protector, was to be produced at the trial of the suspected spy before the forthcoming Diet, and that Warsaw Diet of March 1597 was to be, in general, a first, if not decisive test of the vitality of the Union of Brest. Nuncio Malaspina, though like Cardinal Caetani he continued to be primarily interested in the prospects of the anti-Ottoman league, was quick to realize that the future of the Union would be determined at the same time. As far as the case of Nicephorus was concerned which was, as a matter of fact, a link between the two problems, he wrote from Warsaw during the Diet, on March 2,[29] to Giovanni Francesco Aldobrandini, the nephew of Clement VIII, who commanded the papal auxiliary forces on the Hungarian front, about Zamoyski's views and intentions. The Grand Chancellor had revealed for the first time the proposals which Nicephorus had made to him when, well before the Synod of Brest, he approached Zamoyski, as Grand Hetman of the Kingdom, on behalf of Sinan Pasha, the Turkish Commander in chief in Hungary : the Ottoman Empire was ready to unite Transylvania, Wallachia, and Moldavia under one of the Báthory's, provided that Poland would support such a project. Though obviously the Turkish candidate would not have been Sigismund Báthory, the pro-Austrian Prince of Transylvania, but one of his pro-Polish cousins, Zamoyski was fully aware that this would bring all these principalities under Ottoman control and by removing the Movilas from Moldavia, reduce even there Poland's influence to a mere fiction. By rejecting that offer the Polish leader rendered at the same time a real service to the common cause of Christendom, since otherwise the passage of the Tartars into Hungary would have been wide open and the Christian forces there outflanked.

---

[29] *Borgh.* III 91 d, fol. 178v-179.

In that connection, the support which Ostrogski continued to give Nicephorus, whom Malaspina would incidentally call his *familiaris*, [30] was shocking and dangerous from the point of view of both the Ruthenian Union and the anti-Ottoman league, even if the Prince ignored the latter aspect of the case and wanted to use Nicephorus only to destroy, if possible, the work of the Synod of Brest or at least to confuse its interpretation. It was chiefly through the alleged representative of the Patriarchate of Constantinople and his role in the religious controversy that the Prince troubled and annoyed the pro-Roman Ruthenian bishops. Wise enough not to provoke the King's anger by open acts of violence against these bishops, Ostrogski hoped to mobilize against them the anti-Catholic forces at the Diet, as he had tried to do it on the occasion of the preceding Diet before the Synod of Brest. Now the legitimacy of the decisions of that Synod was to be questioned by those deputies who would speak in defense of the antisynod, directed by Nicephorus. The King had been opposed from the outset to such a transfer of a purely religious issue to the political body of the Diet, but could not prevent that the Palatine of Kiev, just as he had done before the Diet of 1596, tried to persuade as many dietines as possible to give to their deputies formal instructions to raise the whole issue in Warsaw in a sense hostile to the Union.

In doing so he was only partly successful. Already on January 18, 1597, [31] Malaspina could report to Caetani that Prince Constantine's "ambassadors" — as he called Ostrogski's agents — whom he had sent to various dietines to agitate against the Union of the Ruthenians "were not received as he had expected." There were indeed some dietines in various provinces of Poland and Lithuania which under the influence not only of Ostrogski but also of his Protestant friends included in their instructions statements directed against the Union, but other instructions went in the opposite direction, even at Łuck the opinions being divided, while most dietines did not touch the question at all. [32] Obviously public opinion was insufficiently prepared to consider the matter and even less to take any definite stand. But this was just one more reason, why the public debates of the Diet — unavoidable if only a small minority would raise the issue — were to prove of so decisive importance.

The diaries of the Diet of 1597, [33] rich in information as they are in that respect, definitely give the impression that the discussions which directly touched the Union of Brest, did not take too much time, being rather

---

[30] *Borgh.* III 89 d, fol. 29 (March 25, 1597).

[31] *Ibidem*, fol. 149v.

[32] A detailed survey of these instructions is given by Chodynicki, *op. cit.*, 360-366. See also the news received in Rome about thiese instructions, and in general, the opposition against the Union led by Ostrogski "*con gran sequito*" (*Urbin. lat.* 1605 I, 56 v, 144, 175 v).

[33] Published by E. Barwiński in *Scriptores rerum Polon.*, XX, Kraków 1907.

overshadowed by so many other problems on the agenda, including the determination of Poland's policy in the relations with the Ottoman Empire and its opponents. But precisely, therefore, the spectacular case of Nicephorus and his trial [34] attracted special attention and his fate was to determine to a large extent that of the Union. This is best shown by Malaspina's report of March 15, [35] to which a detailed account of the debates of the Diet was attached.

It clearly appears from that source, confirmed by all the others including the correspondence of Arcudius [36] — again a valuable eye-witness —, that the King and the government were decided to make a thorough distinction between religious and political matters and to accuse Nicephorus not on ecclesiastical grounds but as spy of a foreign power. Distinct, too, were the respective roles of the spokesmen of the government, the two most prominent and experienced statesmen of the Commonwealth : Leo Sapieha and Jan Zamoyski, Grand Chancellors of, respectively, the Grand Duchy of Lithuania and the Kingdom of Poland. Both of them opposed Constantine Ostrogski, the former, however, who otherwise had rather friendly personal relations with the old Prince, mainly in the matter of the religious Union, the latter by accusing Nicephorus in spite of his protection by the Palatine of Kiev.

The debate on the Union of the Ruthenians came first [37], at the beginning of March, and started with an exchange of views between Bishop Maciejowski, who recommended the Union on behalf of the hierarchy of Latin rite, and Prince Ostrogski who attacked it. It was then that Sigismund III ordered Sapieha to give a full account of the negotiations in that matter " from the beginning to the end, " that is from the first initiative of the Ruthenian hierarchy to the latest Synod of Brest. Having attended that synod as royal delegate, along with Prince Nicholas Christopher Radziwiłł, now deeply depressed by the death of his wife, [38] and Demetrius Chalecki, active at the Diet, [39] the Grand Chancellor of Lithuania who like the latter was of Ruthenian origin himself, was well qualified to defend the work of the Synod and — according to Malaspina — " did it so perfectly, that the Prince remained confused. " Particularly interesting was that the senators were shown on that occasion " a Ruthenian book written five hundred years

---

[34] Discussed in detail, but with different conclusions, by Chodynicki, *op. cit.*, 368-370, and K. Lewicki, *op. cit.*, 185-209.

[35] *Borgh.* III 89 d, fol. 23v, and particularly fol. 25v-26 of the annex.

[36] In his letter to Aquaviva of March 20, 1597 (A, 3).

[37] To the references in the Diaries (*Scriptores*, XX, 98, 101-104, 153-155, where Sapieha's speech is summarized, 471-472), the account in Malaspina's report, quoted above (note 35), has to be added ; most of the details given in the text are taken from that source. See also other news received in Rome: *Urbin. lat.* 1065 I, fol. 193 v, 224, 262, 280 b, 312.

[38] See the moving references in the letters of his Jesuit friends (Roman Archives of the Society of Jesus, *Epist. Germ.* 117, fol. 79, 103).

[39] *Scriptores*, XX, 85, 158, 425, 451, 464, 497, 513.

ago and considered by the Ruthenians not only authentical but sacred, where it was said that the Pope is the Vicar of Christ and superior to all Patriarchs, especially to that of Constantinople. " The greatest surprise and most valuable contribution was, however, the support which Sapieha and the cause he so ably defended, received from another high ranking senator of Ruthenian origin, that same Palatine of Nowogródek Tyszkiewicz, who until recently had seemed so full of doubts in the matter, as evidenced by his correspondence with Rahoza.

In contradistinction to Sapieha and Chalecki, and to so many other Ruthenian magnates including members of his own family, who had abandoned Greek Orthodoxy already before the Union of Brest and now were Catholics of Latin rite, Theodor Tyszkiewicz wanted to remain faithful to the Eastern rite ; but having been convinced by the Metropolitan that this was possible under the Union of Brest, he immediately joined that Union and at the Diet criticized Ostrogski for saying that the religion of the Ruthenians had been changed. It was no change at all, he asserted, but a return to the religion which their ancestors had professed. In Constantinople, he continued using Skarga's main argument, there is no longer any Patriarch, since he is not elected nor confirmed by those who according to canon law have that power, but chosen and approved by the Sultan and his court, established and deposed at any caprice of the Turks, so that today he is their investigator and " more Turkish than Christian, " noted for simony and many other vices. Therefore, he concluded, it was a shame not only to recognize him as head, but even to call him so.

After that violent attack against the Patriarchate, largely motivated by the disgraceful role of its alleged representative, Nicephorus, the King himself spoke, complaining that Prince Constantine was spreading rumors among the people, that he was forcing them by violence to embrace " the Ruthenian Catholic religion, " that is to adhere to the Union of Brest. He expressed, therefore, his strong resentment, and turning to the case of Nicephorus, ordered Ostrogski to bring that Greek the next day before the tribunal of the Speaker of the Diet. When the Prince asked for another delay of the trial, Sigismund III refused, and it was in vain that Constantine and his Catholic son, the Castellane of Cracow, tried to obtain the interference of the Primate and the Nuncio in that respect. The King had serious reasons not to permit any further postponement of a full clarification of that matter. For, as Malaspina specified in his report, the Greek had written a letter to the Patriarch of Constantinople " in which he let him know that on the occasion of the Ruthenian Union there were discords in the Kingdom, and tried to persuade the said Patriarch through many arguments to make the Turk understand, that now is the right time to occupy that Kingdom. " [40]

---

[40] *Borgh.* III 89 d, fol. 26.

In that brief summary of the charges against Nicephorus, including his relations with the Tartar Khan, the tool which the Ottoman Empire regularly used against Poland, the connection between the struggle against the Union of Brest and the Muslin danger was clearly evidenced. Zamoyski's speech before the Diet and the charges made by the public prosecutor [41] were much more specific. The intercepted letters which a Greek " metropolitan " called " Paphnutinus " had sent from Ostrog, the Prince's residence, to Moldavia, contained a passage saying that " the Polish dogs " were fighting each other and forcing the Ruthenians to accept the Latin faith. Arguing that Paphnutinus was nobody else but Nicephorus himself, the Grand Chancellor revealed that that same Nicephorus during the latest struggles in Moldavia had been a Turkish agent acting against the Poles. Nicephorus was also blamed for his role at the Synod of Brest, where he pretended to represent the Patriarch while the see of Constantinople was vacant, preside over meetings which he called a synod contrary to the laws of the land and the King's interdiction, arbitrarily deposed the lawful bishops and agitated against the Union approved by the King. However, acting in full agreement with Sigismund III, who once more declared that his subjects of Greek religion were free to remain as they had been before or to accept the Union with Rome [42], Zamoyski asked for Nicephorus' condemnation not at all on religious ground but because he was endangering the external security and disturbing the internal peace of the Commonwealth.

This is confirmed by the testimony of Arcudius [43] who served as interpreter at the trial of his countryman and naturally became interested in his fate. The privilege which Nicephorus had received four years before from Patriarch Jeremiah and now so proudly exhibited with a view of justifying his role at Brest, seemed authentical to the Catholic Greek theologian who remarked that it granted to the representative of the late Patriarch the powers of some kind of " Grand Inquisitor. " But this was precisely the reason why Arcudius was so deeply shocked by what he called the decay of the Eastern Church where such powers could be given to a man who, as he admitted himself, had not even been ordained and, as evidenced in the discussions with him, had no theological training at all. Even his religious convictions were not too strong, because when his condemnation for his political activities became imminent, he tried to escape it by declaring himself ready to serve under Arcudius as teacher in the Greek College at Rome.

He humiliated himself, at least privately, in vain, since his trial which took more time at the Diet than the debate on the Union of Brest itself,

---

[41] *Scriptores*, XX, 104-108, 122-124, 156 f., 478-487, 490-491, 522-525.
[42] *Ibidem*, 489.
[43] In his letters of March 20 and July 25 (A 3, A 4).

produced an overwhelming evidence of his role as a Turkish agent. In spite of his denials, that role resulted not only from Zamoyski's charges but also from the statements made before the Diet by the envoys of the Prince of Moldavia where his political activities had started. Worst of all, Ostrogski who first violently defended him, seeing his case lost and resenting that the suspect entanglements of Nicephorus had compromised his protector too, left the Senate before the verdict, and when the Calvinist Prince Radziwiłł who was fighting with the Palatine of Kiev against the Union of Brest, advised him to return and possibly to save the Greek, answered angrily : " Let the King eat him up. " Even so Nicephorus was not definitely condemned After long discussions, it was decided to collect further proofs of his guilt and in the meantime to jail him at the Castle of Marienburg in far away Prussia where, however, he soon died. [44]

In any case, his defeat was a victory for the Union of Brest, and therefore the Nuncio could sum up his report on the whole showdown at the Diet, [45] by saying that the Union was thus " well stabilized. " He even expressed the hope that the Moldavians who had contributed to the indictment of Nicephorus would join that Union along with the Ruthenians. And he was anticipating a great gain for Christendom, since in addition to acquiring so many souls, it now was evident that " the alleged Patriarch of Constantinople exercised more the office of a Turkish explorer than of a pastor. "

Yet, it was precisely the almost simultaneous intervention of a real Patriarch who made Malaspina's high expectations rather illusionary, not only as far as possible extensions of the Ruthenian Union were concerned but even regarding the stabilization of that Union within the limits of the Commonwealth. It was indeed no contradiction when Nicephorus was blamed at the same time for pretending to represent a Patriarchal see which was actually vacant, and for writing anti-Polish letters to the Patriarch of Constantinople. For the situation there was undergoing continuous changes : during the Synod of Brest and at the time of the proclamation of the Union there had been unquestionably one of the frequent vacancies of the see of Constantinople, because Jeremiah's second successor, who had been very busy trying to obtain from Moscow and other Orthodox countries the necessary financial means to satisfy the claims of the Turks, had just died [46], and it was not before November 24, 1596, [47] that a new Patriarch was installed. But he too died very soon, and only then, at the beginning of 1597, a solution was found which gave at last to the Greek Church a head of unusual prominence and versatility. The Patriarch of Alexandria, Meletius

---

[44] *Scriptores*, XX, 124, 525 ; on the role of Radziwiłł see Lewicki, *op. cit.*, 188 f.

[45] *Borgh.* III 89 d, fol. 23v.

[46] State Archives of Venice, *Dispacci Costantinopoli*, vol. 44, report of Oct. 20, 1596, summarized in *Rubr.* 6, f. 98v.

[47] *Ibidem*, fol. 111 (report of Nov. 24, 1596).

Pigas, who already as such had exercized a great influence in Constantinople reaching as far as the Ruthenian lands to the detriment of all attempts towards reunion with Rome, and who already at the earlier vacancies had seemed the most desirable candidate but refused for financial reasons, now decided to accept, if not the formal position of Patriarch of Constantinople, at least that of administrator of this see retaining that of Alexandria. He did so, as he admitted to the Venetian bailo, [48] a keen observer of all those developments, on the order of the Sultan to whom he continued to render very important services. The highly cultivated and astute Greek had no illusions as to the internal decay of the Ottoman Empire, but no illusions either as to the possibility of a victory of the Christian nations in the struggle against that still powerful Empire and therefore considered it expedient to appease its rulers by complete subservience.

He believed to serve at the same time the interests of Greek Orthodoxy against any possible Catholic advance to which he always remained very strongly opposed. He acted, therefore, both against any anti-Ottoman league, doing it, of course, chiefly through Orthodox rulers, like Michael the Brave of Wallachia and even occasionally in connection with the policies of Protestant powers, like England, [49] — and against any movements towards religious union with the Holy See, in particular the only one which was materializing with serious chances of success : the Union of the Ruthenians.

Coming into office at Constantinople soon after the Synod of Brest, he was now in a much better position to fight a movement which he had tried in vain to check when still Patriarch of Alexandria only. It was, therefore, with him that Nicephorus established close contact in both the political and religious field, along with Cyril Lucaris who had represented Meletius at the Synod of Brest.[50] Again it was Arcudius, so familiar with all Greek problems, who first became alarmed and forwarded to Rome[51] a copy of an appeal which the Patriarch had sent, not to the Ruthenian hierarchy, the great majority of which had retified the Union with Rome, but in general to the clergy and people remaining faithful to Orthodoxy. That appeal was followed, on August, 4, 1597, by an encyclical,[52] in which confirmed all what the opposition had done at Brest under Ostrogski's leadership, in particular the deposition of Metropolitan Rahoza and the other bishops

---

[48] *Ibidem,* fol. 150v (report of April 12, 1597 — from vol. 45 of the *Dispacci*), where the whole background of Meletius' appointment is explained in detail.

[49] All this is explained in the Venetian reports of 1597, especially in the part of vol. 45 which has been preserved in a copy made before the complete deterioration of that volume.

[50] See above, in the preceding chapter, p. 367.

[51] With a letter to Cardinal Santori which is summarized in his letter of July 25, 1597, to General Aquaviva (A, 4).

[52] I. I. Malishevsky, *Aleksandriiskii patriarkh Meletii Pigas*, II, Kiev 1872, appendix Nr. 18.

who had ratified the Union : the Patriarch named the layman Ostrogski, in addition to Cyril Lucaris and to one of the bishops opposed to the Union, viz., Bałaban, his representatives or "exarchs" in the Ruthenian dioceses, where they were to exercise the ecclesiastical power in the place of the deposed pastors including the former exarch Terlecki, and where the ambitious Palatine of Kiev now received from Constantinople that authority in religious matters which he had always wanted to exercise and which Sigismund III consistently denied him.

To the King the whole message of Meletius Pigas, followed by similar appeals to the Brotherhood of Lwów — formerly in conflict with Bałaban — and to other Orthodox princes, and by a long message to Ostrogski himself,[53] was an open challenge. Yet the "Pope and Patriarch of Alexandria and President (praeses) of Constantinople" as he now proudly called himself, did not hesitate to send on June 9, 1597, to his "most beloved son in the Lord" Sigismund III, the "unconquerable" King of Poland, with his "apostolic benediction," a Latin letter [54] signed in Greek but otherwise quite similar to a papal bull, in which he treated that Catholic ruler as if he were a follower of the Orthodox Church. Warning him against "the men of the Roman curia," he complained that the King had prohibited clergymen of the Eastern Church to enter his realm. This was, of course, a reference to Sigismund's interdiction to any foreigners to attend the Synod of Brest, an interdiction which anyway had been violated by the representative of Meletius, Cyril Lucaris who still remained in the Commonwealth, as well as by Nicephorus whose trial must have been already known to the Patriarch. If he did not complain on that occasion [55] about that much more serious action of the King, it was probably because, like Ostrogski, he did not want to identify himself openly with the political role of that other Greek. In general, however, his unctuous message was a clear statement that he would continue to defend the cause of Orthodoxy in Sigismund's Kingdom.

In view of the traditional prestige which the Patriarchs of Constantinople enjoyed among most of the Ruthenians, though men like, for instance, Tyszkiewicz were becoming aware of their real role under Ottoman domination, the endorsement by Meletius Pigas of the deposition and excommunication of all pro-Roman members of the hierarchy, was a serious threat to their authority. Even those who were doubtful as to the real powers of

---

[53] Russk. istor. bibl., VII, 1667-1707.

[54] Published by G. Hofmann in Orientalia Christiana, XXV (1932), 260, from the original in the Vatican Archives, Borgh. III 63 bc, fol. 298v.

[55] Shortly before the death of Nicephorus in 1599, Meletius asked the Sultan to intervene in favor of that "Metropolitan" whom the Poles kept in jail, because he wanted "solevare i Rasciani (!) et altri" against the bishops who had submitted themselves to Rome ; see Documente privitore la istoria românilor, XII, 443.

Nicephorus, especially after his recent trial, were now impressed by the utterances of a legitimate Patriarch and well known leader of the Greek Church. Therefore not only the condemned bishops were anxious to receive in that delicate situation the protection and vindication of their present head, the Pope of Rome, but also his Nuncio to Poland [56] supported their request for a papal brief which would annul their excommunication and be for them a well deserved " consolation ". Such a brief was indeed issued by Clement VIII on June 5, 1597, [57] declaring all the decisions of the "false " Patriarch of Constantinople invalid though, pending the approval of the Cardinals, the dispatch of that document had been delayed for a couple of weeks. [58]

That natural step of the Holy See was important not only for the Ruthenian Church now united with Rome, but also for a more general reason. For, strange enough, there had been until then illusions at the Vatican, that Meletius Pigas, the distinguished theologian born on the island of Crete under Venetian rule and educated at the University of Padua, was not irreductibly opposed to a union between the Eastern and the Western Church. Such was the impression of Clement VIII himself when he received in 1594 [59] a very friendly letter of the Greek Patriarch of Alexandria, and the Pope was confirmed in that opinion by the Venetian Giovanni Battista Vecchietti who on behalf of Gregory XIII and Sixtus V had negotiated with the Coptic Patriarch of Alexandria and on that occasion had met there the Greek Patriarch also. When the latter was put in charge of the Patriarchate of Constantinople, Giovanni Battista, instead of continuing the promising negotiations with the Patriarch of the Copts, which now were entrusted to his brother Girolamo, was sent by Clement VIII to Meletius with a rather surprising instruction. [60] He was not only to congratulate Pigas on his elevation to the Patriarchate of Constantinople, but to find out whether the new Patriarch — or rather administrator of that See — would not conclude a religious union with Rome on the basis of that of Florence which was specifically recalled not without a re-examination of the main controversial issues separating East and West. Giovanni Vecchietti was to carry papal briefs in that matter also to the ambassadors of France, Venice, and Ragusa in Constantinople in order to obtain the support of these Catholic powers, which precisely because of their good political relations

---

[56] In his report of April 22, 1597, *Borgh.* III 89 d, fol. 191v.

[57] *Documenta Pontif. Hist. Ucrainae illustr.*, I, Nr. 162.

[58] *Borgh.* III 18 h, fol. 403v, 404v (in the instructions for Malaspina, of May 17 and 31, 1597).

[59] On June 16 he brought that letter to the attention of the Cardinals (Vatican Library, *Barb. lat.*, 2929, fol. 216v).

[60] *Borgh.* IV 269, fol. 127-130 (without date) ; see *ibidem*, fol. 134-137 the instructions for his brother sent to the Coptic Patriarch.

with the Ottoman Empire were time and again of service to the Holy See in religious matters concerning the Levant.

Nothing could better indicate the complete hopelessness of that mission, which was to restore the Union of Florence with the whole Greek Church, than Meletius' violent opposition to that first step in that direction which, in the opinion of the Holy See, was the regional restoration of the Union in the Ruthenian lands. And other events were soon to prove that even such regional unions were possible only where Orthodox populations, ready to turn towards Rome, were under the rule of a Catholic power which could encourage, support, and protect such an initiative.

It is true that even in the Balkan countries which were under direct Ottoman rule, among the Slavic peoples rather than the Greeks, there appeared immediately after the Union of Brest, although without any apparent connection with it, projects of approaching the Holy See through whose policy the liberation from the Turkish yoke was expected. Particularly significant in that respect was a letter which on June 29, 1597, [61] that is precisely at the time when the Patriarch of Alexandria and Constantinople intensified his struggle against the Union of Brest, was sent to Clement VIII by the Metropolitan of Serbia and Novipazar, Archbishop Visarion. Entirely different in his attitude from that other Serbian Metropolitan Lucas, who had attended the antisynod of Brest without, however, playing any active part there, Visarion in his long message written in the Serbian language but in Latin characters, only his signature being in Cyrillic letters, after giving to the Pope any possible titles which would imply full recognition of his supreme authority over all Christendom, and recalling negotiations with his predecessors, resumed these negotiations through his envoys who were to express his obedience to " our Father and Pastor " and to " the Holy Mother, the Roman Church. " And a few months later, a nobleman from Ragusa, Paolo Giorgio, who was sending to Clement VIII regular reports from Bulgaria, [62] forwarded to him a letter which the Archbishop of Tirnovo, Dionysius, who had four bishops under his jurisdiction, had written to that papal agent in May 1597, seeming ready to enter into relations with both Pope and Emperor and hostile to the Turks.

In the Bulgarian case it seemed obvious that liberation from the Turks was the main objective of these negotiations, with even the papal emissary stressing the possibility of Bulgarian participation in the struggle against their Ottoman masters. And the same was true of all the other " miserable Christians " in the Balkans [63] including of course the Serbs. When,

---

[61] *Borgh.* III 96 c, fol. 47.

[62] *Borgh.* III 112 ef, fol. 46-53, 54, 57-59 ; the copy of the letter of the Archbishop of Tirnovo is on fol. 55.

[63] About Archbishop Dionysius of Bulgaria see also *Ms.* 49 of the Polish Library in Paris (pp. 323-326), and about another " Patriarch " of Bulgaria who asked for

therefore, these prospects of political liberation through the anti-Ottoman league, as planned by the Holy See, did not materialize and the war in Hungary was dragging on without much success, the plans of religious union, impossible to carry out as long as Muslim domination lasted, vanished also, even in cases where members of the Orthodox hierarchy seemed as well disposed as was Metropolitan Visarion.

But even in autonomous Moldavia, in the immediate neighborhood of Poland, the hopes of a repercussion of the Union of Brest proved illusionary. Malaspina, who had expressed such hopes in connection with the trial of Nicephorus, returned to that problem at the end of the year in his report of November 2. [64] For Archbishop Solikowski who, for so many years, had been promoting the cause of religious reunion in Moldavia, had just written him from Lwów that Prince Jeremiah was going to send his representatives to the Holy See with a declaration of obedience. Even if this was really Movila's intention, he never succeeded in carrying out that old project: Poland's influence was strong enough to keep him on the Moldavian throne, though even this required another armed intervention of Zamoyski at the turn of the century, but neither able nor willing to force the union with Rome upon a reluctant Orthodox clergy and population. Particularly doubtful was the Nuncio's additional remark that if Moldavia would abandon the schism, the same could be hoped of Wallachia: far from being in any " unity of minds, " the rulers of the two principalities were hostile to each other, and Michael the Brave of Wallachia, against whom Jeremiah Movila needed Polish protection, was in political and even more in religious matters under the influence of Meletius Pigas, [65], and, strange enough, also in contact with Constantine Ostrogski. [66]

But Malaspina's expectations were reaching even farther: he concluded his optimistic survey of the situation by referring to " infinite favorable results " of the growing influence of the Holy See in Eastern Europe " which would be explained by Abbot Comuleo (Komulovich), who had more practice in these matters than myself. " This was a reference to the fantastic projects of the Croat prelate who, in spite of the failure of his first mission to all countries of that part of the world, from the Danubian principalities to Moscow, was now in Moscow again, [67] renewing his efforts to gain that power for participation in the anti-Ottoman league under papal leadership and thus, perhaps, eventually for religious union with Rome. He failed

---

help against the Turks: Vatican Archives, *Arm.* 52, vol. 21, vol. 335 (Dec. 4, 1597), where relations with Georgia through an Armenian agent are mentioned.

[64] *Borgh.* III 91 d, fol. 247v.

[65] See above, Part IV, Chap. III, p. 357.

[66] See Chodynicki, *op. cit.*, 369, where the whole background is well explained.

[67] On his way there he wrote in April |1597 to the Papal Secretary of State (*Borgh.* III 18 h, fol. 413, instruction for Malaspina, of June 19).

once more completely though, in agreement with the ambassadors whom Emperor Rudolph II had sent to Moscow at the same time, he tried to influence the Grand Duke by promising him a royal crown. Neither the last of the Ruriks, crowned as Tsar like his father, nor Boris Godunov who already exercised the real power, was seriously interested in that idea of which Komulovich knew only too well that it was deeply resented by the Poles. [68]

They did not even know that also the papal representative, acting on his own account, was making such an offer, but strongly suspected the " practices " between the Emperor and Moscow, a suspicion which was creating all the time additional obstacles to the Polish-Austrian negotiations in the matter of the anti-Ottoman league, as Cardinal Caetani experienced more than once, and which now even lead to difficulties in the passage of the imperial ambassadors through Polish Livonia. Malaspina was fully informed and reported to Rome [69] about the political reasons of the Polish opposition against any support of Moscow's pretensions by the West : these pretensions, based upon dynastic claims, included all the Ruthenian provinces of the Commonwealth, were apparently even extended as far as the Vistula, and in any case had as main objective Kiev, that is, the very see of the Metropolitan who had just concluded the Union of Brest. No specific reference was made to that Union, neither in Moscow by Komulovich who fascinated by more ambitious projects had not taken the expected part in that concrete achievement, nor by Sigismund III when at the very time of the Croat's second mission to the Tsar in August 1597,[70] he once more discussed with the papal Nuncio the eastern policies of the Holy See. But this time it was clearly pointed out to Malaspina that not only " honoring the Muscovite with a royal crown " would be a serious source of trouble, but also that it would lead to disastrous consequences if " the Muscovite should assume the protection of the schismatics in the Kingdom. " That almost casual remark of the King who pointed out also that Komulovich had not been treated in Moscow " according to the dignity of the Holy See ", was made in connection with the trial of a rather obscure notary in Wilno who confessed " that he had been elected by the schismatic Ruthenians, subjects of the King, as ambassador to Moscow in order to complain that the King hindered the exercise of their religion and violently deprived them of

---

[68] See about his negotiations in Moscow P. Pierling, *La Russie et le Saint-Siège*, II, 364-368. About the hopes of Rome that the " Muscovites " would follow the example of the Ruthenians see *Urbin. lat.* 1064, fol. 776 (news of Nov. 27, 1596).

[69] On April 22, 1597, *Borgh.* III 91 d, fol. 191. To another report, of August 20, 1597 (*Borgh.* III 89 d, fol. 170 v-172 v) in which Malaspina returned to that problem, he added a memorandum explaining the historical reasons why the Poles opposed the granting of the royal title to the Grand Duke of Moscow. See also the news recorded in *Urbin. lat.* 1605 I, fol. 247, 262, 414 ; II, fol. 454, 561.

[70] *Borgh.* III 89 d, fol. 161-162 (August 9, 1597).

their churches ". Apparently he was even instructed to implore the Tsar for his help.

Whether this information of the Nuncio [71] was correct or not, an interference in favor of those Ruthenians, who remained opposed to the Union with Rome, would have been entirely in the line of Moscow's traditional policy since the Union of Florence and was now facilitated by the elevation of the Metropolitan of Moscow to the rank of a Patriarch a few years before. Fortunately, however, for the Commonwealth and for the Union of Brest, such an interference was hardly possible for the time being in view of Moscow's internal situation which was leading her into a long time of troubles. For that same reason her military preparations along the Lithuanian frontier, so frequently mentioned not without alarm in Malaspina's reports, did not result in any open conflict. On the contrary, in 1598, the year of the death of Tsar Fedor, the last descendant of Rurik, and Boris Godunov's highly controversial succession, the same Leo Sapieha who had so successfully worked for the Union of Brest succeeded in concluding at Moscow another prolongation of the armistice of 1582. [72]

In the same year of 1598, Malaspina was recalled from Poland where neither he nor Cardinal Caetani had obtained the much desired participation of that country in the anti-Ottoman league, and made Nuncio in Transylvania where he was to work for that same purpose. In one of his last reports from Warsaw [73] he described once more Ostrogski's action against the Union of Brest, but expressed the hope that thanks to the support of the King, the hierarchy, and many senators, that Union would not only survive but progress from day to day. For his successor as Nuncio to Poland where he had accomplished so much and gained a valuable experience, Malaspina wrote a general report [74] in which, at the very end, he returned to the idea of inducing even Moscow to unite with the Latin Church and to join the Christian powers in view of that liberation of Greece from Turkish tyranny, which the Muscovites themselves seemed seriously to desire. But this time the suggested way of making true that old dream was particularly fantastic : Malaspina suggested that Sigismund III, who had lost his first Austrian wife, should remarry with the young daughter of the present Grand Duke of Muscovy. Noting that among the Poles there were partisans of that project, the Nuncio himself considered it necessary that his successor dis-

---

[71] It was probably about that same case that Arcudius wrote to Rome on July 25, 1597 (A. 4), referring to a notary in Wilno who after violently blaming Metropolitan Rahoza for concluding the Union with Rome, got in trouble because he was convicted of falsifying official records.

[72] K. Tyszkowski, *Poselstwo Lwa Sapiehy do Moskwy* (The Legation of L. S. to Moscow), Lwów 1927.

[73] *Borgh. III* 96 c, fol. 75-76.

[74] Vatican Library, *Urbin. lat.* 837, fol. 479-512.

cussed it with the Pope, since the Muscovite princess was, of course, a schismatic.

Much more important and to the point was another advice which Malaspina gave to the next Nuncio, [75] namely, to watch the possible appearances in Poland of Greek Patriarchs of Constantinople and Alexandria who, through the Brotherhoods established among the Ruthenians, hindered their " perfect Union " with the Latins. Thinking particularly of the powerful Brotherhood of Lwów which continued to oppose the Union of Brest, Malaspina suggested consultation with the Latin Archbishop of that city, the experienced Solikowski, so that any such Patriarch would be expelled from the Kingdom. He considered such an understanding with the Archbishop of Lwów necessary also with regard to the situation in Moldavia, [76] where religious conditions were so confused and the neighborhood of the Tartars so alarming. It is true that the Patriarchs acted in that whole distant region rather through emissaries and written appeals than through personal appearance, but in any case the warning against their influence was only too well justified, especially as it was closely connected with the political influence of the Ottoman Empire. However, in that case too, the danger to the Commonwealth and accordingly to the Union of Brest was considerably reduced as long as the tension in the relations with that Empire, of which the Patriarchs used to be the tools, did not result in any open war. And that was precisely what Zamoyski succeeded in avoiding by not joining the war in Hungary but stopping through a firm attitude and, if necessary, an indirect control of Moldavia both Turkish and Tartar penetration at the border of the Commonwealth. [77] Therefore in these last years of the sixteenth century even Cyril Lucaris, the old collaborator of Meletius Pigas and enemy of the Union of Brest, though continuing his close relations with Ostrogski, tried to persuade men like Solikowski and Nicholas Christopher Radziwiłł that at the Synod of Brest he had advised Nicephorus, the only real enemy of the Commonwealth, to confer with the Catholics, failing merely because of Protestant opposition — a statement which left the King highly skeptical. [78]

It was not before the first Turkish invasions of Poland and Moscow's rebirth after the " time of troubles, " that is around 1620, that both powers with the assistance of Cyril Lucaris, now Patriarch of Constantinople, and of the Patriarch of Jerusalem whom he sent to Kiev and Moscow, successfully started using the opposition against the Union as a dangerous

---

[75] *Ibidem*, fol. 503.
[76] *Ibidem*, fol. 511v.
[77] For a general survey of Zamoyski's policy in that matter see the *Cambridge History of Poland*, I, 460.
[78] See the manuscript sources quoted by K. Lewicki, *op. cit.*, 176 n. 1 and 208.

weapon in their struggle against Catholic Poland which was simultaneously attacked by Protestant Sweden with the connivance of the Elector of Brandenburg, at last established in East Prussia. And it was under that outside influence that the Ukrainian Cossacks entered that struggle against the Union of Brest which only then became a serious source of trouble for the Commonwealth.

But all this is quite another story and was preceded by a score of years which might be considered a breathing space for that Union and made possible its survival, in contradistinction to the fate of the Union of Florence among the Ruthenians, one hundred and fifty years ago. That survival throughout the years which immediately followed the Synod of Brest, is the more remarkable, because in that early phase the Union of Brest had a relentless opponent whom the Union of Florence did not find in that same region : Prince Constantine Ostrogski who, contrary to Cardinal Caetani's expectations, lived twelve more years and died only in 1608, eighty two years old. Why in spite of his age he continued to be the main danger to the Union, disregarding all efforts of the Holy See to appease him, [79] was well explained in Malaspina's final survey. [80] It was an exaggeration to say that he passed from schism to " atheism, " since his interest in religious problems never disappeared, making him sponsor the theological polemics against the supporters of the Union. But it was true that defending Greek Orthodoxy, he was moving farther and farther away from that faith and doctrine, while his relations with all non-Catholic denominations became closer and closer. And while the Synod of Wilno, in 1599, proved once more the impossibility of any doctrinal agreement between Orthodox and Protestant, their anti-Catholic alliance which was formally concluded there, [81] explains how the cooperation of both religious minorities was one of the main reasons why the Union of Brest had to face such difficulties in a Catholic country. Nothing similar had been experienced by the Union of Florence since the unfriendly attitude of the last supporters of the conciliatory movement cannot be compared with the problems arising from the Protestant Reformation. And this leads back to the question how under such conditions the Union of Brest succeeded where the Union of Florence had failed.

When on the eve of Pociej's and Terlecki's mission to Rome the chances of these two movements were compared, it was correctly pointed out [82] that Clement VIII was more interested in Poland than the Popes of the fifteenth

[79] See *Documenta Pontificia historiam Ucrainae illustr.*, I, Nr. 198-206, about the last efforts of Clemens VIII in that matter, 1604-1605.

[80] *Urbin. lat.* 837, fol. 491v.

[81] D. Oljančyn, " Zur Frage der Generalkonföderation in Wilna, " *Kyrios* I (1936), see particularly p. 29; A. Florovsky, *Čechy a vostočnyc Slavjane*, II, 387-390.

[82] *Orientalia Christiana*, III (1925), 163; see above Part IV, Chap. II, p. 310.

century who furthermore did not have any permanent representatives there to promote the regional Union of the Ruthenians. It was said with the same good reason that King Sigismund III was showing a special zeal in all religious matters, and though his power was more limited than that of his Jagellonian predecessors had been, it must be emphasized that the political unification of the Commonwealth and the cultural intercourse of its peoples, which the old dynasty had accomplished, created much more favorable conditions for religious union also. No more than the Jagellonians did their present successor want to enforce that union, as best evidenced by the fact that he did nothing to remove Bałaban and Kopysteński from their sees [83] so that the dioceses of Lwów and Przemyśl joined the Union only one hundred years later. But Sigismund III did not hesitate to declare time and again [84] that the real " Greek faith " which it was his duty to protect, was not the schismatic but the Catholic Church of Eastern rite.

In all this the King was supported by the ablest statesmen of the Commonwealth, like Jan Zamoyski and Leo Sapieha, the two Grand Chancellors who better than any of the high officials at the time of the Union of Florence realized the importance of the Ruthenian Union with Rome. But in their opinion as in that of Sigismund III, this religious matter was primarily the concern of the hierarchy whose attitude constituted the greatest advantage which the Union of Brest enjoyed in comparison with that of Florence. Metropolitan Isidore was not only isolated, as it was recalled with good reason, but a foreigner who soon left the country where no prominent Ruthenian bishop appeared for a long time. Now it was the spontaneous initiative of the Ruthenian hierarchy which made the new Union possible and the leadership of the Metropolitans guaranteed its development. This is true even of Rahoza who, in spite of his age, played such a leading role at the Synod of Brest and courageously faced criticism and even insults in defense of its decisions. [85] Among the bishops, it was of course Pociej who continued to excel in genuine dedication to the Union, so that the diocesan synod which he held in Brest in July 1597, was praised by all witnesses [86] as a great success, since almost all clergymen present voluntarily made the same profession of faith which the bishops had made before. Therefore it was only natural that after Rahoza's death in 1599 it was Pociej who was elected his successor and confirmed by King and

---

[83] *Akty Zap. Rossii*, IV, Nr. 135 ; see Chodynicki, *op. cit.*, 401.
[84] First in his official statement of Dec. 15, 1596, *ibidem*, Nr. 114 ; see also Malaspina's report of Nov. 21, 1597 (*Borgh.* III 91 d, fol. 252) about the King's interpretation of the " *fede greca.* "
[85] See the letter of Arcudius to General Aquaviva, of July 25, 1597 (A, 4).
[86] *Ibidem*, at the end of the letter ; also in Maciejowski's letter of July 16, *Borgh.* III 91 c, fol. 168-169.

27

Pope with the permission to keep as Metropolitan his former see of Brest and Volodymir also. [87]

He vigorously defended the Union at the forthcoming Diets, and if he could not do it as a regular member of the Senate to which, after all, neither the Metropolitan nor the bishops of Eastern rite were admitted, this was, as he well realized himself, [88] only the consequence of the unabated Orthodox and Protestant opposition making hopeless any motion which would have increased the number of the Catholic bishops-senators from fifteen to twenty-one or possibly twenty-three. This was neither the fault of the King nor of the hierarchy of Latin rite which, after assisting in the conclusion of the Union of Brest, supported it without any prejudice against their fellow-bishops of Eastern rite.

The Primate of Poland himself, Stanislaus Karnkowski, who had seemed little interested before and merely authorized the convocation of the Synod of Brest, writing to Malaspina on December 13, 1597 [89] about the necessity of holding a national synod not limited to his own province of Gniezno, emphasized the necessity of inviting also the bishops of Eastern rite : " If we ourselves — he argued — do not support the Union of the Ruthenians with unanimous advice and effort, and if all of us do not consult with them about its stability and continuity, it does not seem that this Union, which has not yet strongly coalesced, could long endure. " The Nuncio who was supposed to preside over such a synod, [90] of course, fully agreed, and it is hardly necessary to point out that Karnkowski's immediate successors felt even stronger in that matter, since the second of them [91] was the same Bernard Maciejowski who as Latin bishop of Łuck had been the most enthusiastic supporter of the Union of Brest. Writing to Malaspina, on September 22, 1597, still from Łuck, he once more recommended to the Nuncio the Ruthenian bishop of that city, Terlecki, with whom, as well as with Pociej, he was discussing the project of extending the privileges of the approaching Holy Year to the Catholics of Eastern rite, in agreement with the Primate who was to communicate in the matter with their Metropoli-

---

[87] *Documenta Pontificia*, I, Nr. 182, 185 (Nov. 15, 1600).

[88] See the interesting comments in *Russk. istor. bibl.*, XIX, 686 (*Antirrisis*).

[89] *Borgh.* III, 91 c, fol. 158-159 (orig., see also the copies, fol. 192-195).

[90] See the comments of Karnkowski himself, *ibidem*, fol. 156 (also in *Borgh.* III 91 d, fol. 118). It was probably in that connection that the King of Poland sent a suggestion to Rome, which was favorably considered there, that a convention be celebrated " *inter Ruthenos unitos cum S. Romana Ecclesia et schismaticos* " and after their agreement the Metropolitan of Kiev be made a Patriarch (*Documente privitore la istoria românilor*, III, suppl. Nr. 98 ; the copy in Bibl. Vallicell., *Ms.* 34, fol. 156, has no date but is placed among the documents of the years 1595-1599) ; that project which never materialized, would require further study.

[91] The first was J. Tarnowski who, died however, a few months after his nomination ; see the biographies in *Sacrum Poloniae Millennium*, I, 483, 508, 569.

tan. [92] Before Maciejowski was promoted to the see of Gniezno, he succeeded George Radziwiłł as Cardinal and Bishop of Cracow, and as such welcomed, in 1603, in the old capital of Poland Metropolitan Pociej who with a large assistance of Ruthenian priests participated there in the Corpus Christi procession and celebrated services according to the Greek rite in the churches of Cracow " to the great pleasure and edification of the peoples who had arrived in large number from all parts of the Kingdom. " [93]

Immediately after the Council of Florence, Metropolitan Isidore, politely received in Cracow by Bishop Oleśnicki, had indeed officiated there in the Polish churches according to the Eastern liturgy.[94] But this time Pociej's similar action, wholeheartedly welcomed by Bishop Maciejowski, was more than a symbolic gesture. Seven years after the Synod of Brest, it was an eloquent testimony that the majority of the Ruthenians of the Commonwealth, under their most enlightened ecclesiastical leaders, had joined the Catholic Poles and Lithuanians in the same faith, and that their traditional Eastern rites were not considered any obstacle to a common way of life under the same federal constitution and in friendly contact with Western culture.

---

[92] *Borgh.*, III 89 d, fol. 229-229 v.

[93] Described in Maciejowski's letter to Cardinal Aldobrandini, Cracow, June, 7 1603 (*Borgh.* III 112 EF, fol. 101; see also *Borgh.* III, 129-1, fol. 233v-234).

[94] How these Florentine traditions were discussed in the polemics at the time of the Union of Brest, has been studied by B. Waczyński in *Orientalia Christiana Periodica*, IV (1938), 441-472. How they continued to influence Pociej, is evidenced in his letters to Pope Paul V, where he even recalled the Council of Lyons, (*Borgh.* I, 512, fol. 25) and summarized Misael's appeal of 1476, a copy of which he discovered in Lithuania hoping that the original would be found in the Vatican Archives (*ibidem,* fol. 65).

LIST OF CONSULTED MANUSCRIPTS

A. ROME

1. *Vatican Archives.*

Regesta Vaticana : vol. 437, 450, 452, 453, 462, 466, 467, 468, 469, 470, 498, 499, 501, 502, 503, 504, 505, 529, 578, 594, 607, 608.

Nunziatura di Polonia : vol. 1, 1 A, 2, 3, 4, 5, 5 A, 5 B, 6, 15 C, 17 A, 22, 23, 24, 25, 26, 27, 27 A, 28, 29, 30, 31, 32, 33, 34, 35, 170 A, 172, 361, 394, 395, Addit. 1, Addit. 2, Addit. 3.

Archivio della Nunziatura di Varsavia : vol. 158.

Nunziatura di Venezia : vol. 10, 25, 26, 27, 28, 30, 31, 32, 41.

Fondo Borghese : I, vol. 34 b, 512 ; II, vol. 475 ; III, vol. 5 c, 6 a, 9 c, 18 a-l, 63 b, 63 c, 66 b, 66 c, 66 d, 67 a, 72 a, 85 c1, 89 a, 89 b, 89 c, 89 d, 90 c, 91 a, 91 b, 91 c, 91 d, 92 b, 96 a-f, 112 c, 112 f, 124 b, 129-1 ; IV, vol. 230, 269, 287.

Fondo Pio : vol. 10, 15, 26, 107, 114, 115, 118, 156, 160, 161.

Principi : vol. 1, 5, 6, 23, 24, 25, 26, 27, 28, 31, 33 A, 41, 47, 49, 50, 51, 52, 53.

Cardinali : vol. 3, 4.

Vescovi : vol. 2, 10.

Secret. Brevium : vol. 372.

Armaria : *29*, vol. 20 ; *31*, vol. 35, 36, 37, 70 ; *32*, vol. 21 ; *38*, vol. 2, 3 ; *42*, vol. 48, 49, 51 ; *44*, vol. 29, 30, 31, 32, 39, 34, 35, 36, 37, 38, 39, 40, 41, 42, 43, 48, 49, 50 ; *52*, vol. 19, 20, 21 ; *64*, vol. 29.

Misc. Armaria : I, vol. 81, 82, 83 ; II, vol. 30, 34, 63, 68, 69, 82, 110, 111, 112, 115, 117, 123, 129, 130, 146, 177.

A. A. Armaria I-XVIII : vol. 1731, 1732, 1733, 1734, 1735, 1736, 1742, 1743, 1744, 1745, 1746, 1747, 1748, 1841, 1842, 1843, 1844, 1845, 1846, 1847, 1858, 1859.

2. *Vatican Library.*

Barber. Lat. : vol. 846, 2808, 2815, 2871, 2886, 2929, 5146, 5798 I-II.

Borgiani Lat. : vol. 450; *Illirici* : vol. 26.

Capponiani : vol. 164.

Ottobon. Lat. : vol. 1088, 2623.

Slav. : vol. 12.

Urbin. Lat. : vol. 837, 854 I-II, 855, 1063 I-II, 1064 I-II, 1065 I-II.

3. *Roman Archives of the Society of Jesus.*

Epistolae Germaniae : vol. 165-177.
Epistolae selectae : III 646, V 648, VI 649, VII 650, VIII 650 a, IX 650 b.
Fondo Gesuitico : 720 A II, 1537 Busta N. 160/9, 1652 Busta 6. 263/3.
Opp. nn. : vol. 331.
Ms. Pol. : 50.

4. *Casanatense Library.*

Mss. 1562, 1563, 1564.

5. *Vallicelliana Library.*

Mss. L 18, N 33, N 34, N 35.

6. *Doria Pamphilii Archives.*

Fondo Aldobrandini : vol. 7, 11, 83 (I was permitted to use the copies in the Papal Oriental Institute).

B. VENICE

1. *State Archives.*

Dispacci Costantinopoli : vol. 41, 42, 43, 44, 45, 46.
Dispacci Germania : vol. 24, 25.
Dispacci Roma : vol. 36, 37, 38, 39.
Dispacci di Residenti in Polonia : Busta 470.
Lettere di Ambasciatori a Napoli : Busta 19 (including a file : *Polonia* 1501-1600).
Lettere (Principi) Polonia : vol. 16.
Deliberazioni Senato : vol. 76, 77, 78, 90, 91.
Senato III Relazioni : F 25, 26.
Esposizioni Principi : Reg. 4, 4 bis, 5.
Cerimoniali : vol. 1, 2.
Biblioteca dell'Archivio Generale : Misc. Cod. 100 (*Annali*).

2. *Marciana Library.*

Mss. 5837, 6032.

3. *Museo Correr.*

Archivio Tiepolo : vol. 114.

C. POLISH LIBRARY IN PARIS.

Mss. 3, 5, 8, 9, 11, 12.

APPENDIX I

The article which is reproduced here, appeared first in the collective publication *Miscellanea in honorem Cardinalis Isidori Kioviensis* (1463–1963), Romae 1963, I, pp. 27–43, under the title "Isidore's Tradition," with somewhat longer introductory remarks and with the complete text of Antonio Possevino's memorandum of 1595 added as appendix.

In my study of the long way from Florence to Brest I stressed the link of traditional continuity between the religious unions of 1439 and 1596 which is frequently questioned. But I also stressed the obvious difference between those two unions; the first was ecumenical and the other regional. That difference explains the well-known fact of the participation of the patriarchate of Constantinople in the Union of Florence, and its condemnation of the Union of Brest. However, in connection with this second uncontroversial point I raised a question which in the light of the available source material could not be definitely answered. It is indeed surprising that the Ruthenian hierarchy, under the leadership of Cyril Terlecki, man of confidence of Patriarch Jeremiah II, started a movement early in 1590, which led directly to the Union of 1596, while earlier plans of reuniting the Ruthenians of the Polish-Lithuanian Commonwealth with Rome had failed. For the Patriarch had left the Commonwealth only a few months earlier, in November 1589, after having reorganized the Orthodox hierarchy.

I could only suggest two contradictory interpretations for this strange development.[1] Either Jeremiah was badly informed about the trend toward Union with Rome among the Ruthenian bishops, or he was himself not too seriously opposed to such an initiative in a country where the conditions for reunion were much more favorable than in Constantinople. I hesitated to decide for one of these two alternatives, and noted only that Jeremiah could hardly show openly any possible inclination toward Rome, after creating the Orthodox patriarchate in Moscow and before his return to the capital of the Ottoman Empire.

I did not foresee that I would soon discover an unknown document which would favor the second alternative and at the same time confirm my views on the survival of a tradition which in that document, as in so many others, is traced back to the famous Cardinal Isidore.

---

[1] See above p. 233.

It appeared highly improbable that new material regarding the origin of the Union of Brest might be found in one of the best known series of manuscripts of the Vatican Library: the *Codices Urbinati Latini*. Thanks to their excellent printed catalogue, where all documents are carefully listed, those volumes seemed to have been sufficiently explored by so many scholars interested in that Union, including myself. When I returned in 1962 to the study of that rich material, I had entirely different problems in mind; but decided to examine on that occasion a *Relatione della Rossia e come introdurre vi si possa la fede Cristiana Catholica*, included in a big volume of *Relationi diverse* concerning the period from 1564 to 1618.[2] Already more than a century ago that collection of manuscripts of every sort and without any chronological order, raised the interest of a Swiss scholar who summarized a fairly large number of manuscript sources, selected from various Roman libraries.[3] In a few lines he also described the *Relatione della Rossia*, without, however, giving a clear idea of its content. His summary gave the impression that the report, after recalling the well-known story of the conversion of Kievan Rus', dealt with the situation in Moscovite Russia and Catholic penetration there. The even briefer notice in the much more recent and systematic catalogue of the *Codices Urbinati Latini*, referring to that abstract,[4] confirmed this impression; the document would seem to be a contribution to the ecclesiastical history of Russia, strictly speaking of Moscovia; and nobody could expect to find there any information on the Union of Brest and the Ruthenians of the Polish-Lithuanian Commonwealth.

To be certain, I started reading the twelve pages of the report, addressed to the Cardinal of San Giorgio, that is to the well-known nephew of Pope Clement VIII, Cinzio Passeri Aldobrandini who was in charge of the affairs of Central and Eastern Europe in the Secretariate of State. This obviously was a contemporary copy without date and signature. The first three pages proved to be nothing but a survey of the history of the Russian Church from Olga and Vladimir to Ivan the Terrible, written during the reign of his son and successor Fedor, without new information and not without inaccuracies. It also appeared that the last four pages dealt with the origin of the Eastern schism, with the growing errors of the Greeks, and with the traditional differences between them and the

---

[2] *Cod. Urbin. Lat.* 839. In that manuscript of 600 fol. which is Vol. XVIII of *Relationi diverse*, and contains 22 of them, the report on "Rossia" which is discussed here and summarized in n. 11, is on fol. 80-85v. And the preceding two: on the frontiers of Hungary (fol. 64–69) and on the Catholics in the Ottoman Empire (fol. 70–79), as well as the following one, on the *"Origo Christianae Religionis in Livonia"* (fol. 86–93), all deal with problems in which Possevino was interested, as does the *"Relatione di Costantinopoli dell'Anno 1593"* on fol. 391–406.

[3] H. Laemmer, *Analecta Romana*, Schaffhausen 1861, 42.

[4] Vol. II, Romae 1912, p. 467: "Historici cuiusdam brevis excursus de Moschovia, de Graecis schismaticis ac de statu Catholicorum in illis regionibus ad dominum Cardinalem S. Georgii".

Roman Church. But the remaining five pages, which constitute the very center of the memorandum, explain the reason why it was drafted—not without some hurry and therefore rather confusing in its arrangement. They describe the situation in the eight Ruthenian dioceses *nel regno di Polonia* on the eve of the Union of Brest and discuss the possible repercussions of their reunion with Rome in the other Orthodox countries. It is precisely in this section, which has been overlooked by the earlier investigators of the volume, that the historian finds at least one entirely new and very important piece of information, as well as interesting interpretations and suggestions.

In order to appreciate the value and reliability of this new source, it is necessary to determine the exact date of its composition and the person of the writer. It was obviously written when the *vladichi*, viz. the two Ruthenian bishops, Pociej and Terlecki, who were delegated to Rome to conclude the union, had already reached their goal, but had not yet accomplished their mission; therefore after their arrival in Rome on November 15, 1595, but before the memorable ceremony in the Vatican on December 23 of that year. Who was the Italian, the closest collaborator in the matter, who had met them on their way through his country, and wanted to convey as soon as possible his impressions and hopes to the Pope?

This question, too, can be answered without difficulty. It is indeed easy to recognize in the whole presentation and approach of the writer the well-known ideas of Antonio Possevino, the Jesuit diplomat who for many years had been so unusually active in the matter of religious union both in the Commonwealth and in Moscow, and who in his earlier reports and publications had frequently expressed the view, stressed also in the memorandum of 1595, that a regional union with the Ruthenians of Poland and Lithuania could be used as an instrument for influencing the Muscovites. Without pointing out all the other similarities it must be noted more particularly that some rather unusual, highly personal comments of Possevino in his *Moscovia*, published nine years before, are repeated in the report sent to Cardinal Passeri Aldobrandini. Thus, in both texts the Greeks are blamed for having changed their mind not less than fourteen times, concluding unions and then returning again to their errors; the Muscovites are criticized for accusing their Catholic neighbors of changing their religious beliefs between the morning and the evening of the same day.[5] Explaining the anti-Catholic prejudice of the latter by the propaganda of "German merchants and English heretics," the report of 1595 clearly reflects the difficulties which Possevino had with these

---

[5] These remarks in Possevino's *Moscovia*, Vilnae 1586, on fol. 7 of the "Alter Commentarius" and on fol. 3v of the "Capita quibus Graeci . . . discesserunt," have been recently recalled by St. Polčin, *"Une tentative d'Union au XVIe siècle: la Mission religieuse du Père Antoine Possevin, S. J. en Moscovie (1581–1582),"* Rome 1957 (Orientalia Christiana Analecta, vol. 150); see particularly p. 24 and 69.

people during his mission in Moscow in 1582. The emphasis of the memorandum in recommending educational activities, especially those of the Jesuits, also recalls so many earlier suggestions of Father Antonio.

Last but not least, it is not difficult to determine why and where Possevino could have met the two Ruthenian bishops on their way to Rome and the reason for his joy at their recent initiative. It is true that after the troubles of the Polish interregnum of 1587 he was no longer used by the Holy See in Polish and Russian affairs[6] and that his latest mission had led him not to Eastern Europe but to France, where he worked for the reconciliation of Henri IV with the Papacy. He returned to Rome in the summer of 1595, and after the absolution of the King of France by Clement VIII on September 17, he was sent back to the Jesuit College in Padua.[7] But it was precisely here that Pociej and Terlecki stopped for a brief rest on their way to Rome;[8] and it is only natural that they got in touch there with Possevino whose activities in Poland they must have remembered very well and who in spite of all his other concerns remained deeply interested in the religious problems of the Ruthenians. When he wrote about these problems eleven years later,[9] briefly discussing the Union of Brest and its origin, though with some confusion as far as chronology is concerned, he still recalled his recommendation to the Holy See to write directly to the Ruthenian hierarchy in the earlier unsuccessful phase of the negotiations. Therefore, he must have been particularly pleased when at last through Pociej's and Terlecki's mission that immediate contact between the Ruthenian bishops and the Holy See was to be established.

If there could still remain the slightest doubt as to the author of the memorandum of 1595, that doubt would be removed by its conclusion which admits that besides the union with Orthodox there were, at the given moment, two other problems of equal importance for Christendom, namely the reconciliation with France and the war against the Turks. No other specialist in the question of the Eastern schism, except Possevino, would have mentioned in that connection not only the Turkish but also the French problem.

It was indispensable to identify the author of the report on the religious situation in the Ruthenian lands, including the whole East European background, in order to evaluate correctly its importance and, above all, its reliability. Knowing that it was written by an experienced,

---

[6] I tried to explain this in my publication *"Possevino's Last Statement on Polish-Russian Relations,"* Orientalia Christiana Perodica, 1953, 257–258.

[7] See L. Karttunen, *Antonio Possevino*, Lausanne 1908, 257–258.

[8] See the notice of 1595, unfortunately without exact date, in the records of the Polish nation at the University of Padova, published in *Archiwum do dziejów literatury i oświaty w Polsce*, VI (1890), 28.

[9] In his: *Apparatus Sacer*, Venetiis 1606, III, 170–173, in the article "Rutheni"; see the reference to this article in Possevino's autobiography, partly published by Polcin, *op. cit.*, 124. See also his *Moscovia*, fol. 24 of the "Alter Commentarius."

outstanding specialist in those matters, we can safely suppose that the long memorandum was studied with due attention at the Vatican; and probably coming from Padua to Rome soon after the arrival of Pociej and Terlecki, contributed to the cordiality with which they were treated. And for the same reason we too must consider it most seriously today, even though one particular, though most significant, is not confirmed by any other source. This information was given to Possevino by the two Ruthenian bishops who would hardly have spoken so openly and sincerely to anybody else about a delicate and confidential matter, and nobody else would have been better qualified to understand fully and to appreciate their rather amazing story which revealed the origin of their initiative and of the Union of Brest in an entirely new light.

After briefly stressing the religious importance of that regional reunion in full agreement with other contemporary opinions and specifying that the eight dioceses which were to be regained by the Roman Church included about ten thousand parishes, Possevino cited the great tradition of Cardinal Isidore who at the time of the Council of Florence had worked for that same purpose. But he added at once that only at the present hour could his undertaking mature, thanks to a development which he considered providential. He then reported in detail the relation of the two *vladichi*.

They said that a few years earlier[10] the Patriarch of Constantinople had visited *la Rossia*—a name which in the context can only mean the Ruthenian lands of Poland and Lithuania under the Metropolitan of Kiev. In his discussion with the local hierarchy he deplored the miseries suffered by the Christians under the Turkish tyranny. He admitted that under such conditions he could not proceed with freedom to remove all the "confusions and abuses," thus confirming an argument which was frequently stressed by Catholic writers and especially by Peter Skarga with whom Possevino had once so closely collaborated. Possevino heard from his Ruthenian visitors, that Jeremiah's complaints had been immediately answered *da alcuni*, i.e. by some Orthodox bishops (and among these was undoubtedly Terlecki, for Pociej was still a layman) in a bold and challenging way. They wondered whether the best remedy to this situation might not be an attempt to conclude "a true union with the Latin Church

---

[10] In the memorandum (fol. 81v) we read that this was two years before (*due anni sono*), which is obviously an error; in 1595 not two, but six years had elapsed since Jeremiah visited the Commonwealth. The mistake was either made by the copyist (Possevino's handwriting is not always easy to read) or by Possevino himself who sometimes was not too careful as far as the chronology was concerned; thus in his article quoted above, in the preceding note, there is an obvious confusion of two different synods held at Brest: in 1594, when it was decided to send representatives of the Ruthenian hierarchy to Rome; and in 1596 when the union was confirmed in the presence of the three royal representatives whose role in avoiding troubles and in defending freedom of discussion is particularly emphasized (*Apparatus Sacer*, III, 171–172).

to have its assistance according to the need." Far from blaming them the Greek Patriarch replied that "the idea was most holy and that those to whom it was not forbidden to execute it, must be considered happy." He added that it was impossible to do this for those who were subject to the Turks in view of various dangers; but his words could only be interpreted as an encouragement to the Ruthenians to go ahead in providing for their salvation. This was the origin, so concluded Possevino after listening to the delegates of the Ruthenian hierarchy, of the plan which finally matured in their coming to Rome, and "with God's grace would result in the conversion of all those peoples."[11]

The same man who had been rather pessimistic with regard to the attitude of the *vladichi* towards Catholicism when he left Poland eight years earlier,[12] now was confident that the reunion of their Church would be accomplished "with vivid hopes of much greater results." He explained that those hopes included similar unions not only with Wallachia and Moldavia, whose Orthodox would follow the Ruthenian example, but even with Moscow where he had had such discouraging experiences, and eventually with the Greeks themselves. This was precisely the reason why he added to his report lengthy considerations, partly historical, partly theological, on the origin and development of the Eastern schism. And Possevino's reborn optimism certainly contributed to the high hopes which appeared in Rome in connection with the regional union of the Ruthenians, considered a promising basis for a union of truly ecumenical character according to the Florentine tradition.

Since all these expectations were soon to prove illusionary, it would be hardly necessary to study in detail Possevino's suggestions regarding Catholic propaganda among the Muscovites and Greeks, though these

---

[11] "Isidoro che uenne al Concilio di Fiorenza, et poi fù fatto Card. le fù Metropolita di Chiouia, ma ritornando non puotè persuadere la uerità alla gente ingannata, perche non era anco gionto il tempo riseruato nell'eterna sapienza per maturare un tanto negotio, al quale hora si uede dato un principio propriam(en)te dal Cielo, perche li Vladichi uenuti qua dicono, che due anni sono sendo il Patriarca di Costantinopoli uenuto a uisitare la Rossia, et piangendo con loro le miserie, che patiuano i Christiani sotto la tirannide Turchesca con le confusioni, et abusi che per ciò nasceuano, non potendosi attendere all'estirpatione di quelli con la debita libertà Ecc(lesiasti)ca fù risposto da alcuni, che per rimediare à questo si doueua tentare una uera unione con la Chiesa Latina per hauer poi aiuti da quella secondo il bisogno, al che il Patriarca replicò il pensiero esser santiss(im)o, et che felici doueuano reputarsi quelli, à chi non era uietato l'esseguirlo, ma che non era licito di farlo à chi staua soggeto à Turchi per uarij pericoli, che si correuano con che uenne (f. 82) quasi ad insegnare alli Rutheni, che non lasciassero di prouedere alla loro salute, et da questo raggionamento si cominciò maturare il consiglio, che in fine ha partorito la uenuta di costoro in Roma, et partorirà con la Diuina gratia la conuersione di tutte quelle genti, et l'unione di quelle Chiese errante alla sua uera madre con uiue speranze di frutti molto maggiori." For the complete text of Antonio Possevino's memorandum of 1595, see *Miscellanea in honorem Cardinalis Isidori Kiovensis* (1463–1963), Romae 1963 I. pp. 37–43.

[12] See his statement of 1587 published in the appendix to the article quoted above, note 6.

supplement in some respects his earlier writings. More constructive were his ideas about the ways and means of strengthening the reunion with the Ruthenians which did indeed materialize as expected, but would require, as Father Antonio rightly anticipated, constant care and support, as well as solicitous cooperation with the *Vladichi*, both the present ones and their successors. In that respect the proposals included in Possevino's memorandum of November 1595, were not particularly original, but in full agreement with the views expressed at the same time by other supporters of the Union of Brest, for example the Catholic Greek Peter Arcudius, well trained in Rome,[13] where Possevino wanted a few more schools for young Ruthenians and even Muscovites to be founded, and particularly by the able Nuncio in Poland, Germanico Malaspina. The latter is quoted in the memorandum which recommended the proposal of the Bishop of San Severo, as the Nuncio is called, to admit the Ruthenian bishops, united with Rome, to the Senate of the Kingdom, along with the Polish bishops of Latin rite. That important point had probably been touched in Possevino's discussions with Pociej and Terlecki who shared, of course, that desire expressed by the Ruthenian hierarchy in all the preliminary negotiations. But later, when that legitimate request did not receive satisfaction, Pociej who had been a member of the Senate as Castellan of Brest when still an Orthodox layman, was the first to realize that the stumbling block was not at all any prejudice or lack of sympathy among the Catholics of Latin rite, but the opposition of the non-Catholic members of the Diet whose unanimous vote was necessary for creating new seats in the Senate.[14]

With regard to the problem which deserves special attention in Possevino's memorandum, viz. the attitude of the Patriarchate of Constantinople, it must be noted that the author returned to consider at the end that same Jeremiah whose favorable attitude Pociej and Terlecki now revealed. He recalled, probably after discussing this question with his visitors, the earlier record of that prominent head of the Greek Church who a few years before visiting the Commonwealth, as well as Muscovy, had rejected all proposals of the German Protestants, defending against them the authority of the Roman Church, and seemed ready to accept the Gregorian calendar. For these reasons he was suspected by the Turks "of feeling with the Latins," and was deposed from the Patriarchate. His very life was in danger. All this is well known from other sources, but makes

---

[13] I discussed the role of Arcudius in my article: *"Unia brzeska w świetle współczesnych źródel greckich,"* *Sacrum Poloniae Millenium*, I, Rome 1954, 71–136 (a Ukrainian translation of that article appeared in the review *Lohos*, XI [1960], 15–25, 93–101, 173–183, 265–269), where four letters of Arcudius regarding the Union of Brest are published in the first appendix.

[14] Thus, for example, a few years earlier, in 1593, a special "Constitution" of the Diet was needed to give a place in the Senate to a new bishop of Latin rite for whom a see had been created in Livonia (*Volumina Legum*, Warsaw 1733, I, 1409).

it understandable that he approved in 1589 the movement toward reunion with Rome, which was developing among the Ruthenians.

Equally understandable are two consequences of his behavior. One of them helps us to understand another apparent puzzle in the history of that movement. Until now it was difficult to explain why the decision which at least some of the bishops had taken already in 1590, was kept secret for several years. They had nothing to fear from the King nor in general from the authorities of a Catholic State, but on the contrary, could be sure that their initiative would be welcomed. They were afraid of Prince Constantine Ostrogski at the time of Pociej's and Terlecki's mission to Rome, which was almost cancelled because of his opposition. But that violent opposition of a powerful magnate who originally seemed to favor the Union, manifested itself not earlier than in 1593–1594; and one of the complex reasons for his change of attitude was precisely his indignation that for about three years the preparation for the Union had proceeded without his knowledge. It was, therefore, another apprehension which justified the strange secrecy: the fear that the initiative of the Ruthenian hierarchy could harm the Patriarch back in Constantinople if it became known that such a pro-Roman initiative was taken immediately after his sojourn in the Commonwealth. There would have been strong suspicion among the Turks, not unjustified, as we see now, that he was not irresponsible for it; and he could have been exposed to dangers similar to those suffered in the past.

This leads to the second consequence. The approval of the Patriarch though secret, was indeed a most valuable encouragement for the leaders of the Ruthenian Church who, as recalled in another passage of Possevino's memorandum, were even more anxious than the Muscovites to maintain the traditional relations with the see of Constantinople. But since that justification of their action had to be kept secret, it could not help them much, even during the lifetime of Jeremiah. In any event, he died before the Union of Brest was concluded. When the synod of 1596 met in that city, the patriarchal see was vacant after two rapid changes following Jeremiah's death. The credentials produced at the synod by the anti-Roman Greek Nicephorus, according to which the late Patriarch had given him practically unlimited powers, were probably spurious—this remained at least Posevino's opinion[15] in contrast to that of Arcudius[16]—but even so they contributed to a confusion which strengthened the opposition among the Ruthenians and facilitated the systematic action against the Union of Brest undertaken by the well known Meletius Pigas who soon took over the Patriarchate of Constantinople.

---

[15] It was a clear reference to the case of Nicephorus, when Possevino in his later account of the Synod of Brest (*Apparatus Sacer*, III, 172–173), after quoting opinion of the royal representatives about that enigmatic Greek, wrote about an imposter coming from Constantinople "cum fictis a Patriarcha litteris falsisque sigillis appositis."

[16] See the third of Arcudius' letters quoted above, note 13.

The entirely different, friendly and understanding attitude of Jeremiah could not help to make the regional union of 1596 an ecumenical one. The situation on the eve of the synod of Brest reminds us, however, of a similar event. Almost one hundred years before[17] a Metropolitan of Kiev who wanted to revive the Union of Florence asked for the opinion of the Patriarch of Constantinople and received from one of Jeremiah's predecessors advice identical to the one given to the Ruthenian hirearchy in 1589.

The discovery of that advice which for the reasons given above contributes to a better understanding of the origin of the Union of Brest, leads furthermore to a conclusion of general significance. The difficulty of dealing with a Constantinople under Ottoman domination, a difficulty which Cardinal Isidore had been the first to experience, ought not to make us overlook the recurring possibilities of saving his heritage, when and where conditions were favorable, with the tacit consent of some at least of the Greek Patriarchs. It is, therefore, worthwhile to study separately the attitude of each of them toward the Roman Church.[18]

[17] For a discussion of the project of Metropolitan Joseph II which in 1500 was referred to Rome by Alexander the Jagellonian, see above, Part I, Chapter V; see p. 112 about the advice of Patr. Niphon II.

[18] Such a systematic study was begun by the late Georg Hofmann in the series *"Grieschische Patriarchen und römische Päpste,"* published in "Orientalia Christiana," Vol. 13 (1928), 36 (1934).

APPENDIX II

Here follows a list of the present writer's latest articles which the reader of this book can use for the further study of the following problems discussed in the text.

For the general background: "Das Problem der Kirchenunion in der osteuropäischen Geschichte," *Österreichische Osthefte*, IV/1 (Jan. 1962), pp. 1–5.

For the eastern policy of the papacy: 1) "Diplomatie pontificale et activité missionnaire en Asie aux XIIIᵉ–XVᵉ siècles," *XIIᵉ Congrès international des Sciences historiques* (Vienna 1965). Rapports II, pp. 5–32; 2) "The Defense of Europe in the Renaissance Period," *Didascalia— Studies in Honor of Anselm M. Albareda* (New York 1962), pp. 123–146.

For the Polish backround: 1) "Kulturgeschichtliche Probleme der polnischen Ostpolitik," *Wiener Archiv für Geschichte des Slaventums und Osteuropas*, Vol. V (1966), pp. 20–40; 2) "Problems of Ecumenism in Poland's Millennium," *The Catholic Historical Review*, Vol. LII/4 (Jan. 1967), pp. 477–493.

For the crusade of Varna (discussed in Part I, Chapter III): 1) Spór o Warneńczyka," *Teki historyczne*, Vol. IX (London Nov. 1958), pp. 16–34; 2) "Angora, Florence, Varna and the Fall of Constantinople," *Akten des XI. Internationalen Byzantinisten-Kongresses 1958*. (München 1960), pp. 216–217.

For the eastern policy of Sixtus IV (discussed in Part I, Chapter V): "Sixte IV et la Chrétienté orientale," *Mélanges Eugène Tisserant*, Città del Vaticano, Vol. II, pp. 241–264.

For the international background of the Union of Lublin (discussed in Part II, Chapter II and III): "Die österreichisch-polnischen Beziehungen zur Zeit der Union von Lublin," *Perennitas—P. Thomas Michels O.S.B. zum 70. Geburtstag* (Münster 1963), pp. 322–324.

For the Croatian background of the Komulovich mission (discussed in Part III, Chapter IV): "The Renaissance Origin of Panslavism," *The Polish Review*, Vol. III (New York Nov. 1958), pp. 1–13.

For the project of an anti-Ottoman league at the time of the Union of Brest (discussed in Part IV, Chapter II and V): "Le projet de ligue anti-ottomane à la fin du XVIᵉ siècle," *Académie des Inscriptions et Belles-Lettres—Comptes Rendus des Séances de l'Année 1960* (Paris 1961), pp. 190–200.

Some of the problems discussed in this volume have also been studied against a general background in my books *The Millennium of Europe*, University of Notre Dame Press 1963 (revised German edition: *Das europäische Jahrtausend*, Salzburg 1966), and *Tysiąclecie Polski Katolickiej* (Rome 1966), which is the last (XIIth) volume of the Series *Sacrum Poloniae Millennium*.

INDEX

OF NAMES AND PLACES

For the painstaking composition of this index I wish to express my most sincere thanks to the Rev. Szczepan Wesoły. Numerous cross references proved necessary in view of the spelling of some Ruthenian names in the text which may seem inconsistent. If in most cases the Polish forms have been used, particulary when dealing with the sixteenth century, it is because those forms usually appear in the sources of that period as far as they are written in the Latin alphabet. The modern transcription or transliterations from the Cyrillic alphabet seem rather strange and have been used almost exclusively when quoting Russian and Ukrainian publications in the footnotes.

201, 274, 280, 284, 297, 299, 367, 369;
see also Arians.
Aquaviva, General Soc. Jesu, 314.
Aquinas see Thomas.
Aragon, King of, 47.
Arcudius, Peter 246, 247, 277, 314, 315, 341, 361, 362, 365, 372, 381, 389, 390, 393, 397, 399, 404, 406, 408.
Arianism, Arians, 150, 168, 185, 299, 367, 399;
see also Antitrinitarians.
Armenia, Patriarch of, 155.
Armenians, 49, 52, 53, 110, 115, 119, 144, 147, 152, 154, 155, 156, 157.
Arsonius, Bishop of Elasson, 229.
Asia, 68, 72, 80, 147, 173, 249.
— Central, 16.
Asiatic, 16, 27, 41.
— Far East, 168.
Asov region, 267.
Astrakhan, 173.
Athanasius, Greek church of St., 315.
Augsburg, Diet of, 131.
Austria, Austrians, 171, 221, 251, 253, 254, 256, 262, 265, 300, 317, 351.
Austria, House of, see Habsburgs.
Avignon, 24, 25.
Avraam, Bishop of Suzdal, 43, 50, 51, 61, 63.

B.

Bakócs, Thomas, Primate of Hungary, 126, 127.
Balkan(s), 17, 36, 41, 56, 65, 71, 73, 76, 168, 219, 251, 254, 255, 256, 259, 261, 326, 411.
Balkan Slavs, 73, 254.
Baltic Sea, 89, 272.
Bałaban, Gedeon, Ruthenian Bishop of Lwów, 220, 232, 234, 237, 238, 243, 269, 276, 278, 288, 296, 303, 309, 322, 329, 339, 345, 368, 371, 374, 375, 378, 382, 388, 399, 409, 417.

Bałaban, Gregory, Abbot, 361.
Baranowski, Adalbert, Bishop of Płock, 316, 317, 318, 320, 335.
Barsum, Archdeacon of Alexandria, 326.
Basel, 33, 39, 40, 43, 44, 45, 47, 48, 49, 56, 64, 146.
Basel, Council of, 16, 31, 33, 39, 40, 41, 44, 48, 56, 58, 59, 64, 65, 69, 76, 90.
Basil I, Grand Prince of Moscow, 27, 35.
Basil II, Grand Prince of Moscow, 37, 38, 41, 42, 43, 44, 51, 61, 62, 63, 64, 73, 74, 76, 91, 92, 94.
Basil III, Grand Prince of Moscow, 112, 128, 129, 130, 131, 133, 134, 172, 216.
Báthory (Batory) Stefan, King of Poland, 186, 191, 192, 195, 202, 203, 209, 213, 216, 218, 219, 220, 221, 223, 224, 236, 256, 280, 365, 395, 401.
Báthory, Andrew, Cardinal, 256, 262.
Báthory, Balthasar, 262.
Báthory, Sigismund, Prince of Transylv. 262, 317, 319, 334, 351, 352, 402.
Batu Khan, 18.
Bayezid, sultan 28.
Belgrade, 137, 367.
Belgrade, Metropolitan of, 367, 411.
Bełz, 69, 70, 233, 234, 238, 239, 240, 268, 276.
Benedictins of Eastern rite, 23.
Berestie see Brest.
Bernardine Franciscans of Polish Province, 110, 119.
Bessarion, Cardinal, 49, 54, 77, 79, 83, 85, 86, 96, 118.
Będzin, 221.
Bielski, Theodor, Prince, 101.
Black Sea, 16, 28, 55, 76, 255, 257, 272.
Bnin, 49. See also Andrew of Bnin.
Bogdan, Prince of Moldavia, 186.
Bohemia, 23, 47, 54, 60, 98, 108, 117, 126, 170, 401.

— 438 —

Casimir, Saint, 107.
Caspar, Nahaj, S. J., 268, 365.
Catherine, Queen of Sweden, 207.
Caves, Monastery of the, 60, 61, 101, 340, 368.
Cedulini, Peter, Bishop of Nona, 213, 253, 254, 255, 256, 258, 259.
Cellini, Livius, 214.
Cerularian schism, 282, 325.
Cesarea, Archbishop of, 215.
Cesarini, Cardinal, 41, 44, 67, 68, 71, 72, 80.
Chalecki, Demetrius, Grand Treasurer of Lithuania, 352, 363, 364, 369, 372, 380, 387, 404, 405.
Chalecki, Gregory, Metrop. of Kiev., 106.
Charles IV, King of France, 191.
Charles VI, King of France, 35.
Chełm, (Kholm), 20, 58, 59, 69, 84, 120, 401.
Chełm, Latin Bishop of, 146, 337, 342, 401.
Chełm, Ruthenian Bishop of, 70, 123, 138, 146, 238, 268, 276, 288, 401.
Chernigov, Michael, Prince of, 18.
China, 168, 204.
Chłopicki, Stanislaus, 264.
Chodkiewicz, family, 149, 155, 160, 187.
Chodkiewicz, Ivan, Palatine of Kiev, 101, 106, 108.
Chodynicki, Kazimierz, historian, 13.
Chreptowicz, Meletius, Bishop of Brest and Volodymir, 238, 245.
Chrysoberghes, family, 28.
Chrysoberghes, Andrew, Bishop, 30, 31, 37, 38, 77.
Chrysoberghes, Theodore, 28, 31, 34, 37.
Chrysoloras, John, 30.
Chrysoloras, Manuel, 28, 30.
Chudov Monastery, 63.
Cicogna, Pasquale, Doge, 260.
Ciołek, Erazmus, 114, 115, 116, 120, 125, 131.
Cizuva, de, see Paul, also Simeon.

Clement VII, Pope, 132, 194, 205, 255.
Clement VIII, Pope, 222, 253, 254, 255, 256, 257, 258, 259, 263, 267, 270, 272, 282, 288, 302, 311, 312, 317, 320, 321, 325, 326, 327, 328, 331, 332, 333, 335, 336, 337, 339, 340, 353, 354, 365, 378, 386, 395, 397, 398, 402, 410, 411, 416 ;
see also Aldobrandini, Ippolito.
Clenck, Rudolph, 192.
Clotilde of France, 207.
Commendone, Giovanni, Nuncio, Cardinal 150, 151, 152, 153, 180, 181, 182, 185, 186, 187, 188, 189, 205.
Commos, John, Bishop of Alexandria, 326.
Como, Cardinal of, see Galli.
Comoli, Alessandro see Komulovich.
Comuleo see Komulovich.
Condulmer, Cardinal, 68, 71.
Constance, 15, 16, 28, 29, 30, 31, 32, 34.
Constance, Council of, 15, 28, 29, 31, 32, 34, 37, 38, 42, 44.
Constantinople, 15, 16, 18, 20, 21, 22, 23, 24, 25, 26, 27, 28, 29, 30, 32, 34, 35, 36, 37, 38, 39, 41, 46, 49, 53, 54, 56, 57, 61, 64, 65, 66, 67, 71, 72, 73, 74, 77, 78, 79, 80, 81, 82, 83, 84, 85, 86, 88, 91, 93, 96, 97, 98, 105, 109, 112, 118, 134, 135, 154, 176, 177, 179, 191, 195, 197, 201, 202, 206, 211, 213, 214, 215, 216, 217, 218, 223, 226, 228, 229, 230, 232, 233, 234, 235, 239, 249, 250, 254, 256, 257, 259, 260, 263, 303, 315, 318, 325, 326, 334, 335, 336, 350, 355, 356, 371, 372, 380, 382, 384, 385, 405, 406, 407, 408, 409, 410.
Constantinople, Emperor of, 30, 34, 36, 38, 41, 44, 47, 49, 63, 68, 74, 100, 105, 108, 201, 230;
see also Greek Emperor.
Constantinople, Empire of, 26, 74;
see also Byzantine Empire and Greek Empire.

G.

Gabriel, Archbishop of Ochrida, 219.

Gabriel, Jacobite Patriarch, 326, 327, 356.

Galektion, Metrop. of Kiev. 106.

Galli, Ptolomeo, Cardinal, 208, 211, 328.

Gamrat, Peter, Primate of Poland, 144.

Garatoni, Christopher, Bishop, 68.

Gasztołd, Albert, Palatine of Wilno, 131, 132.

Gasztołd, John, Palatine of Wilno, 96, 132.

Gembicki, Laurentius, Primate of Poland, 335, 336, 337.

Genoa, 67, 79.

George son of Lingven, Prince, 61, 62.

Georgia, 41.

Germany, 54, 137, 152, 192, 195, 204, 213, 272, 401.

German(s), 31, 37, 47, 48, 53.

German Knights, 90.

Gilbert see Lannoy.

Glinski, Michael, Prince, 130, 133.

Gniezno, 139, 159, 418, 419.

Gniezno, Archbishop of, 29, 48, 120, 126, 129, 268, 291, 306, 338.

Godunov, Boris, Tsar, 230, 413, 414.

Golden Horde, 17, 107, 116.

Gomoliński, Stanislaus, Bishop of Chełm, 220, 337, 342.

Goniądz, Peter of, 159.

Goślicki, Bishop of Przemyśl, 301, 306, 338.

Gozdawa, coat of arms, 279.

Gratiani, Antonio Maria, 180.

Greece, 32, 57, 68, 71, 72, 79, 266, 292, 414.

Greeks, 17, 18, 20, 21, 22, 26, 28, 29, 30, 33, 38, 39, 43, 44, 46, 47, 48, 49, 52, 54, 56, 68, 72, 73, 74, 77, 78, 79, 81, 82, 110, 115, 118, 119, 132, 147, 148, 150, 153, 154, 156, 196, 201, 208, 210, 212, 213, 215, 219, 242, 250, 255, 270, 279, 290, 291, 294, 299, 315, 321, 325, 330, 341, 357, 360, 361, 372, 392, 411.

Greek College in Rome, 13, 196, 215, 246, 361, 372, 393, 406.

Greek Congregation, 196.

Greek Emperor, 37, 39, 47, 53, 54; see also Constantinople Emperor of.

Greek Empire, 24, 61, 74, 77; see also Byzantine Empire.

Greek Orthodox(y), 16, 38, 53, 59, 61, 69, 71, 78, 99, 104, 110, 121, 124, 128, 131, 132, 143, 144, 145, 148, 149, 150, 163, 164, 167, 170, 171, 184, 185, 196, 197, 200, 203, 206, 211, 231, 234, 237, 258, 262, 274, 325, 345, 356, 357, 405, 408, 416.

Greek Patriarch, 19, 20, 21, 81, 93, 96, 97, 110, 135, 201, 213, 217, 223, 224, 226, 230, 235, 325, 255, 356; see also Constantinople Patriarch of.

Greek Rite, 81, 84, 85, 86, 89, 92, 95, 103, 132, 138, 142, 152, 154, 166, 187, 188, 207, 208, 212, 258, 285, 328, 353, 364, 385, 399, 393, 419.

Greek Schism, 19, 78, 197, 386.

Gregory X, Pope, 20.

Gregory XIII, Pope, 190, 195, 196, 203, 204, 205, 206, 209, 210, 214, 215, 219, 223, 246, 254, 255, 256, 325, 372, 375, 410.

Gregory XIV, Pope, 246, 253.

Gregory, Archbishop of Polotsk, see Zahorski.

Gregory, Armenian Bishop of Lwów, 49.

Gregory, Metrop. of Kiev, 43, 51, 63, 85, 86, 87, 88, 89, 91, 92, 93, 94, 96, 97, 98, 99, 100, 118.

Gregory see Tsamblak

Grodno, 149.

H.

Habsburgs, Hause of Austria, 65, 66, 67, 108, 117, 130, 134, 137, 140, 170, 171, 174, 175, 176, 180, 181, 182, 187, 191, 196, 221, 241, 254,

P.

Pac, Nicholas, Bishop of Kiev, 149, 190, 224.
Pachomius, Patriarch of Const., 223.
Pachomius, Archbishop of Cesarea, 215.
Padua, 249, 315, 316.
Padua, University of, 249, 315, 357, 410.
Palaeologus, Andreas, 105.
Palaeologus, Dionysius, 212.
Palaeologus, Zoe, 100.
Palaeologus see Constantine XI, John V, John VIII, Michael.
Paolo Giorgio, 411.
Paphnutinus, Metropolitan, 406.
Parczów, 151, 152.
Paris, 25.
Paruta, Paulo, Venetian Ambassador, 260, 335.
Paul II, Pope, 97, 102.
Paul III, Pope, 177.
Paul " de Cizuva ", 103.
Peloponnesus, 32, 72, 81.
Pelissa, " Cavaliero ", 260.
Pełczycki, Leontine, Bishop of Pinsk and Turov, 237, 238, 268, 276, 288, 303, 331, 349.
Peremyšl see Przemyśl.
Pereyaslav, 21.
Persia(ns) 173, 176.
Peter, Saint, 240, 320, 329, 385.
Peter, Metropolitan of Moscow, 21.
Peter, Bishop of Kiev, 17, 18.
Philadelphia, Archbishop of, 315.
Philanthropenos, Manuel, 34.
Philip I, Metrop. of Moscow, 94.
Philip the Good, Duke of Burgundy, 47.
Phocas Family, 223.
Photius, Patriarch of Const., 27, 28, 34, 35, 38, 39.
Photian schism, 325.
Piast dynasty, 69, 84.
Piccolomi, Cardinal, 86, 90; see also Pius II.

Pigas see Meletius.
Pinsk, Bishop of, 60, 237, 268, 276, 279, 288, 303, 331, 349, 371, 393, 395.
Piotrków, 123, 183.
Piotrków, Synod of, 148, 228.
Pisa, Council of, 26.
Piso, Jacopo, Nuncio, 130.
Pius II, Pope, 86, 87, 88, 89, 90, 91, 95, 96, 98.
Pius IV, Pope, 151.
Pius V, Pope, 152, 169, 172, 174, 176, 177, 179, 181, 190, 258.
Plano Carpini see John.
Płock, Bishop of, 125, 131, 316, 320, 321, 335.
Pociej (Potiy), Adam, castellane of Brest, 225, 243, 245.
see also Pociej Hypatius.
Pociej, Hypatius, Bishop of Brest and Volodymir, 245, 247, 248, 249, 265, 268, 270, 273, 274, 275, 276, 277, 279, 282, 283, 284, 285, 288, 289, 293, 294, 295, 296, 297, 298, 300, 303, 304, 305, 306, 307, 308, 309, 310, 311, 313, 314, 315, 316, 320, 321, 322, 324, 326, 327, 328, 329, 331, 332, 333, 334, 335, 336, 337, 338, 339, 340, 341, 342, 343, 344, 345, 346, 347, 349, 360, 361, 362, 365, 367, 368, 370, 376, 383, 385, 386, 388, 389, 390, 392, 393, 394, 399, 416, 417, 418, 419.
Poczampov, Lord of, 102, 103.
Podlachia, 159, 163, 166, 295, 342.
Podolia, 58, 69, 76, 125, 131, 136, 164, 176, 257, 263, 264, 364.
Podolia, Palatine of, 58, 68, 69.
Poland, King of, Kingdom of, Poles, passim.
Poland, Crown of, 163, 164, 186.
Poland, Primate of, 29, 48, 120, 124, 126, 129, 166, 268, 291, 306, 307, 335, 338, 418.
Polish Chancery, 90.
Polish Hierarchy, 48, 89, 90, 136.
Polish Jesuits, 157, 200, 201, 220, 227.

W.

226, 232, 297, 299, 307, 314, 328, 339, 345, 363, 368, 389, 401, 413, 416.
Wilno, Academy (University), 168, 197 204, 390.
Wilno, Bishop of, 29, 56, 61, 64, 75, 77, 113, 114, 115, 118, 120, 125, 133, 167, 204, 211, 307.
Wilno, Brotherhood, 232, 243, 292, 345, 368.
Wilno, Jezuit College, 157, 167, 168, 197, 204, 365.
Wilno, Palatine of, 297, 298, 307, 345, 346, 367.
Witołd, see Vitold.
Wittenberg, 213.
Władysław II see Jagello.
Władysław III the Jagellonian see Ladislas III.
Włodzimierz see Volodymir.
Wołłowicz, Eustachius, Msgr., 314, 328.

X.

Xanthopulos see Isidore II.

Y.

Yaroslav of Vladimir, Grand Prince, 19, 20.
Yazhelbitsa, Treaty of, 92.
Yurievich Alexander see Soltan Alexander.

Z.

Zagupiti, Nicholaus, 87, 88, 94.
Zahorski, Herman Ivanovich (Gregory), 276, 279, 280, 362, 363, 365, 381, 393, 395, 397.
Zamość, 224, 228, 401.
Zamoyski, Jan, Grand Chancellor of Poland, 209, 221, 224, 226, 227, 229, 231, 233, 241, 250, 256, 245, 268, 269, 270, 271, 272, 273, 277, 278, 283, 286, 301, 317, 319, 334, 335, 338, 352, 355, 358, 400, 401, 402, 404, 406, 407, 412, 415, 417.
Zápolya, John Sigismund, Prince of Transylvania, 186.
Zasławski, Janusz, Prince, 295, 343.
Zbirujski, Dionyse, Bishop of Chełm, 238, 268, 276, 288.
Zielewicz see Herbest.
Zizania, Stefan, 345.
Zydyczyn, Monastery of, 361.